# Hitler and His Generals

# HITLER and HIS GENERALS

## The Hidden Crisis, January–June 1938

BY HAROLD C. DEUTSCH

*University of Minnesota Press* • *Minneapolis*

© Copyright 1974 by the University of Minnesota.
All rights reserved.
Printed in the United States of America
at Edwards Brothers Inc., Ann Arbor, Michigan.
Published in the United Kingdom and India
by the Oxford University Press,
London and Delhi, and in Canada by the
Copp Clark Publishing Co. Limited, Toronto

*Library of Congress Catalog Card Number:* 73-86627

*ISBN 0-8166-0649-8*

The German edition of this volume appears
under the title *Das Komplott: Die Entmachtung
der Generäle* (Zurich: Diana Verlag).

*12-18-78*

*For Marie who has had a vital share*
*in whatever I have written*

# Preface

Opposition took many forms and came from every quarter in the Reich of Adolf Hitler. The National Socialist regime directed its appeals to all sections of the population but also inflicted mortal injury on the interests and ideals of uncounted men and women. The honor role of those who resisted or at least took no part in its support is long and varied.

For those who ventured on the perilous road of conspiracy, the experience became an exercise in futility in most instances. The military sector, which had some control over soldiers, along with its civilian allies alone had any prospect of bringing plans to fruition. This central fact and the high drama of July 20, 1944, explain what some regard as the disproportionate preoccupation of historians with the military elements among those who were in opposition. Doubtless their part of the story has been the most intensively researched. Perhaps for this reason there is also great awareness of what remains to be done.

Except for the immediate background of the bomb attempt on Hitler in 1944, the attention of postwar historians has dwelt most heavily on what is essentially only prelude—the Wehrmacht crisis of 1938 that eliminated from their posts Generals von Blomberg and von Fritsch, the War Minister and the Army commander in chief. Hitler managed at the time to keep the very existence of a major crisis in high military circles hidden from both the public and a large part of the general officer corps. Interest was that much greater when the basic facts became known after 1945. The extensive amount of publication which followed included two excellent studies, those of Fritsch's own nephew, Count Johann Adolf

Kielmansegg (*Der Fritsch-Prozess 1938: Ablauf und Hintergründe,* published in 1949), and of Hermann Foertsch (*Schuld und Verhängnis: Die Fritsch-Krise im Frühjahr 1938 als Wendepunkt in der Geschichte der nationalsozialistischen Zeit,* published in 1951). The impression, in fact, was that the mine had been largely worked out, and though what was now known as the Blomberg and Fritsch affairs (or Blomberg-Fritsch affair) figured largely in many works on aspects of the military Opposition, little new research effort was expended on this period. Yet considerable gaps in the story remained and, in the attempt to fill them without re-examining the entire story, confusion, misunderstanding, and at times utter nonsense were allowed to creep in.

The books of Kielmansegg and Foertsch were written under severe handicaps. The former, for example, was obliged to do his preparatory research while travel in postwar Germany was still difficult. My own study, on the other hand, suffers from the fact that many who were needed as witnesses had died. Yet it still can be said to fall in the "just in time" category. Of the persons listed at the end of this book under "Individuals Providing Oral Information" some twenty are no longer living and, in half of these instances, death occurred within six months after they had last been interviewed.

It has also been my good fortune to receive the generous support of many persons who gave or loaned me documentary material vital to this undertaking. At many a stage of preparation I have had the indispensable assistance of Count Kielmansegg. Most significantly, he made available the entire store of letters, records of interviews, and other data which he had assembled for his own important study or which had subsequently come into his hands.

Hans Bernd Gisevius, Count Rüdiger von der Goltz, and General (ret.) Friedrich Hossbach are the only surviving figures of significance to the Fritsch affair. The help of Dr. Gisevius was of the first importance in piecing together the activities of the group around Admiral Wilhelm Canaris and Colonel Hans Oster working for the cause of Fritsch through the armed forces intelligence organization. He also read the entire manuscript and recorded many hours of criticism and commentary invaluable in clarifying essential points and identifying pitfalls. In four extended interviews Count von der Goltz provided many insights. He also placed at my disposal pertinent sections of his unpublished memoirs.

General (ret.) Gerhard Engel, who became Army adjutant in the

viii

# Preface

Reich Chancellery the very day the Fritsch case went to court, has patiently reviewed with me many problems associated with Hitler's attitude, aims, and conduct. He also authorized my use of portions of his diary which is being prepared for publication by Helmut Krausnick and Hildegard von Kotze. To them I am further indebted for their consent to my use of these parts of the diary.

Ilse von Hassell and her children kindly agreed to my using unpublished parts of her husband's papers that commented on the Blomberg and Fritsch affairs and their sequelae. General Hossbach orally and by letter told me much that pieced out the absorbing story in his memoirs. I much appreciate the help here of my friend Professor Walter Bussmann, who interceded with General Hossbach (whose adjutant he had been) and persuaded him to abandon for this occasion a rule against further interviews.

Franz Josef Huber gave important help in relating the previously untold story of his brief but highly significant association with the Fritsch case. A major contribution to this work is Dr. Erich Schultze's account of his relations with such principals as Generals von Fritsch and Beck and in making available a number of important documents including an extensive manuscript written in the early fifties by Dr. Ludwig Bielschowsky.

My friend Dr. Anton Hoch, director of the Archives of the Institut für Zeitgeschichte, was unfailingly helpful with advice on persons to be interviewed and on documentary materials both at the institute and in private hands. His counsel has further been a great help in discussions of many problems concerning developments in 1938. Robert Wolfe of the National Archives, Washington, D.C., has done much to make research in the Archives pleasant and profitable. Miss Elke Froehlich helped with items of information about Blomberg, whose biography she is preparing. My friend Mrs. Luise Jodl has discussed with me various problems on which she gained insight when secretary to General Beck. She has also been a great help in performing for me several research tasks.

The research on which this study is based was made possible by a Fulbright fellowship in Germany (1969-70) and by a grant from the Office of International Programs of the University of Minnesota.

Once again my most essential support has been that of my wife, Marie Frey Deutsch, on whose critical comment, editorial skills, and constant encouragement I have leaned steadily. I hesitate to

ix

estimate the number of miles she drove me in Europe while in the back seat I typed away with materials spread about me. To her this volume is dedicated.

The National War College                                   H. C. D.
Washington, D.C.
June 1973

# Dramatis Personae

## Principals

Field Marshal Werner von Blomberg, War Minister
Eva von Blomberg, nee Gruhn, his second wife
Colonel General Baron Werner von Fritsch, commander in chief of the Army
Colonel General (after February 4, 1938, Field Marshal) Hermann Goering, Air Minister, commander in chief of the Luftwaffe, Prime Minister of Prussia, etc.
Reinhard Heydrich, creator and chief of the SD, head of the Gestapo
Heinrich Himmler, Reichsführer (leader) of the SS and head of the Reich police forces
Adolf Hitler, Fuehrer and Chancellor of the German Reich

## National Socialist Leaders

Dr. Joseph Goebbels, Minister for Propaganda and Public Enlightenment, Gauleiter of Berlin
Victor Lutze, successor to Röhm as chief of staff of the SA
Ernst Röhm, chief of staff of the SA, executed in 1934

## Adjutants in the Reich Chancellery

Captain Gerhard Engel, Army adjutant commencing March 10, 1938
Colonel Friedrich Hossbach, Wehrmacht adjutant and chief of the Central Division, Army General Staff
Commander Karl von Puttkamer, Navy adjutant
Julius Schaub, personal adjutant of Hitler

Major Rudolf Schmundt, Wehrmacht adjutant after Hossbach
Captain (ret.) Fritz Wiedemann, personal adjutant of Hitler

## Close Associates of Fritsch

General Ludwig Beck, Army chief of staff
Captain Joachim von Both, adjutant
Count Rüdiger von der Goltz, Fritsch's legal defender
Lieutenant Otto Heinz Grosskreuz, adjutant
Major Horst von Mellenthin, former adjutant
Professor Karl Nissen, physician and friend
Captain von Prittwitz, adjutant
Baroness Margrete (Margot) von Schutzbar-Milchling, friend
Major Curt Siewert, first staff officer

## Army Figures

General Wilhelm Adam, chief of the Truppenamt (Troop Office,
   later renamed General Staff) before Beck
Colonel Erich von Bonin, chief of staff, East Prussian military
   district
Colonel General Walther von Brauchitsch, Fritsch's successor as
   commander in chief
Charlotte von Brauchitsch, his second wife
Major General Kurt von Bredow, head of the Ministeramt (principal
   War Ministry department) under Schleicher and murdered with
   him in June 1934
Major General Count Erich von Brockdorff-Ahlefeld, commander
   of the Potsdam garrison
General Franz Halder, vice chief of staff
Colonel General Baron Kurt von Hammerstein-Equord, Fritsch's
   predecessor as commander in chief
Colonel Paul von Hase, regimental commander at Neuruppin
General Erich Hoepner, division commander
General Günther von Kluge, commander of Wehrkreis VI
General Ritter Wilhelm von Leeb, Kassel Army Group commander
General Curt Liebmann, commander of the War Academy
General Wilhelm List, commander of Wehrkreis IV
Field Marshal August von Mackensen, World War I hero and
   legendary figure
Major General Erich von Manstein, vice chief of staff before Halder
   (to February 4, 1938)

# Dramatis Personae

Major General Friedrich Olbricht, chief of staff of Wehrkreis IV
General Walther von Reichenau, commander of Wehrkreis VII
Lieutenant Colonel Edgar Röhricht, first staff officer of Wehrkreis IV
Colonel General Gerd von Rundstedt, commander of Berlin Army Group
General Kurt von Schleicher, Hitler's predecessor as Chancellor, murdered in the purge of June 1934
General Ritter Eugen von Schober, Bavarian corps commander
Major General Viktor von Schwedler, head of Personnel Office
Colonel General Hans von Seeckt, commander in chief to October 26, 1926
General Joachim von Stülpnagel, retired senior general
General Wilhelm Ulex, commander of Wehrkreis XI
General Erwin von Witzleben, commander of the Berlin Wehrkreis

## War Ministry Figures

Colonel Alfred Jodl, chief official in Wehrmachtamt after Keitel
General Wilhelm Keitel, head of Wehrmachtamt, then of the OKW
Lieutenant General Georg Thomas, head of War Economy in the War Ministry
Commander Baron Hubertus von Wangenheim, naval adjutant of Blomberg

## The Abwehr-Associated Opposition Group *

Rear Admiral Wilhelm Canaris, head of the Abwehr
Dr. Hans Bernd Gisevius, official of the Ministry of the Interior
Dr. Carl Goerdeler, former lord mayor of Leipzig and Reich price commissioner
Major Helmuth Groscurth, head of Abwehr II
Captain Friedrich Wilhelm Heinz, Abwehr member
Count Wolf von Helldorf, police president of Berlin
Colonel Erwin von Lahousen, Groscurth's successor as head of Abwehr II
Commander Franz Liedig, Abwehr member

*Though they may later be classified as integral members of this group, Groscurth, Lahousen, Liedig, and Schulenburg were at this stage more in process of becoming associated with it. Helldorf, Schacht, and Nebe are included because, through Gisevius, their principal services to the cause of Fritsch were channeled by way of this group.

Reich Criminal Director Arthur Nebe, head of the Reich Criminal Police

Colonel Hans Oster, chief of staff of the Abwehr and head of its Central Division

Major Alexander von Pfuhlstein, intelligence chief of Wehrkreis XI

Dr. Hjalmar Schacht, Minister of Economics until February 4, 1938, and president of the Reichsbank

Fritz-Dietloff von der Schulenburg, deputy police president of Berlin

Theodor and Elisabeth Strünck, closely associated with Oster and Gisevius in Opposition activities

## SS and Gestapo Officials

Ministerial Director Werner Best, principal legal specialist of the Gestapo

Criminal Commissar Fehling, member of department II-H of the Gestapo

Ministerial Councilor Franz Josef Huber, head of department II-C of the Gestapo, interrogator of Fritsch

Criminal Commissar (later Councilor) Joseph Meisinger, head of department II-H of the Gestapo

Heinrich Müller, deputy head of the Gestapo

Walter Schellenberg, high SS and Gestapo official

Karl Wolff, high SS and Gestapo official

## Tools in the Plot against Fritsch

Cavalry Captain (ret.) Achim von Frisch, the blackmailer's victim

Ganzer and Heiter, associates in the blackmail scheme

Otto Schmidt, the blackmailer

Josef Weingärtner, known as the "Bayern Seppl," male prostitute

## Legal Figures

Military Judge (Kriegsgerichtsrat) Biron, chief investigative judge in the Fritsch case

Hans von Dohnanyi, adjutant of the Minister of Justice

Franz Gürtner, Minister of Justice

Major General Walter Heitz, president of the Reich Military Court

Military Judge Ernst Kanter, attached to the investigative panel

Senate President Rudolf Lehmann, member of the court-martial

# Dramatis Personae

Senate President Sellmer, nominally the presiding judge of the court-martial

Ministerial Councilor Heinrich Rosenberger, head of the Wehrmacht Legal Department

Military Judge Karl Sack, attached to the investigative panel as head of protocol

Colonel Baron von Schleinitz, adjutant of General Heitz

## Peripheral Figures

Colonel Karl Bodenschatz, adjutant of Goering

Ulrich von Hassell, ambassador recalled from Rome on February 4, 1938

Baron Hermann von Lüninck, chief president at Münster

Reich Bishop Ludwig Müller, head of Evangelical Church

Baron Konstantin von Neurath, Foreign Minister to February 4, 1938

Michael Obladen, Hamburg businessman involved in a Navy plot against the regime

Franz von Papen, former Chancellor, ambassador in Vienna

General Admiral Erich Raeder, commander in chief of the Navy

Carl Christian Schmid, government president at Düsseldorf

Dr. Erich Schultze, former East Prussian official and associate of various Opposition figures

Kurt von Schuschnigg, Chancellor of the Republic of Austria

Major General Count Hans von Sponeck, character witness for Fritsch

Count Wedel, police president of Potsdam

August Winnig, former chief president of East Prussia

# Time Chart

A document to which the author was given access too late to permit its use in the narrative of this volume confirms certain of the author's suppositions, refutes a few others. The salient points of the document are discussed in "A Supplementary Note" (see pages 422–423) and the reader is directed to the Note at appropriate points in the chronology below.

| | | |
|---|---|---|
| 1933 | January 30 | Hitler assumes chancellorship. Blomberg, with Reichenau as first assistant, becomes War Minister. |
| | October | Ludwig Beck succeeds Wilhelm Adam as head of Truppenamt (Army General Staff). |
| | November 22 | Incident at Wannsee station. |
| 1934 | February | Werner von Fritsch succeeds Kurt von Hammerstein-Equort in command of Army. |
| | June 30–July 2 | "Blood Purge" of SA and other elements. |
| | August 4 | Death of Hindenburg and institution of military oath to Hitler. |
| 1936 | July 8 or 9 | First Gestapo interrogation of Otto Schmidt. |
| | August 26 | Second interrogation of Schmidt. |
| | August (final days) | Hitler rejects the "dossier on Fritsch." |

| | | |
|---|---|---|
| 1937 | Autumn | Blomberg consults Rosenberger on marriage problem. |
| | November 5 (16:15–20:30) | Hossbach conference in Chancellery. |
| | November 9 | Fritsch's farewell audience with Hitler before departing for Egypt. |
| | November 10 | Fritsch leaves for Egypt. |
| | November 11 | Beck memorandum critical of Hitler's program. |
| | Early December | Blomberg secures Goering's support for his marriage. Goering concerts his plans with Himmler and Heydrich. Gestapo watch set on Fritsch in Egypt. Gestapo watch set on Eva Gruhn. |
| | December 22 | Blomberg gains Hitler's consent to marriage plans. |
| 1938 | January 2 | Fritsch returns from Egypt. |
| | January 10 or 11 | Fritsch and Raeder withdraw as marriage witnesses. |
| | January 12 | Marriage of Blomberg and Eva Gruhn. Hitler and Goering serve as witnesses. |
| | January 15 | Extended talk of Hitler and Fritsch (see Supplementary Note). |
| | January 15–22 | Resumption of interrogation of Schmidt and others. Reconstruction of "dossier on Fritsch." |
| | January 18 (?) | Interruption of Blomberg honeymoon by death of his mother. |
| | January 20 | Funeral at Eberswalde. |
| | January 21 | Telephone effort to activate Army leadership against Blomberg. |
| | (morning) | Gruhn file reaches Helldorf. |
| | (early afternoon) | Helldorf visits Keitel. |
| | January 22 (late morning) | Helldorf visits Goering at Karinhall. |
| | January 23 | Goering, Himmler, and Heydrich concert plans at Karinhall. |
| | January 24 (afternoon) | Blomberg asks Hossbach for conference with Hitler. |
| | (evening) | Encounter of Goering with Hossbach |

|  | and Wiedemann. Hitler informed by Goering of developments. |
|---|---|
| January 25 (2:15) | Hossbach rejects summons to Chancellery. |
| (10:00) | Hossbach with Hitler and Goering. |
| (ca. 11:00) | Goering calls on Blomberg. |
| (noon to 22:00) | Marathon pressures on Hossbach by Hitler and Goering. |
| (afternoon) | Keitel tells Fritsch about Blomberg scandal (see Supplementary Note). |
| (22:30) | Hossbach warns Fritsch. |
| January 26 (ca. 8:00) | Meeting of Hossbach and Fritsch in riding ring. |
| (ca. 10:00) | Hossbach reports violation of orders to Hitler. |
| (ca. 10:30-11:30) | Hossbach telephones von der Schulenburg. Hitler receives Blomberg. Goering asks help of Wiedemann. |
| (11:45) | Blomberg informs Keitel of developments. |
| (ca. 13:30) | Keitel visits Goering. Wiedemann conveys Goering's wishes to Hitler. |
| (ca. 14:00-16:00) | Hossbach with Hitler and Goering. |
| (ca. 16:00) | Hitler squeezes an "opinion" out of Gürtner. |
| (17:00) | First audience of Keitel with Hitler. |
| (ca. 19:30-21:30) | Hossbach with Hitler and Goering. |
| (21:30) | Fritsch confronted with Schmidt. |
| (ca. 22:30) | Fritsch summons Joachim von Stülpnagel. |
| January 26-27 (ca. 23:00-2:00) | Beck twice with Hitler, once with Fritsch. |
| January 27 (morning) | Schacht, Nebe, and Helldorf inform Gisevius of developments. Abwehr group is activated. Beck in Karinhall. Gürtner in Karinhall. |
| (ca. 10:00-14:00) | Fritsch interrogated by Huber. |
| (ca. 11:00-11:40) | Blomberg's farewell audience with Hitler. |
| (13:00) | Keitel's second meeting with Hitler. |

| | |
|---|---|
| (mid-afternoon) | Huber visits Ferdinand Strasse. |
| (afternoon)* | Blomberg departs for Italy. |
| (late afternoon) | Huber takes Schmidt and Weingärtner to Goering and Himmler. |
| (evening) | Huber discovers innocence of Fritsch. |
| January 28 | Wangenheim confronts Blomberg in |
| (morning) | Rome. Huber reports Fritsch's innocence to Best, Heydrich, and Himmler. Fritsch interrogated by Best (see Supplementary Note where doubt is raised about this). Fritsch suspended. Keitel with Hitler. Keitel confers with Rosenberger. Goering and Gürtner interrogate the Bayern Seppl and Schmidt. Goerdeler arrives and is taken to Gürtner. |
| (noon) | Hossbach told of dismissal. |
| (afternoon) | Keitel asks Rosenberger for memorandum on court problem. |
| (evening) | Wiedemann reproaches Hitler on treatment of Hossbach. |
| January 29 | Keitel with Hitler. Puttkamer protests |
| (morning) | treatment of Hossbach. Raeder received by Hitler. Oster's mission to Ulex. Gisevius's mission to Kluge. Goerdeler tries to stir up Wehrkreis IV.† Negotiations of Keitel and Goering with Brauchitsch. Rosenberger confers with Gürtner and Dohnanyi. |
| (afternoon) | Gürtner and Dohnanyi visit Wannsee station. Hitler agrees to court-martial (may have been following morning). Gürtner transmits formal opinion. |
| January 30 | Continued negotiations of Keitel and Goering with Brauchitsch. Schacht calls on Raeder and Stülpnagel. |
| (late afternoon) | Goltz undertakes defense of Fritsch. |

*Deduced from the fact that Wangenheim had to follow that evening.

† This assumption is based on the near certainty that Goerdeler had arrived in Berlin on the 28th. The plans exercise at Leipzig which he interrupted would hardly have been scheduled for the 30th, a Sunday, and the 31st would have been rather late for this action.

# Time Chart

| | |
|---|---|
| January 31 (late forenoon) | Rundstedt received by Hitler. |
| (afternoon?) | Hitler's first meeting with Brauchitsch. Nebe learns of "mistaken identity." |
| February 1 | Further negotiations of Keitel and Goering with Brauchitsch. Hitler's second meeting with Brauchitsch (could have been on following day). |
| February 2 | Negotiations of Keitel and Goering with Brauchitsch. |
| February 3 (morning) | Hitler agrees to appoint Brauchitsch. Fritsch yields to Hitler's demand for resignation (see Supplementary Note). |
| February 5 (early morning) | The media announce great *revirement* (see Supplementary Note on date). |
| (14:00–ca. 15:30) | Speech of Hitler to military leaders. Brauchitsch addresses generals. |
| (evening) | Hitler informs Cabinet. Hitler leaves for Berchtesgaden. |
| February 5 | Brauchitsch flies to Berchtesgaden to secure action on court-marital. |
| February 7 | Keitel and Canaris at Karinhall to discuss court procedure. |
| ca. February 11 | The investigators interrogate the Bayern Seppl. |
| February 13 | Hitler insists on continuation of proceedings. |
| ca. February 20 | Wannsee (third Gestapo) interrogation of Fritsch. |
| February 23 | Fritsch condemns proceedings in protocol. |
| March 1 | Biron and Sack check at Lichterfelde-East station. Gestapo interrogation of grooms and orderlies. |
| March 2 (18:00) | Discovery and interrogation of Captain von Frisch. |
| March 3 | Frisch snatched by Gestapo. Hitler again refuses to quash proceedings. |
| March 4 (late evening) | Hitler pressured into removing Frisch from Gestapo custody. |

| | | |
|---|---|---|
| | March 10 (morning) | Opening and adjournment of Fritsch trial. Captain Engel assumes post of Army adjutant. |
| | March 12 | German entry into Austria. |
| | March 17 (morning) | Resumption of Fritsch trial. |
| | March 18 (ca. noon) | Fritsch acquitted. |
| | (late evening) | Meeting of Brauchitsch with Gürtner. |
| | March 19 | Rosenberger's clash with Keitel. Hossbach-Canaris memorandum proposing demands on Hitler. Formulation of Fritsch's challenge to Himmler. |
| | ca. March 22–31 | Efforts of Gisevius, Helldorf, Goerdeler, and Puttkamer with Brauchitsch. |
| | March 30 | Hitler's letter to Fritsch. Rundstedt persuades Fritsch to drop challenge to Himmler (see Supplementary Note). |
| | April 7 | Fritsch's reply to Hitler. |
| | May 26 (ca. noon) | Lutze offers Ulex SA help against SS. |
| | May 28 | Hitler states intention to destroy Czechoslovakia. |
| | May 30 | Case Green revised to conform with aggressive intentions of Hitler. |
| | Early June | Ulex works on Bock and Brauchitsch. Kluge tries to address Brauchitsch through Keitel. |
| | June 13 (morning) | Hitler, aided by Brauchitsch, rings down curtain on Fritsch affair at Barth. |
| | June 15 | Fritsch appointed honorary colonel of Artillery Regiment 12. |
| | August 11 | Installation of Fritsch as honorary colonel. |
| 1939 | September 22 | Death of Fritsch near Warsaw. |
| 1942 | August | Liquidation of Otto Schmidt. |

# Table of Contents

xxiii

# Table of Contents

Illustrations between pages 228 and 229

# Hitler and His Generals

# CHAPTER I

# Hitler and the Military: The Honeymoon, 1933–36

"It is no exaggeration to say that a domestic incident constituted the prelude to tragedy." This is the verdict of Sir Nevile Henderson, Britain's last ambassador to Berlin, in viewing the turnover in German military leadership during the first months of 1938. In the closely tangled Blomberg and Fritsch affairs—the one involving the marriage of War Minister Werner von Blomberg to a woman of ill repute; the other, trumped-up charges of homosexuality against Army Commander Werner von Fritsch—he saw the overture to World War II.[1]

By exploiting these affairs to rid himself of the two most powerful Army leaders in Germany—and to intimidate those of like mind in the Generalität (the general officer corps)—Adolf Hitler was able to set his course virtually unimpeded on a foreign policy of limitless aggression. The military leadership, notably that of the Army, had been acting as a roadblock to the dictator's program for enlarging Germany's "living space." With his victory over the generals the way was opened to a vast expansionary drive that violated both German tradition and modern concepts of the legitimate use of power. At the same time key members of the military establishment were driven into the ranks of the conspiratorial Opposition: those seeking to overthrow the regime. Hereafter the military Opposition group would be at the center of resistance moves within the Third Reich. Though Hitler's relationship with the Wehrmacht (armed forces) is constantly in the foreground in the annals of Nazi Germany, only in July 1944 was the course of history influenced by it more directly than in early 1938.

[1] Henderson, *Failure of a Mission: Berlin, 1937–1939* (New York, 1940), 105.

1

In forming in 1935 the Wehrmacht from the Reichswehr (Army and Navy) of the Weimar Republic and the new Luftwaffe (Air Force), Hitler had drawn the blueprint for a tool of great capability that he envisioned manipulating to carry out his personal will. By the end of 1937 forging of the tool itself was well on the way to completion. But control of it rested in the hands of men who, for one reason or another, shrank from the use to which the Fuehrer planned to put it. Before we begin the story of how Hitler wrested direction of the armed forces from these men, we need to ask: What, more particularly, were the aims of Adolf Hitler and what was the nature of the instrument he required to realize them?

## Hitler's View of the German Future

No attempt can be made here to analyze in depth Hitler's ideas and intentions for Germany's external relations. This chapter will aim only to review briefly his basic position as a backdrop for the crucial turn in his relations with the Wehrmacht.

It is assumed here that, by the time he achieved power in 1933, Hitler had gone far in formulating his external programs. In all essential aspects these remained fixed in his mind and provided guideposts for every major decision he made in foreign relations. They flouted many realities and in the end they led Germany to disaster. "But," to quote Gerhard Weinberg, "the great burst of activity in Germany in the 1930's that soon spilled over Europe and affected the whole globe was no random excitement, no accidental explosion."[2]

In short, well before Hitler acquired the means to pursue his aims, he knew what he wanted. This is confirmed once more in evidence recently come to light on his outlook as it had been formed by the late spring of 1931: a record of two conversations with Richard Breiting, editor of the *Leipziger Neueste Nachrichten.* What we learn there amplifies the testimony of *Mein Kampf* and of its sequel (suppressed during the Fuehrer's regime but discovered in the postwar years) and the writings of Hermann Rauschning on the consistency of Hitler's outlook as it matured in the twenties and remained constant thereafter.[3] Perhaps most astounding—enough to have raised challenges to the authenticity of at least

[2] Weinberg, *The Foreign Policy of Hitler's Germany: Diplomatic Revolution in Europe, 1933-1936* (Chicago, 1970), 1. The introductory analysis, "The World through Hitler's Eyes," is particularly valuable.

2

part of Breiting's report—is the infinity of detail that jibes closely with what Hitler attempted in later years.[4]

The total impact of these sources concerning Hitler's views and plans leaves little doubt that, far from being an opportunist (except as to means) or a manipulator of power without design, he had both clear and firm ideas on what needed doing. Each major piece of evidence as it appeared has served to confirm and enlarge the existing picture and to support the dictum that, "except when he pledged his word," Adolf Hitler usually meant what he said.[5]

Hitler's closely related concepts of race and space are too familiar to require extended explanation here. What cannot be underscored too heavily is the deadly seriousness of these fantasies and his iron determination to make the solution of Germany's space problem on racial lines the primary objective of his policy. The oft-proclaimed national purpose of abrogating the Treaty of Versailles, notably by restoring part or all of the boundaries of 1914, was useful both in gaining popular support and in keeping attention focused on what was, in any event, a necessary way station. In Hitler's own mind, this aim was insignificant when contrasted with his dreams of Germany's grander destiny. Until 1933 he proclaimed the utter inadequacy of aiming to reacquire lands lost in World War I as a program for German policymakers. Involved was the relative bagatelle of 70,000 square kilometers of territory, when, as a *beginning*, he thought in terms of gaining 500,000 square kilometers.[6] Such a program demanded war on a grand scale. The process of acquiring, depopulating (of its native stocks), and repopulating (with Germanic settlers) successive masses of territory betokened limitless expansion whose only logical climax would have been world conquest.[7]

[3] *Hitler's Secret Book*, with an introduction by Telford Taylor (New York, 1961). See also Hermann Rauschning, *The Revolution of Nihilism* (New York, 1939), *The Voice of Destruction* (translation of *Gespräche mit Hitler*; New York, 1940).

[4] Edouard Calic, ed., *Ohne Maske: Hitler-Breiting Geheimgespräche 1931* (Frankfurt, 1968); English edition, *Unmasked: Two Confidential Interviews with Hitler in 1931* (London, 1971). The extraordinary prescience evidenced by Hitler in some of his forecasts and declarations of intention has led some reviewers to wonder whether there has not been some introduction of extraneous material. Thus Hugh Trevor-Roper in the London *Times*, March 7, 1971. The present writer has little personal doubt about the basically genuine character of the publication.

[5] John W. Wheeler-Bennett, *The Nemesis of Power: The German Army in Politics, 1918-1945* (2nd ed., London, 1964), 461.

[6] Weinberg, 6.

[7] The most convincing demonstration of this is that of Günter Moltmann in his essay "Weltherrschaftsideen Hitlers" in *Europa und Übersee, Festschrift für Egmont Zechlin* (Hamburg, 1961), 197-240.

After Hitler had embraced the premises inherent in the doctrines of race and space, his policy was determined for as long as his reign endured. War was now no longer the last resort in continuing policy but its indispensable instrument. Military conflict was to be delayed only as long as shorter range goals could be gained more cheaply and the arts of propaganda and diplomacy employed to isolate, divide, or enfeeble the selected victims. And of course the Wehrmacht had first to be built up and his own mastery over it fully assured.

Once Hitler had assumed the reins of government, it was no longer expedient to take the world so much into his confidence. Though he did not deny what he had revealed before 1933, he was never again so publicly explicit. And those who yearned to deceive themselves—they were legion both in Germany and elsewhere—welcomed the emphasis on more moderate goals, such as revision of the more onerous and less defensible aspects of the Paris settlements of 1919-20. When it was tactically or propagandistically useful, Hitler for a time continued to observe treaty provisions he had once denounced. Further, he entered into restrictive covenants, such as the Nonagression Pact with Poland (1934) and the Anglo-German Naval Agreement (1935). Needless to say, the instant a treaty obligation became obstructive of his ultimate designs, it ceased to be worth the paper on which it was written.

Hitler planned to move toward his long-range goals by stages which had a distinct form in his mind. Within a single decade he expected to solve both the internal and the external problems of the Reich. A mere five years of power, he predicted, would restore the shattered military might of Germany. "With 20 million workers and our technical heritage," he said to Breiting, "we need only four or five years of financial efforts to achieve military power, a power that will erase Versailles in order to assure the German people within this period the living space and the place on the continent to which from the racial and historical standpoint they are entitled."[8]

Hitler then unfolded to the newspaper editor the phantasma of a reconstitution of Europe which must have left his hearer, conscious of the current reality of a disarmed and truncated Germany, goggle-eyed. Within a year after Hitler's seizure of power Austria would voluntarily join the Reich. (His first and unsuccessful effort to take over Austria was in fact to be made in the year following

[8] Calic, 78-79.

4

that in which he became Chancellor.) The contiguous people defined by the Nazis as "German," such as the German-speaking Swiss, the Sudetenlanders of Czechoslovakia, the Dutch and the Flemings (in Nazi parlance "Low Germans"), and the Alsace-Lorrainers were marked for annexation. The former Austrian was also nothing loath to dispose of the Habsburg heritage. Bohemia would be annexed, Slovakia and Croatia made into separate but scarcely independent states. "Briefly stated," as Hitler laid down his views, "Switzerland, Belgium, Yugoslavia, and Czechoslovakia must disappear as states." Italy, the prospective ally, would receive its share of Balkan loot, while Poland, Romania, Hungary, and Bulgaria were each assigned appropriate places in a Nazi-dominated Europe. The Dutch and Scandinavians were fated at best to achieve the status of protectorates. A solid buffer of German-dominated territory would extend from the North Cape to the Black Sea with Finland and Bulgaria as flank guards. With their homelands swallowed by the Reich, young Danes and Dutchmen would "feel fortunate" to be able to join their ravishers in "ruthlessly" colonizing the East.[9]

The brief span of time the Nazi leader allowed himself to accomplish so much was predicated on awareness of the enormous power potential of the Soviet Union and the United States. By the end of the next decade they would be moving ahead steadily and could become formidable obstacles to his program, "We must complete our rebuilding before the Soviets have become a world power, before the area of 7 million square kilometers which belong to the United States have become the arsenal of world Jewry. These colossi are still sleeping. If they awaken it will be the finish of Germany."[10]

Along the way, as it became necessary, he would make deals with the British, the Vatican, the Americans, and perhaps even with Stalin. Sooner or later there would have to be a crusade against the Soviets. The British were the natural allies of Germany and had many imperial problems. To placate them, Germany must soft-pedal colonial claims and for the time being refrain from building an overseas fleet. With the awakening of Japan the United States sat on a powder keg and would also in time be preoccupied with China. "I am only saying that we find ourselves in a favorable world situation. For that reason we [National Socialists] do not

[9] *Ibid.*, 81-82, 89-91, 100.
[10] *Ibid.*, 71-72.

intend to come to power in order to govern but to embark upon a *Weltpolitik* [world-embracing policy]." As so often in later years, Hitler interlarded threats with assurances that he would take drastic steps only if challenged, or if the parties faced with mutilation or extinction were so unreasonable as to resist. The Soviets would be attacked only "if they should oppose German intentions." France would be partitioned only if she proved difficult.[11]

In this monologic dialogue, whose brutal frankness is exceeded only by his "table conversations" during the war in the East,[12] Hitler revealed how much thought he had already given to the military means for pursuing his wide-flung political aims. "Our ascent is hopeless unless our physical and spiritual powers are placed in the service of total mobilization." What most preoccupied him was the shortest path to the buildup and control of the Reichswehr. He had watched with interest the intrigues in that body during the Weimar period and was much concerned with the Army's leadership. He was familiar with the names of the principal generals and obviously knew something about them.[13] He had already made up his mind that he could never carry out his program with the traditional Army and its leaders. "A new Army will come into existence and that with a new General Staff."[14]

This prophecy was never to find complete realization. Even in the dying days of the Third Reich, the old staff traditions could not be entirely erased. As the 100,000-man Army of the Republic more than quintupled during the thirties and then swelled into the mass armies of World War II, Hitler still found himself unable to dispense with the experienced Generalität.

## Hitler and the Generalität in the Nazi Rise to Power

Unquestionably the relation between sword and swastika will continue to figure among the least resolved of the many disputations on the history of Hitler's Reich. What the role of the Army was in his rise to power, in the march to full dictatorship, and in later conspiratorial activities will have to await the definitive verdict of history. The compass of this study can permit no more than scrutiny of this basic problem that is part of the framework within which the story here must be presented.

[11] *Ibid.*, 77, 79, 88, 91–92.
[12] *Hitler's Secret Conversations, 1941–1944*, with an introductory essay on the mind of Adolf Hitler by H. R. Trevor-Roper (New York, 1953).

6

# Hitler and the Military

Among the major tragedies of the Weimar Republic is its failure to assure itself of the sympathy and ungrudging support of its armed forces. Traditional military prejudice combined with unfortunate circumstances to prevent the democratic order from ever receiving a proper chance to prove itself. For most of the Army and Navy leaders the Republic was a political dead end into which the nation had blundered in its despair after the lost war. They were prepared to protect it from harm during this national sleepwalking while hastening the awakening and perhaps cushioning a possible fall. The centrifugal and divisive forces within Germany worried them and left them skeptical about holding the nation together without coercive means. Since these latter could not be provided on any enduring basis by the military, the ideal of most of the generals was a regime, with or without monarchy, on much the pattern of the Empire. There should again be an authoritarian civil order and the Army should once more constitute "the school for the nation."[15]

There is some relevance in the fact that the officer corps of the Reichswehr was more aristocratic in composition than that of any other military force of the twentieth century. Owing to the severe treaty restrictions on its size (4000 officers), it could be largely staffed by members of old military families devoted to traditional concepts. Most of the officers entertained antirepublican and especially anti-Social Democratic prejudices and were bound to be sensitive to the intermittent challenges to their role in state and society. It proved easy to ignore Western experience in World War I and convince themselves that a democratic order was not suited to dealing effectively with such modern problems as total mobilization in wartime.

[13] Since this contrasts with Hitler's relative lack of concern with the personalities of any but the top figures of the general officer corps in the period 1933-38, these allusions have raised some doubts about the authenticity of this part of Breiting's record. However, it may be argued that in 1931, when the leadership of the Army was in a more fluid state than later, the emerging figures among the generals were of greater interest than they would be under the more settled conditions of the Blomberg-Fritsch era. Also, Hitler was accustomed to bone up on probable conversation topics before receiving visitors he wished to impress.

[14] Calic, 44, 109.

[15] Much of the most searching and informed analysis of the Reichswehr's role in Hitler's achievement of power and the development of dictatorial rule is to be found in pp. 685-966 of the monumental work of Karl Dietrich Bracher, Wolfgang Sauer, and Gerhard Schultz, *Die nationalsozialistische Machtergreifung: Studien zur Errichtung des totalitären Herrschaftssystems in Deutschland 1933/34* (2nd rev. ed., Cologne and Opladen, 1962; cited hereafter as Bracher *et al.*).

7

In National Socialism there was much that the Reichswehr leaders found repellent. They detested its vulgarity and its revolutionary disregard for traditional values. On the credit side was its strength as a popular movement, potentially sufficient so that it could attain power legally and convert the masses, including the workers, to national goals and military resurgence. It also promised the Army a political refuge where it would be guarded against civilian criticism and the constant threat of hostile "reform" moves.

## The Elevation of Blomberg

After Hitler became Chancellor a first consideration from the Nazi standpoint was regroupment of the military leadership. There was the immediate need of a new Reichswehr Minister to take a central role in the transition. The fallen Minister and Chancellor, Kurt von Schleicher, had been the archetype of "political general." Throughout the Republic's history he had been in the middle of every intrigue in the Reichswehr Ministry. In the end his machinations helped to lose him the vital support of the aged President von Hindenburg and, however unintentionally, did much to clear the road for Hitler.

Both the Army commander, Baron Kurt von Hammerstein-Equord, and his chief of staff, the head of the Truppenamt (Troop Office, later renamed General Staff) Wilhelm Adam, were highly suspect figures to the new regime. The former had been a close collaborator of Schleicher's, had leaned toward the use of arms to prevent Hitler's accession to power, and was a reputed "liberal."[16] Adam, a crusty Bavarian not given to compromise or soft speech, was clearly among those least inclined to accommodate himself to the new order. Neither, therefore, was a likely candidate for the Ministry post.

There is still much haziness about the backstage maneuvers by which Werner von Blomberg became Reichswehr Minister. Hitler's first requirement was that the new Minister be drawn from among generals who had stood apart from Schleicher. This also accorded

[16] It shocked many, for example, that Hammerstein would not repudiate a daughter who had turned Communist. According to the late General Vincenz Müller, Schleicher in their last conversation of Arpil 29, 1934, related that Hammerstein had proposed to arrest Hindenburg and to govern with the Reichswehr. V. Müller, *Ich fand das wahre Vaterland,* ed. Klaus Mammach (Leipzig, 1963), 349.

8

with the wishes of Hindenburg, who had the decisive voice in the matter and who desired to "finish with the methods of Schleicher."[17] The names most often mentioned, with Blomberg's, were those of Werner von Fritsch and Joachim von Stülpnagel, who found favor because they eschewed the political dabbling to which Schleicher was so addicted. Blomberg had the kind of showy social presence which captivated the old President. A major recommendation in Hitler's eyes was the strong backing of Blomberg by Colonel Walther von Reichenau. Thus far Reichenau had been the only soldier of some prominence who had committed himself to National Socialism, a flirtation which earned him the censure of Schleicher.[18] Reichenau may well have induced Blomberg to make a secret detour to Hitler's mountain retreat at Berchtesgaden during one of the general's trips to Geneva, where he represented the Reichswehr Ministry in armament discussions, with the aim of getting closer to the Fuehrer.[19]

Blomberg's career had been one of ups and downs. After a meteoric rise to head of the Truppenamt, he had fallen out with Schleicher and had been transferred to the Wehrkreis (military district) command in East Prussia. He was accounted one of the more adaptable members of the Generalität and under the Republic had been credited with democratic sympathies. In East Prussia he had backed his first chief of staff, Colonel Erich von Bonin, called the "red" Bonin because of his republican views, in an effort to persuade the trade unions to set up a reserve system for the defense of the province. The attempt had been aborted by the rooted mistrust of the Social Democrats for the military.[20]

Blomberg next fell under the influence of the dynamic Reichenau, who succeeded Bonin in 1931, and of Ludwig Müller, chief chaplain of the Wehrkreis. Blomberg was persuaded to look to the SA (the party militia) for help with the East Prussian defense system and dispatched Pastor Müller to Hitler's Berchtesgaden retreat to seek his agreement. Hitler was transported at this first sign of renewed contact with the Wehrmacht since the breach of relations at the time of the Beer Hall Putsch of 1923. Too little time remained before the seizure of power for the implementation of the project,

[17] Franz von Papen, *Der Wahrheit eine Gasse* (Munich, 1952), 275.
[18] Interview with Alix von Reichenau, June 23, 1970.
[19] Reichenau was certainly far more eager than Blomberg to move closer to Hitler.
[20] Interview with Dr. Erich Schultze, February 15, 1970.

but the incident helped induce Hitler to try Blomberg as Reichswehr Minister.[21]

## A Soldier-Rebel: Walther von Reichenau

The doom of Hammerstein and Adam was sealed with Hitler's elevation and the appointment of Blomberg. This raised the problem of successors and here the two newcomers had at hand their candidate to take the place of Hammerstein—Reichenau. Of the prominent figures in the Generalität of the Hitler era no other officer more resisted the traditional mold. It would be difficult to imagine a greater contrast than that between him and, for example, Fritsch. Long before 1933 he had discarded the prejudices and habits of thought of his class. Though an aristocrat related to high Bohemian and (by marriage) Silesian nobility, he lacked the early association with large landed property which did so much to form the outlook of the officer corps. As a boy he had accompanied his father to sell Krupp guns in South America. He had toured the United States and other countries, spoke excellent English, and was acquainted with several other languages. All in all, the young Reichenau had thoroughly emancipated himself from any taint of provincialism.

By the advent of the thirties, Reichenau, though sharing the skepticism of his fellows about the Weimar Republic, differed from them in having lost faith equally in the destiny of his class. He never seems to have become ideologically a Nazi or to have fallen a victim of Hitler's famed charisma. What most attracted him may well have been a kinship of spirit and of eagerness to shake off the dead hand of the past. To a man like Reichenau, impatient with outworn ties and shackling habits of thought, Nazism was

[21] Interviews with Dr. Erich Schultze in 1969 and 1970. Dr. Schultze, in 1933 Social Democratic councilor of Königsberg and member of the Provincial Council of East Prussia, was also a "secret" Reichswehr officer and was dispatched to East Prussia in the late twenties by War Minister Wilhelm Gröner to work out a reserve system that in time might extend to the rest of the Reich. A friend of Bonin's and Müller's, he was closely associated with the efforts to solve the reserve problem but, as a dedicated anti-Nazi, refused to undertake the mission to Berchtesgaden. On his larger role in matters related to this study see below, pp. 54–56. General Adam's memoirs relate that in June 1938, during the course of an inspection trip in the Rhineland, Goering commented that it was Hindenburg who had forced Blomberg on Hitler, describing him as the Army's best soldier. Adam himself believed that Reichenau had pulled the strings, counting on moving into the War Ministry with Blomberg. Wilhelm Adam, "Erinnerungen" (in the Archives of the Institut für Zeitgeschichte—referred to hereafter as IfZ), 166.

bound to appear a wave of the future that would sweep away encumbrances to effective political, social, and *military* action.

This should not be taken to imply that Reichenau was even then blind to weaknesses and dangers in the movement. He detested the vulgarity and crude adventurism of many of the brown-clad troops. "I hate these swastikamen," he burst out (in English) to his wife on returning from some party affair.[22] Though striving to bring the Army closer to National Socialism, he did not for a moment brook party encroachment on Army preserves. It may be said that he promoted National Socialism in the Army to make it an organ of the National Socialist state and thus less vulnerable. Least of all was he inclined to promote the SS (the elite security echelon created as Hitler's bodyguard) as a new Wehrmacht arm.[23]

Hitler's leaning toward Reichenau was as much influenced by appreciation of his flexibility and innovative disposition as by his receptivity to Nazi ideas. The Fuehrer later regarded him as the only general who understood motorization.[24] Yet he was uneasy about a soldier who was so politically involved. Undoubtedly he felt more comfortable with men like Rundstedt or Guderian who stuck to their military concerns and left politics to the (Nazi) politicians. The man, in fact, was too independent by half. In East Prussia Reichenau had not hesitated to attend dinner meetings of the organization of Jewish-front fighters and was with difficulty dissuaded from appearing there in uniform.[25] He was disturbed by nationalist extremes in Hitler Youth training and went so far as to dispatch a personal emissary to Britain to look into possibilities for setting up in Germany a separate organization of 100,000 boys under his patronage to be affiliated with the international Boy Scout movement.[26]

In the first months of World War II Reichenau was to carry readiness to oppose Hitler's offensive plans to an extreme paralleled only by such determined Opposition leaders as Hans Oster: Rei-

[22] Reichenau interview, June 23, 1970.

[23] Reichenau's extensive notes from the years 1933–34 underscore his preoccupation with this problem. *Ibid.*

[24] Fritz Wiedemann, *Der Mann der Feldherr werden wollte: Erlebnisse und Erfahrungen des Vorgesetzten Hitlers im ersten Weltkrieg und seines späteren persönlichen Adjutanten* (Dortmund, 1949), 102.

[25] Horst von Mellenthin, "Niederschrift über eine Unterredung zwischen Herrn General a. D. Horst von Mellenthin und Dr. Krausnick" (in IfZ, ZS 105), 2.

[26] As related by Prince Hubertus zu Loewenstein, an anti-Nazi then in exile, who was approached but refused to serve as intermediary with the British. Conversation with the author on June 29, 1971.

11

chenau went to the length of trying to sabotage the attack by notifying the British.[27] Before he died in 1942 he was to take issue with Hitler on so many fronts that the mere mention of his name would sting the Fuehrer to fury.[28]

The more that is learned about Reichenau, the greater force there is in the argument that he alone of the generals of the Nazi era demonstrated the combination of insight, courage, drive, and sheer brutality that could have stopped Hitler before disaster overtook the German nation and the world.[29] But antagonism against him as "the Nazi general" and his offenses against professional decorum closed the minds of many and prevented him from achieving a position from which he could have challenged the dictator.[30] He was charged with having an all-consuming ambition and, with far less justice, being a cynical opportunist. Brimming with life that he savored to the full, he neither could nor would observe the restraints expected of a Prussian officer. Everywhere, too, there were people who smarted from his inability to suffer fools gladly.

Reichenau appears to have been confident that, with the backing of Hitler and Blomberg, he would make the leap from the lowest rung in the generals' ladder, which he had just reached, to the highest. Blomberg went so far as to threaten resignation if his candidate were rejected. Though fading fast, Hindenburg was still stubborn enough to repel this intrusion upon his prerogative. Rei-

[27] For the full story see Harold C. Deutsch, *The Conspiracy against Hitler in the Twilight War* (Minneapolis, 1968), 72-77. Since publication of that study the author has been able to confirm the incident through the testimony of the two British intermediaries, Counsul General Jasper Leadbitter and Peter Tennant, head of the British National Export Council, January 14 and July 7, 1970.

[28] As related by General Franz Halder to General Georg von Sodenstern. Sodenstern interrogation of September 10, 1947, (in IfZ, ZS 149), 11.

[29] It is astonishing how unanimously this view is expressed by those, including Opposition-oriented soldiers, who knew him well, especially from serving under him. Cf. Hans von Salmuth's letter to Dr. Vogelsang of August 6, 1955 (in IfZ, ZS 133); Hermann Foertsch, "Unterredung mit General a. D. Foertsch am 15.10.51 in München" (in IfZ, ZS 37), 4; Edgar Röhricht, *Pflicht und Gewissen: Erinnerungen eines deutschen Generals 1932 bis 1944* (Stuttgart, 1965), 81-82, 115; Walter Warlimont, "Interpretation and Commentary on the Jodl Diaries, 1937-1945," Part I, 1937-39 (unpublished account on microfilm in the National Archives, Washington— hereafter NA), 118.

[30] A fine athlete who loved to show his proficiency while demonstrating his democratic ways, he would participate in cross-country runs, "half naked" (i.e., in a track suit) as Rundstedt disgustedly put it. Rundstedt interview with Baron von Siegler, November 26, 1951 (in IfZ, ZS 129). During the Polish campaign he stripped to swim across the Vistula. He drove his compressor-equipped Mercedes at reckless speed. He would address his men familiarly and his superiors with less than the ceremony they expected.

chenau to him was too young (actually forty-eight), too little "serious," and too inexperienced for the post. "This man has not even commanded a regiment," he said disgustedly to Vice Chancellor Franz von Papen; "how can he then want to step to the head of the Army?" Blomberg, to all intents and purposes, was shown the door.[31] Certainly all other Army influences that could reach the old President were also thrown against "the upstart." The only greater fear among the general officer corps was that Hitler would try to put over Ernst Röhm, the dreaded leader of the SA.[32] So the bitterly disappointed Reichenau was passed by and the choice fell on Fritsch, whom Papen had recommended to Hindenburg.[33] Together with its departing chief, the Generalität heaved a vast sigh of relief. "The cup has passed us by," Hammerstein announced in triumph to his office staff. "It is all over with Reichenau and Röhm. I can lay things into Fritsch's hands."[34]

## The Impact of the Blood Purge of June-July 1934

Reichenau had to content himself with carrying on at the Ministeramt (Office of the Minister) in which he was Blomberg's right hand. There he was to play a fateful role in promoting his aim of making the Army a true organ of the Nazi state, though a force independent of the party and the SA. His task was facilitated by the ardor with which Hitler undertook to woo the Army in the first years of his rule. He was wise enough to make haste slowly in pursuing his design to turn it into an instrument of his will. The first necessity was to mold it into an effective weapon; for that he needed the confidence and unreserved collaboration of the military professionals before whose expertise he still stood in considerable awe. On assuming control of the government he pro-

[31] As reported by Papen to the colloquium of the Europäische Publikation e. V. (referred to hereafter as E.P.), protocol of March 3, 1953, 26.

[32] There was much anxious talk about this nightmarish possibility in offices of the Army high command. Countess Margarete von Hardenberg, then Fräulein von Oven and Hammerstein's secretary, found the perfume-reeking Röhm so nauseating on one occasion that she avoided shaking hands with him and was teased by Hammerstein: "You weren't exactly friendly with your future boss." Hardenberg interview, February 20, 1970.

[33] Papen to the colloquium of the E.P., protocol of March 3, 1953, 26. Papen and Fritsch had been together for three years at the War Academy. The then Captain Edgar Röhricht, who was present when Reichenau received the bad news by a telephone call from Blomberg, testifies that for a moment Reichenau lost his composure, his monocle falling out of his eye onto the desk. Röhricht, *Pflicht und Gewissen*, 54.

[34] Hardenberg interview, February 20, 1970.

claimed his "love of our Army as the bearer of our arms and the symbol of our great past."[35] Four days later (February 7) he made an address at the War Ministry to the principal commanders, the first of the artful appeals with which he was to score so effectively in the six years which followed. The most important step toward the achievement of his goals, he assured them, was to build up the armed forces. Pacifism must be crushed and the fitness of German youth and its readiness to bear arms promoted. In contrast to Italy, there would be no amalgam of the Army and the political militia. Thus flattery, cajolery, and reassurance were interlarded to dupe his hearers.[36]

The artistry of the great dissembler is most fully revealed in the way he disguised the very price he exacted as another element of reassurance. The armed forces were to remain unpolitical and above all party ties. They would never be called upon to subdue internal conflict, for which he had "other means." This promise seemed all to the good but the reverse side of the coin seems to have been lost upon those to whom he spoke: he reserved to himself a free hand in implementing his revolution and in dealing with those who might oppose it!

The following weeks brought more flattering words and gestures. "We wish to educate [the nation] in reverence for our old Army," he proclaimed in an election speech. The opening of the new Reichstag on March 21 was "staged" in the Garrison Church at Potsdam, the burial place of Frederick the Great and a nationalist holy of holies. Hitler also excelled on every occasion in showing veneration for Hindenburg, still potent as a symbol of the imperial military tradition.

For half a generation Germany's soldiers had been largely denied public compliments and honors and Hitler poured balm on their wounded feelings. Still, flattery and promises lose their luster if not accompanied by solid benefits. The new regime was undoubtedly serious about abrogating the military restrictions of the Versailles Treaty. It was soon tooling up for rearmament and evidently determined not to count the cost. Where previous governments had hesitated and skimped, this one was coldly purposeful. They would have been strange soldiers (not merely strange *German* soldiers) who did not welcome ending one-sided restrictions on the

[35] Bracher *et al.*, 710.
[36] A digest of the speech is in the papers of Horst von Mellenthin (in IfZ, ZS 105). It is also summarized by Bracher *et al.*, 710-711.

# Hitler and the Military

forces to which they belonged and gaining full equality with neighboring states. Nor could they fail to rejoice in better conditions of service and more rapid promotions. Hitler for a time also made motions toward bringing back the monarchy most senior officers favored.

For a rounded picture one must further recall that most soldiers, like other Germans, perceived attractions in the new order. Bridging class differences, stressing national unity against petty particularisms, and promoting the simple joys of workers and peasants along cultural and recreational lines appealed to the less castebound officers. Down to 1936 (except for Austria in 1934) there were no foreign adventures. Instead the bonds of Versailles seemed to be loosening without materially worsening relations with the Western Powers.

Even the Blood Purge of June 30, 1934, seemed on balance a plus from the Army's standpoint. Röhm had been disappointed of any hope to succeed Hammerstein that January. However, the Army leaders were still torn by anxiety that Hitler might yield to SA pressures and permit a major encroachment on the military preserve. For a time Hitler tried his customary game of balancing opposing forces. Blomberg later claimed to have warned him that "we German soldiers would defend our position with our lives and that he might soon have to cope with civil war." Only when Röhm seemed inclined to force the dictator's own hand did Hitler join those determined to curb the SA.[37]

Unquestionably Blomberg and Reichenau were heavily involved in the background of the purge, the latter probably even more than it is possible to establish.[38] Yet they can hardly have welcomed the more indiscriminate and revolting aspects of the affair. Of the several hundred persons murdered without pretense of legal pro-

[37] Blomberg interrogation, 7th Army Interrogation Center, September 23, 1945, 3 (in NA).

[38] Letter from Franz Halder to Helmut Krausnick, October 8, 1954 (in IfZ, ZS 240 (V)). Recent studies indicate that Reichenau, though his role was primary, was by no means so isolated as was formerly supposed. Fritsch and his chief of staff, General Ludwig Beck, were apparently neither caught unawares nor standing entirely apart. Whatever they knew of an impending blow at the SA, however, does not imply realization that it was to take the form of a lawless and, in many respects, indiscriminate massacre. Cf. Heinrich Bennecke, *Die Reichswehr und der "Röhm-Putsch"* (Munich, 1962), and Klaus-Jürgen Müller, "Reichswehr und 'Röhm-Affaire.' Aus den Akten des Wehrkreiskommandos (Bayer.) VII," in *Militärgeschichtliche Mitteilungen*, Vol. 1 (1968), 107-144. Fritsch, says his adjutant Mellenthin, was horrified by the manner of proceeding against the SA. "Niederschrift," 11.

15

ceedings, only Röhm and the other SA leaders could, with any show of likelihood, be accused of plotting against the state. Most of the rest fell victim to nothing more than old grudges or rivalries on the part of one or another of the Nazi engineers of the coup. Most shocking from the Army's standpoint was the shooting of General von Schleicher, his close associate General von Bredow, and the wife of the former. Though there is small probability that Blomberg and Reichenau were themselves involved, this put a strain on their relations with their military peers.[39]

Hitler, also, was probably not involved personally in this particular abomination. It would have been too dangerous at a time when Hindenburg lingered on and the Reichswehr continued powerful in the state. Having eliminated his SA as a power factor and with party prestige at a low ebb, he was unprepared to invite a confrontation with the Army. On June 30 itself he had said to one of his adjutants: "It has always been my view that we can achieve our goals only with the Reichswehr and never against it."[40] It was imperative, therefore, to disassociate himself from the crime by voicing condemnation and horror and reporting that the SS men involved had been apprehended and summarily shot.[41]

The generals, no doubt, were eager to believe this and their resentment turned in other directions. Part was understandably aimed at Blomberg, who should have gone to the bottom of the matter and found out who had issued orders for Schleicher's death. Fritsch appears to have been badly perplexed. He might have gone over

[39] Blomberg insisted after the war that he had been assured that Schleicher was to be arrested and properly tried. He also claimed that Schleicher had been a "very close friend of Röhm's." Blomberg interrogation, September 23, 1945, 3. Gerhard Engel, Hitler's Army adjutant from 1938 to 1942, held that the fact that Reichenau was an old regimental (Guards) comrade of either Schleicher or Bredow— he didn't know which—speaks against his having been in any way an accomplice. Interview with General Engel, May 11, 1970. Röhricht ( *Pflicht und Gewissen*, 66) relates how at the Propaganda Ministry he was told by a party member, who was shot later that day, that the Gestapo men sent to arrest Schleicher found him and his wife already dead. This version would support the claims of Blomberg about the intended arrest and would make the murder a "private" enterprise of someone among the managers of June 30, almost certainly SS leaders Himmler and/or Heydrich.

[40] Wiedemann, *Der Mann der Feldherr werden wollte*, 66.

[41] As related to Engel by General Walther von Brauchitsch, Fritsch's successor as Army commander in 1938. Engel was later told a similar story by an SS officer named Breithaupt. Engel interview, May 11, 1970. It is not clear in what manner Hitler conveyed these claims to the generals. The best guess may be that it was done through Blomberg in the address discussed below.

16

# Hitler and the Military

Blomberg's head to Hindenburg to demand an investigation, but he had been to Neudeck, the President's East Prussian estate, only a few days before June 30 and had found him in a mental haze and a physical state that forecast his early demise. Hindenburg could scarcely be brought to talk of anything but his experiences in the wars of 1866 and 1870.[42]

Fritsch does seem to have confronted Blomberg in an exchange that engendered some heat.[43] Blomberg was persuaded that the mood of the generals was sufficiently serious to demand a personal appearance before them. The result was not a happy one since the attempt to justify some proceeding against Schleicher by alleging that he had been in concert with a foreign power did not prove very convincing. "We refused to buy that" is the report of Fritsch's adjutant, the later General von Mellenthin.[44]

The generals' suspicions turned naturally against the SS leaders, Himmler and Heydrich. The former was usually assumed to have given the fatal order.[45] Their presumed accomplice, Goering, was more difficult to assail without striking perilously close to Hitler. However much an intruder, he was also now one of them as the commander of the Luftwaffe.

Fritsch, for one, refused to be satisfied with Blomberg's specious explanations. He now ventured into the lion's den by calling on Goering. Taking his stand as the Army's representative, he asked Goering as a fellow general to intervene with Hitler in favor of a thorough investigation and prosecution of those responsible for the murders (supposedly 478) of the purge. Goering, of course, took umbrage but could not refuse to submit the matter to Hitler.[46]

At this critical point Himmler and Heydrich took a hand. Though our source reports only that they had "gotten wind of the danger,"

[42] Mellenthin, "Niederschrift," 10. Mellenthin, as Fritsch's adjutant, was present at the talk with Hindenburg.

[43] Mellenthin (ibid., 11) states this as a strong supposition. More positive is the testimony of Hans Bernd Gisevius, Bis zum bittern Ende (enlarged ed., Zurich, 1954), 181.

[44] Mellenthin, "Niederschrift," 12.

[45] Engel interview, May 11, 1970.

[46] This account is derived from the narration of two men who were close to one or another aspect of the events of June 30, Goering's cousin Herbert and Hans Bernd Gisevius, at that time in the police section of the Ministry of the Interior. Their accounts, which apparently agreed fully, were recorded the same evening (June 17, 1938) by one of their hearers, Ulrich von Hassell. From the unpublished papers of Hassell (copy in possession of author; cited hereafter as Hassell Papers).

17

it must have been Goering who alerted them to it. They delivered to Hitler a compilation Heydrich had made of hostile foreign comments on the excesses of the purge. This "magnificent weapon" as its author boasted, so roused Hitler that he rejected all pressure for an investigation. But Himmler and Heydrich were given reason for further hatred of Fritsch and seeing in him a personal antagonist. The incident can only have contributed to the common animosity and sense of rivalry toward the Army commander on which the later resurgence of their 1934 alliance with Goering was based.

How do the balance sheets of the parties affected stack up on the June purge of 1934? The verdict is simple in the case of the SA, which was demolished as a significant force in the National Socialist state. Decapitated, it vegetated on under Victor Lutze, whom Reichenau had suggested as Röhm's successor because of his stupidity and lack of dangerous leadership qualities.[47] Insofar as a spark of life lingered in the organization, it was expressed in impotent rancor against the SS that only once threatened to burst into flame: in the Wehrmacht crisis of 1938 the SA was roused sufficiently to make a fruitless offer of alliance to the beleaguered Army.[48]

The Army could feel delivered from a deadly menace. On the eve of June 30 its leaders had felt so threatened that they barricaded the Reichswehr Ministry with barbed wire and instructed department heads to "keep their pistols within easy reach in their desk drawers."[49] It could also tell itself that it had been freed of an aspiring competitor in the military field. Hitler had opted for it against the SA radicals and its monopoly as a bearer of arms seemed assured. "There is only one bearer of arms in the state, the Wehrmacht," he reiterated in the Reichstag on July 12.[50] He had kept his pledge not to call on the Army in internal crises and had given a smashing demonstration of "the other means" to which he had darkly referred. In the process, however, a new competitor was raised for the Army in the SS which in time did not hesitate to strike at its leadership. Hans Oster summed it up in a notation

[47] Foertsch, "Unterredung," 4. Thus Lutze was known to be quite hopeless as a speaker.
[48] See below, pp. 380–382.
[49] General Beck sent around his secretary, Fräulein von Benda, with a note to this effect. Interview with Luise Jodl, June 24, 1970.
[50] Röhricht, *Pflicht und Gewissen*, 73.

18

that fell into the hands of his captors in 1944. "June 30, 1934," he wrote, "was the first opportunity to nip in the bud the *methods of a gang of robbers*. In this struggle between the Wehrmacht and the SS, however, Himmler and Heydrich emerged as victors."[51] The birth of the SS state took place in the bloody labors of June–July 1934.

Much can be said for the view that thereafter the Army carried a crippling psychological burden because of its comparative quiescence after the murder of two of its most highly placed members and the wife of the one. Awareness of this left a self-doubt that endured into and beyond the crisis of 1938. Once it had been so plainly violated, the proud tradition of comradeship in the officer corps was no longer unassailable. The hesitations, inner divisions, and eager rationalizations that were to paralyze the Generalität in the Fritsch affair were thus a carryover from the moral defeat it had suffered in 1934.

## *The* Coups d'État *of August 2, 1934*

After June 1934 the Army was less than ever situated to repel the two strokes by which the now firmly established dictator extended his grip on the Reichswehr (now well along in its evolution into the Wehrmacht; formal establishment was then but a year away). In form and reality his exploitation of the death of the old President on August 2 can be labeled a dual *coup d'état*. However artfully it was camouflaged by official verbiage and the provision of a plebiscite, the absorption of the presidential functions and prerogatives by the "Fuehrer and Chancellor" was subversive of the Reich Constitution. And in his usurpation Hitler not only appropriated a chief of state's command over the armed forces but transformed the bond between commander and soldier into a personal one by requiring an oath of slavish obedience to himself.

Was Adolf Hitler personally the architect of these momentous steps? So far as the oath is concerned, it may have been a welcome but unsolicited gift from Reichenau. Unquestionably the actual formula was decided on and dictated by Reichenau the day before

[51] *Spiegelbild einer Verschwörung: Die Kaltenbrunner Berichte an Bormann und Hitler über das Attentat vom 20. Juli 1944. Geheime Dokumente aus dem ehemaligen Reichssicherheitshauptamt*, ed. Karl Heinz Peter (Stuttgart, 1961), 451. On Oster, see below, pp. 50–51, 53.

Hindenburg's death.[52] Whether this had already been cleared with Blomberg remains undetermined. The best guess is probably that the inspiration was Reichenau's, that he easily converted Blomberg to his view, and that the War Minister thereupon secured the ready consent of Hitler.[53]

From 1919 to 1933 the formula of the soldiers' oath had read: "I swear to be faithful to the Reich Constitution and vow that, as a brave soldier, I will at all times protect the German Reich and its lawful institutions and will be obedient to the Reich President and to my superiors." In December 1933, it had been changed to: "I swear by God this sacred oath that I will serve my people and fatherland at all times faithfully and honestly and, as a brave and obedient soldier, will be prepared at all times to stake my life for this oath." And now the August 2, 1934, formula was: "I swear by God this sacred oath that I will render unconditional obedience to the Fuehrer of the German Reich and people, Adolf Hitler, the commander in chief of the Wehrmacht, and, as a brave soldier, will be prepared at all times to stake my life for this oath."[54]

The new oath violated law and precedent both by its ultrapersonalized form and by being administered not only to newly enlisted soldiers but to the entire Army. It was sprung as a complete surprise on all but the small group directed to work on it in the War Ministry. Blomberg appeared at the Ministry in the afternoon of August 2 before the summoned officers of the capital's military establishment. With a solemn air he acknowledged the formal notification of Hindenburg's death and then spoke only a few sentences. Germany, he proclaimed, by the will of the nation and by destiny

[52] This statement rests solidly on the testimony of Captain (later General) Hermann Foertsch to whom the oath was dictated by Reichenau. *Schuld und Verhängnis: Die Fritsch-Krise im Frühjahr 1938 als Wendepunkt in der Geschichte der nationalsozialistischen Zeit* (Stuttgart, 1951), 64. Röhricht (*Pflicht und Gewissen*, 76–77) relates how that morning Reichenau asked for proposals for a new oath formula based on the union of the offices of President and Chancellor. The suggestions of the three or four officers involved were then carried by Foertsch to Reichenau who dictated the official version. That Reichenau set up the new formula and was the initiating spirit in the affair is further confirmed by his widow. Reichenau interview, June 23, 1970.

[53] Papen (377) was convinced that Hitler and Blomberg had gotten together on the question on August 1. Since Reichenau directed members of his staff to give him suggestions that morning, the agreement of Blomberg and Hitler may have been gained on the previous day. Or Reichenau may have cleared with them after fixing on the new formula.

[54] The first two oaths are given in E.P., *Die Vollmacht des Gewissens* (Munich, 1956), I, 119. The third is in Foertsch, *Schuld und Verhängnis*, 64.

was embodied henceforth in Hitler alone. The Reichswehr was doing no more than it should when it supported this view. He concluded by declaiming the new oath, thus subscribing to it for himself.[55] By his directive, that evening hundreds of thousands of uniformed men in all parts of Germany raised their hands and repeated the formula without foreknowledge of what they were about to say.

Shock and foreboding were expressed then or later by some of the more discerning Army figures.[56] Fritsch's chief of staff, General Ludwig Beck, came back from the meeting in the Great Hall of the War Ministry shaking his head gloomily. "One cannot do things in this way," he said.[57] Returning to his home that evening he described the day to a comrade as the darkest of his life. He felt he had been taken unawares and never rid himself of the thought that he should have refused then and there to take the oath. It was only with considerable difficulty that Fritsch dissuaded him from resigning his post. Beck never forgave himself for having yielded.[58]

There is no concrete evidence to show that Army or Navy representatives took issue with Blomberg on his arbitrary and unlawful directive. The change in the oath formula of December 1933 had been decreed by the Reich President as commander in chief of the armed forces. This time the War Minister acted entirely on his own dubious authority. One witness who was close to military leaders opposed to the regime does testify that Fritsch protested to Blomberg and exerted enough pressure so that it was not until August 20 that a law sanctioning the new formula was enacted.[59]

The compass of this study does not permit a thorough analysis

[55] Röhricht, *Pflicht und Gewissen*, 78.

[56] The reactions of the group of officers serving directly under Reichenau are described in *ibid.*, 78-79.

[57] As recounted by his then secretary, Fräulein von Benda, now Luise Jodl. Interview, June 17, 1970.

[58] Based on a letter of January 15, 1942, from Beck's brother, Wilhelm, to Wolfgang Foerster. Quoted by Foerster in *Generaloberst Ludwig Beck: Sein Kampf gegen den Krieg* (Munich, 1953), 27. This fully confirms the testimony of Gisevius as given at Nuremberg. International Military Tribunal, *Trial of the Major War Criminals before the International Military Tribunal, 14 November 1945-1 October 1946* (42 vols., Nuremberg, 1947-49; cited hereafter as IMT), XII, 194.

[59] Based on statements by Dr. Erich Schultze in various interviews in 1970 and 1971. It is his view that the legalization of the change in the oath was held up because of Fritsch's opposition until after the plebiscite of August 19 approving Hitler's assumption of the powers of the presidency. On Dr. Schultze see below, pp. 54-56.

of the longer range effects of the oath of personal allegiance to Hitler. Unquestionably it had vital consequences at every stage of Opposition activity involving military figures. For the time being it accomplished what Reichenau intended: it was a major move toward making the Wehrmacht more specifically an organ of the National Socialist state and putting Hitler under obligation to it and to Reichenau personally.[60]

Hitler had every reason to be delighted and, on the day the new oath was legalized, he addressed a glowing public letter of appreciation to Blomberg. After a warm expression of thanks he continued: "Just as the officers and soldiers of the Wehrmacht bind themselves to the new state in my person, so shall I always regard it as my highest duty to defend the existence and inviolability of the Wehrmacht in fulfillment of the testament of the late field marshal [Hindenburg] and faithful to my own will to anchor the Army in the nation as the sole bearer of arms."[61]

It was a counter-pledge accepting the mutuality of obligation and was so understood by soldiers of every political inclination. Thus the later General Heinz Guderian wrote at the time: "A fateful oath! May God give that it be maintained by *both parties* with the same faithfulness for the welfare of Germany. The Army is accustomed to keep its oath. May it be enabled to do so in honor."[62] At least this furnished an argument by which, in later days, it could be reasoned that the clear violation of Hitler's promises canceled the oath of obedience to him. To the bitter end, however, Reichenau's fatal play was a principal stumbling block to all who sought to break the bondage of the military to the tyrant.

### Blomberg and Fritsch

After the uncertainties over the position of the Wehrmacht vis-à-vis other forces in the National Socialist state, nearly four years of comparative tranquillity succeeded June 1934. The military leadership was left largely to itself in running the internal affairs of the three services. Hitler gave scant attention even to major appoint-

[60] Members of Reichenau's staff seem to have shared an impression that he was as concerned with binding Hitler to the Wehrmacht as with binding the Wehrmacht to him. Röhricht, *Pflicht und Gewissen*, 78.

[61] Papen, 378.

[62] Elisabeth Wagner, ed., *Der Generalquartiermeister: Briefe und Tagebuchaufzeichnungen des Generalquartiermeisters des Heeres General der Artillerie Eduard Wagner* (Munich, 1963; cited hereafter as Wagner Diary), 67.

22

ments, usually signing unread the documents submitted to him through the Wehrmacht adjutant, Colonel Friedrich Hossbach.[63] There was so much to be done in rebuilding military power that at first there seemed little room for argument about the course to be steered. It was not until 1936 that disagreement and tension began to show themselves. The military establishment was reaching a level where its character and further development needed specific adaptation to ultimate purposes. Hitler's determination to create and control an instrument suitable to his far-ranging aims then clashed with traditional viewpoints. Even the pliant Blomberg became an obstacle in the course the dictator had set for himself.

In the years 1934-36 the War Minister did little to displease the overlord to whom he had literally been the first to swear allegiance. Between him and Reichenau the Wehrmacht was moved closer to the National Socialist state and its ideology. At the Hindenburg obsequies in East Prussia on August 7, Blomberg, seemingly on impulse, turned to Hitler and secured approval for an order that, in place of the plain "Herr Hitler," he should in future be addressed by Wehrmacht members as "Mein Fuehrer."[64] Reichenau, for his part, issued the "Sie-Erlass," a directive specifying the use of the direct address to superiors in place of the traditional third person. Could he have pursued his inclinations all the way, he would, in fact, have opted for the familiar "Du." As it was, the "Sie-Erlass" was opposed by most officers and largely ignored.[65]

Hitler later claimed that sometimes Blomberg had to be checked because of his precipitancy; he himself felt that the "political permutation" of the Army was a matter of time and should only be attempted gradually.[66] Blomberg's and Reichenau's disregard for traditional etiquette and their strivings to foster Nazi concepts and attitudes certainly did not sit well with the Generalität. At the beginning Blomberg had not been so much an outsider as he gradually became. By the time of his disgrace in 1938 the attitude of many generals was reflected in General Adam's acid retort when taunted by one of the more Nazi Ministers, "What do you think

---

[63] Hossbach, *Zwischen Wehrmacht und Hitler 1934-1938* (2nd rev. ed., Göttingen, 1965), 39.

[64] *Ibid.*, 12.

[65] Warlimont, "Interpretation," 132.

[66] Diary of General Gerhard Engel (unpublished manuscript, lent to the present author by General Engel; cited hereafter as Engel Diary), entry of April 20, 1938.

now of your field marshal?" "He is not our field marshal," Adam shot back, "but yours!"[67]

Relations between Blomberg and Hammerstein during the brief period the latter remained in office were not overly strained. Hammerstein was actually believed by a close observer, though mistakenly, to have first recommended Blomberg to Hindenburg.[68] Hammerstein's pessimism and resignation, together with his notorious laziness which the beginning of ill health was compounding into lassitude, led him to tolerate repeated invasions of his prerogative by the Blomberg-Reichenau combine. Thus he failed to protest when office (Amt) and department (Abteilung) heads of the Army command were summoned to confer with Blomberg.[69]

Fritsch was made of harder clay, at least when dealing with service matters, and quickly put them to rights by stringent orders to subordinates that they refrain from direct reports to the War Ministry. He also demanded copies of reports sent in by the Wehrkreis commanders on "political" matters, such as encroachments of the SA. Hammerstein's previous passivity made it more difficult, however, to restore the proper order of things without friction with both Blomberg and subordinate levels of command.[70]

The Army also had reason to feel that Blomberg had put up no real fight in resisting Goering's demand for an autonomous Air Force. The divorce of the two services had come with Blomberg's appointment; he reported on returning from the conference with Hindenburg that he had been unable to prevent air matters being withdrawn from Army control and placed under Goering.[71] A separate Luftwaffe enhanced Blomberg's own position by eliminating the need to go through the Army command in air matters and by making him the direct superior of three services when, in the following year, the existence of the Luftwaffe was publicly acknowledged and, shortly thereafter, he was formally appointed commander in chief of the Wehrmacht.

Clashes on policy and jurisdiction inevitably clouded the personal relations of Blomberg and Fritsch. The latter disliked conferences

---

[67] Alfred Jodl, *Das Dienstliche Tagebuch des Chefs des Wehrmachtführungsamtes im OKW* (cited hereafter as Jodl Diary), which for the period January 4, 1937, to August 25, 1939, is Document 1780-PS in IMT, XXVIII, 345–390; the source here is p. 363, entry of March 2, 1938.

[68] Mellenthin, "Aktenvermerk" (in IfZ, ZS 105), 1.

[69] *Ibid.*, 1–2.

[70] *Ibid.*, 3.

[71] *Ibid.*, 1.

with the War Minister and put them off as long as possible. "Announce me some time over there," he would finally say in a wry tone to his adjutant.[72] In general he found it easier to deal with Hitler, who seemed reasonable in discussing concrete matters. Though their personalities had nothing in common, Hitler still went out of his way to avoid unpleasantness with the Army commander. Fritsch in turn strove conscientiously to discover the positive in both National Socialism and its Fuehrer.[73] But he could not quite forget a prophecy made to him by World War I's famed General Ludendorff after he became commander of the Army in 1934: "Hitler will lie to you and cheat you and in the end drop you just as he did me."[74]

It is time for a more prolonged look at this ill-fated soldier whose destiny so intertwines the story presented in this volume. Werner von Fritsch is no doubt much easier to understand than the more complicated Blomberg. Though he was often described as an example of the classic Prussian officer, in reality his background was not Prussian. On his father's side he was of Saxon, on his mother's of Rhineland origin. Coming from a line of government servants ennobled in the eighteenth century, the father was the first soldier, entering, as his son later did, the Grand Ducal Hessian service. The family was not wealthy and his upbringing was frugal and rather Spartan in discipline. This contributed to his extreme reticence and introversion. "When you further write," he said in a letter in 1938, "that I am often difficult to understand you undoubtedly are right. I have never spoken to others about myself. I simply cannot do that and in case someone tries to force his way in, he only achieves the opposite."[75]

The monocle which seemed to fit Fritsch's personality so perfectly was not, as with so many officers, an affectation but had been adopted to correct a serious weakness of his left eye which had tortured him during his youth.[76] It was also a feature in his personal armor, notably in dealing with Hitler. "I wear a monocle," he

[72] Mellenthin, "Niederschrift," 12.

[73] *Ibid.*, 13. Mellenthin, "Aktenvermerk," 3-4.

[74] Alexander Ulex, unpublished memoirs (in IfZ, EDI; cited hereafter as Ulex ms.), 98. Hossbach (*Zwischen Wehrmacht und Hitler*, 125) reports the same story from Fritsch in somewhat different words.

[75] Count Johann Adolf Kielmansegg, *Der Fritsch-Prozess 1938: Ablauf und Hintergründe* (Hamburg, 1949), 16-17.

[76] *Ibid.*, 17-18.

said on one occasion, "so that my face remains stiff, especially when I confront that man."[77]

Beneath his rigidly controlled exterior the more discerning perceived hidden facets. Only his friends and co-workers gained much insight into them since he shunned society as much as his high office permitted. He would appear only at the most unavoidable ceremonies and was never seen in Berlin salons. The shrewd ambassador of France, André François-Poncet, who met him occasionally at the races, found that his seemingly "haughty and surly exterior covered a human wit and a more amiable nature than appeared."[78] However withdrawn and almost shy he might seem in a larger circle, says Guderian, among trusted comrades he was wholly approachable, showed a fine sense of humor, and exercised a winning charm.[79] "One has the feeling of a son speaking with his father" is another verdict.[80] His speech, whose incisiveness was accentuated by a clipped manner of speaking, had no intentional cutting edge. If he felt a criticism had proved too wounding, he was at pains to say something to revive drooping spirits.[81] A subordinate responsible for bringing disciplinary cases to him lauds his humanity. "Is this necessary?" he protested in reducing a particularly harsh penalty. He always showed awareness that he was dealing with the fate of human beings rather than "ruling in a case."[82] This sense of personal responsibility toward his fellowmen coupled with the absolute confidence he inspired about his probity and the purity of his motives won him a devotion beyond that gained by any German Army commander since the days of the elder Moltke.

A characterization of Fritsch in a British embassy report at the beginning of 1938 does not find him personally impressive but credits him with determination and clear ideas of what was best for the Army. He is described as single-mindedly devoted to rebuilding it and not likely to "meddle in politics" before completing this task.[83]

[77] Interview with Fabian von Schlabrendorff, February 13, 1970.

[78] François-Poncet, *The Fateful Years: Memoirs of a French Ambassador in Berlin, 1931-1938* (New York, 1949), 225-226.

[79] Guderian, *Erinnerungen eines Soldaten* (Heidelberg, 1951), 26.

[80] August Winnig as quoted by Fabian von Schlabrendorff. Interview, February 13, 1970.

[81] Baron Leo von Geyr von Schweppenburg, *The Critical Years* (London, 1952), 173.

[82] Interview with Major General (ret.) Fritz Hofmann, April 13, 1970.

[83] Sir George Ogilvie-Forbes to Anthony Eden, January 6, 1938 (in Public Records Office, London—hereafter PRO; C8s/83/18), 8.

# Hitler and the Military

"Meddling in politics" in any traditional sense was a temptation not difficult for Fritsch to resist. He had no interest in the political game as such and his withdrawn way of life afforded few contacts that could have helped to promote political insights. Estimates of his political capacities vary from the moderately negative to the devastating. "Helpless as a child" is the rather one-sided judgment of the historian Gerhard Ritter.[84] So strong a verdict would seem to fit only if applied to his inability to deal with scoundrels in an arena unfamiliar to a man of his character and experience. There was much that was sound about his judgment of the political scene. His mind was an extraordinarily disciplined one, though tending, as with most highly specialized individuals, to move in restricted channels.[85]

Fritsch's generally negative attitude toward National Socialism was based on more than the prejudices and snobberies of his class. Much in Nazism offended his sense of fitness and his moral and ethical principles. Doubtless his strong religious orientation had a good deal to do with this. His mother was a von Bodelschwingh, a family distinguished in Protestant Germany. He was brought up in strict religious observance and remained habituated to it. Though his religious interests were not obsessive, they were sufficient to make him a member of a circle gathered about the prominent Berlin theologian Professor Schubert.[86]

Fritsch was much concerned about the religious controversies then shaking Germany but he did not feel it advisable to become involved. He did assert himself in what seemed within his province, fostering the care of souls in the Army.[87] He demanded that officers attend services with their men and forbade them to abandon formal church membership.[88] His ideal was to make the Army a port secure in the storm of religious conflict.[89]

[84] Ritter, *Carl Goerdeler und die deutsche Widerstandsbewegung* (Stuttgart, 1954), 136.

[85] Percy Schramm speaks of "a disciplined brain" such as he had observed in only a few other persons. Quoted by Gerd Brausch, "Der Tod des Generalobersten Werner Freiherr von Fritsch," in *Militärgeschichtliche Mitteilungen*, Vol. 1 (1970), pp. 95-112, at 98n28.

[86] Schultze interview, December 5, 1969. Dr. Schultze, who had numbered theology among his studies, was a member of this circle.

[87] Mellenthin, "Niederschrift," 12.

[88] Foertsch, *Schuld und Verhängnis*, 58. Foertsch's information is based on notes provided by General Gotthard Heinrici on a speech delivered by Fritsch on July 25, 1934, to a group of high officers.

[89] Count Lutz Schwerin von Krosigk, *Es geschah in Deutschland, Menschenbilder unseres Jahrhunderts* (Tübingen and Stuttgart, 1951), 281.

The words, then, that best characterize Fritsch's religious attitude are undemonstrative piety. Of a piece with this was a fundamental modesty and a preference for a simple way of life.[90] If he had any controlling passions they were his profession and thoroughbred horses. The disintegration of his personality after his dismissal in 1938 may be laid as much to his separation from constructive activity as to the crushing blow to his dignity.

Though Fritsch's basic conservative leanings have never been questioned, there has been some argument about his views in areas where conservatism at times found common ground with Nazism. There is, for instance, the much-disputed letter which Justice Robert Jackson announced he would submit in evidence before the International Military Tribunal in Nuremberg. The document then could not be produced. It had been claimed that it was one of several score letters addressed by Fritsch to Baroness Margot von Schutzbar-Milchling and sequestered by American occupation authorities. An English translation of it is to be found among translations retained in Washington when the originals were returned to the baroness. The translation is dated December 11, 1938, and has Fritsch saying that after World War I he had decided that Germany, if she were again to be powerful, needed to win three battles:

1. The battles against the working class. Hitler has won this.
2. Against the Catholic Church, perhaps better expressed against ultramontanism.
3. Against the Jews.
We are in the midst of these battles and the one against the Jews is the most difficult.[91]

Fritsch thus is made to appear a man who had much in common with Hitler. German Resistance survivors, who had made something of a hero of him, were dismayed until the prosecution could not produce the original document and the baroness submitted an affidavit swearing that she had never received such an epistle. She

[90] Fritsch's devoted adjutant, Captain Joachim von Both, who was in charge of his purse, on one occasion said to Colonel Baron Leo von Geyr von Schweppenburg: "What do you think are the expenditures of an Army commander?" He then revealed that, after taking care of his mother, Fritsch retained 500 marks monthly (then about $125 in value) for his personal expenses. Interview with General Geyr von Schweppenburg, January 26, 1970.

[91] The translations are part of microfilm roll T84/272, Record Group No. 242/1048, in NA (hereafter cited as Fritsch Letters).

28

further affirmed that its tone and content were utterly alien to Fritsch's sentiments.[92]

The answer to the mystery lies in one of three possibilities: (1) the insertion of a forgery among the English translations; (2) the abstraction of the original of such a letter from American legal files; and (3) loss of the letter in the mountains of prosecution documents. In view of the questionable authenticity of the translations and what we know of Fritsch in general, supposition would lean toward the first explanation.

## Fritsch and the Regime

Fritsch had not sought the office to which he was elevated in January 1934, nor did he enter upon it with a light heart. He had hesitated to accept the appointment and only the urgings of his predecessor twice removed, General Hans von Seeckt, induced him to do so.[93] One version has it that, at this stage, he was one of the generals who gave thought to military action to prevent a Nazi takeover.[94]

Hitler does not seem to have had an active dislike for Fritsch until after he had done him such injury that he could only assume that Fritsch had become his enemy. He had a good deal of respect for the general's abilities and could not ignore the regard, verging on veneration, he enjoyed in the Army. But Hitler had an abysmal antipathy for the type of Prussian officer which Fritsch seemed to epitomize. Austrian sansculotte and artistic dilettante confronted ultra-Prussian professional and neither liked what he saw.[95] Hitler further was prone to write off as soon as he could dispense with them persons who, like Fritsch, were immune to his charisma and suggestive powers.

[92] Letter to Dr. Hans Laternser, June 3, 1946, in papers assembled by Count Johann Adolf Kielmansegg (hereafter cited as Kielmansegg Papers).

[93] Ulex ms., 94.

[94] This is the story related to Dr. Josef Müller by Monsignor Ludwig Kaas, leader of the Catholic Center party. A similar account was given Müller later by Captain Ludwig Gehre. Müller interview, October 11, 1969.

[95] Walter Buchs, party judge, who knew Hitler intimately, spoke of the aversion of the "Austrian artist's soul" for the Prussian officer. Robert M. W. Kempner, *Das Dritte Reich im Kreuzverhör: Aus den unveröffentlichten Vernehmungsprotokollen des Anklägers* (Munich, 1969), 71. Both Hitler's reaction to the Prussian officer generally and the specific application to Fritsch were emphasized repeatedly by General Engel in a series of interviews beginning on May 4, 1970. Wiedemann (*Der Mann der Feldherr werden wollte,* 115) also testifies that Fritsch represented a type against which Hitler had "an inner revulsion."

Gradually a more personal score accumulated against Fritsch in the Reich Chancellery. Party influences, as Hitler frequently told him,[96] were being constantly employed against him. SA resentments because of the 1934 purge were directed mostly against the SS, but many fanatic Nazis saw in it a victory of the Army over the party. They feared Hitler's preoccupation with the military buildup meant closer ties between him and the conservative generals.[97] It was easy for animosity to focus on Fritsch: the symbol of the traditional Army both in his office and in his person. In contrast to Blomberg, he shied from anything that implied a personal relationship to the party, even returning the Gold Party Badge that had been conferred upon him by Hitler.[98] Fritsch was not always circumspect about his audience when making critical remarks.[99] Nazi adherents found it particularly irritating to note the many quarters at odds with the regime where he was regarded as a last hope. Church circles were known to submit complaints to him.[100] Millions felt, and many were overheard to say, that as long as he and the Army were "around" the party would not be allowed to become too presumptive.[101] Up to the highest Army and ministerial quarters there was hope that if things got "too bad" Fritsch would put them to rights, that he was waiting only for the "right moment."[102]

Unavoidably much of this got back to the SS and could only challenge it to find ways of getting rid of him. When a Nazi-oriented general like Reichenau claimed that he could take no step that

[96] See below, p. 210.

[97] Otto Meissner, *Staatssekretär unter Ebert-Hindenburg-Hitler: Der Schicksalsweg des deutschen Volkes von 1918-1945, wie ich ihn erlebte* (Hamburg, 1950), 434.

[98] Walter Bussmann, "Zur Entstehung und Überlieferung der 'Hossbach Niederschrift,'" in *Vierteljahrshefte für Zeitgeschichte* (cited hereafter as *VfZ*), Vol. 16, No. 4 (October 1968), 377.

[99] The foreign correspondents counted Fritsch as an enemy of the party. An occasion on which he did not trouble to hide his sentiments before one of them is recorded by William Shirer, who stood next to him at a parade of troops and SS in Saarbrücken on March 4, 1935: "He kept up a running fire of very sarcastic remarks—about the SS, the party, and various party leaders as they appeared. He was full of contempt for them all. When Hitler's car arrived, he grunted and went over and took his place just behind the Fuehrer for the review." Shirer, *Berlin Diary: The Journal of a Foreign Correspondent, 1934-41* (New York, 1941), 27.

[100] "Niederschrift über Unterredung der Herren Generale a. D. von Sodenstern und Winter mit den Herren Dr. Vogelsang und Krausnick am 23.6.54" (in IfZ, ZS 149; cited hereafter as Sodenstern and Winter), 3.

[101] J. A. Kielmansegg (*Der Fritsch-Prozess 1938*, 103) stresses how much harm such loose talk did to Fritsch.

[102] Testimony of Gisevius at Nuremberg, April 24, 1946, IMT, XII, 194.

was not "registered,"[103] one can imagine the kind of watch Himmler's people maintained over Fritsch! If Himmler and Heydrich had been the least inclined to forgive him for seeking action against them after June 1934, this would have been overcome by new vexations. He was ever holding a protecting hand over soldiers whose indiscretions got them into scrapes. When Hitler demanded his interposition in the case of some officers overheard in a restaurant to refer to the Fuehrer as a "house painter," he wrote the unit commander to warn his officers to speak less loudly.[104]

More directly hurtful to Himmler and Heydrich were Fritsch's moves to limit development of the SS as a bearer of weapons. Frictions constantly arose when Army and SS units came in contact. In autumn 1935 the exercise ground at Altan-Grabow was the scene of conflict between an Army regiment and the Leibstandarte, the super-elite SS guard formation that bore Hitler's own name. From the first day the SS men flouted camp regulations, inflicting damage on barracks, canteens, and other installations. Their rowdyism came to a climax in a battle royal in the camp theater. Fritsch thereupon submitted the records of an investigation to Blomberg and demanded nothing less than the dissolution of the Leibstandarte. After two weeks' delay Blomberg returned the documents with a curt note: "A proposal of this nature may not be submitted to me at all." Fritsch then went directly to Hitler and Himmler, only to be fobbed off by them with excuses and evasions.[105]

The hatred of the SS had received another boost and it was inevitable that an opportunity would be sought to trip up the troublesome general. When, a few months later, a file of material came into Himmler's hands that could be used to make Fritsch appear a homosexual, not surprisingly it soon got to Hitler. "Himmler," says SS General Karl Wolff, "came away from this parley in a downcast mood because Hitler had said that, though Fritsch was doubtless one of the strongest and most important opponents of National Socialism, he could not be dealt with in this fashion."[106]

That Hitler had reached the point where he could describe Fritsch in this way as an opponent of the regime was partly the work of Blomberg. The War Minister's conduct in the 1938 crisis was

[103]Röhricht, *Pflicht und Gewissen*, 102. Reichenau made this statement when Röhricht complained about his own mail being intercepted.
[104]As found in the Fritsch Letters Schlabrendorff interview, February 13, 1970.
[105]V. Müller, 368.
[106]Wolff, "Aktenvermerk des Generals der Waffen-SS Karl Wolff über die Blomberg-Fritsch Krise, 11.8.52" (in IfZ, 1182/53), 2.

to reveal some of the jealousy that had been building up against his principal subordinate. He could not but be aware of the mounting criticism against himself in the Army, the charges of deviousness and ambivalence, and Fritsch's contrasting reputation for integrity. After Fritsch's fall both he and his naval colleague, Admiral Erich Raeder, believed that Blomberg had helped to poison Hitler's mind.[107] But by promoting a rift between Hitler and the leaders of the Army, Blomberg, during his last two years in office, departed from his role of mediator and thus made himself more dispensable to all.

[107] In letters from Raeder to Fritsch (April 25, 1938) and Fritsch to the Baroness Schutzbar (April 14, 1938). Quoted by J. A. Kielmansegg, *Der Fritsch-Prozess 1938*, 103.

# CHAPTER II

# Growing Estrangements, 1936–37

The year 1935 may have marked the high point of Werner von Blomberg's position in the National Socialist state. On June 1, some weeks after Germany had cast off the military shackles of Versailles, he was appointed Reich Minister of War and commander in chief of the Wehrmacht. In command matters his office was later known as the High Command of the Wehrmacht (Oberkommando der Wehrmacht—OKW). To external appearances, the authority he exercised exceeded that hitherto given to any German soldier. None had ever stood above all branches of the military establishment. It was an eminence purchased at great cost—growing alienation from the core service, the Army.

## Weakening of Blomberg's Position

The War Minister was caught in a developing vicious circle. As his prestige and position became more dependent on Hitler, there was a corresponding estrangement from the Generalität, which in turn accentuated dependence on the Fuehrer. It was whispered about Berlin that when the Army asked that a case be presented to Hitler, Blomberg failed to give it loyal support.[1] In OKH (Oberkommando des Heeres—Army High Command) the whispers were not so guarded. Fritsch actually believed that, when he used Blomberg as an intermediary, difficulties were enhanced rather than ameliorated. "When it goes through Blomberg," he would say, "there are always frictions and misunderstandings."[2]

Nor could Blomberg look to the party for backing. However much

[1] Ogilvie-Forbes to Eden, January 6, 1938 (in PRO, C23/83/18), 2.
[2] Foertsch, "Aktenvermerk," 4.

he worshiped at the personal shrine of Hitler or sought to promote National Socialist attitudes in the Wehrmacht, he would criticize the party and its organizations when they got in his way. Though the Army increasingly treated him as an outsider, to the party he remained the corporate expression of the aristocratic military tradition. As for the SS, though Himmler and Heydrich regarded Fritsch as the stumbling block to their designs, Blomberg was also marked for elimination. This was not a personal but a professional matter— he was the head of a rival shop.

Another prominent party leader with whom Blomberg's stock was on a falling curve was Goering. The War Minister sat in a chair which Hitler's egocentric lieutenant coveted. Both in actuality and in the eyes of the world, Goering was second in the National Socialist state. In each of his innumerable functions he stood first, with one glaring exception and that the most important of all—his military status. In this area, too, the external manifestations of rank which were so dear to his heart were most on public display— witness the occasion, full of pomp and show, when Blomberg was made a field marshal (April 1, 1936) and again when he was sent to represent Germany at the coronation of George VI, the kind of glittering pageant which Goering loved. In short, Blomberg's greater prominence in a field where power and parade harmonized so perfectly had, by 1937, become a source of festering irritation to Goering. This had ominous implications for the future of the War Minister.

Blomberg and party leaders had differences on personnel and policy questions also. When he returned from London, he annoyed Hitler and infuriated Himmler by speaking disparagingly of Ambassador von Ribbentrop, then a special pet of the SS chief. Having observed maneuvers in Italy, Blomberg delivered a devastating critique of the Italian Army and thus of Italy as a potential ally. Thereby he greatly upset Goering and Himmler, enthusiastic advocates of an Italian connection.[3]

In August 1935 Blomberg had weakened his position by sending Reichenau to command Wehrkreis VII at Munich. No doubt Reichenau needed the troop experience whose lack Hindenburg had decried. "Some day," said Blomberg, "Reichenau will be the only proper successor for me"; at Munich he would lose the repute of a bureau general and have a chance to gain popularity.[4] Doubtless

[3] Meissner, 435.
[4] Foertsch, "Unterredung," 6.

Blomberg was sincere in this and eager to groom Reichenau as his successor. But he also was not comfortable with Reichenau who was no easy subordinate. The War Minister was a born compromiser while his deputy hated middle courses and drove himself and those about him relentlessly toward any goal he espoused. There may also have been an element of envy in Blomberg's feelings, Reichenau being so obviously the stronger and the only other general who had a personal relationship with Hitler.

In place of this human dynamo, Blomberg took as chief of the Wehrmachtamt (previously the Ministeramt) General Wilhelm Keitel, the epitome of an easy subordinate, a receiver of orders rather than a producer of ideas. With him there would be no more admonitions or prolonged arguments. Blomberg, who may have been sensitive to charges of being influenced by Reichenau, could now feel he was on his own. There was no one to thrust him in directions he did not wish to go but, also, no one to warn of pitfalls. Reichenau was later convinced that Blomberg would never have drifted into his fatal scrape had he continued at the War Minister's side.[5]

### Rising Tensions

Before 1937 Hitler and the Wehrmacht secured from each other much of what they wanted. The rebuilding of German military power made astonishing progress. Every suitable national impulse had been harnessed to this purpose: for example, the fight against unemployment, Hitler having determined that every public measure designated to promote employment would be tailored to the arms program. "This," he had told the Reich Cabinet a week after he became Chancellor, "has to be the dominant thought, always and everywhere."[6]

No doubt the military leaders initially welcomed every argument that would give impetus to rearmament. But by 1936 the soberer among them were seriously disturbed about a precipitancy that ignored economic implications and exalted quantity above quality in the expansion of the forces.

Respected voices prophesied dire consequences if fundamental principles were ignored. The Wehrmacht's chief expert on the interrelation of armament and the economy, General Georg Thomas, took up the cudgels. Beginning in 1936 he campaigned against

[5] Reichenau interview, June 23, 1970.
[6] Weinberg, 30.

ideas of lightning war (Blitzkrieg) that promised combat of short duration and laid all stress on a maximal initial effort. In articles in newspapers and military journals and in addresses to military and business leaders Thomas argued that the next war would again be one of matériel for which Germany's position in finance, raw materials, and foodstuffs was totally inadequate.[7]

Equally emphatic, and muted only as censorship and controlled media demanded, were the protests of the two most distinguished political economists in Germany, Hjalmar Schacht and Carl Goerdeler. As with Thomas, a more thoroughgoing analysis of these men will be made in a forthcoming volume by the present author.[8] But it should be said here that all three were moved from an oppositional to a conspiratorial posture by the events related in the pages to follow.

Schacht, a financier of rather awesome world-wide reputation, had done much to help Hitler in his rise to the chancellorship and in his effort to master the economic crisis while financing rearmament. Schacht wished a restoration of German military power sufficient to provide the means to resist and, if need be, apply international pressure. A man whose thought moved along lines of trade and finance, Schacht was mainly interested in territorial revision of the Versailles Treaty as it concerned colonies. Unquestionably he shrank from whatever threatened international conflict.

Perhaps the best brief estimate of Schacht is that in a British embassy report early in 1938. "Schacht," it said, "is composed of the most diverse qualities. Vanity, arrogance, over-weaning ambition, simplicity, good nature, wit, repartee, malice, technical ability, inconsistency alternate with kaleidoscopic effect in his complex character." The report said further that he was "one of few if not the only man who dares to speak out to Hitler."[9] Of this there is abundant evidence beyond his own complacent writings. The Speer memoirs testify to an incident in 1936 at Berchtesgaden in which an argument between Hitler and his obstreperous Minister of Economics waxed so hot that Hitler rushed fuming onto the terrace to rant about the way Schacht was holding up his rearmament program.[10]

[7] Thomas, "Gedanken und Ereignisse" (written at Falkenstein, July 20, 1945; copy in author's possession), 1-3; "Mein Beitrag zum Kampf gegen Hitler" (prepared in 1945; copy in author's possession), 1; interview with Thomas, September 1945.

[8] In the case of Goerdeler a somewhat more extensive estimate than that given here will be found in Deutsch, 11-15.

# Growing Estrangements, 1936–37

Like Thomas, Schacht did not hesitate to agitate against Hitler's positions. In the spring of 1936 he addressed the senior General Staff officers of the Wehrmacht Academy. He stressed that unproductive expenditures, such as armaments, must not exceed what a sound economy could afford, and condemned current aberrations like some of those practiced by the Luftwaffe. The storm of applause which followed amounted to a demonstration against Hitler's program, so that Blomberg felt it necessary to rise and go on record in its defense.[11]

Goerdeler had on two occasions been Reich price commissioner and was, until 1937, lord mayor of Leipzig, a post he quit in protest against the destruction of a Mendelssohn monument by SA rowdies. The regime then prevented the Krupp Company from following through on an offer of employment to Goerdeler. The concern thereupon made him a compensatory payment which he used to develop foreign contacts and to round out his view of the international scene. Hitherto unknown facets of his multifarious Opposition activities constantly come to light. His indefatigable efforts to rouse the flame of resistance in others and his all-too-frequent indiscretions gave him in some quarters the repute of a "talker." To this it may be replied that without his work in enlistment, agitation, proselytizing, and tying together isolated sectors there would often have been little movement in Opposition affairs.[12]

Goerdeler was of basically conservative and strongly national leanings but Nazi extravagancies and his foreign journeys had opened his eyes to much. Most important, his travels had convinced him that, in the existing world configuration, Germany could secure by diplomatic means most or all of what she could justly claim in the way of treaty revision. By 1938 he was dedicating himself to preach this gospel to his vast acquaintance of military, religious, and business leaders, as well as to innumerable persons at every level of administration.

As much as Schacht, Goerdeler appreciated that Hitler's armament program implied a not-too-distant surge of aggression that threatened the ruin of Europe and was morally bankrupt from its incep-

[9] Ogilvie-Forbes to Eden, January 6, 1938 (in PRO, C23/83/18), 28.

[10] Albert Speer, *Inside the Third Reich: Memoirs* (New York, 1970), 116.

[11] Walter Warlimont, "Zur Persönlichkeit von Dr. Hjalmar Schacht" (October 1, 1945; prepared at the request of the author), 1–2. Further testimony on Schacht's opposition to Hitler's program is found in François-Poncet, 221–223.

[12] This point is developed with particular force by Hans Bernd Gisevius. Recording for the author, July 1971.

tion. Endowed with a missionary zeal that was foreign to the skeptical banker, he threw himself without reserve into the task of converting others to his position.

The reaction of the military to such warning voices was a mixed one. Hammerstein, who unfortunately no longer commanded soldiers, recognized full well the hazards of the situation. In conversation with an old acquaintance in 1936 we find him delivering an analysis of the relation between Hitler's armament policies and a drift toward war. The program was overhurried from the standpoint both of solid results and of the economic pressures it engendered. Lack of raw materials and foreign exchange to import them set limits to production. Once the process of tooling up and filling the magazines was completed, there would be increasing compulsion to go to war if the whole procedure were not to be wasted.[13] Hammerstein concluded that by 1938 rearmament would have reached a point where Hitler could begin to think seriously of having his "big war" and aim toward a convenient moment. But he would not be able to wait beyond a limited period—in no case longer than 1940. The tyranny of the economic bind on Germany would compel him to act, for the burden of armament would no longer be bearable.

Assuredly the higher Generalität from Blomberg on down was eager to avoid risk-taking. Each of Hitler's more daring moves—quitting the League of Nations, declaring universal service for German youth, and sending troops into the Rhineland—had sent the War Minister into a state of nerves that Hitler later compared to that of a "hysterical maiden."[14] A psychological impediment to anyone inclined to issue warnings was created when the dictator's predictions of Western passivity always turned out to be correct, while, on his side, the Fuehrer felt confirmed in his own judgment and lost respect for that of the military. On the question of long-term goals, few of the generals took Hitler's occasional intimations seriously. Before November 1937 such remarks were usually regarded as momentary flights of fancy. Revelations like those in a speech to a military audience in 1935 and to one of peasant and party leaders in the fall of 1937, though shocking enough, were a far cry from the coherent and detailed statement to Breiting in 1931.[15] The appeal for enlarged living space in itself left the generals cold,

---

[13] Hammerstein's views are related by his partner in the conversation, August Winnig, *Aus zwanzig Jahren 1925 bis 1945* (Hamburg, 1948), 105-108.

[14] Engel interview, May 11, 1970, and Diary, entry of April 20, 1938, etc.

## Growing Estrangements, 1936-37

if only because the steps required to achieve it seemed to place such a goal beyond the realm of reality. Blomberg, who reacted so anxiously when the Fuehrer contemplated concrete moves that threatened foreign complications, always discounted sharply what he said about larger aims.

Fritsch seems to have felt a deeper anxiety about the trend in Hitler's policy. To a relative, Lieutenant Count Kielmansegg, he for a brief moment uncovered his misgivings when the young man enthused, "Uncle Werner, you must agree that we live in great times." "I often wish," the general replied with a sigh, "that they were smaller."[16]

Speer relates how, in the autumn of 1937, Fritsch asked to see plans for the rebuilding of Berlin which reflected Hitler's dreams. One wonders what implications the responsible Army commander saw in the gigantic arch of triumph that had been sketched by the future Fuehrer in the mid-twenties. The questions he asked gave Hitler's architect the impression that Fritsch was gauging the time span over which Hitler might be counted on to be interested in preserving peace.[17]

This was a period when the honeymoon between Hitler and the Army was over and the bridegroom no longer felt the need of wooing. Domestically, his dependence on the Army was much reduced from that of 1934, when his position had been shaky. The state apparatus he had firmly in his hands; the party was disciplined and submissive. In external relations the military leadership had become an exasperating brake. Notably the miscalculations of Blomberg and the Army chiefs on the Rhineland action of 1936 had left him with contempt not only for their judgment but for what he labeled their cowardice.[18]

[15]Walter Görlitz, ed., *Generalfeldmarschall Keitel, Verbrecher oder Offizier? Erinnerungen, Briefe, Dokumente des Chefs OKW* (Göttingen, 1962; cited hereafter as Keitel), 81n89

[16]This incident probably occurred in 1936. Interview with General Count Johann Adolf Kielmansegg, September 16, 1969.

[17]Speer, 129.

[18]Hitler himself had been prepared to withdraw the three battalions sent over the river if the French mobilized. "If the French mean business, then I shall pull back." As told to Count Rüdiger von der Goltz by General Beck. Goltz interview, February 17, 1970. Blomberg proposed withdrawal even though the French had not gone beyond the retaliatory gesture of putting eleven divisions on a war footing. Testimony of Field Marshals von Manstein and von Rundstedt at Nuremberg, August 9 and 12, 1946, IMT, XX, 603-604, XXI, 22. Luise Jodl, then Beck's secretary, testifies that he and his staff awaited "with bated breath the reaction of the Western Powers." Interview, June 24, 1970.

Hitler was similarly growing less patient with the disapproving posture of the generals—it can be called no more than that—on much that went on in the Third Reich. He knew that they did not like repressive measures against the churches or excesses of Jew-baiting. He must have had some report of how often Blomberg was urged by people like General Thomas to protest such actions. Blomberg would argue that in a totalitarian state the Ministers had no Cabinet responsibility but had to stick to the areas of their portfolios.[19] Only when a fellow Minister, Schacht, put pressure on him, did he agree to go along to Berchtesgaden to plead for better treatment of the Jews.[20]

The annoyance Hitler derived from even so minor a challenge to his policy was fed by a systematic smear campaign inaugurated against the Army leaders in 1936 by party elements led by the SS. He probably did not believe charges that the generals were conspiring against him. He had no love for them but, as yet, was not afraid of them. His state of mind is probably best expressed by what he said two years later: "The Army is an uncertain element in the state, even worse than the Foreign Office and Justice."[21]

One aspect of the "uncertainty" Hitler referred to was probably distrust of the willingness of the Army leaders to follow and obey wherever his policy might lead—in brief, to the point of a war of which they did not approve. Twice Goering called on Blomberg to quiz him on this. Whether or not Hitler sent him to ask what he did not wish to ask personally, we may be sure that the subject was discussed between them and that Goering encouraged doubts about the rival service.[22] Increasingly the Fuehrer resented the way in which Blomberg and Fritsch dragged their feet in matters of

[19] Thomas, sometimes alone, sometimes with others, repeatedly pleaded with Blomberg to take a stand on behalf of the Wehrmacht. Thomas interview, September 1945. August Winnig, who planned an appeal to Blomberg after his talk with Hammerstein, found him exuding charm but forestalling any serious discussion by leaving the door open and launching immediately into extravagant praise of Hitler. Winnig, 109.

[20] Blomberg interrogation, September 23, 1945. Blomberg claims to have accompanied Schacht on two such occasions. Hitler responded that his policies conformed with popular will and cited in proof the circulation figures of Julius Streicher's contemptible sheet, *Der Stürmer*, which engaged in rabid anti-Semitic attacks. When Blomberg said such figures were a disgrace to the German people, the dictator was taken aback, started to utter a rebuke, but thought better of it and changed the subject.

[21] Engel Diary, entry of October 16, 1938.

[22] Blomberg tells of the two visits in his memoirs written in 1943. Warlimont, "Interpretation," 96.

40

armament and armed forces expansion dear to his heart, such as the order and speed in which particular age groups would receive their training.

In 1931 Hitler had told Breiting that he would fight his big war with "a new Army and a new General Staff." His mind thereafter may have detoured, but by 1937 it was fixed again in the view that the Prussian-German General Staff was something he could do without.[23] This conclusion is drawn by his personal adjutant, Captain Fritz Wiedemann, and shared by Wiedemann's Wehrmacht colleague, Colonel Friedrich Hossbach. The latter found evidence for it in the noticeable decline of consideration for Army concerns and a greater readiness to entertain suspicions and complaints. Trivial incidents were made the excuse for general reproaches. By the end of the year, too, there were indications of an approaching extension of the dictator's totalitarian claims to the Wehrmacht.[24]

### The Wehrmacht on the Eve of Crisis

Politically speaking, the German Wehrmacht on the eve of the 1938 crisis was an amorphous mass in which, at least in retrospect, can be discerned some distinct elements. This situation might have been different if, as it grew side by side with the new state, the mediator between them had been other than Werner von Blomberg. During these critical years he eschewed all influence on nonmilitary matters and confined the armed services strictly to their own preserve.

The Third Reich, a saying went, had a Royal Prussian Army, an Imperial Navy, and a National Socialist Air Force. The last-named knew itself to be, in a general way, the creature of the regime and, in a more particular way, of its crown prince, Hermann Goering. Its origin, as well as the fact that its leadership and officer corps were generally much younger than those of the Army and Navy, inclined the Luftwaffe to favor current rather than traditional ideas and values. In a pinch it could probably be relied on to defend the regime against its own sister services.

Everything in the structure and tradition of the Navy conspired to make it relatively immune to subversive influence from Opposition-minded sources. Requirements of life aboard ship made for exceptional discipline which determined many patterns of thought

[23] Wiedemann, *Der Mann der Feldherr werden wollte*, 115. Interview with Captain Fritz Wiedemann, December 2, 1969.
[24] Hossbach, *Zwischen Wehrmacht und Hitler*, 124.

and conduct. Absolute obedience was taken for granted to a degree never approximated in the other two services. It contrasted, for example, with that aspect of Army tradition and training which, since the days of the elder Moltke, had fostered independence of judgment among subordinates.

The Navy was more unified and more accustomed to a common mold than the Army which, before 1913, did not really exist as a national force.[25] From its birth in the war of 1870 the Navy was imperial in organization and command, a feature that made it the more susceptible to widespread guilt feelings after the mutiny which had launched the revolution of 1918. In Army circles one spoke *sotto voce* of the Navy's "revolution complex" and never mentioned the topic in interservice conversations. The mutiny was held to be a blot on the Navy's record which was all but ineffaceable, and efforts to compensate for it made inconceivable massive penetration of its ranks by elements fomenting subversion against the regime.

Despite this, islets of disaffection appeared here and there in the Navy, operating essentially in isolation and condemned in some instances to flit across the stage of history without gaining enough attention to be recorded. Some such segments of Navy Resistance have found a historian in Walter Baum.[26] That there were others may be inferred from the case of a most unusual group in Hamburg on which a glimmer of light has fallen for the first time.

Our fragment of information stems from the memoirs of Governor Philip La Follette of Wisconsin. Visiting early in 1939 a close friend, Michael Obladen, a leading businessman of Hamburg (head of a chemical firm) and a reserve officer in the Navy, he was introduced to a group of naval officers headed by an admiral at a luncheon on a Hamburg-America liner. A meeting with the admiral's aide took place the next day in a park. La Follette was told that about 100 naval officers could be counted upon to act against Hitler and the principal Nazis provided they received British and American assurance that during the period of turnover no attack would be made by the West, notably France. The governor and his brother, Senator Robert M. La Follette, Jr., called on President Roosevelt,

[25] Under the Empire in times of peace the Army was administratively divided and controlled by the rulers of Prussia, Bavaria, Saxony, and Württemberg.

[26] Baum, "Marine, Nationalsozialismus und Widerstand," *VfZ*, Vol. 11, No. 1 (January 1963), 16–48.

who appeared intensely interested, but nothing more came of the matter.[27]

As in the case of the Obladen Navy circle in Hamburg, new though usually fragmentary information keeps coming to light about Army-related individuals and groups in the Opposition movement. At times seemingly unconnected threads prove to belong to a common fabric.

With few exceptions, of whom Reichenau would be the most pronounced, the army group and Wehrkreis commanders of early 1938 were guardians of traditional values in Germany, lukewarm or hostile toward the regime, and devoted to their commander in chief. Little has been said thus far of General Ludwig Beck, Fritsch's chief of staff. Though the central figure of the conspiratorial group that emerged from the Fritsch affair, Beck's role in the Wehrmacht crisis itself was a secondary one. A later study by the present writer will attempt an analysis in greater depth of his character and capacities. An earlier study had the following to say of him: "It would be difficult to envision a figure more in conflict with popular or Hollywood conceptions of a Prussian general than Ludwig Beck. A West German, a fervent admirer of French culture, so intellectually distinguished as to belong to the famed Wednesday Society of savants, he exhibited none of the stiffness, the fixed ways, and the limited horizons often associated with old-style military professionals. It would not be possible to imagine him in the monocle that suited so well the personality of Fritsch. His portrait mirrors well his personality—a tense, sensitive, finely chiseled face with slightly sunken, rather sad eyes. In religious matters he was a believing Christian with a bent toward austerity."[28]

As between Beck and Fritsch, the former undoubtedly was more

[27] The author was asked by the editor of La Follette's memoirs to comment on this narrative, and, in an effort to unearth more evidence, in May 1970 he conferred with surviving members of the Obladen family. Obladen's former secretary, Dr. Peters, and some of Obladen's friends. The search thus far has yielded confirmation of the close friendship between Obladen and La Follette and the former's association with Opposition elements. A bulky file of correspondence with La Follette was destroyed with other incriminating papers by Obladen after July 20, 1944, when he was in fear of arrest. Obladen died in 1947 from a wound he received on the final day of the war. It is hoped that at a future date this investigation can be pursued further. The La Follette memoirs have now been published by Donald Young, ed., *Adventure in Politics: The Memoirs of Philip La Follette* (New York, 1970). The story reviewed above appears on pp. 259–261.

[28] Deutsch, 28.

profoundly intelligent, more broadly cultivated, and politically more aware. In their own military field, however, Beck was less flexible than Fritsch, who, among top Army figures, was regarded by "innovators" as more open to new ideas in such areas as tank warfare.[29]

It would seem the height of historical irony that Fritsch, the target later of outrageous intrigue, and Beck, the archetype of uncompromising military Resister, were chosen to succeed Hammerstein and Adam by those who sought an accommodation between the Army and the regime. Beck had shared the common underestimate of the Nazis and the equally common delusion that Nazism would gradually mellow and its more distasteful aspects fade away. By 1938 these delusions had eroded before the grim realities of five years of Hitler's rule and the multiplying signs of a drift toward war. There remained to Beck, however, another fallacy, that Fritsch was a guarantee of Army intervention if Nazi excesses passed all tolerance. The Wehrmacht crisis itself rudely swept away this final self-deception; but the awakening was too late to permit utilization of the favorable moment to do what he later saw to be needful.

Moving faster than Beck at this stage, though later to be his closest collaborator, was General Erwin von Witzleben, commander of the Berlin troops. Witzleben stands in a special place of honor among the generals who at one time or another formed part of the military Opposition: he was the first to unreservedly commit himself and never swerved or faltered in his dedication. He lacked the wide horizons and intellectual qualities of a Beck but had much to offer in compensation. He is perhaps best described as an unpretentious, straightforward soldier with a good fund of common sense. To his downright nature answers came simply: Nazism was a criminal abomination, the military oath a swindle, Hitler's chosen path the road to national disaster. Others agonized and procrastinated where he was prepared to act.

Failing contrary evidence, it has usually been assumed that Witzleben, like the majority in the first specific plot against the regime in the summer of 1938, was converted to conspiracy by the Fritsch affair. It now appears that his first moves in this direction came no later than the summer of 1937. The witness thereto is Ursula von Witzleben, wife of a relative, General Hermann von Witzleben.[30]

[29] This is the considered verdict of Heinz Guderian, who was forced to conduct a continual struggle with Beck over setting up tank divisions. Guderian, 25-27.

# Growing Estrangements, 1936–37

On September 11, 1937, the Witzleben clan was assembled in the troop commander's service quarters in Berlin to celebrate the arrival of his first grandchild. While the rest of the company were chatting about other concerns, the general asked her to accompany him to view some changes he was making in the grounds. In the garden he made the usual comment about indoor microphones and then began a discourse on the situation in the Reich. Hitler, he said, was driving relentlessly toward war. His course was a criminal one and all would be held to account if he were not stopped. Witzleben and his "friends" were prepared to assume this burden. But they needed help and would have to decide which military men should be approached.[31] Since she had practically grown up in the Rundstedt household and knew General Fromm well, what did she think about the wisdom of going to these men? She replied that Fromm must be eliminated from consideration, being much too equivocal in his attitude toward the regime. Rundstedt passed muster in this respect but was not the person to commit himself to such an enterprise. Witzleben smiled and said that these were also the views of his friends.

Only a small number of Witzleben's associates in 1937 can be identified with relative certainty. The surest of them is Major General Count Erich von Brockdorff-Ahlefeld, commander of a division at Potsdam and an immediate subordinate. It would have been strange had Witzleben not thought of Brockdorff before all others since he commanded the major force nearest Berlin; indeed, a year later the two were intimately associated in the summer 1938 plot. There is, however, an important piece of supporting evidence permitting us to move beyond the realm of conjecture. Just then, we learn, Brockdorff was making his *own* survey of prospective recruits. It looks, in fact, like a division of labor, Witzleben checking on the men who had command positions in Berlin and Brockdorff doing the same for those who directed troops elsewhere.

A nearly forgotten volume (1953) by August Winnig tells a story which, standing by itself, has seemed to lack special significance

[30] The account which follows was obtained in an interview with Frau von Witzleben on February 10, 1970, in the presence of her husband, who was also at the party described and learned from her immediately thereafter what his cousin had said.

[31] Most important for the Witzleben group would be military men associated with troop command in the Berlin area. Among these would be Gerd von Rundstedt, commander of the Berlin Army Group and the Army's senior general, and Erich Fromm, head of the General Army Office (Allgemeine Heeresamt) in OKH, which was in charge of training units.

and generally escaped notice. Winnig had for a short time (1919-20) been chief president (Oberpräsident) of East Prussia and then had acquired a national reputation as union leader, writer, and lecturer. He also had founded and led a political party known as the Old Socialists. Since 1923 he had lived in Potsdam and made the acquaintance of many officers of the elite Infantry Regiment 9, which carried the tradition of the former Prussian Guard. The officers were mostly ardent young aristocrats and, since so many of them bore the title of count, the regiment was popularly known as "Count Nine."

Winnig had also become the friend and something of a mentor of Count Fritz-Dietlof von der Schulenburg, son of the chief of staff of the crown prince's World War I army group. Like his father and brothers he had joined the party and had seen in it the hope for regeneration of Germany. Two years of government service in East Prussia, under the able but in several ways notorious Gauleiter Erich Koch, had cured him of that fancy. As he put it grimly to Winnig, "I had to make up my mind whether to quit the service or become Hitler's Fouché and I have decided for the second."[32]

In July 1937 Schulenburg was transferred back to Berlin to become deputy police president there. In the capital he was soon a principal figure of the famed "Counts Group" of idealistic young noblemen. Its ten or eleven regulars often invited in others for discussion and there was an affiliate of sorts among officers of Infantry Regiment 9 with whom Schulenburg had resumed intimate contact.[33]

One autumn day Schulenburg appeared at Winnig's home to check whether all was clear for a visit by General von Brockdorff. The count arrived in a service car with a huge bundle of plants for Winnig's garden as a "cover" for his visit. Brockdorff told Winnig of a plot to overthrow the regime and Goerdeler was mentioned as being involved. The discussion dealt with the concrete problems of takeover, in which the regiment would play a major role, and with the most likely recruits to be sought from the higher Generalität. Promising prospects seemed to be General Erwin von Kleist of the Breslau Wehrkreis, a highly religious man, General Erich Hoepner, slated to command one of Germany's first tank divisions

[32] Winnig, 11. Schulenburg was referring to Napoleon's famed police minister who turned against him.

[33] Albert Krebs, *Fritz-Dietlof Graf von der Schulenburg: Zwischen Staatsraison und Hochverrat* (Hamburg, 1964), 157-158.

and a man who refused to allow the customary picture of Hitler in his office, and the two Generals von Stülpnagel (Joachim and Karl Heinrich, cousins). The fact that Witzleben's name was not mentioned indicates that he was "in the bag" so far as Brockdorff was concerned.[34]

To round out the picture, Schulenburg's connection with Witzleben at the time of the Fritsch trial investigation should be noted, together with a plan formed then to make use of the regiment of Colonel Paul von Hase at Neuruppin, about thirty miles northwest of Berlin. It is not likely that this would have been a complete improvisation, so Hase most probably belonged to Witzleben's "friends" a good deal earlier.[35]

### The Abwehr Resistance Group

Those acquainted with Opposition developments, linking both Witzleben and Schulenburg closely with the group around Colonel Oster at the Abwehr (the Wehrmacht intelligence service) will wonder whether these connections also had not been formed before 1938. The supposition would seem strong but what testimony we have points in the other direction. The sole survivor of the Oster circle, Hans Bernd Gisevius, emphatically denies the existence of such a link. As will be noted, Oster and Gisevius were doing their own recruiting late in 1937, and Gisevius would surely have learned of such a promising tie as one with the commander of the troops in the Berlin area.[36]

In all but the final phase of the German military Opposition, members of the Abwehr took a major part. This was due primarily to the convergence of three personalities: Wilhelm Canaris, Hans Oster, and Hans Bernd Gisevius. Each played a leading role in the crisis of early 1938 by coordinating elements hostile to the regime. Thereby they contributed vitally to setting the stage for that concentration of diverse forces which planned to strike for peace and German freedom in September 1938.

It is beyond the scope of this study to trace the long and difficult

[34] Winnig, 111–112. The author's assumption that this meeting took place in the fall of 1937 is based on the facts that it was *before* the Blomberg and Fritsch affairs and that the plants could not be set out in winter.

[35] See below, p. 315.

[36] Gisevius interview, July 11, 1971. It should be noted further that Gisevius only a few months later had a conspiratorial planning assignment in Witzleben's office. Another supporting argument is that Schulenburg's connection with Oster was in itself a product of the Fritsch affair.

road by which Wilhelm Canaris was transformed into a conspirator.[37] He will be depicted here as we find him at the turn of the year 1937-38. Three years earlier he had replaced Captain Conrad Patzig as the head of the Abwehr. Canaris was counted on by the military leaders to deal more effectively than Patzig had done with the Abwehr's SS rivals while avoiding head-on collisions. His capacities as an intelligence chief have been estimated all the way from sheer ineptitude to being "the born head of a Deuxième Bureau,"[38] but for contending with the forces of darkness in the Nazi Reich he was the most perfect selection imaginable. To substitute him for the downright Patzig was for the regime going from bad to worse. This summarizes the judgment of a nonmember of the Abwehr Opposition group, Canaris's deputy, Vice Admiral Leopold Bürkner.[39] Colonel Rohleder, another nonmember and a man little inclined to sentiment, says of Canaris that he was a man of rare goodness and humanity to whom it was a physical torture to learn of outrage or depravity.[40]

Canaris's voluminous diary, which he kept as a historical record of Nazi villainies and regularly showed to Opposition friends, revealed perhaps more than he realized that he was the real initiator and impeller in uncounted Opposition moves.[41] Innumerable threads, the traces of most buried but constantly reappearing, ran through his hands. A master of dissimulation, though open with trusted friends, he relished employing it against those opponents whom he regarded as embodiments of evil. The late Percy Schramm, an observer and keen judge of the OKW scene during the war, asserts that Canaris alone succeeded in thwarting Hitler's uncanny instinct for sensing how people felt about him.[42]

One cannot hope to penetrate all the facets and complexities of this extraordinary character. Joined to nobility and wisdom were strange whimsies and phobias.[43] But he had absolute moral consis-

[37] A brief estimate of Canaris is presented by Deutsch, 55-63.

[38] Albrecht von Kessel, "Verborgene Saat: Das 'Andere Deutschland'" (written in Rome, late 1944-early 1945; lent to the present author by Kessel), 67.

[39] Bürkner interview, February 14, 1970.

[40] Rohleder to the colloquium of the E.P, protocol of December 15, 1952, 10.

[41] Interview with Major General Alexander von Pfuhlstein, February 14, 1970. Pfuhlstein had many opportunities to read at length in the diary whose destruction marks the greatest of many tragic losses of Resistance materials.

[42] Percy Ernst Schramm, *Hitler: The Man and the Military Leader* (Chicago, 1971), 34.

[43] For instance, Canaris was childishly fearful of germs and microbes, and usually disliked men of overwhelming physical presence. "That is a kidnaper," he would say of such robust types.

tency combined with an uncompromising hatred of physical violence and senseless destruction of the heritage of the past.[44]

By 1937 Canaris not only was carrying on his clandestine struggle against the evils of the regime but had come to feel that it must be brought down. During the previous two years he had systematically enlisted for top positions men on whose sentiments he could count. More, he had begun to reach out to the Wehrkreise to identify similar key figures. In most cases these were corps I-C's (intelligence chiefs—G-2's in the American service) with whom he kept in constant official contact. Most of these died in the Nazi terror in 1944-45, but one who survived tells us how Canaris operated.

General Alexander von Pfuhlstein was then a major and the I-C of the 11th Army Corps at Hanover under General Ulex. Among the duties of the I-C were liaison between the corps commands and the party and its formations. Pfuhlstein's outrage at the innumerable encroachments of the party expressed itself in strongly worded reports to Canaris. He rather expected reprimand but none came, not even when Pfuhlstein stated that it was time for intervention from the highest authority (Blomberg?) to end these abuses.[45]

Suddenly, in January 1938, Canaris appeared unannounced at Hanover on an "inspection." He was extraordinarily cordial and highly complimentary. That evening he invited Pfuhlstein and his wife to dinner during which he asked Pfuhlstein to make some unimportant-seeming calls to Berlin for him. On the major's returning to the table it became clear why the admiral had maneuvered to remain alone with Frau von Pfuhlstein. He had wished to ascertain whether the wife of a prospective recruit promised to be a support or a hindrance—perhaps even a danger—to the enterprise. Only after he had reassured himself on this vital point did Canaris drop his mask and, speaking with complete frankness, reveal the intention of Opposition forces to free Germany from its traducers. The meeting ended with Pfuhlstein's agreement to place himself unreservedly at Canaris's disposal. It was also arranged that contact

[44] By 1942 or 1943 Canaris became worried about the fate of Paris when the tide of war should turn. While visiting that city he said to a group of subordinates that, when the critical hour came, there must be Abwehr men in Paris who would save "this unique city" by preventing fighting within it. It is claimed that one of his hearers actually helped persuade General Dietrich von Cholitz to follow the policy he did in August 1944. Friedrich Wilhelm Heinz, "Von Wilhelm Canaris zum NKVD" (written in the first postwar years; copy in author's possession), 6. It is a moving thought that, even from prison and in the shadow of his gallows, Canaris's protecting hand was still reaching out.

[45] Pfuhlstein interview, February 14, 1970.

49

in these matters would hereafter be maintained through Colonel Oster.[46]

Hans Oster must be counted with Canaris, Goerdeler, and Beck among the most significant figures of the German Resisters to Hitler, and some would give him the first rank. His tragedy, and, in some degree, that of the German Opposition, lie in his elimination from an active role in the decisive phase, 1943-44.[47]

In the 100,000-man Reichswehr, minuscule by Continental great-power standards, the 4000 officers got around a great deal. By the time Hitler became Chancellor, Oster had served in a number of Wehrkreis commands, most recently as I-C in Münster, where the successive chiefs of staff were Generals von Brauchitsch, von Witzleben, and Halder, all of them prominent in the events of the year 1938. At Münster Oster had been involved in some affair at Mardi Gras time and had been obliged to leave the Army. In December 1933 he became acquainted in Berlin with Gisevius, then starting his career in government service, who had been assigned to the Political Police which was developing apace into the Gestapo. Gisevius's break with the regime commenced when he realized that he had stumbled into a community of blackguards. This conviction was affirmed and his antipathy extended to the entire SS, foster parent of the Gestapo and creator of the SD (security service), by the bloody orgy of June–July 1934, which he was able to observe from close by. The friendship with Oster was founded on their common disgust and horror toward that gangster episode.

Inside information on the affair, provided by Gisevius, aided Oster, still on civilian status, in securing entrée to Captain Patzig and employment in the Abwehr. It had also been Gisevius who first directed his friend's attention to the buildup of this hitherto small intelligence unit in the War Ministry and indicated that it would make an ideal spot for a Resistance center.[48] The next step in Oster's rehabilitation was his return to the Army through the intercession of General Halder, who urged Hammerstein, then still Army commander, to permit his re-entry as a special officer (E-Offizier).[49] From this category he gradually worked his way back to

[46] *Ibid.*
[47] More because of the mistakes of others than his own, Oster was removed from the Abwehr in the spring of 1943 and placed under restraint.
[48] Gisevius recording, January 1972.
[49] Letter of Halder to Helmut Krausnick, July 14, 1955 (in IfZ, ZS 240 (V)).

regular Army status and something just short of his previous General Staff rating.[50]

When Canaris became chief of the Abwehr in 1935, another rung up the ladder was in the offing for Oster. The admiral's previous duties had involved relations with the staff of Wehrkreis VI at Münster and he had come to know its dashing I-C chief very well. Later he had supported him for the Abwehr post with Patzig.[51]

Meanwhile Gisevius had been removed from the Gestapo because of his ill-concealed distaste for its activities and had found refuge at the Ministry of the Interior. He was not, however, a person who easily escaped notice. His physical presence—the height and bulk of an American football tackle—saw to that. There was also a certain vehemence and impetuosity in his nature, together with strong likes and antipathies. Less ardent spirits among Opposition associates were made uneasy, were sometimes frightened, sometimes repelled. This gave him a reputation for indiscretion he did not entirely deserve.

It got around that here was a man who sought ways to ward off "brown" pressures. The report reached Schacht who asked him to institute a search of his home for hidden microphones. Notations about what he was doing and saying also got to the SS and earned him Heydrich's special animosity. Pressures on the Ministry mounted and in May 1935 he was relieved of his post and sent for a while to Berlin police headquarters. Then, on the day Himmler became head of the Reich police forces (June 17, 1936), Gisevius was notified of his removal from *all* police-related functions. Soon after, he was transferred to Münster to work on price controls in the district administration.[52]

In Berlin, Gisevius had formed a close relationship with Arthur Nebe, founder and chief of the Criminal Police Office (called Kripo). Nebe, an old police specialist with some standing in the party, had been in charge of Gisevius's training for the Political Police. In 1934 Nebe had suffered a vital shock when he was directed by Heydrich to arrange for the "suicide" of Gregor Strasser, Hitler's former rival for control of the party. It turned out that

[50] Canaris's recommendation that he be returned to full General Staff status was rejected by the tight-laced Colonel Hossbach, who controlled such personnel matters as chief of the OKH's Central Division, a post he held in conjunction with his Wehrmacht adjutancy. Letter of Hossbach to Professor Wolfgang Foerster, September 14, 1952 (copy in author's possession).

[51] Halder to Krausnick, July 14, 1955 (in IfZ, ZS 240 (V)).

[52] Gisevius, *Bis zum bittern Ende*, 208, 225. Gisevius's testimony, IMT, XII, 289.

51

the order had come from Hitler with the complicity of Goering.[53] Any last doubts Nebe had about the criminality of the regime had been removed by the wholesale murders, without a shadow of legal procedure, in June–July 1934.[54] This experience pushed him across the line between doubting National Socialist and active Oppositionist. When Himmler assumed authority over the Reich police, Nebe's Criminal Police Office, previously under the Ministry of the Interior, was assigned to the Reich Main Security Office (Reichsicherheitshauptamt—RSHA), henceforth the special preserve of Heydrich.[55] Though a blow to him, this made Nebe a key figure in many situations where the fate of the Opposition stood in the balance.

Gisevius had also become closely acquainted with another powerful police official, Berlin's police president, Count Wolf von Helldorf. He was a man who differed in much from Nebe. Whereas Nebe was moved by revulsion against a political order which violated all the canons of criminology, Helldorf was a revolutionary adventurer, a former SA leader whose comrades had been slaughtered by "the black ones," and a renegade aristocrat who retained remnants of old class loyalties. His motivations were in general more complex than Nebe's and his final conversion to the Opposition was effected as a result of the Fritsch affair itself.

Through these connections, Gisevius again and again gained life-saving insights into threats arising from "the other side." Other pipelines led into the enemy camp but most of them produced driblets compared to the flow of critical information he received. His unique contribution has not always received full recognition. Gisevius's book *Bis zum bittern Ende* (which appeared in English translation titled *To the Bitter End*) steps on many toes and at times turns its back on Opposition saints and shrines. It has helped to make him a "controversial" figure whose writings are searched for flaws and whose services are minimized. Yet, as new evidence is uncovered, it tends more often to confirm his account of things than to raise new challenges.

In Münster, Gisevius's restless spirit led quickly to an extension of relationships with the Wehrkreis commander, General Günther von Kluge, the chief president or governor, Baron Ferdinand von

[53] Hans Bernd Gisevius, *Wo ist Nebe? Erinnerungen an Hitlers Reichskriminaldirektor* (Zurich, 1966), 134-140.
[54] Interview with Elisabeth Strünck-Gärtner, April 18, 1970.
[55] Gisevius's testimony, IMT, XII, 289-290.

# Growing Estrangements, 1936-37

Lüninck, and the Düsseldorf president, Carl Christian Schmid. But his stay was short. A feeling of apprehension in various Opposition sectors late in 1937 led to Schacht's getting in touch with Canaris through Oster, which resulted in an arrangement by which Gisevius would go on indefinite leave. It would have been futile to seek a transfer to a government agency in Berlin since none would risk taking on such a political liability. So, to provide for his livelihood, Schacht maneuvered a sinecure with a Bremen factory in which Gisevius never set foot.[56] For the next two years, supposedly taking time from government service for economic studies, Gisevius was the single full-time promotional worker the Opposition had at its disposal.

When moved by zeal, Oster was no more prone to idleness than was Gisevius. When something needed to be done, his rule of life was to go at it himself rather than look for others to do it.[57] One connection he made that was to be important in the approaching crisis was with Hitler's personal adjutant, Fritz Wiedemann, who provided the Abwehr group a valuable line into the Chancellery.[58] Though the principal results were to be realized later, half a dozen connections already existed between the Abwehr at Tirpitz Ufer and the Foreign Office. Oster had other links in process of formation, such as those with a number of foreign military attachés whom he trusted.[59] In many cases feelers had been extended and soundings made which facilitated more serious overtures when the crisis developed. Ties were also being formed—in part through the good offices of Goerdeler—with individuals and groups in many parts of the business world and in local government administrations.

Soon after Gisevius's return to Berlin, he and Oster went on a December holiday in the Dolomites with Theodor Strünck (a prosperous attorney from Frankfurt) and Strünck's wife, Elisabeth.

[56] *Ibid.*, XII, 195.

[57] Interview with Franz Liedig (with Helmut Krausnick), August 9, 1960.

[58] Wiedemann interview, December 2, 1969. Wiedemann should be characterized as a collaborator rather than a member of the Opposition. He had, of course, a pretty good idea of where his information was going and how it probably would be utilized.

[59] These were, in the front line, the Dutch attaché, Major Gijsbertus Sas, and the Yugoslav attaché, Colonel Vladimir Vauhnik. The relations with Sas receive extensive attention in the author's *Conspiracy against Hitler in the Twilight War*. About those with Vauhnik there seems to be nothing in print except what he brings into his own book without giving names. Vauhnik, *Memoiren eines Militärattachés: Mein Kampf mit dem Fingerspitzengefühl Hitlers* (Klagenfurt, 1967). The story of the relations of Oster and Vauhnik will be developed in a later study.

The Strüncks, who were also in touch with Schacht and President Schmid, had been seeking ways since 1936 to take an active part against the regime. Gisevius had already made them acquainted with Nebe, who told them of ominous clouds he perceived on the horizon. Something, he sensed, was brewing in the Prinz-Albrecht-Strasse, the SS and Gestapo headquarters. "If we are not ready to act soon," he gloomily predicted, "it will prove too late."

It was the Dolomite holiday which decided Oster to suggest to the Strüncks a more intimate collaboration. The couple were spurred to make an early move to Berlin, where, in June 1938, Strünck became a member of the Abwehr.[60]

## The Role of Erich Schultze

The history of the German military Opposition often touches on peripheral figures that sometimes became more central, sometimes faded away without much trace. A notable case is that of Dr. Erich Schultze. He was the son of a Hegemeister or state game-preserve manager at Wöllnau near Halle, and his family was on cordial terms with that of Bruno Heydrich, former opera singer and director of a musical academy. Erich Schultze, born in 1901, became fast friends with Reinhard Heydrich, whose birth was in 1904. During World War I the two boys spent their summers in the woods with prisoner workers and learned Russian from them.[61]

Their paths parted when Heydrich entered the Navy and Schultze, after brief service as an ensign in the Guards Cavalry Rifle Division, studied for the law. The two remained in touch though their political roads diverged sharply. Heydrich, cashiered out of the Navy, entered upon a meteoric career with the SS. Though not yet thirty, Schultze, a Social Democrat, rose to prominence in East Prussia as city councilor of Königsberg and an official (Landesrat) of the provincial administration. As recounted earlier,[62] he also was a "secret" officer of the Reichswehr with the mission of setting up a reserve system in East Prussia.[63]

Having taken the strongest possible public position against the

[60] Strünck-Gärtner interview, April 18, 1970. Gisevius recording, July 1971.

[61] Except when otherwise noted, the story concerning Dr. Schultze is derived from an interview of December 5, 1969.

[62] See above, p. 10n 21.

[63] In the possession of the author is a signed five-thousand-word statement by General Erich von Bonin, dated September 2, 1966, which gives a detailed account of Dr. Schultze's association with the Reichswehr as well as of other significant activities.

Nazis, Schultze became a target for their more ruffianly elements. In the night of January 31, 1933, the day after Hitler became Chancellor, the Schultze home was invaded by a gang of SS toughs who inflicted unspeakable tortures on him, his wife, and his four-year-old daughter and left him for dead.[64] Though unable in his state to accept a proferred candidacy in Germany's last parliamentary election, the indomitable man, on March 17, 1933, wrote a passionate appeal from his hospital bed to six Social Democratic leaders of the Reichstag. Instead of their making the futile gesture of voting "no" on the Enabling Act giving the Hitler government dictatorial powers, he pleaded with them to leave the building in a body. Thus they would preclude the quorum that would give the act legality.[65]

Forced by the SS to leave East Prussia early in 1935, Schultze took up residence in Berlin. Heydrich had provided for his protection in the hospital and had made a trip to his bedside. They now resumed relations, with Schultze a frequent visitor to the Prinz-Albrecht-Strasse headquarters. Heydrich would let himself go with amazing frankness, apparently cherishing this one escape from otherwise dehumanizing relationships. What he did not know about were his friend's contacts with anti-Nazis. Schultze had met General Beck soon after the war when, as a young assessor in Wiesbaden, he roomed with a relative of the retired Lieutenant Colonel Winterstein, a regimental comrade and close friend of Beck's. The latter was a frequent caller whenever Winterstein was in Wiesbaden and the young attorney was often drawn into their circle. Schultze met Hans Oster not long after. As a junior court official (Referendar) in Düben in Saxony, he knew Colonel Martini, husband of Captain Oster's elder sister, who owned an estate nearby. Sometimes his and Oster's visits there would coincide and they found much in common. Schultze's relation to Fritsch developed more than a decade later in Berlin when he resumed theological studies and was

[64] An affidavit of a close friend, Dr. Ludwig Bielschowsky, detailing these brutalities makes gruesome reading. Schultze suffered permanent injuries and bears to this day numerous scars of his harrowing experience. To force admissions from him, he and his wife, among other torments, had the nails torn from fingers and toes. She was pregnant and, of course, miscarried. "Eidestaatliche Erklärung von Dr. Ludwig Bielschowsky" (written at Frankfurt, March 24, 1954; copy in author's possession).

[65] This extraordinary document, together with Bielschowsky's affidavit on how it was delivered and received by the Social Democratic leaders, is being prepared by the present writer for publication.

a frequent visitor at the home of Professor Schubert of the Berlin University faculty. Fritsch also at times frequented this little circle and he and Schultze soon were drawn together by their mutual strong religious interest. Schultze had come to know Blomberg in East Prussia.

Thus Erich Schultze in the years 1935-39 renewed old ties and built new ones that were to play a part in bringing him closer to the vortex of the Wehrmacht crisis of 1938.

## Signs and Portents

As Germany moved into the last quarter of 1937 there were no visible signs of domestic or foreign crisis. In the Army leadership the feeling was one of unresolved problems, unclear leadership responsibilities, and an undefined tension.

For Fritsch mental uneasiness was accompanied by physical discomfort. He was reaching a state of health that demanded attention. Though not interfering with his duties, an old bronchial condition was increasingly troublesome. His physician, Dr. Karl Nissen, told him that a stay of about two months in a dry climate would be required to clear it up.[66] Reluctantly Fritsch decided to go on leave in Egypt and had been asking friends how best to spend his time there.[67]

Fritsch also felt under intensified surveillance. Since spring he had known that his mail was under "control" and he assumed as much for his telephone. He became so jittery about it that he put a cushion over his mother's phone whenever he visited her.[68]

Two of his official relationships were increasingly unpleasant. Goering was noticeably unfriendly. On one occasion he was so disagreeable that when he left, Fritsch rushed to throw open the window to gasp for air.[69] The tension with Blomberg was also becoming worse. Smoldering difficulties over the division of leadership responsibilities had burst into flame that summer. A "Directive on Unified War Preparation of the Wehrmacht" had been issued by Blomberg on June 24 and had led to an explosion in the General

[66] Nissen interview, July 15, 1971.
[67] Colonel Geyr von Schweppenburg, for example. Geyr von Schweppenburg, 172.
[68] J. A. Kielmansegg, *Der Fritsch-Prozess 1938*, 34.
[69] As related by Fritsch's second adjutant, Captain von Both, to Colonel Geyr von Schweppenburg. Geyr von Schweppenburg, 172.

Staff.[70] At bottom the quarrel was over the Army's refusal to accept the principle of equal importance of the three services, the foundation of the OKW's claim to supreme authority in strategic and planning matters. The fear that the Army would be crowded into a kind of military no-man's-land was not without foundation as later experience in the war was to prove. Opponents complained that the Army, as the senior and much the largest service, had a superiority complex which led it to demand a monopoly for itself in planning and strategy.

The Army's views were developed by Fritsch in an August memorandum on "Wehrmacht Leadership and Direction of the Wehrmacht in Wartime."[71] The fur flew and a trial of strength between Fritsch and Blomberg threatened. Fritsch was prepared to stake his post and notified the War Minister accordingly.[72] Blomberg struck back by threatening to resign himself if Fritsch insisted on transmission of the memorandum to Hitler.[73] Hossbach knew well that, if it came to a choice between the two generals, Hitler would never hesitate. During an earlier period of strife between them, the Fuehrer had said that he could then only back Blomberg. The Wehrmacht adjutant did succeed in persuading Fritsch to leave matters at a kind of stand-off.[74] But resolution of the issue was only postponed and would have to be fought through at some later date.

Meanwhile the relationship of War Minister and Army commander had descended to that of "cat and dog," as one observer put it. An effort to clear the air through a prolonged personal discussion only succeeded in patching up things for a few weeks.[75]

Fritsch's situation had become precarious. Rumors of his impending fall multiplied toward the end of the year. Reichenau, always on top of developments in the War Ministry and, in this instance, passionately concerned, hinted to an American correspondent, Carl von Wiegand, that Fritsch's days in office were numbered. He was surely observing events as a runner on the mark listens for the pistol shot. Stories maliciously magnifying Fritsch's ill health

[70] The directive is given in IMT, XXXIV, Document 175-C.
[71] Fritsch's memorandum is printed in Keitel, 123-144.
[72] Hossbach, *Zwischen Wehrmacht und Hitler*, 119.
[73] Keitel, 112. Neither Hossbach nor Keitel mentions the threat of resignation of the other party.
[74] Hossbach, *Zwischen Wehrmacht und Hitler*, 119.
[75] As related by Colonel Otto Heinz Grosskreuz, who had been Fritsch's adjutant after his dismissal. Interview, January 15, 1970.

and claiming that he was no longer fit to carry out his duties were sedulously spread about Berlin.[76]

The German stage was set for a new act in the high drama of the Wehrmacht in the Third Reich. It remained for fate to determine who would be privileged to write the script.

[76] J. A. Kielmansegg, *Der Fritsch-Prozess 1938*, 34.

# CHAPTER III

# Colonel Hossbach Takes Notes

At 4:15 P.M. on November 5, 1937, a gathering unique in the annals of the Third Reich convened in the Chancellery under the chairmanship of the Fuehrer. No such group had previously assembled on Hitler's order and none of like character was ever to be summoned by him again. It consisted of the War Minister (Blomberg), the heads of the three armed services (Fritsch, Goering, and Raeder), and the Minister of Foreign Affairs (Neurath). The inclusion of Baron Konstantin von Neurath gave the meeting a very different character from that anticipated by its military participants. Supposedly this was a session called to debate allocations for armaments among the services, but the addition of the Minister of Foreign Affairs made it a convocation of high officers of state concerned with aspects of Germany's external relations.

To complete the tally of those present, Colonel Friedrich Hossbach functioned as a silent observer. Unbidden, the Wehrmacht adjutant took it upon himself to set down those brief notes which, when expanded later into a summary statement, led to the assignment of his name to one of the more historic councils of the twentieth century.

It was not Hilter who had asked for the meeting. He was responsible, however, for the fact that it developed so differently from what was expected by the man who had inspired it. The real initiator was Blomberg, who had hoped to break through an impasse over the allocation of raw materials. During 1937 shortages in this area had made themselves painfully evident, so that the constant bickering of the Wehrmacht branches over the shares they considered appropriate was becoming serious friction.[1] Goering, since 1936 General Plenipotentiary for the Four Year Plan, was, in his customary ruthless and roughshod manner, exploiting his position and his greater influence with Hitler to steal for the Luftwaffe one march after another on the other services. The saying in the Luftwaffe's upper reaches "No worries about financial problems—the colonel general takes full responsibility!"[2] held as well for raw materials. Though for the most part Blomberg studiously avoided confrontations with Goering as likely to lead to difficulties with Hitler, the situation was becoming increasingly intolerable. The conduct of the always pushing troublemaker was reaching a point of challenge to Blomberg's sacred principle of unity in Wehrmacht direction as well as to the equilibrium between the services. Blomberg hoped that a meeting of the military chiefs, where he could be sure of Army and Navy backing, would lead to a decision by Hitler that Goering himself would have to respect.[3]

Adolf Hitler's peculiar genius for recognizing and pouncing on a purely fortuitous occasion to further personal designs was seldom more in evidence than in the use he now made of the meeting initiated by Blomberg. As chief of state it was entirely in order for him to preside; if he stretched a point by inviting the Foreign Minister also, who was to cavil at his decision? Automatically, however, it was no longer the military family affair the Minister of War had had in mind. National defense was thereby merged with the broad sweep of foreign policy. Such matters as armament and Army expansion would now be considered in terms of their bearing on an international program which, though not exactly news to the participants, had not hitherto been so comprehensively enunciated or related to prospective situations.

With two exceptions this emphasis was a surprise to those who had responded to the summons for the meeting. When by accident or design Goering appeared early (he may well have been directed to do so), Hitler's calculations were quite frankly spread before

[1] How raw materials had come to take priority even over financial considerations in rearmament was stressed by Jodl in a diary notation (350) of February 4, 1937: "The saying, money is no object, has, though in another sense, proven itself. The main role is played by raw materials."

[2] Schwerin von Krosigk, 226.

[3] These aspects of the background of the conference of November 5, 1937, are analyzed in greater detail by Hermann Gackenholz, "Reichskanzlei, 5. November 1937: Bemerkungen über 'Politik und Kriegsführung' im Dritten Reich," *Forschungen zu Staat und Verfassung: Festgabe für Fritz Hartung*, ed. R. Dietrich and G. Oestreich (Berlin, 1958), 60-62.

him. Above all else, the Fuehrer stressed, the conference was designed to needle Fritsch, whose pace in building up the Army was much too dilatory. It would also do no harm if Blomberg could be brought to put pressure on the Army commander. Queried by Goering on his reason for including Neurath, Hitler stated that he did not wish the affair to have a purely military character. What he wanted to bring home to the others, unnecessary in the case of Goering but especially important in that of Fritsch, was that Germany's international position demanded more forced draft in the tempo of rearmament.[4] Just before the meeting opened Goering passed on some of what Hitler had in mind to Raeder.

Scarcely had his audience—for the next two hours it was to be no more than that—been seated than Hitler, speaking from notes, launched forth on a disquisition aimed at delineating his fundamental position on the place Germany should occupy in the world and the requirements this would entail. He began, indeed, with a detailed review of some of the economic problems that were to have been the central theme of the meeting, but used them essentially as a springboard from which to dive into an oration on over-all policy. What he told them, he solemnly proclaimed, was the sum of intense reflection and of the experience of governing during the last four and one-half years. In the event of his death it must be taken as his testamentary injunction to whoever should wield power in the future.[5]

The dictator, Hossbach's statement goes on, then developed what had all the earmarks of his inmost thought on the needs of Germany and the course which must be pursued to provide for them. The fate of the nation would be determined by success or failure in dealing effectively with the problem of living space. Autarchy—an ideal much stressed in Nazi propaganda of that epoch—was not really attainable, particularly not in the vital area of foodstuffs, within the framework of existing territory. There was thus no choice but to enlarge greatly the space currently available. This aim should

---

[4]Testimony of Goering at Nuremberg, IMT, IX, 344-345.

[5]From the notes he took at the conference, Colonel Hossbach, in the following days, prepared the summary that was ultimately dated November 10. The German text may be found in IMT, XXV, 402-413, or in *Akten zur deutschen auswärtigen Politik, 1918-1945* (Baden-Baden, 1950), Series D, I, 25-32. The best English text is in *Documents on German Foreign Policy, 1918-1945* (Washington, 1949-66; cited hereafter as GD), Series D, I, 29-39. The text itself has been questioned in some quarters on suspicion that it may have been abbreviated before or after it got to Nuremberg, but, in the view of the author, is defended convincingly by Bussmann, 373-384.

be pursued not by a return to overseas expansion but by the annexation of regions immediately contiguous to the Reich. Unoccupied land did not exist nearby and it would be necessary to crush the resistance of those presently holding land to get what was needed. Undoubtedly France and Britain would equally oppose such efforts and it would be necessary to be on the alert for situations when they would be otherwise occupied and unable to intervene.

In any event, Hitler announced, the Reich could not afford to wait beyond the period 1943-45. By that time France and Britain would no longer entertain any illusions about German intentions and would be arming to thwart them. If, for example, Germany were ready by 1943 to eliminate Austria and Czechoslovakia by lightning moves, she would then, with her flanks secured, be in a position to deal effectively with France as the major enemy. But opportunity might well beckon earlier if the French Army were occupied with internal disorders or if Italy, by aggressive action in the Mediterranean, should become involved in hostilities with the Western Powers. This latter possibility especially engrossed the hopes of the Fuehrer and he claimed to consider it a possibility for as early as 1938. There was hope that the war in Spain would endure three years more, thus guaranteeing the continuance of Mediterranean tensions. Germany must further encourage Italy to establish herself in the Baleares; this was unacceptable to France and Britain and might conceivably embroil them with the Italians. Britain had already quietly written off Czechoslovakia, and France possibly had also. Poland and the Soviet Union were bound to move slowly and, if Germany acted with great speed, they would be presented with the *fait accompli* of the conquest of Czechoslovakia.

Sufficient has been said earlier in this volume to leave no doubt about Hitler's seriousness in proposing for the future this and, for that matter, a far greater measure of expansion toward the southeast and east. More doubt can legitimately be advanced about his exposition as it dealt with immediate prospects.[6] Clearly the thrust of his argument was all in the direction of magnifying the importance of a stepped-up pace in rearmament and the need of a consid-

[6] In his testimony at Nuremberg (IMT, IX, 344-345), Goering admitted the seriousness of purpose in much of Hitler's statement on fundamental goals but, in line with his persistent efforts to minimize the significance of this conference, he maintained that what was said about more immediate implications was largely rhetorical.

erably more aggressive posture on the part of Fritsch and Beck in organization and planning. To emphasize this point Hitler may well have deliberately exaggerated some of his statements. As he was to indicate later in another connection,[7] a little more or less credibility did not matter if one's aims were advanced.

However sincere Hitler was in enunciating his more immediate anticipations, no one today can doubt his firm determination to seize every opportunity to pounce with impunity on Austria or Czechoslovakia. It is less easy to gauge with confidence the reactions of his individual listeners. They obviously were in no way invited to pass judgment on the announced principles or the general direction of policy. Hitler had presented what he had in mind as immutably fixed and no voice was raised at the time or thereafter in dissent. The meeting, then, resembled in no way a Prussian Crown Council or one of Louis XIV's *Conseils d'État*. For Hitler himself, though not for those who heard him, it may have had a little of the character of a council of war, in which, rigidly within the framework of his proclaimed program, suggestions might be advanced for necessary first steps. As it happened, he got a much more emphatically negative response than he had bargained for, which no doubt contributed mightily to this being the final occasion on which anything resembling "the Fuehrer taking counsel with his lieutenants" was to take place during the last seven years of the Third Reich.

Approximately 85 percent of the Hossbach document details Hitler's revelations and argumentation. The short page and one-third of the Nuremberg publication recounting the following two and one-half hours of discussion scarcely can reflect the viewpoints raised against them. That part of the verbal exchange which dealt with the economic controversy the meeting had been called to adjust is summarized in a single sentence. Blomberg and Fritsch, for once in complete harmony, brought up point after point contradicting Hitler's more short-range calculations. In what, despite the sketchy summary, sounds like a rapid fire of objections, they took issue first with those aspects of Hitler's analysis which dealt with the German position vis-à-vis the Western Powers. Under no circumstances, they maintained, should France and Britain be allowed to become enemies of Germany. The military resources of the former, they insisted, had been greatly underrated in the Fuehrer's discourse. A Franco-Italian war would demand no more than twenty

[7] In his Berghof speech of August 22, 1939.

French divisions on the Alpine front; there would be more than enough others to deal with Germany. Blomberg heavily underscored the poor state of the Reich's western defenses and the contrasting excellence of the Czechoslovak fortifications which had grown into another Maginot Line. The dismaying vision that emerged from his remarks portrayed a German Army gnawing away fruitlessly at the fortresses of Bohemia while the French inundated a denuded frontier in the West.

Fritsch stated that he had just ordered the preparation of a study on the operational problems of a war with Czechoslovakia. In view of what Hitler had said, he thought it imperative to forgo his two-month leave which was due to start on November 10. This Hitler declared to be unnecessary since no conflict was to be expected in the near future. When Neurath commented that an Italian collision with the French and British in no way appeared imminent, the Fuehrer conceded that none was probable before the summer of 1938. In response to Blomberg's and Fritsch's skepticism about France and Britain having all but written off Czechoslovakia, he merely reiterated his conviction that London would stand aside and that Paris would not brave a military involvement with Germany without assurance of British support.

Interesting in the story of November 5 insofar as we have it is the reticence up to this point of Hermann Goering. Thus far he had restricted himself to suggesting that, in view of what the Fuehrer had said, it would be advisable to consider terminating the intervention in Spain; this decision, Hitler said, might have to be made at a suitable juncture. In view of Goering's consistent inclination against risk-taking during the successive crises of 1938–39, it may be concluded that at bottom he shared the misgivings of his two Wehrmacht colleagues. But as they were carrying the ball with so much spirit and at the same time taking on themselves all the odium of obstructing the Fuehrer's aggressive plans, it was natural that he should sit back and conserve his credit with Hitler, especially in view of the personal encounter with the two generals which was now to follow and which, though doubtless surprised by its heat, he must have anticipated.

Students of the period have at times remarked critically on the total absence of any moral tone in the protests raised.[8] The issue as it relates to antagonism to Hitler's aggressive resolves is alluded

[8] Thus Wheeler-Bennett, 361, and Peter Hoffmann, *Widerstand, Staatsstreich, Attentat: Der Kampf der Opposition gegen Hitler* (Munich, 1969), 37.

to at various points in the present volume.[9] It doubtless merits attention in connection with this far-ranging disclosure of both Hitler's ultimate designs and the sinister opportunism with which he surveyed the current international scene. By November 1937, however, those present knew the chief of state sufficiently well to recognize the utter hopelessness of influencing his policies by advancing considerations of right and wrong. The form and spirit of the discourse he had addressed to them that very day were proof enough that he would reject with scorn any discussion on such a plane.

The problem they faced with him is universally encountered among men and hardly restricted to those who had the misfortune to deal with Adolf Hitler. The pragmatic argument is perforce the only resort for advocates of morality if they hope to debate persuasively with less idealistic fellows. To have taken any other line on November 5, 1937, not only would have proved unavailing but would have constituted a declaration of a parting of the ways with the dictator for which none of those present was prepared at the moment. Neurath, for his part, was shortly after to lay his position on the line in a broad-based statement rejecting what Hitler had pronounced.

The Hossbach document, it has been noted, devoted no more than a concluding sentence to the personal confrontation between Goering and his two fellow generals. It was then probably well past seven, much too late for the thoroughgoing discussion on which Blomberg had reckoned. Armament experts who had been waiting impatiently in the antechamber of the Chancellery were never summoned to join the conclave and had perhaps already been dismissed. Yet Hossbach's reference to "a second part of the discussion" dignifies it too much to allow for the belief that it occupied no more than the closing minutes of a meeting concluded at 8:30 P.M. His one summary sentence may largely be explained by his reluctance to derogate from the enormity of Hitler's "testamentary statement" by dwelling at any length on this personal bickering on another topic. Also, a rapid and heated back-and-forth exchange that went on for some time would have been even harder for a man who had no shorthand to record than the less hectic and more broadly formulated previous discussion.

Blomberg and Fritsch seem to have been in a state of considerable

[9] See also Deutsch, 186.

agitation over the course taken by the conference. They could hardly fail to be exasperated by the unheralded switch in the theme of the meeting and were probably, in view of the limited time still left to them, inclined to hit harder and with less circumspection than they might otherwise. In any event, the annoyance they felt necessary to restrain in exchanges with Hitler was vented on the supposedly safer target of Goering. Thus they landed on him with a sharpness that rather took his breath away and at one point (according to Hossbach's memoirs) led him to the half-plaintive, half-furious outburst that he too should be allowed to express his opinion from time to time.[10]

Blomberg, much in the lead but at times seconded by Fritsch, did not confine himself to the allocation of raw materials but ventured comments which could only be taken as impugning Goering's general performance as director of the Four Year Plan. Hitler, though his features indicated surprise at the vigor of the attack, made no move to come to his lieutenant's aid but confined himself to the role of "attentive listener."[11] His neutral posture was in line with his practice of promoting rather than inhibiting clashes among the more prominent figures of his regime by such tactics as giving them overlapping responsibilities. He may also have taken malicious satisfaction in the discomfiture of his overly presumptuous crown prince. In view of the late hour and the constricted form of the discussion, it was hardly difficult for him to avoid ruling on the points at issue.

Blomberg's unexpectedly severe critique, in the presence of Hitler and high dignitaries of the Third Reich, could not fail to be a grievous blow to the vanity of the most puffed-up figure of the Nazi hierarchy. The consequent resentment must have contributed substantially to the ruthlessness that was soon to be demonstrated by the vengeful Goering in his endeavor to unseat the Minister of War and slip into his place.[12]

### Sequelae of November 5

In the history of the Nazi period, there are few events that can yield so wide a range of assessment as the conference of November

[10] Hossbach, *Zwischen Wehrmacht und Hitler*, 120.

[11] *Ibid.*, 120, 191.

[12] In a postwar interrogation Blomberg affirmed that he had always "feared the vengeance of Goering." Otto John, *Zweimal kam ich heim: Vom Verschwörer zum Schützer der Verfassung* (Düsseldorf-Vienna, 1969), 28.

# Colonel Hossbach Takes Notes

5, 1937.[13] Assuredly the related developments of the following months did not lack dramatic impact. To many analysts the simple statement that within a quarter of a year the three men who had ventured to oppose the Fuehrer's position were out of office is sufficient proof of a direct causal relationship. In contrast to this, others have maintained that the meeting of November 5, if it can be called the climax of anything, was so only in a theatrical sense. To them it was no more than a single incident in the confrontation between Hitler and the opponents of his foreign policy. It should not, they argue, be regarded as determining for the leadership crisis that followed in late January, early February 1938.

In the analysis of this problem it is necessary to examine (1) the continuing impact of the conference on Hitler's hearers and on those to whom they communicated something of their experience, and (2) the influence on Hitler himself of the discussion that followed his discourse. There is further the related and, for what was to follow, perhaps decisive question of the effect of the second part of the discussion on Goering.

Undoubtedly for all concerned the sweep and crassness of the Fuehrer's presentation had been a real shock and had left them more or less off balance. Goering himself, despite being forewarned and fundamentally far more familiar then the others with Hitler's thought, was not entirely immune to this. In judging the extent and enduring quality of this impact, it is necessary to make one sharp distinction: that between those who customarily went along with little or no debate on any line the Fuehrer indicated and those who had felt a growing discomfort as his ultimate aims more clearly emerged and his risk-taking became more pronounced. To the former group belonged Goering, Blomberg, and Raeder; in the latter must be reckoned Neurath and Fritsch along with the absent but quickly oriented Beck.

Raeder, as was his habit when participating in conventicles that were not strictly concerned with his professional responsibilities, had sat in silence through both Hitler's exposition and the expression of other views which followed. Goering having told him just before the meeting that Hitler's purpose was to spur the Army

---

[13] The controversy engendered has found reflection not only in the basic literature on the period, notably that concerned with analyzing the origins of World War II, but also in more limited treatises. Among the latter are the previously cited essay of Gackenholz, which tends to minimize the impact of the affair, and the contrary position delineated by Count Peter Kielmansegg, "Die militärisch-politische Tragweite der Hossbach Besprechung," *VfZ*, Vol. 8, No. 3 (July 1960), 269-275.

to greater efforts in rearmament, he took the Fuehrer's rhetorical flourishes with a grain of salt. He was least prepared to take seriously any notion of an inevitable showdown with Britain; risking the Navy which was still in the launching stage of its rebuilding program in such a conflict seemed to him too absurd to contemplate. In this light, at any rate, he described his reactions later before the International Military Tribunal.[14]

Though it was in the interest of Raeder, as it was in that of Goering, to minimize at Nuremberg the importance of the November 5 meeting, there is in his case much to argue for his fundamental sincerity. He seems to have managed to convince himself of what he wanted to believe. Though he had a pronounced stubborn streak and could at times outlast Hitler in some dispute on matters of deep concern to the Navy, his inclination was to avoid confrontation with the dictator on borderline issues, especially such as had a political tinge. From the strictly service standpoint to which he in the main subscribed, it was obviously wise to conserve his ammunition for exclusively Navy concerns. A dash of naiveté facilitated the process of self-deception, permitted him to be fooled repeatedly with the same dodges, and ordinarily made him susceptible to the Fuehrer's dialectic. When contradictions to what he was told could no longer be ignored, he seemed to lean instinctively toward whatever version he found the more reassuring.

Those anxieties which remained to trouble Raeder after the meeting were largely dispelled by an aside directed to him as they were leaving the room by Blomberg, who had apparently rallied considerably from his state of shock. Perhaps as much to reassure himself as the admiral, whose perturbation he may have sensed, the War Minister remarked that Hitler's fanciful and wide-ranging exposition must not be taken too seriously. It was probably at this point too that he let drop an ancient proverb, "Kommt Zeit, kommt Rat [With time comes counsel]." By this he seems to have meant that should this bridge actually have to be crossed, they would have to find ways to thwart any bellicose moves on Hitler's part.[15]

---

[14] IMT, XIV, 34–37. See further Erich Raeder, *Mein Leben* (2 vols., Tübingen, 1957), II, 149–150. Raeder's reactions are convincingly analyzed by Klaus-Jürgen Müller, *Das Heer und Hitler: Armee und nationalsozialistisches Regime 1933–1940* (Stuttgart, 1969), 245.

[15] In an affidavit of February 26, 1946 (IMT, XL, 406), Blomberg deals with this conversation as if it had involved the participants generally after they had left the meeting room. Raeder's memoirs (II, 150) make it clear that the War Minister's comments were addressed to him alone as they walked out together. Neurath and

# Colonel Hossbach Takes Notes

The reactions of Blomberg present a less simple case for analysis than those of Raeder. Where the admiral, if he had allowed himself to face the issue, might have rebelled inwardly against the immorality of Hitler's flaunted program of aggression, it is less likely that Blomberg suffered any such qualms. On the other hand, as a man of far more sober judgment than Hitler, he had been consistent in responding with caution to every critical international situation. If he had remained in office, we may with confidence assume that he would have reacted similarly to any proposals for drastic action in 1938 and 1939. Yet, though he was ever prepared to act as a brake, he did not really anticipate too great a call for it, accustomed as he was to Hitler's exaggerations and histrionics. "These people are so much given to heroics," he said in 1936 to Colonel Baron Geyr von Schweppenburg when that military attaché in London voiced his anxieties about the adventurous trend in German policy.[16] The War Minister, as his remarks to Raeder show, recovered his composure after the adjournment of the meeting and began to retreat from the posture of alarm he had evidenced during its course. His annoyance about the way Hitler had ridden roughshod over the original concept of the meeting had probably stimulated him to a more vigorous expression of his objections than he would otherwise have ventured. Also, once his emotional pitch had subsided, he may have been somewhat appalled by his own temerity. There is no evidence that, until his world collapsed about him three months later, he returned in any talk with Hitler to the topics on which he had voiced opposition. Instead he submitted without further murmur to that part of Hitler's dictate that called for specific measures—the coordination of military planning and preparation with the concept of a resort to arms on short notice against Czechoslovakia if opportunity should present itself in 1938.

On December 7 Blomberg issued a "First Supplement to the Directive on the Unified War Preparation of the Wehrmacht of 24 June 1937." Two appendixes were added on December 1, amending the provisions for Case Green, the plans for a possible war with Czechoslovakia.[17] Whether Blomberg's action really gave Hitler all he wanted will receive attention later. Certainly it was

Fritsch, if they had been among the listeners, would probably have made rejoinders that would have been reflected in Raeder's account. It is noteworthy, too, that Hossbach says nothing of such post-conference exchanges among the military men who had been present.

[16] Geyr von Schweppenburg interview, January 26, 1970.

[17] IMT, Doc. 175-C, XXXIV, 745-746. GD, Series D, VII, 635-638.

all that could be demanded from the War Minister for the time being in the way of concrete steps.

As for Goering, he made an immediate and ostentatious gesture of falling into line by a separate order that amounted to another challenge to the advocates of unified command in the War Ministry.[18] The Luftwaffe was directed to put itself in readiness for a war on short notice with Czechoslovakia. If Goering was aggrieved over the lack of support his chief had given him in his own sphere on November 5, this can only have served to inspire him to make ever more extravagant demonstrations of devotion. It was surely no suitable time for the executor-designate and chief beneficiary-to-be of Hitler's still unwritten will to take issue with what the Fuehrer had called his testamentary statement in the field of external policy, especially since Goering could tell himself that at bottom it reflected no more than pious hopes and might, when the time to inherit arrived, be conveniently ignored. Besides, Goering had set his sights on a goal for realization of which the good will of the Fuehrer was a primary consideration—succession to Blomberg in the direction of the Wehrmacht.

In contrast to the miscellany of naiveté, wishful disbelief, and crass opportunism evidenced by Raeder, Blomberg, and Goering, the reactions of Neurath and Fritsch were governed by a sense of responsibility toward the functions with which they were charged in the state. The Foreign Minister was so deeply shaken that he decided once and for all that he would have no truck with such a policy.[19] Being far more sophisticated in international matters than the military men in Hitler's audience, he realized that the day's pronouncements had implications well beyond earlier statements on foreign policy, often vague and incoherently formulated. Here was, he knew, a completely serious and frightfully consistent assertion of intentions that forecast a program of potentially limitless aggression. Neurath sensed some, perhaps a great deal, of what his fellow listeners had missed: that the very unreality of Hitler's short-term expectations offered the most sinister portent for the immediate future. It was startling enough to be dished up such fancies as a civil war in France and a Franco-British-Italian embroilment in the Mediterranean—both portrayed as conceivable within a few months—accompanied by the demand that the lis-

[18] As reflected in Jodl's diary entry (355) dated November 5 (probably dated after the writing).
[19] Cited from an affidavit of Baroness Ritter, IMT, XVI, 700.

teners of November 5 should attune their thinking and planning accordingly. More irresponsible yet was the sweeping prediction, without evidence or logical underpinning, of French and British *désintéressement* in the face of an unprovoked attack on Czechoslovakia. In effect, the dictator had put up a smokescreen of imaginary opportunities that might be exploited. Beyond this, he did not shrink from the greater risks of creating his own openings for aggression if no convenient ones should present themselves.

Despite Blomberg's criticism of some of Hitler's prognosis, Neurath knew better than to waste his time trying to enlist that "rubber lion" in an alliance for peace that invited a further serious confrontation with the dictator. Instead he turned unhesitatingly to Fritsch in whose basic integrity and steadfastness he had reason to have considerably more confidence. Despite the fact that his agitation was bringing on a series of heart seizures, Neurath called on Fritsch on November 7, showing a dispatch amazing in this rather dilatory and sluggish old man.[20] It is not known which of the two proposed adding Beck to their deliberations on how they might turn Hitler from his fatal path. We may assume that Fritsch had already discussed the problem with his chief of staff and that Beck, who had the closest professional and personal relationship with Hossbach, had already received a preliminary report from the Wehrmacht adjutant.

The Foreign Minister and the Army chiefs were instantly at one that everything possible must be done to divert Hitler from his course. Since Fritsch was already scheduled for an audience of leave-taking on the 9th, it was agreed that he would present the military arguments then. Neurath would follow up with the political ones as soon as he could secure an audience.

Unfortunately the talk with Fritsch, of which we know only the general intention, ruffled the Fuehrer's feathers to a point where, not needing much insight to discern what the Foreign Minister wished to say, he brusquely put off the meeting for two months.

[20] The present writer can perceive no valid ground for such sneers as that of Wheeler-Bennett (362) who says the conference of November 5 had only a "delayed action" effect on Neurath and that the "moral or immoral aspects of the Fuehrer's statement do not appear to have revealed themselves until 48 hours later." When one considers that the meeting lasted until eight thirty in the evening, that, quite apart from the emotional strain under which he labored, it must have been exhausting to an elderly man of far from robust constitution, that Neurath probably had his first heart seizure that evening or on the next day, and that an appointment had to be made for a call that may have taken place as early as the morning of the 7th, it seems strange to accuse him of taking his time about pursuing the matter.

When, finally, on January 14, Hitler consented to receive Neurath, he proved in no way softened. The Minister protested in vain that the announced course would lead to another world war and pleaded that much of what Hitler wanted could be gained, though of course more slowly, by peaceful means. These arguments produced only the cold response that there no longer was time for so deliberate a procedure. In the end Neurath could only say that he would not be an accomplice in such a policy and asked to be allowed to resign his office.[21] This Hitler, thinking no doubt of the Minister's considerable international prestige and the speculations and uneasiness abroad in case of his sudden departure, was not yet prepared to consider. It is a safe guess, however, that his early dismissal was from that moment a settled matter. Thereafter it was merely a question of when it might be accomplished with a minimum of international attention.

Since neither Fritsch nor Beck survived to relate their stories after the war, it is not easy to reconstitute their moves on the days which followed November 5. Beck's reaction to what he learned from Fritsch, Neurath, and probably Hossbach on November 6 and 7 is not directly documented, but can have differed only in degree from his shocked response when Hossbach gave him his written summary on the 10th or 11th. As so often when he was of troubled mind and wished to master his emotions, Beck then reached for his pen to set down his thoughts.

In notes which bear the date November 12 the chief of staff delineated his views on Germany's position in the world. He did not question that she contended with somewhat special problems in her spatial relationships. These derived from both her central position on the Continent and the territorial alterations imposed by the Treaty of Versailles. But a thousand years of history had stabilized the populations of Europe; extensive displacements were conceivable only at the cost of disturbances whose consequences no one could foresee. Minor territorial shifts were always possible but must not be attempted at risks to the integrity of the German nation.[22]

Autarchic aims as furthered by the Four Year Plan, said Beck, could provide only emergency solutions. Reflecting the teaching of Goerdeler, he felt that for the long pull Germany must secure

[21] Neurath's testimony at Nuremberg, IMT, XVI, 701.
[22] The substance of Beck's notes is given by Foerster, 80–82. The originals are in Beck's papers (in IfZ, BAMA, H 08-28 (III)).

the largest possible role in the world economy to escape slow strangulation. An effort to deal with this problem by enlarging her living space by force would run up against too many obstacles. France and Britain would surely opposè any expansion of German territory or power. He did not agree, however, that this opposition was unalterable; heretofore no adequate effort had been made to persuade them by peaceful means. Though mildly stated, this was an undoubted slam at Hitler's tactics of bluff, bluster, and unilateral action and, inferentially, broke a lance for the Republic's policy of reassuring the Western Powers. Politics was the art of the possible, said Beck. One must exhaust all means of achieving an understanding, the wisest policy even if a break should prove unavoidable later.

The British Empire, he admitted, was not invulnerable. Yet, next to the United States, it was still the most influential world power. Therefore Britain could always count on allies in moments of danger. The Fuehrer, Beck noted, was also inclined to ignore the Soviet Union as a power factor. Hitler's historical parallels were without sound foundation. The evaluation of military factors was not his province but that of the responsible professionals. Politico-military, financial, economic, and spiritual considerations were entirely missing from the discourse. Hitler's conclusion that it would be necessary to solve the German space question by 1943–45 at the latest was so lacking in supporting argument as to be "shocking."

Beck expressed doubts about Czechoslovakia and Austria having surplus foodstuffs and raw materials. The thesis that their incorporation would benefit Germany militarily and politically needed thorough evaluation. No doubt German leaders ought to think about and be prepared for opportunities to deal effectively with the Austrian and Czech questions. The idea of going beyond this to create "opportunities" if none offered themselves required far more thorough and wide-ranging examination than Hossbach's summary statement indicated Hilter had devoted to it.

Though Beck often wrote down such reflections on complicated issues solely to help clarify his own thinking, his notes in this instance seem to have been intended also for other eyes. Despite the critical drift of his arguments, they are set down with a restraint he would scarcely have observed had he written only for himself. No more than once or twice does he permit his indignation to break through. That he intended to present his thoughts to higher authority is indicated also by the existence of two typed copies of the notes in addition to the handwritten original. Since Fritsch had left two days before on his scheduled two-month journey, he could hardly have been the target of Beck's argumentation. During his absence the chief of staff conducted Army affairs and Blomberg was for the time being his immediate superior. The fact that the War Minister also had the Hossbach summary made him the only person to whom Beck's comments could be properly addressed. At the moment he was the only channel through which Beck could hope to influence Hitler.

If the staff chief did, in fact, present his reflections orally or in this form to Blomberg,[23] it is scarcely probable that the War Minister passed on the warnings to Hitler. After November 5 Blomberg, uneasy about being so forward in taking issue with Hitler and in his vehement criticism of Goering, appears to have been more inclined to let sleeping dogs lie than to stir them up by making renewed issue of the points raised. Also, and far from immaterial, the time was fast approaching when he had a favor to ask of them both.

Fritsch had stated his objections to Hitler's exposition in plain language at the time of the conference. Even before the meeting he had been of troubled mind about his own position with the dictator and had given thought to forgoing his vacation in Egypt.[24] His offer during the discussion to cancel his leave may have been motivated as much by fundamental anxiety about party machinations as, forewarned by what Hitler had just said, by a feeling that it was necessary to act the role of watchdog against foreign adventures.[25] The task of confronting the Fuehrer a second time to set himself against his pet projects was one he faced on November 9 with little hope and a heavy heart. "Again and again," he wrote to a friend that day, "new and difficult things are brought to me which must be attended to before I leave."[26]

Since we have no record of this conversation, it is necessary to depend entirely upon surmise. Fritsch certainly did not come to it on the eve of his departure to raise basic issues or lay his

[23]This is the guess of Beck's biographer, though he notes that Hossbach did not regard it as probable. Foerster, 168n46.

[24]Gackenholz, 473.

[25]This suggestion of Fritsch's certainly should not be interpreted to mean an eagerness to get the Army ready for what Hitler had in mind.

[26]In a letter to Baroness Schutzbar. J. A. Kielmansegg, *Der Fritsch-Prozess 1938*, 34.

command on the line. Yet his comments can only have been wholly critical, in conformity with what had been agreed with Neurath, and the exchanges may at times have had a stormy aspect. If they did not, Hitler must have shown great self-restraint, for he certainly was much exercised thereafter. Hence his rudeness to Neurath in refusing to receive him until two months later. In the weeks which followed, Colonel Hossbach also had occasion to note increasing outbursts of suspicion against the Army.[27]

Whatever Hitler may have promised himself from the conference of November 5, after the 9th he can have had no doubt that insofar as its main target, Fritsch, was concerned, there was no prospect of realization. He may or may not have gone to the meeting expecting the continuance of a tolerable working relationship with Fritsch if he could produce the proper effect on him. At the very least, he must have hoped to bring Fritsch sufficiently into line to clear the road for the next stage of his program. It was now evident that Fritsch, influenced by Beck and his back stiffened by him, would continue to be the same stumbling block to swift-paced rearmament as heretofore, about which Hitler had so often fruitlessly complained. All the dictator had pleaded for on November 5, with the innumerable implications for the Army in organization, expansion, officer selection, and strategic planning, would continue to be resisted if not sabotaged outright. The impression Hitler must have gained from Fritsch's posture on November 5 and 9 really sealed the fate of the general as the Army's commander in chief. Thereafter Hitler only waited for an occasion when he might rid himself of this incubus with a minimum of complications.[28] What was needed to bring about such a situation was a convenient catalyst, and this, with little delay, was found in Werner von Blomberg.

To what extent did Blomberg's remarks in the discussion of November 5 place him in Hitler's bad graces or make him appear, like Fritsch, an obstacle in the Fuehrer's path? The main anxiety expressed by the two generals had concerned the danger of embroilment with France and Britain. In the view of some writers,[29] this

[27] Hossbach, *Zwischen Wehrmacht und Hitler,* 120.

[28] It has been urged in contradiction of this thesis that Fritsch himself, when he set down on February 1, 1938, his suppositions on why catastrophe had overtaken him, did not mention either date. This objection loses force when we remind ourselves that the general at this stage, unable to conceive of such infamy on the part of a chief of state, could think only of how he might convince the Fuehrer of his innocence and of the machinations of the SS chiefs. The Fritsch notation of February 1 is to be found in *ibid.,* 59-62.

[29] Thus Gackenholz, 474.

could hardly be regarded by Hitler as a fundamental contradiction of his policy since he himself wished to avoid such a clash while moving against Czechoslovakia. This argument evades the more vital point at issue—the element of risk-taking. Hitler believed, or claimed to do so, that the threat of Franco-British intervention was sufficiently negligible to be ignored with impunity. Like Neurath, Blomberg and the Army leaders were convinced that this was a miscalculation and insisted that the danger was indeed great. Most vital of all, it is probably correct to say that, even if they had not disagreed with Hitler on the extent of the peril, they still would have exercised restraint and argued that *any* risk of a world conflict over Czechoslovakia must be avoided. This brings one back again to the ultimate difference of viewpoint on the larger issues involved: all the Fuehrer's eloquence on the subject of living space had failed to elicit a responsive echo. Far from sweeping the generals off their feet, it had merely left them cold and troubled.

Hitler must have known that, despite Blomberg's gingering up of Case Green to give it a more aggressive cast, the War Minister would continue to act in the same alarmed, foot-dragging way that had characterized him at every internationally critical moment since 1935. With a mood of restiveness and an urge toward dramatic accomplishment dominating the dictator again at the turn of the year 1937–38, this prospect was bound to rouse both impatience and a measure of resentment. For Adolf Hitler men tended to fall more and more into two categories: unconditional adherents and opponents. Fritsch had never been counted among the first and no one would heretofore have put Blomberg among the second. As Hitler's egotism and impatience with contradiction grew, he also became less inclined to make in-between distinctions. Blomberg no longer measured up and was at the same time gradually becoming more dispensable. Hitler, as his later relations with Mussolini were to show, was not a man without a sense of obligation. In the dark recesses of what passed with him for a conscience, qualms about the removal of the man who had been his only War Minister were to arise from time to time. He could not forget that for the extensive coordination of the armed forces with his regime he owed more to Blomberg than to any other man alive. The recollection of this continued to assert itself in surges of mixed gratitude and regret long after the Minister left office. More significant than this, however, was the usually accompanying remark that, quite

76

apart from Blomberg's outrageous marriage, the time had come to part from him.[30]

If there is agreement on anything in the history of the Blomberg-Fritsch affairs, it is assuredly that the initiatory role was played not by Hitler but by Goering. At first glance this may seem to diminish rather than enhance the importance of the conference of November 5 in relation to the developments which followed. Close analysis, however, indicates the exact opposite. It is a safe assumption that Goering, furious at the vigor of the attack upon him, was henceforth alert to opportunities to even the score. He also no doubt remained, more than ever, on the lookout for ways to take advantage of his professional rivals. If there was any probability, even some likelihood, of war within a year or two, this accentuated the expediency of getting the Wehrmacht into his hands at the earliest conceivable date. The more immediate portents were favorable: there was the assurance, gained from his knowledge of Hitler and his observations of November 5, that he could count on being permitted wide latitude in any undertaking he chose to launch against the two generals who stood in his path.

[30] As evidenced from conversations recorded in the diary of Captain Engel, entries of April 20, 1938, and September 10, 1939.

# CHAPTER IV

# The Eclipse of Blomberg

In taking up the story of how the two Werners, Blomberg and Fritsch, were thrust from the military summit of the Third Reich, we enter a debate where truth and fable, fact and fancy, and guesses good and bad have long intermingled. What we seek to form into more intelligible shape is a bewildering mosaic, in which, even where the pieces seem to fit together, they do not always make a meaningful pattern. Persistent attempts at rearrangement to make better sense produce varying results. What seems to lead to greater clarity in one sector may distort what had appeared in fair order in another.

The most contradictory interpretations have centered on the problem of how much can be assigned to plot, how much to circumstance. There is no longer much disagreement about the central role of intrigue, but views differ greatly on just where it enters the picture, its relation to the always important time factor, the identification of all the targets, and exactly what was meant to be done to them. Argument also dwells endlessly on the villains in the piece and who among them should be classed as principals, confederates, or only accessories after the fact. On one point there may be a measure of consensus; on a related one the most complete dissonance.

### Perennial Villains: Goering and the SS

Opinion is all but unanimous in assigning a prominent role to Goering and various officials at or near the top of the SS. This is a natural recourse when looking for sources of affliction in

78

# The Eclipse of Blomberg

Hitler's Reich. "Cherchez le SS" is a slogan that leaps to mind when exploring the darker riddles of that period. It applies with special force to misfortunes suffered by the Army and its leadership. For the researcher probing to find what really happened, this very natural habit of assumption creates obvious dangers. The fact that a man or a group may have shown themselves capable of virtually anything does not automatically identify them as the perpetrators of every misdeed that happens to coincide with their interests. On any particular occasion the responsibility may lie elsewhere. Caution is especially demanded when dealing with so ready-made a scapegoat as Adolf Hitler but must be heeded also in assessing the role of other Nazi captains and agencies.

After perhaps seeming to imply the opposite, it is possible to affirm in this instance that the SS leadership was indeed deeply implicated. In laying up trouble for Werner von Fritsch it was certainly chiefly responsible. But it was not the immediate force which set things in motion toward the end of 1937, hitching the action neatly to what was in preparation to entrap Blomberg.

In the move against both of the generals the decisive impulse came from Goering. So flat an assertion on what has been almost universally assumed but usually regarded as lacking conclusive proof may cause surprise, but the reasons for making it will emerge as the story unfolds. The main problem is perhaps that of just when he decided to take a hand. It was certainly no later than December 1937 but may well have been several weeks earlier.[1] More exact determination depends on the question of just when he became absorbed in the private affairs of Fritsch and Blomberg.

Too much that is cut and dried has been propounded about the activities of Nazi agencies. Actually their many overlapping functions and their tendency to trespass on each other's domains teach that it is never safe to accept appearances at first glance. Goering had never forgiven the SS for managing to get such a power-generating tool as the Gestapo away from him. To keep his hand in on cloak-and-dagger operations, he built up and gave the widest possible scope to the Forschungsamt (FA) or Department of Investigation. The researches of this innocent-sounding institution were diverse and far-reaching. It was responsible for much of the dirty work for which credit or blame, as the case may be,

---

[1]According to Gisevius (*Bis zum bittern Ende,* 260), it also was Goering and not Himmler who originally brought the charges against Fritsch to Hitler's attention in 1936. See below, p. 145.

often accrued to one of the notorious SS-controlled agencies—the SD or the Gestapo. Thus it was the FA which had the official monopoly on wiretapping. Some notion of the extent of such activities as monitoring telephone calls and decoding the wireless messages of foreign governments may be gathered from the fact that it employed no fewer than a thousand language specialists.[2]

With good reason, Heydrich believed that whatever Goering preferred to keep to himself he withheld, however much he was charged to pass on any data on civilians that were pertinent to the duties of the SD or Gestapo. In the end he saw no choice but to penetrate the FA with his own people to be sure of getting the information he wanted.[3]

Insofar as there was a continuing surveillance of high military officials, the FA also seems to have been the organization entrusted therewith.[4] There is no evidence of a blanket watch over top-level commanders, though specific individuals no doubt were marked for attention.[5] In view of Goering's solicitude in all that concerned Fritsch and Blomberg, he must indeed have been "specific" in his orders to the FA to keep close track of their movements. It may be assumed that he gleaned what he could about both their public and their private affairs.[6] Thus he may have known more than Blomberg did himself about the background of the young woman in whom the War Minister was developing an obsessive interest in the second half of 1937.

### Blomberg and Eva Gruhn

In December 1937 Werner von Blomberg was in his sixtieth year. His external appearance gave a somewhat mixed impression of aging and vigor. His small, rather worn face, with heavy bags under his eyes, topping a tall, thin body had at times a somewhat jaded

[2] "Vernehmung des Walter Schellenberg, 17.9.47" (in IfZ, ZS 291 (V) ).

[3] This represents the conviction of Franz Josef Huber, former general of police and Gestapo chief in Vienna. Interview, June 3, 1970.

[4] Prominent former SD and Gestapo officials who have been consulted affirm that they cannot think of any department of their agencies which could have been made regularly responsible for such an assignment. Interview with Walter Huppenkothen, May 29, 1970; Huber interview, June 3, 1970. For more specific assignments in this category Huber believes that conceivably Amt (office) II-G of the Gestapo could have been involved.

[5] Engel interview, May 11, 1970.

[6] Fritsch, it has been noted, was so conscious of this probability that even when visiting his mother he put a cushion over her telephone. J. A. Kielmansegg, *Der Fritsch-Prozess 1938*, 34.

aspect. In contrast to this occasional impression, he was usually brisk and lively with a pronounced disposition toward gaiety and humor. Soberer and perhaps somewhat prosaic colleagues such as Fritsch, though not pretending to be immune to his charm, regarded him as too impulsive and easily influenced as well as too much given to "romantic-fantastic notions."[7]

Those who valued such things admired Blomberg's cultivated tastes. He read extensively and kept abreast of foreign literature. It was pleasant to work with and for him and he was popular with his personal staff. Those closest to him were likely to observe a soft streak in his makeup. He was easily influenced by outgoing personalities and was prone to fall under the sway of individuals with charismatic qualities, such as Hitler and Reichenau. His first wife, whom he lost in 1929 after a long and painful illness, had been a splendid woman who played a most beneficent role in his life.[8]

Thereafter Blomberg, though not withdrawn socially, seems to have given little or no occasion for talk about feminine entanglements. Not too long, in fact, before he himself stumbled so badly, he had been prone to lecture others on how those strategically placed to influence the course of history must always be circumspect in their private affairs.[9] The involvement of Edward VIII with Mrs. Simpson had provided him an opportunity to pinpoint this more specifically. Upon receiving a detailed account from the German military attaché in London, Geyr von Schweppenburg, he emitted an eloquent sigh: "You see, Geyr, sex!"[10]

Now this sexagenarian had himself become involved in a highly questionable affair. Somehow he had made the acquaintance of Fräulein Eva Gruhn, a young woman of varied background who had of late risen a step or two in the Berlin half-world.[11] In view of what happened to Blomberg later, it is natural that the story should arise that she had been deliberately thrust in his way for

[7] Fritsch's notation of February 1, 1938. Hossbach, *Zwischen Wehrmacht und Hitler*, 60.

[8] Much of this characterization is furnished by Countess Hardenberg, who was successively secretary to Blomberg, Hammerstein, and Fritsch and a keen judge of each of these men. Interview, February 29, 1970.

[9] Röhricht, *Pflicht und Gewissen*, 113.

[10] Geyr von Schweppenburg interview, January 26, 1970.

[11] Gisevius (*Bis zum bittern Ende*, 260) relates that Blomberg from time to time would leave his car in diverse quarters of Berlin with the apparent intention of sampling the capital's night life. The meeting with his future wife may well have occurred during some such excursion.

the purpose of compromising him.[12] Though this cannot be entirely ruled out, the fact that those who were after Blomberg's scalp were entirely capable of such skulduggery is by itself no proof that they perpetrated it.

Eva (also Erna, Margreth, Margarete) Gruhn had grown up in humble circumstances. She was born in 1913, the daughter of a charwoman of the Berlin Royal Palace and of Paul Gruhn, another servitor (gardener?) of the palace staff who was killed in World War I.[13] Mother Luise was one of numerous members of the palace service dismissed when it was pared down to those needed for public show purposes. She then took up massage, a profession known in Berlin for the wide range in degree of respectability it enjoyed. In this instance, as is attested by a police report prepared during the flurry of interest about the Gruhns in January 1938, there was no hint of unsavory activities in connection with her massage salon. On the contrary, inquiries addressed to departments keeping watch over abortion mills, disorderly houses, medical malpractice, and corrupt trade practices all produced for her a clean bill of health. Most of her clients were found to be physically handicapped persons and the larger proportion were women. It was a hard life, however, and Frau Gruhn appears to have been progressively more soured by it. In time she achieved a fearsome reputation as a scold and a malicious gossip, became increasingly involved in conflict with her neighbors, and on one occasion was sentenced to two months in jail for making out a false affidavit.[14]

Young Eva is said to have worked for a while in her mother's massage salon, but the two did not get along and, at the age of eighteen or nineteen, she left the parental wing for good. How

[12]Thus John J. McCloy II, *Die Verschwörung gegen Hitler: Ein Geschenk an die deutsche Zukunft* (Stuttgart, 1963), 10. McCloy tells of a claim that she was placed in Blomberg's office for this purpose, but the present writer knows of no evidence that she ever worked in the War Ministry. McCloy cites a report of Dr. Ernst Kaltenbrunner (Heydrich's successor as head of the SD) of August 25, 1944, but no such statement is found under that date in *Spiegelbild einer Verschwörung.* Hossbach (*Zwischen Wehrmacht und Hitler,* 118) also states that the girl was used to trip up Blomberg.

[13]Erich Schultze became acquainted with Eva Gruhn's mother when, in 1918, as a seventeen-year-old ensign of the Guards Cavalry Rifles Division, he and his companions did a good deal of lounging around the palace and carried on desultory conversations with members of its service staff. He recalls her as a pleasant and not unattractive person. Interview, December 5, 1969.

[14]Police report of January 24, 1938. It is to be found in a file on "Frau Eva von Blomberg" which survived the war (original in IfZ, Akz. 4490/70; cited hereafter as Gruhn Police File), 37-38.

much this had thus far sheltered her is questionable, for it appears that she had already begun to branch out into activities which brought her increasingly into conflict with the authorities. During the period when the "Blomberg scandal" was exploited by Hitler he referred to her repeatedly as a "convicted prostitute." No proof of this is known to exist and after the war she conducted a suit (settled out of court) against a writer who had referred to her in such terms.[15] Her past life seems to have been pictured by Hitler in 1938 in excessively lurid colors so as to magnify Blomberg's offense in marrying her and to accentuate the embarrassment of the Generalität.[16] On one occasion she was arrested on suspicion of a theft that could not be proven.[17] Most concrete and partially still available are the records concerning her career as a photographic model. The products thereof ranged from forms of comparatively innocent nude "calendar art" to types of pornography which found a ready sale in bars and on crowded boulevards. Some specimens achieved sufficient distinction to leap frontiers for distribution abroad.[18] Be it noted that Eva seems to have done

[15] The volume in question was Gisevius's *Bis zum bittern Ende.* Gisevius interview, July 11, 1971.

[16] This was the view of Ministerial Director Heinrich Rosenberger as expressed after the war to Count J. A. Kielmansegg. Rosenberger, as will become clearer as this account proceeds, was acquainted with many of the less-known aspects of both the Blomberg and the Fritsch affairs. He held that Eva Gruhn's previous life was not so extreme as often pictured but was magnified to serve particular ends. Notes of Count Kielmansegg on a conversation with Dr. Rosenberger, May 4, 1947. Kielmansegg Papers.

[17] Gisevius, *Bis zum bittern Ende,* 265.

[18] At least three collections of varying lack of innocence came ultimately to rest in police files. Franz Josef Huber, who was shown the original file from the Police Presidium when it was passed around Gestapo headquarters, insists that what he viewed was not pornography but ordinary nude poses. Some of his colleagues admiringly remarked that she was indeed "attractive enough to please a field marshal." Interview, November 20, 1969. Dr. Erich Schultze was shown some photos by Heydrich. When he commented that they looked faked, Heydrich grinned knowingly as if claiming credit for a clever piece of roguery. Interview, July 4, 1970. Foreign Minister Neurath's son was shown photos of Fräulein Gruhn by the Brussels chief of police which he reported to be of a coarseness that was "indescribable." Wiedemann, *Der Mann der Feldherr werden wollte,* 110, and interview, December 2, 1969. The much-abbreviated file on Eva Gruhn found in Berlin ruins in 1945 and loaned in 1970 by the office of the Berlin public prosecutor to the custody of the IfZ has six photographs posed by her with a male partner that have an undoubted pornographic character.

To give a more complete account of the materials it is necessary to get a little ahead of our story. The abbreviated file of which a copy, minus the pictures, is in the IfZ, was apparently the file shown Gisevius by Nebe on January 26, 1938. Gisevius, *Bis zum bittern Ende,* 265. It seems to have consisted of "fresh material" discovered in various files of Nebe's department after the scandal had

very poorly as a model from a business standpoint. In what apparently was her first venture along this line in 1931 or 1932, only eight pictures were sold for half a mark each and she did not even receive her promised commission.[19] She is reported to have been given a milder sentence in connection with another offense when she testified that she had received no more than sixty marks for her "efforts."[20]

It is not known just when Blomberg formed his connection with Eva Gruhn, though it is usually assumed that it was not many months before the period under consideration here.[21] Gossip has had the first meeting taking place on a bench in the Tiergarten or in a bar or nightclub and it is assumed to have occurred without benefit of formal introduction. The facts are quite prosaic: Blomberg met her as a customer of the hostelry known as Der Weisse Hirsch (The White Deer) of which she then was an employee.[22]

Before long the field marshal was hopelessly infatuated and striving hard to ward off the attentions of another "suitor." It may well have been he who secured her a clerical position in the Reich Egg Center.[23] In the end the doting lover appears to have concluded

broken within Berlin police circles on January 21 and after the first collection of Gruhn documents had been delivered by Helldorf to Goering on the 21st or 22nd. It was transmitted by Nebe to Helldorf with a covering letter on the 27th. Gruhn Police File, 16. In the Police Presidium it was apparently assumed to add too little of substance to be sent on to Goering, or perhaps it was known that the Blomberg affair was already all but concluded. In any event, it was marked "This envelope is to opened only with the personal approval of the Herr Police President," and locked away. It thus escaped the fate of the more ample file originally brought to Helldorf, shown by him to Keitel, and passed on to Goering. After the affair had cooled, Goering gave the dossier to his adjutant, General Bodenschatz, and directed him to lock it in his safe. Bodenschatz relates that he destroyed it on Goering's order in April 1945. Karl-Heinz Bodenschatz, "Statement on the Blomberg Affair" (in IfZ, ZS 10).

[19] As she recorded in a statement for the police on January 23, 1932. Gruhn Police File, 48.

[20] Gisevius, *Bis zum bittern Ende*, 255. *Bemühungen* (efforts) is also the term she employs in her 1932 statement to describe her contribution to the photographic enterprise of that time. Gruhn Police File, 48.

[21] On the other hand, Gisevius (*Bis zum bittern Ende*, 269) says that one of Blomberg's adjutants reported the relationship to have been several years old.

[22] As related by Dr. Rosenberger to Count Kielmansegg, May 4, 1947. Kielmansegg Papers.

[23] We do not know whether Fräulein Gruhn had already "graduated" fully to this calling before meeting the War Minister or whether this was the first step in a social buildup he tried to effect for her after he became her protector. Wiedemann ("Aufzeichnungen," IfZ, ZS 191, 29) and Keitel (102n175) describe her position as that of a "stenographer." In a statement for the police of January 23, 1932 she indeed gives her profession as that of "stenographer." Gruhn Police File, 47.

84

# The Eclipse of Blomberg

that the only sure way of monopolizing his mistress was to marry her. Reluctant as he was to face the facts, he could not, of course, entirely hide from himself the clash this entailed with the traditional prejudices and standards of the officer corps. At some point in 1937 (summer or fall?) he considered it wise to seek advice on the interpretation of existing regulations by consulting the head of the Wehrmacht Legal Department, Ministerial Director Rosenberger. Alluding to what he described as a "hypothetical case," he asked about the propriety of an officer marrying a woman who had been involved in an "affair." The officer corps, remarked Blomberg, "amazingly enough seemed to be against" such a marriage.[24] Unfortunately Rosenberger in his postwar account did not report on the tenor of his reply. But it appears to have been sufficiently negative in tone either to discourage Blomberg for the time being or to determine him then and there to seek support in higher quarters. His problem, in fact, was steadily becoming more pressing—by the end of 1937 Eva Gruhn was several months advanced in pregnancy.[25]

## The Entry of Goering and the SS

This was the state of affairs when Blomberg, in late November or early December 1937, went to solicit the help of Hermann Goering.[26] It will, no doubt, always remain a subject of wonderment why he chose in this manner to put his head into the lion's mouth. By now he should have had few illusions about his fellow Minister and Wehrmacht subordinate who, however much he was the star performer of the Nazi circus, had amply shown how dangerous he could be when his claws were out. Perhaps like so many others who should have known better, Blomberg counted somewhat on Goering's "human qualities," notably that exuberant bonhommie which cloaked a nature which was anything but *bon homme*. Undoubtedly Goering, if he chose, could be enormously helpful in Blomberg's precarious situation, notably in dealing with Hitler and

[24] As related by Dr. Rosenberger to Count Kielmansegg, May 4, 1947. Kielmansegg Papers.

[25] As related by members of the Blomberg family to Elke C. Froehlich, who is preparing a biographical study of the field marshal. There seems to have been a miscarriage while Blomberg and his wife were in Italy before embarking on a journey to the Far East. Communicated by Miss Froehlich, July 7, 1971.

[26] According to Gisevius, Blomberg had gone to Goering about three months earlier to seek advice on the wisdom of a man in his position having an affair with Eva Gruhn and he was encouraged to continue the relationship. Gisevius, *Bis zum bittem Ende*, 281.

with the Wehrmacht leadership, which would resent the marriage even with the best aspect that could be put on it—a man in the exalted position of War Minister espousing a "simple working girl."

Another, though at first thought paradoxical, explanation is that Blomberg may have gone to Goering for the very reason that he feared him, felt uneasy about having offended him on November 5, and hoped to disarm him by a man-to-man appeal. This would persuade Goering that there had been nothing personal about the position Blomberg had taken and would afford him a chance to parade his magnanimity. It would put their relationship above official controversy. Blomberg may also have felt that he was guarded against knavery by the traditional comradeship among professional officers, a code to which many a scoundrel in the military has continued to render a certain obeisance. This may sound strangely naive for a man who qualified as a sophisticated observer and occasional participant in the high politics of the Third Reich. But it is quite in line with other illusions to which the infatuated general became a prey during the course of his late-blooming love affair.

The field marshal told Goering that he had fallen in love with and wished to marry "a child of the people," humble in background and, to be sure, "with a certain past." He was assured that under National Socialism, which was fighting to put an end to social prejudice, such a marriage would set an example that would help to bridge the gap that, unfortunately, still existed between the classes. He, Goering, would defend it against all critics and was sure that Hitler would give his approval. Blomberg, therefore, need not be concerned about raised eyebrows among "reactionary" elements in the officer corps and among his fellow generals.[27]

The War Minister went away enchanted by so much helpfulness and good fellowship. It encouraged him to come back a few days later with a yet more unusual request. He had a younger rival who refused to bow out and persisted in providing competition. Would not Goering employ one of the varied means at his command to get this man out of the way? In justice to Blomberg, it can be assumed that he left no doubt that this was not meant as a Nazi-type euphemism for "put out of the way."[28]

[27] Bodenschatz, "Statement on the Blomberg Affair."
[28] Though we can safely be charitable up to this point, it is appropriate to note how much Blomberg had adapted himself to the way things were done in the Third Reich. Whatever means short of murder Goering might employ to remove this obstacle to Blomberg's nuptial designs would still be of an extralegal order not acceptable in a law-respecting society.

# The Eclipse of Blomberg

Again Goering was most accommodating. For the master of the Four Year Plan the problem presented no difficulty. He straightway called in Herbert Dassler, president of the Reich Grain Office, and instructed him to find a suitable post in South America for the overly daring rival who ventured to cling to Eva Gruhn (or was it the other way around?). Dassler quickly provided for a well-paid position in Argentina.[29] Meanwhile Goering in convincing terms announced to the startled beneficiary of this arrangement that his health demanded a drastic change of climate. The man seems to have accepted his fate philosophically and with what good grace he could, but made it a point to call on Goering before leaving. He confided that Fräulein Gruhn had a rather more lurid personal history than she had probably told the field marshal and that the latter had better think twice about marrying her.[30]

It should not cause surprise that Goering did not rush to Blomberg with this warning. He was by now much occupied with affairs which followed upon the revelations of the War Minister (or were they such to Goering?). The stakes for which he was preparing to play—control of the Wehrmacht for himself—were indeed high.[31] The lovesick Blomberg was not likely to be able to block his path: the War Minister's folly had set him up perfectly for the low blow Goering was preparing. The really serious obstacle was the person of Fritsch. As the prestigious representative of the senior service, certain of Navy support in any clash with the upstart Luftwaffe and its presumptuous chief,[32] he presented a candidacy that was

---

[29] As related by Dassler in 1946 to his fellow prisoner General Bodenschatz, Goering's long-time adjutant. Dassler spoke of this having taken place "some weeks" before the marriage. Bodenschatz, "Statement on the Blomberg Affair." Investigation by the author has established that Dassler is now dead and efforts to trace in other ways the identity and current whereabouts of the reluctant emigrant and perhaps secure his testimony have thus far proven fruitless.

[30] As related by Goering to Count Helldorf on January 22, and passed on to Gisevius by the latter. Gisevius, *Bis zum bittern Ende*, 282. Goering a few days later also told Keitel of the rival who had been shipped out of the country on Blomberg's solicitation because Fräulein Gruhn wished to marry him. Keitel, 106. Goering did not in this case recount what the man in question had told him about the lady.

[31] This conclusive judgment of Goering's motives is in line with the virtual consensus among both his more closely involved contemporaries and later students of the period. Most notably, it conforms with the categorical statement of the man closest to Goering throughout these years, General Bodenschatz. His chief, he says, had at this time but a single aim, to become commander of the Wehrmacht. Letter of Bodenschatz to Professor Walter Baum, September 2, 1956 (in IfZ, ZS 10).

[32] To judge of this Goering did not have to see it demonstrated when Raeder spontaneously proposed Fritsch to Hitler as successor to Blomberg. Raeder, II, 120.

all but irresistible unless personal flaws could be urged against him. At first glance, this would seem a formidable task when dealing with a man so universally respected for his spotless life. But Goering's fertile imagination when it came to mischief-making may have been stirred by his current involvement with the predicament of the uxorious Blomberg, suggesting an attack in reverse order on the bachelor Fritsch, who was, in marked contrast, so innocent of entanglement with women. Even if he had had no earlier intimation that there might be such vulnerability to be exploited—and it will be seen that this is not completely certain[33]—it required no great inspiration on the part of Goering to perceive this opening.

To devise and spring the traps he planned for Blomberg and Fritsch, Goering stood in need of confederates. The choice of these was virtually dictated by the division of labor among the clandestine-functioning agencies of Nazi Germany. Though Goering had ample machinery under his control to collect information on whoever stood in his way, he lacked the kind of operatives attached to the Gestapo and the SD who could engage in clandestine activities. The men who commanded these agencies could also be trusted to put their heart into anything that had the hated leadership of the Army as a target.

Assuredly there was not then nor did there ever exist any bond of sentiment between Goering and Himmler. In fact, if there was any fundamental rule in the political jungle that was the playground of the Nazi leaders, it was the total absence of enduring or even passing friendships anywhere near the top of the hierarchy. Alliances, however, were formed or broken as opportunities beckoned or common foes revealed themselves.[34] In the contest between "the first paladin of the Fuehrer" and "faithful Heinrich" many close observers had, from early in the regime, predicted the decisive showdown in the rivalries among Hitler's embattled lieutenants. There is no question at all that Goering, and very little doubt that Himmler, aspired ultimately to the first position in party and state. Though he became so officially only on September 1, 1939, Goering had been more or less Hitler's successor designate since the autumn of 1934.[35] To this Himmler, like the other Nazi chief-

[33] See below, pp. 143-144.

[34] Beyond any previous publication, the Speer memoirs offer examples *ad nauseum* both for the prevalence of backbiting relationships and for the, usually, very short-lived marriages of convenience.

[35] Testimony of Goering at Nuremberg, IMT, IX, 344.

tains, had to render formal obeisance, though he must have had his private thoughts on the matter. But his main concern, like that of Goering, was a more immediate one than the eventual power struggle in a still hypothetical post-Hitler Reich. As practical men they were both more interested in the realities of power as it was then and would in future be exercised under the reigning dictator. In these terms the command of the German Wehrmacht, when taken together with the existing and still expanding personal empires of the two rivals, could for one or the other lead to a pinnacle of power that in time could conceivably overshadow that of the supreme leader himself.

Himmler could not fail to recognize this just as well as Goering. He hardly knew Hitler's mind so well that he could foresee with complete assurance what was actually to happen—that the Fuehrer would categorically reject Goering as War Minister. Therefore he had to anticipate the strong probability that Goering, if Himmler decided to throw in his lot with him at this juncture, would further enhance his position in the state by the elimination of the two generals. Why, then, was he willing to help promote an archrival? In the first instance, such a course jibed with his eagerness to humble the Army leadership. The future could also be counted upon to bring other turns of the political wheel that could be exploited to even matters with Goering. Himmler had the consolation of knowing that his competitor was notoriously and, by all signs, incurably lazy; that, in consequence, he rarely if ever developed anything approaching the full potential of his innumerable offices. To control the Wehrmacht he would have to lean heavily on party and SS support. Himmler could afford to wait and of the two Nazi hierarchs he was by far the more patient man.

Well before mid-December the alliance was in full operation and working along three well-defined lines:

1. It set a close Gestapo watch on Eva Gruhn—not, we may be sure, to secure evidence against her that would be used to dissuade Blomberg from taking the final step of marrying her. There is much that remains puzzling about this surveillance. It may already have been under way, with or without Goering's initiative, before Blomberg made his first appeal for aid. Or it may have been undertaken initially at the request of Blomberg himself to ward off his rival before he hit on the idea of asking Goering

to take care of that problem with greater finality.[36] From wherever the inspiration for this watch may have come, it served to give the confederates a much amplified picture of Fräulein Gruhn.

2. At Goering's request, two Gestapo agents were dispatched to shadow Fritsch in Egypt.[37] Being accompanied only by his adjutant, Captain von Both, he might feel himself unobserved and indulge in some indiscretion.

3. The II-H (homosexual affairs) office of the Gestapo's Criminal Councilor Joseph Meisinger was put to work to fabricate or, if it already existed, reconstruct and expand a dossier of "evidence" that could be sprung against Fritsch at the psychological moment.[38]

Regarding the nature of the Gestapo watch on Eva Gruhn, some insight is gained from the testimony of an outsider—Dr. Erich Schultze.[39] About mid-autumn of 1937 the Schultze family began to receive almost daily news bulletins from their housemaid, who lived in an apartment complex in the Eisenacher Strasse of Berlin's Schöneberg district. Arriving one morning with the usual bag of breakfast rolls, she announced importantly: "Our building is becoming very fashionable. We now have a regular visitor in the person of Field Marshal von Blomberg." In the weeks that followed she provided further details of a growing *chronique scandaleuse.*

The housemaid's frequent reports were soon supplemented during one of Dr. Schultze's visits to his friend Heydrich in the Prinz-Albrecht-Strasse. The SD chief was plainly bursting with importance and soon was recounting with gusto an affair between the War Minister and a girl of dubious reputation. Quite obviously his keen interest derived from something more than titillation at an item of gossip about the great in the Nazi Reich.

The truth of this was dramatically revealed before the end of the year when Dr. Schultze one day accompanied his small daughter to the apartment house in the Eisenacher Strasse where she was to deliver some direction from her mother on household affairs.

---

[36] The source for Blomberg's having asked for this "protection" is Gisevius (*Bis zum bittern Ende,* 283), whose information is that Blomberg did not shrink from having an adjutant telephone the request to the Gestapo. The manner in which the War Minister's adjutants were kept in the dark about his relationship with Eva Gruhn until just before the marriage argues against such a version.

[37] As reported to Gisevius by Nebe who also gave him the names of the two agents to pass on to Judge Karl Sack of the investigative panel preparatory to Fritsch's court-martial. Gisevius interview, July 11, 1971.

[38] The citation of evidence and analysis of these latter two features of the "Goering-Himmler plot" will receive more detailed attention in the next chapter.

[39] Interviews, December 5, 1969, and July 4, 1970.

# The Eclipse of Blomberg

It was a cold late December day and the father waited below in the vestibule while the little girl ran up a floor or two to transmit the message. When he next called on Heydrich a few days later, he was greeted by a leering: "What do you have to do in the Eisenacher Strasse? Do you perhaps have a share in Blomberg's girl friend?" "What do you mean?" was Schultze's startled reaction. "Well, here I have you in this picture," grinned Heydrich, showing a photograph of him coming out of the building.

Schultze required no further proof that the Gestapo was up to no good in watching so closely over the field marshal and the lady in the case. There seemed every likelihood of some coup or blackmail against the War Minister in the offing. Schultze was leery about calling on Blomberg at his home or office, for he feared that so direct an approach might elicit a vehement response. He therefore tried to stage a casual-seeming encounter at the entry of the apartment in the Eisenacher Strasse. He planned on first saying something about the girl and, should this offend Blomberg, at least warn him that a Gestapo watch was stationed over him and his mistress.

After several vain attempts to encounter the field marshal in what would look like an accidental meeting,[40] Schultze decided to attempt a warning through a close friend, Reich Bishop Ludwig Müller, the former chief chaplain of the East Prussian military district. Müller had known the Blomberg family well and had officiated at the funeral of the general's wife. When Schultze unfolded his story, the bishop tried on the spot to reach Blomberg by telephone to arrange a meeting but could not get through to him. Further attempts during the following days were similarly unsuccessful.[41]

Needless to say, Goering had meanwhile done nothing to deter Blomberg from his make-or-break talk with Hitler. Though under Blomberg's Ministry the regulations with respect to the marriage of officers had been eased, a review by superiors was still required. For the War Minister there was only one—the Fuehrer himself. "Field Marshal General is unexplainably excited," was the notation on December 15 of the puzzled Colonel Jodl, Keitel's principal

[40] In the last of these attempts Schultze actually did meet the War Minister and saluted him just as Fräulein Gruhn, who had evidently observed the arrival of Blomberg's car from her window, came down the stairs. For a confrontation with the general under such circumstances he was scarcely prepared.

[41] These days very likely fell into the period when the War Minister was passing the holidays with Fräulein Gruhn at Oberhof.

assistant in the Wehrmachtamt. "Reason cannot be ascertained. Apparently is a personal matter. Retires for eight days to unknown place."[42]

Actually Blomberg and his bride-to-be had gone to a retreat at Oberhof. Was he suffering from an attack of jitters about taking the decisive step? Despite Goering's assurances, did he still have some doubts about Hitler's reaction? Was he waiting to be advised by Goering that the door stood open? The fact is that, when he did move, the procedure had something of a taking-the-bull-by-the-horns complexion. It was quite incidental to a meeting in Munich on December 22 at memorial services for General Ludendorff. The day was one of intense discomfort and confusion due to severe cold and heavy snowfall which delayed the special trains and threatened to disrupt the entire program. Somehow the separate trains bearing Hitler and Blomberg did make it in the nick of time and proceedings were kept tolerably close to schedule.

While everyone was hurrying off to get warm after the ceremony, at which Blomberg had delivered the funeral oration, he turned to the Wehrmacht adjutant and requested him to arrange an immediate conference with Hitler. When Hossbach asked whether, as was the usual rule, he should be present, Blomberg said that this was unnecessary since it concerned a personal matter and would take no more than a few minutes. Hossbach having made the proper communication to Hitler, the Fuehrer and his War Minister went off to the former's Munich quarters.[43]

Hitler most probably had already been alerted by Goering about the plea that was to be addressed to him by Blomberg. In fact, if, as is usually assumed, Goering had promised to put in a good word with the Fuehrer about the marriage,[44] this was a necessary prelude to Blomberg's raising the matter. What Goering had said and the manner in which it was conveyed must ever remain a mystery. Whether fully prepared for what he was to hear or not, Hitler responded warmly to the idea of the War Minister's marrying a girl of plain background, "a secretary." He could only approve that Germany's foremost soldier should in this way help to close the gap between the classes.[45] What he did not say but must have thought was that Blomberg, even in the terms in which he described

[42] Jodl Diary, 356.
[43] Hossbach, *Zwischen Wehrmacht und Hitler*, 105.
[44] As related by Goering to Helldorf. Gisevius, *Bis zum bittern Ende*, 281.
[45] Wiedemann, *Der Mann der Feldherr werden wollte*, 111-112.

the antecedents of his future wife, was further dismantling the already shaky bridges between him and the Generalität and putting himself more than ever in Hitler's hands.

If Blomberg had been apprehensive and withdrawn before gaining the sanction of the Fuehrer, his mood now took on an aspect of defiance. He knew that, no matter what Hitler and Goering might say or do, he must still face the disapprobation of his military peers and he did not intend to respond to it with bowed head. On returning from Oberhof after Christmas, he enlarged by one the small circle of initiates regarding his wedding plans. This was General Wilhelm Keitel, to whose son his daughter had just become engaged. After all, he asserted in an almost chip-on-the-shoulder fashion, in National Socialist Germany it was no disgrace to wed "a child of the people." Disparaging chatter in so-called "society" would leave him cold. His children had been taken into his confidence and were placing no obstacles in his path.[46] With this communication the War Minister's course appeared irrevocably set.

## How Hitler and Goering Came to Be Witnesses

The marriage itself, as simple and private as one could make it, was planned for the War Ministry and it was to be a nonreligious affair. One aspect of the ceremony, however, was to achieve a certain historic importance—the choice of witnesses. All published accounts have hitherto assumed without argument that from the beginning these key roles were reserved for Hitler and Goering. The usual tale is that Goering, probably at the time he received Blomberg's first confidence, had volunteered his own services and offered to enlist those of Hitler.[47] The Fuehrer is said to have given his consent, eager to shield Blomberg with his authority against attacks on the marriage as a *mésalliance*.[48]

The facts are dramatically different. It was not Hitler and Goering who were originally scheduled to be witnesses—that was an emergency substitution—but Raeder and Fritsch. So important a problem as the choice of witnesses must have come up in the tête-à-tête meetings of the War Minister and Goering in December, and it is safe to say that the latter either suggested or strongly backed

[46] Keitel, 102. Actually Blomberg's sons and daughters were in varying degrees upset about the marriage and concern about it may have contributed to his mother's death a week of so after the ceremony, a possibility hinted at by Keitel (103).

[47] Thus Meissner, 436.

[48] Wiedemann interview, December 2, 1969.

the selection of the Army and Navy chiefs. It cannot have needed much argument to convince Blomberg that to associate the heads of the traditional services with the marriage would do more to silence censure from the military than the blessing of party stalwarts like Hitler and Goering.

There is nothing to indicate when and how the invitation was extended to Raeder and Fritsch or the spirit in which it was accepted. It can hardly have been before Fritsch returned from Egypt on January 2. The plot to discredit them along with Blomberg was foiled entirely because of the accident of friendship between Heydrich and Erich Schultze. It must have been on or just before January 10 that the SD sachem, clearly in a mood of anticipated triumph, recounted to Schultze how Blomberg was on the point of marrying Fräulein Gruhn and that, luck piling on luck, Fritsch and Raeder had been talked into acting as witnesses. "This will make a real *troika*," he gloated, alluding to their common Russian studies, and boasted that he was about to bring down three choice targets with a single shot.[49]

To fully comprehend the personal element in Heydrich's glee, one must appreciate the fierce hatred he bore not only Fritsch but Raeder. He considered the admiral ultimately responsible for his expulsion from the Navy and pursued him with a ferocity which refused to yield to mediatory pleas from members of his old crew (officers who had begun their service as cadets in the same year as he).[50]

The full compass of the plot against Blomberg was now clear. If Fritsch and Raeder acted as witnesses, the marriage to outward appearances would be an affair within the Wehrmacht, involving it far more deeply than would the personal disgrace of Blomberg and compromising Fritsch and Raeder with him when the story on his wife's background broke. What troubled Dr. Schultze most was the involvement of Fritsch, a man to whom he felt linked by a strong bond of sympathy through their common religious interests. Also, in marked contrast to Blomberg's self-invited afflic-

[49] Schultze interview, December 5, 1969.

[50] As stated by former Gestapo member Bruno Streckenbach to Heinz Höhne. Höhne, *Der Orden unter dem Totenkopf: Die Geschichte der SS* (2 vols., Frankfurt and Hamburg, 1966), I, 164, 382. Though the more radical Nazi leaders detested Raeder as a "reactionary," Heydrich seems to have been alone in his personal antagonism. Hitler at that time wished to retain him. Raeder (II, 126-128) recounts how the Fuehrer went to great lengths to reconcile with him after Hitler's petulance had given the admiral offense.

# The Eclipse of Blomberg

tion, Fritsch and Raeder seemed destined to become the wholly innocent victims of a dirty maneuver.

Heydrich had not mentioned the date of the marriage and Schultze had not wished to betray too much interest by asking questions; however, all indicators pointed to its being no more than a few days off. The matter seemed so pressing that he took a taxi direct from the Prinz-Albrecht-Strasse Gestapo headquarters to the Eisenacher Strasse, fabricating on the way some pretext for stopping to see the family maid. Fortunately, as he had anticipated, it proved unnecessary for him to initiate the subject he had at heart. Almost immediately the girl began an excited chatter about the noisy farewell party that had taken place in Fräulein Gruhn's apartment the night before; the marriage, she said, was but two days off.

Since Schultze assumed that Fritsch at this juncture was probably under close surveillance, he did not venture to go to the general's residence in the War Ministry until after dark. Fritsch's first reaction was that he should warn Blomberg. Schultze strenuously advised against this, urging that the War Minister at this late hour before the marriage would only react explosively. Besides, Reich Bishop Müller as a friend of the family had undertaken to attempt a warning. Fritsch, yielding to this argument, went off in a taxi to counsel with Raeder.[51] Next morning the two service commanders went together to Blomberg to tell him that, having reflected on the matter, they had arrived at the conclusion that Hitler would be offended if he himself were not asked to act as witness at the ceremony.[52]

[51] Raeder's memoirs, which say very little about the 1938 Wehrmacht crisis, are silent on this. Raeder, feeble and mentally and spiritually exhausted at the time the memoirs were prepared, did not write them himself but entrusted the task to a naval friend. The two volumes, notably the first, have many errors and omissions. Interview with Admiral Karl von Puttkamer, June 27, 1970. No doubt some will be highly critical of the failure of Fritsch and Raeder to "warn" Blomberg. Such criticism, however, is likely to be influenced by our fuller knowledge of the past of Eva Gruhn. It should be borne in mind that Dr. Schultze and, at that stage, probably his informant, Heydrich, did not know of her police record or ventures in pornographic photography. To have told Blomberg that she was a woman "of dubious reputation" would hardly have been much of a revelation to him. The clergyman, Müller, must have seemed to them a better counselor at this juncture than his brothers in arms.

[52] Schultze interviews, December 5, 1969, February 15 and July 4, 1970. What is revealed here differs so diametrically from all previously published versions that the author has been at particular pains to secure confirming evidence. The testimony of Dr. Schultze is backed in one way or another by the following: (a) General Count Kielmansegg, who relates that his aunt, Fritsch's sister, Elisabeth

## The Nuptials

At noon on January 12, 1938, Werner von Blomberg espoused Eva Gruhn at his War Ministry in the presence of a wedding party that had been kept to a minimum. It included no member of the Blomberg family and only a single personal friend, Corvette Captain Hans von Friedeburg, a former naval adjutant. The others present to felicitate the couple were Blomberg's three current adjutants, the mother of the bride, and the two last-minute witnesses. None of Blomberg's military peers had been invited and only Keitel, Fritsch, and Raeder knew that a marriage was about to take place.

The shock of the news reverberated through military quarters in Berlin and in the Wehrkreis commands. "Field Marshal General marries completely by surprise Fräulein Gruhn," the next-to-speechless Jodl registered in his diary.[53] The War Minister's old friend, and formerly his closest associate, General von Reichenau learned of the wedding during a luncheon in Munich; dismayed and unbelieving he rushed to the telephone to make inquiries of one of Blomberg's adjutants. The embarrassed reply was that neither he nor his two colleagues knew anything whatever about the lady involved.[54]

Almost as stunned was Goering's own adjutant and intimate, General Bodenschatz, who had been told nothing by his chief until the latter, in glowing spirits, stopped briefly by the Air Ministry just before leaving for the nuptials. Bodenschatz was further mystified by not being asked to go along. The wedding, as Goering

von Werner, told him that Fritsch had received and turned down an invitation to act for Blomberg. Interview, December 8, 1969. (b) Countess Hardenberg had the same story from Hammerstein, who during those days was in constant touch with Fritsch. Interview, February 29, 1970. (c) Frau Ilse Schneckenburger, widow of General Schneckenburger and former secretary to General Adam, says that Adam told her the same story as recounted by Fritsch. Interview, May 27, 1970. (d) Frau Elwine Hevelke, personal secretary to Fritsch at the time of the crisis, was a daughter of Blomberg's first cousin. From her aunt, Frau von Laue, wife of a famous physicist, she learned a few days after the marriage that Blomberg had expressed to her his deep chagrin that Fritsch and Raeder had first agreed to act as witnesses and had then suddenly withdrawn. Interviews, June 11, 1970, and June 27, 1971. (e) General Count Wolf Baudissin affirms that he learned at the time of the crisis, he believes from Blomberg's daughter Dorothee, that Fritsch and Raeder were to have been witnesses but had withdrawn at next-to-the-last moment. Interviews, June 28, 1970, and June 23, 1971. Dorothee von Blomberg, now Frau Karl-Heinz Keitel, cannot recall having received or passed on such information. Letter to the author from Elke C. Froehlich, November 29, 1971.

[53] IMT, XXVIII, 356.

[54] As related by Alix von Reichenau. Interview, June 23, 1970.

described it on his return, had taken place in a strained and awkward atmosphere. "Blomberg's people" (meaning the one former and the three current adjutants) had been unable to hide their acute discomfort and the bride herself had not made a good impression on him. The prevailing mood had been most peculiar after the vows had been spoken and while the ill-assorted company tried to make conversation.[55]

Hitler later confessed himself to have been particularly disturbed by the encounter with Eva's mother.[56] On her face he fancied himself able to read "what she was and from where she had come."[57] It would, no doubt, have been difficult for an observer to discern for whom the occasion was most embarrassing and, in some cases, painful. Everyone must have sighed with relief when the customary decencies of offering good wishes and sipping champagne had been observed so that they could take their leave.

The newly wedded pair departed on a honeymoon that took them first to Leipzig. There, to the disgust of the priggish Keitel, they were pictured a few days later in German newspapers standing before the monkey cage of the zoo.[58] We do not know how long the wedding journey was planned to last, but it was abruptly terminated by the sickness and death of Blomberg's mother who lived with a daughter at Eberswalde not far from Berlin. At the funeral on January 20 the strange concealments which had characterized the marriage and which, at this stage of affairs, perhaps did more to attract than divert attention were continued. Those who attended were given no occasion to meet the new Frau von Blomberg, who stood at the grave next to her husband so heavily veiled as to be unrecognizable. The general mystification was accentuated by there being no opportunity to offer the usual condolences to the next of kin; the field marshal and his wife were the first to leave the cemetery.[59]

[55] Bodenschatz, "Statement on the Blomberg Affair."

[56] Eva and her mother after six years of estrangement had at least outwardly become reconciled shortly before her marriage. She and Blomberg had called on Frau Gruhn on January 9 and it was probably on that occasion that they extended to her the invitation to be present at the ceremony three days later. Police report on Frau Luise Gruhn, January 24, 1938, Gruhn Police File, 37.

[57] Comment made in a midnight conversation with Captain Engel in the night after his birthday, April 20, 1938. Engel Diary.

[58] Keitel, 103.

[59] Ibid.

## The Trap Is Sprung

A problem of some interest on which further light may never be shed is Goering's conception of how the trap into which the War Minister had blundered was to be sprung. The situation was really such that this could be expected to occur without a helping hand from him or his confederates. The furor among the dwellers in the Frau Feldmarschall's former apartment house and the happy excitement in the sisterhood of joy about the meteoric rise of one of their own were not likely to pass unnoticed. The odds thus from the start were prohibitive that within a matter of days the inside story would break in one fashion or another. As will be noted more fully later,[60] the renewed urgency of the Gestapo immediately after the marriage in rounding out the "case" against Fritsch suggests that the time for making use of it was believed to be at hand.

Conceivably, then, Goering just sat and waited for the inevitable moment when the lightning would strike. More likely by far, he or his confederates decided to make doubly sure of things by taking a hand. On the very day (January 21) on which the final chain of developments that swept Blomberg out of office got under way, an effort was made to activate the Army leadership against him. It would have been worth much to the intriguers if the spark that set the well-laid fuse ablaze had originated from that center. The phone rang in Fritsch's outer office and a male voice asked to be put through to him. Fritsch, on his guard following warnings from various directions that something nasty against him seemed afoot, refused to talk without prior identification of the caller. The latter then claimed to be "General von ——," a name not borne by any general officer then stationed in Berlin. When adjutant Captain von Both still refused to put him through, the voice concluded: "Then tell the colonel general that Field Marshal von Blomberg has married a whore." He was asked to come and make

[60] See below, p. 146. That Himmler and Heydrich knew much about the background of Blomberg's bride before the marriage and thus could anticipate what happened was attested by Dr. Werner Best, legal specialist of the Gestapo, in a conversation with Dr. Fritz Neuroth, a judge of the Reich Military Court, later in 1938. As Best put it, Blomberg was "knowingly allowed to slither into the marriage." Neuroth to Kielmansegg, November 23, 1947. Kielmansegg Papers. Best himself denies having made such a statement to Neuroth. Best, "Aktennnotiz des General a. D. Hermann Foertsch über eine Unterredung mit Herrn Ministerialdirektor z. V. Dr. Werner Best über die Vorgänge der Heirat Blomberg und die Angelegenheit Generaloberst Freiherr von Fritsch im Frühjahr 1938, 13.9.52" (five-page statement in author's possession).

an oral declaration at Army headquarters but no one appeared.[61]

Both reported the conversation to Fritsch who discussed the incident with Beck and also called Hossbach into consultation. There was much shaking of heads but no inclination, as those behind the maneuver must have hoped, to launch an attack on Blomberg. It is completely untrue that the Army leaders, as is asserted in some studies,[62] brought their guns to bear on Hitler to force him to remove Blomberg. Fritsch's reaction, despite what he had already heard from Erich Schultze, was, in fact, the chivalrous one of rallying behind the beleaguered War Minister. Others were obviously mobilizing to get his scalp and, thought Fritsch, were probably exaggerating the dubious reputation of the lady in question. It was the duty of the officer corps, he said, to come to the support of its senior representative.[63]

A number of versions, competing in sensation, are offered to explain how the action against Blomberg began. All agree that the file on Eva Gruhn somehow came to move up the bureaucratic chain that ended at the desk of the police president, Count Wolf Heinrich von Helldorf. A frequently repeated account is that of Gisevius, who tells how the wife of a Berlin police inspector related to her husband some of the spreading gossip about Blomberg's new bride and thus spurred him to check in the Residence Registry Bureau in which he happened to be employed.[64] Another version pictures a police official overhearing a little girl saying to another

---

[61] This paragraph is based on the accounts of Hossbach (*Zwischen Wehrmacht und Hitler*, 106) and Gisevius (*Bis zum bittern Ende*, 254). For an analysis of the Blomberg and Fritsch affairs it is particularly unfortunate that the man who observed developments most closely in Fritsch's office, Captain von Both, was killed soon after in a riding accident.

[62] Thus Wheeler-Bennett (366-367), who, giving no source, has Fritsch going to Hitler on Beck's urging to press for Blomberg's dismissal. Craig similarly states that "at Beck's insistence, Fritsch went to Hitler and convinced him that Blomberg must go." He cites as authority for this a January 26 entry of the Jodl Diary, but no such report is to be found there under that date. Gordon Craig, *The Politics of the Prussian Army, 1640-1945* (Oxford, 1955), 493 and n 1. Actually, when in the evening of January 26 Hitler and Fritsch had their first meeting since the return of the latter from Egypt, Blomberg's fate had been determined some thirty-four hours earlier and Fritsch was concerned only with his own defense. Wiedemann states most emphatically that when he heard something of such a claim (it may well have been in connection with Goering's maneuvers to give currency to such a version), he went into the question with various persons who had been close observers of the affair. "Reliable testimony" confirmed that Fritsch had made no remonstrance whatever to Hitler about the Blomberg marriage. IfZ, Document F35, 80334. Wiedemann interview, December 2, 1969.

[63] Hossbach, *Zwischen Wehrmacht und Hitler*, 106.

[64] Gisevius, *Bis zum bittern Ende*, 254.

on the street: "Mother Gruhn has gotten herself a fine new son-in-law, a field marshal."[65] And a third relates how a drunken prostitute who has been arrested is brought to the commissar of the night service to repeat her boast that she is "not so bad," that girls like her can expect to rise to the highest places.[66] The most detailed and specific account, and the only one set down by a person connected with the Gruhn file reaching Helldorf, is that of Criminal Councilor Curt Hellmuth Müller, head of the Reich Identification Center of the Kripo. For reasons Müller does not mention, his secretary, a Herr Burkert, called his attention to several pornographic pictures in a set newly arrived from Gerhard Nauck, an official of the Bureau of Moral Offenses. "When I noted on the two naked bodies their names in ink," testified Müller, "I called Nauck to ask him whether he was concerned with their identification. He thought this was not immediately necessary. I only was struck by the name of the woman which I had read somewhere though I could not recall who it might be." His curiosity aroused, Müller checked his fingerprint files and found the woman recorded there several times. Then he went to the head of the Public Registry Office, Government Councilor Mesch, who drew out of his files the card of the new Frau Feldmarschall von Blomberg.[67]

Now fully alert, Müller rushed to Kripo chief Arthur Nebe, whose reaction was an explosive: "Man, Comrade Müller, and this woman has had her hand kissed by the Fuehrer!" Nebe then brought the matter to the attention of Helldorf.

Müller's authentic-ringing story would seem to rule out any role for "accident" in the sudden disclosure, little over a week after her marriage, of Eva von Blomberg's police record. That a "new" set of pornographic pictures of her should at this psychological moment come into the hands of the authorities would be too amazing a coincidence to be credited. Someone had evidently been instrumental in setting the ball a rolling.

[65] Wiedemann, *Der Mann der Feldherr werden wollte*, 109–110.

[66] As related to Huppenkothen by Gestapo chief Heinrich Müller. Huppenkothen interview, May 29, 1970. In line with this last version is the account given Franz Josef Huber by Criminal Commissar Scholtz. According to Scholtz, the prostitutes of the notorious Friedrich Strasse quarter had seen a newspaper picture of Blomberg and his bride (it can only have been the one taken in front of the Leipzig monkey cage) and recognized in the latter a former colleague. This then came to the ears of an official of the Criminal Police who investigated and found the fateful file. Huber interview, November 20, 1969.

[67] Statement of Curt Hellmuth Müller, December 9, 1949. Quoted by Höhne, I, 238–239.

# The Eclipse of Blomberg

The police president's reaction on receiving the file, as he later told Gisevius, was one of sore anxiety. The regulations by which he worked left no uncertainty about the proper course—report the matter to his superior, the high authority over all Reich police forces, Heinrich Himmler. But Helldorf knew well what a weapon he would deliver into the hands of the SS leaders. Undoubtedly it could be used to compromise or, worse yet, to blackmail the head of the Wehrmacht. Himmler and Heydrich would not scruple to exploit it in promoting such aims as building the SS into a fourth Wehrmacht service.[68]

In the circumstances, Helldorf's bias was all on the side of the established military leadership. But if he were not careful about indulging it, the consequences might well be painful. Only recently he had been called to order for directly informing Goebbels of the homosexual proclivities of the state secretary in the Propaganda Ministry, Walter Funk. It meant some risk for him if so soon and in a situation so parallel he went outside constituted channels. Despite this he determined to carry the problem to Blomberg's closest ministerial co-worker, General Wilhelm Keitel.

Though their personalities were quite different and their relationship without real warmth, Blomberg and Keitel had an association that went back to World War I days. During that conflict they had belonged to the same regiment and had commanded units occupying contiguous sections of trench.[69] After further contacts in various military assignments in the twenties, their association had again become more intimate when Keitel succeeded Reichenau as head of the Wehrmachtamt in 1935, bringing him under the direct command of his old comrade. Always chameleonlike in taking on the coloring of his superiors, he adopted wholeheartedly Blomberg's views on a strong Wehrmacht command and unfailingly supported whatever line his chief laid down.[70] On the very eve of the crisis of 1938 the two men and their families had moved closer to one another by the engagement of young Karl-Heinz Keitel to Dorothee von Blomberg. Helldorf could not have turned to a

[68] Gisevius, *Bis zum bittern Ende,* 255. This is also the source for the following paragraph.

[69] When interrogated by the author in October 1945, Keitel related how they had liked to joke with one another by reference to each other's trench sectors as the Keitel and Blomberg "lines."

[70] Speer relates (129) that on the first occasion he observed the two together, Keitel would obsequiously nod approval to everything Blomberg said. Unfamiliar with insignia designating military rank, the architect judged from his manner that he must be an adjutant.

man who by professional and personal ties was under heavier obligation to rush to the aid of Blomberg as the storm clouds gathered over the head of the War Minister.

The conversation commenced with the police president sparring cautiously, evidently wishing to ascertain just how much Keitel already knew. He showed the general Fräulein Gruhn's picture on a residence registry card and asked whether this was the same person who had just married Blomberg. When Keitel protested that he had not yet seen the face of the lady, Helldorf was incredulous, the engagement of the children of the two men having just been mentioned prominently in the press. He asked Keitel to make immediate inquiry of Blomberg, for there was pressing need for clarification of the matter. The course of history might conceivably have proceeded very differently if the War Minister had then been in his office. Unfortunately he was out of the city, having gone to Eberswalde to attend to his mother's affairs. When Keitel suggested that the card be left to be shown to the War Minister the next day, Helldorf refused on the plea that the matter was too pressing. The dismayed general was then informed that the woman who had reported her move from the Eisenacher Strasse to the War Ministry in the Bendler Strasse, where Blomberg had his official residence, had been repeatedly convicted of moral transgressions.[71]

Keitel, deeply shocked, urged that the file should simply be suppressed. Helldorf objected that the number of police officials already in the know and the rapidly spreading public gossip would never permit the matter to rest.[72] History again might tell a different story had Keitel in this critical moment asked to take charge of the police file and delivered it to the senior officer of the Wehrmacht, Fritsch. In that event the Army commander would have been introduced normally into the chain of affairs and the Blomberg case would have been brought to Hitler by the Wehrmacht rather than the reverse. In every respect developments would have been profoundly and, from the Army's standpoint, favorably affected.[73]

---

[71] Keitel, 103–104, and interrogation, October 1945. Actually Helldorf already had established the identity of Eva Gruhn as the new Frau von Blomberg to his own satisfaction by comparing her police photos with the one taken in the Leipzig zoo. Gisevius recording, July 1971.

[72] Gisevius, *Bis zum bittern Ende*, 256.

[73] Hossbach, *Zwischen Wehrmacht und Hitler*, 115. When Hossbach some weeks later learned for the first time that Keitel had seen the Blomberg file before the crisis broke, his indignation so moved him that in his downright fashion he did not hesitate to make it an item of record with the new chief of the Army Personnel Department, the culprit's own brother, General Bodwin Keitel. His thought was

# The Eclipse of Blomberg

In view of Helldorf's sympathies, one may be sure that if he had thought it at all possible to get away with it, he would have welcomed such a proposal.

But Keitel's loyalties had been too much divorced from the Army by his three years' tenure with the Wehrmachtamt. In charity to him we can assume that he never gave thought to this course of action. In seeking to flee from personal involvement he apparently considered only how he could most quickly wash his hands of the whole distressing business. He suggested carrying the matter to Goering and, as he relates it, called the Air Ministry to make an immediate appointment for Helldorf. He also claims that Goering passed on the information to Hitler that very evening.[74] In his *sauve-qui-peut* spirit of self-centered befuddlement, he callously refrained from warning Blomberg, though five full days intervened before he learned what the course he proposed had produced.

The story as it next develops rests entirely on the contradictory evidence of the two surviving witnesses of the period, Bodenschatz and Gisevius. The former recounts how Helldorf came to the Air Ministry in great perturbation and urgently requested an immediate interview with Goering. When the police president left, Goering called Bodenschatz into his office and "in visible agitation" told him that Blomberg's wife was a repeatedly convicted prostitute who had been under the surveillance of the morals police. He complained bitterly about having to report so unpleasant a matter to the Fuehrer.[75]

In the account of Gisevius as derived from Helldorf, both the time and the locale of the meeting with Goering are very different. The conversation is placed in Goering's country mansion, Karinhall, and the time is given as the morning of the next day, Saturday, January 22.[76] Goering is reported to have been irritated about being

that if the political wheel should turn sufficiently at some future date to permit it, this would provide the basis for a formal inquiry into Keitel's conduct.

[74] Keitel, 104. Keitel, writing in 1945-46 with little more than his memory to rely upon, is often vague or confused about dates and tends to telescope the happenings of several days into one.

[75] Bodenschatz, "Statement on the Blomberg Affair."

[76] The undisputed fact that Goering made his report to Hitler on Monday, January 24, provides a guideline for the time of Helldorf's calls on Keitel and Goering. The police president can only have visited Keitel on the last previous "working day," i.e., Friday, January 21. Whether he called on Goering the same afternoon in the Air Ministry (Keitel and Bodenschatz) or went to Karinhall the next morning (Gisevius), it was in the order of things that Goering should wait until Monday and Hitler's return from his mountain home on the Obersalzberg to make his report. Keitel's account that Goering's talk with the Fuehrer came on the same day as

molested with "business" during his weekend. Helldorf spoke his piece, to which Goering listened with some manifestations of nervousness but none of surprise. In fact, he waxed confidential and related both Blomberg's admission that his intended had "a certain past" and the more frank revelations of the War Minister's rival when he called just before leaving for South America. Helldorf then departed, leaving the Gruhn file in Goering's hands.[77]

Gisevius relates further that Goering, laying aside his distaste for conducting "business" on weekends, invited Himmler out to Karinhall on Sunday (January 23) and that the two of them further summoned the third member of the intriguing triumvirate, Heydrich.[78] Since the next days were bound to be critical ones for their plans, the confederates assuredly had every reason for a close coordination of their movements. They had, at least so far as the SS chiefs were concerned, been alerted a few days earlier that things were on the point of breaking. Quite independently of the line of disclosure that was to put the Gruhn file on the desk of Helldorf, it had come to the ears of a police official that the demimonde of Berlin was agog about the sensational career being made by one of its own. The information had been relayed to Dr. Werner Best of the Gestapo who had made it the subject of a report to Heydrich.[79]

## Hitler and Blomberg

In the early evening of January 24 the Reich Chancellery must have worn an air of somnolent expectancy. The Fuehrer's train was shortly to reach Berlin. He was returning from his retreat at Berchtesgaden and for the Chancellery staff the customary routines when he was in the capital would resume. Thus his personal adju-

Helldorf's call on him in the War Ministry can be dismissed as contradicted by Gisevius, Wiedemann, Hossbach, and Bodenschatz and by the illogic of telescoping within a few hours (1) Helldorf's reception of the file, (2) his call on Keitel, (3) his call on Goering, and (4) Goering's report to Hitler at the Reich Chancellery. There is further evidence in that Blomberg was seeing to his mother's affairs at Eberswalde on January 21 (the day after her funeral) and was back in Berlin on January 24. Thus Helldorf's call on Keitel can only have been on the former date.

[77] Gisevius, *Bis zum bittern Ende*, 256–257, 283. Gisevius is so sure of his account of Helldorf's going to Karinhall for this meeting with Goering because Helldorf, in relating it, complained with much annoyance about the waste of time in making the trip. Gisevius interview, July 11, 1971.

[78] Gisevius, *Bis zum bittern Ende*, 257. This information was picked up by Helldorf from the gossip of the Nazi adjutants. He was warned of Himmler's and Heydrich's annoyance that he had gone first to Goering. Gisevius interview, July 11, 1971.

[79] Letter of Best to General Foertsch, September 13, 1952 (in IfZ, ZS 37).

# The Eclipse of Blomberg

tant, Fritz Wiedemann, was on duty and waiting in the antechamber for his arrival. The Wehrmacht adjutant, Colonel Hossbach, had also appeared and stationed himself in the entry hall to waylay the Fuehrer as he came in. The reason for his presence was an urgent request from Blomberg for a speedy meeting with Hitler.[80] Inevitably one is impelled to speculate: had the War Minister learned or sensed something of what was brewing against him and was he trying to get to Hitler before others who might wish him ill?

Animation entered the drowsy Chancellery scene with the bouncing arrival of Goering and his adjutant, Bodenschatz. The accounts of Wiedemann and Hossbach on what next occurred cannot be entirely reconciled and analysis must rely partly on conjecture. Since Hossbach was positioned at the entry, it stands to reason that his encounter with Goering must have come first. The Air Minister immediately launched into a plaint about what he labeled the "revilements" in Army circles about the new Frau von Blomberg. It was no disgrace, after all, if the War Minister had married a girl of simple background. Hossbach said that rumors were rife about the reputation of the lady, but that, Hitler and Goering having acted as witnesses, he could only assume that things were in order. He recounted Fritsch's feeling that the officer corps would take its stand behind Blomberg. "Are you trying to make me responsible for the reputation of Frau von Blomberg?" growled Goering. Hossbach repeated that the officer corps could only judge the respectability of the lady from such evidence as Goering's readiness to act as witness. "And if the reputation should not be in order?" "In that event," replied Hossbach, "the officer corps would have to reserve its position." Goering thereupon voiced a general lament that it always fell to his lot to bring particularly unpleasant matters to the Fuehrer's attention.[81] He then must have passed on to the antechamber and the observation of Wiedemann.[82]

To Hitler's personal adjutant, Goering seemed in a state of considerable excitement, an agitation possibly accentuated by the en-

[80] Hossbach, *Zwischen Wehrmacht und Hitler*, 106. Hossbach voices no surmise about what Blomberg wanted to discuss with his chief.

[81] *Ibid.*, 107.

[82] As Hossbach relates it (*ibid.*), Hitler appeared at this point and retired with Goering, giving him no opportunity to present Blomberg's request for an audience. Since this conflicts with the story of the exchanges between Goering and Wiedemann, it is assumed to be an error in recollection. Hossbach also says nothing of the presence of Bodenschatz.

counter with the unbending Hossbach. After he had paced back and forth for some time "like an angry lion," Wiedemann, made increasingly curious, finally ventured: "Mr. Prime Minister [of Prussia], no doubt you have many worries with the Four Year Plan and your many other burdens." "True enough," ranted Goering, "but what I have experienced today knocks the bottom out of the barrel." Having made Wiedemann little wiser, he then resumed his pacing. Turning to Bodenschatz, whom he knew well as a former classmate in military school, the adjutant whispered: "What is the matter with him?" "Blomberg will have to get out," was the laconic answer. "How then?" "But I am telling you, Blomberg must get out; he has married a whore!"[83]

At this point Hitler appeared and was closeted for a considerable period with Goering. All accounts of contemporaries that have thus far come to light picture his extreme perturbation. This unanimity of view, including persons normally highly skeptical when there was the slightest reason to suspect him of putting on a show, has persuaded virtually all students of the period that he was genuinely surprised and horrified. This once, at any rate, he is credited with allowing his innermost sentiments to be reflected in word and mien. "Utterly surprised and completely shocked" is the verdict of the then Captain Engel.[84] Goering, coming out of the conference, told the waiting Bodenschatz that the Fuehrer's initial reaction had been a despairing cry: "Nothing is spared to me."[85] And Wiedemann recounts finding him in a state "crushed" as he had never seen him in his four years as adjutant. Like a broken man he walked trancelike about the room, bowed down with his hands behind his back and muttering: "If a German field marshal will marry a whore, then anything can happen in the world."[86]

This near universal acceptance of the sincerity of Hitler's amazement and consternation, including as it does contemporaries and scholars most critical of him,[87] is no doubt highly persuasive. The

[83]Wiedemann interview, December 2, 1969. A brief version is given in his memoirs (*Der Mann der Feldherr werden wollte*, 109), a more extensive one in "Aufzeichnungen" (39).

[84]Engel interview, May 11, 1970. Engel, it is true, was not stationed in the Chancellery as Army adjutant until some weeks later. His judgment is based on what he was told soon after by others then present and on numerous personal talks with Hitler himself during the following months.

[85]Bodenschatz, "Statement on the Blomberg Affair."

[86]Wiedemann, *Der Mann der Feldherr werden wollte*, 111, "Aufzeichnungen," 99, and interview, December 2, 1969.

[87]Krausnick, "Vorgeschichte," in E. P., *Vollmacht des Gewissens*, I, 281-283. Foertsch, *Schuld und Verhängnis*, 141. Hossbach, *Zwischen Wehrmacht und Hitler*,

present writer is inclined to share this view though he harbors certain reservations. He is not prepared to rule out completely the possibility that this was Hitler's most smashing histrionic performance and that, though knowing little about Eva Gruhn before the marriage, he had at least appreciated the likelihood of Blomberg's riding to a fall. Perhaps the following points should be held in mind while recognizing that the probabilities greatly favor the accepted version:

1. Hitler insisted on a secrecy about the marriage so complete that on the day before the nuptials one of his adjutants would say to another only that something of great importance was about to occur.[88] It was no doubt natural that the Fuehrer should defer to the War Minister's plea for maximum privacy. But this concealment also served to avert attention from the bride's character while it would still have been possible to dissuade Blomberg from the marriage. The fact that the secrecy Hitler enjoined served this end is of course no evidence that such was his purpose. But it opens the way to a somewhat more serious consideration that argues against final acceptance of the thesis that he was completely bowled over by events.

2. One is struck by the assiduity with which the dictator henceforth strove to shift to the Army leaders the odium of having allowed Blomberg to slither into the abyss without warning. Why should he go so much out of his way to accuse others of what Himmler and Goering could have done so much more easily? He himself knew of Blomberg's wedding plans no later than December 22 and probably (from Goering) a week or two earlier. The Army leaders could have learned of Blomberg's intentions only after January 2 when Fritsch returned from Egypt and was invited, we have no idea just when, to act as a witness. Though the Generalität had no love for Blomberg, Hitler knew perfectly well that Goering and the SS chiefs had much stronger reasons for getting rid of the War Minister. He also knew that they controlled far more extensive means to learn about the bride-to-be. Hitler's dwelling so much on the lack of a timely warning to Blomberg and trying so hard

120. Though Hossbach shares the general view on Hitler's "surprise," his impression of the Fuehrer's reaction was more one of excitement than of anxiety or depression. Gisevius argues effectively for the sincerity of Hitler's demeanor at this juncture. Hans Bernd Gisevius, *Adolf Hitler: Eine Biographie. Versuch einer Deutung* (Zurich, 1967). Recording, July 1971.

[88]As remarked to Wiedemann by Schaub. Wiedemann, *Der Mann der Feldherr werden wollte*, 109.

to shove the blame onto Army shoulders suggest a defense mechanism that implies that the responsibility rested closer to home. It justifies a query whether he was not protesting too much to be wholly innocent.

The best guess is that Hitler reacted to the news brought him by Goering on January 24 with mixed feelings. As is revealed so often in remarks to his intimate circle in the following months, awareness of what he owed his War Minister competed in his mind with increasing dissatisfactions. It would, of course, help immeasurably to clarify matters if we had an authentic account of what passed between him and Goering that fateful evening of January 24. We must rely instead on logical deduction from what we know went before or followed after and from what Hitler related to Wiedemann who passed it on to his friend Oster and thus to Gisevius. As the latter reports it, Hitler, after an initial scene of great agitation, took a calmer view of things and said that Blomberg must immediately divest himself of this encumbrance by securing a divorce. Or, better yet, he should demand an annulment on grounds of gross deception, thus forestalling any chance that the Gruhn woman could run around with his name for the rest of her life. For the time being, at least, Blomberg was to be barred from the Chancellery and was not to wear a uniform. Goering was to carry these commands and proposals to him the next day.[89]

Did Hitler mention to Goering or at least imply that Blomberg might remain in office if he should consent to dissolve the marriage? The fact that he laid so much stress upon snipping the bond speaks for a readiness at least to consider this. There seems little sense in sending Goering with such an injunction if Blomberg's response was to have no bearing on the central issue. Hitler may well have put things in such a fashion that, while making no promises, his decision would depend on Blomberg's answer. What he told Keitel later was much less equivocal: that the War Minister had, in effect, been given a choice between his wife and his job.[90] That statement, of course, may constitute another of the innumerable deceptions of which the Fuehrer of the German Reich was guilty at this period. It conforms in spirit, however, with what is recounted by Gisevius.

Undoubtedly some ideas—perhaps most of the discussion with

[89] Gisevius, *Bis zum bittern Ende*, 257. Gisevius interview, July 11, 1971, for Wiedemann as the source.
[90] Keitel, 198.

Goering concerned this—were expressed on the problem of a replacement for Blomberg if he did depart from office. Here the name of Fritsch cannot fail to have come up immediately. Except when a civilian was appointed, the Army as the senior service had always furnished the War Minister in Germany. There was also the extraordinary personal prestige of Fritsch. If no other factor entered the picture—Hitler's words during the next days indicate a repeated recognition of this—no one else was even thinkable as a successor provided he was willing to undertake the assignment.

Goering had come prepared for this. Either he already was carrying with him a second file—the "reconstructed" dossier against Fritsch—or he reminded Hitler of the charges that had been raised against the general. At any rate, Hitler had the file in his hands the next morning when he and Goering launched their concerted assault on Colonel Hossbach to win the Wehrmacht adjutant to their view of things.

Hossbach had waited in the Chancellery entry hall until Hitler came out of his workroom with the departing Goering. Once more, however, the Fuehrer had disappeared so quickly that there had been no chance to exchange even a brief word with him. Thereupon the colonel went home to bed, only to be awakened at 2:15 A.M. by a call from one of the dictator's personal adjutants, Julius Schaub, from whose manner it was evident that Hitler was standing beside him. Schaub transmitted an order to come immediately for a talk with the Fuehrer. To this Hossbach, not a man who came running when he felt himself imposed upon, objected that he had retired. He was then bidden to come to the Chancellery at 10 that morning.[91]

Hitler obviously had done much hard thinking since the departure of Goering some three or four hours earlier and since Wiedemann had seen him in the posture of a "broken man." Never in the history of his dictatorship did he more dramatically demonstrate his genius for seizing opportunity on the wing. It is not possible, of course, to assert with full assurance that he had already mapped out the course of action on which he was actually to embark later that morning. But the eagerness he betrayed to start working on Hossbach is evidence that the real target now was Fritsch.[92] He

[91] Hossbach, *Zwischen Wehrmacht und Hitler*, 107.
[92] There is a strong indication here that Hitler already had in hand the dossier on Fritsch which would thus have been either brought by Goering or sent to the Chancellery shortly after he left Hitler.

must have known that, unless he personally were determined to hold him, Blomberg was a finished man. Once the full past of his wife was revealed, neither Hossbach nor any other Army representative would move a finger to save him. Isolating Fritsch was a problem of very different complexion.

At 10 A.M. on January 25 Hossbach made his prompt appearance at the Chancellery. There now began a marathon discussion which, interrupted only by meals and frequent intrusions by Goering, endured until late that evening. The fate of Blomberg was not treated as an issue. Hitler informed Hossbach that he had been misled by the War Minister about the person of the bride-to-be: Blomberg had done no more than stress her humble background and mention offhand that she was a woman with "a certain past." Now it turned out that she had been under police surveillance and had several times been sentenced on morals charges. To Hossbach's overwhelming disgust, Hitler then launched into a "hymn of praise" on Blomberg as War Minister. He had shown himself a paragon of loyalty and done much to bring the Wehrmacht closer to the party. The officer corps had never properly understood or appreciated this. It grieved him deeply to be obliged to part with so trusty a co-worker.[93]

In view of the rumors and strains of the previous days, Hossbach was not caught entirely by surprise. Yet the recital of the more complete story on Frau von Blomberg was still a profound shock. If the guardian-in-chief of Wehrmacht honor gambled with his reputation in this fashion, the officer corps had suffered the loss of a moral battle. To have to listen to attacks on that body for not understanding or appreciating such a man was more than he felt able to take. He was striving with difficulty to master his shame and fury when he was brought up short by a shift of the topic from Blomberg to Fritsch. The Army commander would also have to go, said Hitler; he was compromised as a homosexual. The evidence had been in the Fuehrer's hands for years.[94]

On the seething Hossbach this had the effect of a cold douche. "Blomberg and now Fritsch!" he thought. "This was too much. Instinctively I recognized that here was a base blow against the head of the Army." However much the charges against Blomberg appeared justified, those against Fritsch seemed to him wholly incredible. They could only be a pretext of Hitler's to rid himself

[93] Hossbach, *Zwischen Wehrmacht und Hitler*, 107–108.
[94] *Ibid.*, 108.

of the inconvenient general. The adjutant now realized what he was up against and that during the next hours he would need all the calm and self-control of which he was capable.[95]

Confining himself for the moment to the problem of Blomberg, he stated his conviction that the Wehrmacht would go along with his dismissal if the charges against his wife could be substantiated. Permitting his resentment and suspicion to break through, he went on to say that he was puzzled that the accusation was brought only after the marriage though the police must have had the evidence in hand for some time. The War Minister must be given a chance to examine the documents and take a position on them. Hitler agreed to this and Goering departed to confront Blomberg with his wife's file.[96]

That morning the adjutants in Blomberg's antechamber in the War Ministry were in a fever of curiosity and agitation. They had been bombarded since the marriage from many sides with questions—like those of Reichenau noted earlier—about its antecedents, queries to which they could only respond with embarrassed assurances that they knew next to nothing of them. Far from abating, the atmosphere of tension had been mounting since Blomberg's return from the aborted honeymoon. Goering's telephoned request for a rush appointment with Blomberg heightened the sense of impending drama.

Of what passed between the two men we have only the fragmentary accounts they gave to others then and later. As Blomberg related when a prisoner in 1945, Goering in the most unfeeling and brutal manner imaginable and without the least preliminary to soften the blow, told him of "certain matters in the distant past" of his wife which had just come to light. Because of this the War Minister was to be relieved of his post and discharged from the Army. "It was the greatest astonishment of my life and the worst blow I had ever received." It took Goering no more than five minutes to deal it to him. When Blomberg objected to "such unspeakably unfair treatment" and insisted that he ought to have some freedom in the choice of a wife, he received "the cool reply that I could please myself about the marriage, but the dismissal was absolutely final." With one significant omission, soon to be dealt with, this account probably reflects quite accurately what was said by the two in the course of their brief meeting.[97]

[95] *Ibid.*      [96] *Ibid.*
[97] This was Blomberg's story in his interrogation of September 23, 1945, 4.

Goering's relation, as might be expected, was somewhat different in emphasis, though it was in substance much like that of Blomberg. To Hitler and Hossbach, his report immediately after was only that the War Minister had "admitted everything" and was a "completely finished man."[98] To Bodenschatz he said on returning from the Chancellery later that day that Blomberg had professed ignorance of the charges against his wife. When told that the marriage could be immediately annulled if he so desired, he had asked whether in that event he would remain in office. On receiving a negative answer, he had stated that he loved his wife and would stick to her.[99]

There can be little doubt that at this point Goering exceeded both the letter and the spirit of his instructions so as not to encourage Blomberg to repudiate his wife and thus perhaps open the way for his return to grace. There is no indication whatever that Hitler had directed him to put matters in this light. Quite the contrary. There is the negative evidence of the omission of anything that carries such an implication in the account of Hossbach.[100] On the positive side is Hitler's explicit statement to Keitel that Blomberg had been asked to seek an immediate annulment and that only after he had categorically rejected this had events taken their course to his immediate dismissal.[101] Here is the exact opposite of what Goering had said to Blomberg. What appears likely is that Hitler had left the matter open when he entrusted Goering with his mission, that his scheming lieutenant took it upon himself to tell Blomberg that he was irreparably "finished," and that Hitler

[98] Hossbach, *Zwischen Wehrmacht und Hitler*, 108.

[99] Bodenschatz, "Statement on the Blomberg Affair."

[100] Hossbach, *Zwischen Wehrmacht und Hitler*, 108. Hossbach does not believe that while he was present Goering reported in greater detail than he relates in his book. Interview, July 1, 1971 (with Walter Bussmann).

[101] Keitel, 198. Hitler's testimony—and that of Keitel—is of course never by itself conclusive. There is much to argue, however, that in this instance Hitler believed what he was saying. He had no interest in stimulating further the already overwhelming bitterness against Blomberg in Army quarters. The Engel diary and recent further statements of General Engel (interviews of May 4 and 11, 1970) show how often in conversation with Army representatives Hitler sought to put Blomberg in a more favorable light. Hitler, it is true, would often say to Engel that the time to part with Blomberg, marriage or no marriage, had been approaching. But the manner of the War Minister's departure he still found humiliating to himself and he would no doubt have much preferred to ease him out more gracefully. Gisevius (*Bis zum bittem Ende*, 257-258), writing in 1939-40, was the first to present the story of Goering's dishonest execution of his mission to Blomberg.

was then informed that the War Minister was at all cost sticking to his marriage. In consequence, as both considered the matter settled, neither Hitler nor Blomberg thought of bringing it up in their meetings of January 26 and 27.

Goering's deceptions did not end there. The manner in which Blomberg conducted himself in the next two days, especially in talking with Hitler, raises legitimate doubt whether he had been shown the whole devastating police file on his wife, pictures and all, or perhaps only the residence registry card with its terse summary of Fräulein Gruhn's police record. Here again was a way to block Blomberg's continuance in office. Receiving only the mildest available version of his wife's transgressions, he would be less inclined to cast her off than if he learned the full story. He also was led to shock Hitler by his utter inability to comprehend the extent of his offense in involving the head of state in such a marriage.

Perhaps the most cynical of Goering's dodges in executing his mission was to throw the entire blame for Blomberg's disgrace on the importunities of the Generalität. It was the War Minister's fellow generals, he solemnly affirmed, who insisted on his dismissal.[102] The falsehood was the more impudent as Goering knew well that there had as yet been no communication whatever on the Blomberg situation between Hitler and the Army leadership. It accorded with his purpose to incite Blomberg against his military peers, so that he would be disinclined to recommend any of them when Hitler raised the inevitable question of the succession. Least of all would he be inclined to take up any cudgels for Fritsch, the ostensible spearhead of any Army move against him. Goering's maneuver, it will soon be evident, was to prove a sweeping success.

Goering's call had a shattering effect on Blomberg and for the moment completely unmanned him. As the Luftwaffe commander drove off, one of the adjutants in the antechamber opened the door a slit and saw his usually robust and erect chief tottering

---

[102] As related by Blomberg to Count Rüdiger von der Goltz in June 1945. Goltz interview, February 17, 1970. Letter of Goltz to General Hossbach, May 15, 1947 (printed in Hossbach, *Zwischen Wehrmacht und Hitler*, 114-116n1). No doubt it was this conversation with Goltz which impressed on Blomberg the bad light in which he placed himself by admitting how Goering had deceived him and, by implication, his own vengeful reaction in the advice he gave Hitler (see below, pp. 117-118). This will best explain why he avoided the subject in his interrogation of September 23, 1945.

like a man utterly broken from his workroom into his private chambers in the rear.[103]

During Goering's absence on the errand he was turning so much to his own profit, the discussion between Hitler and Hossbach continued at the Chancellery. On the problem of the succession to Blomberg, the adjutant stated plainly that the position must go to an Army general and not, for example, to Goering about whose competence he proceeded to voice objections. Hitler brusquely cut him short and rejected any mention of Goering in that connection. Swallowing this rebuff, Hossbach turned to the charges against Fritsch and thereby set the pattern of the conversation. Hour after hour Hitler and the returning Goering resorted to every trick of argument to convince him that the case against the Army commander was as clear as that against the War Minister had proved to be and should be treated as a *chose jugé*.[104] Since the issue no longer concerned the fate of Blomberg, however, this aspect of the dispute will be dealt with in the next chapter.[105]

Hossbach left the Chancellery between ten and eleven that evening to return to his own residence. His mind was in a turmoil from the trials and conflicting impressions of that fateful day and from a severe conflict between conscience and the soldier's habit of obedience. Hitler had given him a categorical order not to warn Fritsch of the accusation against him, a command that clashed with his concept of higher loyalty. The gross conduct ascribed to Fritsch in the dossier could not be reconciled in his mind with all he knew about that gentleman. Yet human nature had strange facets and if, by some incomprehensible quirk, there should be something to the charges against the general, he should be given an opportunity to do his duty by the Army.[106] Blood, decreed the officer's ancient code, washed away dishonor. In short order the adjutant made his decision and directed his car to the War Ministry in the Bendler Strasse where Fritsch had his personal quarters.[107]

There Hossbach learned that Fritsch had heard from another source about Blomberg's being on the way out. The problem of

[103] Gisevius, *Bis zum bittem Ende*, 257.

[104] Hossbach, *Zwischen Wehrmacht und Hitler*, 109.

[105] The remainder of the present chapter will continue to center on the Blomberg affair and will deal with problems of the related Fritsch crisis only where they are too closely intertwined to avoid mention.

[106] In this fashion Hossbach put the matter the next day to Wiedemann when that colleague reproached him for so flagrant a violation of a specific order. Wiedemann, *Der Mann der Feldherr werden wollte*, 117.

[107] Hossbach, *Zwischen Wehrmacht und Hitler*, 109.

114

# The Eclipse of Blomberg

the succession was now assuming the center of the stage and the Army commander affirmed spontaneously and categorically that his personal wish was to remain at his post; under no circumstances would he accept the War Ministry. Hossbach then crossed his personal Rubicon by relating the charges which had been dinned into his ears *ad nauseum* that day at the Chancellery. To his vast satisfaction, Fritsch, moved to use uncharacteristically colloquial language, instantly rejected the assertion as one that had been "stunk-up and lied-up."[108]

With renewed determination and confidence, though understandably apprehensive about his own fate, Hossbach sought an audience with Hitler on the morning of the 26th. With all the eloquence of which he was capable, he restated his conviction of Fritsch's innocence and related his conversation with the Army commander. To his relief and astonishment, Hitler listened with complete calm, though he did interject that Hossbach had done him a grave injury by eliminating the element of surprise so far as dealing with Fritsch was concerned.[109] Yet when the adjutant quoted the general's words which repudiated the charges so uncompromisingly, the Fuehrer put on an air of great relief and said: "Why, then things are in order and Fritsch can become Minister."[110] Upon Hossbach's reporting that the general had no other wish than to remain at his post and did not desire to be considered for the War Ministry, the discussion turned to other possible choices. Hossbach mentioned Rundstedt, Beck, and, if a stopgap appointment should seem advisable, the aged Count von der Schulenburg, who had much prestige as chief of staff of the crown prince's army group in World War I.[111] Hitler seized upon this last suggestion with enthusiasm, directing the adjutant to get in touch with Schulenburg and invite him to Berlin.

There was much about this solution to attract the dictator, at least before he was presented an hour or two later with a more alluring idea. It would give him time to work out a more permanent arrangement satisfactory to himself and for the time being ward

[108] *Ibid.*, 110.

[109] As related by Hossbach to Wiedemann. Wiedemann, *Der Mann der Feldherr werden wollte*, 117.

[110] This momentary pose of acquiescence on Fritsch's candidacy can only have been tactical to avoid any appearance of basic prejudice against him.

[111] The figure of Count Friedrich von der Schulenburg (1865-1939) had been built up into heroic proportions in the Third Reich. He had joined the party in 1931 and as a highly decorative "front man" had been given high honorary ranks in both the SA and SS.

off all pressures to appoint a prominent active Army officer. The proposal, however, was fated to be stillborn. When Hossbach got through to the count at a health resort in South Germany, he was told by Schulenburg that his physical state prohibited his coming to Berlin. He was also startled to hear that Himmler's adjutant had called shortly before with a similar request.[112] Hossbach was made painfully aware that other, darker forces were busily taking a hand in the game. His newfound optimism on the course of affairs began once more to fade.

Hitler, indeed, was about to hear a suggestion that was to eliminate from his mind any thought of appointing a new War Minister from within the Generalität he so much distrusted. Unknown to his Wehrmacht adjutant who, if protocol had been observed, would have arranged the meeting and been present, Hitler had summoned Blomberg, who arrived at the Chancellery soon after Hossbach left the Fuehrer's workroom.[113] The account Blomberg gave to Keitel and what he related to Count von der Goltz in June 1945 no doubt constituted a telescoping of what transpired between him and Hitler on January 26 and in the forty-five-minute farewell audience the next morning.

Hitler briefly but gently dealt with Blomberg's own situation, telling him that the burden placed by the marriage on them both was simply too great for them to bear and that there was no choice but to part company.[114] What shocked him most, he later professed, was Blomberg's total inability to comprehend the impossible character of his line of conduct and his extreme surprise that the Fuehrer should address any reproaches to him. The unhappy man spoke again of having married "a simple girl of the people" and protested that this had seemed to him precisely in the spirit of National

[112] Hossbach, *Zwischen Wehrmacht und Hitler*, 111. Schulenburg died about a year and a half later.

[113] Hossbach does not mention the hour of his audience, but Hitler's aversion to seeing anyone before ten o'clock makes that time the most probable. Since Keitel informed Jodl at precisely noon (Jodl Diary, 356) of Blomberg's fall, the meeting of the latter with Hitler must have taken place in the late morning. Keitel and Hossbach, in what they wrote after the war, speak of only one meeting and both refer to the farewell audience of the following morning, the 27th. In the case of Keitel this may be taken as a failure of memory; in that of Hossbach as the result of his having been left in the dark by Hitler, who did not want him present during the talk with Blomberg. It is possible that Hitler only called Blomberg to the Chancellery after the talk with Hossbach, wishing to have the fallen general's thought on the succession before he went farther in that matter.

[114] Jodl Diary, 357, entry of January 26, 1938.

116

Socialism,[115] words that can only raise further doubts about whether Goering had conveyed to him the full record of his wife's past.

Hitler could scarcely condescend to argue on such a matter and he passed as quickly as he could to the live issue of the succession. Fritsch, whom minutes before he had pictured to Hossbach as virtually rehabilitated in his sight and worthy to be War Minister, he now declared to be out of the running because he stood accused of a homosexual offense. Blomberg, whose misery demanded company, evidently found a perverse though understandable satisfaction in seeing the man standing next in the military hierarchy and whom Goering probably had pictured as leading the pack against him in straits so similar to his own. Far from wasting chivalrous words on the need of establishing Fritsch's guilt before disposing of him, he commented that such leanings on the part of Fritsch, a queer fellow in many ways, seemed to him entirely conceivable.[116] As suitable candidates for the position of Army commander he mentioned Reichenau and Brauchitsch.[117]

With Fritsch thus cavalierly thrust aside, Blomberg pointed out that Goering, as "next in rank," was now the logical candidate for the War Ministry.[118] The suggestion hardly stemmed from love of the man who the day before had treated him so heartlessly and in whom he was later to recognize the architect of his misfortunes;[119] that noon, in talking with Keitel, he would accuse him of selfishly refusing to cover up for him because he wanted to be War Minister.[120] Yet whatever resentment he felt against Goering was dwarfed by his animosity toward his fellow generals on whom the intriguer had shoved the odium of his dismissal. He did not

---

[115] In a conversation with Captain Engel some three months later, Hitler recounted this and pointed out that, though Nazi concepts might reject some of the hypocritical morals of traditional "society," he still would never tolerate that a party member in a responsible position should marry a professional prostitute. Engel Diary, entry of April 20, 1938.

[116] As related by Hitler to Hossbach the next day. Hossbach, *Zwischen Wehrmacht und Hitler*, 114. In his conversation with Count von der Goltz in June 1945, Blomberg's troubled conscience was reflected in his defensive attitude. Fritsch, he insisted, had always been an odd character and evidently "not a man for women." It thus was easily understandable, he claimed, that people should conceive that he might have homosexual leanings. Letter of Goltz to General Hossbach, May 15, 1947. Hossbach, *Zwischen Wehrmacht und Hitler*, 116.

[117] Blomberg interrogation of September 23, 1945, 5.

[118] Letter of Goltz to Hossbach, May 15, 1947. Hossbach, *Zwischen Wehrmacht und Hitler*, 114.

[119] In 1945 Blomberg told Otto John that he had fallen for a "scoundrelly trick" on the part of Goering. John, 28.

[120] Keitel, 111.

need to be told how they would detest the idea of Goering as War Minister and must have thought it no more than poetic justice to deliver them into his clutches. They would then soon learn to look back with nostalgia to the comparatively halcyonic days of Blomberg's incumbency of the Ministry.

After the war Blomberg tried to defend himself by arguing that none of the prominent Army figures had been qualified to succeed him. When reminded of such men as Beck, Leeb, and Brauchitsch (the latter "at least better than Hitler"), he could only repeat his verdict. Beck, for example, he characterized as "a man of slow decision, hesitant and irresolute."[121]

Blomberg's mention of Goering sat no better with the dictator than the censure of that worthy by Hossbach a day earlier or the recommendations Keitel and Wiedemann were to make. In the judgment of General Engel, Hitler's biggest worry had become how to ward off his ambitious henchman's many-signaled drive to the military summit. However contrary to what he said in public, Hitler actually had a low opinion of Goering's military qualifications; in moments of strong verbal flow he would express this in no uncertain terms to his entourage. Perhaps because of his Austrian background, or so the North Germans in his entourage thought, he had a weakness for such baroque characters. But this did not mean that he cherished illusions about them. He knew well that Goering lacked military stature in the customary General Staff sense of strategic, tactical, and defense-political insights. His World War I achievements as air squadron commander had been spectacular enough but had equipped him for little else.[122]

Hitler with some heat put it to Blomberg that Goering lacked patience and industry;[123] he labeled him "absolutely unfitted" to be War Minister.[124] The question springs to mind, of course, how he could make his heir presumptive a man whom he considered unqualified even for this lesser post. The answer no doubt lies partly in the common preference of egocentric leaders for successors who lack the capacity to emerge from their predecessor's shadow. It may also be assumed that Hitler had no intention of ever elevating

---

[121] In conversation with Count von der Goltz. When Goltz called to his attention that Beck in the end had been the one of these generals who had not hesitated to act against Hitler, Blomberg agreed and said that for this reason he, in his own mind, had often begged Beck's pardon. Goltz interview, February 17, 1970.

[122] Engel interview, May 11, 1970.

[123] Blomberg affidavit, November 7, 1945. IMT, XXXII, Document 370 PS.

[124] Blomberg interrogation of September 23, 1945, 5.

# The Eclipse of Blomberg

Goering, crown prince or not, or *any* of his more ambitious lieutenants to the military heights. Doubtless the experience with Röhm, who had presumed too far in this regard, was deeply engraved on his memory.

Goering having thus joined Fritsch in the discards of candidates and Blomberg having no inclination to recommend one of the other generals, the fallen Minister was brought by elimination to utter the fateful query: "Why don't you take it on yourself?"[125]

Blomberg went on to say that Hitler was already in an ultimate sense commander in chief of the Wehrmacht under the constitution. If the War Minister's post were simply left vacant he "would be the actual as well as the legal commander."[126] The idea was a novel one and most probably had not popped into Blomberg's mind until that very instant. It does not seem to have counted among the hopes or fears of anyone who then knew of and thought about the problem of the succession to the War Ministry. We may be sure that it registered in capital letters in *Hitler's* mind, though he maintained a noncommittal attitude and said he would think about the matter.[127] He then remarked that if he did decide to follow this advice he would need someone to do the intensive staff work that would be required. "Who," he asked, "is that general you have had at your side up to now?" "Oh, Keitel," was the answer; "he would not come into consideration. He is no more than my *chef de bureau* [office manager]." "That," exclaimed Hitler, "is exactly the kind of man I am looking for." Blomberg further clinched things for his hard-working, submissive chief of the Wehrmachtamt by describing him as well disposed toward Hitler personally and as a man who could contribute constructively to a good working relationship with the Army.[128] Hitler then directed that Keitel should come to the Chancellery in civilian garb that afternoon.

[125] Goltz interview, February 17, 1970.

[126] Blomberg interrogation of September 23, 1945, 5.

[127] When Blomberg let the cat out of the bag in conversation with Count von der Goltz in June 1945, he obviously did not at first recognize what a monstrous thing he had confessed to. Then, noting the count's aghast expression and guessing that he was thinking of the disasters which Hitler's direction of the Wehrmacht had brought upon Germany, he became nervous and begged his listener not to mention to anyone what he had just said. Letter of Goltz to General Hossbach, May 15, 1947. Hossbach, *Zwischen Wehrmacht und Hitler*, 115.

[128] Blomberg interrogation of September 23, 1945. Blomberg affidavits, November 7, 1945, and February 26, 1946, IMT, XXXII, 465, and XL, 408. Warlimont, "Interpretation," 102a.

As if not content with what he had already done to deliver the Army into Hitler's hands, Blomberg, whether in response to a request or on his own initiative, then—or quite possibly during the forty-five-minute meeting on the 27th—identified those generals who, he had reason to believe, were most uncooperative in their attitude toward the National Socialist state. Small wonder that Beck, when he learned of this, branded the former War Minister a "scoundrel" (*Schuft*).[129] Small wonder, too, that Hitler waxed more and more cordial and concluded the meeting with the assurance that, if the hour for war should strike, Blomberg would again be called to his side. Meanwhile he would in outward form "remain in the service" and continue to draw full salary.[130] With these sugarcoated embellishments he formally dismissed Blomberg as War Minister.

Clinging to this last despairing hope of rehabilitation in wartime, but in a state close to collapse, Blomberg returned to the War Ministry and summoned Keitel. To him he gave a brief account of what had transpired in his talk with Hitler, who would enlighten him more fully on what had been said about the succession and about charges against Fritsch which would eliminate that officer as a candidate. With the same strange insensitiveness to the inescapable verdict of his fellowmen that he had shown earlier, and which makes one question again how much Goering had really told him, he kept insisting to the flabbergasted Keitel that his dismissal could have been avoided. If Goering had not been so set on taking over his post, a way could have been found "to cover the affair with the mantle of love."[131] He had been aware before the marriage that his present wife had "a frivolous past," but that, after all, was no reason for ostracizing a woman forever. Moreover,

[129] A notation of April 30, 1938, in the unpublished papers of Ulrich von Hassell quotes Beck as having said in a conversation of April 23 that Blomberg "had had a hand" in the dismissal of many generals on February 4. To his wife, Hassell reported more fully what Beck had told him, relating that Blomberg, in one of his final talks with Hitler, had given him the names of generals who in his book were anti-Nazi. Interview with Ilse von Hassell, April 30, 1970.

[130] To Keitel, whom Blomberg saw immediately after returning to the War Ministry, he related that "old Prussian tradition" decreed that a field marshal theoretically always remained on active service. Keitel, 105. Blomberg later claimed in his largely worthless unpublished memoirs that Hitler, in their last meeting of January 27, "spontaneously promised me with the greatest emphasis that I would take over the supreme command in war-time." Telford Taylor, *Sword and Swastika: The Wehrmacht in the Third Reich* (London, 1953), 151. The memoirs are on microfilm in the IfZ. Most of what he wrote about the 1938 crisis was destroyed.

[131] Blomberg no doubt meant the love Hitler owed him for his loyal service, not a romantic respect that others should have toward his love for his wife.

# The Eclipse of Blomberg

she had for some time been earning an honest living at the Reich Egg Center. When Keitel urged a divorce, he indignantly repulsed him, saying that he loved his wife beyond all measure, that the marriage was a true love match on both sides, and that he would "rather shoot a bullet through his head." Telling Keitel that he was to report to Hitler in civilian clothing at one o'clock, he left him standing and rushed into his private quarters with tears streaming from his eyes.[132]

## Blomberg's Exit

What remains of the story of the eclipse of Werner von Blomberg can quickly be told. Hitler had ordered him to stay away from Germany for a year; for this "vacation," as Blomberg liked to refer to it later, the Reichsbank was directed to provide a sum of 50,000 marks in foreign exchange. Wiedemann, who was sent to pick up this sum and who gave the bank's President Schacht a quick rundown on developments, was treated to some of the choicer of the acid comments at which that gentleman excelled. The combined "vacation" and resumed honeymoon, incidentally, was a gift from Hitler, presumably from his personal funds.[133] Blomberg was at first scheduled to leave that evening (January 26), but the departure was delayed by Hitler's desire to see him once more on the following morning.[134] There is no indication what particular afterthought moved the dictator to ask to see the departing Minister once more.

Two emissaries were yet to pursue Blomberg on the Italian leg of his journey. In the rush of his departure the preparation of official papers relative to his leaving office had been overlooked. Since Oster was one of the very few officers in the War Ministry who was known to be initiated into the details of the scandal, he was selected by Keitel to follow Blomberg to Italy to see to the fulfillment of these formalities. Catching up with Blomberg in Capri, Oster was astonished and rather shocked to find him

[132] Keitel, 104-106.

[133] Wiedemann, *Der Mann der Feldherr werden wollte*, 110, and interview, December 2, 1969.

[134] On this occasion, Hossbach, who had been told nothing of the meeting on the 26th, performed his usual duties of making the appointment and conducting the arriving and departing general from and back to his car. To his astonishment, what he had assumed would be no more than a short farewell audience lasted forty-five minutes. The two brief encounters between Blomberg and Hossbach progressed in icy silence, which the former broke at the end with a sneering "Farewell, my good man." Hossbach, *Zwischen Wehrmacht und Hitler*, 113.

in a lively, almost a gay mood.[135] While Blomberg retired to another room of his hotel to examine and sign the documents, his wife did the honors in a manner which to the handsome Oster seemed rather flirtatious.[136]

More dramatic was the journey to Rome of Blomberg's own naval adjutant, Commander[137] Baron Hubertus von Wangenheim. During the preceding days of turmoil the War Minister's staff had been prey to the most agonizing doubts and confusion over what was happening. In largest part they had to depend on reports and rumors that drifted over from the Reich Chancellery. Distress grew in proportion to the cumulation of shocking information on the past life of their chief's new wife. Gradually the conviction hardened that Blomberg could not possibly have been given the full story by Goering. Finally Wangenheim either decided on his own or was delegated to carry the problem to the head of the Navy, Admiral Raeder.

While Raeder and Wangenheim were deep in discussion, another visitor arrived and was invited to participate. This was Hitler's naval adjutant, Commander Karl von Puttkamer. Wangenheim proposed trying to catch Blomberg while he was still in Rome, make to him a full disclosure about his wife, and, if he should still refuse to part from her, convince him that the only honorable way out of his dilemma was a bullet. Since the three naval men shared a common devotion to the traditional officers' code, there was no disagreement about this and Raeder gave his specific approval. The problem was now one of securing the necessary foreign exchange to make such a journey. Puttkamer had an inspiration. His fellow adjutant, Wiedemann, was the guardian of substantial funds that he might draw upon for a purpose with which he was bound to sympathize. Puttkamer and Wangenheim therefore hurried off to the Chancellery.[138]

As expected, Wiedemann proved to be in a cooperative frame of mind. He first of all confirmed to his visitor the worst that he had heard about Frau von Blomberg. "We adjutants of the field

[135] Gisevius, *Bis zum bittern Ende*, 275. The assumption that it was Keitel who must have made the selection is the author's.

[136] Interview with General Achim Oster, December 17, 1969. Gisevius testifies that Oster did not at the time report anything of this nature about Eva von Blomberg in an otherwise detailed account of the journey. Gisevius recording, July 1971.

[137] This appears to be the best translation of the German rank of "Kapitanleutnant."

[138] Puttkamer interview, June 27, 1970. Jodl, in his diary entry of January 29 (360), also reports that Raeder sent Wangenheim to Rome to demand that Blomberg part from his wife. See also Gisevius, *Bis zum bittern Ende*, 269.

marshal," Wangenheim then said, "are convinced that he does not know what is wrong with his wife. I wish to enlighten him about her."[139] Could Wiedemann provide the foreign exchange needed to get to Rome? Yes, he could; that evening (January 27) Wangenheim was on his way to the Eternal City.

Wangenheim on his return related to Wiedemann and Puttkamer how he had found Blomberg at his hotel and, though sparing him as much as possible, had given him the story of his wife's past. Apparently playing for time to consider the form of his answer, Blomberg said he would have to talk with her and went through the motions of consulting her in the next room. On returning, he said that he could not bring himself to leave this woman in the lurch. Wangenheim then became more explicit and, finally, so vehement that the tortured Blomberg protested, "You are virtually pointing a pistol at my chest." The infuriated officer then pulled a revolver out of his pocket, slammed it on the table, and cried, "I have brought that along with me." As he turned toward the door, Blomberg sneered after him, "Young man, what do you know about *raison d'état* [*Staatsnotwenigkeiten*]?" At this Wangenheim choked out, "I have nothing but contempt for you, Herr von Blomberg."[140]

The sequel threatened to be disastrous for Wangenheim and he might well have been a lost man had it not been for the circumstance of Raeder's preliminary approval. The incensed Blomberg complained to Keitel about the incident by telegram and letter. When Wangenheim had thrust the pistol at him, he said, he had rejected it because he "moved on a different level of life and conceptions."[141] Keitel was naturally offended that an officer who was now under his jurisdiction should undertake such a mission without his knowledge or authorization. He ran with the matter to Goering, who exploded in fury. A dead field marshal, he ranted, was just about all that was still needed in this damnable situation. He called in the overly bold young officer, gave him a fearful dressing down, and talked of having him shot.[142] Finally he demanded that Wangenheim be dismissed from the service for having dared to go abroad without formal leave. Raeder could not but feel honor bound to come to the defense of his man and, when Keitel refused to

[139] Wiedemann, *Der Mann der Feldherr werden wollte,* 110.

[140] *Ibid.,* 110–111. Blomberg's final remark is given here as reported by Admiral von Puttkamer. Interview, June 27, 1970.

[141] Jodl Diary, 362, entries of January 31 and February 1.

[142] Gisevius, *Bis zum bittern Ende,* 269.

retain him further in the War Ministry, gave him an appointment in the naval command. With the doggedness that characterized him when standing up for his own, Raeder actually dared to propose Wangenheim to Hitler as naval adjutant twenty months later, but was told to reassign Puttkamer, who had been away commanding a destroyer.[143]

Goering's fury with Wangenheim appears so excessive in terms of the adjutant's offense that one feels impelled to look for a more personal angle than is at first visible. Why should he be so upset about Blomberg's being told the fuller story of his wife's past and urged to seek an annulment? Did he fear that the former War Minister might yet respond to such pressures and, even at this late date, make a determined play for return to the still vacant office? Was he uneasy about Blomberg's learning that he had been given a somewhat doctored message on the 25th? Wangenheim certainly noted that his former chief seemed to hear much of what he told him for the first time.[144]

Blomberg's purblind hope for a comeback in his military career in the event of war suffered cruel disappointment. With that insensitiveness whose growth had kept pace with his infatuation he would not comprehend the hostility which had swept through the officer corps and especially the Generalität, for which he was a traitor to its most revered traditions. He, whose wife's nude photos or worse had been handed around with derisive remarks in police and Chancellery quarters, refused to understand that the disdain expressed so savagely by Wangenheim differed little in degree from the feeling which prevailed among most of his old comrades.

Probably the ex-Minister never learned how much he owed to Hitler for not having lost much more than his post. The morning after his departure from Berlin, Beck called on Keitel with the severest demands. The sparrows, he complained bitterly, were chirping the full story on the Frau Feldmarschall from the rooftops of Berlin. Her old associates kept placing spiteful calls to generals from public houses where they continued to celebrate the social

[143] Puttkamer interview, June 27, 1970. Wiedemann, *Der Mann der Feldherr werden wollte*, 111, and interview, December 2, 1969. Jodl Diary, 363, entry of February 2, 1938.

[144] Gisevius believes that Goering was so furious because he feared that Wangenheim had told Blomberg things about his bride's past that Goering had not mentioned during his call at the War Ministry on January 25. Gisevius, *Bis zum bittern Ende*, 269. The detailed story of Wangenheim's trip to Rome was given to Oster by Wiedemann immediately after the adjutant's return. Gisevius recording, July 1971.

elevation of their "colleague." If Blomberg would not agree to part with this woman, his name should be struck off the roll of officers of the German Army and he should be deprived of the regiment of which he was honorary colonel. Beck urged that the Wehrkreis commanders act collectively to press such views upon the Fuehrer.[145] In his meeting with Hitler on January 31, Rundstedt, possibly put up to it by Beck with whom he had conferred immediately before, took the same position and went beyond it to demand that Blomberg be summoned before a court of honor.[146]

Such severity toward his fallen friend was more than Hitler was prepared to stomach. Keitel, for whom family considerations harmonized with the Fuehrer's wishes, also seems to have done all he could to nip such proposals in the bud. Blomberg probably never heard of them and thus could the more easily deceive himself on what he might yet induce Hitler to do for his rehabilitation. He clearly persisted in his delusion that all would yet have been well if only Hitler and Goering had been so generous as to "cover the affair with the mantle of love."

Actually not too many weeks passed before the bloom on the marriage had faded sufficiently to make him regret the price he had been compelled to pay. He had not yet left Italy when he wired Keitel a plea to facilitate a visit to him of his second son, Axel, so that they might discuss "matters of the utmost urgency." A week later Axel returned to Berlin with a letter in which his father begged Keitel to submit to the Fuehrer a proposal by which, in return for restoration to favor and his former office, he was prepared to repudiate his wife. Hitler, when shown the letter, responded logically enough that the clock could no longer be turned back. Blomberg, he said, had been given his chance to stay on through a timely annulment of the marriage and upon his refusal events had taken their inexorable course.[147]

Blomberg, in his massive self-deception, conceived the fancy that Keitel, to safeguard himself in his still glamorous new post,

---

[145] Jodl Diary, 360, entry of January 28, 1939.

[146] Rundstedt, "Affaire Blomberg-Fritsch 1938" (in IfZ, ZS 129 (I) ).

[147] Keitel, 198-199. For the sake of the record it should be noted that Finance Minister Schwerin von Krosigk reports (270) that Hitler, after receiving Goering's revelations the evening of January 24, consulted with Minister of Justice Gürtner who confirmed the view that Blomberg had a legal basis for an annulment. Gürtner is said to have thereupon been dispatched to the War Minister to tell him that he could remain in office if he adopted this course. Since Schwerin's account of the affair contains errors and since Blomberg after the war said nothing of such a mission to him by Gürtner, this version may be discounted.

must have sabotaged his reconciliation with Hitler.[148] After the war he complained bitterly that throughout this period there had been a "planned campaign" to spread the false story that he had been given an initial choice between retaining his post and staying with his wife. The intention, as he saw it, was to further exacerbate the resentments harbored against him throughout the Wehrmacht. The principal villain he now saw accurately enough as the initiator of the deception, Goering, but he also threw much of the blame on Keitel. His former man Friday, who, he was sure, knew better, "was unscrupulous enough to impress this infamous lie upon my grown children, which resulted in an extended alienation."[149]

To render justice to Keitel, it is more likely that he was simply repeating in good faith what he had been told by Hitler, who himself, in this instance, may be regarded equally a victim of Goering's chicanery.

When the war erupted in September 1939, Blomberg wrote to Hitler to place himself at his disposal and plead for employment. Through Hossbach's rather artless successor, Major Rudolf Schmundt, a basically decent fellow who sympathized with the fallen Minister's lot, he hinted that he would be content with the command of a corps. Captain Engel, in his official role as Army adjutant, then spoke frankly to Hitler, stressing that the recall to service of Blomberg would give the gravest offense to the Army. Indignation would be the greater in view of Fritsch's not having been offered a command and joining his regiment as an ordinary combatant. This judicious bracketing of the two men was enough to do the trick, though it may not have been needed. Hitler could not ignore the fact that to give a command to the universally despised Blomberg without granting one to the revered and regretted Fritsch would cause an explosion throughout the military and possibly have serious repercussions.[150] There was nothing he wanted less than to be compelled again to employ Fritsch in any capacity and to avert this it was necessary to dispense with Blomberg. He therefore stated that as long as the former War Minister clung to his wife he must remain in the obscurity of retirement.[151]

[148] Keitel, 199.

[149] Blomberg interrogation of September 23, 1945, 5.

[150] It is quite conceivable, for example, that Blomberg's immediate associates, whether superior or subordinate, would simply have declined all dealings with him.

[151] Engel Diary, entry of September 10, 1939. In his rambling memoirs (Taylor, 152) Blomberg states that, on returning to Germany, he was indirectly informed

# The Eclipse of Blomberg

So Werner von Blomberg vegetated in friendless isolation, ignored by his former peers.[152] His ostracism carried over into the brief span of life that remained to him after the war when generals who were his fellow prisoners continued to cut him; some of them who might have visited him as he lay dying made no move to do so.[153] With those persons who did condescend to converse with him in the last months of his life he sooner or later sought an opening for a pathetic assertion that, after all, his seven years of marriage had proved happy ones.[154]

## A Dictator Acquires a New Lackey

Blomberg's grim recital on January 26 had left Keitel in a state of semishock, so that he had to drop into a chair and get a grip on himself before going home for a hasty lunch and change into civilian raiment. Previous to leaving the War Ministry, he did inform his closest co-worker, Colonel Alfred Jodl, of what he had been told. With tears in his eyes he related Blomberg's fall and sadly commented that their common aim of a unified direction of the Wehrmacht had thereby suffered a cruel blow. "The man may fall, his work must remain," Jodl summarized his own reaction in his diary.[155]

Keitel went home so downcast that he lacked the heart to say anything to his wife, however much she was concerned because of the coming family tie. Meanwhile he received a message from the Chancellery postponing his appointment with the Fuehrer from one to five o'clock, and, on the heels of this, an urgent summons from Goering to come as quickly as possible to the Air Ministry.

Goering's keen sense of timing told him that the moment of decision was at hand. Now that the fall of Blomberg was definite that the promise to employ him in case of war "could no longer be realized." This may well have been a confidential communication from the sympathetic Schmundt on the basis of a conversation with Hitler.

[152] This extended to former friends and close associates, such as Reichenau. On one occasion during the war when the two generals and their wives happened to be in the same restaurant, neither made any gesture of recognition. Reichenau interview, June 23, 1970.

[153] Thus Brauchitsch, who truly had little reason to feel superior or self-righteous in relation to Blomberg, shocked his British captors by what seemed to them a callous indifference to the opportunity to ease the passing of his former comrade and superior. Interview with Airey Neave, July 6, 1970.

[154] Wiedemann, *Der Mann der Feldherr werden wollte*, 112. Goltz interview, February 17, 1970.

[155] Jodl Diary, 356-357, entry of January 26 (noon). Keitel's account of that day omits the brief talk with Jodl.

and official, though Hitler had reserved to himself the hour and manner of the public announcement,[156] the matter of succession must be competing in the Fuehrer's mind with the problem of how to speed the exit of Fritsch. He was certain to have raised with Blomberg during their late morning conference the question of whom to appoint and it was important for Goering to learn what had been said. The crafty schemer was mobilizing all his resources and overlooking no bets on how to bring his influence and pressure to bear. It is highly probable that while Hitler was occupied with Hossbach and Blomberg, Goering had utilized this period of waiting to entreat the good offices of Wiedemann.[157]

Goering had evidently decided that in grasping for power there was no sense in being modest. Wiedemann, he urged, should tell Hitler that he, Goering, would like to be made a field marshal, most definitely not an air marshal, a rank much cheapened through its proliferation in Britain. The Fuehrer should also make him commander in chief of the Army. In return for such more attractive plums Goering was prepared to give up his direction of the Four Year Plan.[158]

Wiedemann, much of an innocent and understandably flattered to be enlisted for the role of amateur kingmaker, also saw real merit in the proposal. Goering, as the acid exchanges with Blomberg and Fritsch on November 5 had recently again demonstrated, had been a stormy petrel among the service commanders and a perennial source of annoyance to the War Minister. If another Army man

[156] "Fuehrer has ordered that fact will be made known only after the 30th and in a sense he will determine." *Ibid.*, 356.

[157] In view of the complicated and dramatic interplay of events during these very full days, it was later difficult even for those most intimately placed for observing them to retain a clear concept of the sequence of developments. Hossbach, writing only two or three years after the war, confessed to some uncertainty about the order of affairs between January 26 and his dismissal on January 28. Keitel is guilty of half a dozen obvious slips in time relationships. And Wiedemann can only report that Goering took him aside "one day" to enlist his help. The best guess on the timing in this instance is the late morning of the 26th for Hitler's tête-à-têtes with Hossbach and Blomberg and for Goering, haunting the antechambers of the Chancellery and lining up support, to have buttonholed Wiedemann. The earliest and best time for Wiedemann to have cornered Hitler was immediately after lunch, when he often relaxed with newspapers on an enclosed veranda at the back of the Chancellery.

[158] Wiedemann, *Der Mann der Feldherr werden wollte*, 112. Be it noted that Goering here asked only that the Army command should be added to his responsibility for the Luftwaffe. He thus did not exactly suggest stepping into Blomberg's shoes. The explanation may lie either in his indifference with respect to the Navy or in his assumption that it would in any event quickly fall under his aegis.

were to be promoted to that position, he could never hope to become as solid with Hitler as Blomberg had been. Goering could then with increased impunity take out his frustration on his Army rival and the long-sought unity of command would be farther than ever from realization. If, on the other hand, Goering himself became War Minister, or its near equivalent by absorbing the Army into his vast personal empire, this same ruthless egotism would ensure his utilizing every resource to center authority in the unified command, i.e., himself.[159]

Wiedemann did go to Hitler—probably after lunch on the 26th—to ask whether he might speak about a matter that was not specifically his concern. "Certainly," was the cordial answer; "please come up to my room."[160] There Wiedemann could say no more than a few sentences: "My Fuehrer, Goering would like to become field marshal and to take over the Army. We have always had differences between the Army and the Luftwaffe. Goering was no easy subordinate for Blomberg. There would be an end to that if you also gave him the Army. He is ready to give up the Four Year Plan." At this point Hitler gruffly interrupted and abruptly ended the discussion with: "Out of the question. He does not even understand anything about the Luftwaffe. He cannot do an inspection properly. I actually understand more about that."[161]

If the estimate of the hour of this conversation is correct, Goering, blissfully unaware of how his candidacy was just then unceremoniously being polished off by Hitler, was busily enlisting the support of Keitel. The Air Minister unblushingly exposed both his curiosity and his preoccupation with his own elevation by asking first what Blomberg had told of his talk with Hitler. He then went on to solicit Keitel's ideas on the succession. "For that only you come into question" was the gratifying answer. "You will hardly be willing to subordinate yourself to another Army general." This reply, so much in line with what Wiedemann was saying to Hitler, was of course exactly what Goering wanted and he expressed vehement agreement.[162]

Keitel utilized the hours between his talks with Goering and

[159] Wiedemann interview, December 2, 1969.

[160] In conversation with the author, Wiedemann, though not remembering exactly, agreed that it was most probable that he caught Hitler when he was lounging on the veranda after lunch since he would not have disturbed him during "business hours." *Ibid.*

[161] Wiedemann, *Der Mann der Feldherr werden wollte*, 113.

[162] Keitel, 106.

with Hitler to call on Fritsch and Raeder and seek to impress upon them the importance of preserving the work of Blomberg for the unity of the Wehrmacht.[163] At five o'clock he was at the Chancellery and what he experienced there must have given him the sensation that the great hour of his life had indeed struck.

Before January 26, 1938, the contacts between Hitler and the chief of the Wehrmachtamt had been trivial. Hitler knew so little about the man that he had referred to him that day to Hossbach as "General von Keitel."[164] In Keitel's case the few cursory encounters with the Fuehrer had produced unstinting admiration. A first brief meeting in July 1933 had been followed by ecstatic reports to his wife about "fabulous eyes" and extraordinary facility of speech.[165] Thus he was already conditioned to succumb entirely to what was for many the Fuehrer's irresistible spell.

Keitel's perception of unique opportunity probably came to him only as the talk unfolded. From Blomberg he had heard no more than that the Fuehrer desired his views on the succession. As it became evident that he stood to profit greatly by the turnover, his normally servile manner when facing persons of higher authority must have been accentuated.[166]

Hitler commenced with a version of the Blomberg scandal more calculated to gain sympathy for himself than for the culprit. He then switched to the problem of the succession and asked for suggestions. As Keitel reported it to the present writer, his answer was "I suppose you will want to take Goering." "Never," shot back Hitler, "he is much too easygoing and lazy. I am going to take direct command of the Wehrmacht myself." Keitel, nettled, asked why he was solicited for his opinion if the matter was already so firmly settled.[167]

From all that is known of Wilhelm Keitel's customary demeanor, this sounds much like a piece of latter-day bravado to make him, for once, look less obsequious toward Hitler than he knew himself believed to be. More accurate, no doubt, are his memoirs, where he reports that Hitler, adapting as always his manner of speaking

[163] Jodl Diary, 356.

[164] Hossbach, *Zwischen Wehrmacht und Hitler,* 114.

[165] Letter from Lisa Keitel to her mother, July 5, 1933. Keitel, 53.

[166] Keitel alone among the military figures interrogated by the present writer in 1945 lacked dignity. When, at the close of the second meeting, hope was expressed to him that there might be a third, his response was to bow twice with outstretched palms and a servile murmur, "Ever at your service; ever at your service."

[167] Keitel interrogation, October 1945.

to his listener, replied in a fashion that would have astounded Wiedemann who had just been treated to an outburst of the Fuehrer's contempt for Goering. He had given Goering the Four Year Plan, said Hitler, and wanted him also to keep the Luftwaffe because there was no better man for it. But as the Fuehrer's predestined successor, the great man should devote his energies to familiarizing himself thoroughly with *all* aspects of state business.[168]

When Keitel next suggested Fritsch, Hitler related the charges of homosexuality against the general and added that he wished *in any event* to make a change soon in the Army command.[169] Then, going on as if the fate of Fritsch were settled, Hitler devoted the rest of the discussion to the question of his successor rather than Blomberg's. Thus was launched a prolonged debate that will be covered at a later point and that was to culminate in the appointment of General von Brauchitsch on February 4.

At 1 P.M. on the following day (January 27) Keitel was again received by Hitler for a conference that endured for close to three hours.[170] Hitler put on a show of great agitation and told how Fritsch had been positively identified by his accuser. The general was thus seriously compromised and could no longer remain as Army commander. For the time being he had been suspended from his functions and ordered to remain in his quarters.

While Keitel was still absorbing this, Hitler gave vent to a fierce denunciation of Hossbach for "disgracefully circumventing" his orders about saying nothing to Fritsch. He never again wished to see this man who had violated his confidence. Keitel should on the spot propose a replacement. Since Hossbach was already scheduled for transfer to troops on April 1 and Keitel, pursuant to an order from Blomberg, had been occupying himself with the search for a suitable adjutant, he had a candidate ready in the person of Major Schmundt, who was duly accepted by Hitler.

According to his memoirs, Keitel, puzzled by the omission of any mention of a successor for Blomberg, returned to that topic to break another lance for Goering. He was told that Hitler had decided to be his own Wehrmacht commander and wanted him to act as his chief of staff. To win the impressionable man before

[168] The source of this and the following four paragraphs is Keitel, 107–109.

[169] Jodl Diary, 358, entry of January 27, 1938. See below, pp. 160, 168, for a more complete account of how Hitler twisted matters in dealing with the problem of Fritsch.

[170] This conclusion rests on the fact that Keitel was back at the War Ministry and closeted with Jodl at 4 P.M. Jodl Diary, 359.

him once and for all Hitler was evidently prepared to exert himself. Not having as yet gauged him entirely, he spread it on rather more thickly than was really necessary. The flattering remarks and extravagant cajolery he addressed to him would have left a considerably more sophisticated person than this simple-minded soldier breathless. Keitel was assured that he was "indispensable." But for that Hitler would make him commander of the Army. "I rely entirely on you. You are my trusted and only counselor in problems of the Wehrmacht. The undivided and close-knit direction of the Wehrmacht is sacred and untouchable for me. I am taking it over myself with your help . . . On June 30, 1934, the party had to be ashamed before the Wehrmacht; may the day never come when the Wehrmacht has to be ashamed before the party."[171]

Keitel returned with whirling head to the War Ministry and told Jodl that the unity of the Wehrmacht was assured. Hitler had won him completely by basely flattering his small but starved ego and making him forget for the moment one of his redeeming features—a gnawing awareness of his own mediocrity. The cynical tempter had also taken monstrous advantage of his credulity.

During the following days Hitler continued the game with unvaried success, notably in maneuvers that concerned the appointment of a new Army commander. Meanwhile the details of a directive on "The Leadership of the Wehrmacht" were being worked out between Keitel and Secretary of State (in the Reich Chancellery) Hans Heinrich Lammers. Both Keitel and Jodl had some lingering doubts about the measure of authority that would be assigned the former under the setup. Hitler salved their anxiety by a show of great solicitude about attaching sufficient weight to the new position. Through Lammers they were informed that the normal title, which would have been "Chief of Staff of the Wehrmacht," seemed too trivial to the dictator for so great an office as the one he had in mind. Therefore he was settling on "Chief of the Supreme Command of the Wehrmacht."

Actually Hitler was well aware that in the Prusso-German tradition the chieftainship of the General Staff implied a deputy command function and under the Empire had denoted nothing less than the de facto command under the nominal direction of the sovereign. The headship of a "Supreme Command of the Armed

---

[171] *Ibid.*, 358. A more self-respecting Army representative than Keitel might well have been indignant over this implied parallel between the current situation and the June 1934 Blood Purge.

132

## The Eclipse of Blomberg

Forces" was subject to more flexible connotations. If Hitler should merely copy his fellow dictator Mussolini by accumulating ministerial portfolios without finding the time or energy for a real exercise of functions, the post would indeed be an exalted one, not too much below the office held by Blomberg. If, on the other hand, he thought only to exploit the officeholder as a tool to subject the heads of the three Wehrmacht services more completely to his will, Keitel would be little more than the *chef de bureau* of whom Blomberg had spoken to Hitler. History has had few doubts about the category into which he fell.

# CHAPTER V

# The Fritsch Crisis: Genesis and Preliminaries

"What an influence a woman without realizing it may have on the fate of a nation and thus of the world." With these words the deeply moved Colonel Jodl gave vent to his feelings on January 26, 1938.[1] The harder-headed Schacht put it similarly a few days later: "This woman has made world history."[2] In the end the high (and low) drama of the Blomberg affair had its historic import as the prelude and setting for something with which, at first glance, it had no logical connection—the fateful Army crisis centering about Werner von Fritsch. This was in no sense a mere corollary to what had happened to the more exaltedly placed War Minister; in fact, the Blomberg and Fritsch affairs became linked only because the former facilitated a move against the Army commander that had hitherto been too risky to undertake.[3] There is much that raises doubt, however, whether this hesitation would in any case have endured much beyond the beginning of 1938. One can make a strong argument that had there never been a Blomberg scandal, something resembling the Fritsch crisis would still have taken place at a time not too distant from when it actually occurred. The forces arraying themselves against Fritsch and the Army leadership were already commencing to close in.

### Flashback

A date close to November 22, 1933.[4] Afternoon is fading into evening at the Potsdamer Platz (downtown Berlin) station of the Wann-

[1] Jodl Diary, 357.
[2] Wiedemann, *Der Mann der Feldherr werden wollte*, 115.
[3] Engel interview, May 4, 1970.

134

# Genesis of the Fritsch Crisis

see suburban line. A professional character of the city's half-world is plying his preferred trade. Otto Schmidt—occasional male prostitute and thief, perennial blackmailer and extortionist and, when moved by convenience or necessity, police spy—is standing unobtrusive but close watch over the goings-on in the busy station. He loiters before the show window of a bookshop and is scarcely noticed in the six o'clock rush of persons hurrying home from their day in the city or waiting for the company of friends or relatives before boarding their trains.[5]

A group of Army and Navy officers accompanied by a man of advanced middle age enters the station and lingers for a moment in conversation. The officers then go their various ways. The man in civilian garb, who is wearing a dark coat with a fur collar, dark hat, and white scarf and carrying a silver mounted cane, proceeds to the men's washroom. After a brief time he comes out and stands marking closely the passersby, particularly young men. Instantly Schmidt is alert. Here, experience tells him, are the earmarks of a homosexual looking for a partner.

Surmise moves toward certainty for Schmidt when he notes the entry of Josef Weingärtner, familiar to him and to homosexual circles as the "Bayern Seppl" (Bavarian Joe). Passing the watcher and the watched and entering the washroom, he is quickly followed by the gentleman. Soon after they come out together and disappear into a dark passage that leads to a link fence separating the Wannsee station from the neighboring freight depot of the Reichsbahn (state railway). There amid a tangle of scaffolding takes place the homosexual act to which Schmidt, claiming to have followed on crepe soles and substituting someone quite different for one of the principals, is to bear witness some years later.[6]

[4]Unless and until the protocols of the proceedings of the court-martial that established the innocence of Fritsch can be located, by far the most significant source of information on the case is the verdict of the court as published by Fabian von Schlabrendorff in *The Secret War against Hitler* (London, 1966), 374-416. He had published an abbreviated version in *Der Spiegel* on September 1, 1965, 46-57. The unabridged version contains much omitted in the *Der Spiegel* piece and is indispensable for a close study of the case brought against Fritsch. It will be cited hereafter as Verdict with the appropriate pages of Schlabrendorff's appendix. Of importance also is the unpublished protocol of the interrogation of Fritsch on January 27, 1938, by Werner Best and Franz Joseph Huber to be found in the IfZ archives (cited hereafter as Fritsch Protocol). The November 22 date is pinpointed by Count Rüdiger von der Goltz, "Erinnerungen" (514-page manuscript, lent to the present author by Goltz), 168.

[5]The source of this paragraph and the two following is Schmidt's own story as recorded in the Fritsch Protocol, 30-36, and in Verdict, 379-380.

[6]Schmidt's story, logical enough and not easy to check up to this point, hereafter

Actually Schmidt has not risked discovery by following but has remained in the station waiting for the two to return. As soon as the Bayern Seppl has received his few marks and has taken his leave, Schmidt dashes after and buttonholes him to ask whether he has "done anything" with the gentleman.[7] When the somewhat dazed fellow stutters an affirmative, Schmidt rushes back to where he can see his intended victim out on the platform boarding a train. He manages to make it into the same coach and a station or two later sits down next to him to tell him that his actions have been observed. Claiming to be an SA man and then introducing himself as "Criminal Commissar Kröger" of the morals police, he allows it to be understood that for a round sum he will remain silent. The horrified gentleman, who says he is Cavalry Captain Achim von Frisch, states that he is willing to pay 200 marks. This is scorned as inadequate and 500 marks are mentioned. The two ride to station Lichterfelde-East, near where, as Schmidt later would have it, the officer enters a house at Ferdinand Strasse 21 "to borrow money from a friend." In court the captain is to say that he got the money from his own apartment, which was next door at No. 20. In any event, a down payment is made with the rest of the 500 marks to be delivered the next morning at the Lichterfelde-East station.[8]

The following morning, Frisch, having withdrawn money from the Dresdner Bank near the station, pays over the rest of the 500 marks, treats Schmidt to a few cognacs and cigars in the station waiting room, and hopes he is rid of his tormentor. Two or three days later, however, Schmidt reappears to relate that his "superior" is demanding his cut and is waiting to confer in the station waiting room. They go there and after an hour of haggling the thoroughly intimidated captain agrees to pay an additional 2000 marks to Schmidt and the "superior," a fellow named Siefert. Half is to be paid immediately, the rest on an agreed-upon date in January.

often descends into fable though it was apparently not difficult for so hardened a liar to maintain a certain consistency. What follows is based on the far more reliable testimony of Weingärtner and of Schmidt's victim, Captain von Frisch, as given before the court-martial.

[7] Weingärtner's testimony. Verdict, 391. That Schmidt did not witness the homosexual act is proven not only by his inquiry of Weingärtner but by the fact that, jumping to conclusions, he testified to its being quite different from what it actually was (fellatio rather than masturbation). Fritsch Protocol, 36. Verdict, 380, 391.

[8] This paragraph and the two following are based on the testimony of Frisch as recorded in Verdict, 394–395.

# Genesis of the Fritsch Crisis

A few days before the time arranged for the second installment, Schmidt corners his victim in the Lichterfelde Post Office and says he must have payment immediately. The captain goes home to collect what money he has there and draws the rest that is needed from the bank to make up the 1000 marks. He is very nervous when he discovers that Schmidt has brought along to the meeting place, again the station waiting room, another "colleague," actually a workman named Heiter who has begged for a chance to share in the profits of a blackmailing venture. Frisch is obliged to pay for so many drinks that the awed hostess still remembers the group over four years later. Between rounds he slips Schmidt the 1000 marks and receives a receipt signed "Kröger" for the full 2500 of which he has been bilked.

The supposedly "final" squeeze fails to satisfy the leechlike Schmidt, who keeps hatching schemes for extracting more money from Frisch. He tries to enlist the help of the Bayern Seppl, who meanwhile has served a short term in prison for some other transgression; that basically inoffensive little man shies from so dangerous a game as blackmail.[9] Schmidt makes a number of further calls on Frisch who is now in bad health and under the care of a nurse. Whether he is too worn out to care very much what happens to him or is at the end of his financial rope, all that he is good for now is cognac and cigars. Passing the house with another shady character named Ganzer, Schmidt relates that here lives a man he once "laid on the cross."[10] One can count on him for at least a drink. At the Fritsch trial Goering is to ask the captain about this and harvests the reply: "It is always best to stand well with people of this stripe."[11]

## Origins of the "Dossier on Fritsch"

Only a few months after Otto Schmidt so unfeelingly laid Captain von Frisch "on the cross," the climate for homosexuals underwent a sweeping alteration for the worse in Germany. They could blame

[9] Testimony of Weingartner and Ganzer. Verdict, 390, 392.

[10] Testimony of Ganzer. Verdict, 292. Both the Fritsch Protocol and the Verdict show Schmidt to have made out he did not know where his victim lived and therefore, on various occasions after January 1934, had wandered around the area near station Lichterfelde-East in the hope of running across him in order to set him up for a new extortion. Apparently Schmidt, probably under coaching, sought to avoid mention of a residence address which would immediately exonerate Fritsch.

[11] Goltz interview, November 1, 1969.

the greatly increased harshness of their fate on the Röhm affair of June 1934. Before then the rulers of the Third Reich had evidenced little inclination to abandon the rather easy attitude of the Weimar Republic about the enforcement of Article 175 of the Penal Code which was directed against homosexuality. This laxity had reflected trends prevalent on both the Left and the Right of the political spectrum. Socialists and Communists shared a Marxist tradition of tolerance toward conduct that was largely personal in its implications. Militant nationalist organizations with their heavy stress on masculine fellowship became something of a haven for elements which to some extent idealized sexual relationships among males.[12] Both such persons themselves and the viewpoints and practices they represented carried over heavily into the SA, though not into the SS with its extravagant mystique about fertility and large families.[13]

When Röhm and his fellow SA leaders, many of them heavily tarred with this brush, were liquidated in June 1934, their removal was accompanied by a great to-do about what had long been a public scandal but had been tolerated by Hitler until he had personal reasons for striking at the SA leadership. The Fuehrer having pulled out all the stops in a propaganda splurge aimed at emphasizing the depravity of Röhm and his fellows and at diverting attention from the savagery of their suppression, consistency demanded that the full power of the Nazi state's repressive machinery be directed to stamp out what had been so scathingly denounced. A "Reich Center for Combating Homosexuality" was established as a Gestapo office (Amt II-H) and offenders—if they did not enjoy some sort of personal immunity—were dragged by the hundreds into concentration camps.

Hitler himself does not seem to have had much interest in this. Similar to the way Goering had allowed it to be known that within

[12] Interview with writer Ernst von Salomon, May 5, 1970. Salomon recalls the prevalence of such tendencies in the Organization Konsul and kindred nationalist federations. He also remembers a blackmailer and police spy named Schmidt who made a specialty of preying on such persons; Salomon served in a Free Corps in Upper Silesia with this man and has much to relate about him. The blackmailer Otto Schmidt is described in the verdict of the military court as being thirty-one years old in 1938 and would seem to have been too young to be the same person. Yet it is puzzling that the verdict relates he had been condemned to prison for theft three times as early as 1921-22, which hardly appears likely in the case of a boy who would then have been only fourteen or fifteen years of age. Can his age as given in the verdict have been understated?

[13] Berlin wits of the Nazi period characterized homosexuals as "saboteurs against the Welfare Society Mother and Child."

the confines of his widespread administrative empire he alone would "decide who is a Jew," the Fuehrer in practice permitted the homosexual label, whether applicable or not, to be affixed only to such individuals in his entourage as had lost his favor. Röhm's aberrations had concerned him no whit before the SA leader had become dangerous to him. How indifferent he really was to such failings in those about him is further illustrated by the elevation of so notorious a homosexual as Walter Funk to the Ministry of Economics, one of the highest posts in the Third Reich, on the same day on which he rid himself of the wholly innocent Fritsch.[14]

More than two years pass after the misadventure of Captain von Frisch before the spinning of the thread then begun by Otto Schmidt is resumed. As a matter of fact, as will be seen later, it is impossible to be entirely sure that it was not four years, though in virtually all that has reached print about the Fritsch affair it is assumed without a hint of doubt that the next date of significance came in 1936. The main source of information is unfortunately Adolf Hitler personally and in all that concerned the Fritsch case he indulged in extremes of mendacity unusual even for so pathological a liar. The safest rule is to accept nothing he said that lacks solid confirmation or fails to conform fully with the logic of the situation.

Otto Schmidt had emerged unscathed from his profitable encounter with the luckless captain. Perhaps the ease with which he had managed that affair inclined him to overreach himself in his next flyer in the field of extortion. At any rate, by 1935 he found himself in the familiar toils of the law and in 1936 he was condemned to seven years in prison.[15] But Schmidt had rarely sat out the full term of any sentence. The explanation lies in his readiness to purchase the shortening of his confinement by relating the goings-on in circles in which he moved and by continuing to play the role of informer after his release.[16] On this occasion he soon gained interested listeners in more exalted quarters than the Criminal Police.

The Gestapo had been drawing rather exceptional dividends from its pursuit of homosexuals. Information gathered from those caught

---

[14] Reference is to the announcement of appointments and dismissals of February 4, 1938.

[15] Verdict, 386.

[16] J. A. Kielmansegg, *Der Fritsch-Prozess 1938*, 55–56. Goltz interview, November 1, 1969.

within its net had swelled the files of more than one person of consequence. The head of the II-H department, Criminal Councilor Joseph Meisinger, was a corrupt, repulsive,[17] sordid figure, addicted to the cruder methods of conducting investigations and detested by more fastidious associates.[18] Capable of any skulduggery in pursuit of his aims, he was not likely to be deterred by scruples where personal profit or the opportunity of gaining credit in the higher echelons of the SS hierarchy beckoned. From merely exploiting information gained from culprits who fell into the hands of his department, he was soon initiating fishing expeditions among already jailed offenders.[19] For such purposes no better catch could be made than a professional informer such as Otto Schmidt—impudent, boastful, without conscience, and, withal, knowledgeable.[20]

When handed over to the Gestapo in the early summer of 1936, Schmidt had already babbled at length to two police interrogators about personages he claimed to be homosexuals. Among the "several hundred" names he listed for his questioners was of course that of "von Frisch," though he may conceivably have recalled it as "von Fritsch," a more common form of the name. It is also possible that, taking satisfaction from attaching as much importance as possible to his victims and thus to himself, he promoted the obscure and decrepit captain to "general."

Be that as it may, in one form or another a name that called to mind the commander in chief of the Army was included in the file that was routinely passed by the Criminal Police to the Reich Center for Combating Homosexuality. For what then occurred the main source, as recorded in the verdict, is the testimony

[17] Gisevius speaks of him as of an "Auch äusserlich widerlicher Dreckfink" (externally repulsive, filthy person). Recording, July 1971.

[18] Gestapo and SD officials interviewed by the present writer, though reluctant to be quoted in critical remarks about former associates, left no doubt about the disgust with which they regarded Meisinger. Best calls him a "rather primitive man of clumsy methods." Best, "Aktennotiz," 2. Walter Schellenberg (*The Schellenberg Memoirs*, London 1956, 13) calls him "one of the shadier characters in his [Heydrich's] service."

[19] Heydrich and Meisinger tried to make out that their pursuit of homosexuals was both a highly laudable "clean-up" operation against vice in Berlin and an activity that paid dividends in police matters. As told by Gisevius, who was present, they on one occasion visited Minister of the Interior Wilhelm Frick to impress this upon him. Gisevius recording, July 1971.

[20] In a written statement to the court-martial, one of the Gestapo witnesses (Meisinger or his subordinate Fehling?) testified that Schmidt would have to be considered "one of the best experts on the homosexuals of Berlin." Verdict, 387.

of Gestapo officials before Fritsch's court-martial. Meisinger is described as all attention when he saw this name and ordered that Schmidt be delivered into the custody of the Gestapo. There on July 8 or 9 he was interrogated by a police captain named Häusserer. Violating all traditional police canons, Meisinger provided for this occasion a photograph of Fritsch in full regimentals and surmounted by his name, title, and military rank.[21] As might have been, and perhaps was, anticipated, the self-complacent Schmidt welcomed the chance to claim new distinction for himself. Yes, he affirmed, this was the man whom he had blackmailed. The Gestapo record of the interrogation as recalled by Dr. Ernst Kanter of the investigative panel of the court-martial that tried Fritsch showed also how, by the use of further suggestive techniques, the vague form of the "higher officer" with whom Schmidt had begun was made more and more to assume the configurations of that general.[22] According to SS General Karl Wolff, Meisinger from the start was aware of the falsity of any association between Schmidt's victim and Fritsch but was propelled by ambition along this course.[23]

At this juncture the standard accounts of the Fritsch affair relate how the triumphant Meisinger rushed to Heydrich who relayed the exciting news to Himmler. And Himmler is described as losing no time in reporting to Hitler. The summary of the testimony in the verdict of the court-martial as first published in 1965 in *Der Spiegel* provides a very different chronology. There we learn that seven weeks passed before Schmidt was subjected (on August 26) to a second grilling by Criminal Secretary Löffner. Heiter was also questioned a few days earlier (August 20) and confirmed "part" of the Schmidt story. The summary of evidence does not state whether this "partial confirmation" pertained to the general facts of the 1933 extortion or involved a specific identification of Fritsch, again from a photograph, as the victim.[24]

These newly revealed facts put a new aspect on the situation. Given what is known about Meisinger's disposition when on a hot scent, it is most unlikely that he should have delayed apprising

[21] Dr. Best relates that this procedure provoked sneers from the more professional figures in the RSHA. Best, "Aktennotiz," 2.

[22] Kanter to Kielmansegg, November 3, 1947. Kielmansegg Papers.

[23] Wolff, "Aktenvermerk" of a statement for Hermann Foertsch, August 11, 1952 (in IfZ), 2.

[24] Verdict, 378, 396. The first to make extensive use of this summary to correct earlier versions was Höhne, I, 235–236.

141

Heydrich and Himmler of the prospect of tripping up the hated Army commander. Rather than any delay on the part of Meisinger, therefore, the explanation may lie in hesitation of the SS chiefs about informing Hitler before beefing up the "case" against Fritsch as much as possible. But why should weeks have passed before the second more intensive interrogation of Schmidt and the questioning of Heiter? A clue may be found in the fact of Heiter's being brought in for examination *before* the second grilling of Schmidt. It would lead to the thesis that there was need of a corroborating witness and one whose story could serve as a guideline in the further interrogation of Schmidt. It may well have taken some time before the footloose Heiter, who seems often to have had good reason for avoiding the police, could be located and brought in. It can only have been after he was heard on the matter and after the Gestapo's second Schmidt interrogation that Hitler was finally advised of developments.

Hitler in 1938 described his reactions of two years earlier somewhat differently depending on the person or group to whom he was speaking. Most commonly he told of a wave of disbelief and revulsion that had led him to thrust the dossier aside and order its destruction. "I do not want to know anything of this swinishness," he claims to have exclaimed. But in talking to Hossbach, the first to whom he spoke of the matter on the morning of January 25 after receiving the "reconstructed" file and before he had the foregoing story down pat, there was no sign of revulsion or incredulity. Quite the contrary, he launched an immediate and sustained effort to persuade the Wehrmacht adjutant that the evidence was so conclusive that it was proper to dismiss Fritsch unheard. As will be seen, it took all of Hossbach's exceptional store of determination to procure a hearing for the general some thirty hours later. Nor, as will also be noted, could it be argued that Hitler's new-won faith in the "evidence" sprang from its having become more impressive since it was shown to him in the first instance. For the only "new" factor produced by the revived Gestapo investigation had been the (quickly suppressed) proof positive of Fritsch's complete innocence. In charity to Hitler we shall assume that he had not been informed of this proof, but neither can he have been told or shown anything that would make the charges substantially more convincing than they were in 1936. To Hossbach there was no word of his ever having entertained the slightest doubt about the general's guilt. When the adjutant pointedly asked Hitler why he had continued to work with the Army commander after receiving material which he now considered so damning, the reply was only that Fritsch had been indispensable during the period of military buildup.[25] This, assuming that the dossier was actually brought to Hitler as early as 1936, is no doubt the real answer why it was thrust aside or, better, "put on ice."

This raises more immediately the question of the date of the "original" dossier. The evidence on this, both specific and inferential, can be summarized as follows:

1. As has been noted, the principal witness is Adolf Hitler himself. In 1938 he told all and sundry that the file had been brought to him in 1936 by Himmler and that he had ordered its destruction. Then, he usually went on, a new one had to be put together when the possibility arose of advancing Fritsch to the War Ministry. Shaken in his former confidence in the unchallengeable probity of high military officers by the abominable conduct of Blomberg, he now felt compelled to eliminate any shadow of doubt about the blameless character of his successor. This all had a plausible ring and rarely failed to achieve considerable impact on his hearers.

2. The 1936 version is supported by the testimony of Meisinger who claimed that he followed orders insofar as the original documents were concerned but did keep carbon copies, apparently at the direction of Heydrich. These in turn, he said, were the basis for the "reconstruction" effected in 1938.[26] There is also the more trustworthy testimony of other Gestapo officials on the interrogations of Schmidt and Heiter in July and August 1936.

3. Startlingly contradictory, as if they had never heard of a 1936 version, is the seemingly disinterested testimony of three surviving high SS or Gestapo officials, Werner Best, Karl Wolff, and Franz

[25] Hossbach, *Zwischen Wehrmacht und Hitler,* 109. Wiedemann in his rather hastily thrown-together "Aufzeichnungen" (101) tells a story, not repeated in his published work, of Hitler's having responded when the material was presented to him: "I have no use at this time for a Fritsch affair. The two fellows are to be shot and the file destroyed." The author's hope to ascertain the source of this statement in a second interview with Wiedemann was frustrated by the latter's death. The second "fellow" (*Junge*) referred to here was no doubt Heiter. In his talk with Rundstedt on January 31 Hitler also said nothing of his disbelief in the charges in 1936 but spoke only of "reasons of foreign policy" for his taking no steps at that time. Foertsch, *Schuld und Verhängnis,* 102.

[26] Wiedemann interview, December 2, 1969. Foertsch, *Schuld und Verhängnis,* 90.

Josef Huber. Severally they report the origin of the file to have been in *December 1937.*[27]

4. Some significance may be attached to the surmise of Hossbach that the sloppy manner in which the dossier shown him by Hitler was put together indicated that it was made to order for the January crisis.[28]

5. What is the import of any internal evidence to be found in the dossier? Like all official documents of the Fritsch case, with the exception of the protocol of the first Gestapo interrogation and the final verdict, it has never come to postwar view. It is necessary, therefore, to fall back on the testimony of survivors of the period whose responsibilities gave them extensive insight. These are in first line Count Rüdiger von der Goltz, the legal defender of Fritsch, and Franz Josef Huber, the general's principal interrogator. According to the recollection of the former, the basic statement of Schmidt came to him in the form of a carbon copy and bore a 1936 date.[29] Huber is convinced that all the documents handed to him the day before his interrogation were originals.[30]

What is to be made of this welter of conflicting surmise or testimony? What Hitler said, as already noted, must be viewed very skeptically. He wished to claim credit for being trusting and magnanimous. He also had good reasons to forestall any impression that the charges against Fritsch were based on revelations which had come opportunely just before the breaking of the Blomberg affair. That would give them too much the appearance of having been manufactured for the occasion. Yet there is much to support the plausibility of the version he sought so eagerly to propagate. It is scarcely conceivable that at precisely the appropriate psychological moment at the end of 1937 the Frisch case should pop up in Meisinger's office so that it could be transmuted conveniently into one applicable to Fritsch. There is also the testimony of the Gestapo and police officials before the court-martial to strongly support the 1936 version.

In the view of the present writer, something like the following

[27] Best, "Aktennotiz." Wolff, "Aktenvermerk." Huber interview, July 1, 1970. Despite repeated communications with Dr. Best's attorney, efforts to secure an interview with him while the author was in Europe in 1969 and 1970 proved unavailing. Best was then in investigative custody in Moabit Prison of Berlin and declined to make any statement while he was under arrest. He was later freed. Efforts to reach him in July 1971 also failed. He has since then been rearrested.

[28] Hossbach, *Zwischen Wehrmacht und Hitler,* 109.

[29] Goltz interview, November 1, 1969, and "Erinnerungen," 166–167.

[30] Huber interview, July 1, 1970.

procession of developments will best reflect both the available evidence and the logic of the situation. Meisinger, exploring in 1936 some of the darker reaches of the Berlin demimonde, stumbles on a potential political gold mine and, through Heydrich and Himmler, brings it to the attention of Hitler. The Fuehrer, we may be sure with every reluctance, recognizes that the time is not ripe for a showdown with the Army. The Rhineland occupation and the Berlin Olympics, when an appearance of domestic tranquillity was at a premium, are in the recent past and the German intervention in the Spanish Civil War is just getting under way. An order is given to destroy the "incriminating" material but it is transmitted in such a way that Meisinger, encouraged by a hint from Heydrich, feels safe with a token compliance. No wider investigation is undertaken at the time and the information is confined to a small circle; to such highly placed SS figures as Best and Wolff it is all new when the matter is taken up again almost two years later and appears to them as something just then arisen. The only "outsider" initiated into the affair is Goering, who stores the item in his mind for possible later use against the rival shop of the Army leadership.[31]

Some sixteen months pass. Then, late in November or early in December 1937, Goering has a caller—Blomberg—whose message opens to him vistas of attaining new pinnacles of power. This leads to a renewed alliance between him and the SS chiefs, the Gestapo watch over Fritsch in Egypt, and the "reconstruction of the file to be used against the general," i.e., the effort to add substance to it.[32] What speaks strongly for work on the latter being

---

[31] Gisevius (*Bis zum bittern Ende*, 260), in fact, has Goering as the one who informed Hitler in 1936.

[32] Gestapo representatives later showed themselves extraordinarily sensitive about what they knew to be the widespread assumption that the harassment of Fritsch had been their idea. To clear themselves as much as possible of this imputation they thrust the entire blame on Goering. Thus, in a wartime conversation with Wiedemann in Tokyo, Meisinger specifically stated that Goering had given the order to reconstruct the 1936 dossier. Wiedemann, *Der Mann der Feldherr werden wollte*, 120, and interview, December 2, 1969. In an exchange with the outraged Goltz late in the summer of 1938, Best on his part claimed that the affair had not really been a Gestapo concern, the orders having come from a "high placed personage." Aside from Hitler, the only Nazi hierarch more highly placed than Himmler was of course Goering. Goltz interview, November 1, 1969. Further evidence of SS sensitiveness about involvement in the affair is a claim of Heydrich to Canaris late in 1938 that he "had not fought against Fritsch." Helmuth Groscurth, *Tagebücher eines Abwehroffiziers: Mit weiteren Dokumenten zur Militäropposition gegen Hitler*, ed. Helmut Krausnick and Harold C. Deutsch in association with Hildegard von Kotze (Stuttgart, 1970; cited hereafter as Groscurth Diaries), 163. This accords also

resumed in December and not, as is most often assumed, in mid-January is that such officials as Best, Wolff, and Huber gained the unanimous impression that the entire file had originated in that month. It was apparently then that the former two became aware of this activity and jumped to the conclusion that it was proceeding from scratch. This conception was also passed on to Huber, probably by Best, when he was unexpectedly inducted into the affair for the Fritsch interrogation.

Other interesting things occur in the waning days of December. Otto Schmidt is taken back into closely guarded custody. Despite his conviction and sentence in 1936, he has been allowed a certain liberty for having once more proved his value by his wholesale depositions on the wrongdoings of others. During the following year he serves in a corps of *Vigelanten* (stool pigeons) under the wing of Georg Kaczmarek, an official in a subsection of Amt II-H headed by Criminal Secretary Löffner. In *late December 1937* Kaczmarek is suddenly arrested and speedily put away on what he claims today to have been trumped-up charges in order to get him out of the way for "knowing too much." What does he know that might make his fate of interest in our present story? He knows all about Schmidt and he is thoroughly aware that Criminal Commissar Fehling, Meisinger's closest assistant, stands guard over a "dossier on Fritsch" which is kept locked in his safe.[33]

The rebuilding and extension of the dossier, if begun as is here assumed in December, does not seem as yet to have been pursued with exceptional energy. There was at the moment the prospect of getting rid of Fritsch by the simpler and less hazardous fashion of having him act as witness for Blomberg's nuptials and thus sharing in the disgrace. Only after he avoids this trap is the "investigation" stepped up to a more lively pace.

At this point we move from educated surmise onto somewhat firmer ground. The renewed questioning of Schmidt is this time

with another claim by Heydrich that the revived investigation against Fritsch was undertaken "auf Höheren Befehl" (on higher command). J. A. Kielmansegg, *Der Fritsch-Prozess 1938*, 100.

[33] Kaczmarek claims he was tried and convicted of actions which, though illegal for the ordinary citizen, were a regular part of his duties. Thus, as Gestapo contact man with sections of the underworld, he perforce had to deal with criminal elements and make payments to some of them. He was sentenced to seven years in prison but in 1942 was released as suddenly as he had been arrested in 1937 and was re-employed by the Gestapo. Interview with Georg Kaczmarek (conducted for the present writer by Edouard Calic), June 1, 1970. Letter of Kaczmarek to the author, June 25, 1970.

associated with a more, wide-flung investigation. In 1936 the only character-in his story picked up for questioning appears to have been Heiter. Now the Gestapo for the first time lays hands on the Bayern Seppl, who denies that the man of the 1933 incident is the same person as the one in the picture of Fritsch shown him. This leads to further, more intensive grilling of Schmidt and yields the admission that his entire story applies to the retired cavalryman, Captain von Frisch. How else would it have come about that on January 15 Fehling and a Gestapo colleague visit the ailing captain? What they learn from him sends them to the Dresdner Bank where they get a statement of withdrawals that coincides with the payments cited in Schmidt's allegations. All is now dismayingly clear: there is no Fritsch case at all but only one involving the totally uninteresting Frisch![34]

But Heaven forbid that at this late date and with the goal in sight the fact that the real culprit was shown to be *Frisch* should be allowed to interfere with such well-laid plans against *Fritsch*. Goering alone can have made the decision to proceed, despite this revelation, with the attack on the Army commander. He had not yet seen Schmidt personally but must have been assured that the fellow was an impudent liar who could be trusted to stick brazenly to his story if provided with the right incentives. If the matter were now allowed to drop no such opportunity to blacken Fritsch was likely to arise again. If Schmidt were only careful not to mention Frisch it seemed unlikely that anyone would stumble across the role he had played. Least of all was Hitler apt to ask embarrassing questions or to look this particular gift horse too closely in the mouth.[35]

[34] Gisevius (recording, July 1971) does not believe that Goering could have given thought to the problem of the witnesses for Blomberg's wedding until, at the earliest, December 22, when Hitler consented to the marriage. In the view of the author, Goering was so intensely concerned with drawing the maximum benefit from Blomberg's folly that he must have reviewed in his mind all aspects of the matter from the moment he learned the War Minister's intentions. It would appear further that the subject of the type of wedding and the vitally related problem of witnesses would arise naturally during the course of his discussion with Blomberg.

[35] Gisevius (recording, July 1971) takes sharp issue with any version by which higher-ups, notably Goering, were made aware in mid-January of the role of Frisch. He holds that Goering was too clever an intriguer to proceed in the face of such knowledge, not so "stupid." It is his view that, in the absence of Meisinger, Fehling or other underlings working with him botched matters by failing to report their "discoveries." But was Meisinger absent from Germany in the second and third weeks of January as he undoubtedly was during the fourth? Goering, with all his intelligence, was an archadventurer prone to take big risks when the stakes were sufficiently high. Once Blomberg was excluded, compromising Fritsch was

147

## Revelation of the Charges

Colonel Hossbach in later years considered it probable that Goering had come to the Chancellery in the evening of January 24 to present Hitler all at once with the double-barreled charges against the spouse of Blomberg and against Fritsch.[36] At first thought such a procedure seems rather too crass even for the often crudely operating Goering: that he would appear before Hitler with ready-made cases against both of the men who stood in his path to the military summit. A less revealing self-serving way would have been to wait until Hitler alluded to the problem of the succession and then remind him (if such a reminder were necessary) of the accusations against Fritsch. At this point Goering could also relate his "discovery" that copies of the incriminating documents had "somehow" been preserved and could quickly be put into proper shape. There is a story of reconstructing the file "in intensive night work" that would fit the thesis that Hitler thereupon called for it and that it was delivered to him in the early morning hours.[37] In any event, the initiative in stimulating the Fuehrer to pick up the cudgels against Fritsch came from Goering, and Hitler was to say as much in reminiscing in the months ahead.[38]

The fact that Hitler at 2:15 A.M. had his persónal adjutant, Schaub, ask Hossbach to come to the Chancellery, a summons the prickly colonel simply refused to obey at such an hour, can be interpreted both ways, once it is assumed that the Fuehrer would not have

the vital step to the accomplishment of Goering's ambition to take over control of the Wehrmacht. It must be held in mind that his aim was to blacken Fritsch enough to eliminate him as a rival, not to initiate an elaborate investigation and trial which would carry the risk of uncovering his own villainy. These he resisted with all the means at his disposal. Be it admitted that at first glance it is difficult to believe that Goering should deliberately take such a chance as to go to Hitler with a dossier he knew to be based on falsified evidence. But the present writer finds far more challenging to logic the only alternative thesis: that the Gestapo staff assigned to "reconstitute" the dossier, which was working feverishly on January 22 and whose final flurry of activity may well have been during the night of January 23-24, should not have informed Goering of the most vital fact in the case. It was precisely Fehling who was in charge of this working group. Though recognizing force in Gisevius's argument, the author is therefore inclined to maintain his original version.

[36] Hossbach, *Zwischen Wehrmacht und Hitler*, 121. This is also the view of Gisevius (*Bis zum bittern Ende*, 258) and J. A. Kielmansegg (*Der Fritsch-Prozess 1938*, 37).

[37] Wolff, "Aktenvermerk," 2. Wolff also claims that it was Himmler who was instructed by Hitler to have the file "reconstructed" and who then delivered it to the Fuehrer.

[38] In remarks to Captain Engel. J. A. Kielmansegg, *Der Fritsch-Prozess 1938*, 100. Engel interview, May 4, 1970.

tried working on Hossbach until his ammunition was in hand. On the one side, it can be argued that the file must have arrived that very minute.[39] On the other, and rather more likely, it would appear that even the farce of a "reconstruction" would have been hard to put over in the four hours or so since Goering had left the Chancellery. The "intensive night work" may well refer less to what was done that very night than Gestapo overtime activities undertaken at the order of Goering either (1) immediately after Helldorf had brought him the Gruhn file on the 22nd, or (2) after his conference with Himmler and Heydrich on the 23rd. Most probably Hitler was told that the file had never been destroyed and the story of its restoration was his own embellishment for the benefit of the gullible. In that event Goering would either have had it with him or ordered it to be sent to Hitler just before or after leaving him. Supporting this, too, is what seems a valid assumption that the dictator would have wished some time to study it to prepare himself for the assault on Hossbach.

The one thing that is certain is that Hitler had the dossier before him when the adjutant arrived at 10 A.M. At this juncture it is necessary to grasp fully the key position Hossbach occupied in that historic hour. It was worth the utmost efforts of Hitler and Goering to win him to their position. As head of state Hitler had undoubted authority to select or dismiss any of the service commanders. Form, however, required that the adjutant should set up the order of dismissal. If he could be convinced of the truth of the charges against Fritsch, the fate of the latter was sealed and his fall would be largely justified in the eyes of the Army.[40] Hossbach's personality and high standing in the profession were a guarantee of that. For this very reason winning him over to the desired course was a formidable task and in the end proved a total failure.

The adjutant was regarded as a stiff Prussian type with some of the usual General Staff snobbery and a profound reverence for the traditions of the officer corps. Though he was highly respected and rather liked by his fellow adjutants, they stood somewhat in awe of him and among themselves gave him the nickname of his namesake, the great Frederick, "der alte Fritz" (old Fritz).[41] His unbending principles and somewhat martinet devotion to the regu-

[39] This is the view of Höhne, I, 239-240.
[40] Hossbach, *Zwischen Wehrmacht und Hitler*, 121. Letter of General Hossbach to the author, January 1, 1972.
[41] Puttkamer interview, June 27, 1970.

lations had also given him the repute of being the "last Prussian." One could expect to gain nothing from him by cajolery and, as men went, he could be regarded as all but immune to intimidation.

The dismissal of Blomberg, it has been seen, had been decided by noon of January 25 when Goering reported on his call to the War Ministry. Except for a few brief interruptions, the entire afternoon and evening were spent in an interminable wrangle over the charges against Fritsch. Hour after hour the iron-willed Hossbach stood up against the arguments which Hitler and Goering loudly and insistently directed against him. From long personal acquaintance, the officer knew too well the high-minded, fastidious gentleman about whom the discussion raged to conceive of his involvement in the gross conduct related in the file. To rush him off his feet, Goering twice left the room for the ostensible purpose of going to Gestapo headquarters to "recheck" the evidence and the staunchness of the "witness." On each occasion he returned vowing that the latter, with whom, in actual fact, he spoke for the first time *two days later*,[42] was unmovable: "Fritsch is guilty!" To get ahead with the stymied dispute, Hossbach proposed that he simply ask Fritsch about the matter. This, as indicated earlier, was emphatically forbidden by Hitler, though Hossbach immediately made it clear that such a prohibition would conflict with his conscience in view of his close personal relationship with the Army commander. At the end of nearly ten hours of vehement debate, Hitler repeated his order to say nothing to Fritsch and Hossbach responded in the same vein as before.[43]

The story of Hossbach's late evening drive home and his sudden determination to call on Fritsch has already been told. The general having received the news of the charges against him with a categorical denial but with much of his usual self-possession, there was a good deal of speculation on the identity of the hostile forces working against him. At this time, and basically through the following days of crisis, neither Fritsch nor Hossbach could believe that Hitler was personally involved in a plot against the Army commander. In consequence, Fritsch and most of his partisans were to suffer from a fatal inhibition which did much to cripple the Generalität in responding to the assault on the head of the Army and, through him, on itself. It proved impossible for them to throw off their traditional conception about what one might expect from a head

[42] See below, p. 180.
[43] Hossbach, *Zwischen Wehrmacht und Hitler*, 109.

of state. Fritsch, and even the Hitler-wise Hossbach, could not comprehend that so exaltedly placed a man would lend himself to the machinations believed to center about Goering and Himmler. Fritsch was the more strengthened in this feeling by the fact that it was palpably superfluous for Hitler to employ such gross methods to bring about his ejection from office. "If he wants to be rid of me," he said to Hossbach that evening, "a word is sufficient to bring about my resignation." That Hitler should aim at something so outrageous as the personal ruin of his Army commander and the compromise, through him, of the military leadership corps did not for some time occur to them. Therefore it seemed imperative to bring home to the Fuehrer as quickly as possible the total falsity of the charges and to drive a wedge between him and the initiators of the intrigue. In any event, they agreed, it would be necessary to strike back at the calumniators.[44]

As he left the War Ministry, Hossbach felt with some relief that the fate of Fritsch was now in his own hands. But how much confidence could he place in them? His impression was that the general was highly indignant about the abominable machinations directed against him and that he would put up a firm, carefully considered defense.[45] At the same time the Wehrmacht adjutant could not suppress the disturbing feeling that there was some inadequacy in Fritsch's response. Secretly he had hoped that the Army commander would simply say: "Hossbach, you will now stay here."[46] Thus the gage of battle would have been thrown down to the Reich Chancellery. Hitler, whether associated with the plot in some way or not, had dealt with Fritsch's fate and the honor of the Army in a fashion that was an unmistakable challenge. Asked (in the summer of 1971) how he would have reacted in Fritsch's place, Hossbach's answer was a restrained but significant: "I should have put up a fight."[47]

The severe limitations under which Fritsch labored as man and soldier decreed his failure in this critical hour of his life. That night and the following day, until summoned to the Chancellery in the evening, he spent in tortured self-examination and gloomy inaction. Though virtually surrounded by potential allies he turned to none of them for advice or support. A few doors away was

[44] *Ibid.*, 110.
[45] *Ibid.*
[46] "What I felt painfully at the time was that one [i.e., Fritsch] did not rouse oneself to more [than Fritsch did]." Hossbach interview, July 1, 1971.
[47] *Ibid.*

his fellow service commander, Admiral Raeder. Within immediate call at Tirpitz Ufer was his own chief of staff and trusted personal friend, Beck. Berlin, too, was the headquarters of the army group commander, General von Rundstedt, and the head of the area troop command, General von Witzleben. For legal advice Fritsch could turn to General Walter Heitz, president of the Reich Military Court. And there was Admiral Canaris, whom he knew to be an expert on Gestapo intrigues and who could be assumed to have means in his Abwehr establishment quickly to learn more. None of these men were taken into his confidence by Fritsch.[48]

The Army commander's unpreparedness for attacking his problem head-on is the more difficult to comprehend since he had been so thoroughly alerted to the precariousness of his position. Beck and Goerdeler had for months been warning him that something seemed to be brewing in Gestapo quarters. Beck had expressed grave doubt about the wisdom of an extended absence from the country, but Canaris had urged him to attend to his health; "We will watch over things."[49] Fritsch had yielded reluctantly to the advice of his physician.[50] Neither Canaris nor Beck had occasion to sound an alarm while he was in Egypt. On the other hand, Fritsch himself had been observant enough to note the scrutiny of the two Gestapo agents who had been sent after him in December.[51] In view of what he had known for at least a year about the watch maintained over his mail and telephone, this was not too much of a shock, but it may have contributed to his decision to shorten his vacation by a week and return to Berlin, after a brief stay in Italy, on January 2. The atmosphere he found there increased his sense of uneasiness about impending events. The very next day he wrote to a friend, the Baroness Schutzbar: "My mistake was to stay away much too long." And on the 7th he followed this with: "It looks to me as if I have returned from there just on time."[52] The warning voices, in fact, now multiplied. In mid-January Goerdeler came to Berlin for a conference with him and Beck to relate impressions of a tour of West European and North American capitals from which he had just returned.

[48] Gisevius (*Adolf Hitler*, 390; recording, July 1971) develops these points with particular force.

[49] Gisevius, *Wo ist Nebe?* 280, and interview, July 11, 1971.

[50] Nissen interview, July 15, 1971. Fritsch soon reported from Egypt that his bronchial ailment seemed to have disappeared completely.

[51] As related by Fritsch to Dr. Nissen shortly thereafter. *Ibid.*

[52] J. A. Kielmansegg, *Der Fritsch-Prozess 1938,* 36.

# Genesis of the Fritsch Crisis

The political climate in Germany seemed to him even more ominous than it had to Fritsch. In particular, he had a presentiment that something in the way of a blow by the Gestapo against the Army was in the wind.[53]

A final note of warning was sounded on the very eve of the jumble of events which overwhelmed Fritsch after January 24. Two or three days previous to this, a close friend, retired General Joachim von Stülpnagel, received a mysterious telephone call. A masculine voice said only: "You are a friend of General von Fritsch. He is in the greatest danger." As the general was asking, "With whom am I speaking?" he could hear the click of the other's receiver.[54]

The alarmed Stülpnagel immediately went to see Fritsch to relate what he had heard, he believed from "a decent member of the Gestapo." The two agreed that some attack from the party might be in the offing but Fritsch did not seem particularly disturbed. A man in his position, he gave as his opinion, was always precariously placed in such times.

All in all, Werner von Fritsch, short of being told exactly what he might expect, had been alerted thoroughly both to the threat against him and to the direction from which it was to be expected.

At an early hour in the morning of January 26 Fritsch rang Hossbach and requested a meeting at the riding ring in the War Ministry. He had evidently passed a restless, quite possibly a sleepless, night seeking explanations for what might have given the intriguers a lead for the campaign against him. He finally recalled that, like other bachelors of prominence, he had been asked to show paternal interest in fatherless boys of the Hitler Youth. Several times a week he had first one and later another youngster to dine with him and had followed the meals with simple lessons in such subjects as map-reading. Occasionally he had whacked them on the fingers with a ferule when they had not paid attention. Perhaps some gossip had got around about these acts of charity and been picked up by those who were now moving against him.[55]

This tale struck Hossbach with apprehension. Hitler-boys regular visitors in Fritsch's residence! Here was something that troublemakers would leap to exploit. His heart was much heavier as he

[53] Ritter, 163.

[54] Stülpnagel, "75 Jahre meines Lebens" (550-page manuscript in Militärarchiv/Freiburg, N5/27), 356.

[55] For this and the following two paragraphs the source is Hossbach, *Zwischen Wehrmacht und Hitler*, 110-111.

proceeeded to the Chancellery to deliver to Hitler the tidings that his express commands had been disobeyed.

It has been noted that Hitler surprised Hossbach by receiving the account of his disobedience with initial calm and that he had seemed relieved Fritsch had so firmly rejected the charges against him. Nothing, he had gone on to say, then stood in the way of the general's becoming War Minister. After Hossbach responded that Fritsch had no other wish than to remain at his post, the adjutant asked whether the dispute of the previous day implied that this would not conform with Hitler's wishes. If it did not, a mere word would suffice to produce the Army commander's resignation. At this the Fuehrer protested that he was entirely aware of the great services of Fritsch to the Army and, unless compelled by circumstances, had no desire to part with him.

This relaxed atmosphere was not fated to outlast that morning. Hitler's cynical hypocrisy in what he solemnly affirmed to his Wehrmacht adjutant is reflected in what he said minutes later to Blomberg and a few hours after to Keitel. It will be recalled that the sour-tempered departing War Minister fostered rather than put a damper on the notion that Fritsch was a type in whom one could well imagine a perverse inclination. On that day, too, Hitler was under virtual siege by Goering and by Himmler, who, as Hossbach later put it, sneaked past him at the entry of the Chancellery as if he were the "embodied bad conscience."[56] If there had been any brief impulse toward generosity on Hitler's part—and this is much to be doubted—one may be sure that between them his intriguing lieutenants took good care to choke it off. Within two or three hours after Hitler had given the impression of softening, Hossbach found that he was reversing himself again and saying that homosexuals were congenital liars, a thought that had been passed on to him by Himmler.[57] The SS chief further envenomed matters by asserting that there was, in contrast to this, a special kind of "rogues' code of honor" (*Ganovenehre*) which should inspire confidence in the assertions of Schmidt.[58] The contradiction between this claim and its application specifically to a man with a record for male prostitution after the supposed mendacity of homosexuals had been stressed was, of course, conveniently ignored.

[56] *Ibid.*, 111.

[57] Wiedemann, *Der Mann der Feldherr werden wollte*, 116.

[58] In an interview with Heinz Höhne on February 5, 1966, Dr. Werner Best related that Himmler had made the same claim to him when he (Best) raised doubts about Schmidt's reliability. Höhne, I, 244, 308.

# Genesis of the Fritsch Crisis

The incredulous Hossbach was informed that even Fritsch's word of honor would not suffice in the existing circumstances to set the Fuehrer's mind at rest. The general, in fact, was to refrain from carrying out his duties until matters were cleared up.[59]

Once again hours of altercation rolled by, interrupted only by meals and Hitler's talks with Blomberg, Wiedemann, Gürtner, and Keitel. Hossbach's proposal that the senior generals, notably Rundstedt, who was on a service trip to Königsberg, should be called to Berlin for consultation received short shrift. An equally flat rejection met his recommendation for the constitution of a court of honor, which would have consisted of high Army generals. Finally Hitler accepted a suggestion to seek the opinion of the Minister of Justice and Gürtner was summoned to the Chancellery for a conference from which the Fuehrer, who had further tricks up his sleeve, was careful to exclude Hossbach.[60]

Franz Gürtner was thoroughly representative of those bourgeois Ministers Hitler had taken over from previous Reich or state governments. They had proven themselves amenable up to a point and been kept on largely for bureaucratic window dressing. Like others who had managed to stay on after 1933, Gürtner had a considerable talent for survival, never permitting his aversion for much about the regime and its works to tempt him into direct confrontation with the Fuehrer. Undoubtedly he had a cool, composed way of dealing with Hitler which avoided irritation and could thus exercise a limited influence in matters where the Fuehrer was not already set on his course.[61] His habit was to bide his time while doing what he could to ameliorate abuses, reports of which kept piling onto his desk.[62]

Those who knew Gürtner well could have predicted with confidence his reaction to the issues which confronted him in the Fritsch crisis. Hitler counted heavily on his lack of backbone and would hardly have consented to call him in at this stage had he not expected him to yield to his wishes once these had been made unmistakably clear.

At first glance the available evidence on the next developments appears to add more confusion than clarification. There would seem to be almost hopeless contradiction between the following:

[59] Hossbach, *Zwischen Wehrmacht und Hitler*, 111.
[60] *Ibid.*
[61] Wiedemann, *Der Mann der Feldherr werden wollte*, 149.
[62] Ritter, 66.

1. The verdict of the court-martial cites a formal opinion of Gürtner which is described as requested by Hitler on the 27th. Though it has no date itself, a passage referring to the Gestapo interrogations of Fritsch on "the 27th and 28th of this month" establishes beyond argument that it was completed between the 29th and 31st.[63]

2. A shorter and somewhat different version is given us by Wiedemann.[64]

3. Perhaps an hour after the departure of Gürtner, Hitler showed Keitel a paper signed by the Minister that he claimed to have had in hand for some time. Keitel relates this in his memoirs and Jodl records the story as Keitel told it to him in a diary entry of the 28th.[65]

The solution to these seeming contradictions lies in there having been two "opinions" wormed out of Gürtner by Hitler: the first brief and tentative in approximately the form given by Wiedemann, the second more extensive and formal, requested by Hitler on the following day and delivered about three days later.

Hitler handed the dossier on Fritsch to Gürtner and asked him for an immediate written opinion. Most probably the Minister of Justice was simply hurried into an adjacent room for a hasty perusal of the documents that were so unceremoniously thrust on him.[66] To give the dossier the greatest possible weight, he was told that the witness in the case had proved reliable in testifying correctly "in all other cases."[67] This formula was to be repeated again and again by Hitler and the Goering-SS clique during the following days. It was in total conflict with the facts set down in Schmidt's criminal file as it had rested since 1936 in the hands of the Gestapo.[68] There he figured as a professional liar and perjurer who had never scrupled to testify falsely when money or other advantage was to be gained.[69]

[63] Verdict, 405–406.

[64] Wiedemann, *Der Mann der Feldherr werden wollte*, 116.

[65] Keitel, 108. Jodl Diary, 358.

[66] This seems a safe guess in that there would hardly have been time for anything more, Gürtner having been summoned to the Chancellery during a break in the afternoon debate between Hitler and Hossbach and Hitler having the opinion in hand to spring on Keitel at 5 P.M.

[67] As related by Gürtner three days later to Ministerial Director Rosenberger. Heinrich Rosenberger, "Die Entlassung des Generalobersten Freiherr von Fritsch," in *Deutsche Rundschau*, Vol. 69, No. 8 (November 1946), 93.

[68] *Ibid.*, 96.

[69] As related to Captain Engel by Canaris and Brauchitsch severally. Engel interview, May 11, 1970.

# Genesis of the Fritsch Crisis

Himmler and Heydrich, though trying hard to make their prize witness look trustworthy and even somewhat respectable, thus were entirely aware that he was a conscienceless rascal who could be manipulated as freely as pressures could be applied or temptation held out to him. Gürtner and his adjutant, Hans von Dohnanyi, were to learn this when the police file was finally extracted from Gestapo hands at the start of the official investigation. Far from "standing up in all cases," his testimony was then found to have done so only when it dealt with little people. As soon as more prominent persons were involved, Schmidt's vanity was aroused and he tended to embroider and at times to make stories out of whole cloth.[70]

In the Fritsch case both carrot and stick were to be employed freely by the Gestapo. Schmidt's life was to be threatened from at least two quarters if he should fail to stick to his testimony, and in May SA leader Lutze furnished General Ulex "proof" that Schmidt had been pressured into testifying as he did.[71] And Fritsch was later told on the authority of a "high police official" (Nebe?) that Schmidt had received a large sum of money to testify against him.[72]

Was Hitler's statement to Gürtner about Schmidt's reliable testimony "in all cases" a barefaced lie or was he merely passing on untested what he had been told by Himmler and Heydrich? The latter appears the more probable. Almost certainly only the Gestapo interrogations of Schmidt and not the rogue's own police record had been delivered into his hands. There is no indication that the dictator ever called for and perused the latter. It fitted in with his interests to accept what his SS lieutenants told him. Gürtner himself was bothered by the omission and he was later to complain about not having been given the relevant material then available.[73] Thus neither he nor Hitler can have been shown anything on the negative outcome of the interrogations of the Bayern Seppl.

[70] As reported by Dohnanyi to Rosenberger soon after the formal investigation began. Schmidt's list of supposed homosexuals included Count von der Goltz himself and the Bishop of Berlin (and later Cardinal) Count von Preysing. Dohnanyi could not ascertain whether Himmler had given the true story on Schmidt to Hitler. Rosenberger to Kielmansegg, September 1, 1947. Kielmansegg Papers.

[71] See below, p. 382.

[72] Fritsch on several occasions told this to his adjutant, the later Colonel Grosskreuz, who in turn reported it to Count Kielmansegg after the war. Keilmansegg to Goltz, August 25, 1947. Kielmansegg Papers.

[73] Wiedemann, *Der Mann der Feldherr werden wollte*, 116. Further substantiated by what Gürtner said to Rosenberger. See below, p. 188.

For the further elucidation of the nature of the Fritsch crisis and of the period which followed, this appears to be a proper place to express the conviction that Hitler *at no time* personally believed in the validity of the charges against Fritsch.[74] The consistency with which he lent himself to the crassest maneuvers of the Goering-SS combine betokens both awareness of the weakness of the case against the general and determination to employ every artifice coming to hand to make it stick. The very show of utter conviction on Fritsch's guilt which he put on during the marathon debate with Hossbach on the 25th argues against his sincerity. He was now insisting on dismissing Fritsch *unheard* on the basis of the very same evidence which he had supposedly rejected out of hand in 1936. Whatever shock he suffered from the conduct of Blomberg falls far short of explaining so complete a *volte-face.*

Whether Hitler at some stage before or during the crisis was expressly informed by Goering or Himmler how fully the assault on Fritsch was a put-up job can thus only determine the *degree* to which he must be counted their accomplice. He knew more than enough about the roguery of his lieutenants and about Goering's ambitions to apprehend what lay behind the entire affair. Except for Goering's aspirations to assume control of the Wehrmacht, Hitler was entirely ready to lend himself to machinations that accorded so closely with his own interests.

Should Gürtner have refused to dignify the accusations by saying that they did not provide the basis for any legal measures? Military law certainly required formal investigation of any such charges that could be taken at all seriously; Gisevius, in particular, insists that the Minister really had no choice but to recommend this course.[75] Such a decision, however, would depend on the estimate of the character of the accuser. Here Hitler's totally inaccurate ploy about the reliability of the witness having been established "in all other cases" had made an impression. Undoubtedly it did much to persuade Gürtner to take a legalistic position on the accusation, holding that it did provide grounds for judicial scrutiny. How much he continued to feel uneasy and defensive about his position is indicated by his later protest to Fritsch's attorney that the official

[74] Particularly impressive on this point is the firm view of General Engel who had unique opportunities to observe Hitler during the weeks and months which immediately followed and to whom the dictator spoke with great vehemence and frankness about the problem he had had with Fritsch. Interviews, May 4 and 11, 1970.

[75] Gisevius recording, July 1971.

inquiry was the only way that could lead to the general's unchallengeable rehabilitation.[76]

The opinion which Gürtner dashed off under so much pressure is reported by Wiedemann to have made the following points:

1. In the documents made available to me Colonel General von Fritsch stands accused of an offense under Article 175.

2. From these documents it is not evident that the colonel general has cleared himself of the charge. (Had Hitler implied that Fritsch had already had some opportunity to clear himself? At the time of the conference with Gürtner, Hitler had no more than Fritsch's assurance, communicated through Hossbach, that he was innocent. Fritsch was not received, and confronted with Schmidt, until some hours later.)

3. In the form in which the documents lie before me they can provide the basis for a charge by the public prosecutor.[77]

Anything less than this Gürtner would scarcely have ventured to present to Hitler. He felt, however, that there was something that did not smell right about the papers in the form he had received them. He also already had in mind the possibility of mistaken identity.[78] Here a date, there a signature was missing. If we are to believe what he shortly after told Wiedemann, he strongly urged Hitler not to proceed on such an uncertain basis against the commander in chief of the Army.[79] But by the instrument he had put in the dictator's hand he himself ensured that such advice would not be taken. With this weapon, one that he could use or misuse to great effect, Hitler was in no mood to call off the dogs that bayed at Fritsch's heels. Instead he told Gürtner that the legal action for which the way had now been paved should be commenced directly and proposed as the most appropriate vehicle a special court constituted under Gestapo auspices. The response of the dismayed Minister escapes our knowledge; he was probably too taken aback to attempt more than a holding action that put

[76] Goltz, "Erinnerungen," 171.

[77] Wiedemann, *Der Mann der Feldherr werden wollte*, 116, and interview, December 2, 1969. Wiedemann stated that the version in his book had been recorded contemporaneously on a slip of paper which accompanied him when he left the employ of the Chancellery.

[78] Gürtner had in mind Standartenführer Fritsch, a notorious SA ruffian who had come a cropper in another connection in 1935. Gisevius, *Bis zum bittern Ende*, 101, 296.

[79] *Ibid.* Gürtner, of course, may have given Hitler the advice to go slowly on one of the following days.

off a decision.[80] Hitler then dismissed him with the unmistakable hint: "You will know at which end of the rope you are to pull."[81]

The ink could scarcely have been dry on Gürtner's statement before Hitler was drawing his first check on the political account which it represented for him. At 5 P.M., probably not many minutes after he bade goodbye to the Minister of Justice, he received Keitel for the first of those meetings "lasting for hours" which were to have such fatal consequences for the Wehrmacht. After dwelling briefly on the departure of Blomberg and polishing off in short order the general's proposal to replace him with Goering, Hitler reacted to Keitel's next suggestion of Fritsch by going solemnly to his desk and digging out the "opinion" he had just extracted from Gürtner as if it had lain there for a long time. Dashing it off under pressure, the Minister had forgotten to put a date on it and Hitler gave Keitel the impression that the origin of the document was contemporary with the raising of the first charges two years earlier. Let us spell out the difference this made to his naive listener:

*The way things were.* Something hatched years before in Gestapo quarters is brought to Hitler's attention for the second time less than forty-eight hours earlier and is used in somewhat doctored form to pressure an "opinion" out of the hesitant Minister of Justice an hour or so before Keitel's arrival.

*The way they were made to look to Keitel.* The evidence goes through regular official channels to the Ministry of Justice at the time of the discovery of the alleged offense in 1936. Hitler nobly refuses to believe it and forestalls an action by the public prosecutor which even Gürtner considers appropriate. The Fuehrer still does not believe the charges in 1938 but can no longer keep them to himself; the problem of the possible succession of Fritsch to Blomberg's office now obliges him to clarify matters. The whole action against Fritsch is made to look like something initiated and pushed by the Minister of Justice which the generous and trusting Hitler has held back as long as he possibly can.[82] Allowing this to sink

[80] Though we nowhere learn specifically that Hitler put this proposal to Gürtner as early as this meeting of the 26th, there is more than mere logic to support this assumption. We know definitely that Hitler expressed the same intention shortly after during that same afternoon.

[81] As related by Gürtner to Dohnanyi. Interview with Christine von Dohnanyi, June 26, 1958.

[82] Keitel, 108. On the basis of what Keitel reported to him about this conversation, Jodl on the 28th noted in his diary (359): "Material about him [Fritsch] lies with the Minister of Justice (suspicion of offense under Article 175—[it has been there]

160

in, Hitler went on to say that he would see Fritsch the next day and surprise him with the charges; he would then know "instantly" by the general's reaction whether there was anything to them.[83] Meanwhile Keitel must maintain absolute silence.

Then, proceeding as if the fate of Fritsch were already settled, Hitler, dropping the question of the successor to Blomberg, gave all his attention to the problem of a new Army commander. Though Keitel understandably skipped over it when he wrote after the war, he reported at the time to Jodl that the Fuehrer, *in any event,* wanted a replacement for Fritsch.[84] This in cynical contradiction of the earnest assurances that had been given to Hossbach in mid-morning!

### The Confrontation with Schmidt

Hitler had told Keitel that he expected to have his talk with Fritsch on the next day (the 27th). No doubt he and Goering since the evening of the 24th had been contemplating a dramatic scene in the course of which Fritsch was expected to be utterly befuddled and give every appearance of guilt. The hope of catching the general entirely off guard had of course been frustrated by the intransigence of Hossbach. There remained the prospect of staging such a shattering confrontation with the blackmailer, Schmidt, that Fritsch would be put out of countenance and at a psychological disadvantage. Everything argues that the *mise en scène* for this was directed by one of the masters of Third Reich political theatricals, Hermann Goering,[85] with Heinrich Himmler in support. The first stroke would be followed by another in which Fritsch was to be subjected to the humiliation of a Gestapo interrogation.[86]

At this point there was summoned onto the stage a man who, though himself a high official of the Gestapo, was in this affair an outsider—Franz Josef Huber. Huber was one of those experienced police professionals who had been brought from Bavaria when Himmler took over control of the Reich's police forces. Hey-

for two years). He [Gürtner] is charged by the Fuehrer with the investigation and maintains that he has known of these things for two years."

[83] What Hitler said here is the more strange because he had known since mid-morning that Fritsch had already been warned by Hossbach and could hardly be "surprised" by suddenly being confronted with the accusation.

[84] Jodl Diary, 358; entry of January 27, 1938.

[85] This is also the view of J. A. Kielmansegg, *Der Fritsch-Prozess 1938*, 99.

[86] That the Gestapo interrogation was already in the cards is proven by the instructions that had been issued by Heydrich to Franz Josef Huber before the confrontation. Huber interview, November 20, 1969.

drich, in particular, had a lively respect for men of this stamp, treated them with marked consideration, and used them to hold within some limits the inundation of the Political Police by amateurs of uncertain competence from the party.[87] In Munich under the Republic, Huber had been charged with surveillance over parties of the Right, including, interestingly enough, the National Socialists themselves. As head of Amt II-C of the Gestapo he now broadened these functions, adding to the conservative elements and political leaders of the Nazi party under his watch the Austrian Nazis who had sought refuge in Germany and were a most troublesome lot.[88]

During the ordinary course of affairs, Huber would never have been brought into the Fritsch affair in any manner. Both from a personal standpoint, as one who from the beginning had been in on the trumped-up charges against Fritsch, and in line with his official responsibilities, Joseph Meisinger, head of Amt II-H, should have had the assignment now given Huber. It was an example of ineptness on the part of those who managed the intrigue that he was beyond reach just then on a sea voyage aboard one of the Strength through Joy steamers.[89] Someone of at least equal status in the official hierarchy was needed to function as interrogator and, for reasons which he himself has never been able to fathom, the choice fell on Huber, who then held the rank of ministerial councilor. Perhaps from the standpoint of the impression to be made on Fritsch, it seemed best to proceed with someone thoroughly professional in manner and background. At the same time it was not without risk to entrust the interrogation to a person not initiated into the intrigue and of uncertain sympathies concerning its objectives. As Huber recalls, it was Heydrich who summoned him one afternoon and handed him the file, with instructions to study it and prepare himself for the role of interrogator.[90] As will be seen, this can only have been on the 26th.

Huber's recollection of the succession of events during the next few days is somewhat hazy; he lacks such props of memory as

[87] Other prominent examples of such police specialists were Heinrich Müller, chief of the Gestapo, who had a great reputation as a specialist in fighting Communism, and Dr. Werner Best, the Gestapo's principal legal expert.

[88] The latter involved especially the so-called Austrian Legion which at times seemed to cause more trouble than it was worth. Huber interview, June 3, 1970.

[89] Both to afford them a pleasant vacation and to enable them to pick up useful information, Gestapo officials were regularly sent along on such trips as "passengers." Ibid.

[90] Ibid.

would have derived from a wider association with the affair. The more dramatic aspects of his experience, however, stand out for him in crystal clarity. He was given only the rest of the afternoon and evening to familiarize himself with the dossier and even in that brief period suffered a melodramatic interruption.[91] Hitler and Goering had finally given way or, having already decided, pretended to give way, to Hossbach's urging to grant a hearing to Fritsch. Most probably they had concerted, perhaps with Himmler, to move the meeting, which Hitler had told Keitel would be on the next day, to that evening. The form of confrontation with Schmidt must have been cooked up during a brief absence of Hossbach when Himmler ducked into the library to check with Hitler and Goering on the course of developments. It was undoubtedly he who directed Huber to fetch Schmidt. Hossbach saw Himmler furtively leaving the Chancellery as he was waiting at the entry to receive Fritsch.[92]

The adjutant had summoned the general by the telephone in Hitler's library and then proceeded to the entry to greet him. There he informed Fritsch of the state of affairs and of the impending confrontation with the "witness." Growling, "This swine I must see by all means," Fritsch then walked toward the library. Hitler was well advised to instruct Hossbach to wait in the small dining room nearby,[93] for the mere presence of the sturdy soldier would have meant strong moral support for the general. Furthermore, the adjutant could be worked on more advantageously if he did not personally witness Fritsch's treatment and his reaction.

After a considerable interval, Hossbach heard someone running noisily from the library; the door of the dining room was torn open and Goering, yowling as if in agony of soul, burst in and threw himself on a sofa. Holding his hands before his face he howled repeatedly: "It was he, it was he, it was he!" For such histrionics Hossbach was the last man in the world to provide a receptive audience and he confined himself to asking coolly what

[91] This provides an additional indication on what was happening to the Schmidt criminal file at this stage of affairs. Since Huber in the afternoon of the 26th was handed a full and, in his recollection, original set of documents, what Hitler at approximately the same time was showing to Gürtner can only have been copies and, as argued above, carefully screened ones.

[92] Hossbach, *Zwischen Wehrmacht und Hitler*, 112. A strong indication that the decision to have Fritsch come that evening was made *before* Hitler "conceded" this to Hossbach may be found in the fact that there would hardly have been time in the brief interval between the call to Fritsch and his arrival to bring Schmidt over from the Gestapo prison, shave and clean him up, and have him waiting.

[93] *Ibid.*

had happened. The incriminating witness, related Goering, keeping up his show of distracted agitation, had recognized Fritsch and was holding firmly to his story. Hossbach said quietly that he was not at all surprised that a "hired informer" should make such a charge. Goering thereupon showered him with reproaches, saying that telling Fritsch of the accusation had only increased the difficulties and brought the general's nerves to the breaking point. Hossbach put an end to the comedy by stating that any officer of the Luftwaffe would have acted just as he did if it had been Goering who stood in Fritsch's place.[94]

Much that is bizarre and fanciful has been told and retold about the confrontation of Fritsch with Schmidt. Accounts compete in sensationalism, such as the blackmailer being revealed to view by the drawing aside of a curtain or by Hitler tearing open a door.[95] Such tricks of staging might have been employed if the element of surprise had not been eliminated and Fritsch had not expected to be confronted. The reality as described by Huber, the sole known surviving witness, was less dramatic. The arrival of Schmidt was announced to Hitler and, with Goering and Fritsch, he went out on a landing above one of the Chancellery staircases. With two Gestapo officers Huber had conducted Schmidt to the Chancellery, where the rogue's slovenly appearance so scandalized Hitler's personal adjutant, Schaub, that he insisted on his being shaved and made generally more presentable before entering the Fuehrer's presence.[96]

Huber with his two officers and Schmidt had been stationed at the bottom of the staircase shortly before Hitler and his two companions came out upon the landing. The officers then led Schmidt to the top of the stairs where Hitler, pointing to Fritsch, addressed him in some such manner as "Was this the man?" Seemingly more stimulated than abashed by the presence of the

---

[94] *Ibid.*

[95] Thus Foerster (87) has Schmidt emerging out of a side door "as out of submersion."

[96] Huber interview, November 20, 1969. Wiedemann (*Der Mann der Feldherr werden wollte*, 118) relates that Weingärtner was also brought along and that he and the other adjutants saw to their being spruced up. He goes on to say that both were involved in the confrontation (which Wiedemann did not witness personally) and that Weingärtner affirmed that Fritsch was not the man involved in the November 1933 offense. The solution of the contradiction between this and the account of Huber is probably that Weingärtner was actually brought along (a point that could easily slip Huber's recollection) but, being a witness who had not responded favorably to coaching, was in the end left out of the confrontation.

great, Schmidt replied with his customary impudent assurance, "Yes, it was him." Fritsch at the moment appeared too confounded to utter a word.[97]

No full or entirely consistent story of what passed between Hitler, Goering, and Fritsch in the following half hour or so of their meeting has ever been recorded. The former two reported to one or another listener whatever suited them, whereas the introverted Fritsch seems never to have brought himself to dwell in detail on so shattering an experience. There is no doubt that the general made things much more difficult for himself by mentioning the Hitler-boys to whom he had been a kindly host. In his first Gestapo interrogation and at his trial he stated that Hitler had asked him whether he could think of anything that could have given rise to a suspicion of homosexuality against him.[98] Too innocent to recognize the leading character of this question, he had then alluded to the two lads. As Hossbach had foreseen, though he had expected it less from Hitler than from the ultimate authors of the intrigue, the dictator grasped at this as if Fritsch had already half confessed an additional homosexual involvement. The color he sought to put upon the matter is illustrated by his remarks to Wiedemann that same evening. Fritsch, he claimed, had entered the room saying, "My Fuehrer, I suppose it can only be a question of the two Hitler-boys." "Just imagine, Wiedemann," Hitler solemnly continued, "now it is suddenly not two but four fellows with whom he has had to do. Now this matter can no longer be kept secret. All I wanted was to hear from his own mouth the proof [of his guilt]; then I would have sent him off to some command, perhaps as military adviser to China or somewhere. That would have covered up the whole business."[99]

Once Schmidt had "identified" him, Hitler and Goering chose to treat Fritsch as if his guilt were established and as if the only problem now were "What next?" The general's offer of his word of honor on his innocence was brushed aside. Instead Hitler advanced the (for him) typical proposal that all maintain silence and that Fritsch simply resign and fade out of the picture, no doubt on the plea, usual when the real facts needed to be hushed up,

[97] Huber interview, November 20, 1969.
[98] Verdict, 400. Fritsch Protocol, 2-3.
[99] Wiedemann, *Der Mann der Feldherr werden wollte*, 118. The "four fellows" to whom Hitler referred were evidently Schmidt, Weingärtner, and the two Hitler-boys.

of "reasons of health." This Fritsch sharply rejected. Such a course would, in fact, have been considered by all who sooner or later heard of the affair as an admission of guilt.[100] At one point, Hitler related to Wiedemann, Fritsch's indignation mastered him sufficiently so that he burst out: "I refuse to account for myself in this way. These are criminals. I demand a court of honor."[101] This no more suited Hitler and Goering than when Hossbach had suggested it earlier in the day. It is not known for certain but likely enough that at this point Hitler mentioned as a substitute the special court he had proposed to Gürtner a few hours earlier.[102]

Except for his one outburst, there is no indication that Fritsch responded with energy to the abominable treatment inflicted on him. It would indeed have been entirely out of character for him to rave or stamp his feet. He could never have reacted like the tough and belligerent Schacht who could (and at times did) shout back at Hitler and generally gave as good as he got. It was not a meaningless boast when Schacht later said that in a case like this he would have struck his fist in the face of his accuser or of the man who dared to confront him with such a one.[103]

Perhaps Goering was not entirely wrong when he said it was unfortunate for Fritsch's state of nerves that he had been advised by the well-meaning Hossbach of what was going on. It had cost the general a restless and possibly a sleepless night as well as uncounted hours of brooding and wracking his mind. It seems also to have endowed him with a grim resolve to keep an iron grip on himself during the anticipated ordeal. This was a course exactly opposite to the one he should have taken to convince his hearers of his innocence or, since they needed no such conviction, of the need to deal with him considerately. They had half expected him to arrive breathing fire and brimstone. Instead they found him confused and puzzled, trying every which way to find an explanation for how such suspicions could have fallen upon him in the first place.

Though Goering knew well and Hitler, in the present author's

---

[100] J. A. Kielmansegg, *Der Fritsch-Prozess 1938*, 44. Goltz, "Erinnerungen," 167.

[101] Wiedemann, *Der Mann der Feldherr werden wollte*, 118.

[102] J. A. Kielmansegg, *Der Fritsch-Prozess 1938*, 44.

[103] "If someone confronts me with such a criminal out of prison, then I strike him or the man who places him before me in the face even if it is my own father." Schacht to the colloquium of the E. P., protocol of January 3, 1955, 3. In an interview with the present writer (October 9, 1969) Schacht expressed himself in a similarly forceful vein.

166

view, was aware that the charges were false, Fritsch's tame response made the worst possible impression on men who themselves often gave way to real or simulated rages. As a Prussian officer, Hitler later said to party intimates, Fritsch should have torn his sword from its scabbard and cast it at the Fuehrer's feet.[104] It was Fritsch's failure to react in anything approaching this manner, Hitler claimed, which made him take the charges so seriously. In the general's state of extreme tension (his "nerves at the breaking point," as stressed by Goering to Hossbach), the harried and exhausted man was an easy mark for the next assault on his emotional fortitude: the Gestapo interrogation which had already been decided upon and for which Huber was hurriedly preparing himself.

Hossbach heard Fritsch leaving the library and went to exchange some words with him and escort him to his waiting vehicle. He reports the general to have been highly indignant, saying he had never seen the supposed witness in his life and that he had given his word of honor accordingly. Apparently Fritsch was too worn and shaken to linger longer and in an agony of shame too great to dwell at greater length on what had occurred.[105]

The adjutant went next to Hitler who stated that he was now convinced of Fritsch's guilt. Especially impressive, he claimed, was the way Schmidt had recognized him from a characteristic shrug of the shoulder. Hossbach stood firm in his position that the word of the Army commander had a rating far above the testimony of such a witness. Although it was close to midnight, Hossbach secured permission to call Beck into consultation and sent his car to pick up the general at his home. He met Beck, who had been instructed to come in civilian clothes,[106] at the entry for a brief orientation and to conduct him to Hitler.

When Beck emerged, it was evident to Hossbach that he had been exposed to Hitler's full powers of persuasion. The scene, as Beck in the following years repeatedly described it to Gisevius, had certainly been dramatic enough. Hitler and Goering were in a state of excitement carried over from the recently concluded parley with Fritsch. The agitation of the jittery, pacing Goering was more

---

[104] Huppenkothen interview, May 29, 1970.

[105] The account as given in this and the following paragraph is based on Hossbach, *Zwischen Wehrmacht und Hitler*, 112-113.

[106] Gisevius, *Adolf Hitler*, 393. Except where otherwise indicated, the following six paragraphs are based on the account of Gisevius in *Bis zum bittern Ende*, 262-263, in *Adolf Hitler*, 393-394, in an interview of July 11, 1971, and in a recording made that same month.

than matched by that of Hitler, who, drenched in sweat, rocked and twisted on a sofa. The dictator began by flinging at Beck the startling question of when and where he had last lent money to Fritsch. The reason for this strange query seems to have been that the Gestapo had failed to locate an account in Fritsch's name in any of the banks near station Lichterfelde-East. Since Beck resided in Lichterfelde, the thought had occurred, or had been suggested, to Hitler that he could have placed his funds at Fritsch's disposal.

Beck indignantly denied ever having lent money to Fritsch and only then was told of the developments affecting him and Blomberg. Of the latter he knew only the first vague reports, whereas what he was told about Fritsch came as a true bolt out of the blue. The way in which Hitler dealt with the charge against the Army commander may be imagined from what he had told Keitel a few hours earlier (the Minister of Justice being made to appear in an initiatory role, etc.), with whatever capital could be drawn from a Hitler version of the confrontation with Schmidt. His aim clearly was to deal with the two cases on the same plane by treating that of Fritsch as if its outcome were as much a foregone conclusion as that of Blomberg. Beck, to the visible annoyance of his listeners, insisted upon making a sharp distinction. Blomberg, he said, had excluded himself from the Army by his outrageous conduct. In contrast, the situation of Fritsch was far from cut and dried and demanded an exhaustive investigation by the military judicial authorities. Beck noted that Goering appeared to be particularly put out by this proposal.

The chief of staff could not but hope to move an issue of such vital concern to the Army as the fate of its commander from the Reich Chancellery to the Bendler Strasse. Such was implied by his suggestion that a General Staff tour just beginning in East Prussia should be canceled and the principal commanders summoned to Berlin for consultation. He could scarcely have thought of anything more distasteful to Hitler and it was roundly rejected as entirely unnecessary.

Coming from the library notes in hand and rather dazed, Beck was met by the anxious Hossbach. The adjutant earnestly presented his argument that the whole business was nothing but a vicious intrigue.[107] This somewhat restored the balance of the chief of staff and he went for a heart-to-heart talk with his commander. He found Fritsch in a state verging on shock, staring uncompre-

[107] Hossbach, *Zwischen Wehrmacht und Hitler*, 113.

hendingly before him, and in such despair and dejection that at one point he queried plaintively whether Beck also did not believe him. Told that Beck could not imagine how he could have given rise to such doubts, Fritsch recovered somewhat and the two were quickly at one on the necessity of an investigation by the Reich Military Court. Their talk ended with a firm handshake.

Beck returned with revived spirits to the Chancellery to report that Fritsch stood firmly by his word and to stress once more the need of a judicial review. It was reluctantly agreed that Goering would meet with the Army commander the next day to work out an understanding on this issue. It was probably at this stage of Beck's two talks at the Chancellery that Hitler, if he raised the subject at all, mounted his last gun in dealing with the chief of staff by holding out the prospect of his becoming Fritsch's successor.[108]

As he was driven home in the early morning hours Beck must have contemplated sadly the collapse of so much of his own particular world. His most immediate worry, however, was whether the badly shaken Fritsch could summon the energy to deal decisively with so merciless a tormentor as Goering. His continued personal intervention seemed so imperative to him that he decided to go himself to Karinhall that morning. But on arriving there he was told by an insolent Goering that the proposed meeting with Fritsch had already been called off. A heated discussion followed in which the Air Minister brazenly insisted that Fritsch was so irremediably compromised that a legal investigation would be an entirely superfluous formality.

Beck's mind must have been more heavily burdened than ever during the return trip to Berlin. It would have been in far greater turmoil had he known that at that very moment Fritsch was submitting to interrogation in the Prinz-Albrecht-Strasse. The final decision on this can only have been made between Hitler and Goering as Beck was departing from the Chancellery. The order was telephoned to Fritsch later that night.[109] Preoccupied as he was with

[108] See below, pp. 216-217.

[109] Gisevius, *Bis zum bittern Ende*, 264. That this order only came to Fritsch in the late night hours and well after he had left the Chancellery may further be deduced from the fact that he said nothing about such a thing to Stülpnagel or to Beck in their talks in the immediately following hours. Despite his reticence with both Beck and others in all that concerned his going to the Prinz-Albrecht-Strasse, he could hardly have failed to mention the matter to these close friends when discussing the next moves.

avoiding any appearance of evasiveness, he was foolish enough to comply.

That Fritsch yielded in this vital matter is the more difficult to comprehend in view of the strong language he had heard from Joachim von Stülpnagel directly after returning from the Chancellery. His first thought on reaching home had been to have an adjutant summon the friend who had warned him but half a week earlier of the blow that had now crushed him. Stülpnagel found him sitting at his desk in a posture of utter despair. He described the nightmare scene to which he had been subjected and replied most positively to the query whether, "as a friend," he could give assurance of his innocence. Stülpnagel did not hestitate to tell him that his response to the way he had been treated was entirely wrong. When Hitler confronted him with this grotesque situation and then failed to throw out the calumniator after receiving the general's word of honor, he should, having no other weapon, have attacked the criminal with a chair. Stülpnagel then suggested two steps: (1) Immediately assemble the top generals, give them his word of honor that the charges were a mess of lies, and call upon them to express their solidarity with him in defense of traditional concepts of military honor. (2) Request Count Rüdiger von der Goltz to undertake the legal side of his defense.

Fritsch straightway agreed to the second of these proposals but raised doubts about the first. Having been suspended from his functions as commander in chief, he at the moment exercised no authority over the Army and felt he had no choice but to wait upon whatever steps should be determined by the Generalität. Its senior representative was Rundstedt and he alone could now take the lead.[110]

To this viewpoint Fritsch was to cling throughout and beyond the period in which the situation retained a certain maleability. Thereby he sealed not only his own fate but that of the Army and, in some measure, of Germany. He had missed his great hour and allowed it to turn into that of his humiliation. After the evening of January 26 the efforts of those who, unsolicited by and often unknown to him, fought for his cause were a desperate striving to recover the ground he had then abandoned.

[110] Stülpnagel, 356.

# Genesis of the Fritsch Crisis

## The Dismissal of Hossbach

Hossbach, whose three talks with Beck that night bracketed those of the general with Hitler, continued to press on the chief of staff the insights he had gained in the two days of constant altercation. No doubt Hitler owed the total failure of his blandishments in the case of Beck to the intervention of the tough-minded officer. Beck, like Fritsch himself, had to do violence to the thought habits of a lifetime to visualize so vile a plot as that pictured by the adjutant. It required another long talk in Beck's office at Tirpitz Ufer the following morning before his last doubts could be erased about the forces which were actually at work.[111]

It was this aspect of Hossbach's role at that critical juncture of Third Reich history, more than his disobedience of the 25th, which most probably was decisive in determining Hitler to rid himself of this troublesome drag on the course he had set. If the adjutant by constant pressure could have been worn down and rendered less resolute in blocking the two Nazi chieftains at every step, he might have been left at his post. But both their argumentative powers and their theatrical talents had gone for nought in overcoming his icy rejection. The man, in fact, was really threatening to spoil everything! If during the next critical days he continued to belabor with counterargument every Army leader who came to the Chancellery, it could spell the ruin of their enterprise. Hitler surely made up his mind that night of January 26-27, when the story of the confrontation with Schmidt had left Hossbach completely unmoved and when every argument addressed to Beck was nullified as soon as he left the Fuehrer's presence and related what he had been told to the waiting adjutant. Before noon on the 27th Hitler's determination had reached the point where he ordered Keitel to arrange an immediate change in adjutant.

Hossback's removal having been settled on, a certain grace might have been expected in dispensing with the services of a man who, for over three years, had been the personal link between Hitler and the Wehrmacht. With his customary cowardice in such matters Hitler shirked this responsibility, being unwilling to face the embarrassment of making the communication himself. The situation was particularly painful because Hossbach could infer that he had

[111] Hossbach, *Zwischen Wehrmacht und Hitler*, 113.

171

been forgiven after having been allowed to continue his functions for two days following his confession to violating orders. The delayed penalty was that much more of a blow and could not easily be justified. Hitler, therefore, simply turned over the unpleasant business to Keitel.

In his memoirs Keitel complains about the thankless task dumped on him and implies that he carried it out with a heavy heart.[112] What he passes over is that he really did no more than imitate his master's ungracious example. Instead of informing Hossbach as considerately as possible in a personal meeting, he merely sent to his office an official notice that he was relieved from duty.

The upshot of this double evasion of the customary decencies was that Hossbach received the notification in the most humiliating way conceivable. At noon on January 28 he appeared at lunch in the Chancellery and was greeted by Hitler with uncommon cordiality. During the meal he was summoned to the telephone and told by the officer next in rank in his own Central Division of the General Staff that he had an order to transmit concerning him.[113] Sensing instantly what was in the wind, Hossbach said that the matter should wait until he called back and returned, outwardly unmoved, to the table where Hitler betrayed his nervousness by prolonging the meal and engaging in spurts of monologue. When luncheon was finally over, Hossbach begged Wiedemann, with whom he had a harmonious working relationship, to listen in on a second receiver while he called his office. The order, as the previous call had led him to expect, specified his immediate dismissal as adjutant. It was signed by Keitel.[114]

So stouthearted a man as Friedrich Hossbach was not one to spare Hitler the direct encounter he had maneuvered to evade. He straightway interrupted Hitler reading his paper on the veranda and stated formally: "I report that my three years of service with you have been terminated. I have just learned it from a subordinate officer of my department over the telephone." "But not in such a way, Hossbach!" was the embarrassed reaction.

[112] Keitel, 109. Keitel obviously did not count on Hossbach's also publishing memoirs and telling the story of his dismissal.

[113] Hossbach had an unusually heavy load of duty, being at the same time Wehrmacht adjutant to the chief of state and head of the important and burdensome Central Division of the General Staff.

[114] This paragraph and the two following are based on Hossbach, *Zwischen Wehrmacht und Hitler*, 116-117.

# Genesis of the Fritsch Crisis

There followed an emotionally charged scene in which Hossbach burst into tears of rage, stamped his foot, and protested that an officer could not be chased out of the door like a dog. Hitler responded that he had not wished this rude form of dismissal; he had only sought to free Hossbach from his conflict of loyalties between Fritsch and himself. Hossbach had not obeyed the order to keep silent. "As I reported to you both before and after the offense," the adjutant reminded the Fuehrer. "I could have had you shot for it." "For which I was prepared." Mincing no words, Hossbach maintained that, though he had violated the letter of the rules on military obedience, such action contrary to orders was sanctified by military law itself when there were moral or legal grounds.

Hitler, increasingly abashed, then deluged him with fair words. He voiced his appreciation of the adjutant's services, made the cheap gesture of asking whether the dismissal could be canceled, assured Hossbach that he would always have free access to him and, with his family, would continue to be invited to Chancellery activities, and promised to write him a testimonial which would in the future clear all obstacles from his path. All of which cost no more than the breath expended in uttering it and proved to be worth about as much.

The churlish sacking of Hossbach produced more of a stir than Hitler can have bargained for among the non-Nazi members of the fraternity of adjutants in the Chancellery. That evening in Hitler's workroom the outraged Wiedemann dared greatly: "My Fuehrer, you have today much wronged a man." "How so? Whom do you mean?" "Colonel Hossbach." Hitler, much taken aback, admitted that he had been at fault and confessed that he had for the first time come to know Hossbach the man behind the mask of staff officer. The colonel should go on a Mediterranean cruise, would be further welcomed at lunch, and would receive an exceptional testimonial. Wiedemann was elated and hurried to carry these consoling words to his departing colleague at the War Ministry.[115]

A completely independent but equally plucky foray on behalf of Hossbach was undertaken by the naval adjutant, Commander von Puttkamer. Although, unlike Wiedemann, he had not been in

[115]Wiedemann, *Der Mann der Feldherr werden wollte*, 121. Wiedemann also tells (120) of inducing Goebbels to plead with Hitler for a more considerate treatment of Hossbach.

on the uglier aspects of the dismissal and knew nothing as yet of the Fritsch affair, Puttkamer was thoroughly distressed to learn about Hossbach's being sent away. An officer whose term of service in the Chancellery largely paralleled that of his Wehrmacht colleague, he entertained a profound respect and admiration for Hossbach's judgment and integrity. His exit at so critical a juncture in the relations between Hitler and the military appeared to him an unrelieved misfortune.[116]

On the day after Hossbach's dismissal (January 29) Puttkamer was no longer able to restrain his sense of urgency. The fact that Hossbach, though without conveying the reasons for his departure, had handed over Wehrmacht business to him until the new adjutant should take charge may have influenced him to proceed with greater boldness. Buttonholing Keitel as he emerged from one of his interminable conferences with Hitler, he insisted on being informed about what was going on. "I am sorry," said Keitel, "but I am not allowed to say anything." When Puttkamer stated that he would then have to go to the Fuehrer personally, Keitel simply shrugged and told him to do as he felt compelled.

Going to Hitler, Puttkamer had hardly begun when the ever-suspicious dictator interrupted him with, "Who sent you?" With the assurance that he came entirely on his own, the naval adjutant related the exchange with Keitel and then said earnestly: "I deeply regret that Colonel Hossbach in whom you had confidence should leave. In my view he would be the best equipped to advise you at this critical time." "You may be right," said Hitler, and repeated what he had told Wiedemann about having only now gotten to know the man Hossbach. But the thing was done and could no longer be recalled.

It was soon clear that the assurances Hitler gave Hossbach and the protesting adjutants were to be wholly without consequence. Whether or not Hitler had briefly been moved by a more generous impulse, it was quickly buried under the animosity he entertained against the future general. Later, a mere mention of the offender's name would suffice to set off fulminations against him with the frequent assertion that his former adjutant would never again be admitted to the General Staff.[117] That this was no idle threat was

[116]This paragraph and the two following are based on the account of Admiral Puttkamer. Interview, June 27, 1970.

[117]Wiedemann, *Der Mann der Feldherr werden wollte*, 121.

demonstrated on November 5 of the following year when Hitler, learning that Hossbach held the post of chief of staff of a corps, harshly intervened to transfer him to a troop command.[118]

## The Gestapo "Investigation"

The initiatory phase of what is known in the annals of the Fritsch case as the "preliminary investigation" was an assignment given the Gestapo by Hitler after, as he put it, the problem of the succession to Blomberg had "compelled" him to make a more serious check of the charges raised in 1936. Officially it constituted the December–January searches insofar as they were acknowledged to have occurred, though with the inference that they had taken place after January 24. Attention within this framework has largely centered on the Gestapo interrogations of Fritsch. It is not completely certain just how often the commander in chief of the Army submitted himself to this crowning indignity. It has been stated categorically but without allusion to source that he was interrogated three times between January 28 and 30.[119] The senior Gestapo official having any association with the Fritsch case,[120] Dr. Werner Best, claims that there were only two questionings.[121] He further maintains that these were both conducted by himself, the first "in the presence" of Huber on the 27th, the second in association with

[118] Deutsch, 230.

[119] Foertsch, *Schuld und Verhängnis*, 100. Writing in 1950 and 1951, Foertsch devotes but a single sentence to this painful episode and does not indicate where he gained the information. J. A. Kielmansegg's report (*Der Fritsch-Prozess 1938*, 57–58) of three interrogations is derived from what Rosenberger and Goltz told him from memory of their 1938 readings of the protocols; it includes such errors as the inference that the first two were conducted by Meisinger supported by Fehling. The lengthy protocol of the interrogation by Franz Josef Huber and the role played by him were apparently forgotten by them. No protocol or record of testimony by participants was available in 1949, Kielmansegg interview, July 12, 1971. The consequent failure of the two well-known works of Foertsch and Kielmansegg to mention him explains the astonishing neglect of Huber as a witness since then. Now in his vigorous late sixties, he was never questioned systematically on his experience in this affair before his meetings with the present writer.

[120] It may be a surprise that the name of the chief of the Gestapo, Heinrich Müller, never arises in connection with the Fritsch case. He might well have been in the foreground of the affair had he not been incapacitated during this period by an attack of and operation for appendicitis. He was later to say loftily that had he been in charge, things would never have gotten out of hand. As matters stood, Meisinger was given his head too much and had "shot over the mark." Huppenkothen interview, May 29, 1970.

[121] Best, "Aktennotiz," 3. The verdict of the court (405) also speaks only of interrogations by the Gestapo on January 27 and 28.

the confrontation of Fritsch with Schmidt on the 28th.[122] In actual fact, the roles of Best and Huber were reversed in the first interrogation and the second confrontation with Schmidt (after that staged by Hitler) took up the major part of it. Best, as will emerge directly, had pressing personal reasons for diverting the attention of students of the Fritsch crisis from Huber, who, if he spoke out, was sure to be a painfully embarrassing witness. In his various statements made previous to an interview with Heinz Höhne in 1966, Best did not mention Huber at all and in 1966 only in the most offhand manner.[123] He was then, of course, and perhaps still is, unaware that the eighty-two-page protocol of the Huber interrogation had survived.

On the morning of January 27 Huber and Best were waiting uneasily for Fritsch at Gestapo headquarters, Prinz-Albrecht-Strasse 8. There was anxious speculation about whether Fritsch would actually appear; there seemed every likelihood that he would have second thoughts and refuse to come. The Gestapo had no jurisdiction over the military and the only motive the general could have in submitting himself to its inquisition was to convince Hitler of his innocence. In view of Fritsch's habitual reticence, which in these days of pressure and shame approached a mania, it seems unlikely that he had mentioned to anyone professionally linked with him what he was about to do. Certainly he failed to confide in the two whose duties entitled them to a most unquestioned concern—Beck and Hossbach.[124] Fritsch felt the humiliation of what he did keenly and must have known that his going would rouse vigorous protests. This secretiveness best explains how confusion could arise about such simple facts as how many interrogations there actually were.

As the appointed hour approached, Best went down to the portal of the building and Huber retired to the third-floor room which

[122] Höhne, I, 243. As reference the text here cites (309n139) Foertsch (*Schuld und Verhängnis*, 100), who makes no such statement. Obviously there is a typing error and the source is doubtless a verbal communication from Best that is, in fact, cited in the two immediately following footnotes.

[123] Best's mention of Huber in the interview with Höhne, which departed from his previous practice of ignoring him entirely, may be ascribed to a growing awareness of the unfavorable light in which he would be placed when attention was inevitably drawn to Huber's role.

[124] Beck, for his part, was overwhelmed when he received the news from Canaris to whom it had come by way of Nebe-Gisevius-Oster. See below, p. 202. Hossbach knew nothing of the interrogations until after they had occurred and has no idea how the order to go to the Prinz-Albrecht-Strasse was transmitted to Fritsch. Interview, July 1, 1971.

had been selected for the interrogation. The role of the former in the entire affair is a somewhat ambiguous one. In Heinrich Müller's absence he was the senior official of the Gestapo as well as its legal expert and could hardly escape taking considerable responsibility. There can be no doubt that he was uncomfortable and apprehensive and perhaps somewhat abashed. He had probably not been initiated into the inner motives of the intriguing combine, but knew his bosses sufficiently well to be thoroughly aware of the "end of the rope" at which he was expected to pull. Best was a man of whom it is known that in many questionable particulars of Gestapo business he did much to maintain "professional" standards and hold down abuses. In the Fritsch affair he apparently hoped to restrict his own role to a minimum, the most logical explanation of why the key interrogation assignment was foisted on Huber. Best's postwar statements on his part in the affair are full of twists and turns that betray his embarrassment. There can be no doubt that he intentionally distorts the picture at various points.

Best had not long to wait. Promptly at the appointed hour (10:00 or 10:30?)[125] Fritsch appeared in civilian garb and was conducted to the third floor. Hidden in niches and window wells in the long corridors of the old building were the Bayern Seppl and others of his stripe who had been hastily assembled to scrutinize the general as he passed in the hope that he might be recognized as a "customer."[126]

As they climbed the stairs the Gestapo official directed the attention of the Army commander to the fact that his bureaucratic rank approximated that of a general officer and that, since other officials would be present at the interrogation, he should be aware that at any time it would be possible to reduce the audience to "a talk under four eyes."[127] Best made a similar comment at least once during the interrogation.[128] He later argued that this was not a clumsy attempt to worm confidences of a compromising nature

[125] Since the protocol of the Huber interrogation covers eighty-two pages and since Best and Fritsch continued alone for a time, the stay in the Prinz-Albrecht-Strasse on the 27th must have occupied three to four hours. The time of Fritsch's arrival is deduced from the fact that Schmidt was brought in at exactly 11:35, a point reached in the protocol on p. 23.

[126] Gisevius, *Bis zum bittern Ende*, 264. For the presence in this fashion of the Bayern Seppl we have his testimony before the court-martial. Verdict, 51.

[127] Best, "Aktennotiz," 3. Best's rank was that of "Ministerialdirigent," which is below that of "Ministerialdirektor." Since the English equivalent of both "Dirigent" and "Direktor" would be "director," the distinction is not reflected in translation.

[128] Huber interview, June 3, 1970.

from Fritsch, but a well-intentioned effort to make the interrogation as considerate and "gentlemanly" as possible.[129]

What is otherwise known about Werner Best might incline one to take this at face value were it not for his omission of the fact that everything said was secretly recorded and that the apparatus would scarcely have been chivalrously turned off if the two men had continued alone. In fact, since the proceedings were also taken down stenographically, it seems fair to assume that the main purpose of the recording was to catch *precisely* what would have been said had Fritsch accepted the invitation to go "off the record" by talking "under four eyes" with Best.[130]

Whatever Best's attitude, in the case of the uninitiated Huber there was merely a professional job to be done. Schmidt had made the worst possible impression on him the previous evening and he was more than ready to believe that the charges against Fritsch were absurd. Both he and Best, however, were astonished and somewhat shocked by the spiritless posture and lack of sovereign poise of a man of such exalted position. They had expected that the general would openly resent being confronted with Schmidt for a second time and that he would refuse to say anything in the presence of a professional criminal. On three occasions, absorbing two-thirds of the time of the interrogation, the blackmailer was introduced into the room for extensive questioning. During the periods of his absence, Fritsch, Huber, and Best would go over the ground repeatedly, seeking an explanation for the firmness and consistency of the testimony in face of continual and severe reminders of the consequences of a false accusation. To the Gestapo men it was painful to see Fritsch from time to time descend to the level of argument with the impudent rogue.[131]

The protocol of the interrogation bears out Huber's claim that he treated Fritsch with all possible consideration and tried repeatedly to animate him to the point of "forgetting himself and crashing his fist upon the table."[132]

Of course nothing in the way of admissions or of statements that might be twisted by his behind-the-scenes persecutors was

[129] Best, "Aktennotiz," 4.

[130] Huber himself was not aware, as Best assuredly was, that the interrogation was being recorded. Huber interview, June 3, 1970. To give Best the benefit of the doubt, it is probable enough that he was acting under orders from Heydrich for whom this kind of procedure would be characteristic.

[131] *Ibid.* Best, "Aktennotiz," 4.

[132] Huber interview, June 3, 1970. Fritsch Protocol.

178

gained from Fritsch. He could in fact only deny everything and try to offer items of information about himself which controverted this or that allegation made by Schmidt. But his demeanor fell so far short of what his interrogators had looked for in a colonel general that they did not quite know what to make of things. In the end Best said he would have some private words with Fritsch, upon which Huber, Fehling (who had conducted Schmidt), and the stenographer left them alone.[133]

This must have been the point where, according to SS General Karl Wolff, Best represented to Fritsch that, as a bachelor without known feminine connections, appearances were against him. He would benefit his case by confidentially telling of earlier relationships with women and thus weakening the fundamental assumptions of the charges against him. Fritsch resolutely declined to make any such revelations; he did not indicate whether there was nothing to reveal or whether he regarded such an invasion of his privacy as a crowning indignity.[134] If there was anything he preferred to keep hidden it was fortunate that he was silent, for, while Best was assuring him of the confidential nature of what was being said, the recorder was inexorably spinning on. In an encounter with Best that summer, Fritsch's defender, Count von der Goltz, did not spare him a reproach. "The protocol of your talk with the colonel general," he told the abashed official, "in which you begged for his trust and asked him to speak frankly, noting that you had the rank of a general and that the conversation was under four eyes, he has taken much amiss. The protocol shows every word of this 'confidential talk' was recorded." Best's only response was an embarrassed silence.[135]

Huber left the interrogation troubled in mind and spirit. He did not know what to make of Fritsch's tame comportment; yet he felt strongly that the general could not be guilty and sensed that something was wrong with the testimony of Schmidt. He paid a visit to Meisinger's department and talked for a while with some of the men attached to it. They seemed to him peculiarly evasive and his suspicions grew accordingly. He therefore resolved to do some further investigating of his own. Taking along some subordi-

[133] Huber interview, June 3, 1970. Fritsch Protocol, 82.

[134] Wolff, "Aktenvermerk," 3. Wolff argues that Best's suggestion was well intended and meant to be helpful. It is noteworthy, however, that Best, after the war, was reticent about this and omits mention of it in his statement for Foertsch.

[135] Goltz interviews, February 17, 1970, and July 8, 1971.

nate officials, he picked up Schmidt and conducted him to the house in Lichterfelde to which he claimed to have followed Fritsch. Under intense questioning Schmidt related once more how the blackmailed man had drawn money from a bank nearby. It was this allusion which alerted Huber to the possible evidence of bank statements and which was to have significant consequences that evening. Meanwhile his impressions of Schmidt and his veracity continued to decline and his uneasiness grew more pronounced.[136]

Though Huber cannot recall with confidence the exact order of developments at this juncture, it may be judged that it was on his return to the Prinz-Albrecht-Strasse after this excursion that he found a summons from Goering.[137] With him he was to bring both Schmidt and Weingärtner. Again Huber collected his men and went off with the two miscreants. Goering received them in flamboyant huntsman's garb and stared in disbelief at the miserable object which was the Bayern Seppl. Then, shaking his head in disgust and addressing no question to him then or later, he turned to Schmidt.

About this point at the latest, though Huber thinks he may have been there from the beginning, Himmler arrived. Both of the Nazi hierarchs had already received copies of that morning's interrogation and both of course had previously studied the dossier on Fritsch. Goering took pride in showing off how thoroughly he had mastered the latter. He seemed to take a malicious glee in discomfiting Himmler before his own people, sneering at him repeatedly: "See, I and Huber, we know our documents and you don't." To such sallies Himmler reacted only in flushed embarrassment. Meanwhile Goering gave Schmidt an intense grilling. From the slant of his questions it was impossible to discern whether he took the blackmailer's story seriously or not.

What was Goering's purpose in staging this encounter? Its course showed clearly that he and Himmler were in no way concerned with establishing facts; if that had been the case questions would surely have been addressed to Weingärtner as well. But since he,

[136] The source of this and the following six paragraphs is interviews with Huber, November 20, 1969, and June 3, 1970.

[137] Huber is certain that the visit to Goering was in the late afternoon or early evening. All circumstances point to this still being the day of the interrogation, January 27. After his trial, Fritsch told friends (Hassell Papers, notation of April 30, 1938) that he had learned that Goering had interrogated Schmidt *before* the confrontation of the evening of January 26. Everything by which Huber could judge, however, indicated that the grilling of the 27th was the first of Schmidt by Goering.

after being posted to observe Fritsch that day in the corridor of Gestapo headquarters, had denied ever having seen him, the prosecution would prefer to ignore him as much as possible. Goering probably just wanted to take a look at him and perhaps judge whether, if he could be made to change his testimony, he was likely to become too rattled to be an asset in the case. One glance was enough to take his measure. Schmidt, however vile, was made of tougher fiber and Goering had reason to ascertain how color-fast he was likely to remain in his story. As will shortly be seen, Goering had that day met with Gürtner and the Minister of Justice had asked to see Schmidt and Weingärtner before rendering a more formal opinion on proceeding with the case than the one he had dashed off at the Chancellery on the 26th. Here was sufficient motive for Goering to look them over in anticipation of their appearance before him and Gürtner the next day.

This interlude concluded, Huber returned with his men and their charges to Gestapo headquarters. It was still early or mid-evening and what had been preying on his mind gave him no rest. Before leaving the building, he decided to take another turn in the now deserted and silent offices of Meisinger's Amt II-H. That official's own sanctum he did not venture to enter, but he did not hesitate to glance over the desks of subordinates. There, lying within sight on one of them, was a bank account book or statement on which appeared the name of Captain von Frisch. Paging back to 1933 and 1934, Huber found a record of withdrawals that tallied exactly with the payments listed in the dossier on Fritsch.

Huber felt "as if he had been stung by a tarantula." On the instant he knew that Fritsch was innocent and that someone had deliberately confused the two names or was suppressing the fact after discovering the mistake in identity. The next thought to flash through his mind was: "Either this is some dirty business on the part of Meisinger or it leads all the way to the top."

Both bureaucratic procedure and common sense dictated his next step—report to Dr. Best, who, Huber assumed, would "take it from there." This, then, was his first order of business the following morning (the 28th). He told what he had learned and proposed that Best should pass it on to Heydrich. Best agreed that the information would have to be relayed to their chief but startled Huber by directing *him* to make the report. It was obvious to the dismayed Gestapo official that, whether Himmler and Heydrich had a personal hand in the matter or not, the tidings he was asked to bear would at the very least prove disconcerting. Things might go badly with a too forward underling who dared to bring such unwelcome news to their attention.

What Best did not tell Huber was that since the previous morning he had received reaffirmation, if it was needed, of Himmler's reluctance to allow the "case" against Fritsch to be weakened in any form. Like Huber, the Gestapo's legal expert had been of unquiet mind after Fritsch departed and had reviewed to himself the entire morning's experience. Despite his perplexity and shock at the general's lack of spirit, he could not develop any confidence in the story of Schmidt. At some points it did not seem to hang together and Best knew, too, what had been withheld from Gürtner, that accusations made by the malefactor against others had *not* always stood up.[138] So troubled had Best been that he gathered his courage and went to Himmler with his doubts. In the course of an argument which lasted the entire evening his skepticism was countered with references to a "rogues' code of honor" and the claim that a man in so precarious a position as Schmidt would not venture to lie.[139]

How little Himmler was inclined to allow the charges against Fritsch to lose potency may be inferred from his intense preoccupation with the course of the interrogation. In view of his well-known addiction to all that savored of quackery and the occult,[140] a fantastic tale related in the memoirs of Walter Schellenberg is entirely plausible. Happening to enter the room adjacent to that in which the interrogation was in progress, Schellenberg was astonished to find himself in the midst of a mystic séance presided over by his chief. Twelve of the most trusted SS leaders had been assembled and were sitting in deep concentration in a circle. At Himmler's direction they were focusing their thoughts to exert a suggestive influence on Fritsch "to induce him to tell the truth."[141]

After the previous evening's experience with Himmler, Best was understandably reluctant to beard him a second time with the proof of what the SS chief shortly before had so vehemently rejected. He may have quieted his conscience with the thought that Huber,

[138] It should be noted, however, that during the interrogation Fritsch had been repeatedly assured that all of Schmidt's testimony that involved others than himself had never been shaken. Fritsch Protocol, 4, etc.

[139] Verbal communication of Best to Heinz Höhne, February 5, 1966. Höhne, I, 244, 308n141.

[140] Himmler's inclination to superstition, including an addiction to astrology and divination, is attested to by virtually all his top subordinates. Thus Huber interviews, November 20, 1969, and June 3, 1970.

[141] Schellenberg, *The Schellenberg Memoirs*, 14.

not having already been repelled, would be risking less than he.

It was with a heavy heart and muttering gloomily, "The big fellows go free, the little ones get hung," that Huber ascended the stairs from Best's office on the ground floor to where Heydrich held sway on the story above.[142] The SD chief was in his office and Huber was able to gain quick access to him. On learning what had been unearthed, Heydrich turned chalk-white but said only, "We must immediately inform the Reichsführer." The two thereupon went down the hall to Himmler. More phlegmatic than his mobile-visaged lieutenant, Himmler kept whatever agitation he felt under better control. Hearing Huber's story to the end, he merely commented, "Thank you, you have done well," and dismissed him.

Huber was relieved to escape so easily from what could have turned into a personal catastrophe. But from that moment he had nothing further to do with the Fritsch case. He himself doubts that he was intentionally sidetracked because of his "soft" attitude. Though he is not sure, he believes that Meisinger returned about then from his badly timed journey, so that it was in the nature of things for him to resume charge of the Gestapo's side of the investigation. What does, however, speak for the view that Huber was shunted aside because he threatened to become troublesome is that he was left out of and told nothing about the second interrogation of Fritsch which Best conducted by himself that very day.[143] It also speaks for Best's willingness, however reluctant, to toe the mark that he went through with what he now *knew* to be no more than a brutal farce.

Needless to say, there is nowhere a hint that Himmler and Heydrich said anything to anyone of a "discovery" that indeed can have been no revelation to them. Meisinger, asserts General Karl Wolff, knew from the start that the case he had built up against

---

[142] Huber has never quite forgiven Best for ducking responsibility on this occasion and exposing him to what might have been the ruin of his career. Otherwise Best, both before and later, always treated him with decency and consideration.

[143] Perhaps another interrogator took Huber's place in the second interrogation. Best always states that he conducted it alone, but the way he leaves out Huber or discounts Huber's role in his accounts of the first makes it unwise for us to accept his word without question. In fact, since the questioning this time seems to have been a good deal rougher on Fritsch, one would like to think someone other than Best was responsible. We know (Hossbach interview, July 1, 1971) that Fritsch thought Best's treatment of him to have been considerate. It was, of course, bad enough for Best to go ahead with the interrogation after what he had learned from Huber shortly before.

Fritsch had no foundation. Heydrich, he adds, must also have known or guessed "the entire manipulation." Himmler, at some stage, may have been one of their dupes, though a most complacent one.[144] But he can have been one no longer after the snoopings of mid-January had uncovered the existence and role of Frisch. At that time he and Heydrich (most probably in conjunction with Goering), though dismayed at the way Huber had stumbled onto the facts, must have decided to brazen things through. In addition to still hoping to complete the ruin of Fritsch with all it meant to them in terms of the Army-SS rivalry, they had to reckon with the reaction of Hitler if he were now informed of Huber's discovery of the existence of Frisch. In the view of Huber, the Fuehrer would assuredly have branded them incompetents for the sloppy security that reigned in the offices of their subordinates.

Was the man on whose desk the offending bank statement was found punished for his carelessness? Though Huber does not recall to whom the desk belonged, it was almost certainly that of Criminal Commissar Fehling. Since mid-January he had been working on the reconstruction of the case and he was later disciplined for several slipups in his manner of operating.[145]

Himmler and Heydrich sought by every means in their power to inhibit even within the highest levels of the RSHA complex any inkling of a connection between the Fritsch case and that of another officer. Yet within forty-eight hours the waves engendered by Huber's findings had somehow penetrated to Arthur Nebe, the Abwehr Opposition circle's extension within the SS empire. The consequence was an alert to the Oster group at Tirpitz Ufer stimulating a search that served in the end to break the case.[146]

## The Conflict over the Court

On January 26 Hitler had told Gürtner that if it should come to a trial for Fritsch, the best instrument would be a special court instituted by the Gestapo. On the following day Hitler advanced the same idea in his second meeting with Keitel and directed him to concern himself with the matter. Accordingly, Keitel, on the morning of the 28th,[147] called in the head of the Wehrmacht Legal

[144] Wolff, "Aktenvermerk," 2.
[145] See below, p. 147.
[146] See below, pp. 206, 294-295.
[147] J. A. Kielmansegg (*Der Fritsch-Prozess 1938*, 44) gives the 27th, Foertsch (*Schuld und Verhängnis*, 99) the 27th or 28th, whereas Keitel entirely skips over his meeting with Rosenberger. Since Keitel (from the nature of the discussion) can only have

Department, Dr. Heinrich Rosenberger, to inform him of the dismissal of Blomberg and the problems raised by the possible succession of Fritsch. The Army commander's elevation, he said, could not be effected until an old charge under Article 175 had been cleared up.[148] It would therefore have to be taken up in a special court.

Rosenberger was a man of whom surviving friends speak with a respect that is akin to reverence.[149] To them he was one of the most courageous fighters for the basic values of that "other Germany" which was striving to preserve the rapidly fading *Rechtstaat* (state based on law) and for which the Fritsch case was a major battle. In response to Keitel's words, he expressed astonishment that such a charge should be allowed to lie dormant for years. He reminded Keitel of Article 147a of the Manual of Military Penal Law by which a superior was liable to punishment if he failed to take action on a criminal charge brought to his attention by a subordinate. To this Keitel replied that from the standpoint of "our decent Prussian and German tradition" Rosenberger was undoubtedly in the right. "You must remember that these men come from the revolution and use a different measuring stick than we do." Perceiving Rosenberger's skeptical expression, he continued, "Or do you doubt that this is the mightiest revolution of history?" "The answer," returned the jurist, "might well be left to history itself." It was said, he went on, that the Fuehrer was a glowing admirer of Frederick the Great. Why did he not follow the example of that monarch in his devotion to impartial administration of the law? Frederick had won immortal fame by that sentence in his 1752 testament which stated: "I have resolved never to interfere in the operations of the courts. The law must speak and the sovereign keep silent."

Keitel looked thoughtfully before him for a time and then returned to the problem of the court to be constituted. Rosenberger

been told of the problem of the court by Hitler in their second meeting (that of the 27th), Keitel's first talk with Rosenberger must have taken place the morning of the 28th. Rosenberger (91-92) specifically relates that all three talks occurred on the same day.

[148] In view of Keitel's silence, our sole sources for this conversation are J. A. Kielmansegg (*Der Fritsch-Prozess 1938*, 44-46), on the basis of information given him by Rosenberger, and what the latter himself published in 1946 in the form of his all-too-brief article. Rosenberger, 91-92.

[149] Thus General Fritz Hofmann: "One of the two or three men in my life whom I revere. Highly cultivated, devoted to the arts, deeply grounded in history." Interview, April 13, 1970.

said emphatically that a special court was ruled out since the law allowed only for a military tribunal. In the case of general officers from the rank of lieutenant general upward, it provided that the Gerichtsherr (ultimately responsible judge) and membership of such a military court must be designated by the Fuehrer as head of state. Keitel agreed to support this position in reporting to Hitler. Having done so, he asked Rosenberger that afternoon to prepare a brief memorandum on the topic for Gürtner. The jurist complied and the memorandum was delivered by Keitel to Hitler. In the evening Rosenberger was told that the Fuehrer had agreed in principle and had passed the document to Gürtner with whom Rosenberger should now get in touch directly.

The next morning (the 29th) saw Rosenberger closeted at the Ministry of Justice with Gürtner and his close adviser and adjutant, Hans von Dohnanyi. The Minister had decided to make Dohnanyi, whose ardent anti-Nazi sentiments were perfectly familiar to him,[150] his confidant and delegate in all that concerned the Fritsch case. The Fuehrer, he related to Dohnanyi, had told him he would know the end of the rope at which to pull. With a twinkle and a wink he added: "All I can do is repeat these words to you."[151] With this injunction an association of Dohnanyi with the Fritsch affair was launched that was to link him inextricably with conspiratorial elements and finally carry him to the gallows.

There is much confusion about Gürtner's role and deportment at this critical juncture. As so often, his principles were at war with an instinct of self-preservation that was ever close to the surface. He had soon sensed that a sinister game whose target was the Army high command was being played. It was no less evident that Hitler, whether directly involved or not, was entirely in sympathy with its objectives. This necessitated caution, especially since it was immediately manifest that the ruthless and vengeful Goering was working against Fritsch. Gürtner must have been directed on January 26 to proceed in close community with the Air Minister in all that pertained to the case. For on the next morning Beck observed him waiting nervously to be received at Karinhall, something Goering tried to conceal from the chief of staff.[152] The verdict

[150] As Dohnanyi later related it to Dr. Josef Müller, there never was any doubt in his mind that Gürtner meant to do what he could to thwart the persecutors of Fritsch. Müller interview, October 11, 1969.

[151] Dohnanyi interview, June 26, 1958.

[152] Gisevius, *Bis zum bittern Ende*, 263-264.

of the Fritsch trial, as finally published in 1965, reveals the two ministers cooperating in an interrogation of the Bayern Seppl on what will be shown to have been the following day.[153] This leads, in turn, to the conclusion that Gürtner joined Goering in the latter's second questioning of Schmidt.[154] Equally valid in this string of assumptions is that Gürtner had insisted on seeing these two "witnesses" before complying with a directive of Hitler of January 27 for a second and more official "opinion" on the case. The order probably came to him through Goering that morning and, as Gürtner made his statement on the 29th, the two interrogations can only have taken place on the 28th after Goering had put Schmidt through his paces in the presence of Himmler and Huber the previous evening.[155]

According to the verdict, Weingärtner did not on this occasion state "with the same certainty" as in the later investigation and trial that Fritsch was not "the man," but said that "he could not take an oath on it."[156] In view of what will be learned later about Goering's management in the formulation of the text of the verdict, this supposed initial "uncertainty" should be taken skeptically. One can imagine Weingärtner's befuddlement under Goering's stern challenges, "Can you take an oath never to have dealt with this man?" For that matter, the much-tried Bayern Seppl later proved equally unable to identify Captain von Frisch as having been among the hundreds he had served since 1933.

The interrogations of the 28th induced Gürtner to push his personal investigation farther by checking with Dohnanyi the locale of the supposed homosexual act at the Wannsee Station. He later told Ambassador von Hassell that this observation had convinced him of "absolute impossibilities" in Schmidt's story.[157]

If this truly represented Gürtner's conclusion on the 28th, his actions of the following day—the opinion he sent to the Chancellery and his talk with Rosenberger—underline how much he was intimidated by Hitler and Goering. Hearing something of his state of mind, Gisevius had on the 28th mobilized the newly arrived Goerdeler, driving him personally to the Ministry of Justice. Goerdeler

[153] Verdict, 391.
[154] There would have been little sense in Gürtner's questioning Weingärtner without first having interrogated Schmidt.
[155] See above, pp. 180-181.
[156] Verdict, 391-392. ᵛ
[157] Hassell Papers, notation of April 30, 1938.

had returned hopeful that Gürtner would oppose anything resembling the special court Hitler and Goering were promoting.[158] Once more they were to be disappointed by the vacillating Minister.

In talking with Rosenberger, Gürtner began by reviewing for the puzzled and poorly oriented official the background of the case. His account of how Hitler had affirmed that Schmidt had told the truth about "all other cases" tells us that he still had not been shown the blackmailer's police file. In the vital matter of the court Gürtner tried to steer a middle course, asking whether one could not include in an otherwise military tribunal the Gestapo's principal legal specialist, Dr. Werner Best.[159] Undoubtedly he hoped by this "compromise" suggestion to placate Hitler and Goering. Rosenberger flatly rejected the idea of including Best.

During these days in which Goering and Himmler were constantly in and out of the Chancellery, the major subject of their meetings with Hitler must have been the problem of the court and, if it had to be a military one, the circumstances under which it could be made to operate. The topic was a burning one in those party circles oriented to what was going on and whose influence made it all the harder for Hitler to abandon his pet project of the special court. That he finally did so can be ascribed only to pained awareness that to insist on so suspect a body in defiance of all military precedent might prove the breaking point both for those who were rallying about Fritsch and for the Generalität as a whole. It would confirm what was being said by persons like Hossbach, who from the first had insisted that the evidence was contrived; the finger of accusation would then point more than ever at the Gestapo which Hitler himself had designated as the originator of the charges. The fact that even the subservient Keitel went along with the objections to the special court must have made a particular impression.

No doubt Hilter was sensitive to any charge in party ranks that he had allowed himself to be overborne by Army pressures. The extent of this anxiety is shown by a confidential circular addressed to party leaders in which he related that he was greatly annoyed over the opposition to the special court but thought it best to give way on this issue.[160] We do not know whether he made some refer-

[158] Gisevius recording, July 1971.
[159] Rosenberger, 92-93.
[160] Rosenberger was told this by a journalist friend who by accident secured a look at a confidential party notice addressed to the editors of his paper. Rosenberger to Kielmansegg, September 1, 1947. Kielmansegg Papers.

ence to built-in controls which, in the second talk with Gürtner, he had included in the proposed arrangements for the court-martial. The desire to add Best to the list of judges would most naturally have come up in that connection.

Such a "compromise solution" ran into the rocklike resistance of Rosenberger. Under the law, he pointed out, only officers and officials of the Wehrmacht were eligible to constitute the court. No doubt Gürtner was glad to pass on so absolute a negative. It was harder, however, to oppose Hitler's other desires that would give him and the Goering-SS combine an influence on the course and outcome of the further investigation and the trial. These in the end were four in number and represented a far from negligible weighing of the scales against Fritsch. However, since their final delineation was reached only after February 4 and after Hitler had made a last gesture of withdrawal, they will be dealt with as the Fritsch case assumes the center of the stage.

It was probably in either the afternoon or evening of January 29 that Hitler approved in principle the constitution of a court-martial. Despite the devices by which he hoped to steer the course of development, he must have given way with reluctance and a feeling of frustration. The substitution of the court-martial for the Gestapo-dominated instrument he had wanted could only be interpreted as a defeat and this he never took gracefully. At the same time he must have looked forward to the outcome with some confidence. It is most unlikely that anyone had yet told him of the existence of Captain von Frisch and the seemingly remote chance that, if his role were disclosed in the investigation, it would break down the testimony of Schmidt. As long as the blackmailer held to his story there would be an indelible stain on Fritsch. The best the defense could then hope for would be a verdict of "innocent on the basis of inadequate proof." From Hitler's standpoint that was all that in the strictest sense was needed, though of course his purpose and that of the cabal would be achieved with far less éclat than from a pronouncement of "guilty." In any event, the eventual outcome of the trial was becoming secondary. That was now the "Fritsch case." The vital issues of the "Fritsch crisis" were to be determined in other ways during the course of the immediately following days.

# CHAPTER VI

# Development of the Fritsch Crisis

On or by January 30, 1938, it appeared a settled matter that there would be a court-martial to try Werner von Fritsch on charges of an offense under Article 175 of the Reich Penal Code. The trial would be preceded by twin investigations, one by officers of the court, the other by the Gestapo. These were bound to continue for weeks if they were not interrupted by some outside agency. Both the investigations and the trial proved grim, dogged struggles between foes and well-wishers of Fritsch and the results were to bear on the affairs of the Third ·Reich in multifarious ways. No matter what the outcome, however, there was small likelihood of the trial's exercising a determining influence on the continuance of Hitler's rule. Insofar as that may be claimed to have been at stake, the Fritsch crisis covered a much briefer period than the case that also bears his name. At most it may be said to have spanned about a week between January 27 or 28 and February 4.

## Hitler's Position and Aims

One of the uncertainties of the Fritsch crisis is the extent to which Adolf Hitler was aware of its implications from the standpoint of peril to himself and his regime. From his deportment during these days there is little to indicate confusion or hesitancy and, least of all, fearfulness or apprehension. If those who were physically closest to him read him correctly, he really had been hit hard by the shocking news of the past life of the new Frau von Blomberg. But within a few hours of receiving it we find him on the offensive. Wiedemann, for example, was convinced that he regarded the mar-

190

riage as a severe blow to his prestige and conceived him that evening to be in a state of dejection unparalleled in the four years of the adjutant's service to him. But whenever the Fuehrer was depressed by events, says Wiedemann, it was never necessary to wait long before there was a strong positive reaction. The discomfiture he had suffered was to him a challenge to balance it with some outward success.[1] This was to lead to the extraordinary *revirement* of February 4 and then to the mounting pressure against Austria. More immediately and directly it was instrumental in giving weight and point to the action against Fritsch.

After January 26 Hitler's problem in dealing with the Army commander altered greatly. Let us assume that he had known nothing of the intrigue in his entourage against Fritsch and Blomberg and had suddenly been confronted with the prospect of almost irresistible pressure to make the former his War Minister. The reverse side of the coin was a probably unique opportunity to get rid of him even as Army commander. The meeting with Hossbach on the morning of January 26 should have brought reassurance on both points. Fritsch, he was told by the Wehrmacht adjutant, had no interest whatever in the War Ministry and also was ready to step down from his current post if he were given the word.

Why, then, did Hitler and Goering become more fixed than ever in their purpose of hounding the Army commander to his personal ruin? Pure spite, in Hitler's case at least, is no satisfactory explanation. The answer can only lie in the determination to exploit to the limit the situation created by Blomberg's folly by undercutting the Army as a semiautonomous power factor.

The scandal of the War Minister's marriage may have been a blow to the Fuehrer's prestige. The compensating feature was that for the reputation and morale of the officer corps it was no less than a disaster. Hitler adroitly barbed the point in speaking to Army representatives during that period, when he would sometimes say outright, sometimes insinuate, that his faith in the integrity of the Generalität had been severely shaken. The immediate purpose of such remarks was to justify going more deeply into the charges against Fritsch which he claimed originally to have rejected. The impact of such comments could be further compounded if the second most prominent member of the military hierarchy could be involved in a disgrace that duplicated or exceeded that of the first. Since Hitler's aim, in short, was nothing less than

[1] Wiedemann, "Aufzeichnungen," 99, and interview, December 2, 1969.

the humiliation of the Generalität and of the entire aristocratic officer caste, it was imperative not to be content with a parting of the ways which could be interpreted to result from simply a clash of views or of personality between the dictator and the Army commander. Accordingly, the charges against Fritsch must, if at all possible, be made to stick. At the very least, the shadow of doubt must be made to hover over the head of the harassed general.

A factor that cannot have failed to carry weight in hardening Hitler's purpose was Fritsch's tepid reaction to the outrage of confrontation with Schmidt and to the crowning indignity of interrogation by the Gestapo. This man was clearly no formidable antagonist in the arena in which he was now forced to defend himself. Hitler had an uncanny sense of how far he could push certain people that was fully matched by the inhuman ruthlessness with which he exploited their vulnerabilities. That Fritsch, after so pathetic a showing, should rally and transform himself into the hub of a generals' Fronde could be dismissed from the dictator's calculations. He and Goering can be described as having tasted blood the evening of January 26. From then on, if not before, they were determined to move ahead for the kill.

This did not imply a heedless rush forward without thought of consequences. As will be seen, there were men in Fritsch's entourage about whose inability to act decisively Hitler was less confident. In particular, it was necessary to avoid raising an issue which would challenge the Generalität to close ranks and seek a showdown. Here is the explanation for Hitler's so reluctant concession in the matter of the court. He could hardly fail to realize that if there were anything that would fix the resolution of the most irresolute among the generals, it would be insistence on a tribunal that was under the aegis of the Gestapo.

## The Men about Fritsch

Perhaps the most fateful aspect of the impasse Werner von Fritsch encountered in defending himself in the crisis which bears his name was that basically he was a lonely and intensely introverted man. He seems to have experienced the greatest difficulty in revealing himself fully even to those closest to him. During these tortured days he kept his thoughts and feelings as much as possible to himself. Insofar as there were exceptions, these seem to have been in his relations with a few military peers who had been his superiors in the past. For such a fine-nerved, highly sensitive man, merely recapitulating the gross charges against himself would be inexpressibly painful. He could not get over the shock of having his word treated as a thing of no account by the head of state. When he went to the Chancellery the evening of January 26, it probably had not occurred to him that more than a categorical denial would be needed to clear up matters. Beyond anything else that entered into the shattering trauma of that meeting, the contemptuous rejection of his word of honor unmanned him. He had thought himself prepared for whatever might be sprung on him by the Nazi hierarchs. What happened was the one thing totally unexpected.

The mortal wound dealt the inner fortress of the man Fritsch made him take too personal and introspective an attitude in all that was still to confront him. It was doubly difficult for him to perceive the larger implications of the attack of which, in actuality, he was only the immediate and observable target. This contributed, probably decisively, to the collapse of the half-formed resolution, made at the time of his orientation by Hossbach, to enlist the backing of the principal Army leaders. In retrospect, it is easy to see that he should have gotten in touch with them that very hour, so that he could go to the Chancellery with the full assurance of their solidarity in his behalf. Few doubt that at this juncture it would have been readily forthcoming. To both Hossbach and him, however, such action looked at the moment like overreacting. Hitler, though behaving abominably, was believed to do so in ignorance of the intrigue against Fritsch. The problem was conceived to be one of persuading him of the falsity of the charges. The two did discuss and agree in principle on the use of force if this should not prove possible.[2]

The men closest to Fritsch in the following days of sore trial were probably his first staff officer, Major Siewert, and one of his adjutants, Captain von Both. Curt Siewert, who combined solidity of character with intense loyalty to his chief, proved a firm support who could ever be reckoned at his elbow. He was likely to look askance at whatever smacked of rashness and was not to be counted among those who constantly pressed for "action." What he has said or written on the Fritsch issue in recent years is essentially an apologia for the failure of "the generals" then and in following years to call for a showdown with Hitler or to attempt some kind of coup.

[2] Hossbach, *Zwischen Wehrmacht und Hitler*, 122.

Joachim von Both was a man of another stripe—much younger than Siewert and with a temperament whose ardor contrasted with the more restrained ways of the first staff officer. General Geyr von Schweppenburg, who once commanded a cavalry regiment to which Both belonged, paints a most attractive picture of him, as do fellow officers and the secretaries in Fritsch's office who had daily contact with him. Adjectives which arise constantly in their characterizations are chivalrous, gallant, buoyant, imaginative, and spirited. He was commonly regarded as Fritsch's favorite and the general is said to have loved him as a son. He was perhaps the finest gentleman rider in Germany and Fritsch, the most passionate of horsemen, was from the start drawn to him by this.[3] The young officer repaid his chief's kindness with a full measure of devotion and responded instantly when there was need of service or support.

Hammerstein and Adam, men belonging more to Germany's past than to her current military constellation, rallied strongly to Fritsch when they became aware of the state of affairs. We do not know at what point Hammerstein learned of them, but he soon was a regular visitor at his successor's office to keep abreast of developments as well as to call on him personally.[4]

Adam had been snatched from the verge of retirement in 1935 to set up a new Wehrmacht Academy dedicated to strategic studies. The first intimation of a crisis at the military summit reached him on January 31 during a reception at the Swiss legation. There Wiedemann confided to him Blomberg's situation. Adam was still digesting these shocking tidings when he was ostentatiously waylaid by Hans Frank, the future hangman of Poland, with a sneering, "Well, so your Minister is now honeymooning in Capri." To the vast edification of the bystanders, the infuriated soldier flashed back, "Excuse me, he is not our Minister but yours."[5]

[3] By strict rule Both should not have continued in competition after becoming Fritsch's adjutant, but the general was so partial to him that he made an exception in his case. His death in a steeplechase a few months later was a shock to his many friends. Geyr von Schweppenburg interview, January 26, 1970.

[4] Interview with Countess Hardenberg, February 20, 1970. She had been successively the principal secretary of Blomberg, Hammerstein, and Fritsch. Though she was on other duty in January–February 1938, her great concern about Fritsch induced her to spend much time in his outer office during this period. Fritsch, so reticent even with his closest male friends, was much too inhibited to breathe a word about the nature of his difficulties to a woman. But Hammerstein, as outgoing as Fritsch was introverted, spoke with her almost daily and gave her a running account of what was transpiring.

# Development of the Fritsch Crisis

It was not until a day or two later that Adam first learned of a crisis revolving about Fritsch having attached itself to that concerning Blomberg. Its full compass, however, was only brought home to him at the meeting of military leaders called by Hitler on February 4. Thereafter Adam's office became one of the resorts for conventicles of Fritsch's friends that often endured for hours.[6]

Fritsch seems to have been somewhat less reticent with these two men who were his contemporaries, equals in rank, and close acquaintances of many years standing. To them he appears to have confided more than to others about the background of the affair, such as the abortive maneuver to get him and Raeder to act as the witnesses at Blomberg's wedding.

Professionally the man who stood closest to Fritsch was of course Ludwig Beck. The two were also bound together by ties of mutual respect and confidence. Beck, it has been noted, was the more intelligent, more broadly cultivated, and by far the more politically aware. Over the years he had gained steadily in appreciation of the irreconcilability of the National Socialist regime with the traditional values of Western society. He had managed to restrain, if not quiet, his fears by hope that a mellowing process would, in time, set matters to rights. Above all else, his faith in the steadfastness and prestige of Fritsch had made him perceive his commander as the ultimate guarantee that the Army would intervene if abuses exceeded all tolerance.

The situation had grown in complexity and seriousness owing to the ever clearer revelation of Hitler's aims in foreign policy that had culminated in the conference of November 5, 1937. It had become harder for Beck to resist the awareness that a definitive break was rapidly approaching. Be that as it may, events early in 1938 had not yet made enough headway in this direction for Beck to respond instantly and positively to signs that a showdown situation was at hand. The night of January 26-27 furnished ample proof that he was still a prey to confusion and indecision. He permitted Hitler's playacting to throw him off balance and for

[5] Adam, "Erinnerungen," 388, entry of February 2, 1938. Jodl Diary, 363. For the Jodl version of this remark, see above, pp. 23-24. Adam states (319-320) that Fritsch and Blomberg made a special flight to Munich to persuade him to accept the appointment, though Fritsch had largely nailed things down by a special telephone appeal that morning. Luise Jodl, then Beck's secretary, believes that it was Beck who made the flight with Fritsch. Letter to the author, April 16, 1971.

[6] Adam's secretary was Ilse Schneckenburger. Adam confided extensively in her as a close friend of his family, in whose home she had been married. Interview with Ilse Schneckenburger, May 27, 1970.

the moment seems not quite to have known what to make of the charges against Fritsch. It took all the resolution of that stern Prussian, Colonel Hossbach, to fully convince him of the existence of a base intrigue.

Having reached this stage, Beck, like Fritsch, still found himself short of the point of crediting Hitler with more than a sort of eager gullibility. In Beck's eyes the approach for Fritsch's friends was not to conduct their fight on his behalf by an open revolt against the head of state. The job, as he then saw it, was to liberate the Fuehrer from his cheka and prevail upon him to render justice to the ill-used general. This all-too-persistent illusion also prevented Beck's timely conversion to the views of that group of Fritsch's supporters who wished to coerce Hitler by a threat of the collective resignation of the top officers in the Generalität.[7]

Beck's inability at this time to gauge fully Hitler's capacity for evil served to reinforce his qualms about seditious or rebellious action against constituted authority which clashed with the military and, above all, Prussian tradition. It was during these troubled days that he uttered to the more impetuous General Franz Halder the dictum: "Mutiny and revolution are words that do not exist in the lexicon of the German soldier."[8] The maxim was apparently quoted by Beck as having been laid down by General Count Alfred von Schlieffen, whose disciple he considered himself to be.[9] It is not clear whether he cited it as one he had made his own or only to stress the momentous character of any decision that controverted this rule. He certainly did not resurrect it at this juncture, however, in order straightway to repudiate it.

In view of Fritsch's self-immobilization, Beck's persistent inhibitions during this period are the more fateful in their consequences since he occupied the sole high position from which it would have been possible to organize a solid front of the Generalität and perhaps the entire Army. If he had acted with a clear perception of what was at issue, he might have proved even better situated to move vigorously than the commander in chief himself. By joining his personal prestige and that of his own office with those of Fritsch, he could have spoken out in a manner of which Fritsch,

[7] Foerster, 89.

[8] Peter Bor, *Gespräche mit Halder* (Wiesbaden, 1950), 113. Confirmed to the author by General Halder. Interview, August 9, 1960.

[9] Max Pribilla, "Die Fritsch-Krise 1938 als deutsche Schicksalswende," *Stimmen der Zeit*, Vol. 147 (1951-52), 211.

restrained by qualms about seeming to appeal to others to right personal wrongs, was incapable. Important, too, was the fact that Beck, as his commander's deputy, acted as locum tenens in conducting the Army's affairs during Fritsch's suspension and the brief vacancy between his resignation and Brauchitsch's official takeover of the Army on February 4. During this all-too-short period the chief of staff could have professed to speak for the Army and called upon it to rally behind its aggrieved leader.

Hitler saw these possibilities far more clearly than did Beck and also tended to take more seriously than proved necessary the likelihood of the chief of staff's arriving at some positive decision. When, at one point during the crisis, Gürtner was pleading with the dictator to moderate somewhat the proceedings against Fritsch because of a dangerous mood prevailing in the Generalität, the response was: "I want to tell you something. The only one I fear is Beck. That man is capable of undertaking something."[10] However Hitler may have meant to employ it, "capable" at the time the word was spoken by him applied in actuality more to the means at Beck's disposal than to a disposition to make use of them.

Somewhat paradoxically, whatever capacity for political assertion Beck perceived in his direction of the General Staff proved an additional inhibiting factor. Having put aside the thought of striking at this time and making future decisions depend on developments, he became absorbed with the importance of maintaining himself in his position. All we know of Beck and of the manner in which he laid his post on the line six months later confirms that his attitude was anything but that of a placeholder. He was thinking of the rapidly approaching time when the issues, as he could discern them, would be more clearly drawn. If the effort to induce Hitler to shift his support to the commander in chief should fail, this single remaining foothold at the military summit would be vital. Its importance, in fact, would be progressively enhanced as the conflict between Hitler and the Army leadership moved further into the area of controversy over foreign policy.

Because of these calculations Beck held himself somewhat in the background, avoided a stance of pronounced partisanship for

[10] As reported by Gürtner to Dohnanyi and by the latter to his wife. "Aufzeichnungen von Frau Christine von Dohnanyi, geb Bonhoeffer" (n.d.; copy in author's possession), 3. Dohnanyi took this to mean that Hitler thought Beck was the only general who might summon the determination to attempt a coup. It led to the jurist's decision to move closer to Beck. Cf. Deutsch, 90.

Fritsch, and exposed himself only when needed to give aid to the defense. This concept of his role he expressed most succinctly to Count von der Goltz, when that old friend from General Staff duty during World War I accepted the formidable assignment of being Fritsch's defender. For the time being, said Beck, he must maintain reserve and avoid compromising himself. Because of reasons he did not feel able to elucidate, he considered it important to stay at his post. He would help wherever he was needed but it must be done as discreetly as possible. Goltz, therefore, when he found it necessary to confer with Beck, avoided going to his office. Instead he would have his wife invite the general to visit the son of the family who was his godchild.[11]

Fritsch himself bolstered Beck in conserving for current and future needs this last remaining military power center. As long as it was held by Beck it could be utilized against any final extravagance of outrage attempted against the commander in chief. It was considered entirely conceivable, for example, that Fritsch should suddenly be arrested by the Gestapo.[12]

For an understanding of Beck's role and, as will be developed shortly, that of Fritsch in the 1938 Wehrmacht crisis it is vital to give due attention to a factor rarely assigned adequate weight in historical analysis: the limitations of the human body and spirit. The relentless snowballing of the military establishment had imposed demands on the chief of staff which bore heavily on his far from robust constitution. Since 1933 General Staff expansion was reflected in the growth to eleven departments from four plus the creation of no fewer than four quartermasters general. Just at the time of the crisis particularly difficult organizational problems clamored for attention. And, to cap it all, Beck's burdens were now doubled by the devolution upon him, through the suspension of Fritsch, of the duties of acting commander in chief.[13]

What has been said here should not be construed to imply that Beck's avoidance of the forefront of the battle betokened a completely passive role. The firmness with which he had rejected Hitler's obvious inclination to depose Fritsch before he had been adjudged guilty by a full-fledged judicial proceeding was not without effect. It did not save Fritsch from dismissal before his case

[11] Foerster, 90. Goltz interview, November 1, 1969.
[12] Goltz interview, November 1, 1969.
[13] Interview with Luise Jodl, then Beck's secretary, June 24, 1970. Gisevius (recording, July 1971) lays particular stress on the role played by Beck's great preoccupation with his duties.

had been tried, but it did contribute to Hitler's yielding in the matter of the court.[14] Beck also protested energetically to Keitel about the participation of the Gestapo in the investigation and tried to get him to intervene with Hitler to have it eliminated.[15] Keitel evidently felt he had exposed himself enough in pushing for the court-martial and had no inclination to forfeit his newfound favor with the dictator on an issue where he had reason to believe there would be no further concession.

Of first importance, both in the definition of Beck's role during the Fritsch crisis and in his emergence as the leader of a conspiratorial circle during the next months, is his developing relationship with the action group whose heart and soul for the next five years were to be centered in the Abwehr headquarters at Tirpitz Ufer.

## The Widening Abwehr Circle

In the Abwehr Opposition group the last weeks of 1937 had been a period of growing uneasiness. Outwardly a state of unusual quiet prevailed at the turn of the year. There were no signs of rising international controversy, no party campaigns to whip up public sentiment on one issue or another. The very calm that prevailed was later conceived to have had about it something foreboding. At least when looking back, some were reminded of a similar atmosphere before June 30, 1934.[16]

Despite this feeling of indefinable unease, Canaris, Oster, and their intimates of the Opposition group were caught unaware by developments in late January. In view of the numerous signals of which we now have knowledge, this may appear strange. It was a sign that Oster's efforts to develop sources of domestic intelligence had thus far borne only moderate fruit. On this occasion, indeed, agencies that possessed means for gathering such information and with whom he had fostered contacts through Gisevius were themselves caught by surprise. It has been noted how assid-

[14] Foerster (91) states that Beck's "repeated use of his influence" with Brauchitsch contributed mightily to Hitler's giving up his resistance to the military court. Since Hitler seems to have given way on this issue on January 27 and Brauchitsch's appointment did not take place until February 4 this can only refer to Brauchitsch's intervention after February 5, when Hitler seemed inclined to draw back. Brauchitsch was isolated from the OKH and did not see Beck during the intervening days. There is no evidence that the issue of the court played a role in the negotiations that led to the appointment of Brauchitsch.

[15] Foerster, 90.

[16] Karl Heinz Abshagen, *Canaris, Patriot und Weltbürger* (Stuttgart, 1949), 177. Gisevius recording, July 1971.

uously Gisevius since 1933 had cultivated the chief of the Reich Criminal Office, Arthur Nebe, and, beginning somewhat later, the police president of Berlin, Count Helldorf. Both of these sources of information were now and in the tense weeks ahead to prove highly rewarding. But neither of them had been able to provide more specific warning than did any of the other quarters where Oster customarily sought insight about affairs in high places.

On what was almost certainly January 27 Gisevius returned to Berlin early in the morning from a trip to western Germany to find an urgent message from Schacht telling him to hurry to the Reichsbank.[17] There he was conducted by a mysteriously acting Schacht to a large meeting room behind his office and told in whispers that a fantastic story had reached him about Blomberg. The banker had been pledged not to reveal his source but he urged Gisevius to rush to his friend Helldorf and learn what he could about the strange doings at the War Ministry.[18]

Gisevius hurried off to police headquarters in the Alexander Platz, reflecting on the way that it would be well to call first on Nebe whose office was in the same building. Since Nebe's functions led to almost daily contact with the SS chiefs, he was likely to gain early inside knowledge on anything exceptional that was stirring in the black-uniformed corps.

Nebe was visibly surprised and a little aghast that Gisevius should so quickly have gotten wind of the scandal about Blomberg. Conducting his friend to a remote corner of the building and earnestly entreating him to observe the utmost discretion, he showed him a set of papers he had received from the "Central Office for

[17] The assumption that it was the 27th is based on the following calculations. As will be noted directly, that same morning Gisevius was to learn that Canaris, and perhaps other selected department heads of the War Ministry, had by this time heard something about Blomberg's predicament from Keitel. Keitel would never have breathed a word of this in official quarters solely from what Helldorf had told him on the 21st, but only after Blomberg had confided to him at noon on the 26th and the subsequent talks with Goering and Hitler that afternoon. This would place what Gisevius relates no earlier than the 27th. An argument can also be made for the 28th but would face the difficulty of Gisevius's then leaving the same evening for Münster to orient Kluge. Unless otherwise indicated, the account in this and the following eight paragraphs is derived from Gisevius, *Bis zum bittern Ende*, 264-271. In conversation with the author on July 11, 1971, Gisevius agreed with the reasoning outlined above, accepting January 27 in place of the 26th he had given in his book.

[18] Schacht's informant was Wiedemann, who told him something of the background of the new Frau von Blomberg when he called at the Reichsbank (probably during the afternoon of the 26th) for the foreign exchange which was to finance the ex-Minister's resumed honeymoon. Schacht interview, October 9, 1969.

the Suppression of Pornographic Pictures and Literature," which formed a division of his department. Gisevius's startled gaze fell on five *pikant* photos of the new Frau von Blomberg attached to a report of her past encounters with the morals police. In addition there was an account of an arrest for alleged theft which Nebe had personally dug out of the records.

After hearing from Helldorf what the police president had experienced during the previous seven days, Gisevius went back to Schacht with his bag of sensations. The two decided that no time should be lost comparing notes with their friends at Abwehr headquarters. At Tirpitz Ufer Gisevius straightway ran into Oster conversing with other officers in the hallway. Pulling him aside, he could not forbear a whispered, "I have just seen the fingerprints of your Feldmarschallin." "What, has that already gotten about?" was Oster's astonished retort. The utmost caution was imperative; Keitel had issued the strictest injunction for silence.

Oster then took Gisevius upstairs to Canaris, who at first mention of the matter at hand gave vent to an exclamation of the deepest distress, "Is this not all terrible?" As on so many occasions, the civilian was struck by the intelligence chief's capacity for moral indignation. Canaris's years of experience in a business not distinguished for sentiment or fine ethical distinctions had clearly failed to immunize him against strong human feeling.

Gisevius detailed to the two Abwehr men what he had learned from Nebe and Helldorf—Keitel had given Canaris only the vaguest outline. His attention was arrested, however, when Canaris, who had evidently received no more than a slight hint from Keitel, added that it seemed as if something was also being raised against Fritsch.

In the light of the more intelligible picture which Gisevius's informants had provided about the bride of Blomberg, this had the effect of an alarm bell. It put them well along the road to a conviction that the War Minister's troubles had not sprung entirely from accident. For years the slogan "look for the hand of the SS" had been second nature to them when there were signs of knavery at work. The intimation that Fritsch was threatened with some kind of defamation served to confirm them in the surmise that a larger plot against the military was afoot.

Whenever their problem was to ascertain whether and in what form the SS leaders were taking a hand in some game or other, the unfailing resort of the Abwehr Oppositionists had been Nebe.

As head of a department that was a branch of the RSHA on the same level as the Gestapo, he had routine access to the front offices of Himmler and Heydrich. There much could be picked up from the gossipy adjutants in the antechamber. For them the Reich's criminal director was one of their own before whom they could speak freely.

Duly informed of what was surmised at Tirpitz Ufer, Nebe set to work. One evening Gisevius heard over his telephone the grunting sound which was the signal to hurry to a familiar corner. The news awaiting him there was sensational enough. Nebe was convinced that something big in the way of a blow at the Wehrmacht was indeed under way. Fritsch, to all intents and purposes, was on the way out and, most staggering in its impact, had been interrogated twice by the Gestapo.

To gauge the effect of this insolent intrusion on the military preserve, one need only think of the uproar a few weeks later when the Gestapo took into custody for questioning a mere Army stablemaster.[19] If previously there had been apprehension and puzzlement at Tirpitz Ufer, it was now succeeded by a fever of excitement. Receiving the dire tidings from Gisevius, Oster in mingled fury and distress rushed off to tell Canaris, who in turn hurried to Beck. The chief of staff was roused to intervene so forcefully with Fritsch that the Army commander agreed to make no further visits to the Prinz-Albrecht-Strasse.[20] His next—and last—encounter with the Gestapo was to take place weeks later and on supposedly neutral ground.

Gradually the picture of what had been and was now going on was being rounded out. Oster invited over Captain Hans Böhm-Tettelbach, Blomberg's Air Force adjutant, and questioned him closely on the background and developments associated with the War Minister's marriage. Nebe and Helldorf kept sending items which here and there shed additional light on the course of affairs. Odds and ends of information also trickled over from the War Ministry. The Abwehr group learned of Wangenheim's dramatic expedition to Rome and Oster was delegated to carry Blomberg's termination papers for signature to Capri. Virtually by the hour the need of counteraction and of energetic direction was becoming clearer.

With Fritsch and Beck for the time being standing aside, the

[19] See below, p. 329.
[20] Gisevius recording, July 1971.

# Development of the Fritsch Crisis

natural leader would certainly have been Witzleben. His command of the forces in and near the capital and the initiative he had taken during the previous half year in looking for prospective allies against the regime virtually dictated this. Of the many "ifs" which feature the Wehrmacht crisis of 1938 not the least concerns the difference it might have made had he been available at this time. But, as on more than one later critical occasion, Witzleben's health had badly failed him. Just then he lay ill in a sanatorium in Dresden. The one man in a pivotal position who had some conception of an approaching and inevitable break with the regime and who had devoted intense thought to whom he might count on for assistance was at this vital juncture eliminated. The challenge fell instead to men who, alas, commanded no one—the Abwehr Oppositionists at Tirpitz Ufer.

Canaris and Oster were, each in his own way, moved as they gained comprehension of what was going on and all that was at stake. Canaris at last became aware that his undercover warfare against the excrescences of the regime had been the labors of a man on a treadmill. He had been contending against symptoms while the cancer was eating into the moral and spiritual fiber of the German nation. The actions of Hitler and Heydrich in the initiation of the Tukhachevsky affair that had launched Stalin's military purge in 1937 had made him realize to what unconscionable lengths they would go to achieve their ends. He may at that time have tried to console himself with the thought that men have always tended to abandon their sterner habits of self-discipline when a conflict in which they were engaged was on an international plane. The shameful intrigues which now were gradually revealing themselves to him were wholly on home ground. The admiral was overwhelmed by what he learned about the antecedents and current aspects of the Blomberg scandal and the treacherous attack on Fritsch.

Oster, unlike Canaris, had never gone through a phase of illusion about the Nazi movement and where it might lead Germany. He had long considered Hitler and his followers capable of any crime and thus saw only confirmation of well-established convictions in what now unfolded before him. What most profoundly affected him was that the target of this particular intrigue was the man he most revered, his former regimental commander, Werner von Fritsch. This strong personal involvement expressed itself in a consuming mission: to devote himself unreservedly to Fritsch's defense

203

and then to avenge him when, as a man, he had been destroyed.

The shock of having been caught off guard by the intrigue converted Canaris to a wholehearted acceptance of Oster's concept of a domestic intelligence net. In the weeks that followed his enlightenment, he bent every effort to meet the needs of the existing situation, mobilizing particularly the resources of Abwehr III (Counterespionage) to trace the evolution of the intrigue, identify the plotters, and develop appropriate countermeasures to defeat their machinations.[21] It was the admiral who, prodded and kept *au courant* by Oster and Gisevius, now served in high military quarters as peripatetic informant and gadfly, essaying everywhere to drum up support for the beleaguered Fritsch.

The Fritsch crisis thus proved the vital catalyst which, radiating its influence outward from the Abwehr Oppositionists, fused enduring links between previously scattered and heterogeneous elements that had often been only vaguely aware of each other's existence and goals. Where cautious soundings had revealed a basic solidarity of views and aims, more direct and bolder initiatives now proved the readiness to participate in concrete measures against the regime.

Unfortunately, both during the few days that most accurately may be called the "Fritsch crisis" and in the following weeks during which hope for "action" continued to flicker, it was never possible to attain unanimity on what was at issue or on any single course of procedure. Those minded to utilize the occasion for a showdown with Hitler or his SS leaders were confronted with a formidable task. Except on information gathering, where past omissions were repaired systematically and speedily, and on the preparation of Fritsch's defense, history can record little better than what was perforce a string of improvisations.

The equivocal positions of Fritsch and Beck exercised a fatal influence here. As long as the former remained head of the Army, though suspended from his functions, he could count on a wide, perhaps a universal, response to whatever appeal he might make to the upper level of command. It is inconceivable that Beck, who held back when left to himself, would not have rallied instantly. For some days, and to a lesser extent for a number of weeks, those pleading for "action" clung to the hope that Fritsch could yet be persuaded that the vital concerns of the nation, and not merely his personal fate, were at stake. As long as there existed any prospect

[21] As Canaris himself related it to his official deputy, Vice Admiral Leopold Bürkner. Bürkner-Krausnick interview (in IfZ, ZS 264 (I) ), 5.

of rousing him to take the lead himself, any other course must have looked feeble by comparison.

## Argument over Fritsch's Guilt

Those who thus sought to animate Fritsch had to include in their calculations the problem of his innocence or guilt. The fact that he was completely exonerated in the end and the insight we have continued to gain into the machinations against him have dominated too greatly the interpretation of the events of early 1938. On the one hand, there has been a tendency to discount the role of accident and circumstance and to overstress correspondingly the element of conspiracy. On the other, a charitable mantle of oblivion has been cast over the real doubts concerning Fritsch's innocence which were manifested even in circles dedicated to his defense. Those who later spoke or wrote about their experiences found it easy to forget or ignore their own contemporary bewilderment.

It was inevitable that the shock waves engendered by the revelation of Blomberg's folly should have some impact wherever they penetrated. That the elegant, wordly-wise War Minister should allow himself to get into such a scrape was almost too unthinkable to grasp. In some instances this gave pause to men whose initial reaction would otherwise have been an uncompromising rejection of any thought that the charges in Fritsch's case might have validity.

Other rapidly accumulating news items reinforced this uncertainty. Wiedemann's account of Fritsch's tepid reaction to the confrontation with Schmidt was relayed to Tirpitz Ufer by Oster and was received with mixed horror and incredulity.[22] This was compounded by Nebe's report of the general's similarly lame conduct during the course of the two Gestapo interrogations. Nebe had listened to the tape recordings and was at a loss for words to describe the impression they had made on him. In one of them Fritsch had not even reacted strongly to an insolent: "But Colonel General, a man with such a squeaky voice must be a homosexual."[23] It seemed inconceivable to some that an innocent man could behave in so feeble a fashion.

A considerable impression was also made by Raeder's account to Schacht of what Hitler had told him. More than anything else, the admiral had been shaken by Hitler's dramatized recital of

[22] Gisevius recording, July 1971.
[23] Gisevius interview, July 11, 1971. This can only have been the second interrogation of which nò protocol has thus far come to light.

Fritsch's reference to the two Hitler-boys. It was this which had made him think there might be something to the charges.[24] Canaris and Gürtner are reported by Gisevius to have been especially troubled to have Raeder take the charges so seriously.[25]

Taken together, these sidelights, coming rapidly and reinforcing one another in the three days after the first tidings of Fritsch's troubles had reached Tirpitz Ufer, served to make a considerable impression. By twos and threes Canaris, Oster, Gisevius, Goerdeler, Nebe, Schacht, and Helldorf debated their import. Only two were inclined to reject out of hand any possibility of Fritsch's being a homosexual. The chivalrous Oster simply refused to allow anything so gross as the account given by Schmidt to be associated with the image of his former regimental chief. Nebe, though greatly exercised over the way Fritsch was conducting himself in this hour of trial, reflected the judgment of the experienced criminologist in his conclusions. The close linking between the cases of Blomberg and Fritsch convinced him that the charges against the latter had been manufactured for the occasion and would sooner or later collapse. The others of the group were beset by doubts in varying measure but gradually succumbed to Nebe's argument.[26]

Hesitations yielded to conviction when, on the morning of February 1, Gisevius cautiously disclosed what he had learned from Nebe the previous evening, that the "evidence" applied to an entirely different person. From that moment the issue was reduced simply to the exoneration of Fritsch who, it was hoped, would then finally strike back.[27] Ironically, it was most probably that very day that Fritsch took the fatal step of acceding to the demand for his resignation. Thereby ended any likelihood of his taking the lead in a counterblow at one of the alternative targets—Hitler or the SS.

Something can be said for Gisevius's view that it might have been for the best if establishing the innocence of Fritsch had never become so much the central issue. In his debates with Canaris and Oster, he went so far as to argue that it would be advisable to proceed from the assumption that Fritsch was probably guilty. Thus it would be impossible to obscure the basic issue: the naked contest for power of which so few on Fritsch's side of the affair were aware. The vital point was that the SS was exploiting the

---

[24] Puttkamer interview, July 10, 1971.
[25] Gisevius recording, July 1971.
[26] Gisevius, *Wo ist Nebe?* 284.
[27] *Ibid.*

# Development of the Fritsch Crisis

crisis to steal a decisive march on the Army. As long as Fritsch, whether momentarily exercising the duties of the office or not, stood at the head of the Army, he was in a position to take some kind of lead. The challenge to his friends then was to persuade him to see things through in seeking some form of showdown.[28] Once the issue had been narrowed to legally establishing his guilt or innocence, the outcome, however important in human terms, was no longer very material in relation to the larger meaning of the affair. The history of the following months was to provide ample illustration of this.

## The "Resignation" of Fritsch

In terms of what has been said above, the most critical issue of the Fritsch crisis concerned his response to Hitler's demand for his resignation. Lack of evidence makes it impossible to fix with absolute exactitude just when and how Hitler called for this, whom Fritsch may have consulted among his friends, and exactly when he sent it in. Hitler had probably intended that Fritsch would leave the Chancellery stripped of his high office after the confrontation with Schmidt the evening of the 26th. The scene, in fact, may well have been staged by him and Goering to provoke, then and there, a definitive break that would make it impossible for Fritsch to continue. If, as the Fuehrer told Nazi intimates, the general acted as a Prussian officer ought and cast his sword at the dictator's feet, his post, in effect, would thereby have been vacated. If he reacted weakly it would provide a pretext for dismissing him. He was thus damned if he did and damned if he did not. It will be recalled that Hitler did, in fact, propose that Fritsch resign in return for the charges against him being hushed up. Fritsch had refused indignantly and demanded a court of honor. It remains unanswered whether Hitler, before the general left, made it clear that the request for his resignation stood. Fritsch, in leaving the Chancellery, certainly did not mention anything of the kind to Hossbach.[29]

Hossbach, in fact, asserts most emphatically that no demand for Fritsch's resignation was made before the 28th, the day his own assignment in the Chancellery came to its abrupt end.[30] His state-

[28] Gisevius interview, July 11, 1971.
[29] See above, p. 167.
[30] "Fritsch definitely was not asked to hand in his resignation before the 28.1.38." Letter of Hossbach to Kielmansegg, September 22, 1947. Kielmansegg Papers.

ment seems based on the natural assumption that such a demand would have followed the prescribed route through his own hands. He did not know that Hitler was already going around him in such matters as the January 26 meetings with Blomberg and Keitel.[31] Certainly the dictator would prefer to work directly on Fritsch and seek to rush him into a precipitate resignation without himself having to go on the record. He would be the more eager not to have his demand documented because of the crassly intimidating form in which it was couched. Fritsch, he told Gürtner, would be dismissed out of hand "because of unfitness" if he did not depart of his own volition.[32]

It is conceivable that Hitler reiterated his demand in the telephone message later that night in which Fritsch was ordered to go to the Gestapo for interrogation. Or there may have been such a communication in the afternoon after the first interrogation had taken place. Either story would fit in with Keitel's account that Fritsch had his completed letter of resignation, including a demand for a court-martial, lying before him on his desk that evening (the 27th).[33] Yet such a letter was not delivered to the Chancellery for at least four days! For on January 30, a date which will be seen to be absolutely fixed, Count von der Goltz had his first meeting with Fritsch and accepted him as his client. The count, who speaks of Fritsch's sending in his resignation "at the beginning of February," had urgently entreated him not to do so. Why make things easy for Hitler, he argued, and give the outward appearance of resigning on his own volition which the dictator desired? "Make him throw you out!"[34]

If all the evidence is in and Fritsch actually wrestled for four to six days with his conscience and the importunities of such friends

[31] Letter of General Hossbach to the author, January 1, 1972.

[32] As told to Rosenberger by Gürtner on January 28. Letter of Rosenberger to Kielmansegg, September 1, 1947. Kielmansegg Papers. Rosenberger, 93. Goltz in a communication to the *Deutsche Rundschau*, which had published Rosenberger's article, states his conviction that Fritsch would never have resigned if Hitler's demand had been framed in such terms. Vol. 70, No. 3 (March 1947).

[33] Keitel, 110.

[34] Goltz, "Erinnerungen," 173-174, and interviews, November 1, 1969, and July 8, 1971. J. A. Kielmansegg (*Der Fritsch-Prozess 1938*, 120) also speaks of Goltz's being among those who urged this course. He holds (144), however, that it was not before the 28th that Fritsch was asked "in an ultimatum-like form" to submit his resignation. Goltz points out in a letter to Kielmansegg of September 9, 1947, that if Fritsch had decided on resignation before January 30 there would have been no occasion for him to advise the general to the contrary. Kielmansegg Papers.

# Development of the Fritsch Crisis

as Beck, Hossbach, Both, Goltz, and Siewert,[35] a new and more dramatic light is thrown on the extent of his hesitations and the struggle that went on around him on the question. At Tirpitz Ufer this "contest for Fritsch's soul" was followed with burning anxiety. Gisevius vividly recalls the "wave of anguish" which went through the group when Oster came one morning to announce in great distress, "Fritsch has handed in [his resignation]."[36]

None of the friends who urged upon Fritsch one or another of the more daring courses can have overstated what was at issue. Once the commander in chief had formally left his post he could no longer speak to the Generalität with the authority of that great office. Any appeal he might thereafter address to it would have the personal tinge he so much wanted to avoid. It would have more the character of a voice from the grave—perhaps deeply moving but no longer very compelling. Specific measures for the preparation or execution of a military coup could then only emanate from a successor—one who was asked to repudiate therewith the very authority which had just elevated him to this high post. As long as Fritsch, however nominally, figured as commander in chief, Beck would also be functioning as his locum tenens and, if he so decided, could on his own initiative attempt to rally the Generalität or issue orders on military moves.

It had to be reckoned, of course, that on a refusal of Fritsch to submit his resignation, Hitler would counter with his outright dismissal. Such a step, however probable, cannot be assumed with absolute certainty. If at all possible, Hitler had to avoid being forced into it. All his moves during these days were studiously directed at hiding from the German people and the world generally the existence of anything like a crisis in his relations with the Wehrmacht. Therefore he might have tried some other tack to bully Fritsch into submitting to the appearance of a voluntary retirement and thus camouflage the circumstances of his departure.

To proceed with the dismissal of Fritsch would further have about it something of a call to a showdown on the part of the dictator. The Army commander, once he had gone so far as to defy the head of state to dismiss him, would simultaneously have

---

[35] J. A. Kielmansegg (*Der Fritsch-Prozess 1938*, 120) speaks of Hossbach, Both, and Goltz. The first-named is also mentioned by Siewert as having jointly with him implored Fritsch not to send in his resignation. Interview with Curt Siewert, January 15, 1970. Gisevius (interview, July 11, 1971) states that Beck also opposed Fritsch's resignation.

[36] Gisevius interview, July 11, 1971.

moved closer to the next logical step of appealing to the Generalität to back him in a trial of strength. The fate of the regime itself would then have been at stake.

In view of such formidable considerations, it seems entirely conceivable that Hitler would have reversed directions and, realizing that he had erred in his estimate of his opponent, let matters ride for the time being. Unfortunately he proved all too correct in taking his measure of the man. Fritsch could not fail to link a refusal on his part to relinquish his post with a broader challenge to the regime for which he was neither psychologically nor otherwise prepared. At least two of the men who were urging him to stick it out, Hossbach and Both, were also in favor of an appeal to force. No doubt others whose position is less well documented, like the tough Hammerstein, took a similar line. Goltz, who came into the situation cold and thinking mainly of the best tactical position for the approaching investigation and trial, seems not, at this stage, to have been confronted with the larger issue. Fritsch himself was still clinging to the delusion that his real persecutors were the SS leaders and that Hitler, though showing a lamentable lack of faith in his Army commander, was not himself involved in the plot. Nor was he even now fully convinced that Goering was among the actual initiators.

All this emerges from the extensive notation on his situation which Fritsch set down just then (February 1). He was most grateful, he said, for the confidence Hitler, "except in this single instance," had always shown him. From the Fuehrer's own mouth he knew that the party had never ceased to agitate against him and that its importunities had thus far always been resisted.[37] For Fritsch, then, his problem after nearly a week of brooding and argument was still one of convincing Hitler how cruelly he had misjudged his Army commander. One is aghast at so much simplicity and reminded of a verdict passed by Friedrich Meinecke on high military professionals: "These technicians of war lacked a full understanding of the totality of historical experience. Therefore they were capable of fatal mistakes in their estimates of happenings outside the area of technical-military perceptions."[38]

[37] Ludwig Beck, "Nachlass des Generaloberst a. D. Ludwig Beck" (in IfZ, BAMA H 08-28 (III)). Hossbach, apparently distressed by such a demonstration of naiveté on the part of a man he revered, omits this section of the notation as published by him (*Zwischen Wehrmacht und Hitler*, 59-61).

[38] Meinecke, *Die deutsche Katastrophe* (Zurich and Wiesbaden, 1946), 68.

# Development of the Fritsch Crisis

The situation would have been dramatically different, of course, if Werner von Fritsch had been a man capable of thinking like a contestant for power. But nothing was more alien to him than the ambitions and mentality of a "political general" of the type exemplified by Kurt von Schleicher or, in a parallel but different sense, a Walther von Reichenau. The restrictions of his· outlook were illustrated in his reply to those who urged him so passionately to refuse his resignation. There was no longer any way in which he could go on serving Hitler, he told them. "I cannot work with this man any longer."[39] To cling to his office thus made no sense to him unless it presupposed an attempt at a change of regime which he was not yet prepared to contemplate.

Fritsch had weighed an appeal to force seriously when Hossbach, in the evening of January 25, had apprised him of the dangers of his situation. In the following days of frayed nerves and exhaustion he was less and less ready to contemplate such a course. In agonies of self-examination he turned up one argument after another against "taking action." The considerations which moved him were of the highest ethical order but intensely personal in character. Pride and conscience rebelled against what might appear the deed of a disgruntled commander who, to fend off or avenge personal injury, summons his subordinates to take action on his behalf. Perhaps most painful of all, he would be in the equivocal position of a man who, when accused of transgression against the law and after demanding a fair investigation and trial, seemingly embarks on a course aimed at forestalling a verdict.[40]

Weighing most heavily with Fritsch was undoubtedly the awesome responsibility of launching what, in all likelihood, would develop into a civil war. Compared to the situation a few months after or in such later rounds of military conspiracy as in the autumn of 1939 and the summer of 1944, there was a total lack of planning or preparation. It is highly doubtful whether Fritsch had an inkling of the soundings that Witzleben had been making since the summer of 1937 and there is no evidence that he knew anything at this stage of the Abwehr Opposition group and its half-formed links

[39] Siewert interview, January 15, 1970. Goltz interview, July 8, 1971. To Grosskreuz Fritsch said a few months later that after Hitler had rejected his word of honor, he would in any event have found it impossible to work further with him. Grosskreuz letter to the German Institute for the History of the National Socialist Period, December 28, 1950, 2.

[40] J. A. Kielmansegg, *Der Fritsch-Prozess 1938*, 120.

with anti-Nazi nuclei in other agencies and in the Wehrmacht. What Fritsch could have legitimately contemplated in the waning days of January and in early February would not have approached an organized and purposeful *coup d'état*. In a state of "highest excitement" he rejected this idea in an exchange with Hossbach on January 28. It would have been more like a clarion call of "à moi" to which a considerable proportion of the Army from the Generalität down to the rank and file would assuredly have responded.

How considerable would this response have been? More, probably, as will be developed later, than many have believed possible. But it would scarcely have been unanimous. Since Hitler's achievement of power the Army, and especially the officer corps, had undergone progressive inflation. Between 1933 and 1938 (October) the number of general officers alone jumped from 44 to 275 (not counting medical and veterinary generals).[41] From a political standpoint there had been a negative selection in terms of elimination of many passionate anti-Nazis. The traditional solidarity of the officer corps was undermined by the far-reaching dilution and the Fritsch affair itself was to create an outright split that endured to the end of the Third Reich.

In effect, the grip on the Army of its leaders was weakened in proportion to its penetration by elements less solidly professional in attitude than those which had made up the Reichswehr of the Weimar Republic. The reactivated officers of the World War I period, the former Free Corps and Black Reichswehr[42] members who had joined the colors, the radicalized youth—all these had been primary targets of Nazi agitation. It has been noted how far the Luftwaffe under Goering's leadership had proceeded down the road to Nazification. With much justification it felt that it owed all to the new regime. The Navy, as we have seen, was more divided but could at best be counted as neutral.

As for the population generally, Fritsch, if anything, overestimated the degree to which it had yielded to the enchantments of Hitler

[41] Hoffmann, 61. Hossbach, *Zwischen Wehrmacht und Hitler*, 125.

[42] In the early twenties, efforts to circumvent the restrictions of the Versailles Treaty on Germany's military establishment had included improvisations such as establishing a semitrained manpower reserve by secretly organized and drilled units of volunteers.

[43] J. A. Kielmansegg (*Der Fritsch-Prozess 1938*, 120) believes that Fritsch's pessimistic appraisal of public sentiment was for him the most compelling argument against his calling for a showdown with Hitler

# Development of the Fritsch Crisis

and the appeals of National Socialism.[43] A conversation he had had in 1935 on the prospects of a coup at that time reflected considerations that must have continued to carry weight with Fritsch in 1938. Confessing that many urged him to take action against the regime, he cited arguments that militated against this. "Ninety percent of the Germans," he maintained, "run after this man." Pointing to the recent naval agreement with Britain, he concluded that "the outside world was accepting him." The only chance to overturn the regime lay in a favorable psychological moment, some development that would turn the public against him. "Do you think this man will be able to hold on?" he asked. Sooner or later France or Britain would step into his path. Then his prestige would be impaired and his public support jeopardized.[44]

In 1938 Fritsch seems to have believed that Hitler's public backing, if anything, was stronger than before. To use force, he felt, would array German against German; as put in the famed expression of Seeckt, his predecessor twice removed, Reichswehr might be called to fire on Reichswehr. As long as he persisted in the illusion that only his own fate was at stake, however unjust the treatment meted out to him, this was more than he felt he could take on his conscience. It seemed to him more fitting to withdraw, nurse his wounds, and see to his defense in the ordeal of investigation and trial that lay ahead. For him, as for so many who rallied to him, the extended investigation culminating in the proceedings of the tribunal was therefore a psychological diversion that distracted attention and energies from issues that were ultimately more decisive. This factor may also have played a role in Hitler's calculations when he yielded so grudgingly on the question of the court.

To a degree which, in the view of the present writer, has hitherto lacked adequate emphasis, the resignation and pessimism which characterized Fritsch's reasoning and conclusions derived from physical, mental, and emotional exhaustion. The constant brooding manifested itself in such cries of despair as he uttered one day in the presence of Hammerstein who was trying to cheer him: "They have cut off my honor. I cannot get over that." "Nonsense, my dear Fritsch," retorted his more elastic predecessor, "such swine cannot cut off a man's honor."[45]

[44] As related by Fabian von Schlabrendorff who was present. Interview, February 13, 1970.

[45] As related to the later Countess Hardenberg by Hammerstein at the time of the exchange. Hardenberg interview, February 20, 19⁻0.

213

By the turn of the month Fritsch's state so closely approached collapse that he required the almost daily ministrations of his physician and close friend, Karl Nissen. The famed internist and wartime doctor of the OKW testifies that Fritsch's condition was wholly psychosomatic, deriving entirely from his acute mental distress. It involved a depression so profound that at one stage of the crisis he confessed to thoughts of suicide. Nissen had to impress upon him that such a course would be exploited by his persecutors as a confession of guilt. The logic of this was too compelling to permit debate, but the harried doctor felt it imperative to stay for dinner and remain at the side of his patient until close to midnight.[46]

A report on Fritsch's dangerously low spirits reached Oster on February 2 from Captain von Both. The situation was regarded as so serious that it was agreed between them that Captain Friedrich Wilhelm Heinz of the Abwehr would spend the night with the general. It proved a rudely disillusioning experience for Heinz, who had looked up to Fritsch "as to a god," to perceive his idol in so pitiable a state.[47]

No doubt there was much that was valid about Fritsch's doubts over proceeding in any manner that would deepen the crisis. But his persistence in marshaling arguments against anything that smacked of "taking action" implies a trend toward rationalization that arose out of his personal condition. At bottom Werner von Fritsch does not seem to have felt up to the trials which a more positive response would have demanded of him.

The general also implored those who, like Hossbach and General Viktor von Schwedler, pressed for countermeasures not to undertake anything on their own. In this fashion he largely immobilized the core in the OKH which could have attempted to meet the moves of the intriguing combine. It is safe to assume that he did what he could to confirm Beck in his role of bystander. Those loyal representatives of the Generalität who rushed to his side when they learned of his troubles were cooled in their ardor and enjoined to avoid both the employment and threat of force. It was thus left to Oster and his friends to attempt, from outside Fritsch's

[46] Dr. Nissen is no longer able to pinpoint the date of this occurrence but he is certain that it was on the occasion of one of his first visits, making it the end of January or during the first days of February. He had arrived about 5 P.M. Interview, July 15, 1971.
[47] Heinz, 72.

214

entourage, to mobilize counteraction against the intriguers. While these brave but necessarily improvised and haphazard efforts were under way, Hitler went about slamming the door on a return of Fritsch to the leadership of the Army. He searched for—and found—a successor.

# CHAPTER VII

# The Elevation of
# Walther von Brauchitsch

That the hour had struck when he could rid himself conclusively of Werner von Fritsch probably flashed through the Fuehrer's mind as he listened to Goering's argument that the old charges should disqualify him from consideration as successor to Blomberg. Whether or not such accusations could be made to stick, it was imperative to exploit them in such fashion as to eject him from office and close the door to his return. The surest—perhaps the only—way to make his dismissal irreversible was to establish firmly another general in his place.

### An Offer to Beck?

The circumstances of the new appointment demonstrate at every stage how determined Hitler was to make the departure of Fritsch irrevocable. This emerged unmistakably in the course of his two meetings with Beck during the night of January 26-27. According to Beck's biographer, Wolfgang Foerster, the dictator went so far as to attempt a cynical assault on Beck's loyalty to his chief by proposing that he step into Fritsch's shoes.[1]

[1] The sole source on this reported aspect of the two Hitler-Goering-Beck meetings is Foerster's recollection of a statement prepared by Beck and entrusted to him for safekeeping. The document was lost "through circumstances associated with the war." Foerster, 87. Hossbach's account (*Zwischen Wehrmacht und Hitler*, 115) of what passed between Hitler and Beck provides nothing on this point and he cannot believe that such an offer could have been made. Interview, July 1, 1971. General Engel is convinced that Foerster's memory of the Beck statement must be at fault in this particular. The dictator, he maintains, at this stage of affairs already felt about Beck in a fashion that would make even a gesture of offering

216

# Elevation of Brauchitsch

No one who learned of this alleged offer then or later seems to have taken it seriously. The one central thought of Hitler as Beck stood before him must have been, "Now, how do I rid myself of this fellow too?"[2] From every standpoint it was better for him to leave things as they were rather than move Beck up a notch. From what we know of his estimate of Beck as a soldier, it is clear that he regarded Fritsch as the better man. Politically speaking, the exchange would have been even worse in Hitler's judgment. In this matter we may be sure that the dictator was well informed, the last item of information coming to him only a few hours earlier. No doubt Beck had figured high on Blomberg's list of generals lukewarm or hostile to National Socialism. But Hitler could feel safe about making such an offer. Skeptical as was the master cynic about the integrity of his fellowmen and incapable of esteeming properly the sensitive and high-principled man who stood before him, he would still have known that Beck had no choice but to decline. Any general engaged as was Beck on an errand for his commander could scarcely utilize the occasion to slip into his place. Foerster claims that the chief of staff flatly refused, stating that the case would have to be investigated by a military court before a replacement for Fritsch could even be considered.[3]

Far from contemplating for so much as an instant the exchange of Scylla for Charybdis, Hitler, if he did make the offer to Beck, pursued entirely different aims. He would have hoped to put at least some strain on Beck's loyalty to his chief by awakening within him the thought of taking over the Army once the latter was out of the way. Or, by being able to cite Beck's refusal to be considered under the prevailing circumstances, he could, if pressure in Beck's favor became troublesome, make out that the chief of staff had said he was not interested in the position. In any event, blandly ignoring Beck's insistence that there should be no question of replacing Fritsch until the charges had been substantiated, he went to work with a will on finding a successor. A promise he made Beck to consult him during the further course of developments was conveniently forgotten.

him the Army command unthinkable. Interview, May 11, 1970. Gisevius points out that the entire experience made so deep an impression on Beck's mind that he returned to it repeatedly in the following years; yet he never mentioned what would seem to have been so significant an aspect of the story. Recording, July 1971. In sum, this part of Foerster's account can be accepted only with reservations.

[2] Engel interview, May 11, 1970.
[3] Foerster, 87.

## Hitler's Talks with Keitel and Rundstedt

The search for a new Army commander, it will be recalled, had already begun; Hitler had told Keitel on the 26th that it was his intention to part with Fritsch *in any event*. Adding a blatant dose of flattery about how he now utterly depended on Keitel, he had then launched upon an exposition on the problem he faced with the Army. He described it as the decisive element in German defense; the Navy and the Luftwaffe could play no more than supporting roles. So he was now deeply absorbed in the problem of revising its command structure and would have to begin with the choice of a new commander in chief.

Keitel, not at all inclined to break a lance for Fritsch, showed no inhibition about discussing matters on this basis. Beck, to whom he had always been cool, was apparently not even mentioned by him.[4] The suggestion of Rundstedt was dismissed by the Fuehrer on the grounds that he was too old and "used up." If he were five or ten years younger he would have been the undoubted choice. Joachim von Stülpnagel, who must have been featured on Blomberg's list of anti-Nazis, was rejected as "disloyal." Since Keitel clearly was not inclined to mention him, Hitler, as if spontaneously, asked, "Why not Reichenau?" Keitel described him as not running very deep and too headlong, and, for the moment, Hitler left it at that.[5] But by the following morning his purpose had hardened and Keitel was now inundated by a veritable stream of arguments on behalf of the black sheep of the Generalität. The problem of a successor to Fritsch, dealt with the day before as not very pressing, was now pictured to Keitel as demanding immediate solution in view of the commander's having shown up badly in the confrontation with Schmidt. The only satisfactory candidate, said Hitler, seemed to him to be Reichenau. This was too much even for the complacent Keitel, not yet the complete sycophant he was later to become. Such an appointment, he knew well, would collide with the solid resistance of the military hierarchy. It would, he

[4] Though Keitel does not mention it, it appears that Hitler had already expressed opposition to Beck, which would have made less likely any gesture of offering him a post a few hours later. Klaus-Jürgen Müller (*Das Heer und Hitler*, 271) holds that Keitel's antagonism to Beck was so great that it is quite possible it was he who dissuaded Hitler from considering him as a successor to Fritsch. This conflicts with the author's view that Hitler never for a moment gave thought to Beck in this connection.

[5] Jodl Diary, 358. Keitel's account (107-108) lumps this exchange with Hitler with that of the following day to which it in large part refers.

told Hitler, create the impression that a sweeping change in military policy and not merely one of persons was contemplated. That was, of course, exactly what the dictator had in mind but he was not deaf to the argument that, for the time being, it ought to be disguised.

Keitel went on to raise further objections to Reichenau personally, holding him to be neither thorough nor industrious, too superficial, not popular (by which he must have meant with his fellow generals and not the troops), and prey to an ambition that extended into the political field. Hitler, conceded this last point but said that the other strictures were "too sharp." Keitel then switched the discussion to other names, mentioned Leeb, who received short shrift, and then Brauchitsch, who, he knew, had already been suggested by Blomberg.[6] Brauchitsch he lauded as strictly a soldier and an outstanding authority on matters of organization, training, and command. He was also a man highly regarded in the Army. Hitler, showing no enthusiasm, agreed to confer with the general at an early date so as to form his own estimate.[7]

Whether he took this as implied permission, or, greatly daring, decided to move ahead on his own, Keitel straightway telephoned Brauchitsch at his Leipzig post and summoned him posthaste to Berlin. There he revealed to his startled nominee the conditions which he thought would make him acceptable to Hitler. But the Fuehrer had by no means given up on Reichenau. During the following days he kept up the pressure to wear down Keitel's objections. At the same time he ran a course for his favorite with Rundstedt, whom he received on January 31. Rundstedt, when the problem of a new commander in chief was raised, began with a warm recommendation for Beck. This Hitler icily took under advisement, additional proof, if it were needed, that Beck had never figured with him as a candidate. In return, he fared no better with his own aspirant. Rundstedt flatly rejected Reichenau "in the name of the Army."[8] So drastic a turndown from the Wehrmacht's senior

[6] Keitel, 105. Blomberg had suggested both Brauchitsch and Reichenau. Blomberg interrogation of September 23, 1946, 5.

[7] Jodl Diary, 359-360. Keitel, 107-108.

[8] This is the way Rundstedt put it in his testimony at Nuremberg. IMT, XXI, 30. More complete reports on the conversation were prepared by him previous to this in Britain, a later one in the same year (1946) in Nuremberg, and a third written in the early fifties for Baron von Siegler (in IfZ, ZS 129 (I, II)). The first of these versions is reprinted in larger part by Foertsch, *Schuld und Verhängnis*, 103. Rundstedt says he was called by Beck on February 3 in Königsberg and that he arrived in Berlin the next morning. All the sources that we have for the events

and, after Fritsch, most prestigious general appears to have been too much even for Hitler's stubborn will. There is much to argue that, though he continued to give vocal support to Reichenau during the following three days, this was essentially a tactical maneuver calculated to keep the pressure on Brauchitsch and his Wehrmacht-amt backers (Keitel and Jodl) to induce him to make the maximum concessions on the points at issue.

As things turned out, the road to the top for Reichenau was henceforth blocked. On the next occasion (November 1939) when a change of Army commander was seriously under consideration, Hitler's erstwhile military favorite had so lost in standing with him that the mere mention of his name elicited a gesture of imperious refusal.[9]

With Reichenau fading out of the picture, Hitler solicited Rundstedt's opinion on Brauchitsch and met a cordial reaction. Brauchitsch, affirmed Rundstedt, was a man of distinction, had an excellent reputation as a leader, and was entirely acceptable to the Army. As Keitel also never ceased to beat the drums for Brauchitsch, Hitler began to treat his candidacy more seriously. On the same day Brauchitsch, who had been cooling his heels in virtual isolation in the Hotel Continental, was received for the first time and the negotiations, if so they may be called, commenced in earnest. Before looking further at the rather curious exchanges which determined the command of the German Army for the next four years, it will help to simplify the solution of more than one later puzzle if we take a glance at the situation of the man who was to be their somewhat doubtful beneficiary.

## The Predicament of General von Brauchitsch

General of Infantry Walther von Brauchitsch, as Rundstedt had stressed in his remarks to Hitler, was regarded in the Army as a distinguished representative of the Prussian aristocratic tradition. His gentlemanly background was underscored by his having passed through the Corps of Pages and the Guards Field Artillery. Socially he was sufficiently ornamental to have been the personal page to the Empress Augusta Victoria and to be widely admired for

of these days including the diary of Jodl (362) speak of January 31. Asked at Nuremberg why he so flatly rejected Reichenau, Rundstedt replied: "For us he was too much the Nazi general."

[9] Reichenau once and for all forfeited Hitler's support by his intrepid and vociferous stand against the Fuehrer's decision to attack in the West in the autumn of 1939. See Deutsch, 72-77, 264-265.

blending a soldierly bearing with an elegant appearance. More recently he had been commander of Wehrkreis I, the important East Prussian military district, and he was currently in charge of Group Command 4 (the armored group of the German ground forces) at Leipzig. Such posts obviously placed him in the front rank of those generals from whom a successor to Fritsch would most naturally be selected. So eminent a judge of military talent as the later Field Marshal von Manstein rated him just after the top group of Fritsch, Beck, Rundstedt, Bock, and Leeb.[10] General Adam, whose immediate subordinate he had been for three years, called him "an intelligent man of determined and self-willed character." He was by no means to be counted among the generals with leanings toward Nazism. Only a few months before he succeeded Fritsch he had felt so repelled at the Nuremberg party rally that he had sighed to Adam: "Oh, if it were only possible for me to live abroad."[11]

Far from anticipating promotion to a more exalted place, Brauchitsch had for some time been entertaining the idea of retirement. As early as October 1936, he had sadly handed to Fritsch, who was then on the point of returning to Berlin from military exercises in East Prussia, a letter stating that an approaching divorce made continuation in the service inadvisable. Reading it on the plane, Fritsch had remarked to Major Siewert that he was loath to lose his "best horse" and hoped that ways could be found by Brauchitsch to deal with his marital problem short of quitting the Army.[12]

Fritsch obviously had gained no idea, nor has it hitherto been known to more than a few, about the real extent of the social quagmire that was threatening to engulf the distressed general. Some twelve years before, he had met in Breslau the captivating though flighty Charlotte Rüffer, divorced wife of a brother officer, and had become one of a series of her "protectors."[13] His wife's refusal to consider a divorce and his transfer to another station

[10] Erich von Manstein, *Lost Victories*, ed. Anthony G. Powell (Chicago, 1958), 75.

[11] Adam, "Erinnerungen," 395. Adam expected Brauchitsch to demonstrate considerable backbone in dealing with Hitler but was soon disappointed.

[12] Siewert interview, January 15, 1970.

[13] Without a doubt the future Frau Feldmarschall was a fine-looking woman with exceptional feminine appeal to which Hitler himself was to prove far from indifferent. Engel interview, May 11, 1970. In intelligence and cultivation she contrasted unfavorably with her future husband. Interview with Ambassador Hasso von Etzdorf, June 26, 1970.

had ,then interrupted the relationship.[14] Before they met again in the early Nazi period, Charlotte had married a bank director named Schmidt, who died by drowning in a bathtub while on a visit to Berlin. When the liaison was resumed, Brauchitsch, now deeply infatuated, pleaded for a divorce, but his wife would grant one without scandal only at the price of a financial settlement that exceeded his means.[15] By 1938 he had, to all intents and purposes, not lived with his wife for some five years and was in a mood to make almost any sacrifice, including that of his career, to liberate himself from this intolerable condition. Matters were in this state of tension when Brauchitsch without warning was summoned to Berlin where fortune beckoned.[16]

## Preludes to Capitulation

The bargaining which eventuated in Brauchitsch's appointment consisted of four-cornered exchanges between Hitler, Goering, Keitel, and Brauchitsch. One close observer and, at that time, confidant of Keitel, Colonel Jodl, sweated the negotiations out on the sidelines. Hitler and Keitel, and no doubt also Hitler and Goering, would confer on the terms to which Brauchitsch was expected to subscribe, Keitel would then carry these to the Hotel Continental and endeavor to soften Brauchitsch's resistance.[17] From time to time Keitel, or he and Brauchitsch together, would visit Goering in the Air Ministry. Finally, on January 31, the day on which Rundstedt administered the final cold douche to Hitler's hopes for Reichenau, the Fuehrer had the first of three meetings with

[14] The first Frau von Brauchitsch has been described as a not very feminine "governess type," a woman lacking in warmth. "Unterredung mit General a. D. Curt Siewert, Hannover, 13.10.51" (in IfZ, ZS 148; cited hereafter as Siewert, "Unterredung"), 4.

[15] Brauchitsch was prepared to devote a major portion of his income to the payment of alimony but his wife, mindful of the uncertainty of life, insisted on a capital sum, which he found himself unable to raise.

[16] This account, involving as it does in the second Frau von Brauchitsch a person still alive, is presented with reluctance. It is, however, so pertinent in explaining the hitherto inexplicable—Brauchitsch's crippling inhibitions in his dealings with Hitler—that it can scarcely be omitted. It is derived from an informant who figured intimately and over a long period in the life of the second Frau von Brauchitsch. The testimony in question has been deposited by the author in the restricted files of the IfZ under the number ZS 1992.

[17] Brauchitsch always stayed at the Continental when in Berlin (Strünck-Gärtner interview, April 18, 1970) and it was at this hotel that, as will be noted later, he made arrangements for Fritsch to meet him on September 27 of that year. Grosskreuz interview, January 15, 1970.

Brauchitsch. In between Keitel would bring Jodl up to date on developments and draw from him occasional advice as well as strength and encouragement.[18] Insofar as circumstances permitted, the entire procedure was covered with a cloak of secrecy; Keitel, for example, was instructed to make his visits to the Chancellery in civilian dress.

It was, of course, not possible to hide completely what was going on from high Army officers. Beck, who as chief of staff considered himself acting commander while Fritsch was suspended and after he had been bullied into resigning, was furious that Keitel should insert himself or be inserted as the promoter of a new appointment. A violent quarrel erupted between the two which was finally mediated by Rundstedt.[19] No doubt Beck felt, and justifiably so, that Keitel was acting as the cat's-paw of Hitler in closing the door on Fritsch by rushing a replacement.

It must have been plain to all participants from the start that Hitler would not content himself with mere changes of personnel, but was resolved to move closer toward the long-aspired "coordination" of the Wehrmacht, notably the Army, with the political system. Keitel, now thoroughly in line, was fully prepared to further such an aim.

The commitments, or should we say the price, to be exacted from Brauchitsch for his elevation to the top post of the Army had been outlined by Keitel to Jodl on January 28. Most probably the general features had been delineated by Hitler and then formulated more precisely by Keitel.[20] They initially comprised moving the Army closer to the National Socialist state and its ideology, bringing in "if necessary" a chief of staff amenable to such a shift (Beck's days in office were thus clearly numbered), and endorsing the new Wehrmacht command structure. Brauchitsch promptly accepted the first two conditions but hedged somewhat on the third, pleading that he was not yet able to oversee the situation and needed to adjust himself. In the main it looked like a good start toward putting over Hitler's program.

During the course of the next days, Jodl's diary recorded a pendu-

---

[18] Apart from Keitel's sketchy account, our sole but, from all appearances, very reliable source on these exchanges is the Jodl Diary, 360–366. Except when otherwise indicated, the analysis that follows is based on this source.

[19] Keitel, 111.

[20] Klaus-Jürgen Müller (*Das Heer und Hitler*, 264n46) is inclined to believe that in large part the conditions were actually suggested by Keitel on the basis of what he had gathered of the Fuehrer's intentions.

lation between confidence and despair as the prospects for the preferred candidate appeared to rise and fall. Brauchitsch was initially reported as "ready for anything," and Goering, coming more and more into the foreground, seemed at first to favor him and be leery about Reichenau. Very early in his talks with Keitel, most probably on January 29,[21] Brauchitsch confessed his inability to take on new, far-reaching responsibilities while his private affairs were in so muddled a state. Keitel was properly sympathetic. After, no doubt, securing Hitler's approval,[22] he summoned one of Brauchitsch's sons (most probably the later Colonel Bernd von Brauchitsch) and dispatched him to Leipzig to plead with his mother to consent to the divorce she had thus far refused. Though available sources are silent, it would seen a safe guess that the message stressed the interests of the state and a tentative commitment on the financial settlement she had demanded.

During the following days the subject of Brauchitsch's personal affairs continued to compete in Jodl's chronicle with the more public aspects of the compact under consideration. The general appears to have brought up the subject of his marital problem once more on January 31, the first of three occasions on which he conferred with Hitler. Since it was merely a matter of money, the Fuehrer assured him, he might put his mind at rest. All that would be necessary would be to name, at the proper time, the sum required.[23]

Brauchitsch was then referred to Goering for a discussion in greater detail. The next day Keitel went with him to the Air Ministry, where Goering, in his turn, voiced sympathy and pledged that, *if other points were settled satisfactorily*, he would shield him against criticism within the Generalität about the divorce.[24]

[21] The manner in which Jodl (363) deals with the problem on the 30th, the dispatch of the younger Brauchitsch on that date to work on his mother, and the necessity of clearing this step with Hitler before taking it—all speak for Brauchitsch's opening his heart to Keitel on the previous day.

[22] Though Keitel at this period assumed what was for him a rather extraordinary degree of initiative, he could scarcely have gone so far as to mediate between Brauchitsch and his wife without authority from Hitler. This was the more imperative because of the financial aspect. Brauchitsch, of course, would have been in a more odious position than ever if now he had failed to become commander in chief. In effect, we may think of him as trapped from the moment he permitted Hitler or his agents to take a hand in his personal affairs.

[23] Engel interview, May 4, 1970.

[24] The divorce itself was no longer a problem, *assuming always* that Brauchitsch received the appointment and the financial support that would go with it. His son had returned from Leipzig with a letter from his mother in which she conveyed her agreement.

# Elevation of Brauchitsch

The reaction he might expect from his fellow generals was obviously a point about which Brauchitsch was much worried and it proved necessary for Goering to again reassure him on February 2. Brauchitsch must steel himself to brave things through, urged the Air Minister, and must not come back later claiming that he should resign because of disagreeable talk. From a purely personal standpoint, in fact, the best of all worlds seemed to be opening up for the previously so harassed general. He, who had been half reconciled to quitting the service and living in a state of semi-disgrace and straitened circumstances, saw now before him the promise of being raised to the military heights, screened against scandal by the most powerful men in the state, and with a guaranteed solution of his family problems. The reverse of the coin if he now failed to secure the appointment need scarcely be stressed. Once he had been privileged to emerge from the shadows and allowed to stand for a moment in the light, it was not to be borne that, his hopes blasted and looking rather ridiculous, he should be forced back into darkness.

The prospects before him if the deal were made were thus all but irresistible and it should be reckoned to Brauchitsch's credit that he still hesitated about some of what was demanded of him. By now the fuller implications of what Hitler expected must have become fairly clear. This was a sweeping purge of the higher Generalität to eliminate those whom Hitler regarded as politically most tainted or as saboteurs of such pet projects as maximum Army expansion and unified Wehrmacht command. The blow would fall hardest on those closest to Brauchitsch in rank and past association. It further threatened to be more than a single-shot affair, for the Fuehrer was adamant about a clean sweep of the officers directing the Army Personnel Office. There General von Schwedler had stood intrepidly against every Nazi inroad.[25] Hitler insisted on nothing less than removing Schwedler and his two principal department heads. He had often complained about them to Blomberg, who would promise to raise the matter with Fritsch and then lack the courage to do so.

It was useless for Brauchitsch to protest that he had already yielded so much and make out that he would in any case do on his own volition most of what Hitler wanted. The changes in the Personnel Office were put to him as a *conditio sine qua non*—so far as Hitler was concerned the most vital part of the package.

[25] P. Kielmansegg, 273.

On February 2 and 3 the screws were progressively tightened on him and his two worried sponsors. Hitler put on a great show of returning to the candidacy of Reichenau and Goering played along with a pose of shifting to his support.

The dodge, as it almost certainly was, proved effective. On the 2nd, Jodl, shocked by Hitler's wholesale gusto for jettisoning "irreplaceable" army and army group commanders, still advised Keitel to urge restraint. By the next morning such a turnover had begun to look to both like a lesser evil when measured against taking Reichenau. The latter, sensing his make-or-break opportunity, had rushed to Berlin where he was impatiently pacing in the wings and frantically importuning the foot-dragging Keitel to secure for him an audience with Hitler. Jodl, a man not given to whimpering, came close to it when contemplating the catastrophe which appeared to threaten. "I support," he lamented, "this [Keitel's] view that every means must be attempted to avert this disaster. Many of the senior generals will leave. General Beck will not remain. General Halder will not condescend to be chief of staff to Reichenau. They will not be able to work together."[26] Such an appointment, the two Wehrmachtamt leaders gloomily agreed, would be a worse blow to the Army than the two it had already received in the cases of Blomberg and Fritsch.

Jodl's diary, its cryptic comments so eloquent in depicting the tension of those days, is silent on just how Brauchitsch did surrender. From his standpoint, Jodl was able to proclaim, "The battle is won." That it probably was no more than a sham battle appears not to have crossed his mind. The real loser, in any event, was the Army, in whose name Brauchitsch had capitulated all along the line. His decision to carry on the uneven contest alone, with Keitel, far from backing him up, persistently counseling appeasement of the dictator, can hardly be explained except by his embarrassment over the intensely personal aspects involved. (As things turned out, some outsiders did catch a glimpse of one or another side of these.) To maintain maximum privacy, he had consulted only with Hitler's representatives, Goering and Keitel, in entering a compact decisive for the most vital concerns of the Army. Thus, to all intents and purposes, Brauchitsch had sold out his fellows when he sold himself. However much he may have salved

[26]Jodl Diary, 365. At Nuremberg Jodl stated that Reichenau had the repute of a "political general" and that it was feared he might "unscrupulously sacrifice the entire old tradition of the Army to the new regime." IMT, XV, 338.

his conscience by telling himself that he had, after all, "saved the Army from Reichenau," he henceforth carried a burden from which, even after he left office four years later, there could be no complete escape.[27]

## The Servitude of Brauchitsch

All in all, Adolf Hitler had every reason to be content with the outcome. Not only had Brauchitsch yielded on the major issues, but he had been led to compromise himself by the attitudes he expressed on such subjects as National Socialism, the church, and the replenishment and expansion of the officer corps.[28] In effect, he undertook to do all and perhaps more than could have been expected from Reichenau. From the dictator's standpoint, there was also assurance of a greater deference to himself than could have been anticipated from the strong-minded and personally less vulnerable "Nazi general."

With respect to this greater dependence of Brauchitsch, there was in the first instance the monetary obligation Hitler had assumed in connection with the appointment. By August the outlines of a settlement calling for a capital sum of RM 80,000 had been agreed upon.[29] The divorce itself came on August 4 and the marriage to Charlotte Schmidt-Rüffer followed on September 23. Final details were regulated in several meetings between Brauchitsch and

[27] In the view of the present writer, this psychological burden and perhaps the continuing fear of personal "exposure" alone can explain the dastardly article Brauchitsch wrote for the *Völkische Beobachter* after July 20, 1944, in which he denounced so many former comrades. The action was the more abominable since Brauchitsch had known of the conspiratorial activities of the group involved at least since September 1938 and had been informed of them repeatedly in the years which followed. In November 1941, just a few weeks before losing his command, he had pledged himself to cooperate with the conspirators once Hitler was assassinated. (On this latter point see Ulrich von Hassell, *Vom anderen Deutschland: Aus den nachgelassenen Tagebüchern 1938-1944*, Frankfurt, 1946, 207; cited hereafter as Hassell Diaries.) At Nuremberg the flustered general tried to justify himself to Halder by claiming that the article was written in the hope of saving a condemned relative, whose fate, it had been intimated to him, would be favorably influenced by such a repudiation of the conspirators. Helmut Krausnick, "Aktenvermerk über eine unterredung mit Generaloberst Halder am 25. September 1954" (in IfZ, ZS 240 (III)). If it is true that he yielded because of this blackmail, it must still be characterized as another sacrifice of his comrades to his personal concerns.

[28] Keitel, 111.

[29] The sum involved has been variously reported up to a quarter of a million marks. The RM 80,000 figure was attested to Major Siewert by Captain von Both, Fritsch's adjutant. Siewert interview, January 15, 1970. In one of a string of perjuries committed by Brauchitsch at Nuremberg after the war, he denied that he had received any monetary gift from Hitler. IMT, XX, 583.

Reichsleiter Philip Bouhler, the manager of Hitler's financial affairs.[30] Perhaps innocence more than a lack of delicacy will explain the general's going to Bouhler's office, which served as Hitler's personal chancellery, in his official car with his command flag flying and leaving it parked before the building.[31]

Curt Siewert, previously Fritsch's and then Brauchitsch's first staff officer, believes the latter did not then really comprehend the position he was placed in by Hitler's gift, conceiving it to conform with traditional grants awarded from time to time to Prussian military leaders for services rendered.[32] However much one may wish to be charitable, it is necessary to adduce against this view that Brauchitsch knew well that the money came out of Hitler's personal pocket and that whatever services the dictator had in mind lay in the future.[33] The types of servitude to be exacted from him should have been clear enough from the conditions to which he had been obliged to subscribe to gain his appointment.

More serious from the standpoint of the hold Hitler was to exercise over his new Army commander was the murky background of the second marriage itself. Except for the additional encumbrance of the prolonged previous adultery, it did not differ too much from that of Blomberg, who, like him, had been determined at all costs to marry a lady "with something of a past." Brauchitsch had just witnessed the grim fate of the War Minister and was soon

[30] Engel interview, May 4, 1970. Letter of General Engel to Dr. Heinrich Uhlig, April 12, 1952 (in IfZ, ZS 10). Engel Diary, entry of October 18, 1938.

[31] As observed by Engel, who knew about the arrangement from Hitler personally. Interview, May 4, 1970.

[32] Curt Siewert, *Schuldig? Die Generale unter Hitler. Stellung und Einfluss der hohen militärischen Führung im nationalsozialistischen Staat: Das Mass ihrer Verantwortung und Schuld* (Bad Nauheim, 1968), 86. Halder, like Siewert always inclined to take a generous, protective attitude toward Brauchitsch, maintains that Hitler's gift did not influence him in professional matters and otherwise only insofar as a natural feeling of gratitude was concerned. Letter of Halder to Dr. Heinrich Uhlig, May 25, 1953 (in IfZ, ZS 240 (V)). However laudable the intention, this persistent effort to present Brauchitsch as a man of unfailing distinguished sentiments simply does not accord with the facts as revealed in this chapter. Siewert's mother-hen impulse whenever Brauchitsch came under attack led him for many years to deny strenuously that Hitler had provided financial support for the divorce ("Unterredung," 3, and supplement 1 to it, as well as an oral statement to Klaus-Jürgen Müller as communicated by the latter to the author). More recently, as in *Schuldig?* and in conversation with the author, he has admitted the facts as here stated. Interview, January 15, 1970.

[33] Hitler's huge fortune was derived from such sources as tax-free book royalties and payments from the postal service for the use of his picture on German stamps, a type of emolument that certainly would never have occurred to previous German heads of state. See Speer, 104.

Heydrich and Himmler, chief figures (with Goering) in the
intrigue against Fritsch (courtesy Bundesarchiv Bestand)

Blomberg, Goering, Fritsch, and Hitler at the Nuremberg
party rally of 1935 (courtesy Bundesarchiv Bestand)

Colonel General Baron Werner von Fritsch

Field Marshal Werner von Blomberg (courtesy Bundesarchiv Koblenz;
copyright A-B-C)

Hans Bernd Gisevius

Hans Oster

Theodor Strünck

Gisevius, Oster, and Strünck
in the Dolomites in 1937

General Ludwig Beck

Rear Admiral Wilhelm Canaris

The Wehrmacht adjutant, Colonel Friedrich Hossbach, accompanying
Hitler on an official visit (courtesy Bundesarchiv Bestand)

General Wilhelm Keitel
(courtesy Bundesarchiv Bestand)

Colonel General Walther von Brauchitsch
(courtesy Bundesarchiv Koblenz;
copyright A-B-C)

Colonel Alfred Jodl
(courtesy Bundesarchiv Bestand)

Count Rüdiger von der Goltz                  Judge Karl Sack

Brauchitsch confers on Fritsch the honorary colonelcy of Artillery Regiment 12 at Gross Born on August 12, 1938 (courtesy Bundesarchiv Bestand)

to learn what was in process of being done to the wholly innocent Fritsch. The bitter and frightening example of colleagues who had somehow come to stand in the way of Nazi hierarchs must have lain heavily on his spirit. He could hardly fail to feel trapped by a man so pitiless in exploiting the infirmities of others for the promotion of his designs. There was no way of telling when Hitler might learn more about the antecedents of the second marriage or of ascertaining how much he already knew. Such anxieties can only have been shared and further stimulated by those of his new wife,[34] who was in the habit of reminding him, whenever he seemed swayed by his subordinates to stand up to Hitler, of "how much we owe the Fuehrer."[35]

As a matter of fact, Hitler already knew more than he needed to. Just a year later when a case was appealed to him in which Brauchitsch wanted to dismiss from the service a young officer despite his readiness to marry a girl of good family whom he had made pregnant, the Fuehrer flew into a towering rage and reversed the decision. Such conduct was typical of these aristocratic generals, he ranted. Here this man Brauchitsch dealt unfeelingly with a lowly lieutenant. Yet he himself, as the Fuehrer well knew, had consorted in such and such places with his later second wife while he was still married to the first. He had, when appointing Brauchitsch, regarded this as his private affair. But the same rule should then apply equally to the offending young officer.[36]

[34] Whatever the anxieties of the second Frau von Brauchitsch, her extravagant pro-Nazi attitudes were not assumed by her as a protective covering. Ulrich von Hassell exaggerated little when he labeled her "a 200 percent Nazi." Hassell Diaries, 71. She had strongly manifested such sentiments well before Hitler's accession to power. Restricted file of the IfZ, ZS 1992.

[35] That his wife importuned Brauchitsch in this fashion was common knowledge in the upper circles of the OKH. It was presumed to be her influence that frequently made Brauchitsch abandon positions overnight to which he had committed himself, with every indication of earnestness, on the previous day. Etzdorf interview, June 24, 1970. The same is attested to in more veiled fashion by Halder, who relates that her influence was "unmistakably acting in the same direction," i.e., by reminding her husband of their debt to Hitler. Letter of Halder to Dr. Heinrich Uhlig, May 26, 1952 (in IfZ, ZS 240 (I)). Etzdorf further recounts how she would naively defend Hitler's shabby treatment of various persons by saying that they had "annoyed [ geärgert] the Fuehrer." Her questionable background was far from a well-kept secret and was, at least in some measure, well known in Opposition circles that were trying to work on Brauchitsch. Interview with Countess Charlotte von der Schulenburg and Irmgard Langbehn, June 19, 1970.

[36] Captain Engel, who presented the case to Hitler, had urgently entreated Brauchitsch and others in the OKH who were concerned with it not to oblige him to do so, predicting exactly what the reaction was to be. Interviews, May 4 and 11, 1970.

A feeling of deep personal obligation joined with a gnawing sense of vulnerability to pressure and blackmail provides much of the answer to why this soldier of repute, in the words of his own chief of staff, was so often to stand before Hitler "like a little cadet before his commandant."[37] Soon his extreme inhibitions when confronting the dictator seemed, even to remote observers, to betoken some hold the latter had over him. "Hitler," noted Sir Robert Vansittart in a memorandum of August 9, 1938, "has a stranglehold on Brauchitsch of some private and discreditable kind; whether it is connected with the fact that Brauchitsch is billed for divorce or for something dirtier and rifer still, I am at present unable to say."[38]

It was no more than an educated guess but Sir Robert's prognosis could not have been more accurate. Awareness of his perilous situation could not fail to impose on Brauchitsch strict limits to his self-confidence in all dealings with the Fuehrer.

When Hitler, concluding their third meeting on the morning of February 4, extended his hand and announced the appointment as commander in chief, a relationship was inaugurated that was fateful for the future of the German Army. The dictator had gained for this high office a nonpolitical soldier whom he had shackled to himself by both personal and professional chains. The cynicism of selecting a man in Brauchitsch's personal situation to supplant one of so spotless a life as Fritsch requires no comment. The exchange was an all too appropriate climax to the unscrupulous maneuvers by which Adolf Hitler propelled himself into dominance over the military leadership of Germany.

[37] As characterized by Halder in November 1939. V. Müller, 374.
[38] PRO, FO371/21736.

# CHAPTER VIII

# Hitler Masters
# the Fritsch Crisis

As long as the resignation and replacement of Werner von Fritsch hung fire, there was a measure of reality about proposals to counter the intrigue of which he was plainly a target though certainly not the only one. During the week before February 4 every conceivable expedient was propounded on his behalf. Suggestions covered the range from comparatively feeble to veritably desperate measures. Some were the quickly abandoned or rejected brain children of individual supporters. Others were seriously considered by evolving Opposition sectors and possible implementation was explored.

There were many impediments to achieving agreement and a measure of coordination in trying to thwart the rulers of the National Socialist state. Merely to disseminate basic information to concerned quarters involved grave hazards. Hitler had done his utmost to inhibit discussion of the situations of Blomberg and Fritsch. Orders to maintain the strictest secrecy were given to all those to whom he spoke of the affair. It was easy to make this appear a show of consideration for the two unhappy generals and was thus almost invulnerable to criticism. The dictator's purpose was further aided by the natural reluctance of the military to call public attention to the shame of Blomberg and the mud thrown on Fritsch. The alternative course of giving maximum publicity to developments in concert with an appeal to the Army and the nation was considered but never adopted.

Keitel, in particular, had strong family reasons for hushing things up as much as possible and getting them over with. In his key position—until February 4 he virtually sat in the War Minister's chair—he proved a zealous collaborator in conveying and adding weight to the Fuehrer's injunctions to silence.

231

But the rumor mills of Berlin were not to be held in check—too much, even before his departure from office, had been stirred up by Blomberg's marriage. In government, party, and other circles attuned to political crosscurrents, there was soon awareness of a trial of strength of some sort between Hitler and the Army. In an effort to disguise their visits, generals like Keitel, Beck, and Rundstedt might be directed to come to the Chancellery in civilian garb and enter through back doors, but somehow their appearance there came to be bruited about. Most vital, the small Opposition group in the Abwehr was feverishly engaged in disseminating, through one channel or another, the information it had gathered.

### Efforts of the Abwehr Activists in Berlin

By the end of January the Abwehr enemies of the regime had made substantial progress in picking up information, evaluating its significance, and transmitting the results to wherever they hoped to stir action. They had also moved to formulate proposals on courses which intervention in affairs might take.

The one thing that the men who, in some form or measure, were linked with this group had anticipated for years was a major attempt by the SS to intrude in the military realm. It was unsettling that this invasion, now that it had come, was not the climax of a series of visible, largely predictable moves on such a familiar issue as transforming SS elite formations into a new branch of the armed services. Instead, owing to the wholly fortuitous surrender of Blomberg to an ill-directed passion, a situation had arisen in which both the War Minister and the Army's commander in chief, the key figures of the military hierarchy, were being ousted from their high offices at the same critical instant.

A further complicating aspect of the crisis was that while the individual targets were all too painfully evident, the identity, modus operandi, and more specific aims of the attacking parties had thus far been only partially revealed. The lineup was soon clear enough, but it remained something of a puzzle just who was initiator, accomplice, or (perhaps) a partial dupe.

The group of men who during the Fritsch crisis per se can be said to have composed the roll of those actively concerned with counterattack was a pitifully small one. In the Abwehr itself it included with certainty only Canaris and Oster, with Gisevius, though still a civilian outsider, to be classed a virtual third. Heinz played no more than a peripheral role and that mainly in the post-February 4 period. Perhaps half a dozen other officers, such as Franz Liedig, Hans Piekenbrock, and Helmuth Groscurth, head of Abwehr II, the sabotage division, though uninitiated, were sufficiently well known to their activist colleagues to be counted upon if needed. Later mainstays of what could more legitimately be called an Abwehr Opposition circle such as Theodor Strünck and Erwin von Lahousen were not as yet members of the intelligence organization.

Sufficiently closely linked with Oster and Gisevius to be classed within the core group were Goerdeler, Schacht, and Nebe, whose activities during the Fritsch affair can be regarded as largely in step with their own. As the Fritsch case itself developed, one can further add Dr. Sack and, to an increasing degree, Dohnanyi. No more appropriate designation for so loose and mixed a grouping presenting itself, one is reduced to speaking of an "Abwehr-associated group" or, more simply, an "Abwehr group." Though inadequate and at times somewhat misleading, in view of the as yet infinitesimal and highly personalized Abwehr base at that period, the term, for want of any better, will be employed hereafter to designate the core group from which the German military Opposition was gradually to evolve.

The role of Canaris, often so qualified and nebulous in later days of active conspiracy, can almost be labeled conspicuous both during the Fritsch crisis and subsequently when it shrank to no more than the Fritsch case. The meager surviving contemporary documentation, such as Jodl's diary, as well as the testimony of postwar survivors reveals his hand at point after point where there were efforts to stir up feeling or enlist support. It was he who established and maintained intimate contact with Hossbach in the days which immediately followed the adjutant's dismissal from the Chancellery (January 28), keeping him *au courant* with each new discovery about the nature and course of the intrigue.[1] In these days there also germinated a new intimacy and sense of solidarity between the admiral and Beck. From their consultation and the deliberation of Canaris, Oster, and Gisevius on more concrete steps sprang whatever there was in the way of broader direction

[1] Hossbach, *Zwischen Wehrmacht und Hitler*, 112. Canaris usually looked in on Hossbach when visiting the OKH; at other times Hossbach would go to him. Hossbach interview, July 1, 1971.

in the counteroffensive launched against the Goering-SS combine.[2]

Canaris is also credited with exerting himself to stiffen the back of Raeder and, after Hitler's decision on the Army command, that of Brauchitsch, by feeding them information on current and anticipated moves by Fritsch's persecutors.[3] His ambiguous position with the commander in chief of the Navy, who had been so unenthusiastic about his appointment, no doubt was something of a handicap in that quarter.

Another person whom the admiral kept needling was Keitel. The head of the Wehrmachtamt and busily emerging chief of the High Command of the Armed Forces was obviously proceeding full sail into the opposite camp, but older loyalties still exercised some claim on him. In the course of his dealings with Hitler, for example, he did represent the Army's position on the court-martial for Fritsch. Canaris also tried to light a fire under Keitel's immediate subordinates and advisers in the Wehrmachtamt by shocking Jodl and the newly arrived General Max von Viebahn with an account of Fritsch's Wannsee (third) interrogation by the Gestapo.[4]

From the Abwehr Opposition enclave in the War Ministry the lines of communication ran to the OKH and other points in Berlin where past experience had indicated a disposition to move against the regime or where the immediate crisis gave hope of translating the rising indignation into action. In the Army command itself, Beck, despite his decision to remain out of the foreground, could be counted on to back any really serious move against the forces behind the attack on Fritsch. Close to him, General Halder, both then and during the following months, was the major spur to action within the staff. In Fritsch's own office, Captain von Both was heart and soul for whatever smacked of positive courses. Hossbach, who continued to direct the Central Division of the OKH while awaiting a troop assignment, was also on deck throughout these fateful days and grimly advocating strong measures.

## Efforts of Schacht and Goerdeler

Army leaders, however, were confined to a peripheral role at this juncture. Whatever there was of concrete proposals and of initial moves, in one direction or another, came from the small Abwehr group in collaboration with two outside civilians, Schacht and

[2] Abshagen, 179.
[3] *Ibid.*, 179-180.
[4] Jodl Diary, 368, entry of February 26, 1938. See below, p. 249.

# Hitler Masters the Fritsch Crisis

Goerdeler. During the Fritsch affair the role of Schacht was a more limited one than that which he had played as a high-level agitator and recruiter in 1936-37 or what it was to become during the following spring and summer. From the time (January 27) when he had alerted Gisevius to the state of affairs in the War Ministry until the conclusion of Fritsch's trial in mid-March, his part in Opposition affairs was restricted to rather isolated attempts to reach key military figures. Beyond this he was significant for the hopes and plans of the Abwehr activists because of his known advocacy of positive courses, his important and far-reaching foreign connections, and his availability for a post-Hitler government.

It was through a message from Gisevius that Goerdeler was warned about the witches' brew that had been stirred up in Berlin. In view of his innumerable contacts with persons hostile to the regime, the signal of alarm may also have reached him through other channels. By January 28 he was in Berlin,[5] where in the following days he evidenced a feverish activity. He first tried through Beck to arrange a meeting with Fritsch, who in his rattled and heartsick condition (it was probably the day of his second interrogation in the Prinz-Albrecht-Strasse) turned down his request. He next was taken by Gisevius to see Gürtner who, in typical fashion, wrung his hands in distress but shrank from any course that could lead to a personal collision with Hitler.[6] He also met individually with Schacht; the Reich Minister of Finance, Count Schwerin von Krosigk; the president of the Reich Military Court, General Heitz; and Rundstedt's chief of staff, General Högner.[7]

Though there seems to be no record on the reaction of any of these gentlemen, it is a safe guess that the only contact which bore fruit was that with Schacht. The activities of the Reichsbank president during the next days indeed imply that something like a division of assignments was worked out between them.[8] It was in the nature of things that he should exploit his intimate contacts with the War Economy Department of the War Ministry to stir

---

[5] This assumption is based on Gisevius's statement (*Bis zum bittern Ende*, 271-272) that Goerdeler saw Gürtner after failing in an effort to get through to Fritsch and *before* the Minister of Justice had delivered his formal opinion to Hitler (the 29th).

[6] Gisevius, *Bis zum bittern Ende*, 271-272. Gisevius recording, July 1971.

[7] From a notation by Goerdeler cited by Ritter, 471n40.

[8] The fact that Schacht's name leads the list of those whom Goerdeler notes among those he called on during these days at least implies that the visit to him came first. It definitely antedates Goerdeler's trip to Leipzig. See below, pp. 255-258.

things up there. We find him sending Lieutenant Colonel Drews, liaison officer to the Economics Ministry, to tell General Thomas of his "impression" that the SS was employing all means to "cast suspicion upon the Wehrmacht and utilizing its moment of weakness to drive it against the wall."[9]

Schacht's first personal target was Raeder, whom he hoped to persuade that some united counteraction to the attack on Fritsch was imperative. The Navy commander had taken some hand in developments since he had been told by Keitel on January 26 of the Blomberg situation.[10] His indignation about such an offense to tradition surpassed that of the Army leaders and led him to the extraordinary step of sanctioning Wangenheim's trip to Rome to demand the suicide of the man he had served as adjutant. On the developments concerning Blomberg and the dismissal of Hossbach, Raeder was briefed by Commander von Puttkamer, who also reported to him on the talk he had initiated with Hitler on the 29th to help Hossbach. It must have been immediately after hearing this that he himself hurried to the Chancellery to look into matters more deeply and apparently to put in a good word for Fritsch as successor to Blomberg.[11] Raeder of course knew that only an Army man was likely to be considered for the position and he had always had the highest opinion of Fritsch, whose choice as commander in chief he had warmly welcomed and sought to further in 1934.[12]

The frustrating inadequacies of Raeder's memoirs are nowhere more evident than in the little he tells about his encounter with Hitler and his own reactions then and in the days which followed. Asked by Hitler whom he recommended to succeed Blomberg, he unhesitatingly endorsed Fritsch, only to be told that the general could not be considered because of a morals charge against him. Hitler then indulged in the cheap but flattering gesture of offering Raeder the Wehrmacht command he had, two or three days earlier,

[9] Jodl Diary, 365, entry of February 3, 1938.
[10] *Ibid.*, 357, entry of January 26, 1938.
[11] The timing given here is based on the fact that, according to Puttkamer (interview of June 27, 1970), his talks with Keitel and Hitler were the day after Hossbach's dismissal (the 28th) and that his second call on Hitler as related below came before the arrival in the Chancellery of Schmundt, almost certainly in the afternoon of the 29th. This would crowd Puttkamer's two meetings with Hitler as well as Raeder's visit into a few hours of the 29th. When this was pointed out to Puttkamer in a second interview (July 10, 1971), he considered it more probable that the exchanges took place over a period of two days (January 29 and 30).
[12] Raeder, II, 120.

decided to take himself and received the expected negative reply.[13]

This is the whole of Raeder's own story and it is necessary to piece it out from other almost equally fragmentary sources and by a good measure of deduction. According to an account which reached Abwehr headquarters, Raeder pointed out to Hitler that there would be much raising of eyebrows if a Blomberg scandal were immediately followed by one concerning Fritsch, especially since the Gestapo seemed to have a hand in both cases. Hitler was said to have simply shown the admiral the Fritsch dossier, after reading which Raeder refrained from further comment.[14]

A reminder of how Hitler had manipulated Keitel in this matter suggests a vital gap in this story. Hitler can hardly have failed to show Raeder the undated "opinion" he had got from Gürtner on the 26th (the longer, more formal one was delivered to him only on the 29th itself or on the 30th). It may further be assumed that he played the same trick on the rather unsophisticated sailor that had worked so well with the naive chief of the Wehrmachtamt—conveying the impresssion that it was Gürtner who had initiated the whole business concerning Fritsch two years before.

Raeder, who was never up to Hitler's wiles, was said to be thunderstruck and at least half convinced. His reaction is another strong argument that he had been given the full treatment including the Gürtner fable. Standing by itself, the dossier which had looked so questionable to Hossbach and to Gürtner would hardly have scored such a devastating effect on him. As with so many others, the dictator also had conjured up a specter from Fritsch's reference to the two Hitler-boys. To Puttkamer the admiral confessed to having been more struck by this aspect as dramatized by Hitler than by the reported assertions of Schmidt. He seemed completely horrified and expressed himself so.[15] Albert Speer, who was entering Hitler's workroom as Raeder was leaving, describes him as utterly distraught, pale, and staggering like someone on the verge of a heart attack.[16]

We do not know whether Hitler pressed Raeder for suggestions regarding a new Army commander; if so Raeder had been too

[13] *Ibid.*

[14] Gisevius, *Bis zum bittem Ende*, 270.

[15] Puttkamer interviews, June 27, 1970, and July 10, 1971. Admiral Puttkamer cannot recall whether Hitler made a particular point of the Gürtner "opinion."

[16] Speer, 128. Speer places this incident on February 2, but it seems most unlikely that Raeder should have been thrown into such a state on that date, for which there is also no record of his having called at the Chancellery.

shocked to respond. After gathering his wits on returning to his quarters, the importance of getting in a word on this issue must have been brought home to him. No doubt he, like others, had appalling visions of Hitler's choosing Goering, whom he detested, or Himmler, whom he feared. It does not seem to have occurred to him, as it had immediately to the generous-hearted Beck, to insist that the problem of a successor should not even be raised until Fritsch's guilt had been determined by a proper investigation and trial. Still too upset, perhaps, to go back to the Chancellery himself, he sent Puttkamer to submit a strong vote for Rundstedt, whom he lauded as a general who enjoyed most completely the confidence of the officer corps. By selecting him for a stopgap appointment, Hitler would gain the necessary leisure to make a more long-range choice among younger candidates.[17]

Hitler received Puttkamer cordially and put on an effective act of a puzzled leader besieged by contradictory advice. "What should I do?" he said. "On one side I am asked to take Rundstedt. On another the recommendation is for Brauchitsch. There we would immediately have a divorce problem. I am not supposed to take Reichenau because he is reputed to be too much of a National Socialist." It would all have been so simple if only this business had not arisen about Fritsch. Otherwise he would have been the clear choice for War Minister and could have himself selected the new Army commander. Hitler then took a list of generals and ran his finger down it one by one. Several times he asked Puttkamer his opinion until the amazed officer protested, "This is too much for me. I do not know these gentlemen that well. Please ask Rundstedt and Beck to come advise you. They are able to speak for both troop and General Staff officers."[18] Therewith the naval adjutant took his leave and reported back to his chief.

Such was the state of affairs with respect to Raeder when Schacht came to make the first of his calls on major figures of the military firmament. In the year of his death Schacht could only recall of this one that Raeder had listened with a sympathetic air to what he had to say about the intrigue that seemed to lie behind the assault on Fritsch and about the need of embarking on countermeasures. The future grand admiral had merely responded that the

---

[17] Puttkamer interview, June 27, 1970. Puttkamer believes that Raeder's vote for Rundstedt was entirely his own initiative and not a second-thought response to a request for advice by Hitler. Interview, July 10, 1971.

[18] *Ibid.*

responsibility for such moves did not rest with him; it was really a problem for the Army.[19] It was the same fainthearted retort he was later to make in repelling the importunities of Commander von Puttkamer in the matter of Fritsch's rehabilitation.[20]

Having failed to make any significant impression on the head of the Navy, Schacht next decided to try his hand with the senior general of the Army, Gerd von Rundstedt. Rundstedt, however, was out of the city and did not return until the 31st. It was probably at this juncture, therefore, that Schacht called on Joachim von Stülpnagel, who though no longer on active service was next in seniority to Fritsch and known to be his closest personal friend among the top officers of the Generalität.

Stülpnagel received Schacht cordially and listened sympathetically to his plea for intervention on Fritsch's behalf. The general pointed out to the Minister of Economics that he not only commanded no troops but had not done so for seven years. Thus he had few connections with younger officers and had largely ceased to have any contact with such contemporaries as Bock and Rundstedt.[21] What Stülpnagel must have said about the latter can hardly have offered much encouragement about the results of an appeal to him. Schacht was already doubtful: after years of discussion with Opposition associates about the relative promise of prominent military men as prospective recruits to their cause, he did not allow his hopes concerning Rundstedt to rise too high. There seemed a chance, of course, that the shock of what was happening to Fritsch, with whom Rundstedt was on excellent personal terms, had made some impact. Schacht guessed, however, that at such a delicate juncture of affairs Rundstedt might try to evade a meeting if one were requested over the telephone. The banker therefore chose the somewhat arbitrary course of simply writing a note to the general's wife announcing his call for the following morning,[22] probably February 1 or 2.[23]

In Rundstedt's case, as in that of Raeder, the prior meeting with Hitler helped to make Schacht's visit a fruitless one. The general

---

[19] Schacht interview, October 9, 1969. Much the same account is given by Gisevius, *Bis zum bittern Ende*, 271.

[20] See below, p. 388.

[21] Stülpnagel, 358.

[22] Gisevius, *Bis zum bittern Ende*, 271.

[23] Since Schacht was determined to see Rundstedt as soon as he heard of the general's return to Berlin, his note to Frau von Rundstedt would have been written on January 31 or February 1.

had been on a tour of inspection in Königsberg when, on January 30, he was reached by the plea from Beck to return to the capital immediately. Rundstedt declined to fly but agreed to take the night express. At the station he was met by the chief of staff who gave him the astounding news of the departure from office of Blomberg and Fritsch and told him that he was expected at the Chancellery at eleven. Beck's question on whether he would consider assuming the command of the Army Rundstedt answered with a firm negative.

After a quick call on Fritsch to assure him of his complete confidence, Rundstedt went to the Chancellery, as ordered, in civilian clothes and through a back entry.[24] Hitler received him in a state of agitation bordering on hysteria. The overwhelmed general was utterly convinced of his sincerity, so that even after the war he insisted that this had not been playacting. No doubt the tensions of the previous days had also taken their toll on the dictator and he hardly needed his extraordinary histrionic talents to feign excitement. He had been facing one challenge of persuasion after another all week and now had his line down pat. Certainly what he moaned to Rundstedt about the blow to his moral sensibilities was nonsense.

Hitler first dealt with the Blomberg affair and emitted a stream of invective about the laggard attitude of the generals on the issues of rearmament and the Rhineland occupation. He sharply rejected a demand that Blomberg be summoned before a court of honor but finally agreed that his name should be stricken from the roll of officers.

The Fuehrer then turned to the case of Fritsch, asserted that Himmler had presented the charges relating to him several years before, and once more affirmed that, except for this, he would have given him the War Ministry. Rundstedt indignantly protested the way that such slanders against a high officer had been kept secret without giving him a chance to clear himself. In his opinion Fritsch had been blackened by "certain quarters" (clearly meaning Himmler) for political reasons, just as he—Rundstedt—had at times been accused of working to restore the monarchy. Hitler defended his own conduct by saying that external factors had dictated his silence; only now had the problem of Blomberg's successor obliged him to take up the matter. Fritsch by his cold, reserved manner,

[24] This account of Rundstedt's meeting with Hitler is based on statements prepared by him when a prisoner in Britain and at Nuremberg and an interview in the early fifties with Baron von Siegler (in IfZ, ZS 129 (I, II) ).

240

instead of flying into a passion, had made his guilt believable. Rundstedt retorted that, as a true gentleman, Fritsch could only react with icy contempt to such charges. He then demanded in his own name, and in that of the Army, an immediate legal clarification and, in the certain event that Fritsch's innocence was established, an appropriate satisfaction. To this Hitler agreed with obvious reluctance.

Hitler then said that, since he could not expect the Army to put up with Goering, he was himself assuming the direct command of the Wehrmacht with Keitel as his chief of staff. Rundstedt approved with the strongly expressed proviso that Keitel's sphere be confined to administrative matters and involve no command function. To this Hitler assented, adding that for later he had in mind a "generalissimo à la Gamelin." "Very good," retorted Rundstedt; then after his certain exoneration this post should go to Fritsch. The dictator, clearly taken aback, digested this in silence.

Hitler concluded by taking up the choice of a new Army commander. It will be recalled that in the following exchange he rejected Beck, found Rundstedt adamant in his opposition to Reichenau, and elicited a cordial reaction to Brauchitsch. The general then took his leave after being strictly enjoined to secrecy.

On leaving the Chancellery, Rundstedt went to relate to Fritsch and Beck what had taken place. He also asked for another meeting with Hitler for the next day with the thought of nailing down more securely the concession on the court-martial and the understanding on the functions of Keitel. Hitler used the occasion to inquire about other high officers, to all of whom Rundstedt was careful to give a good character.

The sum total of the impression made on Rundstedt by these two meetings left only a meager chance that Schacht could win him for any positive action. Hitler had thoroughly succeeded in convincing this key figure of his own sincerity and at the same time in reassuring him to a considerable degree on the points of his greatest anxiety. Blomberg had been delivered to a deserved disgrace though he had been spared the worst. Army fears about Goering's receiving the War Ministry had been allayed and Hitler's own tenancy made to look like merely a temporary measure before the choice of another general. The muddleheaded Keitel seemed to have been rendered sufficiently harmless so far as the Army's interests were concerned. Rundstedt had been added to the array of innocents, headed by Fritsch himself, who counted Hitler and (somewhat more doubtfully) Goering among the dupes of the intriguers. It was assumed that they only needed to be enlightened through the legal procedure that Hitler, however reluctantly, promised to place in the hands of a court-martial. Fritsch had been assured an appropriate rehabilitation once his name had been cleared. Finally, there was the hope that the SS leaders would receive their due once Hitler had been made to realize the iniquitous role they were playing.

When Schacht appeared at the residence of the Berlin group commander the morning of February 1 or 2, Rundstedt seems to have looked on him as an interloping busybody. "Mr. Minister, my lips are sealed," was his haughty greeting. Schacht, understandably put out and also in consternation over so much naiveté, rejoined that he had not come with the thought of gaining information, that he probably knew rather more than might be welcome to his reluctant host. He only wished to *tell* him something—how vital it was to launch some counteraction rather than to leave all initiative to the other side. Thereupon he was given the huffy answer that Rundstedt did not need to be told what he had to do.[25]

The story about Rundstedt deserves this measure of attention because it is typical of the situation and sentiments of many of those high officers of the German Army who, in their minds and hearts, had not yet come to a parting of the ways with the regime. Equally decisive for what happened, or failed to happen, in January–February 1938 were the perplexity and helplessness of others who had reached this point or were on the threshold of doing so. These more determined spirits were confused and inhibited by uncertainty or disagreement about just what could be done. Of the various courses which at one time or another were proposed, particularly in the Abwehr Opposition center, the most frequently discussed was some kind of common action on the part of the principal generals. This obviously had the greatest assurance of success if Fritsch himself issued the appeal and this was urged upon him by a number of his closest friends. It will be recalled how Joachim von Stülpnagel, one of the few to whom he felt sufficiently close to unburden himself on his shattering experience in the Chancellery, had begged him to appeal to the principal generals to declare their solidarity with him. Fritsch's reply had been to defer to whatever the Generalität should be prepared to do on

[25] Gisevius, *Bis zum bittern Ende*, 271. Schacht interviews, October 9 and November 6, 1969.

its own. Thereby he played directly into the hands of Hitler, who wanted nothing so much as to make the whole affair appear a private and personal matter without political overtones.[26]

Fritsch similarly took the wind out of the sails of the faithful General von Schwedler, whose fate, unknown to both, was just then a major issue in negotiations between Hitler and Brauchitsch. Fritsch himself, Schwedler told the later General Horst von Mellinthin, did not want anyone to try to mobilize the Generalität on his behalf. Mellinthin pleaded that it was up to the Generalität to take the initiative by placing itself unreservedly at Fritsch's disposition. The difficulty lay in the vast expansion of the Army and the corresponding ballooning of the officer corps at all levels: it had not, since about 1936, been possible to count even on the top commanders. For some time Fritsch himself had lacked confidence in the completeness of their support and occasionally he had expressed to Mellinthin his disappointment with this state of affairs.[27]

One of the shortcomings of any plan for a strike of the Generalität was that, once Hitler had consented to the court-martial, it was no longer easy to define or secure agreement on specific demands that might be addressed to him. The assurance that Fritsch would not be railroaded on trumped-up charges did much to satisfy many of those who were in on the crisis. The secrecy which Hitler had so largely succeeded in imposing shrouded at the critical moment the vital issue of Fritsch's expulsion from office. Few knew anything of the pressure to force his "resignation," even fewer about the hassle surrounding the appointment of Brauchitsch. Once Fritsch had resigned, and a successor who was basically acceptable to the Generalität was well on the way to appointment, a common action of the generals had lost much of its point.

No doubt this played something of a role in Hitler's breaking the promise he had made to Beck during the night of January 26-27, that the chief of staff would be heard on all personnel actions relating to the Army. Not once during the crisis was Beck summoned to the Chancellery.[28] He would have been certain to raise again his objection to any successor's being considered as long as Fritsch's guilt had not been established. This was one

[26] K.-J. Müller, *Das Heer und Hitler*, 265.
[27] Mellenthin, "Niederschrift," 13.
[28] As related by Beck personally. Hassell Papers, notation of April 4, 1938. Gisevius recording, July 1971.

viewpoint which Hitler was determined to eliminate entirely from the discussion.

## The Issue of Civil War

Both during the course of the Fritsch affair and in all later situations in which an appeal to force was considered or urged by Opposition elements, the most unfailing curb on a decision to act unquestionably was uncertainty about what wider support could be anticipated. Even when there was the most confidence in the cooperation of key military leaders, doubts invariably would be advanced about whether orders would be obeyed by company grade officers and the rank and file. Furthermore, even when this assessment was on the optimistic side, there would still remain a question about the reaction of the Navy and a most pessimistic view about the Luftwaffe. Added to this were nightmare visions of civil war in which the Army would be arrayed against large sections of the nation led by the uniformed formations of the party.

Much of the postwar review of the period has given support to the legitimacy of such doubts and apprehensions. Particular weight must be attached to judgments voiced by men who originally counted among the advocates of an appeal to force. Among these is General Hossbach. Speaking in the mid-fifties, he confessed that new insights had persuaded him that he had been mistaken in 1938; that neither the contemporary state of the Army nor that of public sentiment justified a hope of success. The Army, and this remains his view today, was too divided, the nation too negatively conditioned by the weaknesses and errors of the Weimar period and by five years of National Socialist rule, to allow the clock to be turned back through force of arms.[29]

As one might expect, such judgments are well nigh universal among those survivors who already entertained them when, at one stage or another of the period 1938-44, they were solicited for and withheld their support in connection with whatever putsch project might be afoot at the particular time.[30] Against this it may

[29] Letter of Hossbach to Helmut Krausnick, March 8, 1955 (in IfZ, ZS 74). Much the same view was expressed by the general in the second of two interviews with the author, July 1, 1971.

[30] A striking example of this is the unanimity of five prominent German generals who were enlisted as critics of a paper presented by the present author at a symposium on military history in 1968. In their several ways Generals von Manstein, von Manteuffel, Warlimont, Geyr von Schweppenburg, and Heusinger all maintained the thesis that neither the rank and file of the Army nor the nation would

be urged that, insofar as they pertain to the situation in February 1938, such verdicts are excessively influenced by the inevitably fresher recollections of later and decreasingly favorable stages of development, notably during the war itself. Assumptions that may have more or less validity for much of the period *after* September 1938 are often highly questionable when applied to the preceding months of that year.

One of the strengths of totalitarian systems in defending themselves against a multiplicity of discontents lies in the suppression of their manifestations. It is virtually impossible for opposition elements to evaluate with confidence their own power or the degree of potential support. The monotonous litany of praise which alone is tolerated in the media and in all public expression has in time a hypnotic effect on those who are forced to be silent. Except for such extravagant optimists as Carl Goerdeler, this applied very largely to the Opposition in the Third Reich. The hazards of sounding out even the most likely prospects and of clandestine communication were crippling impediments to recruitment and the formation of alliances between already existing groups of Resisters. Consequently every analysis of the support for or antagonism against Hitler's rule had to be heavily interlarded with question marks.

Under such circumstances it was unavoidable that in the sea of external approval islands of sentiment hostile to the regime were not charted by the Opposition. Some of these were to be found within the National Socialist party itself where resentment had arisen against excesses which originated within the SS. The sinister reputation which had clung to it since the 1934 bloodletting had become steadily more intertwined with the extension of the police state. Year after year the SS-controlled Gestapo and SD went on consolidating their power and expanding their functions. Where there still were formal boundaries, these were increasingly overstepped and the dividing lines themselves were steadily fading. Signs of "off limits," as in the case of the Wehrmacht, were ignored in such matters as the secret surveillance over its leaders.

No doubt old Field Marshal von Mackensen spoke for millions when, in 1936, he carried a protest to Hitler personally. "Herr Reich Chancellor," he had said, "you are embarked on the wrong

have "marched." Cf. William Geffen, ed., *Command and Commanders in Modern Warfare* (2nd enlarged ed., United States Air Force Academy, Colorado, 1971), 189-222.

course. Pull back the police and let law and the courts return to what they formerly were. The omnipresence of the police leads to calamity and is not German." Hitler had been silent for a time and then had answered, "Perhaps you are right. But I cannot do otherwise. I no longer can turn back."[31]

In by far the largest party formation, the SA, there was fierce hatred of the SS. Neither the upper echelons nor many of the rank and file had forgiven, or would ever forgive, the savage purge they had suffered four years earlier. Goering, who had been Himmler's close associate as lord high executioner in June 1934, also was a target for this resentment. Even the inbred devotion to Hitler had suffered a severe shock from that experience. A bitter jealousy of the organization that had shaken off the SA's earlier suzerainty and become the central executive arm of the totalitarian state compounded the thirst for vengeance. Nowhere were the necessarily hushed maledictions against the SS more heartfelt than in the top circle around Victor Lutze, Röhm's successor as SA chief of staff.[32]

During the Fritsch crisis itself and in the following weeks of investigation and trial, Lutze and his chief lieutenants remained on the sidelines. Perhaps they at first did not see clearly the situation and its possibilities for themselves. Perhaps, contrary to this, they recognized them fully and hoped that the Army would take the lead and the risk of striking a blow at Himmler's empire. Only after it became evident that "the generals" were hanging back was Lutze to enter the arena.[33] His trustworthiness as an ally would have been highly debatable, but his readiness to proceed to such lengths as to offer the Army an alliance against the SS serves to underline that the SA in their millions would have done little or nothing to oppose a putsch whose proclaimed target was the hated offshoot and its terror apparatus.

Those in the military hierarchy who were then or later forced to weigh the chances of a coup were of course primarily preoccupied with what they might expect of their troops. Both

---

[31] As related by Mackensen in 1938. Winnig, 115. Unless one happened to touch Hitler somewhere on the raw, he was prone to backpeddle when confronted with determined criticism if no third parties were present. Then, as in this case and in that of Wiedemann's plea for Hossbach (see above, p. 173), he would say that "perhaps" the critic was right but that it was too late to change course.

[32] Gisevius (*Bis zum bittern Ende*, 220-224) relates a series of exchanges with Lutze in which the latter's detestation for the SS found fervent expression.

[33] See below, pp. 380-382.

# Hitler Masters the Fritsch Crisis

the little that is available of contemporary auguries and postwar testimony indicate that here too the fresher recollections of later periods have led to a frequent underestimate of sentiments receptive to a "call to arms" in 1938. The SS was either unpopular or out-and-out detested in all ranks. A part of this was professional snobbery toward an upstart intruder generally assumed to be aiming at a place as the fourth weapon-bearer of the state. Political police are never popular, even among adherents of an authoritarian regime. It should also not be forgotten that it was precisely at the lower levels of the Army, from private to company grade officers, that thousands, perhaps tens of thousands, of representatives of the "inner migration" were to be found. These were men who despaired of finding other refuge from the threat of the concentration camp or to whom joining up had offered the last chance of a dignified livelihood in a state to which they were suspect.

Such factors served to create a reservoir of anti-SS feeling in the Army that would surface in any situation in which black uniforms could plausibly be associated with an aggression against the military. General Franz Halder, who was usually conservative in estimating support from the lower ranks for any coup attempt which left Hitler among the living, had no doubt that the troops would unhesitatingly fire and aim well when the target was the SS.[34] It is noteworthy that he passed this judgment almost two years after the Fritsch crisis and at a time when the issue of Army versus SS was less sharply drawn than, with a little publicity, it could easily have become in February 1938.

Little by little rumors that something deeply injurious to the Army and its commander was going on and that the "black ones"[35] were in some fashion behind it trickled out over the military grapevine. Some units were reached quite early and with considerable accuracy. Others received them late or not at all. Wherever they did penetrate it was manifest that Fritsch enjoyed enormous respect and, where he was in some degree personally known, there was an attitude of regard that was akin to reverence. The depth of response no doubt related closely to the professional background of the soldiers concerned. With respect to the ranks involved this was by no means always uniform. Thus in Cavalry Regiment No.

[34] Groscurth diaries, 241, entry of January 13, 1940.
[35] The contemptuous reference to the SS as the "black ones" (*die Schwarzen*) by elements hostile to the regime was sometimes meant to retaliate for use of the term by fanatic Nazis in referring to the Catholic clergy.

14 (Ludwigshorst) the company grade officers were mostly new-comers (reservists or recently reactivated men) who did not feel very involved personally. On the other hand, the majority of the noncommissioned officers were old hands from the 100,000-man Army and were thrown into a state of feverish excitement. All in all the regiment is judged, by one surviving officer, to have been ready to march if the issues had been clearly enough drawn.[36]

In the case of another cavalry regiment (No. 9 at Fürstenwalde) the commander, Colonel Reiche, felt sufficiently sure of his troops to send a blazing letter to Beck through regular service channels. Reports had reached the regiment, he stated, that things were going on in Berlin which the officer corps could not accept. He wanted it understood that he and his unit stood unreservedly behind their commander in chief.[37]

Another officer of like views, who himself was to defy the Nazi hierarchs during Fritsch's trial and later às corps commander in the East, was General Count Hans von Sponeck. This intrepid man had just a month or two earlier left the command of Infantry Regiment No. 48 (Döberitz) in order to transfer to the Luftwaffe. In contemporary discussion with friends of similar political orientation, he stated unequivocally that his old regiment would march if it were called upon to do so.[38]

Two prominent generals of the present West German Bundeswehr agree on the reaction of Armored Regiment No. 2 (Eisenach), a part of the division of General Maximilian von Weichs, in which they were then lieutenants. In this instance the story that dark forces in the regime were at work in some plot to discredit Fritsch came down directly from the OKH. The officers, most of them professionals as was likely to be the case in a tank unit, were greatly exercised and agitatedly discussed the implications of what they had learned. Neither of the generals doubts that they and their comrades would have responded to an appeal or orders from Berlin to intervene. It is further their view that the men, many of them also old hands, would have followed at this period without hesitation.[39]

[36] As related by Baron Kunrat von Hammerstein-Equord, who was an ensign in this regiment and who, as a godchild of Fritsch, paid close attention to the sentiments of officers and men. Interview, May 9, 1970.

[37] As related by Luise Jodl, then secretary to Beck, through whose hands this letter and a number of similar missives passed at that time. Interview, June 17, 1970.

[38] Interview with Colonel Eberhard Einbeck, December 2, 1969.

# Hitler Masters the Fritsch Crisis

Probably the surest unit in the German Army from the standpoint of minimal Nazi penetration and of devotion to Fritsch was Infantry Regiment No. 9 (Potsdam), whose role in the earliest known project for an armed assault on the regime has been dealt with previously.[40] It should thus go without saying that at this juncture it would have lived up to the expectations of those who looked to it as the first resort if it came to a clash in the crisis that revolved about the attack on Fritsch. The wartime mortality among the ardent young aristocrats who largely composed the officer component of this elite formation left few who could tell about the role destined for it at various times in the year that followed the autumn of 1937. One of these is the later Lieutenant General Count von Baudissin of the Bundeswehr. Though he knew nothing at the time of what others in Berlin may have had in mind for his regiment, of which he then was adjutant, he has no doubt whatever that it would have flown to arms if it had been called upon in the name of the commander in chief.[41] It was definitely among the units from which assurances of support were forwarded to Beck.[42]

Obviously no pattern that may reliably be assumed to reflect the state of mind of the German Army can be claimed to emerge from such later estimates of local situations. If this inability to generalize too much applies to cases where there was some awareness of developments in Berlin, it holds even more for the infinitely larger number of units which pursued their routine tasks in ignorance of what was happening to their commander in chief. Of some significance are contemporary judgments from men in a position to estimate the reactions of the average soldier. Especially interesting here is Jodl's account of the shock suffered by General von Viebahn, and, by implication, himself, when Canaris on February 26 told them something about Fritsch's interrogations by the Gestapo. Viebahn, who had just come from a post in the provinces to enter the OKW, was so horrified that he asserted that if the troops learned this story there would be a revolution.[43] The assessment gains in weight when it is noted that Viebahn could by no means be numbered in the camp of ardent anti-Nazis.

[39] Interviews with Lieutenant General Baron Bernd von Freytag-Loringhoven (November 3, 1969) and Lieutenant General Baron Peter von Butler (February 27, 1973).

[40] See above, p. 46.

[41] Interview with Count Wolf Baudissin, June 28, 1970.

[42] Interview with Luise Jodl, June 17, 1970.

[43] Jodl Diary; 368.

A more telling verdict because it comes from a man lower in rank and of keener perception is that rendered in retrospect in the summer of the following year by Captain Engel. Confiding to his diary his view of the relative chance of a military coup then as against early 1938, he wrote: "We, in the Army, have missed out on everything it was imperative to do. In February 1938 I was with the troops. The fury of the officers was tremendous. At that time the troops would still have obeyed us. Now it is all over, for the successes [of Hitler] have been too great." This verdict of July 1939 remains the judgment of General Engel. Assuming that the generals themselves were prepared to "risk their necks" and, as before February 4, were in their accustomed commands, troops made properly aware of the treatment meted out to Fritsch would have "obeyed and used their weapons." The many frictions with party formations at garrison posts and exercise grounds had conditioned officers and men to regard them as interlopers and at least quasi-adversaries.[44]

It should be stressed that the feeling among officers and men described here resulted from only the most general idea of what was being done to Fritsch. The difference between what was then known and the reality is demonstrated by Engel's reaction when he came to Berlin in March to become Hitler's Army adjutant and learned more, though far from the whole story. He felt like a man thunderstruck and wanted to rush to Fritsch's side. From this it may be argued that a cry of rage would have swept through the Army if the full story had become known to it. There is thus much to support the conclusion that it is Hitler's achievement in confining knowledge of affairs to the smallest possible circle, not a demonstrable lack of receptivity to a potential call to arms on behalf of Fritsch, which best explains the course of affairs. For that success, of course, the weaknesses and errors of key military leaders from Fritsch himself downward must bear a major share of responsibility.

Partial confirmation of this analysis may be claimed from odds and ends of information—it could hardly be called more—about the marked apprehensions on "the other side." As the initiators of so much that had been planned and in preparation for many weeks, Goering and his SS colleagues can hardly have failed to weigh conceivable countermoves and to calculate the resources that might be available against them. They must have been aware of

[44] Engel Diary, entry of July 5, 1939. Engel interview, July 15, 1971.

such vital moments of decision as when Hossbach warned Fritsch of his danger (January 25) or when on the morning of the 27th it remained to be seen whether Fritsch would obey Hitler's order to go to the Gestapo. A refusal to do so would certainly have brought matters to the verge of a showdown.

There seems to be no clue on how much the SS chiefs knew, during the two or three days following, about the coalescence of elements in support of Fritsch, but they cannot have failed to be aware of the agitated comings and goings at the War Ministry. They must similarly have appreciated that in some of the aroused quarters the use of force was bound to be considered. Measures to meet a number of contingencies had to be concerted and to some degree initiated. Reports coming to the Abwehr action group spoke of a state of feverish preparation in the Prinz-Albrecht-Strasse that denoted anticipation of a coup or counter-coup.[45]

After the war, Goering's adjutant, General Bodenschatz, told Count von der Goltz that Goering and his associates had directed the concentration of 20,000 SS about Berlin.[46] Bodenschatz no doubt played only an observer's role throughout the crisis and his figure for the SS is in any event too large.[47] But he had no discernible reason for making up a tale of this kind; one would indeed question the foresight and competence of the intriguers if they had not adopted some such measures. Interesting and somewhat puzzling is the lack of any evidence concerning something like an alert to elements of the Luftwaffe.

More conceivable than a full-fledged Army putsch, which would have demanded too much unanimity among the generals, was a smaller scale raid or *coup de main* by an elite troop on such a target as the Gestapo. Such designs were repeatedly weighed at Tirpitz Ufer and advocated with particular ardor by Gisevius. Heydrich seems to have gotten wind of these projects and perhaps of initiatory, but in the upshot abortive, moves to implement them. At one point he learned that the scales of decision were delicately poised and that elements of the Potsdam garrison (one thinks immediately of Infantry Regiment No. 9) were alerted for a move to Berlin.

However many queries may be raised about the authenticity of

---

[45] Gisevius, *Bis zum bittern Ende,* 268.

[46] Goltz interview, November 1, 1969, and "Erinnerungen," 188.

[47] It is, for example, strongly questioned by Huppenkothen, who indeed denies any knowledge of such a concentration. Interview, May 29, 1970.

the memoirs of SS and SD member Walter Schellenberg, there is nothing inherently unreasonable in his story of a strange evening he passed with Heydrich. Having the repute of a crack pistol shot, he was asked to report, suitably armed, during one of the critical phases of the Fritsch crisis. During dinner Heydrich fidgeted and gave other signs of extreme tension which continued throughout the evening. At one point he burst out, "If they don't start marching from Potsdam during the next hour and a half, the greatest danger will have passed." Somewhat later he relaxed and recounted what he had learned from Army informants. Certain General Staff officers had become so roused over the proceedings against Fritsch that they wished to use force and had got into close touch with officers of the Potsdam garrison. If the decision was for action it would almost surely have come that night.[48] Heydrich said nothing of his own defensive measures, but one can assume that any SS formations at his disposal were strategically placed and that he was waiting for a signal that the threatened move from Potsdam was actually under way. Meanwhile he welcomed having at his side an expert gunman in the event of a sudden threat to him personally.

Schellenberg furnished no hint that would help to fix more precisely the specific stage of affairs at which Heydrich saw his greatest peril. It appears most likely that it coincided with one of the crucial points in the pretrial investigation. It was then that the sense of outrage among Fritsch's adherents was most fully focused on the Gestapo and less broadly on the regime. The incident could, in fact, have occurred immediately after the exoneration of Fritsch and at the time of the last desperate pleas from activists to settle accounts with the Prinz-Albrecht-Strasse. In the Fritsch crisis itself the aims of the Abwehr's action-minded group were fixed in another direction—that of reaching out from Berlin to start fires which in turn might ignite a flame in the capital.

## Efforts of the Abwehr Activists in the Provinces

Because of the near paralysis at the summit of the military pyramid, a situation which derived in part from a lack of confidence in the solidarity of its base, the action-seeking elements of the Abwehr group turned in desperation to the expedient of trying to induce selected corps commanders to move in some fashion. At least three

[48] Schellenberg, The Schellenberg Memoirs, 14–15.

252

such missionary ventures, each basically the initiative of a single individual, were directed to provincial headquarters at the end of January and there may have been further essays of which we thus far lack record.

Except in the case of Goerdeler, whose primary thought always was to set the generals to "marching," these efforts represented no extravagant hopes of inspiring a major action against the regime from one or another provincial center. Insofar as it is possible to generalize, they were conceived as a circuitous way of "getting at" Fritsch, perhaps also Beck. The thought was to persuade corps commanders to work on Fritsch, perhaps utilize them to rouse their fellows to a show of solidarity behind their chief. If there was anything which could sweep him out of his lethargy and stimulate him to some positive step it would be this. At a minimum these missions would ensure that the generals reached, and perhaps others whom they would enlighten in their turn, would not be caught entirely off guard by whatever course Hitler might adopt in the days ahead.

In perusing the roll of corps commanders, a name that would quickly catch the eye of a searcher for anti-Nazi allies was that of General of Artillery Alexander Ulex who headed the 11th Army Corps in Hanover. Ulex, a Mecklenburger whose tall, gaunt, ramrod figure seemed to reflect firm principles and devotion to traditional codes and concepts of honor, was known both for his lukewarmness to the regime and his fidelity to Fritsch. An important factor must also have been the presence in his headquarters, so to speak at his right hand, of Major von Pfuhlstein, the I-C (intelligence chief) of the 11th Corps, whom Canaris had personally recruited as an Oppositionist only a few months before.[49] There was also General Vierow, the chief of staff, who was known to stand close to his commander and to enjoy his confidence.

It is still the view of Pfuhlstein that in this case it was Canaris who determined that Ulex should be sounded out and confided the task to Oster, who had already taken over the maintenance of the link with Pfuhlstein. Gisevius, who learned about the trip from Oster when he returned from his own visit to Münster, is sure that the initiative proceeded entirely from his friend and that Canaris almost certainly knew nothing of it.[50] In any event, Oster

---

[49] See above, pp. 49-50.

[50] Gisevius recording, July 1971. In a brief postwar statement Ulex affirmed that no reference to Canaris had been made in the meeting (in IfZ, ZS 627).

was here building on a foundation that had been laid by Canaris.

Arriving in Hanover on the 29th, Oster first surveyed the ground with Pfuhlstein and then went with him to Ulex to apprise him of developments in Berlin. He appealed to him to put himself at the head of the twelve corps commanders for the purpose of confronting Hitler with an ultimatum. They were to threaten their collective resignation unless he called off the action against Fritsch. Ulex, deeply disturbed, pointed out that a united front of the commanders was not attainable—Reichenau and Friedrich Dollmann of the 9th Army Corps would surely refuse to go along. As matters stood, the proposal looked to him like a political adventure of which no one could fully foresee the consequences.[51]

Thus Oster had to return to Berlin with his purpose unaccomplished. That he had not failed by too great a margin is indicated by the sequel related by the later General von Pfuhlstein to whom the outcome had been as sore a disappointment as it had to Canaris's chief of staff. On the day after Oster's call it was discovered that Ulex had disappeared from his headquarters, going, as it turned out, to nurse his troubled conscience at the exercise ground of Bergen. When nothing was heard from him for two days, the anxious General Vierow sent Pfuhlstein to beg him to return. The major found his chief sitting in profound depression in a darkened room. On receiving Vierow's message, he rose slowly and said sadly: "It is a great burden to me to have the feeling of having failed at a decisive moment."[52]

Looking ahead, it is possible to conclude that Oster's mission, whether self-appointed or not, gained more than he can have realized at the time. No doubt Ulex's more positive response to a stimulus from a very different quarter—the SA—a few months later stemmed in part from his abiding sense of having failed at a vital moment in January.[53]

Parallel to Oster's visit to Hanover were missions by Gisevius and Goerdeler. It has been noted how assiduously the former had been promoting his contacts with Kluge and Lüninck, the Wehrkreis commander and the chief president of Münster. Kluge had been steadily more fortified in his anti-Nazi orientation, while Lüninck was one of the staunchest among the dwindling number of critics

[51] Pfuhlstein interview, February 14, 1970.
[52] *Ibid.*
[53] See below, pp. 399–400.

of the regime who still held high posts in the civil administration.[54]

Gisevius reached Münster early in the morning of January 29 and put through a call to Kluge. The general was on the point of departing for a weekend of hunting and was not at all enthusiastic about receiving a visitor. But he yielded to the plea that there was a most important matter to discuss. Gisevius, who had expected to find him at least partially oriented about affairs in Berlin, was taken aback when it turned out that not the merest hint of them had reached him. He had hoped to discuss possible concrete steps with Kluge, but now felt that a man caught so completely unawares required time to reflect and recover. He therefore said that he would leave the general to think over the problem and hurried off to organize support that would exercise the right kind of continuing influence. Before returning to Berlin he made two side trips which assured that Lüninck and the Düsseldorf government president, Carl Christian Schmid, would call on Kluge on the next day and urge him in the desired direction.[55]

Meanwhile the impassioned Goerdeler had managed to stir up things in the higher reaches of Wehrkreis IV, whose command was staging a plans exercise with the staff of the 14th Division at Leipzig at the end of January. Goerdeler had for years fostered the anti-Nazi sentiments of the chief of staff, General Friedrich Olbricht, and, through him, those of the more recently arrived first staff officer, Lieutenant Colonel Röhricht.[56] It is from the memoirs of the latter that we gain the detailed story of Goerdeler's impetuous intervention to rouse the military to action.

The hour for the plans exercise was at hand when Röhricht was mystified by instructions from Olbricht to accompany him in civil garb and in a car without the usual military markings. In a quiet residential neighborhood they halted to admit a gentleman whom Röhricht recognized as Goerdeler. Arriving at the officers' casino where the exercise was scheduled, Olbricht took over an appropriate chamber and had the neighboring rooms vacated to assure greater privacy. Meanwhile Röhricht had the difficult task of separating the Wehrkreis commander, General Wilhelm List, from the already

[54] Actually Lüninck was then in his last year of office. He remained closely associated with the conspiracy and was among those who lost their lives after July 20, 1944.

[55] Gisevius, *Bis zum bittern Ende*, 272-273.

[56] Röhricht, *Pflicht und Gewissen*, 110.

running exercise so that he could be included in the discussion.[57]

Goerdeler commenced with his now well-rehearsed report on what was transpiring in the capital. He told of the circumstances surrounding the marriage of Blomberg and the maneuvers ascribed to Goering and Himmler to exploit it for their own sinister purposes. Fritsch was the victim of a base slander. In the Wehrmacht leadership and specifically in the OKH there was for the moment no coherent direction, as was evident from the fact that there had been no effort to apprise the Wehrkreise of what was going on. He and Schacht were acting in conjunction to rouse selected military leaders to action. The principal enemy seemed to be Himmler. He, Goerdeler, was prepared to take on major responsibility if it came to a *coup d'état*.

While his listeners sat in dazed silence, Goerdeler went on in a low voice to give details. Finally List said that he was hardly in a position to take a stand on the matter. Disappointed, Goerdeler pleaded for at least a move to "smoke out" Gestapo headquarters; further steps would then determine themselves. One could hope to seize so much incriminating material that, with the help of the courts, it would be possible also to clean up elsewhere in the regime. His feeling clearly was that, if one could start a stone rolling, forces hostile to the Third Reich would reveal themslves in such numbers as to release an avalanche.

Olbricht now interjected that for an action in Berlin the troops in Potsdam, Spandau, and Döberitz were most strategically situated. Goerdeler protested the lack of any purposeful leadership in Berlin. Beck was doing nothing. Therefore it was imperative that the initiatory impulse come from the outside.

The first rule of a military intervention, stressed Olbricht, was unified direction. No doubt the other Wehrkreise were as unsuspecting as that in Saxony had been. Smoking out the Gestapo could hardly be attempted as an isolated action, for it would undoubtedly inspire resistance by the regime all along the line. And where were the political forces on which a coup must base itself? The people in general backed Hitler.

Olbricht then, with a tortured expression, looked at Röhricht

[57] The story as here related is based on Röhricht's *Pflicht und Gewissen* (111-117) and on a report he wrote about the incident in 1951: "Bericht über eine Aussprache mit Goerdeler während der Blomberg-Fritsch Krise, 22.2.51" (in IfZ, ZS 96). Gisevius (*Bis zum bittern Ende,* 272) and Ritter (146) relate no more than the bare fact of Goerdeler's trip to rouse the military in Leipzig.

in mute appeal. Responding, Röhricht reminded his hearers that they no longer had to deal with the tightly integrated body of professional soldiers who had composed the Reichswehr of the Republic. What looked like an Army was now a loosely structured formation of men drawn from the entire nation and with several years of party indoctrination behind them. The officer corps itself no longer could show a uniform outlook, being a conglomerate of a handful of regulars with reactivated and reserve officers. Most of the lieutenants came from the ranks of the Hitler Youth.

In view of these hard facts, the only assured way to move against the regime would be with a specifically constituted force. Because of the omnipresent internal political espionage, such a body could only be formed with the greatest circumspection and would demand time. The whole propaganda and communications apparatus was in Hitler's hands as was the control of transport. Moving a division by rail to Berlin would require three days and would have to be arranged in the capital. The Luftwaffe was heavily Nazi-indoctrinated and the Army had no adequate means of defense against it. If he were dispatched to one of the Wehrkreis divisions to alert the troops for a putsch no one would take him seriously. He would not be sent to a court-martial but to a psychiatrist. And what was to be understood by "smoking out the Gestapo"?

The officer concluded by proposing that it was necessary to discover in Berlin just what kind of game was being played there. This appeared to be in line with the thought of General List, who rose and told Röhricht, as one who had recent experience in the War Ministry, to accompany him on a flying visit to Beck.

The drive to the capital proceeded in silence while the two men strove to digest and gauge for themselves the meaning of what they had heard. Evening was coming on when they reached OKH headquarters and trooped through the gloomy corridors to Beck's sanctum, which somehow gave Röhricht the impression of a house of mourning. Beck himself looked worn and tired. While the two generals were closeted together, Röhricht was filled in on details by the aide on duty, a former regimental comrade.

The return journey again proceeded wordlessly until they halted at a hostelry where the driver was delegated to pick up some sandwiches. Then, at last, List broke the silence to relate what Beck had told him. Blomberg would have no successor since Hitler himself was taking over the Wehrmacht. The rest was confusion with Fritsch rendered impotent at this critical juncture of the Army's affairs because of the charges against him. By the time the legal proceedings he had demanded were completed, a new pattern would have emerged whose outline no one as yet could clearly perceive. It looked as if the Army would not play much of a part in determining its own fate.

Beck, it is clear, had not shared in whatever deliberations preceded Goerdeler's impetuous dash to Leipzig. It is further evident that the chief of staff made no move to back the civilian's initiative or to exploit List's call in any way. Apparently there was no enumeration of possible countermeasures, no concerting of signals by which the leadership of Wehrkreis IV might later be alerted to take a hand in affairs.

The story of Goerdeler's attempt to ignite a fire in Saxony that might in turn have an incendiary effect in Berlin is very revealing of the realities that shaped affairs in early February 1938. It illustrates graphically the indecision and disarray that reigned in the upper levels of the OKH, the unawareness that prevailed in provincial commands of what was transpiring in Berlin, and their helplessness when, by the heroic but rather clumsy intervention of outsiders, they were apprised of what was going on. It also serves to bring home some of the almost insurmountable difficulties that faced any attempt to initiate effective action against the regime from anywhere but the natural center of the Reich. Only a clear call from the top level of the OKH which ruthlessly laid bare the situation, sharply defined the issues, and proposed concrete measures would have had some prospect of throwing the weight of the Army into the political scale. But neither Fritsch nor Beck in the brief space of time available to them was able to summon the insight and resolution that were indispensable to such a role. Thus the critical days were allowed to pass in uncertainty and inaction while the wheel of fate was making its decisive turns. The dictator was driving relentlessly forward, becoming every day more sure of his purpose, and widening the sweep of the scythe with which he was decapitating the Army's traditionalist leadership. By February 4 he could feel that he was succeeding in mastering the most severe crisis he had faced since June 1934.

## The Revirement of February 4, 1938

From every standpoint it would have been advantageous for Adolf Hitler to announce to the German nation on January 30 a sweeping change of personnel in high position. This would have done much more for him than merely to endow with dramatic color the fifth anniversary of his accession to power. It would have detracted greatly from any semblance of internal crisis, an impression he wanted at all cost to avoid. The turnover could have been made to look as if it had been some time in contemplation and could have had the trappings of a rather routine "changing of the guard," such as Mussolini had led the world to expect from time to time in a Fascist type of dictatorship. It would also have cut down sharply on the period available to any elements that might be inclined to come to the aid of Fritsch in which they could gain insight into what was going on, oversee the situation, rally their sympathizers, and conceive measures to take in his behalf.

The obduracy and resolution of the unbending "last Prussian," Hossbach, had ruined this scenario. His refusal to allow Fritsch to be railroaded unheard and his readiness to lay his career, perhaps even his life, on the line by his defiance of the order to say nothing to his commander in chief had wrecked the design to finish with the whole affair in short order. Hence it was necessary for Hitler and the cabal to move with greater deliberation and to risk that the disconcerted Army leaders would recover their poise, break through the iron curtain of secrecy the dictator had erected with the collaboration of Keitel, and set out to enlighten and rally military leaders in Berlin and in the Wehrkreis commands.

The more intelligent and imaginative of the Nazi chieftains appreciated somewhat the extent of this risk. The apprehensions of Heydrich that some kind of coup might be attempted have been noted. Similarly illustrative is the distress and, for at least a passing moment, the near panic of Goebbels. At the critical juncture of the expulsion from the Chancellery of Colonel Hossbach, itself a challenge to the officer corps, Goebbels evidently feared that a wave of indignation would sweep through the Army. To the adjutant himself the Propaganda Minister expressed his profound regret about his departure.[58] When Wiedemann indignantly protested that the Fuehrer had dismissed a General Staff officer as he would a house servant and said that unless Goebbels undertook to bring this home to Hitler he would do it himself, the little man wrung his hands in agitation and wailed: "Herr Wiedemann, Herr Wiedemann, you are entirely right. I shall tell him. . . . If tomorrow

[58] Hossbach, *Zwischen Wehrmacht und Hitler*, 117-118.

twelve generals should take their departure we are finished."[59]

The dreaded generals' strike did not eventuate. Hitler had taken, and was continuing to take with diabolical insight, the measure of his men. His contempt for the aristocratic officer caste, "these antique knights with dusty conceptions of honor,"[60] battened on the observations in these hectic days. The infatuation of Blomberg, the helplessness of Fritsch and Beck in the rough-and-tumble political game at which he was a master, the insensitivity of Rundstedt to what was at stake, the ease with which he led Keitel by the nose and enslaved Brauchitsch—such demonstrations of the vulnerabilities of the men with whom he had to deal determined him to make a clean sweep while the initiative was still so fully in his hands. No longer was he content to surmount the crisis that might well have threatened the foundations of his regime. He now sought a more far-reaching victory and one more enduring in its consequences. The stake was nothing less than the direct control of the Wehrmacht!

The stubborn rectitude of Hossbach prolonged the crisis, multiplied the hazards of the attack on the Army, and spoiled the dramatization of the fifth anniversary of the regime. In compensation Hitler had five additional days in which to deal with his problems in a more decisive fashion. In place of a precipitate, largely improvised operation, it was now possible to make a more studied elimination of obstacles that had hitherto set limits on his unrestricted exercise of power.

The special beauty of the situation for Hitler was that the more wide-ranging the action, the more it fulfilled the aim of distracting attention from its real purpose. Never before or later was he so favorably placed to cast restraint to the winds with impunity. By dealing potential opponents so many blows at one time, he encountered less difficulty than if he had struck them one at a time. The German public and the world generally were left largely at sea as to what it was all about. Thus, while the *revirement* of February 4, 1938, resembles the murderous orgy of June 30, 1934, in that so many birds were accounted for with a single stone, it differed in that the variety of targets tended to lessen rather than increase the negative side of its impact.

Hitler disguised his absorption with changes at the military sum-

[59] Wiedemann, *Der Mann der Feldherr werden wollte*, 120.

[60] Siegfried Westphal, *Heer in Fesseln: Aus den Papieren des Stabschefs von Rommel, Kesselring und Rundstedt* (Bonn, 1950), 79.

mit and at the same time cleaned house among the "undesirables" by a wholesale removal or transfer of lesser generals. We know that he had begun to occupy himself with the problem no later than his last talks with Blomberg on January 26 and 27 and that the departing War Minister, in venting his spleen against the Army, had given the Fuehrer a list of top members of the Generalität who were thought lukewarm or hostile to the regime.[61] It is safe to assume that Goering's comments were solicited and probable enough that Himmler provided additional names from personal knowledge or secret files. The subject recurred constantly in those interminable daily conferences between Hitler and Keitel in which every aspect of the Wehrmacht picture was under scrutiny. Either Hitler himself, or Goering and/or Keitel on his behalf, went deeply into the matter with Brauchitsch, though one would like to think that the latter did not personally make additions to the purge list. At any rate, Brauchitsch, acting as Hitler's emissary and before his own appointment, on February 3 had an extensive conference with General von Schwedler of the Personnel Office.

Brauchitsch began by naming the officers whom Hitler wished to see removed from their current posts. Schwedler himself and two of his department chiefs, Colonels Kuntzen and Behlendorff, figured at the top of the list of those who were to be sent from General Staff posts in Berlin to the military wilderness of troop commands. Beck's deputy chief of staff and chief quartermaster I, General von Manstein, was to be given a divisional command. The axe was to fall hardest on Generals Kress von Kressenstein, a Wehrkreis commander, von Porgrell, the inspector of cavalry, and von Niebelschutz, the inspector of training, all of whom were slated for retirement.

Thereby was concluded the tally of prominent officers expressly designated for dismissal or transfer as a result of Hitler's talks with Blomberg, Keitel, Goering, and Brauchitsch. Hitler further insisted, however, that for good measure one of the group commanders and a number of Wehrkreis chiefs should also be removed. It was, of course, simplest and least painful to select men who by normal procedure would have been slated for the earliest retirement. In the case of the group commander Brauchitsch personally intervened to exempt Rundstedt as one who "got along well with

[61] See above, p. 120.

the Fuehrer," choosing in his place to eliminate General von Leeb.[62]

To further throw dust in the eyes of interested observers, Hitler enlarged the purge circle beyond the confines of the Wehrmacht. It was now to include inconvenient figures in the Foreign Office, among them the Foreign Minister, formerly so complacent, but who was too much inclined to pull back now that expansive pressures began to exceed his limits of tolerance. Little more than two weeks before, Hitler had refused Neurath's offer of resignation because he wished to avoid any impression of inner conflict on foreign policy. He had also valued the reassurance which Neurath's presence in the government had represented abroad at a time when anxieties about Reich policies were everywhere on the rise. The solution he worked out was a brilliant piece of political legerdemain. The venerable baron was made head of a "Secret Cabinet Council" whose existence was to be strictly confined to paper. In effect he was kicked upstairs to a landing which was not there. The membership of the mythical body was worked out with Goering and solemnly proclaimed.

Hitler's decision to rid himself of Neurath appears to have been made quite late, though not so late as to excuse the manner in which it was sprung on the Foreign Minister. On February 3 Stülpnagel heard on his telephone the warning voice which two weeks or so before had alerted him about the menace to Fritsch. Neurath, said the mysterious caller, was in imminent danger of dismissal. Stülpnagel straightway drove to the Foreign Minister's residence to find that he had returned home only a few minutes before from a festivity honoring him for his term of service. Hitler had been present to congratulate him and had personally conducted him home. On the way he had been full of assurances that he would never part with him.[63] Small wonder that Neurath said bitterly to Wiedemann, "That is the greatly famed fidelity of the Fuehrer."[64]

Hitler condemned to an even greater oblivion than that of Neurath the ambassador in Rome, Ulrich von Hassell, who, as an advocate of restraint, stood out sufficiently among diplomats to have earned in the Eternal City the sobriquet *Il Freno*—the brake.[65] Brakes were what Adolf Hitler was now recklessly casting aside right and

[62] As related after the war by the then General Kuntzen. J. A. Kielmansegg, *Der Fritsch-Prozess 1938*, 123–124.

[63] Stülpnagel, 359.

[64] Wiedemann, *Der Mann der Feldherr werden wollte*, 115.

[65] Hassell interview, December 2, 1969.

left. To avoid too much the appearance of weeding out "moderates," the more innocuous Herbert von Dirksen was recalled from Tokyo.

Franz von Papen was also called home from Vienna but was actually to receive a dramatic reprieve to be dealt with in a later chapter. More fortunate than others struck by the same lightning, he was informed by a telephone call from Berlin, "so that he would not learn about it from the papers."[66] The fate of Hassell was exactly this with the rudeness compounded by his being in Berlin at the time, where he read the news of his recall over his breakfast coffee at the Hotel Adlon.[67]

Long overdue from the Nazi standpoint, Schacht was replaced as Minister of Economics by Walter Funk.

By evening of Feburary 3 the last pieces of the sinister game were falling into place and only the final agreement with Brauchitsch remained to be nailed down the following morning. This could now be sufficiently taken for granted to permit the show to go on. During the evening summonses to top Wehrmacht figures for a meeting at 2 P.M. on the 4th went out to all parts of the Reich. They were not being called to council but to be presented with a *fait accompli.* Midnight radio and morning papers were the media by which the world was informed of the sweeping *revirement.*

At 2 P.M. on February 4 the dictator and his new Army commander entered the main assembly hall of the War Ministry in an atmosphere charged with high tension. Hitler immediately began to thunder against Blomberg, whose story was presented in a fashion that was little complimentary to the fallen Minister. Hitler professed to have soon recognized his weakness of character and for that very reason to have done his best to strengthen the authority of the War Minister. But Blomberg had never proved the prop that was needed. In all critical situations, such as the Rhineland occupation, he had lost his nerve. Goering could testify that it was not the War Minister but the Fuehrer himself who had pushed toward rearmament. Blomberg had been dismissed from his post and "of course" would be deprived of the regiment of which he was honorary colonel. But it would hardly do to afford the world the spectacle

---

[66] Papen, 458.
[67] Wiedemann, *Der Mann der Feldherr werden wollte,* 114.

of the first field marshal of the Third Reich being sent off in disgrace.[68]

As for Fritsch, "of course" no one but he would have been considered as successor to Blomberg had it not been for the cloud hanging over him. Only after the Fuehrer's confidence in the officer corps had been shaken by the conduct of Blomberg and—a barefaced lie—by the addition of so much more incriminating material when the charges had recently been reexamined had he felt compelled to dignify the charges by an investigation, for, "of course," he could not appoint as War Minister anyone over whom there hung the threat of scandal. Then Fritsch had shown up very badly when he was called in and told what was at issue. He had said that the suspicions raised against him must have been in connection with two Hitler-boys to whom he had given hospitality. This to Hitler had been proof that Fritsch had also made homosexual advances to these boys and, when the original accuser had stuck to his story in confrontation with the general, there had been no choice but to put matters into the hands of the Minister of Justice. After careful study Gürtner had given an opinion that the material submitted to him would not permit the case to be quashed but demanded judicial investigation. This was now to be entrusted to a court-martial. Fritsch, "of course," could not meanwhile continue in his funtions and was being replaced by Brauchitsch.

By now the repeated rehearsals and constant reworking of the version he wished to put over on military listeners had made him letter-perfect. If he was nervous it apparently only heightened the impression of sincere and spontaneous emotion. In sum, this "most elegant actor of history," as the keenest of his adjutants describes him,[69] performed so brilliantly that only the most skeptical were able to escape being influenced. Before this many of those present had learned little or nothing of these dramatic and shattering developments. "When one hears it this way one can almost believe it," a fellow general whispered to Kluge as they left the presence.[70]

Hitler had managed to make the guilt of Fritsch appear virtually

[68] The account of Hitler's address is based on the later notations of Generals Adam, Ulex, and Liebmann. Adam, "Erinnerungen," 391–394. Ulex ms., 95–96. "Persönliche Erlebnisse des Gen. d. Inf. a. D. Curt Liebmann aus den Jahren 1938/1939" (copy in author's possession; cited hereafter as Liebmann), 1–2.

[69] The verdict of General Engel, who for four years observed him from the closest proximity. Interview, May 11, 1970.

[70] As related by Kluge. Gisevius, *Bis zum bittern Ende*, 277.

proven, although he was to be given every opportunity to clear himself. His own assumption of the War Ministry was presented as a temporary solution of a very complicated problem. Doubtless to make it more palatable and allay fears of future SS encroachments on the military, he labeled rumors that it was his intention to make Himmler commander in chief of the Wehrmacht as "crazy talk." He gave his "sacred pledge" that he would *never* appoint a nonprofessional to a military post, a promise violated six years later in the case of this same Himmler when he was made commander of the Home Army and of Army Group Vistula. When General von Manstein ventured to ask whether at some later date an Army man might be named generalissimo, Hitler replied with great presence of mind that the way to this "at the right moment" stood open.

All in all, it was a masterly performance and produced just the right mixture of shame, consternation, and reassurance in his audience. The Army men were in most cases thoroughly intimidated. "We all had the feeling," wrote General Curt Liebmann a year and a half later, "that the Army—in contrast to the Navy, the Luftwaffe, and the party—had suffered an annihilating blow and that in future any measure directed against it would be defended with a certain justice on the plea that the generals did not deserve any confidence."[71]

How much this was exactly the effect he wished to achieve may be judged from Hitler's concluding remarks: "After such sorrowful experiences I must consider anyone capable of anything. The 100,000-man Army has failed to produce any great leaders. From now on I shall concern myself with personnel matters and make the right appointments."[72]

At this final piece of impudence, Adam and perhaps others looked at Rundstedt to see whether as the senior in service he would not speak up, but he made no move in that direction. As the generals and admirals filed out Adam attached himself to his friend Beck and the two went off for a lengthy exchange. The chief of staff related how Hitler had promised during the night of January 26 that he would do nothing in winding up the Fritsch affair or make any changes following from it without consulting him. "And yet," said Beck resignedly, "he has not done so even once." This was too much for the toughminded Adam who had never minced words

[71] Liebmann, 2.
[72] Adam, "Erinnerungen," 393.

in talking to his friend about Hitler. "You are still a plain fool; how much longer will you let yourself be deceived by this swindler?" Far from resenting this forceful language, Beck some weeks later confessed that this "friendly reproof" had done much to finally open his eyes to the situation.[73]

That evening Hitler paraded his model of a "changing of the guard" before the last meeting of the Reich Cabinet over which he was to preside. Brauchitsch and Keitel were introduced and the formula on the latter's functions as well as the order on the Secret Cabinet Council was read by State Secretary Lammers. On the antecedents of the entire *revirement* the Cabinet was less fully oriented than had been the generals. No opportunity was given for questions or discussion. Shortly after the meeting adjourned, Hitler concluded eleven busy and momentous days in Berlin by taking his special train back to Bavaria. He had made history apace during this brief period! The martyrdom of Werner von Fritsch, on the other hand, was to drag on for further tortured weeks.

[73] *Ibid.*

# CHAPTER IX

# Attack and Counterattack

February 4, 1938, stands among the major landmarks in the history of the Third Reich. It signified so pronounced a shift in the power relationships within Germany that it has with small exaggeration been labeled a *coup d'état.* Hitler, in effect, usurped the immediate direction of the armed forces of the state and took a long step toward emasculating the leadership of the senior service—the Army. It is not surprising that more and more the image of the "Fuehrer and Chancellor" tended to give way to "Fuehrer and Commander in Chief of the Wehrmacht." By 1938 the office of Chancellor had been largely obscured by the personal dictatorship of Adolf Hitler. After February 4 the inexorable consolidation of military leadership in the Fuehrer's hands continued to its completion nearly four years later with the assumption of the direct command of the Army.

The coup of February 4 carried far in other directions than those immediately visible. The central issue of the Fritsch crisis had been at bottom the simple one of which would fall: the general or Hitler.[1] At stake was the role that would be played in future by the Generalität. Only the small circle around the Abwehr Opposition group had realized this and then but dimly. To all intents and purposes, the outcome had been decided on approximately February 1 by Fritsch's resignation. At this time, also, Hitler's own position between the contending forces was definitely established. The basic interpretation presented in these pages is that, despite whatever shock Hitler may have suffered through the revela-

[1] J. A. Kielmansegg, *Der Fritsch-Prozess 1938,* 40.

tion of Blomberg's folly, he quickly rallied to meet the challenge. The blow to his pride and the setback he perceived in the debacle of a Minister he had imposed on a reluctant military establishment determined him the more to cull fortune from misfortune and turn loss into profit. From that moment, it is held, Hitler, tacitly or otherwise, became an accomplice of the initiating cabal and strove with complete consistency to utilize the occasion for a far-reaching invasion of the military sphere. His assumption of the functions of the War Ministry was an improvisation that he might never have hit upon had it not been suggested by Blomberg. The elimination of Fritsch, however, he pursued relentlessly from the night of January 24. Eager to believe, and make others believe, the worst, he may momentarily, because of the general's feeble response to the confrontation with Schmidt, have been inclined to take the charges seriously. But his unswerving endeavor to stack the cards against Fritsch argues against any conviction on his part that the case could stand up on its own. Far from having even the most fleeting intention of making Fritsch War Minister, Hitler utilized such a pretense as an excuse for going more deeply into the once-rejected charges. The problem of finding a successor to Blomberg was thus used to eliminate Fritsch also as Army commander.[2]

Not in contradiction but somewhat differently slanted stands the viewpoint advanced with much force by Gisevius that the dictator was genuinely overwhelmed by the concatenation of unheralded events. He argues that Hitler teetered back and forth between guilt and innocence in his assessment of Fritsch as well as between support for the intriguing cabal and sympathy with those who rallied to the Army commander. The indecision is believed to have been so pronounced that it would have been possible for Fritsch's friends to force the Fuehrer's hand if only the general himself had taken the lead. What in the end determined Hitler was the clarity of purpose on one side contrasted with the confusion and divisions on the other. In effect, about February 1 he came out on the side of "the larger battalions."[3]

Whatever these differences of view regarding Hitler's outlook and intentions in late January, after February 1 the lines of interpretation converge. From then on there is agreement that his course was straight and consistent—he had determined the direction in

[2] This was very much the conviction of Rosenberger. Notes on a conversation with Rosenberger. Kielmansegg Papers.
[3] Gisevius recording, July 1971.

268

# Attack and Counterattack

which he was going and pursued it without further hesitation to the end.

## The Forces against Fritsch

As the Fritsch crisis faded into the Fritsch case, the lineup of elements that, in one way or another, had chosen sides underwent further transformation. In general the lines appeared to become more clearly defined.

Since January 25 contacts between Hitler and Himmler in matters concerning the Fritsch affair had been almost as frequent and intimate as those between the Fuehrer and Goering. We know that before mid-morning of the 26th the two (whether alone or with Goering also present) had been closeted together discussing the succession to Blomberg. Himmler was deeply enough involved either (1) to be delegated to sound out Count von der Schulenburg or (2) to feel free to get in touch with him on his own.[4] From Hossbach and Wiedemann we gain glimpses of his appearances at the Chancellery during these critical days. Wiedemann, however, was persuaded by him that he had nothing to do with the antecedents of the Blomberg affair and very little with pushing matters against Fritsch.[5] Himmler was obviously afraid that he and his shop were being ticketed with the major responsibility for the troubles of one or the other general. "Himmler is said to be depressed," Jodl noted in his diary, "that high officers of the Wehrmacht are making the most unheard of reproaches against him."[6] Small wonder that he was trying desperately to make his own role appear peripheral at most.

Actually that role was becoming more central as the action against Fritsch moved into the foreground. Himmler joined with Goering in staging the confrontation with Schmidt he had himself suggested and it is a safe guess that it was his proposal that led to the Gestapo interrogations of the general. His responsibility is much enhanced

[4] See above, p. 116.

[5] Himmler complained with a lugubrious air that he had not been permitted to watch over Blomberg as he did over the other Ministers. Had this not been the case he would surely have learned about the past life of Eva Gruhn before it was too late to issue a warning. Wiedemann also was made to believe that, with respect to Fritsch, Himmler had gone no further than to say that homosexuals were habitual liars and to suggest a surprise confrontation with Schmidt. Wiedemann, *Der Mann der Feldherr werden wollte*, 116-117. The present volume should offer ample evidence that the captain was overly credulous on both counts.

[6] Jodl Diary, 367, entry of February 10.

if, as we may assume, he told Hitler nothing of Huber's discovery about Frisch and brazenly went ahead with the second interrogation. No one doubts that he joined with Goering in fighting against the court-martial and in advocating in its place a special Gestapo-dominated tribunal. We may further assume that it was his idea that at least Dr. Best should be added to the former.

The SS chiefs and their Gestapo instruments redoubled efforts when the latter continued their investigations in the weeks which followed the turnover of February 4. During this period Himmler and Heydrich were constantly dodging in and out of the Chancellery.[7] Their hands can be discerned in innumerable Gestapo moves that betoken more than the initiative of such underlings as Meisinger. Every vital maneuver in this grim game must have been blueprinted in the higher reaches of Prinz-Albrecht-Strasse 8.

The unremitting drive exhibited by the SS leaders in the pursuit of their quarry testifies to their lively appreciation of the challenge to their prestige and indeed safety. Once it was settled that the charges against Fritsch would be submitted to legal examination, their entire course with respect to these charges since 1936 was under scrutiny. Any misstep would have painful consequences; the risks covered a wide range up to an actual attack on their headquarters by outraged Army elements. In their case the danger of the game they had been playing continued beyond the settlement of the larger issues of the Wehrmacht crisis in early February.

The situation for Himmler and Heydrich was the more hazardous because of Goering's somewhat equivocal position. That political gambler had failed in his throw for the larger stake—the War Ministry. The elimination of Fritsch had not brought him that prize, but Hitler had bestowed on him the frosting without the cake by the award of a field marshal's baton. The Fuehrer knew that Goering was at least as much entranced with the trappings as with the actuality of power, that what he coveted especially were "show positions." In this case the distinction was enhanced by the relegation of Blomberg to the shadows, making Goering the only active soldier who could boast such an honor.

Hitler was somewhat in awe of his touchy lieutenant and had, no doubt, felt it important to placate his vanity.[8] He may have

[7] Engel interview, May 4, 1970.

[8] Dr. Nissen, in his years as physician to the OKW, had frequent occasion to note how Hitler would go out of his way to show consideration for Goering. This continued into a period when relations between him and his "premier paladin" had begun to cool. Hitler at times would interrupt a meeting when told that Goering

felt, too, that Goering had earned some reward for his *sangfroid* during the graver moments of the crisis when his own nerves had failed him more than once. He must have had in mind January 1938 (perhaps also June 1934) when years later he spoke of Goering's being "brutal and ice cold in times of crisis." Whenever there was a crucial situation, he could be "ruthless and hard as iron."[9]

Goering's situation contrasted with that of his SS allies. For the moment he had achieved the ultimate he could expect in the way of personal advancement. The conviction of Fritsch would not open a new road to power. In fact, pushing matters to extremes to attain it now promised considerable danger without commensurate reward. Goering, though endowed with a tougher hide than Himmler, was by no means insensitive to the questions being raised about his role in both the Blomberg and the Fritsch affairs. In addition, it was now imperative that he curb all overt hostility toward Fritsch. As one of the judges-designate of the court-martial he had to do his best to adopt a pose of impartiality.

Goering, therefore, was delighted to see the SS and Gestapo getting the lion's share of the blame that was being widely voiced even in party (notably SA) quarters. With equal faithlessness, Heydrich, seconded by Best and Meisinger, was later to seek to clear himself at Goering's expense. Yet the marriage of convenience held after a fashion until the Fritsch case was settled. If Goering were to cover up for himself during the trial, he had to do likewise for the equally or more outrageous activities of the Gestapo. But he had no intention of exposing himself unduly in the process.

While the Fritsch case was being adjudicated, a rather ambiguous role was played by two new figures in the foreground of the capital's military stage—Keitel and Hossbach's successor, Schmundt. Much has already been said about the former, notably in connection with the elevation of Brauchitsch to the exclusion of Reichenau. He has appeared as a man of mediocre talents who, on ability alone, would have found it difficult to gain entry to the General Staff. He owed his advancement to being an awesomely industrious worker and to his faculty for effacing himself in the service of his superiors. In a first meeting his frank, open glance and stalwart soldierly figure were likely to make a favorable impression. He was also not lacking in a certain persuasiveness combined with a pleasant

was arriving in order to go out to receive him. He would himself joke about this excessive mark of recognition. Nissen interview, July 15, 1971.

[9] Gisevius, *Adolf Hitler*, 411.

if ingratiating manner. His underlying insecurity was symbolized by the hasty, somewhat faltering gait that was his trademark.[10]

It is highly questionable to what degree this soldier of limited understanding recognized the basic issues of the Wehrmacht crisis and of the Fritsch case that followed on its heels. There is no indication of personal animosity toward Fritsch and certainly none that he wished to inflict injury on the Army from which he had sprung. But his close association with Blomberg since 1935 had bred a deep concern for the maintenance and further extension of the united Wehrmacht command. His first professional anxiety as the War Minister rode to his fall had been that the principle of Wehrmacht unity might collapse with the man. Hitler's success with him had been in some measure due to the persuasiveness of his argument that assumption of personal command by the dictator was the salvation of this situation. At the same time, Keitel was both caught in the spell Hitler had been at such pains to weave and dazzled by an office which had been outwardly embellished to disguise its limitations.

Hitler's mounting disdain for those in high military places had been accelerated during the 1938 Wehrmacht crisis, notably through his experiences with Blomberg, Fritsch, and Brauchitsch. It can only have been further compounded in his daily and prolonged sessions with Keitel, whom, except for the candidacy of Reichenau and the debate over the court-martial, he bent almost effortlessly to his will. One aspect of the cruel streak in Adolf Hitler manifested itself in his overbearing treatment of subordinates whom he felt he could safely abuse. Once when he had rudely berated and dismissed one of his servitors, the amazed Frau von Dirksen expressed her wonderment that the man had tolerated it. "I know exactly," he said cynically, "with which of my people I can allow myself this and with whom I cannot."[11] Small wonder that Keitel, though kept on because he was "faithful like a dog," was also picked on as a whipping boy and often had to bear the brunt of the Fuehrer's altering moods.

Unquestionably Keitel possessed organizational powers useful

[10]Walter Warlimont, "Zur Persönlichkeit des Generalfeldmarschalls Keitel" (prepared at the request of the author, September 28, 1945), 1.

[11]As related by Wiedemann who overheard the exchange. "Aufzeichnungen," 45. He tells how Hitler would call out, "A pencil," and Keitel would jump to get one. On one occasion when it was Hitler's whim not to receive him at the Berghof for three days, Keitel had his adjutant call every few hours to beg for an appointment.

in areas where other shortcomings could be balanced by extraordinary application. In a period of massive Army expansion and sweeping reorganization, this capacity could lead to real contributions. Against this, his kindest critics were unable to credit him with strategic insights or qualities of leadership.

It was, however, the deficiencies inherent in his office which put Keitel in such an impossible situation. In certain respects, he had stepped into the shoes of Blomberg; yet he was without a clear legal status in relations with the head of state and the commanders of the three services. Hitler, who had no personal interest in such matters, permitted him to carry out some of the customary ministerial duties. But at bottom he treated him as a *chef de cabinet*, a bare cut above the *chef de bureau*, the job for which Blomberg had recommended him. The prestige of the office was too minimal to make up in any degree what he lacked in abilities and personality. Under such a head there was no question of building up the OKW into the sort of Wehrmacht structure Hitler pretended to envision but never consistently furthered.

Fortunately for the OKH, Keitel for a time clung to the ingrained loyalties of the professional staff officer. During and somewhat beyond the period covered by this volume, his relationship with many of his old associates of the General Staff remained cordial. It was possible for them to find fault frankly with affairs in the OKW and to warn him against Hitler's hypnotic influence. He might remain unconvinced but would at least listen patiently and give thought to the problems. In turn he would pass on friendly warnings about moods and plans in Hitler's entourage, especially about hostile machinations of the SS. When Halder became OKH chief of staff in the late summer, he ventured at times to bring home to Keitel privately the utter indignity of his position, only to be met with tears and protestations that this was all endured for the sake of his beloved Army. Needless to say, there was never the slightest sign of a real effort at amendment.[12]

As the last pathetic remnant of Keitel's independence faded over the following years and, particularly, as he sensed more keenly the boundless contempt with which he was regarded in General Staff quarters, his consciousness of inferiority and insecurity took a malicious turn. Thereby ended the mediatory role he had sought to play between Hitler and the Army, as well as some of the other

[12] Letter of Franz Halder to a member of the IfZ, March 29, 1955 (in IfZ, ZS 240 (V)).

Wehrmacht agencies. In later years this change of attitude was to express itself in petty spite and trickery.[13]

The only way Keitel could escape being broken by his unceasing humiliation was to habituate himself to self-deception. To manage this he sought to convince those about him of what he himself only half believed. Those closest to him who, conscious of his difficulties, tried to understand and sympathize, eventually turned against him as, lashing out in his misery, he betrayed them all. With the one exception of Jodl, they sought to cut their ties and escape from him. In the end, utterly demoralized and a prey to self-contempt and self-commiseration, he would emit such cries of unhappiness as "I am no real field marshal at all" or "I no longer have any friends."[14] On both points he spoke no more than the bitter truth.

To all intents and purposes Keitel thus was becoming Hitler's man. The adherents of Fritsch were made aware of this in many ways, but they counted on his residue of Army loyalties to neutralize any tendency to become the tool of those who sought Fritsch's ruin. Up to a point Keitel had probably found some satisfaction in having the furor over Blomberg yield to that over Fritsch. For family reasons and perhaps because of guilt feelings at having helped to unleash the dogs on Blomberg by sending Helldorf to Goering, he must have found it a relief not to have the Blomberg affair stand alone. This may have put a damper on any inclination to exert himself greatly on behalf of Fritsch. It did not mean, however, that he wished to see the Army commander hounded to utter ruin. In the Fritsch case, therefore, Keitel was somewhat on the fence.

Schmundt at his own humble level is rather a pitiable figure. Basically a man of decent instincts, amiable, and of weak will, he was also something of an idealist and hero-worshiper. His idol hitherto had been Beck, his teacher at the War Academy. He now yielded completely to Hitler's manic influence and quickly trans-

---

[13] *Ibid.* General Engel relates an instance in 1942 when Keitel deliberately provoked an eruption of vexation on the part of Hitler that led to an order for Canaris's dismissal. When Canaris, entreating Engel's help, detoured around Keitel to secure a meeting with the dictator in which he managed to re-establish himself both in his office and in Hitler's good graces, Keitel veered with the wind. In virtually the same breath in which he reprimanded Engel for arranging the audience, he telephoned his congratulations to Canaris, pretending that the admiral's rehabilitation was the product of his own good offices. Interview, May 4, 1970.

[14] Warlimont, "Keitel," 3.

ferred his devotion to him. Instead of functioning as an extension of the Wehrmacht, notably the Army, in the Fuehrer's entourage, he became a docile instrument through which the dictator steadily extended and hardened his grip on the armed services. Despite his considerable capacity for rationalizing what he was too feeble and too entangled to escape, the psychological morass in which he found himself led to progressive disintegration of his personality and alcoholism.[15] His death in the explosion of July 20, 1944, may be judged to have come as a release.

In the Fritsch affair the role of Schmundt was at least as equivocal as that of Keitel. He had had little contact with the general and thus was free of any particular personal bias. But from the viewpoint of Fritsch's friends he started off badly by allowing himself to be maneuvered into a position of keeping hands off from which he never really emerged. Either Hitler or Keitel (at Hitler's orders?) had directed him on his arrival in Berlin to stay clear of the entire affair. When he called on Hossbach for the customary orientation by his predecessor, he rejected all attempts to bring him up to date on developments concerning the Army commander. The furious Hossbach then declined to proceed with the orientation which, from the Army's standpoint, had lost much of its meaning if the problem of greatest immediacy was to be excluded.[16] Thereupon Keitel ordered Jodl to orient Schmundt as best he could with respect to his duties, omitting all mention of "personal matters" (i.e., the situation regarding Fritsch).[17]

Schmundt maintained this hands-off posture throughout the adjudication of the Fritsch case, a position which could only be inimical to Fritsch's interests. Hitherto the Wehrmacht adjutant had been considered so much the particular representative of the Army that the OKH had never troubled to imitate the Navy and Luftwaffe in appointing a man of its own. For someone in Schmundt's position to remain aloof in all that pertained to the proceedings against Fritsch was a rank impropriety and a psychological and tactical handicap to the general's case. It roused so much bitterness in high Army circles that even Brauchitsch made an exasperated com-

[15] As related by a number of well-informed persons who would prefer not to be quoted.
[16] Hossbach, *Zwischen Wehrmacht und Hitler*, 123.
[17] Jodl Diary, 361, entry of January 29, 1938.

ment.[18] One consequence was a decision early in March to send a separate Army adjutant to the Chancellery.[19]

## The Defenders of Fritsch

Except for the intriguing cabal, whose members, in varying degree, knew that a showdown with the Army leadership was in the cards, the Wehrmacht crisis of 1938 caught all affected parties unprepared. Of those who emerged as "the friends of Fritsch" some few had been troubled by a rising foreboding and had gone so far as to identify him as the target of a coming attack. Still, the form and direction of the assault had left them confused and breathless. Only the more politically sophisticated, such as Schacht, Goerdeler, and Gisevius, had quickly recognized what was at issue. Hossbach, who had begun his extended tour of duty in the Chancellery believing implicitly that he should eschew anything that smacked of "politics," had over the years gained sufficient wisdom in the ways of Nazi hierarchs to recognize their aims quickly. When Wiedemann had commenced his duties in the Chancellery early in 1935, his remark to Hossbach that the Wehrmacht leaders could not afford to ignore political factors in such revolutionary times had been met with a firm: "We are soldiers. We do not want to have anything to do with and understand nothing about politics. We occupy ourselves only with military affairs."[20] Three years later Hossbach would surely have framed a less negative response. Certainly he came to recognize what then was at issue.

Of the other military figures, only the worldly-wise Canaris and, coached by Gisevius, the uncompromisingly anti-Nazi Oster had some appreciation of the situation. To Beck realization came but gradually and it was not until after the Fritsch affair that he fully got his bearings. The other soldiers, including Fritsch himself, saw the affair basically as an intrigue against the Army commander personally. The pernicious consequences of such an intrigue and of the Blomberg scandal for the Army in its relation to the state and the other services were recognized but were seen more as inherent in the unfortunate course of events than as objectives of the attack. It should further be recalled that, outside of Berlin, the

---

[18] To Captain Engel, Brauchitsch voiced not only annoyance but positive distrust concerning the role of Schmundt in the Fritsch affair. Engel interview, May 11, 1970.

[19] See below, pp. 389–391.

[20] Wiedemann, *Der Mann der Feldherr werden wollte*, 98–99.

number of prominent military men who before February 1 had even heard of the furor about the two generals could be counted on the fingers of a single hand.[21]

The efforts of those who wished to counter the assault on Fritsch were, as we have seen, characterized by uncertainty and indecision during the crisis period; but they did not go for nought, for they helped to pave the way for a more purposeful and, in the end, successful course of action in the Fritsch case. The individuals and elements rallying to Fritsch, though varying greatly in the form and intensity of their oppositional impulse, began to coalesce. The stress of the crisis crystallized a number of Opposition nuclei that might otherwise have taken months or years to evolve. In many instances, also, individuals who had swayed between resisting specific aberrations of the Nazi dictatorship and making a commitment to eliminate it were brought by their indignation to take the decisive plunge.

This was notably the case with the two basically incompatible noblemen who headed the police of the capital, Counts von Helldorf and von der Schulenburg. Their affiliation, which had begun inauspiciously when Schulenburg took over his new post in July 1937, had toward the end of the year undergone considerable improvement. One benign influence had been the transfer to the Berlin police (in October 1937) of Paul Kanstein. He had been a friend of Schulenburg's even before their extended association in the East Prussian administration and also had earlier professional relations with Helldorf. Some months later Kanstein himself was to become involved in their conspiratorial designs. At this stage he seems to have played a mediatory role on a more purely personal basis.[22]

Though the aristocratic political gambler, Helldorf, and the idealistic aristocrat, Schulenburg, could never be expected to find each other congenial, Kanstein at least succeeded in dispelling the cloud of mutual distrust that had hovered over their initial meeting. Another guardian spirit presided over the next step—the formation of a political alliance in which both turned their backs on former loyalties. This was the artist Hugo Kükelhaus, who just then was in daily contact with them while refurbishing and refurnishing

---

[21] Aside from the three commanding generals who were oriented by members of the Abwehr group, the only one who seems to have learned much was Reichenau, who set out to inform himself after being startled by Blomberg's strange nuptials. No doubt he had one or more lines leading into the War Ministry, probably directly into Blomberg's office.

[22] As related by Kanstein. Krebs, 156.

police headquarters on the Alexander Platz. Kükelhaus was an amiable fellow who achieved cordial relations with both the police president and his deputy. What Schulenburg learned about Helldorf through two other new acquaintances—Oster and Gisevius—encouraged him to take the initiative in sounding his chief out further. The personalities of Schulenburg and Gisevius clashed too greatly to permit their relations ever to be free of strain and eventually their paths diverged considerably in the pursuit of Resistance goals. But in the aim of winning Helldorf to a more unqualified stand against the regime they were at one. Through Kükelhaus, Schulenburg suggested to Helldorf a confidential meeting for an exchange of ideas. A rendezvous was arranged in one of Berlin's natatoriums, where the unceasing din eliminated all danger from eavesdropping microphones and the general nudity served as the best imaginable disguise.[23]

Helldorf at this stage still held back from a total commitment, though moving steadily toward a wider rejection of the regime. As long as the fate of Blomberg was all that was at issue, he had maintained a certain reserve. Thus he had not confided all he knew to Gisevius on the morning of January 27, withholding the significant detail of Goering's having shipped the War Minister's rival to Argentina. It was a point which, if known in time, would have revealed much about the depth of Goering's involvement in the affair and helped the Oppositionists to put pieces together. Helldorf seems to have been uncomfortable about revealing such an example of Nazi skulduggery to his anti-Nazi collaborator.[24]

The shift of the spotlight to Fritsch evoked a greater concern in Helldorf. He still felt enough the soldier and officer to resent this attack against the Army and Gisevius skillfully nourished his resentment with items of pertinent information. Gisevius also passed on to him Nebe's report of the rage of Himmler and Heydrich because Helldorf had carried the Gruhn file to Goering rather than to them.[25] Any retreat to Nazi loyalties by Helldorf was thereby

[23] *Ibid.*, 157.

[24] Gisevius, *Wo ist Nebe?* 278. Gisevius recording, July 1971.

[25] Gisevius (*Wo ist Nebe?* 279) argues that the fury of the SS leaders derived from the lost opportunity to blackmail Blomberg on their own account. In view of the opinion presented in these pages that Himmler and Heydrich were as much Goering's allies in the plot against Blomberg as in that against Fritsch, and that they knew about as much about Eva Gruhn as he did before the marriage took place, it would follow that there was no such reason for this outburst. In that case their resentment against Helldorf sprang from the simple fact that once again he had dared to go around them to another Nazi hierarch.

## Attack and Counterattack

made more difficult, at least insofar as his relations with the SS were concerned. Correspondingly his inclination to cast off final restraints in collaborating with the Abwehr enemies of the regime was reinforced.

Schulenburg, for his part, seems to have known and appreciated so little of what was afoot in late January that he went ahead with a scheduled vacation on the ski slopes of the Arlberg at the beginning of February. It is not known how much he learned about events during his absence from Berlin, but he was back in the capital and deeply immersed in the discussions of Fritsch's friends by the middle of the month.[26] By then the meaning of February 4 was so deeply engraved upon his consciousness that it was for him the final turning of the road. Six years later, when incarcerated in Gestapo cages, he was to profess that this day had marked his complete repudiation of the National Socialist regime.[27] The odious intrigue against Fritsch signified for him, as for so many others, the shattering of the last foundation stone on which Prussia and the Reich had rested. The "coordinating" process that had leveled workers, burghers, farmers, and public servants had now been extended to soldiers. As Schulenburg now saw it, the only salvation for the Reich and even for whatever National Socialism had contributed to Germany henceforth depended on an overthrow of the dictatorship.[28]

Though he had been absent during the immediate crisis and entered upon the scene only after the Fritsch case had ben under way for about two weeks, Schulenburg was not deterred from contributing substantially to the defense. His hitherto rather loose tie with Oster became firmly knotted during this period.[29] The course of the investigation will reveal the count's hand at more than one significant juncture.

### The Dilemma of Brauchitsch

As could have been foretold by anyone who knew the circumstances of his appointment, Walther von Brauchitsch found himself beset by external pressures and inner conflicts from the moment of his

[26] It is certain that this was the case by the time of Fritsch's Wannsee interrogation (approximately February 20).
[27] *Spiegelbild einer Verschwörung*, 87.
[28] Krebs, 163.
[29] His wife, who with her children had moved to Berlin in January, testifies to the multiplication of Schulenburg's contacts with Oster during these weeks. Interview with Countess Charlotte von der Schulenburg, June 30, 1970.

279

entry into office. On the one hand, he had been maneuvered into concessions which impinged on traditional concepts of the Army's place within the state. On the other, his peculiar personal situation had inhibited him from making any attempt to assure himself of the solidarity of the higher Generalität in his support. These two features of the negotiations were closely related. If Brauchitsch had felt able to call in his more prominent colleagues to reinforce his arguments, it is inconceivable that Hitler could have imposed so much of a straitjacket on the senior branch of the Wehrmacht.

As things were, Brauchitsch stood desperately in need of assuring himself as quickly as possible of the confidence of his peers if his position were to be at all tenable. For that very reason he had to keep a sealed book on some of the commitments he had made. His situation was not calculated to allow him to sleep easily. Whatever he did to live up to the agreement with Hitler would be interpreted by the Generalität as new signs of weakness in defending Army interests. If he fell too far short of the terms he had accepted, estrangement from the merciless dictator would result with the possible loss of his dearly bought post as well as a more personal form of reprisal. In his own affairs there was still ample chance of a slipup of one kind or another. Months of negotiation loomed ahead before the details of his divorce settlement were ironed out and the promised gift of money paid over.

Thus Brauchitsch could scarcely avoid being caught in the middle. He evaded as much as he could implementing the concessions he had made and sought to take the edge off others in application.[30] But, harassed by the importunities of his Hitlerite wife-to-be, he yielded enough to offend many of his Army colleagues.

At the very beginning he was the victim of a grievous dilemma. There was no way of avoiding moves that bore on the affairs of his beleaguered predecessor. He knew enough by then about Hitler's real disposition on the Fritsch case to shy from any demonstration of great zeal in his behalf. This realization was underscored by Keitel's counsel that he "should not straightway put a burden on his prestige with Hitler in this delicate matter."[31] At the same time he was made painfully aware—indeed it was conveyed to

[30] K.-J. Müller, *Das Heer und Hitler*, 272.

[31] Keitel, 275. The context indicates that this advice was tendered on the issue of Fritsch's rehabilitation. It was already Keitel's attitude, however, when the focus was still on the Fritsch case. With so transparent a man it must have been made amply manifest to Brauchitsch.

[32] *Ibid.*, 274.

him in unmistakable terms by fellow generals—that his conduct in dealing with the cause of Fritsch was the decisive test in gaining the confidence of his peers.[32] Brauchitsch must have known as well as did his sponsor, Keitel, that he was accepted by them only on sufferance. On top of the handicap of the manner of his appoint-ment, he entered office with the burden of further liabilities. Not the least of these was resentment at the blatant nepotism in appointing Keitel's brother, Bodwin (known because of the contrast in their statures as "the little Keitel"), to take the place of the respected General von Schwedler as head of the Personnel Office.[33] It was, no doubt, to avoid an additional and perhaps fatal irritant to the Generalität that Brauchitsch had resisted Hitler's demand for the immediate sacking of Beck. On the plea that the chief of staff was needed to familiarize him with OKH procedures and current problems, he was able to persuade Hitler to let Beck stay until autumn.[34]

Brauchitsch did commence with a fervent appeal to his subcommanders to give him their confidence. Immediately following Hitler's talk to the assembled generals on February 4, the newly appointed Army chief requested them to adjourn to the Bendler Strasse where he addressed them in turn. He protested that he was entering upon his post reluctantly and with serious reservations. Certain actions of the Fuehrer, notably the dismissal of a number of high officers announced that day, he had been obliged to accept as "accomplished facts."[35] His next remarks implied that what had occurred thus far with respect to Fritsch would have to be accepted similarly. In addition, Brauchitsch peremptorily forbade discussion of these matters, indicating that violations could lead to disciplinary measures.[36] Fritsch's fate would be decided by a court-martial.

In giving this assurance, which repeated only what Hitler had just told the same assembly, Brauchitsch must have felt on safe ground. The next obvious step was the constitution of the court. But Hitler departed for Berchtesgaden without attending to this vital detail and it suddenly began to look questionable whether

[33] Keitel (*ibid.*) confesses to having suggested this appointment but says that it did not rouse criticism on the part of most generals.

[34] *Ibid.*, 273. Keitel reports his presence during the debate about when to remove Beck which seems to have continued through the first two Hitler-Brauchitsch meetings before Hitler grudgingly yielded.

[35] Liebmann, 2.

[36] Geyr von Schweppenburg, 174. Confirmed by Warlimont, interview, February 7, 1970.

he intended to proceed at all. Since things had gone without a hitch in the Fuehrer's meetings with the generals and the Reich Cabinet—perhaps better than he had dared hope in the former instance—he may have wondered whether he was not secure enough to consider hedging on his promise. In any such second thought he was fortified by the urgings of Goering and Himmler, who never ceased to insist that a trial was wholly superfluous as well as undesirable for reasons of state.[37]

Brauchitsch on February 5 yielded to the exhortations of Beck and others and flew to Berchtesgaden to confront the dictator.[38] Some hours of argument are said to have followed before Hitler was brought round to standing by his word. A decision was also reached by Hitler on the key appointment of the investigative judge and prosecutor.[39]

The record is a blank on what Goering and Himmler were doing during these critical hours, but they must have made for Berchtesgaden, if they were not already there, as soon as they learned of the turn taken by events. Their influence can be discerned in several of the more salient provisions now laid down for the investigation and trial.

The final decisions on the constitution and procedure of the court-martial were made in consultation with General Heitz, president of the Reich Military Court, and Dr. Biron, the chosen investigative judge, who were both summoned to the Berghof for that purpose. Perhaps "consultation" is not the most accurate term for what was more in the nature of an extended orientation and tutorial. Hitler himself acted as instructor with a detailed review of the evidence and past developments and laid down extensive guidelines for the anticipated procedure.[40] Perhaps he also allowed his visitors to perceive at which end of the rope it would be wise to pull. In the case of General Heitz, at least, some appreciation of this was later evidenced at several critical points.

[37] Gisevius, *Bis zum bittern Ende*, 277.

[38] Beck's role is emphasized by Foerster, 91. Aside from Gisevius (*Bis zum bittern Ende*, 278), the pressure on Brauchitsch and his intervention are attested to by Hossbach (*Zwischen Wehrmacht und Hitler*, 123) and in a notation by Hassell of April 30, 1938, in his unpublished papers. Goltz (letter to the author, January 21, 1972) says that Brauchitsch followed Hitler "very soon" to Berchtesgaden. Verdict (378) gives February 5 as the date on which Hitler named the judges and ordered the investigation to proceed.

[39] Gisevius, *Bis zum bittern Ende*, 278.

[40] *Ibid.*

# Attack and Counterattack

## The Court and the Defense

Relieved as were Fritsch's friends to see the end of uncertainty about the establishment of the court-martial, close analysis of the stipulations Hitler laid down could only give rise to anxious moments. Insofar as the circumstances permitted, the dictator had encumbered the course of the defense. In brief:

1. Hitler reserved to himself the role of Gerichtsherr or ultimate judicial authority in the case. It was an office peculiar to German military in contrast to civil justice.[41] The function of the Gerichtsherr was to determine the procedures for the court, confirm the verdict, and, if he chose, reject it and decree a new trial. Rosenberger had assumed that this assignment would go to General Heitz as the supreme judicial authority of the Wehrmacht. In view of the high rank of the accused, however, it was difficult to quarrel with a decision which, though unprecedented, was supported by a certain logic.

2. Goering, who by virtue of his new dignity as field marshal had become the highest ranking officer of the Wehrmacht, was named a member of the court. In view of his known bias against Fritsch it was a scandalous appointment. Besides his role in the intrigue, which some surmised without concrete evidence, he had unquestionably revived the charges against the Army commander and brought them to Hitler's attention, had moved heaven and earth to have him declared guilty out of hand, and had resisted having the case go to the very tribunal in which he was now to function. Heaping outrage upon outrage, Hitler delegated to him also the more specific arrangements for the proceedings against Fritsch. This must be inferred from the fact that Keitel and Canaris, on February 10, had to go to Karinhall to discuss them with Goering.[42]

3. On Goering's insistence,[43] a prominent judge of the Luftwaffe, Dr. Biron, was selected for the key function of investigative judge and prosecutor. Goering did not know the man well but could assume that a person under his command and dependent on him for advancement would "pull on the right end of the rope." The fact of his party membership may also have given hope that he would "know how to work with the right people."

[41] A somewhat similar office is provided in the military judicial procedures of a number of other countries.
[42] Jodl Diary, 367, entry of February 10, 1938.
[43] J. A. Kielmansegg, *Der Fritsch-Prozess 1938*, 49.

4. Hitler abused his position as Gerichtsherr by directing that the Gestapo investigation should continue parallel to that of Biron and his staff. The two inquiries were to make available to one another the protocols of interrogations and to permit each other's representatives to be present at them. Each team was to convey to its opposite number any information that otherwise came to hand. The justification for this totally unprecedented procedure was the argument that the Gestapo was already in full career with its own "preliminary investigation." In fact, it had fought hard to retain a monopoly on this function, but this had been opposed successfully by Gürtner under the influence of Rosenberger.[44] The "compromise" was still a neat arrangement for Himmler's people. It gave them full license to keep up their own snooping to ferret out anything that could be made to look damaging to Fritsch. It also enabled them to keep abreast of what "the other side" found out or was trying to do, afforded them opportunities to cover up their own tracks, and opened the way to intimidation, perhaps even "elimination," of unwanted witnesses on whom Fritsch's friends might stumble.

The independent and free operation of the court could hardly fail to be influenced negatively by this directive. The forces rallying to Fritsch could only attempt to balance matters somewhat by influencing the selection of others associated with the court. Hitler himself had but limited leeway in naming the other judges. The choice of Goering dictated that of Raeder and Brauchitsch as heads of the other services. In conformity with legal requirements, the tally was completed with appointment of two military jurists, Drs. Sellmer and Lehmann, the Senate presidents of the Reich Military Court. In the natural course of affairs, Sellmer, the senior of the two, would have acted as presiding officer but, as it turned out, Goering impudently usurped that role without anyone's daring to take issue with him. By far the most important step from the standpoint of the defense, for which the credit belongs to Rosenberger, was establishing at the side of Biron as keeper of protocol Dr. Sack, the military jurist who had been Rosenberger's candidate for the post of chief investigator. In the view of the present writer, Karl Sack is the most underrated figure of the military Opposition.

[44] Interview with Ernst Kanter, May 9, 1970. Gisevius asserts (recording, January 1972) that Hitler further alleged that the Gestapo's part in the investigation was not really directed against Fritsch but was necessitated by the pursuit of its regular charge to deal with the problem of homosexuality, in this case to establish the extent of Schmidt's reliability.

# Attack and Counterattack

In the judgment of Rosenberger he was indeed "one of the great historical personalities of that epoch."[45] His role from this point on is vital in the struggle against the forces mobilized to ruin Fritsch and is significant in numerous later crises in Opposition affairs. Only the men in the developing Abwehr Opposition circle are in the same category of guardian angel for friends in trouble. In such cases no risk was too great for him and he operated at times with a daring that took away the breath of less resolute associates. Like Canaris he would respond without hesitation to appeals on behalf of total strangers who were beset by one or another manifestation of Hitlerite tyranny. Rare among those of his profession, he was a man of genuine revolutionary élan who stands with the activists of the Opposition.[46]

After a war record of extraordinary distinction (he was wounded five times), Sack had studied law and in time gained prominence in the Hessian administration of justice. From there, like a number of other distinguished jurists, he went over to the military legal system and was eventually to become the Army's judge advocate general. He achieved some prominence opposing the Nazis in the twenties, making speeches against them and being a strong supporter of the Stresemann "fulfillment" policies they hated.

In Sack's case, bravery on the battlefield was fully matched by far rarer civil courage. He was astute and enterprising and of a steadfastness and determination exceeded by no other figure of the Opposition.

Sack's qualities of leadership were to come into the foreground during the Fritsch case, where, in one situation after another, he was the moving spirit and initiator in steps that helped to clear the general. Without a doubt his influence was the essential factor in stiffening Biron, a man of no great strength though honorable and well intentioned, in the pursuit of his duties. By instinct and past association Biron's heart no doubt was on the Army's side. In his first meeting with Goltz he was to assure Fritsch's defender: "I know that Colonel General von Fritsch is an outstanding personality and conceive my task to be establishing his innocence."[47] These sympathies, however, on occasion seemed in danger of being overborne by his fears, for he could not fail to appreciate the hazards

[45] As expressed in a letter addressed in 1948 to General Fritz Hofmann. Hofmann interview, April 13, 1970.
[46] Interview with Judge Wilhelm Weinheimer, February 15, 1970.
[47] Goltz interview, November 1, 1969.

to his position in the Luftwaffe. At times he might have faltered under pressure had there not been Sack's steadying presence at his elbow.

Sack's task was much lightened after mid-February by the addition to the investigative panel of Dr. Ernst Kanter, another military jurist and his colleague in the military court at Giessen.[48] By then the investigation was in full swing and the only two senior officials of the court-martial charged with this function, Biron and Sack, were hard put to it to attend to the most necessary of their duties. Working as a team, they had more than enough to occupy them in conducting their interrogations and had no one competent to observe those of the Gestapo. Or better, as Kanter puts it, "those of which the Gestapo chose to notify them." It was always to be assumed that Himmler's people carried on as they saw fit when they wished to proceed without the presence of outside observers.[49]

Sack had appealed to General Heitz and, with the help of the general's adjutant, Colonel Baron von Schleinitz, had persuaded him to petition Hitler to add another judge to the panel. Here is a further striking illustration of how the official court-martial investigators were handicapped because Hitler, as Gerichtsherr, reserved all dispositions with respect to the case to himself.[50] The Gestapo, of course, could invest whatever it chose from its unlimited resources to buttress its own position in the race with the rival group. As things were, the defense and the official investigation would have fallen badly behind if it had not been for the volunteer help provided by the Abwehr circle and by Nebe from Himmler's own police empire.

The new assignment went to Kanter and at first was strictly limited to attending those Gestapo interrogations of which the court representatives received notice. Heitz, who by now was moving with reserve in any action that might incur the ill will of the SS, was at first reluctant to bring Kanter more fully into the case. It was only after further importunities from Sack and another appeal to the good offices of Colonel von Schleinitz that Kanter was empowered to assist the others in studying the basic materials for

[48] Kanter, who now lives in Cologne, retired several years ago as a Senate president of the German Federal Court.

[49] Kanter interview, May 9, 1970. A known example of the Gestapo's failing to give the required notice was its arrest and interrogation of Captain von Frisch after he had been discovered by the court-martial investigators.

[50] Letter of Kanter to Kielmansegg, January 17, 1949. Kielmansegg Papers.

the case, such as the Gestapo files that had thus far accumulated.[51]
Needless to say, the Gestapo was vexed to perceive the addition
of another member to the rival team. In various ways Kanter was
made aware of this. There would be harassing telephone calls late
at night or seductive feminine voices over the phone suggesting
a rendezvous at nearby corners.[52] Sack and Kanter worked with
complete unity of mind and purpose throughout the case. This
solid front of his fellow jurists could not fail to exercise a strong
influence on Biron.

Of vital import for Fritsch was, of course, the choice of his
defender. Here, as we have seen, his attention had as early as
the evening of January 26 been directed by Joachim von Stülpnagel
to Count Rüdiger von der Goltz. The count, Stülpnagel had pointed
out, was a man of high mind who, as a National Socialist, would
be especially qualified to deal effectively with party personages.[53]

Goltz was a member of a distinguished military family whose
father gained world attention as commander of the major German
operation in the Baltic area after the conclusion of World War
I. Other bearers of the name made their mark in Turkey and elsewhere. He himself had served in a Prussian Guard regiment and
had suffered an incapacitating leg wound at the very beginning
of the conflict. He then entered upon the study of law but, because
of the increasing dearth of officers, returned to service on the staff
of the crown prince's army group. There began his acquaintance
with the family of the chief of staff, Count Friedrich von der Schulenburg, resulting later in his becoming a close friend of the fourth
son, Fritz-Dietlof. He also established a cordial personal relationship with another member of the staff, Ludwig Beck, whom he
served as adjutant and who later became the godfather to one of
his sons.[54]

Like Fritz-Dietlof, Goltz joined the National Socialist party and
was in time elevated to the post of president of the Reich lawyers'
organization. He became a member of the Prussian Council of
State and something of a persona grata in the Reich Chancellery,
where Wiedemann, among whose duties it was to stage such little
affairs, was accustomed to invite him and his nine (later ten) children for a ceremony of congratulation on Hitler's birthdays.[55]

[51] Letter of Kanter to Keilmansegg, November 8, 1947. Kielmansegg Papers.
[52] Kanter interview, May 9, 1970.
[53] Stülpnagel, 356.
[54] Goltz interview, November 1, 1969.
[55] Wiedemann, *Der Mann der Feldherr werden wollte*, 92.

Fritsch had the more readily agreed to ask Goltz to be his defender because he knew the count quite well, probably better than any other attorney in Berlin. He had been a General Staff officer of the 1st Guards Division in which Goltz's father had commanded an infantry brigade and, when he was commander of an infantry brigade in Stettin, had been a guest in the Goltz home there. Goltz believes further that Beck probably seconded Stülpnagel's recommendation.[56] All personal considerations aside, Fritsch agreed with Stülpnagel on the advisability of choosing a man who stood well with the regime and at the same time could be trusted to show understanding and concern for concepts of military honor.

Fritsch evidently waited to approach Goltz until Hitler had agreed, on January 29 or 30, to his trial by court-martial. On the afternoon of the latter date, a Sunday, Goltz and his wife were entertaining out-of-town friends whom they had not seen for years. This pleasant gathering was interrupted by a telephone call from Captain von Both who asked that Goltz come immediately to the Bendler Strasse. When the count described his situation and asked whether the matter really required such instant attention, he was told that Fritsch nevertheless begged him to come.[57]

Goltz found Fritsch withdrawn in manner as usual but visibly in a state of great excitement. He began with the startling query whether Goltz would be willing to represent him in a matter which must bring him into the sharpest conflict with Himmler, Heydrich, and the entire SS. The astonished caller replied that he could not imagine how an attorney could be of any use in a controversy with the SS. Fritsch thereupon explained that his difficulties with the Black Corps had led it to raise charges against him under Article 175 and related briefly his experience in the Chancellery. Goltz must realize, he said, that to represent the Army commander in this case could lead to personal reprisals for him. The count replied that he was entirely at the general's service.[58]

Late the following morning Goltz was back in the Bendler Strasse for a more thorough briefing on all that Fritsch had thus far learned and experienced. His visit happened to coincide with Rundstedt's return from the Chancellery with the story of his talk with Hitler.

[56] Goltz interview, July 8, 1971.

[57] Goltz interview, November 1, 1969. Goltz, "Erinnerungen," 164. This chapter of Goltz's memoirs is a restatement with some amplification of his "Darstellung Prozess Generaloberst von Fritsch" (prepared in 1945-46; in IfZ, ZS 49). Except where differences may occur only the memoirs will hereafter be cited.

[58] Goltz, "Erinnerungen," 164-165.

# Attack and Counterattack

Rundstedt had apparently already called on Gürtner to impress on him also the Army's concern for the earliest possible clarification of the matter to the benefit of Fritsch.[59]

The next call made by Goltz took him to the Ministry of Justice where he had successive talks with Gürtner and Dohnanyi. From the first exchange there was no doubt that the Minister's personal sympathies lay entirely with Fritsch. He could not hide embarrassment and a defensive attitude about submitting the opinion he had delivered to Hitler two days earlier, protesting that he really had no choice about the investigation and trial since it was the only way Fritsch could clear himself. Later, after February 5, when he agreed to the coincident Gestapo investigation and the exchange of protocols, he excused his action to Goltz on the plea that, had he failed to compromise, the Ministry of Justice would simply have been booted out of the entire affair. In parting he gave the attorney sage counsel: "Count von der Goltz, I am giving you some good advice. Read the documents with greatest care. I have learned from experience that the man who knows the documents best wins his case."[60]

Goltz knew Dohnanyi better than Gürtner because that official's wife, Christine, a Bonhoeffer, was the count's cousin. In his case, too, it was immediately obvious that he supported Fritsch and with greater personal dedication than was the case with the more fainthearted Gürtner. Gürtner and Dohnanyi had by now become so skeptical about the witness, Schmidt, that they had gone beyond the bounds of their function and made a personal visit to the Wannsee station at the Potsdamer Platz. Their observations there, they said, had not served to increase their confidence in Schmidt's testimony. Goltz and Dohnanyi agreed to remain in constant contact for the coordination of their moves while the investigation was under way.[61]

As Fritsch's defender sat down to study the various files made available to him by the Justice Ministry, he was struck by one startling revelation after another. There was Schmidt's record of highly questionable testimony, so contrary to what Hitler had assured Gürtner, Hossbach, and others. Before him also was the supplementary protocol of Schmidt's interrogations, undertaken with such curious haste on and after January 20, the very eve of the

[59] *Ibid.*, 165.
[60] Goltz interview, November 1, 1969.
[61] *Ibid.*

289

breaking of the Blomberg scandal.[62] There were the protocols of Fritsch's Gestapo interrogations—and a notation (assuredly an oversight by the SS) stated that they were transcripts of a recording. Here the attorney's eyes fell with indignation on the bald words of Werner Best: "We are among ourselves." Further, there was the avidity with which the Gestapo had leaped to grill the two Hitler-boys who had enjoyed Fritsch's hospitality plus the completely negative results of this questioning.[63] It was all of a pattern—a desperate effort to exploit every resource to pin something on Fritsch. Everywhere were signs of hands working through the Gestapo, always the strong hint of puissant forces lurking in the background.

As the lawyer perused the Schmidt police file an incident he had all but forgotten flashed into his mind. Back in October of 1936 he had been called to the door to speak to a poorly dressed, starved-looking fellow who claimed to have just been released from a concentration camp. There, he said, he had made the acquaintance of a rogue named Schmidt, a man who had engaged in extortion practices even in the camp, and who had boasted of "holding in his hand" State Secretary Funk and Councilor of State von der Goltz. The man said Schmidt had claimed he would see to it that these two highly placed miscreants would also land in the camp in short order. Wary of blackmail, the count had sent the man packing without even giving him the few pfennigs he had spent on suburban fare, a severity which later caused him some regrets. At the time he suspected that it might be a trick of the Gestapo and decided to dispatch a letter the next day to Werner Best reporting the incident. No reply had come from Best.[64]

Goltz determined to bring the situation to the attention of Gürtner and to make a plea for suspension of the case. Was it not best, he urged, for him to make a deposition under oath in the matter touching him personally and then be confronted with Schmidt? Thereby could be established once and for all the mendacity of the pretentious scoundrel and a stop could be put to the farce of an investigation. But Gürtner, who knew well that Hilter would not relent even if the Minister summoned the courage to face him

[62] Goltz, "Erinnerungen," 168.
[63] Ibid., 169.
[64] When challenged about this at the time of the Fritsch case, Best excused himself on the grounds that pressures of work and the certainty that Goltz was above such suspicions had led him to neglect the matter. Goltz interview, November 1, 1969.

on the issue, insisted that pursuing things to the bitter end was
the only way Fritsch could be cleared. He praised the widsom
of Goltz in having written to Best: "How good it is, how happy
I am that you wrote the letter."[65]

Goltz could only resign himself to driving ahead on a road strewn
with obstacles. He continued his efforts to demonstrate the general
unreliability of Schmidt and to find an absolute alibi for Fritsch,
but knew that his central problem was making the blackmailer
repudiate his own testimony.

It soon became evident how much the dual investigation was
a handicap both to the defense and to the attempts of Biron's court
investigators to get at the facts in the case. The mere circumstance
that witnesses were subjected to two teams of questioners, and
thus quickly learned what others had said, interfered at every point.
Goltz became so vexed with the consequences of this absurdity
that he went to Keitel, entreating him to induce Hitler to direct
a return to a more normal procedure. Beck was also so exercised
over the situation that he lodged a similar complaint with Keitel.
Neither intervention had the slightest positive result.[66] In fact, it
is highly questionable whether Keitel, knowing how adamant Hitler
was on this point, ever raised the matter in the Chancellery. Thus
the investigation settled down into a grim race between two competing state agencies charged with striving along parallel lines but
persistently operating at cross-purposes.

### Activities of the Abwehr Group

Meanwhile, at a constantly accelerating pace, the elements dedicated to the exoneration of Fritsch were getting to know each other
and drawing closer together. Save for the inner circle already clus-
tered about the core group in the Abwehr, few of those concerned
had hitherto formed close relationships among themselves. An exception was the friendship between Rosenberger and Sack, who
have been described as being "one head and one soul." Rosenberger
had originally brought Sack over into military justice; for years
they had been comrades in a campaign to humanize the Army's
disciplinary code and had achieved such reforms as the abolition
of punitive drill and of confinement in the dark on bread and
water.[67]

[65] Goltz, "Erinnerungen," 183.
[66] *Ibid.*, 185.
[67] Hofmann interview, April 13, 1970.

Sack seems to have become acquainted with Canaris and Oster in the mid-thirties. At any rate, their mutual antipathy for Nazism formed the basis for a working relationship of sorts by the time of the Wehrmacht crisis of 1938. There was much besides their political outlook to draw Sack and Oster together. They were both the sons of Protestant clergymen with a strong religious orientation. Another bond was their common disposition to translate deep convictions and public concern into action. Sack was as ardent in spirit and could be as daring as Oster, but was the cooler and more self-controlled of the two. He was less inclined to plunge ahead all the way in a once chosen direction and was more bound to traditional conceptions. He could not, like Oster, have brought himself to follow a course that, in established terms, would be defined as "treason to the country."[68]

More intimate, no doubt because they were personally more attuned to one another, was the friendship between Sack and Dohnanyi. The military jurists frequently had business with the Ministry of Justice, where Dohnanyi as principal aide to Gürtner often spoke for the Ministry in dealings with other agencies. The acquaintance between the two ripened rapidly into friendship when, in 1937, they were members of a Commission on Penal Law. Sack felt much drawn to the clear-thinking, fine-nerved Dohnanyi, who seemed to him to embody the judicial conscience. The decisive bond between them was forged by their cooperation in the Fritsch case, where Sack was mainly responsible that Dohnanyi, who had at first been somewhat disoriented with respect to contending forces and issues, moved with fuller insight and purpose as the proceedings advanced. It was Sack, also, who in the process made Dohnanyi acquainted with Oster and thus helped to initiate a working partnership of great moment in the history of the German Opposition.[69]

In the later stages of the Fritsch case it was Oster, Sack, and Dohnanyi who, together with Gisevius, furnished the vital linkage between clusters of support for the general. From Oster the line ran over Canaris to Beck, whom Sack as yet knew slightly or not at all. The close direct relationship of Beck and Oster was to blossom only during the spring and summer months. Canaris also pro-

[68] Hermann Bösch, *Heeresrichter Dr. Karl Sack im Widerstand: Eine historische-politische Studie* (Munich, 1967), 50.

[69] Weinheimer interview, February 15, 1970. Bösch, 51. According to Josef Müller, Canaris, Oster, and Dohnanyi in their conversations always stressed how much their association had grown out of the Fritsch affair. Interview, January 19, 1970. See also Gisevius, *Bis zum bittern Ende*, 279-280.

vided a line to Hossbach, whose severity in dealing with the problem of Oster's rehabilitation after his Mardi Gras escapade made difficult any cordial communication of a more personal type between the two.[70] There was further a direct line from Oster to Captain von Both in Fritsch's immediate entourage.[71]

Oster thus functioned as the vital exchange and motor center for very nearly all who were prepared to "do something" to thwart manifestations of Nazi tyranny. Through Fritz-Dietlof von der Schulenburg ran his connection with officers of Infantry Regiment 9 at Potsdam. Most essential to the entire campaign on Fritsch's behalf was the constant stream of information about the doings "on the other side" which reached Gisevius from Nebe and, to a lesser but still important extent, from Helldorf and was passed on to Oster. Failing this source of insight into Gestapo activities and stratagems, those who worked for Fritsch would most often have floundered in the dark.

From the moment of Sack's entry into the case, Oster worked closely with him, according to one account, and Rosenberger.[72] The flow of intelligence on "the enemy" which came through Gisevius was now directed especially to Sack who passed on what was of immediate use for the defense to Goltz.[73] This revealed much of the pattern of the intrigue that had been mounted against both the War Minister and the Army commander. From Nebe came the first signal about the watch kept on Fritsch in Egypt, including the names of the agents who had performed that assignment.[74] Gisevius also learned from Carl Christian Schmid, the government president of Düsseldorf and a man with a keen nose for inside news, that Goering had obliged Blomberg by shipping his rival off to Argentina. As has been noted, this item was then confirmed by a reluctant Helldorf.[75]

By far the most significant single piece of information dealt with the existence of a "double" to whom the story as related by Otto

[70] This lack of personal contact alone can explain Hossbach's continued conviction that Oster was no more than "a peripheral figure" during the Fritsch affair. Hossbach interview, July 1, 1971. The present study shows this view to be much in error.
[71] Heinz, 72.
[72] Ibid., 75.
[73] It is evident that the Oppositionists at Tirpitz Ufer were somewhat leery of Goltz because of his party membership and prominence in National Socialist affairs. Certainly Goltz was told nothing of the role of Nebe as a source of information. Goltz interview, July 8, 1971. Goltz, "Erinnerungen," 197.
[74] Gisevius recording, July 1971.
[75] Ibid. Gisevius, Wo ist Nebe? 278.

Schmidt actually applied. As usual when some SS deviltry was afoot, it was Nebe who managed to learn of it in the antechambers of the Prinz-Albrecht-Strasse. The circumstances convey more than a hint that the news he picked up was a repercussion of the furor following the discovery made in the deserted offices of Meisinger's department by Franz Josef Huber. Huber's successive reports to Best, Heydrich, and Himmler, it will be recalled, were made the morning of January 28, a Friday, releasing a chain of reactions which, though unrecorded, can safely be guessed at and whose full impact can only have been felt the next Monday.

To begin with, the number of those who knew of Captain von Frisch had been increased by at least two—Huber and Best. The annoyance of Himmler and Heydrich must have manifested itself in divers ways, notably in calling on the carpet Fehling or whoever else had been guilty of such sloppy security.[76] If Meisinger returned from his cruise that weekend, as seems likely, he must have been included in any conventicles that fixed blame and determined the next steps. All in all, a number of offices in the Prinz-Albrecht-Strasse must have buzzed like so many nests of disturbed hornets. Small wonder that this intruded on Nebe's attention and that he soon ferreted out the reason behind this perturbation.

On the evening of January 31 Gisevius heard on his telephone the guttural sounds which told him that Nebe would await him at one of their points of rendezvous. On this occasion he was summoned to a dimly illuminated corner in the Zehlendorf suburb where Nebe resided. There Gisevius was picked up by a car with dimmed lights which careened up and down various streets before Nebe was convinced that all danger of being followed had been excluded. They finally halted at a dark park where Nebe, pistol in hand and nerves ajangle, went to scout out the environs. Then, at last, he divulged that the so-called Fritsch case was turning out to be one of mistaken or deliberately misplaced identity. Himmler and Heydrich knew of the "error" but were set on driving ahead anyway and moving heaven and earth to hide the facts.[77]

Nebe implored his friend to exercise the most extreme caution in utilizing this information. If Heydrich heard of the least indiscre-

[76] If, contrary to the view expressed here, Gisevius is correct in believing that Himmler, Heydrich, and Goering had not been apprised of the Gestapo's discovery of Frisch in mid-January, the tremors at Prinz-Albrecht-Strasse 8 can only have been the greater, affording that much more occasion for them to reach Nebe.

[77] This paragraph and the two following are based on the account of Gisevius, *Bis zum bittern Ende*, 274.

tion he would go berserk and "shoot like mad about him." Insofar as at all possible, those on Fritsch's side must appear to discover the truth by their own devices.

Gisevius hastened to Oster and early the next morning the two conferred with Canaris. It was agreed that the admiral would advise Beck and Keitel. Others to be less directly alerted would be given a statement prepared by Gisevius in which the charges against Fritsch would be so analyzed as to argue for the probability of a confusion of persons. Copies were carried to Beck and Raeder by Canaris and during the succeeding days were brought to the attention of other generals.

After February 5 Sack received a copy from Gisevius.[78] The statement seems to have been withheld from Goltz, though all concerned with the defense or the court investigation were alerted in one way or another to watch for evidence indicating misplaced identity.[79]

Thus the pulling and hauling on the part of both groups of contestants gathered momentum. All this went on under cover of the severest security regulations. The case had been officially placed in the category of a "secret Reich matter," which prohibited not only advising the public of its existence but any private mention by those who were initiated. Goltz, for example, judged it imperative to say no word of what he was doing to his office staff, which must have been greatly mystified by his frequent and unexplained absences. There was some absurdity about this since he was regularly called for by a military service car, but he had to avoid giving the least excuse for being dismissed from the case. This condemned him to the tedious and time-consuming task of typing all that related to it himself.[80]

Goltz's caution was well advised, for he soon learned from his friend Fritz-Dietlof von der Schulenburg that he was under close Gestapo watch. Schulenburg arranged to have two technicians from the Abwehr examine his telephone for hidden microphones.[81]

So far in our story of the formal investigation phase of the Fritsch case something has been said about all of the principal and many of the secondary figures with a noteworthy exception—Werner von Fritsch himself. Apart from a statement he was to have inserted

[78] Gisevius interview, July 11, 1971.
[79] Thus Beck made it a point to bring such a "likelihood" to Goltz's attention. Goltz, "Erinnerungen," 178–179.
[80] *Ibid.*, 199.
[81] *Ibid.*, 188.

in the protocol on February 23, a step to which he was persuaded with some difficulty by Sack, the ousted Army commander never emerges into the foreground. Both investigation and trial are to show him in an invariably passive role, responding negatively to challenges and only on this one occasion yielding to an impulse to strike back.

Hitler's official letter of dismissal, which had reached Fritsch on February 5, had taken a form which could only further humiliate and wound. It consisted of two brief paragraphs. One contained the obligatory words of appreciation about his service in rebuilding the German Army. The other was a flagrant misstatement of the reasons for his departure. It asserted that Fritch had for reasons of health begged to be relieved of duty some time before. The trip to Egypt had held out hopes for improvement but, these not being realized, Hitler had no choice but to defer to the general's wishes. Fritsch can only have been consumed with bitterness as he affixed his initial to record the reception of the document and laid it away.[82]

Aside from his extreme exhaustion, Fritsch's impassivity in face of the many-pronged attack which continued to be directed against him sprang from a crushing pessimism for which there was all too much justification. Since the confrontation on the evening of January 26 he had sensed what Goltz found difficult to grasp until he surveyed the accumulated files at the Ministry of Justice. In a clash between the assertions of the Army commander and of a notorious criminal, if the chief of state saw fit to reject the word of honor of the former, his case became all but hopeless. There was small possibility of locating adequate proof that over four years before on a day that could not be fixed exactly a certain action had *not* occurred. Had he learned of the charges when they were first raised in 1936, Fritsch told Goltz, there might still have been some prospect of doing this. With the passage of two more years such chances had become minimal.[83]

To Fritsch it seemed that all he could do as the official inquiry got under way was to repeat monotonously the denials he had made in the Gestapo interrogations. Meanwhile he was imprisoned in a dreary routine of existence which reinforced his tendency toward erosive introspection and his sense of hopeless isolation. He is at times described as subject to a form of house arrest which

[82] Text in J. A. Kielmansegg, *Der Fritsch-Prozess 1938*, 42.
[83] Goltz interview, November 1, 1969.

did not strictly enjoin confinement to quarters. The formal restrictions seem to have been limited to suspension of official duties and of normal social life, already so self-restricted. The diplomatic corps buzzed with rumors of his "arrest" when a dinner scheduled for February 3 to which prominent members had been invited was canceled.[84] For the time being he seems to have abandoned his beloved morning rides.[85] His excursions seem to have been confined to long walks in the Berlin environs with Hossbach or in the parks of the Potsdam palace complex with Joachim von Stülpnagel.

Perhaps unknown to him, Stülpnagel always carried a well-loaded revolver.[86] Fritsch's friends were beset by anxiety about a possible *coup de main* by which he would be snatched away into Gestapo custody.[87] They were mindful, too, of the innumerable instances in which the Gestapo or some other ill-famed arm of the regime or party had been credited with staging "suicides." So a special guard of devoted junior officers under Both's auspices was set to watch over Fritsch night and day.[88]

About eight persons were allowed regular access to the general. Even these, until they became personally known to the individual guards, would be received with drawn pistols and closely escorted to the adjutant on duty, Captain von Prittwitz.[89] Fritsch's physician, Dr. Nissen, related graphically to the present author his own sensations of discomfort when he was conducted in this fashion.[90] The young men who volunteered for this duty had instructions to shoot without warning at the slightest sign of anyone's trying to evade their surveillance.[91]

However wise and necessary such precautions, they inflicted on Fritsch a regimen which could not fail to increase his tendency toward gloomy introversion. It severely restricted his contacts with all but his most intimate associates among his military peers and inhibited whatever impulse he may have felt from time to time

[84] François-Poncet, 230.
[85] Letter of Hossbach to the author, January 1, 1972.
[86] Stülpnagel, 358.
[87] Affidavit of one of the officers concerned, Baron Hans von Koskull, September 20, 1947. Kielmansegg Papers.
[88] Goltz interview, July 8, 1971.
[89] Prittwitz fell in the war as a lieutenant colonel.
[90] Nissen interview, July 15, 1971.
[91] Koskull affidavit. Kielmansegg Papers.

to strike back at his tormentors.[92] His mood, on the contrary, was more to seek escape from the sea of troubles which threatened to engulf him. It was probably under the impact of humiliations which inundated him in late February (his third Gestapo interrogation and the questioning of former grooms and orderlies) that his thoughts once more turned to suicide. Goltz was asked whether it would be well to forestall further painful experiences by choosing death. Like Dr. Nissen before him, the count replied that this was the one thing to avoid since it would appear an indirect admission of guilt. As a soldier he must bear what came his way. Goltz believes this declaration to have conformed entirely with Fritsch's basic feeling but he was glad to have the matter put so forcefully.[93]

Gradually Fritsch did become aware how Adolf Hitler, whatever his role may have been in the initiatory stages of the affair, was now not only tolerating but actively backing SS machinations. The dictator's perverse insistence on the dual investigation, his leaving Schmidt in the hands of an agency which in plain fact had the power of life and death over him, his fiat that, despite these circumstances, the case must continue until the blackmailer defied his jailors and repudiated his own testimony—all this betokened the fullest measure of connivance.[94] But appreciation came too tardily and, before February 23, too gradually to produce the kind of shock effect that would rouse him to retaliation.

## Progress of the Investigation

The first phase of the investigation was marked by a sorting out and drawing together of elements ready to play an active role on behalf of the former Army commander. Something like an improvised network of communication had sprung into existence to link the points of support in ministries and Wehrmacht agencies. Persons who had hitherto largely lived the restricted lives of sober citizens attending to their own affairs found themselves caught up in a web of clandestine relationships.

For the first time since Germany had become a nation, a conspiratorial atmosphere reigned in significant sectors of her governing apparatus. In view of Hitler's stringent security injunctions in all

[92] Thus Captain Engel, on becoming Army adjutant and learning for the first time the extent of what had been going on, wished to rush to Fritsch to whom he was personally devoted. He was told that there was no chance of his securing access to the general. Engel Diary, entry of the night of March 11-12, 1938.

[93] Goltz letter to the author, January 21, 1972.

[94] Goltz interview, July 8, 1971. Nissen interview, July 15, 1971.

# Attack and Counterattack

that pertained to the Fritsch case, ordinarily innocent forms of activity could be classed as intervention in the proceedings he had ordained. In effect, if the friends of Fritsch were to thwart the forces arrayed against him, they were condemned to the role of plotters against authority. Persons who merely sought to be helpful were thus not many steps behind associates who were consciously crossing the threshold of conspiracy against the state.

As a consequence, the Fritsch affair was something of a rehearsal for the more genuine conspiratorial enterprise that blossomed during the following summer. Lines of communication and habits of cooperation were formed which became established features of the Army-related Opposition. Like all plottings against an existing order, this one manifested itself in nocturnal flittings that frayed nerves even among the less amateur of those who worked for the exoneration of Fritsch.

Best equipped by professional background for such cloak-and-dagger encounters were the police and intelligence specialists grouped about the Oster-Gisevius partnership. In addition to their occasional association at the Abwehr offices, where caution put restraint on free exchanges, the two friends met frequently in the evening. This was much facilitated by proximity of residence; Oster lived at the Bayrischer Platz and Gisevius in the Duisburger Strasse close by. Often Gisevius would carry Oster's messages or other information to Sack, whose apartment was only a few minutes' walk away.[95] Sack also kept Oster generally informed of significant developments in the investigation and regularly provided copies of the protocols of the proceedings. These would then be carried by Canaris to Beck,[96] usually by way of Hossbach, whom it was also important to keep *au courant*.[97]

In many instances it proved difficult or hazardous for these principals to deal directly with one another. Here an enduring link was provided by Elisabeth Strünck. Her husband had not yet joined the Abwehr, but he was then in Berlin on an extended exercise as a reservist. He and his wife stayed at the Hotel Continental and she had the regular use of their automobile. It was during the proceedings in the Fritsch case that she began that devoted and tireless activity that enmeshed her more than any other woman

[95] Gisevius interview, July 11, 1971.
[96] Weinheimer interview, February 15, 1970.
[97] General Hossbach relates that Canaris regularly brought him the protocols which he then passed on to Beck. He does not recall whether they ultimately were deposited in his or Beck's files. Interview, July 1, 1971.

299

in the affairs of the Opposition.[98] In February–March 1938 she carried messages between Nebe and the Oster-Gisevius duo. After a suitably camouflaged telephone call, she would meet Nebe at Im Kornfeld on the edge of the city or at the home of a Dr. Hildebrand near the War Ministry.[99] Her other major activity which later assumed great importance, that of providing a place for meeting and exchange of information, was as yet inhibited by the Strüncks' residence in a hotel.

The investigation had not gone far before a direct connection was also established between Oster and Goltz. It was Dohnanyi who called to the count's attention the unstinting support which anyone associated with the defense could be sure of finding at Tirpitz Ufer. On some half-dozen different occasions Goltz went to Abwehr headquarters to entreat Oster for one form of help or another with invariably positive results. On one of these visits Oster made him acquainted with Gisevius, but the relationship did not develop beyond that point. All in all, it was brought home to Goltz that the Canaris-Oster shop was at his disposal when aid was needed.[100]

Goltz, indeed, had need of all the assistance he could summon to his side. His task obliged him to follow innumerable leads to undermine the dependability of Schmidt and to refute the particulars of his testimony against Fritsch. The police files furnished ample material for instances of falsehood or outrageous exaggeration on his part. Goltz sought to dramatize this by demonstrating the absurdity of the charges Schmidt had raised against other prominent persons. Of their number Ambassador Leopold von Hoesch was already dead. Count Wedel, the police president of Potsdam, who stood high in the party, was called in for interrogation and declared under oath the falsity of the accusation in his case.[101]

Most telling by far was an examination of Schmidt to investigate his concentration camp boast that he "had in his hand State Councilor von der Goltz." The blackmailer was first questioned at length on the supposed circumstances of his relations with the count.

[98] Her extraordinary role in this regard is attested to by all survivors of the military and associated Opposition, notably Gisevius, who had the most occasion to observe and benefit by it. Interview, July 11, 1971.

[99] Strünck-Gärtner interview, April 18, 1970.

[100] Oster's form of introduction was typical: "This is a time when all decent people should know each other. Dr. Gisevius, Count von der Goltz." Goltz interview, November 1, 1969. Goltz letter to the author, January 21, 1972.

[101] Goltz, "Erinnerungen," 181.

# Attack and Counterattack

Besides numerous other details that in no way fit his supposed quarry, he asserted that the man wore glasses and was small, square-built, and brunet—all features opposed to the facts. When Goltz was brought in, Schmidt then affirmed that he had never seen him in his life. In the end it turned out that the actual victim was a deceased lawyer named Goltz, a commoner without distinction, whom Schmidt had ennobled and promoted in the world to enhance his own importance.[102] The parallel to the situation of Fritsch appeared so obvious that the defense could only feel sustained in its efforts to discover a similar "double" in his case.

Unfortunately, in view of his wide-ranging connections in the Berlin demimonde, Schmidt had found it easy to give some plausibility to his lies by telling the truth about a number of other notable persons. It could only hurt Fritsch's case that one of these was now arrested by the Gestapo amid much public sensation. This was no less a personage than the man who, next to boxer Max Schmelling, was Germany's most world-famous athlete, tennis champion Baron Gottfried von Cramm, just then returned home from new international triumphs. Apparently the blow to Germany's prestige abroad mattered little to Himmler and Heydrich if thereby they could harden the case against Fritsch.

Thus progress and setback alternated in the endeavor to discredit Schmidt as a witness. Clearly truth and untruth were blended in his many charges. What was imperative was proof that he was lying in the particular case at issue.

The search for such evidence took many forms. The memories of Fritsch's secretarial staff were strained and the files of his office thoroughly searched for details of his daily movements during the period in question. It was not too difficult to establish that official travel, tours of inspection, lengthy meetings, and related activities in that part of November 1933 would have made such an involvement all but impossible. Unfortunately an "all but" was insufficient for the needs of the defense. It was always remotely conceivable that an interlude of this nature could have been squeezed in during an early evening. After all, the date given by Schmidt had to be regarded as approximate, so that the most perfect alibi imaginable for November 22 could do no more than further lower the probability of the accuracy of Schmidt's claims.[103]

[102] *Ibid.*, 183-184. Goltz interview, November 1, 1969.

[103] Goltz, "Erinnerungen," 175. Countess Hardenberg, Fritsch's principal secretary in 1933, relates how in 1938 she recalled circumstances which led to a searching

Another hope was to discover in the situation at the Wann-see station circumstances which could incontrovertibly refute Schmidt's account of the incident. The railway authorities were able to attest that during the period in question the trellised gate between that station and the neighboring freight depot had regularly been locked after business hours. But, again, there could be no absolute proof that it had not accidentally been left open on a particular evening. Here too "all but certain" was not enough for the purposes of the defense.[104]

A third line of inquiry dealt with the residence associated with the first payment reported by the blackmailer, Ferdinand Strasse 21. All persons residing at this address or in a neighboring dwelling of the same housing complex were questioned on whether they had any acquaintance with and might have been visited by Fritsch. The turnover in German as in most European apartments being far slower than in the United States, all who had lived there in 1933 were still in residence, save one. The exception was the owner of the building, a Jew named Duenkel, who had migrated to Palestine in 1934.[105]

Faced for the third time with the prospect of a situation where one flaw in the chain of evidence might impede the clarification of an angle in the case, Goltz made the first of his calls on Oster. By utilizing means available to the Abwehr, it proved possible to locate the emigrant in Tel Aviv and to have him questioned by a German vice counsul. The man was shown a photograph of Fritsch and quickly stated that the individual depicted was completely unknown to him. But he threw a new element of confusion into the situation by raising doubts about a man named Bauer, one of his former tenants with whom he had been at odds. This person, he said, had from time to time received doubtful-looking visitors and was himself the kind of person who might well have had to do with homosexuals. This apartment house grotesquerie actually carried on into the trial where the enraged suspect branded it as an attempt at revenge for past differences.[106]

Besides wishing to exclude the possibility of any person at Ferdinand Strasse 21 being visited by Fritsch, the defense was interest-

out of travel vouchers of Wehrkreis commanders who had met with him that day and eliminated any chance of his having been involved in such an incident on November 22. Interview, February 20, 1970.

[104] Goltz, "Erinnerungen," 175.

[105] *Ibid.* Verdict, 393.

[106] Goltz, "Erinnerungen," 176. Verdict, 393.

ed in establishing whether any of the residents there could have been a "double" to whom the blackmailer's charges might actually apply. It soon was evident beyond any doubt that no one living on these premises could have played this role. Goltz was so eager not to overlook any openings, no matter how remote the chances, that he fastened on the fact that one resident did have a brother of high military rank, a retired General Staff member named von Waldow. Beck, who had been more directly alerted than Goltz to the possibility of misplaced identity, regretfully gave his opinion that the matter would have to be pursued. Goltz therefore went ahead despite the personal wish of Fritsch that General von Waldow should not be disturbed. Biron's interrogation of the general and his brother, had, of course, the expected negative result.[107]

While these curiously assorted inquiries were under way, Goltz and the court investigators were also working along a dozen other lines. The two fatherless Hitler-boys and their mothers, though already interviewed by the Gestapo even before the official investigation had begun, were again heard and repeated that nothing the least questionable had ever occurred. At Fritsch's request all who had served as adjutants or General Staff officers with him were called in and with one voice proclaimed wrathfully that he had never shown any homosexual tendencies. His military identity cards of past years were pulled out of the files and found to be of a color and format that entirely contradicted what Schmidt had described.[108]

In short, every line of inquiry undermined both Schmidt's story and any notion of the "rogues' code of honor" Himmler had tried to propagate for him. There remained no shred of *probability* that Fritsch was the man of Schmidt's story, but nothing as yet had been found to eliminate absolutely its *possibility*. Proving his innocence therefore still required a refutation of Schmidt's testimony so devastating that he himself must admit his lies. It became more and more imperative to locate the "double" of whom Nebe had told. If he could be identified and Schmidt's elaborate structure of testimony fully applied to him, it seemed inconceivable that, despite Schmidt's amazing gall and ready imagination, he would be able to construct a new story about Fritsch to replace that which would have been refuted.

So the search for the original figure of the tale that had been

[107] Goltz, "Erinnerungen," 177.
[108] *Ibid.* 178-179.

fitted to Fritsch continued and with it the race that grew from Hitler's decree for a dual investigation. The Gestapo, of course, had not been idle and at this juncture it reached out to deliver a new and, it may have hoped, literally mortal blow. It announced that, on the basis of what it had learned since questioning Fritsch on January 27-28, the time had come for a third interrogation.

## The Wannsee Interrogation

However great the frustrations of those whose goal was the complete exoneration of Fritsch, the outlook of the opposing forces in the third week of February was increasingly grim. One by one the defense and the official investigators were assembling the pieces of evidence which, when the case came to trial, would make it difficult to avoid a verdict of "proven innocence." At any time the still missing piece—the role of Captain von Frisch—might be uncovered. In that event the danger to Himmler and Heydrich would be considerable. February 4 had been a personal triumph for Hitler and had its compensations for the disappointed Goering. The position of the SS leaders, in contrast, continued precarious. If things went badly for them in the Fritsch case, there was no guarantee that Goering and the Fuehrer would not worm their way out by sacrificing them.

Least of all can Himmler and Heydrich have had much faith in their quondam ally, Goering. In conformity with his studiously nurtured pose of "impartial judge," he had perforce withdrawn from his advanced position on the attacking line. The odium of being the persecutors of Fritsch was falling more and more on them.

The threat of full exposure moved perilously close to the SS leaders when, on approximately February 11, the defense "discovered" the Bayern Seppl. Weingärtner had been in the hands of the Gestapo since at least mid-January, had been interrogated by it well before January 27, and had on that day been contemptuously looked over by Goering. The following day he had then been questioned by Goering in company of Gürtner. Since he kept insisting that Fritsch was not the man who had been his partner at the Wannsee station in November 1933, the Gestapo had every reason to act as if he did not exist and to violate the rules of the game by withholding the protocols of his examination. The much-embarrassed Gürtner had his own reasons for concealing from

Fritsch's friends the personal investigations in which he had engaged on the 28th and which had not prevented him from rendering his formal opinion the next day.

The court investigators can have learned of Weingärtner's presence in Gestapo hands either (1) from Dohnanyi or a repentant Gürtner, or (2) through an intentional or unintentional indiscretion from within the SS. The explanation in the latter case may lie in a string of reactions following one of Nebe's reports to Gisevius, on this occasion dealing with Fritsch's Gestapo interrogation of January 27. This related the ugly trick on the Army commander of posting a batch of male prostitutes in corridor recesses of the building in the hope that he would be "identified" as a customer. Passed on immediately to Canaris and Oster, the information must have been relayed by the former to Beck and Hossbach. Sack must have learned of it soon after taking up work on the investigative panel. Sack, argues Gisevius, would have had little difficulty learning from Fehling that Fritsch's supposed partner of the 1933 incident was currently in Gestapo custody.[109]

Interrogated by Biron, Weingärtner gave the same story as before, confirming the general facts of the 1933 incident as given by Schmidt but denying that the partner involved was Fritsch. In the face of this clearly disinterested testimony, which established the case for misplaced identity, Biron and Sack could only assume that the further prolongation of the proceedings against Fritsch had passed all limits of absurdity. This was also the impression of General Heitz, who agreed to accompany them to Berchtesgaden to urge Hitler to dismiss the case on the basis of established innocence. To their astonishment and dismay, Hitler, who received them on February 13, refused to declare himself satisfied and insisted that the case be carried through to the end.[110] There was nothing for it but to return to Berlin and concentrate on the identification of Schmidt's actual victim.

Before defense and investigators could progress much farther in their search, their attention was diverted to the next countermove of the Gestapo—the demand that Fritsch present himself for another interrogation. Perhaps a certain courage of despair was taking over in the Prinz-Albrecht-Strasse. True, Hitler had gained additional time for the men there by directing that the investigation continue. But with the testimony of Weingärtner now available to the court,

[109] Gisevius recording, January 1972.
[110] Bösch, 30.

the chance of a favorable outcome from the SS standpoint had become slim.

Since no concrete evidence has come to light on just what Himmler and Heydrich promised themselves from another interrogation of Fritsch, we are once more 'reduced to conjecture. A partial answer may be detected in the fact that during the interrogation an attempt was made to needle Fritsch into a political indiscretion. This would hardly by itself be enough to explain .the staging of the affair. Hopes for some kind of coup seem to have been entertained and the one recommending itself most logically would have been an attempt at murder thinly disguised as suicide, which Fritsch's friends actually anticipated.

Even had there been nothing of this nature to fear, Fritsch's advisers felt it incumbent to resist the demand on procedural grounds. Since learning of Fritsch's having gone to the Gestapo on January 27 and 28, the group about Oster and Canaris had worked strenuously through Beck to prevent further visits to the Prinz-Albrecht-Strasse.[111] Goltz also advised his client to refuse any further dealings with the Gestapo, basing his stand on the exemption of the military from its ministrations. As before, however, Fritsch, still harboring some remnant of his illusion that Hitler needed to be convinced of something, insisted that he must avoid the impression of having anything to hide.[112]

After much back-and-forth, Keitel inserted himself into the discussion and proposed a compromise. Fritsch should be spared the humiliation of again having to go to Gestapo headquarters. Instead the meeting should take place on "neutral ground" in an unoccupied villa in Wannsee, an attractive lake, park, and fine residence area on the western edge of Berlin. Actually it was a place at the disposition of the SS, but no doubt to be much preferred to the Prinz-Albrecht-Strasse from the standpoint of military dignity.

The proposal rang a new bell of alarm concerning a possible attempt at assassination. Out-of-the-way Wannsee seemed to lend itself better to malignant designs than the relatively congested Gestapo headquarters in Berlin. An especially sinister portent was seen in what Oster learned, almost certainly from Nebe, about the character of the SS men who were to staff the villa for the occasion

[111] Gisevius, *Bis zum bittem Ende*, 269-270.

[112] Goltz, "Erinnerungen," 187. Goltz to Kielmansegg, October 1947. Kielmansegg Papers.

of the interrogation. They were ruffians who had functioned in the execution squads that had shot the SA leaders in Lichterfelde during the Blood Purge of 1934.[113] Oster had also been warned that the Gestapo seemed prepared for the most desperate extremes, including the shortcut of a staged "suicide."[114] The picture conveyed to the world would be one of a despairing general resigning all hope of covering his transgression further and resorting to the soldier's traditional escape from dishonor.

A problem for the Gestapo was the inescapable presence of the respected jurist Dr. Kanter. By the rules of the investigation he would as usual represent the court-martial as an observer. If there had been any doubt where his sympathies lay, these had been eliminated by this stage of affairs. The rather feeble attempts to intimidate or compromise him had gotten nowhere, only serving to put Fritsch's friends more fully on their guard and to enlighten Kanter further about the forces at work.

As usual when something out of the ordinary needed doing, the responsibility fell to Oster. Before the departure for Wannsee, Fritsch was carefully searched in the presence of Oster, Kanter, and Siewert. They could thus attest that he had gone to the meeting totally unarmed. Kanter, on the other hand, was given a seven-shot pistol by Siewert with some quick instructions on how to use it. It must have been a strained moment for the peaceful jurist when he was told by Oster that if things came to the worst he should account for as many of the black-uniformed scoundrels as possible.[115] The main purpose of any shooting he might do, however, would be to signal Captain von Both to summon assistance. To provide the necessary muscle, Oster had arranged for a tank company under dependable officers to "exercise" in an immediately adjacent area. Both, whom the rules did not permit to be present at the interrogation, was to remain with the car and provide the connecting link between Kanter and the nearby force.[116] The setup was obviously not calculated to protect Fritsch against an actual attack but could be counted on to make the SS men seriously hesitate about the efficacy of such an attempt.

Arriving at the villa on what seems to have been February 20,

[113] As related by Oster to Dr. Kanter the day before the meeting. Kanter interview, May 9, 1970.

[114] Letter of Kanter to Kielmansegg, November 8, 1947. Kielmansegg Papers.

[115] Letter of Kanter to Kielmansegg, January 17, 1949. Kielmansegg Papers. Kanter interview, May 9, 1970.

[116] Kanter interview, May 9, 1970.

Fritsch, Kanter, and Both found it centered within parklike grounds behind a brick wall that separated it from the street. While Both remained at the car with the driver, the two principals approached the building and were met at the door by Meisinger. The presence of this crude and insolent official in place of the professional-mannered Huber and the finicky (by SS standards) Best was an unpleasant augury for what was likely to come. Here was a man who had a reputation for sticking at nothing to trip up or wear down his victims.

Fritsch and Kanter were conducted into a large, bare salon. Some ten sinister-looking figures in nondescript civilian clothes appeared as if out of nowhere, most of them standing around while two busied themselves with the visitors' coats. Kanter felt it required little imagination to see them as typical SS hangmen. Meisinger then led the way into a small, scantily furnished room with a barred window. Fritsch and Kanter exchanged glances and the latter wondered whether the bars had been installed for this occasion. The mastering sensation was one of profound isolation—it seemed a locale where anything could happen. Nothing had been seen or heard of the standby troops on the way in. Small wonder that Kanter was glad to feel the reassuring bulge in his clothing that signified the presence of his pistol and he believed that Meisinger was also aware of it.[117]

Meisinger began with a certain diffidence, obviously impressed to sit opposite a man who had the exalted rank of colonel general. He first went over the ground of the previous interrogations and of the confrontation with Schmidt. Since Fritsch could only respond with his usual litany of denial, the Gestapo official gradually became more offensive, going into the business of the Hitler-boys and Fritsch's relations with orderlies and horseboys. The general's irritation mounted visibly and his answers were increasingly abrupt though he did manage to control his temper. Meisinger, obviously aiming to goad him into compromising outbursts, finally shifted into the wholly extraneous political field and raised questions which, if tolerated, could transform the whole case from a criminal into a political action and make Fritsch a candidate for the People's Court. It was a line of attack that troubled Kanter almost as much as it did Fritsch. He had the strictest orders from General Heitz

[117] J. A. Kielmansegg (*Der Fritsch-Prozess 1938*, 72–73) on the basis of an early postwar account of Kanter. Additional details given by Kanter in an interview, May 9, 1970.

to remain absolutely silent no matter what outrageous question the Gestapo representative might put. But Fritsch only reddened and floundered instead of categorically rejecting the whole line of inquiry. When the impertinent Meisinger finally sought to push him into saying outright that he was "against things," Kanter risked his judicial neck by intervening, protesting that such matters were completely outside the legitimate area of interrogation.[118]

Meisinger was taken aback and, after a moment's hestitation, said that he would pause and call RSHA headquarters for further instructions.[119] He left the room and the minutes ticked by in ominous silence as Fritsch and Kanter sat there frozen. They were too aware of the likelihood of hidden microphones to address remarks to each other. After a time the tension became too much for the nerves of the military jurist. He got up and left the building taking good care to leave all doors open behind him. Outside he was relieved to see the faithful Both circling nervously around the parked car and, after apprising him briefly of developments, Kanter returned to Fritsch. Some twenty minutes after his departure Meisinger finally returned from a telephone conversation which one would mortgage one's soul to have on record. He seemed deflated and, after a few rather meaningless questions and one nasty flick back to the topic of the stableboys, he concluded the interrogation. One more but not yet the last ordeal for Fritsch had been surmounted.[120]

There seems little likelihood that it will ever be possible to reach firm conclusions on this incident, which must be counted among the major mysteries of the whole affair. No one can doubt that Himmler and Heydrich were fully capable of trying to end in this way a proceeding that from their standpoint was commencing to go thoroughly sour. Goering may have been as ready as they to stoop to murder but no longer was subject to the same pressures as before February 4. It seems unlikely that Hitler had been initiated into any sinister SS plans, but, from its standpoint, he had shown a reassuring readiness to accommodate himself to accomplished facts that squared with his purposes.

If an assassination plot was actually in operation, the countermea-

[118] Kanter interview, May 9, 1970.

[119] J. A. Kielmansegg (*Der Fritsch-Prozess 1938*, 73) places the shift in the line of questioning *after* Meisinger's call to Gestapo headquarters. Kanter's version today is the reverse of this. Interview, May 9, 1970.

[120] J. A. Kielmansegg, *Der Fritsch-Prozess 1938*, 73-74. Kanter interview, May 9, 1970.

sures devised by Oster were well calculated to forestall it. The demeanor of Both and Kanter revealed that they came forewarned and, in Kanter's case, forearmed. In point of fact, Both and the driver were also provided with pistols and these may have been as intentionally discernible as Kanter's weapon. The ten or more SS men in or about the villa and grounds must as well have perceived some evidence of the soldiers "exercising" in the neighborhood. To proceed with a coup under such circumstances would have meant calling for a showdown with the Army rather than evading one. Just as the first shift in Meisinger's line of interrogation showed an inclination to push matters to extremes, his change of manner after, no doubt, conferring with his fellows at the villa and after his call to the Prinz-Albrecht-Strasse, indicated that he had been informed of what confronted him and had been instructed to abandon what had become too great a hazard.

The impact of the Wannsee interrogation on the further course of the investigation and on the Resistance tendencies engendered by the Fritsch affair gains importance the more one learns about it. Tidings of it penetrated more quickly and farther in military quarters than those of any other incident of the 1938 Wehrmacht crisis, if only because the communications system of the Abwehr Opposition group was becoming more effective.

On his return to the inner city, the furious Kanter proceeded without delay to report to Oster who straightway took him to Canaris. All characterized the treatment of Fritsch as outrageous and agreed, as Kanter wrote in 1949, "that it was imperative to act against Himmler and the Gestapo.[121]

From what Kanter learned the next day, Oster and Canaris must have responded like runners dashing off the mark to carry the intelligence to wherever it was needed. How rapidly the news flowed through the military arteries of Berlin became clear when the jurist was summoned imperiously to Keitel. On arrival at the War Ministry, he was first conducted to General Heitz, who deluged him with reproaches for having gone to the Abwehr on his return from Wannsee. This had already created "unrest" and was likely to lead to "the most serious difficulties."[122] Heitz plainly was not to be counted among those who would associate themselves with a move against any agency connected with the regime.

[121] Letter of Kanter to Kielmansegg, January 17, 1949. Kielmansegg Papers. Kanter interview, May 9, 1970.
[122] *Ibid.* Kanter interview, May 9, 1970.

# Attack and Counterattack

The general next took Kanter to Keitel to whom the jurist recounted the previous day's happenings in much the form and spirit that he had to Oster and Canaris. Keitel, turning no hair, requested him to step outside while he conferred privately with Heitz. When Kanter was again admitted, he found that the two generals had concocted for him three questions so devised as to pass over all aspects of the story damaging to the Gestapo. His efforts to reintroduce them in his answers were brusquely repelled, as was his assertion that, after all, it was "the tone that made the music." The end result was a picture of the treatment received by Fritsch as perhaps not particularly noteworthy for courtesy but basically "correct." The dumbfounded Kanter was dismissed by Keitel with an ungracious: "Well, then everything is in order. You just are not familiar with the Gestapo's way of doing things." He was also instructed in no uncertain terms to observe silence in the future about his experiences in the investigation, *particularly toward Canaris and Oster.*[123]

Unmistakably Keitel and Heitz were concerned with a formulation aimed at soothing importunate generals and belittling the authentic account of the Wannsee meeting put out by Canaris and Oster. The effort to silence Kanter and constrain him to cut his line of communication to the two Abwehr chiefs miscarried badly. His contacts with them were far less frequent and intimate than those of Sack, but to Sack he confided daily all that pertained to the case. His first thought as he seethingly left the War Ministry was indeed to speed with the account of his experience there to Sack, "who assuredly saw to its dissemination."[124]

There are other echoes of the endeavors by Canaris and Oster to spread the tale of the crowning Gestapo outrage. It will be recalled that Canaris invaded Keitel's own sanctum to relate the facts about the Wannsee incident to the dismayed Viebahn and Jodl.[125] Captain von Both, who had the full story from Kanter, probably did more than the reticent Fritsch to enlighten the latter's own entourage. The loyal Both's patience was now at the breaking point. At a dinner at Goltz's residence, where he sat beside the countess, he startled and rather horrified that good lady by bursting forth: "There will simply have to be some shooting between the contend-

[123] Letter of Kanter to Kielmansegg, January 17, 1949. Kielmansegg Papers. J. A. Kielmansegg, *Der Fritsch-Prozess 1938*, 72.
[124] Letter of Kanter to Kielmansegg, January 17, 1949, Kielmansegg Papers.
[125] See above, p. 249.

ing groups. Unless we shoot we will never get rid of the SS and this whole gang."[126]

The exertions of the Abwehr group to rouse selected military men and others now received a boost from an unexpected quarter— Werner von Fritsch. What he had endured at Wannsee not only had shaken him once more to his inner being but seems to have been a turning point in his gaining a deeper understanding of the issues, along the lines observed by Dr. Nissen in his regular calls.[127] The gradual erosion of his conception that fundamentally *he* was the target of attack gave way to a surge of comprehension, especially about Hitler's essential involvement in the plot as it had now developed. The Abwehr group and Sack, who by this stage of affairs can be regarded as its extension into the investigative panel, had hoped for a sign of such recognition that could be utilized to drive the same point home to his military peers. The resolute Sack had baldly put it to Kanter that, if necessary, one would have to *compel* Fritsch to make a statement to such effect.[128] It is not known how long and in what ways he had been working on Fritsch, but it was the Wannsee experience which gave the convincing force to his arguments.[129]

At the close of the proceedings of the investigative panel on February 23, Fritsch asked to have a statement inserted into the protocol. Dictating to the rapidly writing and innerly triumphant Sack, he delivered words of crystal clarity: "Never before has a people permitted a commander in chief of its Army to be dealt with so disgracefully. I am having this entered specifically in the protocol so that later historical writing will know how in the year 1938 the commander in chief of the Army was treated. Such treatment is not only humiliating to me; it is also dishonoring for the entire Army."[130]

Since the German "people" knew nothing of any Fritsch affair

[126] Goltz interviews, February 17, 1970, and July 8, 1971.
[127] See above, p. 198.
[128] Bösch, 31. Kanter interview, May 9, 1970.
[129] J. A. Kielmansegg, apparently basing his conclusions on mistaken information from Goltz, holds (*Der Fritsch-Prozess 1938*, 31) that Fritsch was moved by an upsurge of indignation roused by the questioning of his former orderlies and stablemen. Goltz ("Erinnerungen," 186) presents the same version. However, we now know from papers left by Sack that the first of these men were not interrogated until March 1. Bösch, 31. Kanter, in a letter of June 17, 1961, to Bösch, also stated that it was the Wannsee experience which spurred Fritsch to move. Bösch, 31, 96n62.
[130] J. A. Kielmansegg, *Der Fritsch-Prozess 1938*, 75.

or trial, the indictment could only be directed against the head of state. The jittery Biron, appalled by such temerity, pleaded with Fritsch not to put such a bombshell into the protocol, but the general remained firm and could not be denied the right to have his remarks recorded.[131]

For the first time Fritsch thus plainly joined with his own tragic fate that of his office and of the Army he had made, which revered him. Together, he said, they were being attacked and dishonored. Assuredly it was a cry of outrage and anguish. But it was also, though indirectly, "a summons to the Army, a warning, and an appeal for help."[132] What he was saying in effect was that, just as the sinister forces at work had dealt with him, so would they also deal with the Army to misuse it for their purposes. The time patently was a quarter to twelve. It it were allowed to run out in his case it would also do so for the once proud Wehrmacht.

What did Fritsch hope would follow from his belated appeal? Neither then nor later, so far as the historical record tells us, did he say or write exactly what he had in mind on February 23. Obviously he was not speaking into the wind for the relief of long pent-up emotions. That he was seeking to evoke a response may be inferred from the approval he gave to Goltz for having the statement extracted from the protocol and duplicated for distribution to Beck, Canaris, and selected members of the military hierarchy.[133] The specific inclusion of Canaris speaks volumes for what Fritsch had in mind. He must have known from various sources what the admiral and his associates had been agitating for during these several weeks. Since Hossbach on January 25 had revealed the charges formulated against him in the Reich Chancellery and Stülpnagel had counseled him the following evening, others had urged much the same course. Hitler must be confronted with a demand from something resembling a united front of the higher Generalität to end the indecent farce of pursuing so frivolous a charge as that raised by Schmidt. Closely bracketed with this proposal was the concept of a counterstroke against the SS.

What the longer range consequences of such a course for the character and continuation of the regime would be had never been spelled out by its advocates and it is improbable that Fritsch thought deeply on the matter. However, the need for intervening

[131] *Ibid.*
[132] *Ibid.*, 76.
[133] *Ibid.* Goltz, "Erinnerungen," 186–187.

in the proceedings, which with each new insight gained in the investigation had lost further in justification, had been re-emphasized by the Wannsee episode.

In one respect nothing had changed since the period of crisis before February 4. The rigidities of the military command system made it all but impossible to initiate anything requiring a united response otherwise than from the top. It has been repeatedly emphasized that Fritsch and, while he acted as his commander's locum tenens, Beck could almost certainly have engineered something of this kind as long as the former was, even nominally, head of the Army. Now the situation depended similarly on Brauchitsch, who was under increasing pressure to exert himself in the cause of his predecessor. A line of communication had been thrown out to him by the Abwehr activists and he was receiving a flow of information paralleling that going to Beck. The chief of staff was ever at his elbow pushing Fritsch's cause with an urgency which set Keitel bleating in distress.[134] Together these influences were having an effect on Brauchitsch, but at the time of the Wannsee incident and the statement by Fritsch which it evoked, the new commander was far from prepared to move vigorously.

Though coming only faintly through, an echo to Fritsch's plea for help did resound within the small group which had thus far gathered around Witzleben. By mid-February he had recovered sufficiently from his illness to return to his duties in Berlin. It would be hard to believe that he was not included among those who were provided with copies of Fritsch's declaration, which he would be the first to greet as a call to arms. This was the more certain as he and some of the men closest to him had already been roused by the furor created by the Gestapo's summons of Fritsch for a third interrogation. The consequence was the first sign of something like concrete plans for a seizure of Gestapo headquarters. Involved with Witzleben at this stage were Colonel von Hase, commander of an infantry regiment at Neuruppin, and Fritz-Dietlof von der Schulenburg. Hase is said to have been ready to bring his troops to Berlin for the action and Schulenburg is claimed to have joined in the plan in close cooperation with Helldorf.[135] The police president of Berlin, who was daily falling

[134] Keitel, 274-275.
[135] Krebs, 163-164. Gisevius greatly doubts this since he is convinced that Helldorf would surely have told him of such a development. Gisevius recording, January 1972.

314

more under the influence of Gisevius, was undoubtedly in the process of crossing his personal Rubicon. At this very time, he and his Potsdam colleague of similar Nazi background, Count Wedel, had amazed Stülpnagel at the annual meeting of the Schlieffen Society (February 28) by voicing without reserve their indignation over the treatment accorded to Fritsch.[136]

That Oster must have had a hand in whatever was under consideration goes without saying. He and Canaris had received Kanter's tidings on the course of affairs at Wannsee with the most positive declaration that action against the SS was long overdue. Oster also told the jurist that the corps commanders must be induced to give Hitler an ultimatum to halt the proceedings.[137] Perhaps to test how far Goltz was inclined to go, Oster, as if spontaneously, asserted to him that "the whole shop in the Prinz-Albrecht-Strasse would have to be cleared out and occupied." Hitler had heretofore always recognized accomplished facts.[138] Goltz, with some amusement, put this down as an outbrust of Oster's well-known temperament, but it may have been a sign of the colonel's hope that things were at last coming to a head.

Nothing, of course, came of these discussions. General Thomas, who also testifies to Witzleben's having been prepared to move at this juncture, states that the troop commander (i.e., Hase) began to have doubts about the younger officers of his regiment going along.[139] Such misgivings were, of course, fully justified, but they were probably compounded in the mind of Hase, who was chronically indecisive and perhaps somewhat on the timorous side. This was to be amply demonstrated on the fatal day of July 20, 1944.

Meanwhile the score against the Gestapo was mounting through two new developments of the continuing investigation: the mysterious "double" was at last found and Fritsch was subjected to a final and crowning outrage, the calling in of his former orderlies and riding attendants.

### The Discovery of Captain von Frisch

Though the furor over the Wannsee interlude and Fritsch's indictment of February 23 had its distracting effect, the confirmation, won from Weingärtner's testimony, of the existence of a "double"

[136] Stülpnagel, 358.
[137] Kanter interview, May 9, 1970.
[138] Goltz, "Erinnerungen," 187.
[139] Thomas, "Gedanken und Ereignisse," 3.

had given a more decisive focus to the investigation. New angles kept appearing which provided additional impetus to the search. The Gestapo's Criminal Commissar Fehling, who was no more than moderately bright, was guilty of another slip. In casual conversation with Kanter, after one of the Gestapo interrogation sessions which the latter attended as an observer, the topic had turned to Schmidt's conceit and braggadocio. Without realizing the implications of what he was saying, Fehling cited as an example the rogue's tendency toward upward valuation of his victims. Then, becoming aware of the inference which could be drawn, he hastily insisted that "of course" nothing of this nature could apply in the present case.[140]

Kanter straightway reported this exchange to Sack and the two, mindful of the parallel of the two lawyers named Goltz, agreed that it would be well to look for someone with a name resembling that of Fritsch.[141] Accordingly, Biron and Sack concerted an inquiry at the waiting room in the station Lichterfelde-East, where the blackmail payments had been made. It seemed remotely possible that someone attached to the food and drink service had observed something of the transaction. It was likely that the man who had been bled by Schmidt at times frequented the place and had therefore suggested it as a meeting ground. If he was indeed a military man, that would further enhance the chance that he could be recalled by one of the attendants.

March 1 probably is the date on which Biron and Sack embarked on this long-shot endeavor.[142] At first their inquiries seemed to fall on barren ground. Then the hostess remembered a retired officer who occasionally came to the waiting room, usually in the company of a lady. She thought she perceived some resemblance between him and the picture of Fritsch which had been shown her. (At the trial she was to recall further the amazing consumption of cognac by this man and two companions some five years before.)

[140] Bösch, 32. J. A. Kielmansegg, *Der Fritsch-Prozess 1938*, 70.

[141] Bösch (32) holds that Sack was the first to hit on the idea that the story told by Schmidt and applied to Fritsch did deal with a real person. It is no discredit to Sack's very keen perception to remind ourselves that he had already heard of the "double" from Gisevius and knew that, in order to safeguard Nebe and his informants, it would be necessary to watch for clues which would make the discovery look like the result of clever deductions.

[142] This is inferred from the fact that the almost immediate sequel, the call on Frisch, definitely took place on March 2.

# Attack and Counterattack

In any event, she felt certain that the gentleman lived nearby, quite possibly in the Ferdinand Strasse.[143]

Biron and Sack in some excitement returned to the Reich Military Court building to discuss the steps to be taken next. It was probably late afternoon and a decision was postponed until the following day. The next morning they determined to canvass the neighboring houses in the Ferdinand Strasse in the same way as they, two weeks before, had investigated No. 21. Sack is also said to have talked about looking in the Berlin address book[144] for a name similar to Fritsch's.[145] At the moment, however, no one seems to have thought this likely enough to make an immediate check.

Biron next called Goltz, who was at Fritsch's quarters, to tell him of the progress they had made and what they intended to do. Goltz, too impatient to wait for the results of what could be a protracted survey, decided to take a quick look at the address book himself. He asked Both to bring him Fritsch's copy and turned to the appropriate block in the Ferdinand Strasse. Veritably leaping from the page he saw for No. 20: "von Frisch, Achim. Cavalry captain (ret.)."[146] A flash of anticipated triumph shot through Fritsch's defender. Within minutes he was on the wire giving Biron the news. The chief investigator promised that he and Sack would see this key witness that very afternoon.[147]

There followed first a ludicrous interlude which again throws light on the ineptness of the Gestapo. In view of the rule that each investigative team must notify the other of significant developments, Biron put through a call to the Prinz-Albrecht-Strasse to have "the witness von Frisch" brought to the Reich Military Court building for immediate interrogation. Shortly after (about noon) a Gestapo official appeared in Biron's office to report that Frisch's nurse declared him too sick to be questioned. Biron then asked the name of Frisch's doctor and, when given it (we can imagine

---

[143] Bösch, 32. Goltz, "Erinnerungen," 190.

[144] The German telephone system prints two sets of books, one based on its clients' names, the other on their addresses.

[145] Bösch, 33.

[146] Goltz, "Erinnerungen," 190. Goltz interview, November 1, 1969.

[147] Goltz says (interview, November 1, 1969) that it was then about noon and that Biron told him that he and Sack would go to see Frisch about three o'clock. In view of a notation by Sack made later that month indicating a Gestapo representative called on them about noon in response to a telephone notice concerning this development in the case (Bösch, 33), we must place Goltz's call somewhat earlier. "Notation for the Record" (prepared by Sack on March 21 and signed also by Biron and Kanter; copy in author's possession; cited hereafter as Sack, "Aktenvermerk").

317

with what reluctance), got in touch with him by telephone. The physician confirmed that his patient was indeed incapable of coming to the court building but stated that nothing stood in the way of interrogating him in his residence.[148]

The afternoon was waning when Sack (about 5 P.M.) called Fehling to inform him of the doctor's verdict and said that he and Biron were on the point of leaving for Frisch's apartment.[149] The message had obviously been delayed until the last minute to forestall any attempt by the Gestapo to get at Frisch first or perhaps even remove him. The reaction of the slow-witted Fehling was one of blind panic. It had been a frantically busy day for him and this seems to have been the first hint which had reached him about what was afoot. Ironically, the extraordinary preoccupation which led the Gestapo to bungle things at this critical juncture seems related to the most crushing humiliation concocted for the general since his confrontations with Schmidt in January. From cavalry depots and military posts all over Germany it was seizing upon and hauling to Berlin orderlies, grooms, and stablemen who had served Fritsch at one time or another during his long military career. Since the previous day it had been interrogating these flabbergasted men. That very morning a batch of nine had been sent on to Biron's panel for a second questioning. Others were coming in and continued to do so down to the last stages of the trial. Fehling and his Gestapo team were too busy with this congenial activity to bother with sending the customary observer for the interrogation of these men by the court investigators which followed their own. His preoccupation seems to have been so profound that he had not been interrupted by underlings who had but a dim if any notion of the calamity which was impending.

In his surprise and mental deshabille, Fehling quite lost his poise and let one cat after another out of the bag. Captain von Frisch, he pleaded, did not come into question as a witness in the Fritsch case. He was a seriously sick man of nearly seventy years. Withdrawals from his bank account at the time in question had been insignificant. In short, every word he uttered screamed verification of the Gestapo's extended knowledge and concern with the affairs of the unfortunate captain. Sack, it need hardly be stated, was neither persuaded nor intimidated. Despite Fehling's frenzied efforts to dissuade them, he and Biron immediately departed and

[148] Sack, "Aktenvermerk."
[149] *Ibid.*

318

arrived at their destination about 5:40. Kanter who, like them, was consumed with curiosity, went along but remained seated in the car.[150]

Biron and Sack found the captain in his bed and under the care of a nurse, but he was able to rise to receive them. They then waited for twenty minutes to observe the rules and give a Gestapo representative time to arrive. That Fehling did not rush to Lichterfelde or see to it that, at all cost, one of his colleagues did so is astonishing and eloquent testimony to his befuddlement. He seems to have sat in frozen consternation and let events take their fatal course. Perhaps he did try to reach Himmler or Heydrich and was unable to do so at what was close to the dinner hour. By now, he must have thought, the interrogation was well under way; so it seemed best to remain silent and hope against hope that Frisch, as Himmler so strongly claimed about homosexuals, was stoutly denying his part in the 1933 affair. In any event, the chance of taking a hand in the game passed and, in a desperate gamble that they would not hear of his ineptitude, Fehling decided to say nothing to his superiors.

By 6 P.M. Biron and Sack felt that they had waited long enough to observe the requirements and commenced questioning Frisch. With brief interruptions to spare the sick man, this continued for two hours. In all essentials the details recounted by Schmidt were confirmed as applying to the captain. An exception was his refusal to admit that he had shown his identity card: "So foolish," he protested, "I could hardly have been."[151] The captain, who seemed a broken and sorely ailing man, even gave Biron for the record the receipt he had exacted from Schmidt when making his last payment.[152]

The impact of the incident òn the course of affairs—and, as it happened, on the survival of Frisch—was essentially the fruit of a master stroke on the part of Sack. The uncertainties of life in the case of an elderly and sick man—especially one who stood in the path of the Gestapo—made it imperative that Frisch's testimo-

[150] Kanter interview, May 9, 1970. For the rest of the paragraph, Sack, "Aktenvermerk."

[151] It seems, however, that he must at least have told Schmidt who he was. The fact is that Schmidt did know his name and would certainly not have released him from his clutches at the end of their first meeting had he not learned the captain's identity.

[152] J. A. Kielmansegg, *Der Fritsch-Prozess 1938*, 81. Bösch, 34. Goltz, "Erinnerungen," 191. Sack, "Aktenvermerk."

ny be taken in such a way that it could by itself be utilized in court. Sack, therefore, risked an act of highly questionable legality by placing the captain under oath.[153] In the view of the present writer he thereby saved Frisch's life since the Gestapo, though still finding him an incubus, no longer was under such overriding compulsion to do away with him. The damage, in effect, had largely been done. Biron, by the way, would never have found the courage to adopt so determined a course.

As the housekeeper-nurse conducted them to the door, the two men were startled to hear her complain plaintively that such official visits were hard on so sick a man—here now was the second one within a few weeks, the Gestapo having been there on January 15! Biron and Sack found it difficult to believe their ears. January 15? Was she sure? Yes, she insisted, that was the exact date.[154]

Relating what they had learned to Kanter, Biron and Sack returned to the inner city and at once conveyed the triumphant results of their mission to the impatiently waiting Goltz. Picking up a huge bunch of roses on the way, the count then rushed to the Bendler Strasse, where he was received by Both and conducted to his client. Too eager to trouble with the formalities of greeting, he burst out: "Colonel General, you can have a salute fired to victory. The real 'Fritsch' has been found and the case is completely cleared up."[155]

To Goltz's chagrin Fritsch's expression changed little. His lips, if anything, assumed a somewhat harder line. Then he said slowly and solemnly: "That will never be enough for the Fuehrer. He does not want to believe anything like that." His defender could only protest that such a position was no longer tenable. But though Fritsch did give voice to his pleasure and appreciation, he persisted in his skepticism.[156]

It was probably before retiring or the first thing the next morning

---

[153]The problem of legality in this instance is examined by Ulrich Stock in his study on legal issues raised by the Fritsch case. Both he and Sack's biographer, Bösch, though by somewhat different argumentation, arrive at the conclusion that Sack's action was technically illegal. Ulrich Stock, "Der Fritsch-Prozess 1938: Seine rechtlichen Beurteilungen und seine Lehren," in *Festschrift für Heinrich Lehmann zum 80. Geburtstag "Das deutsch Privatrecht in der Mitte des 20. Jahrhunderts"* (Berlin, 1956), 925-937. Bösch, 34-35.

[154]Gisevius, *Bis zum bittern Ende*, 284. Gisevius recording, January 1972. In Goltz's recollection she said that two Gestapo agents had come on January 15 or 16. Letter to Kielmansegg, September 30, 1947. Kielmansegg Papers.

[155]Goltz, "Erinnerungen," 190.

[156]*Ibid.*, 191. J. A. Kielmansegg, *Der Fritsch-Prozess 1938*, 82.

that Fritsch dashed off a note to his friend Ulex, who after February 4 had written a letter assuring him of his continued devotion: "A miracle has occurred. Count Goltz and Captain von Both[157] have been able to prove that the criminal has lied. My fight against the party continues. More later by word of mouth."[158]

Shortly after Goltz had departed in a somehat deflated mood, Hossbach arrived and was met by Both with an enthusiastic: "We have him, we have him." With glowing eyes he pointed out the place in the address book where the name of Frisch had been found. Hossbach at once expressed alarm about a probable counterstroke of the Gestapo to do away with the irreplaceable witness. Before retiring he got in touch with Canaris to urge that the Abwehr find means to put Frisch into some kind of protective custody. The admiral, who already had been given a detailed picture of developments by Sack,[159] saw no way of accomplishing this and for once was less apprehensive than another about SS machinations: "This time you are too mistrustful."[160]

Hossbach was to prove far from alone in his fears. Rosenberger, when Sack visited him early on the 3rd, as he did almost daily to report on affairs, congratulated his friend on his foresight in putting Frisch under oath. Because of this, Rosenberger said, Himmler would have far less incentive to do away with him. His disappearance would no longer be of sufficient value to the prosecution to be worth the sensation it would cause and it might have disagreeable repercussions.[161] Rosenberger apparently feared most what was actually to occur, a stroke by the Gestapo to get hold of Frisch, keep him away from further questioning by the court investigators, and put him under pressure to change his testimony.

To forestall such a coup, Rosenberger in his turn got in touch with Canaris while Sack went on to inform Hossbach, whose orientation by Both must have been unknown to him. The upshot was that Canaris joined Sack and Hossbach at the latter's residence, where the three debated at some length what was to be done about

---

[157] The reference to Both makes it appear that Goltz had not that morning told Fritsch of the discovery in the address book, probably hoping to give him the good news all at once. Fritsch may thus have learned about it first from Both and received the impression that he participated in it with Goltz.

[158] Ulex ms., 96.

[159] Bösch, 36.

[160] J. A. Kielmansegg, *Der Fritsch-Prozess 1938*, 82.

[161] Letter of Rosenberger to Kielmansegg, September 1, 1947. Kielmansegg Papers. It is noteworthy that Hossbach and Rosenberger independently thought first of Canaris when the pinch was severe.

Frisch. The former Wehrmacht adjutant kept insisting that no effort should be spared to put him into safekeeping before the Gestapo could lay hands on him. Canaris, for his part, continued to argue that Frisch should be left in his own dwelling.[162] In the end Hossbach's viewpoint prevailed to the extent that it was agreed Canaris and Rosenberger should appeal to the highest judicial authority of the Reich, the Minister of Justice. They found that Gürtner had no doubts whatsoever about the need for alarm. "Your anxiety," he said meaningfully, "is completely justified, for the Gestapo will shrink from nothing. You must understand my words in the most extreme sense." But he insisted that his Ministry lacked jurisdiction, which lay entirely in the hands of the Wehrmacht. It was there they would have to seek recourse.[163]

Both Canaris and Rosenberger can have had little confidence as they left Gürtner to proceed to Keitel. At the OKW they may at first have gained encouragement from finding the latter closeted with Brauchitsch on whose moral support (at least) they may have reckoned. But as they must have anticipated from the way Keitel had fobbed off Kanter shortly before in the matter of the Wannsee incident, he shied from intervening in anything that implied confrontation with the SS. Brauchitsch, far from assisting them, sarcastically quoted a saying which implied they were eager to have Keitel do their work for them: "Hannemann, geh Du voran."[164]

While these wild-goose chases were being pursued, Sack returned to his duties on the investigative panel. He must already have fulfilled the necessary requirement of providing the Gestapo with a copy of the previous evening's interrogation. The congenial task that morning was to trip up Schmidt by inducing him to recommit himself to the story of a *single* incident in Lichterfelde in November 1933. In previous questionings he had insisted that there could be no possible confusion between Fritsch and another man. Biron led him skillfully over the familiar ground and he seemed more emphatic than ever in confirming what he previously had said. Yes, only once had an incident of this kind taken place in Lichterfelde. Only once had he received money in the waiting room of

[162] Bösch, 36.

[163] J. A. Kielmansegg, *Der Fritsch-Prozess 1938*, 83. Letter of Rosenberger to Kielmansegg, September 1, 1947. Kielmansegg Papers. Goltz (interview, November 1, 1969) quotes Gürtner in a similar vein, warning what the Gestapo was likely to do. Gisevius (recording, January 1972) points out that Gürtner really did lack any jurisdiction.

[164] J. A. Kielmansegg, *Der Fritsch-Prozess 1938*, 83. Bösch, 36.

station Lichterfelde-East. Never had he been there otherwise in his life. A receipt of the kind he had then written was unique in his career. It was quite inconceivable that he could have confused Fritsch with anybody else; such an incident in this area and at this time could not have occurred twice. Fritsch and Fritsch alone was the party concerned.[165]

Thus Schmidt got himself deeper and deeper into the mire. When he seemed beyond going backward or forward, Biron exploded his bombshell by laying before him the incriminating receipt he had the previous evening received from Frisch.

At this moment observers of the scene must have found it difficult to deny the rogue a certain measure of admiration. We do not learn that he was as much as put out of countenance. Of course, he said, the case of Fritsch had nothing to do with that of Frisch. If he had told Biron that the incident in Lichterfelde was unique, it was only because the remote business with Frisch had slipped his mind. In any event, he added impudently, why should he further incriminate himself: "Why should I tell you any more?" The resemblance between the two cases was pure accident. Moreover, the man to whom he had given this receipt had never been with him in the waiting room of the Lichterfelde-East station. He had no idea where Frisch might live, having never been in his dwelling.[166]

It was, be it admitted, a remarkable exhibition of *sangfroid*. But at the time it seemed to accomplish no more than to save Schmidt's face—a little. His performance, however brazen and quick-witted, did not seem likely to persuade even the most naive. General Heitz agreed with Biron and Sack that the case was cleared up and ready for adjournment. It was probably on that same day (late afternoon?) that he with Sack and Biron went to the Chancellery to report in this vein to Hitler and secure his formal concurrence as Gerichtsherr.

When Heitz and his two companions entered Hitler's workroom, they could have seen an ominous augury of what was in store in the unanticipated presence of Himmler. How did he come to be there? We can assume that it had been a day of furious discussion in the Prinz-Albrecht-Strasse. Since Fehling, hoping to hide his

[165]Goltz, "Erinnerungen," 191.
[166]Verdict, 397–398. J. A. Kielmansegg, *Der Fritsch-Prozess 1938*, 86. Gisevius (recording, January 1972) is more skeptical about the presence of mind with which Schmidt is credited here. He considers it probable that the accuser had been coached to insist straightway that there were two separate cases if Frisch somehow were uncovered.

foreknowledge, had kept quiet about what had occurred the night before in the Ferdinand Strasse, the first inkling of the perilous state of affairs must have come to Himmler with the arrival of the protocol dispatched by Sack. This probably led to an immediate decision to snatch Frisch away from further questioning by the court investigators and to see what could be done to make him change his story. It is interesting to speculate whether his arrest was taking place while Heitz and the two military jurists were meeting with Hitler.[167]

Himmler's presence in the Chancellery can have been either (1) the result of a determination to be at Hitler's side when the inevitable demand for a halt to the proceedings was presented, or (2) his response to a summons from the dictator after the request from Heitz for an appointment was received. In any event, the SS chief was very much in evidence when Heitz's little group arrived. Perhaps most important, the two Nazi hierarchs already knew that Schmidt had kept his poise and, no matter how absurd the situation, stood by his testimony.[168]

When Heitz had spoken his piece, Himmler, taking his cue from what Schmidt had maintained that morning, insisted that there were two distinct cases and that nothing was really changed. He may also have utilized the occasion to charge in all good faith that his people had not been notified, as required, of the approaching interrogation of Frisch.[169] The discussion, if so it can be called, ended with a definitive declaration by Hitler that so long as Schmidt held to his story the Fuehrer could not dismiss his doubts about Fritsch and that the investigation would have to be concluded and the trial proceed.[170]

Dismay mingled with incredulity as the tale of the repulse in the Chancellery spread among Fritsch's partisans. Like Goltz, vir-

[167] It is, of course, possible that Himmler and Heydrich with Hitler's specific approval determined on Frisch's arrest only after the meeting in the Chancellery. The presence of Himmler at this meeting is attested by the account of Field Marshal Maximillian von Weichs (in IfZ, ZS 182), who heard it half a year later from Heitz at the Nuremberg party rally.

[168] Himmler and Hitler knew this from the report of the Gestapo representative who had attended that morning's interrogation of Schmidt.

[169] It seems more probable that Himmler made this complaint in a separate communication to Heitz on the following day (the 4th). It could not have been made later in view of the sharp reprimand Sack addressed to Fehling early on the 5th. If Himmler had made the charge to Heitz in his presence, Sack would not have been the man to remain silent.

[170] Goltz (interview, November 1, 1969) quotes Hitler as having said: "As long as the witness has not withdrawn his charge the case for me remains unsettled."

tually all who were in the know had assumed that to carry on the proceedings in the face of such conclusive proof of their absurdity was unthinkable. They failed, however, to comprehend that, in a situation of sufficient desperation, the Fuehrer of the German Reich could be as brazen and impudent as the blackmailer Schmidt. Very few of them had any conception of the full compass of the concerns Hitler had developed in the Fritsch affair. During its course his prestige had been linked with carrying the matter through to an unfavorable verdict for Fritsch, at the very least an acquittal "for lack of proof." On this depended the continued persuasiveness of the Nazi slogan, "The Fuehrer is always right." Another hazard of acknowledging defeat lay in the problem of how to deal next with Fritsch, whose honor had been challenged and who had been dismissed summarily before being given a chance to vindicate himself. Full rehabilitation would demand re-employment at a high level in the service of the state. This on the basis of a relationship that had been shattered beyond repair!

To accept any measure of defeat at this stage presented real dangers. The specious argumentation with which he had gulled the higher Generalität on February 4 might recoil upon him. The generals might in fact go so far as to demand the sacrifice, at least the severe curbing, of one of the pillars of the state—the SS. Every new ploy attempted by the Gestapo to humiliate or wear down Fritsch increased the likelihood of a concentrated attack on the SS if and when it failed to make its charges stick. With the clearing of Fritsch one could expect the real counteroffensive to begin.

A story related by Goltz of an entirely friendly encounter with an official named Neumann, one of Goering's state secretaries, is illustrative of how even a high party functionary regarded the situation. In discussing the progress of the case, Goltz mentioned that proof was forthcoming that not Fritsch but another person had been Schmidt's victim. Neumann was horrified and ejaculated, "Why, that would be awful!" When the startled Goltz inquired why that would be awful (he could imagine nothing better), Neumann replied that to persecute a man of Fritsch's stature on false charges was itself an appalling thing. But then it also would be necessary to deal drastically with the people who had raised the accusation and inspired the steps against the general.[171] In brief,

[171] Goltz, "Erinnerungen," 193-194.

one of Goering's own men accepted without argument the thesis that Schmidt would never have ventured to attack Fritsch on his own account.

How much better under such circumstances for Hitler to brazen things through. The case of the prosecution, though seriously compromised and in danger of collapse, was not yet hopeless. Schmidt had shown astonishing poise. As long as he was in the persuasive hands of the Gestapo there would be no lack of motivation for him to stick to his story. At least until the trial got under way, Hitler could be sure that his condition for canceling it—Schmidt's repudiation of his testimony—would not be met. At that time "iron Hermann," whose nerves stood up so magnificently in times of crisis, would manage to prevent the worst. Meanwhile the Fuehrer could devote himself to preparing the international success which was so desperately needed to surmount a domestic setback if such proved unavoidable.

On top of the bad news from the Chancellery for Fritsch's friends came the tidings on March 4 that Frisch had been taken into custody by the Gestapo. Sack had gone to the Ferdinand Strasse to flesh out with more detail the story which had been held to its essential points two nights before to spare the infirm witness. He found no one and needed little imagination to divine what had happened. To parry this counterstroke Sack called on the energy and circumspection which were so characteristic of him. He instantly realized how Frisch's disappearance enhanced the importance of the protocol of his interrogation. A raid by the Gestapo upon the files at the Reich Military Court was now a serious possibility. Sack sought the never-failing help of Oster and arranged through him for a reinforced guard at the building.[172] Sack also took advantage of the ineptitude of Fehling in two further defensive measures. On the morning of the 3rd, when Fehling happened to be at the Reich Military Court, Sack had renewed the subject of the captain's bank account and maneuvered the Gestapo official into reaffirming positively that the late 1933-early 1934 withdrawals had been minimal. Fehling was then requested to provide a copy of the account book entries "for the court record." Needless to say, when the trial ended

[172] Based on information provided Bösch by Dr. Kraell, another military jurist whom Sack had brought over from the Hessian administration of justice. Bösch, 136. Gisevius (letter to the author, January 3, 1972) is highly skeptical of this account, holding that the building, because of the high-security information stored there, was already strongly guarded.

on March 18, no such document had been delivered.[173] Biron and Sack, it should be noted, had in reserve by the time the trial opened the relevant data on Frisch's account which the former had personally gone to procure at the Dresdner Bank. Frisch's withdrawals of 1933–34 were found to tally exactly with the figures in his own and Schmidt's story. Further, the bank manager officially attested that Gestapo agents had called on January 15 and had been given the same information.[174] Two days later (March 5) Sack bearded Fehling in the presence of Biron and Kanter on Himmler's complaint about a supposed failure to notify the Gestapo before talking to Frisch. By this time Himmler, fancying that for once his opponents had placed themselves at a disadvantage, was trumpeting this about. Caught off guard the embarrassed Fehling could only admit that Sack had given him the information and that the "misunderstanding" resulted from his failure to report this to his superiors.[175]

These, of course, were but skirmishes in the battle which raged meanwhile over the disposal of Frisch. Driven as it was into a corner, the Gestapo was indulging in new extremes of effrontery. Already its representatives were at work minimizing the import of the protocol of March 2. It was stigmatized as fragmentary and as having been pressured out of a sick man.[176] Frisch's arrest was sustained on the basis of his confession to Biron and Sack of illegal conduct under the 1933 homosexual act. To give color to this course, a court action for the initiation of legal proceedings was formally scheduled. Actually the Gestapo, in one of its perpetual lapses into amateurism, overlooked a good bet in the existence of a police file of sorts on Frisch. This was extracted from the records by Helldorf and secured in some fashion by Nebe, who dispatched it to Oster by the hand of Elisabeth Strünck.[177]

As a counter to the disparaging observations of the Gestapo on the validity of the existing protocol, Biron demanded the delivery of Frisch for more intensive examination. The Prinz-Albrecht-Strasse insolently alleged humanitarian grounds for refusal. Frisch, it solemnly asserted, was in its own hospital and much too sick

[173] Sack, "Aktenvermerk."

[174] Gisevius, *Bis zum bittern Ende*, 286. Gisevius recording, January 1972.

[175] Sack, in recording it in his "Notation for the Record," had Biron and Kanter attest in writing their presence during Fehling's admission. Sack, "Aktenvermerk." The spreading of Himmler's charge, probably as told him by Keitel, is reported by Jodl. Diary, 369, entry of March 4, 1938.

[176] J. A. Kielmansegg, *Der Fritsch-Prozess 1938*, 84.

[177] Strünck-Gärtner interview, April 18, 1970.

to be questioned. (It is quite conceivable that he was being brutally knocked about at the precise moment this claim was advanced.) In fact, it was necessary to reckon with his early demise. So sick Frisch certainly was not; he was, in truth, to live four more years.[178] Biron and Sack did not need to be told that, if he died at this time, it would not be from natural causes.[179] Actually, as is sometimes the case with invalids, the old captain revealed an astonishing toughness. Though fearfully mistreated for a man in his condition—the bruises on his face were still clearly visible at the trial two weeks later[180]—he resolutely refused to change one iota of his story.

Once again Sack had to take the lead in a precarious situation. Since the frightened Biron hung back, there was nothing for it but to go himself to General Heitz. Probably with the aid of Colonel von Schleinitz,[181] Sack so assailed him that Heitz finally agreed to accompany him in calling on Hitler. It was already late at night,[182] a fact that may have added solemnity to their pleas for the Fuehrer's intervention. With Sack at his elbow, Heitz put the case in such strong terms that Hitler agreed to order that Frisch be made available to Biron's panel. It was further arranged that he should be transferred to the custody of the Ministry of Justice where any interrogations were to take place.[183] Thereby he was delivered from the physical abuse to which he had been subjected in the privacy of the Gestapo's quarters. With a new and unassailable record of his testimony, any remaining motives for removing him from this world were also eliminated.

Fritsch, a man of deep compassion, a quality accentuated by his personal misfortune, felt during these days a greater concern for the miseries of Frisch than for his own. It moved him infinitely that this pitiful wreck of a man should be made to suffer for his frankness and integrity and, in a sense, on Fritsch's behalf. He followed the captain's fate closely and after the trial requested

[178] Goltz saw a newspaper notice of his death in 1942. Goltz interview, November 1, 1969.

[179] J. A. Kielmansegg, *Der Fritsch-Prozess 1938*, 84.

[180] Kanter interview, May 9, 1970. Sack also told a friend that Frisch had been "terribly mistreated." Letter of Fritz Neuroth to Kielmansegg, November 23, 1947. Kielmansegg Papers.

[181] J. A. Kielmansegg (*Der Fritsch-Prozess 1938*, 84) assumes that it was Schleinitz who persuaded Heitz to act. The initiatory role was certainly that of Sack (Kanter interview, May 9, 1970), but there can be no doubt that Schleinitz gave his support if he was at all drawn into the matter.

[182] Kanter interview, May 9, 1970.

[183] Gisevius, *Bis zum bittern Ende*, 284-285.

Goltz to intervene with the Ministry of Justice to have the proceedings against him quashed.[184]

As already noted, these very days saw a new and heavy burden placed on Fritsch by the Gestapo examination of his former grooms and orderlies. As a passionate horseman he had ridden extensively at every military post where he had been assigned. The Gestapo's demand for a list of those who had done personal service for him was received with inward gnashing of teeth but with every show of compliance. It simply would not do to appear to be hiding anything.

The situation gave the Gestapo a much-sought opportunity for an entering wedge into the military preserve that had hitherto been so strictly off limits. It sent its agents with obvious relish to the various military posts where the individuals in question were then in service to take them into custody for transportation to Berlin. In several instances this led to flare-ups in temper or outright resistance. In Potsdam the adjutant of Infantry Regiment 9, Lieutenant Count Baudissin, a man highly sensitive to Nazi encroachments, did not mince words with the Gestapo agents who came to carry off a stable boss. They were told in no uncertain terms that the man would be issued a pistol and directed to use it, if necessary, to prevent his being taken away. Himmler's men were obliged to leave with their mission unaccomplished, but were soon back with a stern order from Keitel to let the man go.[185] A somewhat similar incident occurred at Fürstenwalde.[186] After much dispute and friction a compromise was worked out whereby the Gestapo no longer went into the military units to remove the men. Instead they were handed over by the military authorities.[187]

Aside from the new humiliation for the unhappy general, this maneuver proved an utter dud. It may be regarded as something of a miracle that this was so. Could not someone be found who had a grievance against Fritsch and wished him ill? Could not these unsophisticated men be trapped into saying something, perhaps relating some incident, that could be blown up to absurd proportions?

Kanter, who as court observer attended these as well as other Gestapo interrogations of which he received notice, had much to

[184] Goltz, "Erinnerungen," 194.
[185] Baudissin interviews, June 28, 1970, and June 23, 1971.
[186] Gisevius, *Bis zum bittern Ende*, 278.
[187] Goltz, "Erinnerungen," 187.

say in an interview with the present author about the leading questions put to these witnesses and the remarks of their interrogators which implied that Fritsch's guilt was virtually established. Meisinger and Fehling employed every imaginable trick to ferret out something that could be made damaging to Fritsch. Had any of the witnesses seen Fritsch naked or unnecessarily exposed?[188] The eight or nine men of the first group all spoke of the general's friendliness and affability. Did it not seem strange to them that a man of such exalted rank should be so familiar with humble folk like themselves? Had Fritsch ever touched any of them in a manner out of the ordinary? At this one man stepped forward and said that, since he had sworn to answer everything fully, he felt compelled to mention that Fritsch had occasionally pulled his ear humorously when he had done something a little wrong.[189]

Thus it went on for hours with the men in anything but a cooperative spirit. In their fury they turned to Kanter, in whom they recognized not only a neutral but a sympathetic observer, to ask whether they had to answer questions of this type. He told them kindly that they should just tell the truth as they saw it. Their mien indicated that they would have liked nothing better than to do violence to the interrogators.

Not the tiniest item was uncovered that could be used to make Werner von Fritsch seem less than the immaculate gentleman he was. But the inferences of the questions were of a coarseness that the absent general now knew enough to imagine vividly. What most twisted the knife in the wound was awareness that, with all the good will in the world toward him on the part of these men, there would be talk in military stables throughout Germany. This was, no doubt, among the more lasting injuries to his sense of dignity that he suffered in the tragic affair.[190]

---

[188] This question was also reported to Baudissin by the stablemaster of Infantry Regiment 9 when he returned to his post. Baudissin interview, June 23, 1971.

[189] Kanter interview, May 9, 1970. Goltz interview, February 17, 1970.

[190] Goltz particularly emphasizes the mortal offense done to Fritsch by the interrogation of the orderlies. Goltz interview, November 1, 1969. Goltz to Kielmansegg, September 9, 1947. Kielmansegg Papers.

# CHAPTER X

# Too Little and Too Late: The Exoneration of Fritsch

The trial of Werner von Fritsch was scheduled to commence on March 10, 1938. On the eve of this next-to-the-last round of the contest revolving about him (the final one was to be the struggle for rehabilitation) tension had risen to its highest point. The bitter feelings generated by the Gestapo's crass manuevers in the hassle over Frisch and the sense of outrage evoked by the Wannsee interrogation and the affair of the orderlies and stable attendants—these threatened to find relief in drastic fashion. Witzleben had entertained plans for a move against the Gestapo in the final days of February. Pressures continued to build up around Brauchitsch. Little is known about this beyond the account of Gisevius, the sole survivor of the inner group of activists. Goltz and Kanter, though able to recount details of the investigation and trial, were peripherally placed insofar as discussions of any kind of coup were concerned. Goltz's sole flashes of insight, we have noted, derived from what Schulenburg had told him of Witzleben's plans and from a possibly calculated outburst of Oster's which he did not take very seriously. Kanter heard strong words from Oster and Canaris at the time of the Wannsee questioning of Fritsch. That was about the extent of their involvement.

## The Final Preliminaries

As Gisevius relates it, Brauchitsch, in the week or ten days before the trial, was beset by attempts to thrust him into one or another confrontation with the forces persecuting Fritsch. Since his elevation to Army commander, every effort had been made to bring

331

him up to date on all thus far learned about what lay behind the troubles of Blomberg and Fritsch. He had been told about obscurer aspects of the Blomberg scandal and how it seemed of a piece with the attack on Fritsch. Such revealing details as the dispatch abroad of Blomberg's rival and the watch over Fritsch in Egypt, while Blomberg was making his marriage arrangements, were brought to his attention. He was also informed of what Nebe had heard about the existence of a "double" for Fritsch. Further, he was kept *au courant* on all that pertained to the progress of the investigation. The channels of communication to him were Canaris and his own chief of staff, Beck.[1]

This was all enormously helpful to a fledgling commander in chief who had much to catch up on after being kept all but incommunicado in the Continental Hotel from January 29 to February 4. During that period he had ventured forth only for conferences in the Chancellery or Air Ministry. The negotiations which led to his selection had shown Hitler's interest in keeping his new Army commander as much as possible isolated from all that swirled about the fate of his predecessor. On the background of affairs he had probably been given no more than the official story. Brauchitsch was not so dull as to fail to be struck by the contrast between this and the more authentic information that was flowing to him from the chief of staff and the head of the intelligence service.

Like other better informed figures of the Berlin military scene, Brauchitsch could have no doubt that, whether there was anything to the charges against Fritsch or not, the forces working to ruin him were seeking to influence the balance in the state to the disadvantage of the Army.[2] At this stage it needed no persuasion to convince him that the prime movers sat in the Prinz-Albrecht-Strasse, the source of the abominations that marked the turn of the month. There lay the target of those entreating him to "act" and he seems to have declared himself ready in principle to do so at an "appropriate" time. What he liked least were what he regarded as "outside pressures" in Army concerns. When Schacht, urged by Gisevius, took the occasion of beginning a new term as president of the Reichsbank to call on Brauchitsch and tried

[1] Gisevius, *Bis zum bittern Ende*, 278, 285-286. Gisevius recording, July 1971.
[2] Thus Puttkamer told the newly arrived Army adjutant, Captain Engel, that it was "a perfidious blow by the party against the Army." Engel Diary, entry of the night of March 11, 1938. Rundstedt later claimed to have regarded it as a long-range intrigue of Himmler's. Rundstedt, "Affaire Blomberg-Fritsch 1938."

to introduce the subject of Fritsch, the Army commander broke off the conversation as soon as he recognized its drift.[3]

The problem seemed to be agreement on when the time would become "appropriate." In the opinion of the Abwehr-associated group of activists, four or five such occasions had been missed since late January. Against this, Brauchitsch reasoned that the Gestapo was daily getting itself deeper in trouble. Once the trial had established the facts clearly and definitely so that the SS leaders stood fully exposed, the hour to strike would come. Then the Generalität would see how things stood and rally solidly behind him.[4]

Brauchitsch is not known to have confided to anyone, if he knew himself, just what he then expected to do. From what we already know of him, it is hard to conceive of anything very forceful, such as the Oster-Gisevius project of a sudden armed descent on the Prinz-Albrecht-Strasse. What comes to mind is more in the nature of "strong representations" to Hitler on the need of curbing the SS, perhaps in the form of replacing Himmler and/or Heydrich.

Such an estimate tallies with Gisevius's report that Brauchitsch was decidedly in favor of going through with the trial. Goering and Himmler are described by Gisevius as despairing, at this stage, of carrying the case to a "successful" conclusion in the face of such testimony as that of Frisch and Weingärtner and concluding it would be best to call off the trial on the grounds that the investigation had shown the charges to be in error.

Two considerations raise doubts about such a version. According to it, Himmler would be diametrically reversing his position of a few days earlier when he had been in the Chancellery and helped thwart Heitz and his two military judges. It would also oblige us to discover why Himmler, when after the trial he searched for every imaginable alibi for his part in the affair, did not make the point that he *had* tried to clear Fritsch without resorting to this final ordeal.

Be that as it may, Hitler did decree that the trial should proceed and all who were a party to it girded for the final showdown. A last signal of alarm came to the Abwehr group late in the evening of the 9th. Gisevius received a call from Helldorf to meet him in all haste. The police president came in his own car and told

[3] Schacht interview, October 9, 1969. Gisevius, *Bis zum bittem Ende*, 287. Gisevius says that Schacht reproached him bitterly for having persuaded him to make the visit.

[4] Gisevius, *Bis zum bittem Ende*, 278, 287.

him they must pick up Oster, whom Gisevius alerted from a public telephone. The colonel had already retired or was on the point of doing so. In pajamas and dressing gown he entered the car at the curb before his residence and Helldorf hastily drove away while relating what he had learned. The SS chiefs and Goering were said to have put their heads together to concoct a final artifice. A former officer and friend of Fritsch, no less a person than Prince Eitel Friedrich, second son of the Kaiser, who was reputed to be a homosexual, was to be arrested and a "confession" got out of him. This would be sprung at the trial with the particular purpose of confusing Brauchitsch and Raeder. The three agreed that the two service chiefs would have to be notified so that, if something of this nature were attempted, they would not be caught unprepared.[5]

As the trial approached, the Abwehr actionists sought to reach Fritsch with urgings that he emerge from his role of defendant to assume that of inexorable accuser. They hoped he might carry on in the spirit shown during his moment of resolution on February 23, beginning with a denunciation of Goering's presence among the judges on the score of manifest prejudice. It was a legal point that, if anyone ventured to raise it, Hitler would find difficult to reject. At least, the newly made field marshal would immediately be driven onto the defensive.[6]

However, in view of the lack of aggressive spirit Fritsch had thus far shown (with the one exception), it seemed imperative to coach Brauchitsch and Raeder on how they might most effectively put those behind the prosecution at a disadvantage. Gisevius was delegated to compose for them a list of questions of military conciseness. This was carried in the evening of the 9th to the two service chiefs by Beck and Canaris, who added an oral commentary elucidating each point.[7]

## The Aborted First Day

The trial of Werner von Fritsch on charges under Article 175 of the Penal Code began in the so-called Preussenhaus, once the home

---

[5] *Ibid.*, 288-289. Gisevius recording, January 1972. Since no such trick was actually attempted, Helldorf probably picked up rumors of some last-minute deliberations in the Prinz-Albrecht-Strasse. Tempted as the Nazis always were to strike a blow at the house of Hohenzollern, there would be hesitation about stirring up monarchist resentments too at so critical a juncture. The veto may well have come from Goering.

[6] Gisevius, *Bis zum bittern Ende*, 288.

of the Royal Prussian House of Peers in Berlin. While the capital must have been vibrating to the tensions at Tirpitz Ufer and the Prinz-Albrecht-Strasse, the principals and a miscellany of guards, witnesses, officials, and high-level hangers-on assembled in the courtroom or the adjacent corridor. Tempers flared in some instances where partisans of one side and the other rubbed shoulders. As Fritsch and his defender entered the corridor together, Goltz overheard the parting shot of a heated exchange between Goering's adjutant, Bodenschatz, and General Count von Sponeck, who was to testify for Fritsch. "Unheard of to treat such a man in this fashion," Sponeck was heard to grind through his teeth as he turned away.[8]

Fritsch and Goltz, the former in full regimentals, went into the courtroom and took their appointed places. The general's face wore that look of stiff impassivity which was so habitual with him. Since only those witnesses and attendants who were immediately required were in the chamber at any particular moment, the "audience" was never very large. Biron now functioned as prosecutor and Sack was there in his usual role as keeper of protocol. Kanter did not attend this first session. Fritsch's former orderlies and other minor witnesses were still being brought in for interrogation and he was kept busy as observer.

Two men attended the proceedings as a result of wires pulled by Fritsch's partisans; the sources differ on whether they were there on March 10 or only came into the resumed session of the court on March 17-18.[9] One was the Minister of Justice; the other, head of the Reich Office of Criminology. It was felt that the presence of Gürtner would have a disciplinary effect on Goering and make him stick more closely to accepted forms. There may also have been some thought that, under certain circumstances, he might intervene with Hitler if things were done improperly. His presence was engineered by Canaris through Brauchitsch, acting in his capacity as one of the judges, and was cleared through Dohnanyi with Gürtner.[10] Actually Gürtner solemnly occupied himself with

[7] *Ibid.*

[8] Goltz, "Erinnerungen," 196.

[9] Goltz, who usually does not concern himself too much with detail (he gives the date of the trial opening as March 12 instead of the 10th), speaks (*ibid.*, 197) of Gürtner's and Nebe's being present from the start. Gisevius's account (*Bis zum bittem Ende*, 290) has them enter the picture as a kind of last-minute reinforcement for the defense on the 17th.

[10] Gisevius recording, January 1972. Goltz (letter to the author, January 21, 1972) affirms that Gürtner's presence was meant to exercise restraint on Goering.

335

voluminous note-taking and never uttered a word during the trial.

The part taken by Arthur Nebe turned out to be only a trifle more active. Here Brauchitsch had been persuaded to propose his inclusion as a resource person in the field of criminology, an area in which he certainly was the chief authority in Germany. Actually the initiated among Fritsch's friends expected him to function more as an expert in "Gestapology," where he could claim equal expertise. In this character he was to be an auxiliary to Goltz, sitting beside him and whispering suggestions on how to embarrass Himmler's people. It was an expedient which at the time seemed to have everything to recommend it. Certainly no one else knew so much from his own observations about the background and interrelation of the Blomberg and Fritsch affairs.

But Nebe was to feel ill at ease and inhibited. Though as an old Nazi and one of Himmler's first-line subordinates he was scarcely suspect as a Fritsch partisan, Goering sensed that his inclusion was a maneuver of the defense. He yielded most unwillingly to the suggestion of inviting him as a consultant, kept him uncomfortable by his close scrutiny, and avoided calling on him except for a purpose of his own at the very end. Goering managed to give the uneasy man a sense of being superfluous and something of an intruder.[11] As for Goltz, he seems to have resented having this unknown and unasked adviser sprung on him without warning at the last minute; he appears to have ignored him as much as possible. His friend Schulenburg had assured him that here was a "decent fellow" who was expert in all police matters, but this was not enough to free Goltz from the feeling of an intrusion.[12]

Jauntily swinging his newest toy, the showy baton of a German field marshal, Goering led the members of the court into the chamber. Behind him came Raeder with a friendly but unrevealing expression. There followed Brauchitsch, betraying discomfort in a somewhat pinched countenance and the two military judges, Dr. Sellmer and Dr. Lehmann. All in the chamber rose with one dramatic exception—the defendant. It was, in effect, a direct challenge to the court and to the legitimacy of the proceeding. Even Fritsch's defender was surprised though he completely approved. As Goltz put it, Fritsch's estimate of Goering proved correct: the Luftwaffe

[11] Gisevius, *Bis zum bittern Ende*, 290.

[12] Goltz, "Erinnerungen," 197. Goltz interviews, November 1, 1969, and July 8, 1971. Goltz does not put the situation in the specific terms employed here but his feeling is unmistakable.

head did not venture to make an issue of this conspicuous affront.[13]

Both sides had been assiduous in coaching "their men" or those they hoped would turn out to be so. The final essay of Beck and Canaris with Brauchitsch and Raeder has been alluded to. Apparently ignorant of this, Sack initiated a separate set of suggestions in concert with Kanter and Rosenberger, himself preparing the first draft, and asking the others to add to or improve on it. Kanter believes that Gürtner was delegated to deliver copies to Brauchitsch and Raeder, who put them in their pockets—and left them there.[14]

Canaris, at least, seems to have entertained some hope of driving a wedge between Goering and his SS confederates. He therefore tried to provide the former with convincing data that the case they had fabricated had small prospect of standing up under attack, but Goering proved evasive. Either by arrangement with Himmler or by a more direct order, Fehling was given the responsibility of filling Goering in on all that might be of use to him. The vain fellow was so pleased with himself to be acting as mentor to so mighty a man that he fell to boasting during his talks with Kanter. He claimed to be continually with Goering just before and during the days of the trial, "always hammering into him the facts that were important to him." During the sessions of March 17-18 he would lean over to Kanter with ecstatic whispers, "He has that from me," or "Isn't he doing it well?"[15]

The procedures began with Goering immediately seizing the direction from the frustrated but unresisting Sellmer. The defendant had to submit to the customary initial query whether he admitted his guilt. Fritsch having affirmed his innocence, the principal witness, Schmidt, was called in. He repeated the details of the story he had now so often recounted and identified the general as the person he had blackmailed. In Goltz's cross-examination, the absurdity of the testimony that there were two supposedly identical cases was demonstrated with devastating clarity. Under normal cirumstances, the defense could have rested and the case been determined then and there, but of course Hitler's requirement that the witness repudiate his own story had not been met. However, interruption came in a startling and dramatic form. It was almost

[13]J. A. Kielmansegg, *Der Fritsch-Prozess 1938*, 88. Goltz's observation is made in a letter to the author, January 21, 1972.

[14]Kanter interview, May 9, 1971.

[15]*Ibid.*

noon when an adjutant from the Reich Chancellery (as Wehrmacht respresentative, Schmundt appears likely) rushed into the courtroom and whispered with Goering. After a moment of flurry among the judges, they announced importantly that, "for reasons touching on the interests of the Reich," it would be necessary to adjourn the trial for a number of days. The chamber buzzed with conjecture. Only Fritsch was taken aside and informed confidentially of the reason for this new blow: the German forces were being readied for a move into Austria and the chiefs of the Wehrmacht services were urgently required to attend to the duties this entailed for them.

## Austrian Interlude

During the course of the previous evening (March 9) Hitler had learned of Austrian Chancellor Schuschnigg's call for a plebiscite calculated to elicit popular support for his country's independence. Under the prevailing circumstances it could only look to the world as an act of defiance against Hitler and a repudiation of an agreement the two dictators had concluded at Berchtesgaden on February 12.

There is much that remains to be learned about the interplay of Hitler's foreign and domestic policies in February–March 1938. Few insiders then entertained any doubt that he welcomed a crisis over Austria both to divert attention from the domestic scene and to find compensation for any loss of prestige he conceived himself to have suffered because of the Blomberg scandal. What has not been established is the degree to which he may, for these reasons, have accentuated the external crisis and speeded the developments that were more or less in the cards.

The first evidence of a conscious linking on his part of the Fritsch affair and relations with Austria came as early as January 31, when Jodl, after hearing Keitel's recital of Hitler's intentions, recorded in his diary: "Fuehrer wishes to divert the spotlight from the Wehrmacht, keep Europe in a ferment, and, by a turnover in various offices, create the impression of a concentration of power rather than a moment of weakness. Schuschnigg should not gain courage but tremble." [16]

In the weeks that followed, the signs of Hitler's preoccupation with using the Austrian situation as a lightning rod to carry off

[16] Jodl Diary, 369.

the dangerous flashes engendered by the proceedings in the Fritsch case became more pronounced. He, who had never found it easy to contain himself when full of a subject, hardly tried to conceal his intent from those about him. What is less clear is the degree to which he was moved by the broad desire to rebound from his setback over Blomberg and the degree to which he was moved by a more specific aim of minimizing the adverse impact of the increasingly probable exoneration of Fritsch.

There is abundant testimony with respect to the former. His adjutants took note of and discussed animatedly among themselves the number of occasions on which he remarked that he must soon score a new success in foreign policy. Wiedemann, Puttkamer, and Engel were all later convinced that, though a move against Austria sooner or later appeared fated, the Wehrmacht crisis induced him to bring matters to a head earlier than would otherwise have been the case.[17]

When Adolf Hitler's mind was aboil with concentrated thought, he was prone to unburden himself with amazing frankness to whoever was handy, even to a comparative stranger. After a breakfast given for foreign military attachés in late February, he happened to be alone in a corner for a time with Colonel Moritz von Faber du Faur, the German military attaché in Belgrade. The meeting with the foreign military representatives had evidently set him to cogitating feverishly on the European scene much in the vein of his Chancellery address of November 5. "In the immediate future," he announced, "I shall launch an undertaking against Austria. It will go smoothly. I have come to an understanding with Stoyadino-vich [the Yugoslav premier]. He prefers the Anschluss to the Habsburgs. Mussolini will grin and bear it as he has little choice since his Abyssinian excursion has estranged England and France."[18]

There is a temptation to look for and "discover" close parallels between the periods of highest tension in the domestic and foreign scenes during the five weeks following February 4. As the proceedings in the Fritsch case unfolded, can one discern an interrelation-

[17]Wiedemann, *Der Mann der Feldherr werden wollte*, 115, and interview, December 2, 1969. Engel interview, May 11, 1970. Puttkamer interview, June 27, 1970. General Engel states that he commenced to hear such remarks directly after he assumed his post in the Chancellery on March 10. From what he learned from his fellow adjutants, it was evident to him that Hitler's attention had been preoccupied with this problem for weeks.

[18]Moritz von Faber du Faur, *Macht und Ohnmacht: Erinnerungen eines alten Offiziers* (Stuttgart, 1955), 204.

ship between them and the mounting pressures against Austria? It is, no doubt, possible to determine dates on which there seems a linkage between what was going on in the two spheres. In one instance only are there the earmarks of more than a coincidence. This, however, has significance.

We have noted Hitler's retreat to Berchtesgaden the evening of February 4 after eleven days of furious activity on the Berlin stage. There, two days later, he received his just-dismissed ambassador in Vienna, Franz von Papen, one of the three diplomats involved in the February 4 turnover. The envoy found a distracted and weary, almost an exhausted dictator: "His eyes stared into vacancy and his thoughts were entirely elsewhere."[19] In his mind must have whirled both the recollection of the turbulent scenes he had experienced in Berlin and the problem with which he was most immediately confronted. This was the issue of the court-martial. He had yielded to the importunities of Brauchitsch that one must be staged but now had to consider how it could best be constituted and influenced to serve his purposes.

Only a week before, Papen had been in Berlin to suggest a meeting between Hitler and Schuschnigg to try to clear the air between the two Germanic capitals. He had been authorized to pursue the matter, though Hitler, intensely preoccupied as he was then with the high point of the Wehrmacht crisis, had betrayed no great interest. The ambassador now reported that Schuschnigg had expressed himself ready for a frank exchange of views. Hitler's reaction was like that of a man coming out of a trance and finding himself instantly in full career. Papen could only assume that his original proposal had hardly registered and that something must have transpired since that made Hitler so suddenly catch fire. "This is an excellent idea," he exclaimed enthusiastically; "please return immediately [to Vienna] and arrange for a meeting on one of the next days."[20] The somewhat dazed envoy, as abruptly reinstated as he had been discharged, departed on his errand. Once again Hitler had shown his instinct for recognizing the whir of opportunity on the wing.

The chance to bring relations with Austria into the foreground came too pat to hand for the dictator to fail to appreciate what it offered in the way of distracting attention from domestic troubles. From this hour, it is safe to assume, his course was fixed with

[19] Papen, 460.
[20] Ibid.

respect to the specific "foreign success" that was to be sought. This must not be understood, however, to indicate a proven tactical connection between bringing matters with Austria to a head and the day-to-day shifts in the prosecution of the Fritsch case.

In view of the remarkable coincidence in time between the climactic move against Austria and the adjournment of the trial that had scarcely begun, it is tempting to perceive at this point the culmination of steps inaugurated on February 6 with the mission entrusted to the reprieved Papen. Yet the catalyst—Schuschnigg's fatal announcement of a plebiscite in which Hitler was bound to see a challenge—can hardly have come otherwise than fortuitously. From this it would follow that the fact that the external crisis reached a high point just when it could serve to impose a pause in the trial was for Hitler a true gift of fortune. It gave him the opportunity to rearrange the pieces in the larger game being played.

At this critical point it was not Hitler but Goering who most fully commanded the situation and recognized its essential implications. Whether or not he had shared entirely in Hitler's hopes to create a large-scale foreign diversion, at the decisive moment he again had the steadier nerves and the firmer resolve. His role in aggravating the crisis when things were poised on the razor's edge is well known and thoroughly documented. It stands, too, in glaring contrast to his line of action six months later, when, in the crisis over Czechoslovakia, Goering was to exercise a braking and moderating influence. The part he played on March 9-11 therefore cannot be explained on the score of sheer recklessness or bellicosity.

Goering's intervention, if so it can be called, commenced in the evening of the 9th directly after he had been informed in excited telephone calls from the Chancellery about the plebiscite and Hitler's reaction. Hitler fumed over the "treason" of Schuschnigg and feverishly issued not always coherent orders. Goering's tactics were to exacerbate the dictator's fury and push him in the direction of military action. Goering was aware that this would at least furnish an unassailable pretext for interrupting the court-martial proceedings the next day virtually as soon as they began. He must also have known that if the rape of Austria were carried through to a triumphant conclusion, the Fritsch trial would resume in an entirely different climate.

Goering's part deserves all the more emphasis since the martial climax of the move against Austria was not entirely predetermined. Hitler was to have more than one moment of indecision before

341

the march was actually launched. To the consternation of the Army leaders, he had on the morning of the 10th, just as the trial was getting under way, ordered Keitel to bring him a plan by which the troops would be in their assembly areas on the 11th and cross the border on the 12th. The flabbergasted Keitel hurried to OKH to lay the problem in the lap of the General Staff. He was received by Beck with icy coldness and told in no uncertain terms that there was not the slightest preparation or even blueprint for such an operation.[21] Keitel asked Beck to accompany him to the Chancellery to report accordingly. They were told by Hitler that an operational plan would have to be ready by late afternoon.[22]

The next hours and the night that followed had a nightmarish quality rare in the peacetime annals of the German General Staff. In helter-skelter fashion the orders for an improvised march had to be thrown together. Beck, whose lunch had as usual consisted of a cup of coffee taken at his desk, this day also went supperless and it was only with difficulty that Hossbach coaxed some food into him late in the evening.[23] Keitel later described that night as a real martyrdom for himself. His telephone kept ringing with calls from Brauchitsch, from the General Staff, and from the head of his own plans division, General Viebahn. The single refrain was that he must persuade Hitler to give up the invasion. He solemnly promised to try his best and did—nothing. "I never considered asking the Fuehrer even once," he writes. "I indeed promised but a little later I would convey a negative answer without having done so. The Fuehrer never learned anything of this. His judgment of the Army would otherwise have been devastating. I wanted to spare both parties."[24]

March 11 dawned in the Chancellery with its chief inhabitants too excited to feel the full weariness of two nights of little sleep. From Papen's pen we have a graphic description of the atmosphere he encountered there. Hitler he pictures in a state bordering on hysteria. "Everybody seemed present whom service and curiosity, duty and intrigue had called there. I saw Neurath [filling in for Ribbentrop, his successor, who was making his official farewells in London] with several gentlemen of his office, saw Minister of the Interior Frick with his state secretaries, Goebbels with a

---

[21] Hossbach, *Zwischen Wehrmacht und Hitler*, 128.
[22] Keitel, 179.
[23] Hossbach, *Zwischen Wehrmacht und Hitler*, 128.
[24] Keitel, 179.

cohort of propagandists and journalists, party chiefs high and low, Himmler surrounded by a dozen tall SS officers, and not least the Wehrmacht with Brauchitsch, Keitel, and several adjutants."[25]

Goering alone among the mighty of the Nazi hierarchy is not mentioned as one who watched and waited. He was much too occupied directing the show and most of the twenty-seven telephone calls made that day to Vienna from the Chancellery were his. Hitler, as usual, was beset by doubts and hesitations as the climactic moment approached. Despite his bravado to Faber du Faur, he was not completely sure what Mussolini would do. When Papen, entreated by Neurath, urged Hitler to countermand the marching orders, the Fuehrer grasped at the advice to draw back. "Yes, yes, that can be done." And to Keitel: "Let Brauchitsch know immediately that the order to march is canceled." The Army commander later thanked Papen effusively: "Thank God that we will be spared this."[26]

That the march nevertheless did take place on March 12 was due in large measure to Goering, who grasped with both hands the lead vacated by the vacillating Hitler. Seldom in his adventurous life can he have shown himself more purposeful; and his purpose cannot be divorced from his unique relationship to all that pertains to the affair bearing the name of Fritsch. He alone could see fully all that was at stake. It is unimaginable that calculations with respect to it failed to be a major factor in the dominant role he seized for himself in the Anschluss.[27] If the union of Germany and Austria in 1938 can be labeled, from the Austrian standpoint, a shotgun wedding, to Hermann Goering must go much of the honor or odium of having brandished the weapon.

The hiatus in the trial caused Fritsch's partisans the greatest uneasiness. A march into Austria threatened further international complications that might be used as a pretext for additional postponements, perhaps even for canceling the trial altogether. Few if any doubted that the entire action, notably its timing, was meant as a "diversionary maneuver." If was felt necessary to mount new

[25] Papen, 485.

[26] *Ibid.*, 486–487.

[27] The author here fully associates himself with the analysis of Gisevius (*Adolf Hitler*, 408–409). K.-J. Müller (*Das Heer und Hitler*, 269n71) correctly points out that no final proof can be advanced for so close a linking between Goering's role in the Anschluss and his personal interests in the Fritsch affair. But it could scarcely be more logically certain.

pressures to assure the resumption of the court-martial at an early date.[28]

There were grave reasons, too, for worries about Fritsch himself. To face what he had supposed to be his final ordeal, he had called on his last reserves of nervous energy. The sudden adjournment of the trial meant not only an inescapable letdown but the strain of new threats and uncertainties. Hossbach was so concerned that he felt it imperative to spend every hour he could spare with him;[29] other friends must have applied themselves similarly to raising his flagging spirits. His almost apathetic performance in the second phase of the trial can be ascribed in part to this further nervous exhaustion.

## The Final Stage: March 17–18

Germany blazed in triumph and the reflected glow beat on the staid walls of the venerable Preussenhaus when the trial of Werner von Fritsch resumed on March 17. The auspices and implications were dramatically different from those of a week before. Fritsch's partisans could only move grimly ahead with the business at hand.

The composition of the court was altered only by the presence of Kanter, who now sat with it in the character of a "specially assigned judge." Twice on this and the following day he was called away to act in his customary capacity at interrogations. These were minor witnesses and included the last of the orderlies and grooms who had been ferreted out in obscurer portions of the Reich. Each time he had the secret satisfaction of returning to report negative results which Goering had to read to the court.[30]

The proceedings commenced on the 17th with a review of the charges of Schmidt that featured him in the role of unwavering accuser. Next a number of Gestapo officials testified on his record as a police informer. He had identified over one hundred persons as homosexuals and "in most instances" this was claimed to have led to convictions. His memory was described as excellent and, in these cases, he had spoken the truth. A written statement from an absent official of the Gestapo was introduced which charac-

[28] Hossbach, *Zwischen Wehrmacht und Hitler*, 128. Rosenberger also believed that the timing in the Austrian crisis was wholly dictated by the desire for a diversion. Notes on a conversation with Rosenberger, May 4, 1947. Kielmansegg Papers.

[29] Hossbach, *Zwischen Wehrmacht und Hitler*, 128.

[30] Kanter interview, May 9, 1970.

terized him as a leading authority on the homosexuals of Berlin.[31]

Goltz strove to erase any positive impression created by this commendation by showing how often Schmidt's claims had failed to stand up. His proposal that he (Goltz) should take the stand concerning his own case was brushed aside by Goering as "super-fluous" in view of its having been shown to be one of "mistaken identity."[32] Goering thus passed over as a bagatelle a highly compromising parallel to the case at issue. Schmidt was made to appear guilty of no more than a confusion of names.

The defender next introduced a potential bombshell in asking for an examination of the new Minister of Economics, Walter Funk, whose name had been bracketed with his own in Schmidt's concentration camp accusations. With a straight face but a biting irony that cannot have been lost upon his audience, he commented that Funk must have been regarded as innocent since he was still in office rather than having shared the fate of Fritsch. Again Goering played his lifesaving role for the prosecution by turning this down.[33]

The same short shrift was given Goltz's proposal to call to the stand those of the "over one hundred" persons accused by Schmidt who had been found *innocent*. This, Goering said testily, still would not prove that Schmidt had lied in other cases. In fact, there was no sense in wasting time attempting to show Schmidt's general mendacity; establishing that he had lied in other cases would not prove he was doing so in this one.

In the matter of showing Schmidt's unreliability, the defense was thus confined to submitting an analysis of his police record which Goltz had laboriously written out himself and to presenting a single witness who was already on deck. This was Count Wedel, the police president of Potsdam and a prominent party member.

[31] Verdict, 386–387.

[32] Goltz, "Erinnerungen," 198.

[33] *Ibid.*, 199. Gisevius (recording, January 1972) holds that to have summoned Funk to testify would have made Schmidt's story look better and have hurt the position of Fritsch. Funk was commonly derided as "die Schwule Walli" ("anxious Walt," using the feminine article). His denials of what many in the courtroom knew to be true would, Gisevius believes, have shored up Himmler's claim that homosexuals habitually denied everything. This might well have been the effect of Funk's appearance, but Goltz could safely assume that Goering would never permit such an ordeal for a man who always toadied to him and was in Hitler's category of "untouchables." To have brought in Funk would also have underscored the outrage of his appointment as Economics Minister on the very day the Fuehrer had dismissed the falsely accused Fritsch.

When Judge Sellmer inquired whether he had ever committed an offense under Article 175, he furiously rejected such a query. Goering intervened to remind the witness that he had to answer all questions, upon which he growled out an indignant negative. Sellmer, made sensitive about the way he had been shoved aside as presiding officer, was much offended and declared that he must insist that *his* questions, too, should be answered as he put them.[34]

Fifteen of Fritsch's former orderlies and stable attendants were then called up in a body and affirmed in chorus that they had never experienced the least questionable word or act on his part. Since he apparently felt that humble folk should, like others, take an interest in the world and its affairs, he had on occasion addressed to them simple queries on geography or a commemorative date. He might tweek their ears in humorous reproof when they did not know the answers. The two Hitler-boys and their mothers were not called since their interrogation by the Gestapo had yielded nothing of interest. Only the protocols were admitted in evidence.[35]

A dramatic, though somewhat aborted, interlude was provided by an extraordinary display of courage—indeed, of heroism—on the part of General Count Hans von Sponeck. This intrepid soldier had only shortly before been transferred from the Army to the Luftwaffe. A former adjutant of Fritsch's, he had volunteered as a character witness but was determined not to let matters rest with a mere statement on the man he revered. Kanter, who has given us the only eyewitness account of the incident,[36] met Sponeck for the first time before the opening of proceedings on March 17 when he entered the antechamber of the courtroom. The general was grimly parading up and down with a face set in bitter lines. Sack made them acquainted and a conversation developed among the three in which Sponeck revealed what he intended to do as a witness. He began by saying he knew well that after he had testified he no longer would be welcome in the Luftwaffe but that this would not deter him. He was enraged that Fritsch had been dismissed on the mere presentation of charges and a groundless case carried on against him. He followed with an expression of hatred and contempt for National Socialism as lacking in respect for all traditional morality and values.

[34] Goltz, "Erinnerungen," 198.
[35] Verdict, 401–402.
[36] Ernst Kanter, "General Graf Sponeck" (a five-page statement of February 7, 1968, lent to the author by courtesy of Colonel Eberhard Einbeck). This is the source of the account here presented of Sponeck's role in the Fritsch trial.

# Too Little and Too Late

What Sponeck proposed to do was breathtaking in its scope and daring. It was nothing less than to "tear the mask off the face of the prevailing regime." He intended to strike out immediately with a denunciation of "powers that set themselves above the state"; these, he would charge, had conspired to arrange the fall of Fritsch and the defamation and emasculation of the Army. He had in mind Goering, Himmler, the Gestapo, the whole RSHA, and such other persons and forces in the Nazi state which sought power and advantage in defiance of established law and concepts of right and justice. In this way he hoped to shift the entire proceedings onto another plane and reverse the position of attacked and attackers.

Though Sack and Kanter agreed wholeheartedly with Sponeck's analysis, they argued vehemently against the course he wished to take. They felt it tactically inadvisable for him to begin with charges that were not subject to immediate proof. The inquiry about those behind the affair ought not to be initiated by him; it could have dire personal consequences and might actually prove disadvantageous for Fritsch. Instead he should first confine himself to what he had to say about the defendant and wait for a signal from the bench. They would try to induce Brauchitsch and Raeder to raise questions that would enable him to point his finger at those responsible.

Unfortunately neither of the service chiefs would agree to expose himself to the enmity of the very forces Sponeck was eager to challenge. They may also have thought of the man behind these forces—Adolf Hitler. Kanter believes that the count learned of their refusal (no doubt, from Sack), felt left to his own devices, and went back to the game as he had first planned it. But he had not reckoned sufficiently with the ruthlessness and presence of mind of Hermann Goering. Hardly had he begun with his allusion to "forces that set themselves above the state" than he was cut short and in loud and sharp tones "called to order." His remarks were labeled irrelevant and he was told that it was "not the business of a general" to intervene with "irresponsible political conceptions." Sponeck was not permitted to resume the forbidden topic but was directed to answer concisely a few rudely put questions. Goering then ungraciously and abruptly dismissed the witness.

Sponeck did indeed pay all and more than the expected price. Immediately after the trial he was dismissed from the Luftwaffe and virtually thrown back to the Army. That he did not fare worse at the time is probably due both to the need to deal carefully with Army feelings just then and to the wish of Goering, glowing with self-satisfaction about his performance in the case, to appear magnanimous. We can only conjecture whether and in what degree long Nazi memories of Sponeck's daring challenge played a part in his murder at Himmler's direction and with Hitler's consent on July 23, 1944, while he was serving a six-year sentence in a fortress for disobeying orders in South Russia in 1942, where he sought to save the force he commanded from being sacrificed by Hitler's erratic generalship. Animosity pursued him even beyond the grave; his widow was arrested and, upon her release deprived of all but the merest pittance of her pension.[37]

It is not known at what stage proceedings were adjourned on the 17th and resumed the next morning. The first day was largely given over to basic testimony and the second more to cross-examination and the confrontation of witnesses with one another. Next to Schmidt, the greatest interest was aroused by the appearances of the Bayern Seppl and Captain von Frisch. Though visibly feeble, Frisch had drawn on hidden reserves of energy, was able to move about freely, and gave his testimony in a firm voice.[38] No mistake, insofar as the Fritsch trial had heroes, the pathetic old captain, beaten by fate and Gestapo truncheons, deserves his place among them.

Throughout Goering kept the threads of the proceedings firmly in his hands. The Fritsch partisans present were convinced that his aim was to "keep something hanging" on the general. As the course of the trial made this appear less and less likely, his pose of "correct" impartial judge was accentuated. To the end, however, he was quick to intervene in any line of questioning that spelled trouble for the Gestapo. Thus at one point, when Schmidt faltered under Goltz's relentless pressure, Goering roared at him in a fashion calculated to make him recover and maintain his story.[39]

Unquestionably Goering's presence exercised an intimidating influence on Brauchitsch and Raeder. The notes that were supposed to enable them to take a hand at critical junctures never came

[37] For these and other facts about this brave soldier the author is indebted to his biographer, the late Colonel Eberhard Einbeck, who permitted the prepublication use of his study on Sponeck: *Das Exempel: Graf Sponeck. Ein Beitrag zum Thema Hitler und die Generale* (Brennen, 1970).

[38] Goltz interview, November 1, 1969.

[39] Notes on a conversation with Rosenberger, May 4, 1947. Kielmansegg Papers. Hassell Papers, notation of April 30, 1938. The account of Goering's helping Schmidt to recover was given by Fritsch to Ulex. Ulex ms., 96.

out of their pockets. There is no evidence that Raeder opened his mouth even once,[40] and Brauchitsch did little better. He maintained an air of icy nonpartisanship and at no point made a visible effort to support Fritsch.[41] He later claimed to have asked questions aimed at delving into the antecedents of the affair. At one point, as he related it, he asked whether Schmidt stood in some special relationship to the RSHA, but desisted from pressing further when Meisinger gave the inevitable reply that he knew nothing of anything like this.[42] Whatever Brauchitsch may have said, it produced so small a ripple that Kanter, for one, could not recall his having said *anything*. Asked later (by Beck or Canaris?) why they had made no use of the material furnished them, Brauchitsch and Raeder could only indicate that they feared the course proposed to them did not accord with "the will of the Fuehrer."[43]

The trance-producing impact of Goering on the other members of the court derived not only from having to do with a ruthless and brutal adventurer, confronting whom spelled danger writ large, but from being exposed to the crude exuberance and animal spirits of the man.[44] In fine, not only the Austrian Hitler but prosaic North Germans as well were unable to withstand entirely the fascination of Goering. Their sense of propriety may have been scandalized when he ignored all the accepted legal forms and dismissed a befuddled witness with a contemptuous, "disappear, idiot."[45] But he kept things in flow and enlivened even the dullest moments. In short, he ran the show with an éclat that could not fail to impress his most staid associates. Fritsch himself could not escape the sway of Goering's personality. At least, he participated in the conspiracy of silence, sticking strictly to the immediate issues of his defense and making no effort to open topics Goering clearly regarded in the category of unmentionables. An entire avenue was also closed to the defense by the absence from Berlin of Himmler and Heydrich, whom it had summoned as witnesses. For the regime this

[40] General Engel (interview, May 4, 1970) says that this later evoked bitter comment from Army men. Admiral Puttkamer found no occasion to contradict the author when he expressed his distress over Raeder's passive conduct in the Fritsch trial. Interview, June 27, 1970.

[41] "Correct and ice cold without exerting himself for Fritsch." Notes on a conversation with Rosenberger, May 4, 1947. Keilmansegg Papers.

[42] As related to Captain Engel by Brauchitsch. Engel interview, May 11, 1970.

[43] Kanter interview, May 9, 1970.

[44] This was Nebe's analysis as given to Gisevius the evening of March 18, a few hours after the conclusion of the trial. Gisevius, *Wo ist Nebe?* 288.

[45] As related by Gürtner. Hassell Papers, notation of April 30, 1938.

was one more dividend of the Anschluss, for it was able to claim that they were occupied in Austria with urgent public business.[46]

Since Brauchitsch and Raeder hung back, it must have been the two regular judges, Sellmer and Lehmann, who made the lone stabs aimed at the Gestapo. Sack, who went to so much trouble to brief the service chiefs, can hardly have failed to fill in his own colleagues on the military bench. One of them now needled Fehling, asking whether it was true he had been in Frisch's apartment as early as January 15 and had also seized the captain's account records at the Dresdner Bank? Yes, was the reply, but unfortunately *there had not been time to read them!*[47]

The other military judge then took the court onto thin ice by raising the perilous topic of the surveillance of Fritsch in Egypt. The Gestapo offical thus questioned (Fehling again?) vigorously asserted that no such watch had taken place, but he was saved from further perjury by Goering: "Why don't you rather say that you know nothing about it?"[48]

Schmidt's story was not made to look any better by the maladroit effort of his colleague Heiter to second him in constructing two nearly identical cases. In relating how he acted the role of Schmidt's superior in the Lichterfelde-East waiting room, he was so awkward in trying to give an impression of two similar cases that he entangled himself completely and had to admit that he had never seen Fritsch.[49]

Where would the case have stood if prosecution and defense had been obliged to rest at this juncture? Count Kielmansegg fears that his uncle in that event would have had to face the prospect of an acquittal because of "insufficient proof."[50] It is difficult to believe that Goering's domination over his judicial colleagues extended so far. Though Hitler could insist on a continued investigation and trial unless Schmidt recanted his testimony, he did not

[46]Gisevius *Bis zum bittem Ende*, 291. J. A. Kielmansegg, *Der Fritsch-Prozess 1938*, 95.

[47]Gisevius, *Bis zum bittem Ende*, 291. Gisevius (recording, January 1972) states that Nebe at this point whispered to Goltz that he should leap in with sharp questions on how the visit came to be made but that the attorney, leery about coming so directly to grips with the Gestapo, hung back.

[48]Gisevius, *Bis zum bittem Ende*, 291, and recording, January 1972. The anonymity in Gisevius's account on who put the questions argues that it was neither Brauchitsch nor Raeder.

[49]Goltz, "Erinnerungen," 200. Verdict, 389. Heiter may well have been the "idiot" whom Goering directed to "disappear."

[50]J. A. Keilmansegg, *Der Fritsch-Prozess 1938*, 92-93.

and could not direct a verdict on such a basis. It had been an outrage to every conception of logic and justice for the dictator to proceed after the discovery of Frisch had demonstrated the absurdity of Schmidt's claims. Any other verdict than "proven innocence" after this had been spelled out in the court-martial would have associated the judges with this outrage. The outcome could thus hardly be doubted, but if the proceedings had ended at this stage there would have been debate and probably not a unanimous vote. From Fritsch's standpoint this had to be prevented at all cost.

It was time for Goltz to introduce a witness he had held in reserve. This was another of Schmidt's associates, Ganzer, whom the count had located in an obscure protocol of a proceeding against Schmidt several years earlier. In his deposition, Ganzer had related how he had strolled with Schmidt through the Ferdinand Strasse and been told by him of a "high officer" there whom he had once "laid on the cross." From what Goltz knew there could be no question but that this was the unhappy captain.[51]

Goltz had Ganzer interrogated and the simple facts confirmed. The man had further declared that no name for the officer had been mentioned. The attorney then wisely decided to let matters rest until the trial. He hoped to trap Schmidt by giving him an opening for applying the story to Fritsch. Almost certainly this prospect would be nullified if he tried to make this point during the investigation. In that event the double investigative procedure would ensure that Fritsch's ill-wishers were fully alerted, would afford them a chance for their usual game of leading and sometimes intimidating witnesses, and thus would lead to protocol confronting protocol. Goltz had had more than enough of that. If more intense quizzing of Ganzer were left for the trial, the situation would be out of the Gestapo's hands and words once spoken could not be recalled.[52]

Hence it came about that at the trial Ganzer was the final hope for Goltz to break down the story of Schmidt. After having Ganzer repeat his story, the attorney turned to Schmidt to ask whether what the witness had told applied to Frisch or Fritsch. And Schmidt, perceiving a chance to give more substance to his tale about the latter, allowed himself to be enmeshed. Assuredly, what he had told Ganzer referred to *Fritsch*. For good measure he added

[51] Goltz, "Erinnerungen," 201.
[52] *Ibid.*, 201-202.

351

that here was proof that the business with Fritsch had actually occurred, for otherwise how could he have told Ganzer about it?[53]

A flash of triumph shot through Goltz, the first since he had gone, roses in hand and believing his task accomplished, to congratulate Fritsch on the finding of his "double." It was now the moment to press Ganzer for details and item after item that could only apply to Frisch was laid before the court. Schmidt had told him that the officer was a cavalry captain, an old man who lived upstairs in an indicated house with his nurse. Ganzer had also been shown the bank where the officer had his account and had been told that, since Schmidt himself had gone the limit in what he could squeeze out of the man, his colleague should try his luck. He should pose as the Bayern Seppl, imitate his slight limp, and wear the kind of sports outfit he affected. If he called on the captain in this guise he would at the very least get cognac. Yes, Frisch interposed, he had given Schmidt a drink the last time he had called to blackmail him. "Cavaliers keep their agreements," he had told him.[54]

From the net into which Schmidt had now gotten himself there was no escape. He had been caught in a specific lie about Fritsch before the entire court-martial and the verdict was now only a formality. No one recognized this more instantly than Hermann Goering. He had followed the testimony of Ganzer with increasing interest.[55] From the way things were going he now saw the need of grabbing the lead in the indicated direction. Thereby he fully embraced the principle "If you can't lick 'em, join 'em." He knew that it was he and no other who must now drive Schmidt to admit that the entire story about Fritsch was a fabrication. Schmidt, still doggedly trying to escape from his entrapment, was put under more pressure than his stamina could resist. He claimed to have told Ganzer of several cases of blackmail in Lichterfelde-East and to have shown him a number of places where victims resided. Ganzer had simply become confused.[56] Certainly he had not been told about a cavalry captain. In this fashion he stumbled on with Goering now making every effort to trip him up further with repeated injunctions to tell the truth. When he still refused to change his story, Goering roared at him: "Why, you are the worst liar

[53] *Ibid.*, 202.
[54] *Ibid.*, 202-203. Verdict, 389-390.
[55] Goltz, "Erinnerungen," 203.
[56] Verdict, 390.

I have ever encountered. Do you still think you can keep lying to us?"[57]

At this Schmidt reached his limit and gave up. "Yes," he confessed without a show of emotion and in broad Berlin dialect, "I have lied." For a brief moment there was absolute silence in the courtroom. With this admission the last barrier to an uncontested exoneration of Fritsch had fallen. The general, who had exhibited an iron self-control and outward detachment while others were contending over his fate, struggled to maintain his composure. Goltz beamed across at Biron, and the judges, who, like everyone else, had followed Goering's inquisition with tense faces, sat back with a serious but relaxed mien.[58]

After climax soon followed anticlimax. The standard accounts say little about further questions or exchanges, conveying the impression that virtually no allusion was made to the problem of why Schmidt ever came to direct his charges against Fritsch. The verdict and its summary of the proceedings show that this was not quite the case. The point was indeed raised and dealt with at some length, though none of the judges or interested parties followed through with any tenacity.

Only Goltz made any significant effort to tear away the curtain. Ending the breathless pause which had followed Schmidt's confession, he asked whether anyone had threatened him if he should change his testimony. Schmidt was at a loss to answer and hesitated so long and so meaningly that Goering considered it wisest to interpose. In a grilling which had followed that of January 27 in the presence of Himmler and Huber, he had himself threatened to have Schmidt shot if he turned out to be lying. Schmidt had clearly been made to feel that his life depended on making his story stand up. Considering it best to be the first to allude to this and at the same time give it an innocent twist, Goering now related how he had threatened the direst consequences if Schmidt's tale turned out to be a fabrication. He solemnly withdrew this monition and in that august assembly that included his service colleagues and the Minister of Justice pledged his word of honor that Schmidt's life would be in no danger if he now told things as they were. Thereupon the blackmailer reluctantly testified: "Yes, this morning, Criminal Commissar Meisinger had me brought to him and said if I did not stick to the truth, then . . ." Therewith

[57] J. A. Kielmansegg, *Der Fritsch-Prozess 1938*, 94.
[58] *Ibid.*

the fellow raised his right fist with the thumb extended upward. "What do you mean by 'then'?" queried Goering, imitating the gesture. "Then I would go to heaven," said Schmidt in a deep and clear voice.[59]

Goltz believes that Goering had not expected this answer, particularly not in the presence of Meisinger, when he assured Schmidt his life would be spared.[60] He may have anticipated that Schmidt, provided an out in the face of Goltz's question by Goering's own statement, would revert to his original scenario and cover the Gestapo. And this he would almost certainly have done if Goering's own switch had not made him unsure of the game being played.

Meisinger, of course, hurried to explain his words as no more than a drastic admonition to "tell the truth." "Schmidt," says the verdict, "was then quizzed on why he had named the colonel general." With his usual quick uptake, he had already tried to make himself look better by saying that, though he had lied about Fritsch, there had *really* been a second case parallel to that of Frisch. It had occurred three or four weeks later, had involved a man who gave his name as Fritsch, who had had dealings with the Bayern Seppl and who, just like Frisch, had a fur coat, a cane, a monocle, and a scar on the side of his face. They had taken a train to Lichterfelde and there, "I'll drop dead, we really went into the house at No. 21. I thought that night: What do you know!" Asked why he had stuck to his lies after seeing his error during the confrontation with Fritsch, he replied that there was really some likeness.[61]

At this point Meisinger was asked or, seeing the need of muddying the waters, volunteered to speculate on "the reasons Schmidt could have for his false testimony." The Gestapo official gave "detailed attention" to this problem. In the beginning, he thought, Schmidt just wanted to seem important. Then, "in his pathological way, he had lied himself into the story to such an extent that, in the end, he believed it himself." Meisinger, not surprisingly, ruled out the possibility that "certain political circles" had any interest in inducing Schmidt to testify as he did. He had made his statement only after arrest, so "there was no conceivable way for anyone to reach Schmidt with such a proposal" (!). His account had con-

[59] Goltz, "Erinnerungen," 204-205. Gisevius, *Bis zum bittern Ende*, 291-292.
[60] Goltz, "Erinnerungen," 205.
[61] Verdict, 398. The summary at this point is extremely confusing, it not being clear what Schmidt is supposed to have said during the investigation and what at the trial.

tained so many details that he could not have concocted them with someone else and it seemed certain that he had actually experienced them.[62]

Meisinger concluded his effrontery with a dose of praise for Goering. Schmidt, he insisted, would surely have persisted in his story had it not been for the expert quizzing at the end of the trial.

With small hope Goltz then made a final move to secure the presence of Himmler and Heydrich. Goering did the expected in repeating the claim that they were too much taken up with affairs arising out of the Anschluss; moreover, the objective of the proceedings had been achieved with the clarification of the guilt question and what lay behind this was no longer "of interest."[63]

Goering did not need to be told that speculation would continue in many quarters on how Hitler could have insisted the charges against Fritsch be pursued. Was it not true, Goering asked the startled Nebe, that even "serious persons" were likely to deny accusations under Article 175? The implication of the question was all too evident. It implied that even a man with so honorable a name as Fritsch could be expected to lie in such a case. It would follow that no one should be reproached for going into such charges until their falsity was established. "Here again is impertinence," Fritsch whispered indignantly to Goltz. Nebe, of course, had no choice but to answer the question in the affirmative.[64]

The hour had now arrived for the final pleas of prosecution and defense. In the circumstances they were understandably brief. After a short review of the evidence, Biron moved for acquittal on the basis of proven innocence. For this he was later to harvest a furious reproof from Goering. The closely observing Kanter believes that the field marshal felt cheated of the opportunity to take an ostentatious lead himself in the matter.[65] Goering may also have felt that for himself and Hitler it was important to have on the record that, at the end of the trial, Fritsch's innocence had still not been entirely beyond debate. As a complete amateur in law Goering seems also to have labored under the delusion that it was the business of the prosecutor to strive to the end for conviction.

[62] The sole source for Meisinger's statement is Verdict, 398–399.
[63] Goltz, "Erinnerungen," 206.
[64] Goltz (*ibid.*, 206) takes umbrage at Nebe's response but it is hard to see what else he could have said. J. A. Kielmansegg (*Der Fritsch-Prozess 1938*, 95) holds that Nebe's reply did conform with professional experience.
[65] Kanter interview, May 9, 1970.

It was "incomprehensible," Goering thundered at the dismayed Biron, that the respresentative of the state should not act in its interests and should simply take it on himself to propose the verdict most favorable to the accused. At most Biron should have asked for an acquittal by reason of insufficient evidence.[66] The utterly crushed jurist was apparently given no chance to expound the realities of the law which fixed the duty of a prosecutor to make his plea in conformity with the facts in the case as he saw them.[67]

Goltz's remarks made up in pungency what they lacked in length. He declared roundly that after all the court had learned there was no purpose in wasting a word on the question of guilt. Something else, he implied, was in greater need of being said: Days of misfortune had been experienced and endured by the German Army after days of victory. Days of shame not yet. The monstrous insult to the entire Army through a uniquely monstrous procedure against its commander in chief by criminal hands had faded into nothing. The shield of honor of the Army and of its commander in chief was clean.[68]

Goltz had deliberately used the expression "by criminal hands" to discover whether anyone would feel that the shoe fit. The answer was not long in coming. After Goering had announced the verdict and before entering on its justification, he turned to take issue sharply with the remarks of the defending counsel. The honor of the Army, he emphasized, had never been touched. Something like what Fritsch had been accused of could happen on occasion without such conduct and the reproach attached to it reflecting dishonor on the Army as a whole.[69]

To Judge Lehmann, with whom he later drove off, Goering expressed himself with greater vigor. "That was unheard of," he growled. "That man in his plea actually dared to attack the Fuehrer, though it was very skillfully formulated." Then on a softer note, "But you know, he still is a splendid fellow."[70]

Before taking a brief recess to permit the judges to confer on the formulation of the verdict, Fritsch was asked if he had any

[66] *Ibid.* Kanter recounts that Biron was deeply depressed. He was about due to come up for promotion and feared that he would never receive it.

[67] Stock's study on the legal aspects of the Fritsch case underlines (932-933) this duty of the prosecutor.

[68] Goltz, "Erinnerungen," 207.

[69] *Ibid.*, 207-208.

[70] As reported to Goltz by Lehmann. Goltz interviews, February 17, 1970, and July 8, 1971. On the first part also Affidavit of Dr. Rudolf Lehmann, August 4, 1947. (Copy in author's possession.)

# Too Little and Too Late

concluding remarks. Here was the final opportunity for him to emerge from the role of accused into that of accuser. The trial, having placed in high relief the entire course of action against him, formed a proper backdrop against which to extend his declaration of February 23 and the just concluded trenchant comment of his defender. Ignoring the challenge, Fritsch reverted to his more usual posture during the entire affair—responding as if to purely personal injury. In sharp words he denounced his abrupt dismissal before being given a chance to vindicate himself and commented bitingly on the disgracefulness of the proceeding.[71] The remarks were in every sense appropriate but not of the sort that would echo into history. Small wonder that accounts of the trial rarely as much as allude to them.

In the short pause before the announcement of the verdict, the judges seem to have exchanged only a few words in reaching agreement. The rest of the time was utilized by Goering to walk up and down with Fehling for a final review of points he might stress. The court was then recalled into session to hear a highly articulate and well-structured exposition on the factors making for an acquittal by reason of proven innocence. It was a first-rate performance and Fehling had no lack of cause for self-congratulatory whispers to the neighboring Kanter ("Isn't he doing beautifully?" etc.). The latter felt that Goering was employing every trick of phrase to salvage something of the flavor of an acquittal by virtue of insufficient evidence.[72] This tied in well with the apologia he was offering for the institution and carrying through of the proceedings. There had been, he stressed, strong suppositions against Fritsch which had necessitated serious examination. Schmidt had been too impudent and adept a liar. Fritsch himself had simply given cause for doubt by his demeanor during the confrontation in Hitler's workroom. In fact, and he felt compelled to say this for the historical record, nothing less than his own effective method of questioning could have achieved the final clarification through the collapse of Schmidt.[73] On this lusty note of self-congratulation Goering brought the trial of Werner von Fritsch to its conclusion.

There remained the formal statement of the verdict with its summation of evidence and justification. The task of formulating this

---

[71] J. A. Kielmansegg, *Der Fritsch-Prozess 1938*, 96.

[72] Kanter interview, May 9, 1970.

[73] Gisevius, *Bis zum bittern Ende*, 292. Goering's self-congratulatory effusions were also inflicted on others. He asked Best whether he had not done a fine job of "laying Schmidt on the cross." Best, "Aktennotiz," 5.

357

was entrusted to Judge Lehmann, who called on Kanter for help. They had only one day for the job and spent the entire night in dictation.[74] The mark, however, is that of Hermann Goering. As already noted, he' left the building and drove off with Lehmann. During the drive he impressed on the judge the "guidelines" for the statement he was to indict. In truth, Goering, whose presidency of the court had been legitimized by the submission of his colleagues, could claim every right to give instructions of this kind. The document therefore goes out of its way to justify the proceedings against Fritsch. The section devoted to "The Evaluation of the Result of the Collected Evidence" is inaugurated by three pages of excuses, stressing points like the accuracy of Schmidt's testimony against various convicted persons and the tendency of individuals "mentally and culturally outstanding and irreproachable in other respects" to lie when it was a matter of denying charges of homosexuality. Thus even an accusation against "a blameless man of great merit" had to be taken seriously and "the trial became necessary."[75]

It was an appropriate epilogue to a drama that had been so dominated by elements of grim farce.

[74] Kanter interview, May 9, 1970.
[75] Verdict, 404-406.

# CHAPTER XI

# Echoes and Sequelae

Though known only to a restricted audience in Germany, the trial of Werner von Fritsch had taken its place in history. The dexterity and verve of Goering, the timorousness of Brauchitsch and Raeder, and the inertia of Fritsch himself had decreed that the larger issues entangled with the affair would be skirted in the trial. Only here and there were hints of what might have eventuated if, instead of tiptoeing around them, the parties concerned had come to grips with these essentials.

With such exceptions as the queries raised by Goltz after Schmidt's confession, those well-wishers of Fritsch present had confined themselves to dealing with the case constructed against him. Others had, however, from the first thought of counterattack. Since becoming aware of a Fritsch crisis, they had pursued this aim with every argument at their command and in every quarter where there seemed promise of support. Unfortunately they had been caught wholly unprepared and in the most critical period—the week before February 4—had to concentrate on circumventing the decree of silence issued by Hitler, on seeking allies, and on developing communication among those willing to help.

These efforts had prevented a complete victory for the forces arrayed against Fritsch. Hitler had been obliged to grant him an opportunity for legal vindication and to yield on the nature of the court to sit as a fact-finding body.[1] He had appointed himself the ultimate judicial authority, had contrived every conceivable handicap for the defense, and had tolerated or himself perpetrated

---

[1] Fritsch's court-martial was a "special court" in the sense of having power only to determine his guilt or innocence, not to take punitive action.

a long list of chicaneries and illegalities designed to make a verdict wholly favorable to Fritsch difficult to obtain.[2] All this had proved inadequate against the strivings of a few intrepid men who surmounted the additional hindrance of working almost entirely from behind the scenes.

In focusing so narrowly on Fritsch's exoneration and forgoing a more direct counterattack, those of the general's partisans who perceived the larger issues had paid a heavy price. They had, indeed, sought repeatedly to seize upon particularly outrageous incidents to urge that the proceedings be cut short by a concerted intervention with Hitler or by using force against the SS. But the hesitations of Brauchitsch, who alone could lead such an action, had made this impossible. The investigation and trial furnished him an alibi to postpone any decision until they were over. The delay gave Hitler leisure to bring off his coup against Austria and create a situation very different from what had previously prevailed.

## The Morrow of Fritsch's Exoneration

With Hitler riding the crest of a new wave of adulation in Germany and many of the generals dazzled by the bloodless triumph of the "campaign of flowers," a direct assault on the regime as a whole was for the time unthinkable. At the moment Hermann Goering was almost as invulnerable. Though the extent to which he had spearheaded the Austrian takeover was scarcely known to a wider public, there was much awareness of it among the prominent figures of the Third Reich who had crowded the Chancellery antechambers on March 10-11. He was basking now in the reflected glory of the Fuehrer's (and his own) achievement. The masterful way in which he had presided over the Fritsch trial left both Fritsch and his sympathizers who had been present confused and somewhat dazed. His sudden *volte-face* had left them, like the blackguard Schmidt, at sea on just what kind of game was being played. Quite contradictory reports on his conduct were being passed around and Fritsch added to the uncertainty by giving somewhat different accounts. To some he reported that Goering had acted with considerable decency.[3] Others were given a version which more approximates that reflected in these pages. To Hassell and to Ulex, Fritsch

---

[2] Ulrich Stock's study of the legal aspects of the Fritsch case furnishes an extensive list of illegalities beyond those dealt with in the present narration.

[3] Thus Rundstedt, "Affaire Blomberg-Fritsch 1938," 4.

# Echoes and Sequelae

said that Goering had clearly started with the intent of achieving a *parti remise* in the form of an acquittal by reason of lack of evidence. When he recognized the way things were going, he had switched about and "steered energetically toward the truth."[4]

There also remained much doubt about Goering's part in the whole affair. To Hassell, Fritsch said that Goering had "played no clear, untainted [*saubere*] role." Many regarded him as at least an accessory after the fact, who, to get rid of Fritsch as a rival in the succession to Blomberg, had in some measure and at certain stages seconded the chief villain and primary initiator—Himmler. Others, again, such as Captains von Both and Engel in a conversation of May 15, concluded that Goering was the originator (*Urheber*) and Himmler the cat's-paw (*Handlanger*).[5]

Goering's role, in fact, was viewed as so wholly opportunistic that there was some hope of inducing him to change sides completely and join in the attack on his erstwhile ally. The existence of such a conjecture is evidenced in a memorandum, "Position on the Case of Colonel General Baron von Fritsch," which was put together by Canaris and Hossbach at the instance of Beck immediately after the trial. The document was meant for Brauchitsch and commenced with a declaration that the outcome of the trial was not in itself enough to restore the honor of Fritsch or free the Army and the entire Wehrmacht from the nightmare of a cheka-type organization. If Hitler, as the Wehrmacht's commander in chief, did not soon take proper measures, it would be necessary to consider whether *the Army,* as the most directly attacked and defamed service, *under the leadership of its commander in chief,* should undertake a special demarche with him.[6] Suggested participants were Rundstedt, List, and Bock. In the event that it appeared desirable to go outside the framework of the Army, the inclusion of Goering, Raeder, and Keitel should be considered.[7]

Under the rubric "Proposal for Demands" the paper favors an initial step for the rehabilitation of Fritsch in the form of a well-publicized visit of the Fuehrer to the sorely abused general. For the Gestapo a drastic turnover in leadership is recommended, men-

[4] Hassell Papers, notation of April 30, 1938. Ulex ms., 96. The quotation above is from Hassell.

[5] Hassell Papers, notation of April 30, 1938. Engel Diary, entry of May 15, 1938.
[6] Italics in original.

[7] A copy of the document is in the possession of the author. Its more essential parts are quoted by Foerster, 92–93. Gisevius (letter to the author, March 20, 1972) is most insistent that it was Beck who inspired the memorandum.

tioning in first line Himmler, Heydrich, Joost (an SD official), Best, Meisinger, and Fehling.

The memorandum next provides more detailed argumentation in support of the demarche and proposed demands and concludes with a six-page appendix spelling out the sins of the Gestapo from the visit to Captain von Frisch on January 15 to the trial. Needless to say, this register of transgressions was but a thin compendium compared to the record as it now stands.

How did Brauchitsch respond to the memorandum of the chief of the Abwehr and the head of the General Staff's Central Division? We know that no such demarche as they advocated took place. Whether Brauchitsch went so far as to consult some of the generals listed as potential associates or whether he sought to advance some of the proposed "demands" by personal initiative in the Chancellery—on these points we lack information. If he spoke to the top figures on the list, it is quite understandable why he would stop then and there. Rundstedt and Bock at this period, as later, were among the least likely candidates for the role intended for them.[8]

Meanwhile, in a more immediate sense and on behalf of a considerably more drastic proposal, Brauchitsch was being importuned to move directly against the foe. In late February and early March he had warded off pressure by promising to take action against the Gestapo once the trial had revealed its full iniquities. The moment the verdict was delivered (about noon on the 18th) a series of visits and telephone calls with this end in view got under way. We pick up the story about 4:30 P.M., when Gisevius returned to his residence weary from a day of tension and excitement. Earlier that afternoon he had conferred with Nebe, who had left the court in a mood of crushing disillusion and pessimism. His observations of Brauchitsch, Raeder, and Fritsch over a day and a half had deprived him of all confidence in the resolution of the military leaders. He had ended by predicting to Gisevius that they would do nothing.[9]

Gisevius had scarcely relaxed when he was summoned to the

---

[8] Stülpnagel (358) indicates his own small faith in the steadfastness of these two contemporaries of his. In February, General Hans von Salmuth, then Rundstedt's and formerly Bock's chief of staff, tried without success to work on them severally to lead a collective action on behalf of Fritsch. Salmuth to Helmut Krausnick, August 7, 1955 (in IfZ, ZS 133).

[9] Gisevius (*Bis zum bittern Ende*, 293-295) is the only surviving source for the story as related here. In his recording of January 1972 he adds details to what is covered on p. 365 in paragraph 13.

phone by a call from Oster. The badly camouflaged message was an urgent request to ask Schacht to arrange an immediate meeting between Brauchitsch and Gürtner. Feeling that he ought to be filled in better before attempting this, Gisevius went first to Tirpitz Ufer. There Oster and Canaris told him that Brauchitsch had in principle declared himself ready to act but wanted to confirm his judgment of the trial by a talk with the Minister of Justice. The Army commander was reported averse to making a telephone call that might be overheard.

Harboring his own thoughts about the ability of some men to make simple things complicated, Gisevius hurried to the Reichsbank where a grumpy Schacht could understand no better than he why such a roundabout way was needed to effect a meeting between the commander in chief of the Army and the Minister of Justice. Since Schacht was leaving for a conference and did not expect to return to his office that day, he agreed to stop at the Justice Ministry and ask Gürtner to call Brauchitsch. What took place during the following two hours is a classic illustration of the problems of clandestine communication which, on a less extravagant scale, were the daily lot of opponents of the Third Reich:

1. Gisevius returns to the War Ministry and tells Oster that Brauchitsch may expect a call from Gürtner shortly.

2. Gisevius returns home. Soon come frantic calls from Oster: Brauchitsch is still waiting for the call from Gürtner. His adjutants keep asking about it.

3. Gisevius again goes to the War Ministry to talk with Oster. On the small chance that there may be a message for him if he again goes to the Reichsbank he proceeds there. Schacht has actually come by and left a note for him. Gürtner will be delighted to meet with Brauchitsch but thinks it wisest to have the general call *him*.

4. Gisevius returns to Oster whom he finds again closeted with Canaris. Brauchitsch has left for his suite at the Hotel Continental to change for a session of the Reichstag scheduled for eight o'clock to hear Hitler's report on the Anschluss. It is now about six thirty and Gisevius decides he himself must take a hand to arrange the desired meeting. Oster first telephones Brauchitsch to prepare him for his caller.

5. Gisevius arrives at the Continental and is admitted to Brauchitsch's suite. The two have not as yet met but the general has

heard enough about this man who has served as a vital channel of information during the past weeks to have a good idea of his role. He comes out of his bedroom in shirtsleeves and carrying his uniform coat.

6. Gisevius delivers Gürtner's message. As he has anticipated, though he also finds it difficult to believe, Brauchitsch says he cannot possibly call Gürtner at such a critical time. (Apparently neither he nor Gürtner wishes to be revealed as the initiator of a conference between them.) Such a conversation is sure to be overheard by Goering's or Himmler's people. Why should this cause such anxiety, wonders Gisevius. After all, Gürtner is not to be classed as an enemy of the state. Why should there be danger in a simple meeting? Brauchitsch sticks to his anxieties.

7. Gisevius next suggests that at the Reichstag the two will be sitting on the government benches. This should provide the occasion for an inconspicuous exchange on a time and place of meeting. Out of the question, protests Brauchitsch; even so brief an exchange will be noticed.

8. Gisevius at his wit's end proposes that, right after the Reichstag meeting, Brauchitsch should drive to Gürtner's residence. Brauchitsch fears the house may be watched. Gisevius earnestly reassures him. Gürtner's home lies in a neighborhood of villas and gardens where a close watch would be difficult. Also, Brauchitsch can leave his car at a nearby corner.

9. Gisevius rushes to the Ministry of Justice. It is now about seven thirty. The streets are lined with crowds waiting for the passage of the mighty men of Nazi Germany. Gisevius must leave his taxi and proceed on foot. He is relieved to see that Gürtner's car is still before the Ministry.

10. Gürtner is upset about the idea of the nocturnal visitor. Like Brauchitsch he fears Nazi spies who may lurk in the neighborhood and suggests instead a meeting for the next day. Gisevius fears it may be too late for him to catch Brauchitsch to tell him this. He suggests that Gürtner buttonhole the general briefly at the Reichstag to tell him of the proposed change of plan. Gürtner is as much worried as Brauchitsch about this being observed. Gisevius in desperation returns to the idea of the late evening call and promises that Brauchitsch will leave his car some distance away. Gürtner reluctantly consents.

11. In leaving, Gisevius refers to the sloppy work of the Gestapo which inaugurated the whole nasty intrigue. Gürtner expresses sur-

prise that this was not obvious from the start. "My dear colleague," he says, "I have not for an instant doubted that it was a case of mistaken identity." His first thought had been of a notorious SA leader named Fritsch who had ended a misspent life on June 30, 1934.

12. Gisevius dashes back to the Continental. As he weaves through the crowds he reflects on how Gürtner, having thought this right along, yet provided Hitler with the first so misused "opinion" and sat in silence through the farce of the trial. Even now he seems to have no strong views on what must be done. Out of breath Gisevius arrives in the lobby of the hotel in time to intercept Brauchitsch going to his car. A quick word makes it clear that Gürtner will await his visitor. Then the exhausted mediator sinks into a chair and allows his thoughts to interrupt the radio transmission of Hitler's speech to the Reichstag.

13. On the morning of the 19th Gisevius eagerly calls up Oster. His friend's voice vibrates with joy. All seems to have gone well. Brauchitsch's adjutant reports that the meeting has taken place. A few hours later Gisevius joins Oster and Canaris. With consternation he notes their long faces. What has come of their maneuvers? Nothing! Once again two timorous men have failed to add up to a single resolute one.

Such could be, and often were, the vicissitudes and frustrations that were the lot of the activists of the Opposition to the Third Reich.

### A Duel with Himmler?

While the elements aiming to rouse Brauchitsch to action against the Gestapo regrouped for their next assault on the reluctant general, another line of advance upon the same enemy was pushed with great fervor. Since the turn of the month it had been more or less settled that Fritsch would challenge Himmler to a duel. Though he had fixed more on Heydrich as the moving spirit of the affair,[10] an encounter with this underling would be regarded as demeaning and would have had the aspect of a personal vendetta rather than a challenge to the SS leadership as such.[11]

What were the objectives of a meeting between Fritsch and Himmler on "the field of honor"? The anticipation that the SS

[10] Hassell Papers, notation of April 30, 1938.
[11] There is no hint anywhere that Heydrich was even considered as an opponent for Fritsch. The reasons cited above for not doing so are the author's deductions.

chief, less weapon-wise than his opponent, would take leave of life there can hardly have been a primary consideration. Rather it was undoubtedly thought that a symbolic confrontation of the Army and the SS in such highly dramatic fashion would lead to a wider showdown. "The enemy" would be clearly identified, bringing therewith a psychological identification of the officer corps, and much of the rank and file, with the cause of Fritsch. Direct demands on Hitler to curb the SS-dominated agencies, notably the Gestapo and SD, would naturally follow. Those Fritsch partisans who aimed for a thrust at the regime as a whole also perceived the prospect of something of this character developing from the encounter.[12]

It was the coadunation of outrages emanating from the Prinz-Albrecht-Strasse in late February and early March (the Wannsee interrogation, the effort to "suppress" Captain von Frisch, and the quizzing of Fritsch's former grooms and orderlies) that gave rise to the idea of a challenge. The element of personal injury to Fritsch was at this point in the foreground. Fritsch was reported to be brightening his dreary hours by pistol practice with his adjutants and the news of a challenge was expected almost daily by the Abwehr Opposition group.[13] That it was postponed until after the trial is claimed to have been due to the importunities of Brauchitsch, who sought to put off anything calling for a showdown until then.[14]

The moment the trial was concluded the concerned parties went to work to draw up the challenge. Fritsch prepared a draft in consultation with Hossbach who then carried it to Rosenberger for legal scrutiny and comment.[15] The chief of the Wehrmacht Legal Divi-

[12]John (30) states that this was the hope of Sack and Dohnanyi and that they encouraged Fritsch to issue the challenge. Christine von Dohnanyi relates that her husband assisted with an early draft of the challenge. "Aufzeichnungen von Frau Christine von Dohnanyi," 5.

[13]The source stating that a challenge was contemplated for issuance before the trial is Gisevius, Bis zum bittem Ende, 285. Rundstedt ("Affaire Blomberg-Fritsch 1938," 4) does imply that he was given the letter of defiance before the trial for delivery immediately after its conclusion. Hossbach (Zwischen Wehrmacht und Hitler, 122-123) and Rosenberger (letter to Kielmansegg, September 9, 1947, Kielmansegg Papers) infer that the challenge was drawn up only after the trial.

[14]Gisevius (Bis zum bittem Ende, 296) says that Brauchitsch secured a postponement after the trial on the plea that Hitler should not be afforded any pretext for holding up the rehabilitation of Fritsch. If Brauchitsch did urge a delay then, he failed since, so far as Fritsch was concerned, the challenge was out of his hands a few days after the trial. Rosenberger gives the date as "about March 23." Letter to Kielmansegg, September 27, 1947. Kielmansegg Papers.

[15]Hossbach, Zwischen Wehrmacht und Hitler, 122-123, and interview, July 1, 1971.

sion made a number of suggestions aimed to "sharpen" the indictment against Himmler, such as, at the very least, mentioning his negligence in raising the charges against Fritsch. He also called his visitor's attention to the possibility that the SS might respond with a coup of its own against Fritsch's most prominent partisans. Gürtner had told him recently, "The Gestapo will shrink from nothing." "Are you aware," Rosenberger said solemnly to Hossbach, "that some morning a number of high officers may be dead?" Hossbach, after reflecting a moment, replied that he was thoroughly aware.[16]

We know in a general way of the role of Sack and Dohnanyi in encouraging Fritsch to challenge Himmler and, possibly, assisting at one point or another with the formulation. That they knew of the intention and strongly approved is certain.[17] The hope that Himmler would accept the challenge and that the duel would actually take place was, of course, never very high. Hitler would almost certainly have intervened to save his minion from being stretched on the grass. Down to the winter of 1935-36 he had taken a positive attitude toward duelling as a test of manhood. At that time the fatal ending of an "affair of honor" between a former Austrian cavalry captain and a prominent SA leader had roused so much adverse comment that this position was reversed.[18] Party members in high office were forbidden to engage in duels.[19] Why then was the idea still pursued? On the one hand, there was a desperate determination to ensure that *something* was attempted.[20] On the other, even the alibi of Hitler's order would not serve to free Himmler of embarrassment and some loss of personal prestige. A rejected challenge, once it became widely known, also would call as much for a political showdown as would an actual encounter.

The revised document was given by Fritsch to Rundstedt for delivery. Certainly he could have picked no more prestigious second nor one who would have underlined better the character of the affair as a confrontation between the Army and the SS. There

[16] Letter of Rosenberger to Kielmansegg, September 9, 1947. Kielmansegg Papers.

[17] Aside from the story of John (30), there is the recollection of Frau Helle Sack and of Kanter as related in a letter of the latter to Bösch, June 16, 1961. Bösch, 47.

[18] Hofmann interview, April 13, 1970.

[19] Winnig (113) claims that this order was not issued until the Fritsch affair, when it was specifically aimed at averting the threat to Himmler, of which Hitler had gotten wind.

[20] Bösch, 47.

is no evidence that at the time Rundstedt raised objections either to delivering the challenge or to the idea of the duel itself. But he did not rush to accomplish the errand and what doubts he had grew. Knowing that by Hitler's directive Himmler was forbidden to comply, he was apprehensive that the matter "would only stir up dust to the disadvantage of the Army." To stir up as much dust as possible was, of course, exactly what the proponents of the duel were trying to accomplish. Rundstedt, in contrast, was eager to bridge the threatening abyss between the Army and the regime. After carrying the challenge in his pocket for a considerable time he went back to Fritsch and persuaded him to abandon the idea.[21]

The failure to follow up in one way or another on the psychological advantage derived from the outcome of the Fritsch trial is the more regrettable in view of the vulnerability of the SS leadership at this time. Never before or after was the morale of Himmler and Heydrich at lower ebb. On the eve of the trial the latter, expecting little that was good from it, had gloomily remarked to associates that he would probably be made to "jump over the knife,"[22] an expression meaning about the same as "be cast to the wolves."

As for Himmler, he had by now come to reckon the entire Fritsch affair as a debacle. He was especially resentful over the way Goering in his *sauve-qui-peut* maneuver had precipitately abandoned what threatened to be a losing game and had elbowed his way into the front rank of the victors. The tension between him and Goering must have been little less than that which Schellenberg reports to have prevailed between the field marshal and Heydrich.[23] If the latter two had been the prime movers in the affair, Himmler from the start had been an abettor.

Precisely this somewhat secondary role must have made Himmler the more sensitive about the onus falling so largely on himself. He could hardly fail to note that the generals closest to developments saw in him the villain of the piece. Brauchitsch, though unable to summon the resolution for a frontal attack on the Gestapo, was not sparing with his words in more intimate conversation, using such terms about Himmler as "this pigsty."[24] Rundstedt simi-

---

[21] Rundstedt, "Affaire Blomberg-Fritsch 1938," 4.

[22] Gisevius, *Bis zum bittern Ende*, 290. Gisevius was told of this remark by Nebe, but does not know whether it was made to the latter, to Schellenberg, or to one of the SS adjutants. Letter to the author, January 3, 1972.

[23] Schellenberg, *The Schellenberg Memoirs*, 13.

[24] See below, p. 382.

larly laid the blame on him.[25] If Himmler's antennae were not sufficiently attuned to catch such private expressions of resentment, he could not fail to be shaken by direct snubs such as that administered to him by General Ulex.

At an exercise of motorized troops in the Harz mountain area Himmler appeared unannounced as an observer. Major von Pfuhlstein reported his presence to Ulex and commented that as commanding general and director of the exercise he could not evade greeting so high an official. "No, I won't do it," was the sharp retort; "I will not shake hands with that fellow." Himmler stood around for a while in flushed embarrassment and then abruptly departed.[26]

Small wonder that the SS chieftain tried every way he could to ward off this hostility and to give no further cause for suspicion or offense to the Army. When one of his group leaders was investigating the case of a subordinate about whom the military had complained, he was admonished: "Investigate everything, do not omit anything, so that I will not be accused again of incorrect conduct toward the Wehrmacht." He saw to it that even internal pronouncements in meetings of SS leaders were toned down. As late as January 1939 he was waspishly bluepenciling ironic remarks on the Blomberg-Fritsch affair in addresses submitted to him before delivery. In one of his own speeches he whined that he had been the victim of "incompetent subordinates."[27]

Heydrich may not have been exempt from this accusation and the relations of the two SS leaders for a time seem to have been somewhat strained. Schellenberg implies that it took all of Heydrich's "skill and cunning" to reinstate himself in his chief's confidence.[28] He was himself no less busy shoving the blame on underlings. Meisinger, whom in any event it was well to get out of the sight of the Army, was dispatched to Vienna and kept abroad thereafter in occupied Poland and in Tokyo.[29] Another removed from the Berlin scene was Franz Josef Huber, over whose continued

[25] Rundstedt, "Affaire Blomberg-Fritsch 1938."
[26] Notation of Alexander von Pfuhlstein (in IfZ, ZS 592).
[27] Höhne, I, 247.
[28] Schellenberg, *The Schellenberg Memoirs*, 15.
[29] Franz Josef Huber doubts (interview, November 20, 1969) whether Meisinger's transfer to Vienna was meant to get him out of the way and points out that the assignments to Warsaw and Tokyo involved promotions. Schellenberg (*The Schellenberg Memoirs*, 15) takes the opposite view about Meisinger being removed as head of the Reich Center for Combating Homosexuality. That is also the conclusion of Höhne, I, 247.

discretion about uncovering and reporting the presence of Captain von Frisch's bank record on Fehling's desk there may have been some anxieties. He, too, was sent to Vienna where he remained as head of the Gestapo until temporarily disabled by a heart attack in 1944.[30] Best, who had acted as a mild brake in the Fritsch business, landed on his feet, being appointed to a higher post in the Gestapo.[31]

All the SS figures involved seem to have welcomed every opportunity to even the score with Goering by pointing to him (quite correctly) as the real initiator of the assault on Fritsch. This fact was actively disseminated in higher SS circles not themselves involved or overly conversant with the affair.[32] Here and there efforts were made to convey it to the more notable partisans of Fritsch. "It is not we who on our own dug out this file," Best, it has been noted, assured the general's defender; "it was demanded by a higher quarter." "Goering?" asked the intensely interested Goltz. "I cannot tell you that," was the fully revealing answer.[33]

The axe officially, though with a very dull cutting edge, fell on Fehling, whose string of blunders richly deserved the censure of his superiors. According to Gisevius, the action resulted from Brauchitsch's urgings that something must be done to assess responsibility for the injustice dealt Fritsch. Goering was induced to order a disciplinary inquiry against the maladroit Gestapo member.[34]

The indictment presented against the criminal commissar was indeed formidable. He was directly accused of "negligent handling of the documents" in the case and with failure to give heed to the high probability of mistaken identity. Aside from the parallel in Schmidt's story about Goltz, the trial had uncovered a similar confusion of identity in that about Count Wedel. It was held that what Fehling had learned on January 15 about Captain von Frisch should have shown that the "Fritsch case" could be explained in the same way. And what of the visit he had made to the Dresdner

[30] It will be recalled (see above, p. 183) that this is not Huber's own view. He regards his transfer in the nature of things after the takeover of Austria. As the official hitherto responsible for keeping watch over the Austrian Legion, he was, no doubt, the logical choice for the Vienna assignment.

[31] Schellenberg, *The Schellenberg Memoirs*, 15.

[32] During his postwar captivity this view was strongly urged on General Warlimont by Waffen-SS General Sepp Dietrich. Warlimont, "Zur Persönlichkeit des Generalfeldmarschalls von Blomberg" (prepared at the request of the author, October 2, 1945), 3.

[33] Goltz interview, February 17, 1970. See also above, p. 271.

[34] Gisevius, *Bis zum bittern Ende*, 297.

Bank the selfsame day which provided the unquestionable link between Frisch and Schmidt's story?[35]

A ministerial councilor from the Police Section of the Reich Ministry of the Interior was entrusted with the investigation but understandably moved with caution. Unless Brauchitsch continued to show interest and followed up with concrete questions requiring clarification, there was small likelihood of "revelations" on the role of the SS chiefs. The limited charge to the nervous official indeed did not include the pursuit of larger game. Nebe urged him to look into such matters as why Fehling opened his inquiry ten days before the "reconstituted" Fritsch file had officially become of interest through the problem of the succession to Blomberg. The councilor could not be persuaded to tread on such dangerous ground without formal inquiry from higher quarters. Canaris then tried to prevail upon Brauchitsch to provide suitable questions, telling him that this was all the investigator was waiting for, but his needling remained without result.[36]

The inquiry thus culminated in a report tailor-made for the purposes of those who should have been its targets. It was again established that Frisch's housekeeper-nurse had testified to the presence of Fehling and another Gestapo official in the captain's residence on January 15, that he had acknowledged this before the court-martial, and that he had not denied having sequestered Frisch's bank records on that day. But Fehling now insisted that the nurse had lied, that he had never been in the Ferdinand Strasse, and that he *had not been of right mind* when he had testified to the opposite in court. He and those working with him, he maintained as he had before the tribunal, had lacked the time to examine the bank statement on 1933–34 withdrawals and thus to gauge their import.[37] Fehling got off with a reprimand for "negligence" and a transfer to another—it turned out a better—position.[38]

So far as the "investigation" had gone, the Gestapo emerged with one of the major blots on its escutcheon to all appearances erased. It was made to appear that, owing to "carelessness" of subordinate officials, the "mistaken" identification of Fritsch with Frisch had not been cleared up, as it should have been, in mid-Jan-

[35] J. A. Keilmansegg, *Der Fritsch-Prozess 1938*, 115. Gisevius recording, January 1972.

[36] Gisevius, *Bis zum bittern Ende*, 297. Gisevius recording, January 1972.

[37] Gisevius recording, January 1972.

[38] Letter of Kanter to Kielmansegg, October 3, 1947. Keilmansegg Papers. Foertsch, *Schuld und Verhängnis*, 129.

uary. Thus it had not been reported to the SS leaders, who inferentially had embarked on the steps they took thereafter in good faith! Once again insolence had proved one of the major and most effective weapons in the arsenal of the Gestapo.

## Expansion of the Abwehr Center

While the farce of "investigating" Fehling's conduct ran its dismal course, the emerging Abwehr Opposition center was continuing its consolidation. The Army elements on which it could expect to draw were still very much limited. Knowledge of the dramatic developments from January to March remained spotty. Among officers of intermediate and lower rank the larger proportion had thus far learned little or nothing of either the Blomberg or the Fritsch affair.[39] The shock to those who had gained greater insight was in many cases profound. An illustration may be found in the case of Count Baudissin, the adjutant of Infantry Regiment No. 9 at Potsdam, who was so shaken with fury that he came within an inch of resigning his commission. He first discussed the problem with his regimental commander, the future Field Marshal Ernst Busch, who, understandably in view of his record of subservience to Hitler, belittled what had taken place. Next he consulted his predecessor and friend, Henning von Tresckow, one of the noblest Opposition figures of later days, who was then at the War Academy.[40] Finding that they felt as one, the two friends went to Witzleben, of whose sentiments they knew enough to feel confident. After hearing them out, the Berlin area commander countered with a question pregnant with meaning: did they feel that the abominations of which they had learned demanded active resistance? When they replied with an emphatic affirmative, he told them to "stay with it," that their chance was sure to come.[41]

The most assiduous in recruiting wider support and firming up existing ties was as usual the circle about Oster. "Of course you

[39] Thus General Warlimont, who at this period was a colonel commanding an artillery regiment at Düsseldorf, heard nothing of any crisis concerning Fritsch before February 4. He never learned anything through official channels and very little at a General Staff discussion in Berlin in the summer. When he temporarily took Jodl's place with Keitel in the autumn, he was no better informed. General Hermann Hoth, who commanded a division, did orient his senior officers after hearing Hitler's address of February 4. Foertsch, *Schuld und Verhängnis*, 233n32.

[40] Tresckow in 1942-44 was the heart and soul of Opposition planning at the Army Group Center on the eastern front.

[41] Baudissin interview, June 28, 1970.

are coming to us," he said to Kanter on the day after the trial.[42] The sheer number of connections he established and fostered, especially in this period, is incredible. As additional insight into his activities is gained, new significant relationships keep appearing. Even more impressive than their multiplicity is how close many of them were and the measure of devotion he was able to inspire.

Hans Oster had a rare gift of intimacy in the sense of achieving a quick meeting of mind and heart. Those to whom he held out his hand in trust needed no assurance of his honesty and sincerity. He tended to a high estimate of those he liked and inspired them with the desire to live up to it. Friends and acquaintances might have doubts about his judgment, style, or manner of procedure. They were not likely to have any about his motives and integrity. This explains why such basically divergent and rather incompatible personalities as he and Canaris could maintain a thoroughly solid relationship throughout their long association in the Abwehr. It also makes more comprehensible his close friendship and collaboration with associates who clashed among themselves or shied from one another.

Oster's experience with the Fritsch affair intensified his dedication in working for the downfall of the regime. It did much to enhance his sense of personal grievance and of mission. In Gestapo hands in 1944 he stressed the intensity of his feeling about the injuries to the honor of the Wehrmacht and his former regimental commander. The cause of Fritsch, he said, he had made his own.[43]

Oster's stature among enemies of the regime was vastly enhanced by the fire-brigade role he played in one emergency after another from January into March. With the indispensable backstopping of Gisevius and his police connections, he had provided by far the greater part of the essential information that made an effective defense possible. Canaris had been forced to recognize the vital importance of an internal intelligence service and to withdraw his objections to building it up from the rudimentary form which it had thus far attained.[44] This was to provide his lieutenant with further means to seek out potential allies and weak spots in the Third Reich.

Relationships developed during this period also gave Oster and Canaris new impetus in utilizing Abwehr personnel policy to en-

[42] Kanter interview, May 9, 1970.
[43] Spiegelbild einer Verschwörung, 430.
[44] Gisevius, Bis zum bittern Ende, 266. Abshagen, 178–179.

large the cadre of Oppositionists. In 1936 Franz Liedig, a Munich attorney, had welcomed reactivation as a naval officer as a means of "inner migration." Canaris, who had known him and his political orientation for years, had been happy to arrange his entry into Abwehr Section I-M (naval intelligence). Liedig had also long been a friend of Heinz, who seized upon the drawing together of enemies of the regime during the Fritsch crisis to make him acquainted with Oster. They soon developed a warm personal friendship with perfect harmony in outlook and intentions. Liedig was in time to become important as a coup planner and as a formulator of proposals for the rebuilding of Germany after a change of regime.[45]

The presence of the Strüncks in Berlin in the period of crisis in early 1938 was also decisive for making their move to the capital a permanent one by his introduction into the Abwehr. The Opposition thereby gained two indefatigable members, whose home in the Nürnberger Strasse, after they had moved from the Hotel Continental, became the primary rendezvous of the Abwehr-associated group. The next months were to see a further enlargement in Elisabeth Strünck's services as messenger, post office, chauffeur, and general confidante that was to help make things move.[46]

The takeover of Austria provided at least one top-flight recruit for the evolving Abwehr Opposition center. Canaris had been most explicit that any officers transferred from Austrian intelligence to the Abwehr must be anti-Nazis. "Bring me real Austrians," he said, "and not Ostmärker,"[47] The emissary delegated to look over possible candidates was Major Helmuth Groscurth, who rivaled Oster in the fierceness of his anti-Nazism and could be trusted to have his heart in such a mission. Groscurth was head of Abwehr II (sabotage) and, being slated for early transfer, was looking for a suitable officer to recommend to Canaris as a replacement. In Vienna his eye quickly fell on the chief of intelligence, Colonel Erwin

---

[45] Liedig interview, August 9, 1960. "Sonderbericht einer Vernehmung (CSIR) No. 6" (an interrogation of Liedig, October 4, 1945; copy in author's possession; cited hereafter as Liedig interrogation).

[46] Survivors of this group such as Josef Müller, Liedig, and Gisevius are eloquent in recognition of her great service. Details of her activities were gained from interviews of April 18 and 20, 1970.

[47] Abshagen, 182. Ostmark or "eastern march" was the Nazi way of describing the annexed territory. Lahousen and other Austrian intelligence officers had already been closely observed by Count Rudolf von Marogna-Redwitz, Abwehr chief in Munich and responsible for operations in Austria, who belonged to Canaris's anti-Nazi group of subordinates. Canaris met Lahousen for the first time on a visit to Vienna in 1937.

von Lahousen, who promised to pass every political and professional test.[48]

In effect Lahousen was recruited for the Oster-Canaris circle of the Abwehr before he left Vienna. When he succeeded Groscurth later as head of Abwehr II, this assured the necessary Opposition continuity in the control of a department which dispensed explosives and the expertise for handling them. He was to take over a magazine which Oster and Groscurth had been stocking to serve a variety of plans for takeover.[49]

Hans von Dohnanyi was another who emerged from the Fritsch affair as a virtual enrollee of this circle. As the crisis and the case unfolded, he had devoted himself with mounting fervor to the general's exoneration. He had worked closely with Sack and Goltz and so obviously had pulled at their end of the rope that he had gained the unfavorable notice of Nazi hierarchs. A letter from Martin Bormann, the deputy of Rudolf Hess as head of the party chancery, informed Gürtner that it was no longer permissible for him to have an adjutant who was not a National Socialist. The backbone of the Minister of Justice was not equal to the pressure and a few months later Dohnanyi went back to the Reich Supreme Court at Leipzig from which he had come.[50]

The change of residence did not cut the threads recently spun between him and the Opposition group at Tirpitz Ufer. A particularly firm relationship had blossomed between him and Oster. An invitation to lecture every Thursday at the Hochschule für Politik provided occasions for weekly visits to Berlin during which he regularly conferred with Oster, Goerdeler, and Hassell—soon also with Beck.

The Fritsch affair also established a stronger bond between Oster and Fritz-Dietlof von der Schulenburg and was a determinant in finally aligning Count Helldorf with the Abwehr circle through his closer connection with Gisevius. It was an additional incentive for Oster to foster further his link with Wiedemann, who in turn had become better acquainted with Goerdeler, Schacht, and Doh-

[48] Müller interview, May 28, 1958. Lahousen's name is rather indiscriminately given in the sources with and without the aristocratic particle. Titles were forbidden in Republican Austria but permitted as part of a surname in both Weimar and Nazi Germany.

[49] Erwin von Lahousen, "Eidesstattliche Erklärung" (June 27, 1948; copy in author's possession).

[50] "Aufzeichnungen von Frau Christine von Dohnanyi," 3. Dohnanyi interview, June 26, 1958. A more detailed account than that presented here is given by Deutsch, 80-91.

nanyi. Despite his mounting disgust with much that went on in the Chancellery, the captain would not join directly in a conspiratorial enterprise. To the arguments of Dohnanyi he replied: "I agree with you. The only thing that would help here would be the revolver. But who is to do it? I cannot help murder someone who has entrusted himself to my care."[51] Despite this ultimate inhibition, Wiedemann must be counted as a conscious well-wisher of the Abwehr circle, supplying it with information for purposes of which he was increasingly aware.

The regrouping, widening, and tightening of the elements that had found their way together and discovered common aims in the Fritsch affair were to bear significant fruit in the months that lay ahead. In the weeks which immediately followed the conclusion of the trial there was still much hit-or-miss individual initiative, as evidenced in the final efforts to induce Brauchitsch to move against the Gestapo.

## The Last Assaults on Brauchitsch

The initial foray into the Army commander's camp was ventured by Gisevius, whose patience was no longer equal to standing by in the hope that something would happen. Having encountered the general only briefly in arranging the talk with Gürtner on March 19 and recalling how skittish he had proved on that occasion, he could hardly attempt a direct approach. Their meeting must appear casual and to engineer this the stay of the Strüncks at the Hotel Continental was made to order. They had observed the hour Brauchitsch was accustomed to take his dinner and one evening, with Gisevius in tow, they entered the hotel dining room shortly after him, taking their places close by in such a fashion that Frau Strünck faced him. Some years before she had been his table partner at an official dinner in East Prussia and it was inevitable that their eyes should meet and greeting be exchanged. When Brauchitsch completed his meal, he stopped for a moment at their table for civilities. Frau Strünck introduced her husband and Gisevius, who begged for a few words with him. Brauchitsch being agreeable, they went into the neighboring smoking room, where the Strüncks later observed them from the lobby in animated conversation.[52]

---

[51] "Aufzeichnungen von Frau Christine von Dohnanyi," 3. Wiedemann interview, December 2, 1969.

[52] Strünck-Gärtner, interview, April 18, 1970. At Nuremberg Brauchitsch added to his string of perjuries by insisting that the meeting to which Gisevius had testified had never taken place.

# Echoes and Sequelae

For close to two hours Brauchitsch and Gisevius were absorbed in the frankest exchange of views which the former was likely to have had thus far with a member of the Opposition. The discussion turned on the misdeeds of the Gestapo in the recent affairs and what could be done about them. For a time Gisevius, guarding against his inclination to vehemence, strove to retain a certain reticence. Then, finding his *vis-à-vis* surprisingly receptive, he brought all his powers of persuasion to bear. Brauchitsch was entirely agreed in principle on the necessity of cleaning out the Prinz-Albrecht-Strasse and only questioned its feasibility. Gisevius argued passionately for both the workability and legality of such a move. He saw no question here of a *coup d'état* or even of an act of disloyalty toward Hitler. It was a problem of self-defense for the Army—of protecting its leaders from further intrigues of the sort recently witnessed. The strongest imaginable legal case, he insisted, could be made for direct action against the Gestapo; in short order he would dig out of its files enough damaging material to make every German approve of the action.[53]

Brauchitsch seemed to find special satisfaction in this theory of legality. Only when Gisevius proposed to widen the front of attack by taking on Goering also did he raise objections from the standpoint of attempting too much at one time. He had the same view as Gisevius of this archrascal, but considered it wise to try to get him to join forces. He had no more that was good to say about Hitler, to whom he referred contemptuously as "that fellow" and whom he claimed to have warned that the Gestapo probably kept files on him too.[54]

Gisevius concluded the conversation by stressing the need to curb the terror apparatus of the regime while it was still possible. In the recent affair, as Brauchitsch well knew, some of the civilian enemies of the SS and Gestapo had rendered yeoman service to the Army. It had been shown that the Wehrmacht could still count on allies in the bureaucracy, the intellectual world, and the economy. Hitherto it had existed in a sort of "splendid isolation" guarded by its uniform from party encroachments. The Fritsch affair, however, was a foretaste of what the future held in store. If the civilians, worn down by years of unremitting and heightening pressure, succumbed to a spirit of resignation, the Army would find itself delivered up to the party.[55]

[53] Gisevius, *Bis zum bittern Ende*, 298.
[54] *Ibid.*, 298-299.
[55] *Ibid.*, 299.

Brauchitsch seemed to follow this argument with approval and reacted most visibly when Gisevius spoke of the thrust of internal developments being in the direction of another world war. At this point the general made expressive gestures at his temples with his index fingers to indicate the insanity of this. All in all, Gisevius saw reason to be elated. As they parted he was firmly convinced that Brauchitsch would move, a conclusion he passed on to the Strüncks.[56]

The promising course of Gisevius's exchange with Brauchitsch encouraged two of his associates to follow with overtures of their own. A voice from the Nazi camp, especially one that could claim expertise on SS villainies, appeared particularly appropriate for removing any lingering doubts on that score. Helldorf, now fully committed to working with the group at Tirpitz Ufer, decided to call on the Army commander. He took with him his file on the Blomberg affair as well as data on a whole string of Gestapo misdeeds bearing on that of Fritsch. Brauchitsch listened attentively and indicated that neither affair could be considered closed.[57] He scarcely needed much persuasion that, as he put it to a relative, the "cancer lay in Himmler."[58] But could he be induced to apply the scalpel?

That, at least, was the impression gained by Goerdeler, ever eager to take the optimistic view of things, who followed on the heels of Helldorf. The contrast between the recital of crimes by the Berlin police president and the high-minded disquisitions of Goerdeler must have been striking and for that reason the more effective. Goerdeler delivered an unsparing analysis of the domestic and foreign situations and, having just returned from a survey of opinion in the West, laid particular stress on the danger of war. To avert this a drastic housecleaning was imperative which must begin with the elimination of the Gestapo. Brauchitsch seemed to agree with everything and to be deeply moved. He assured his visitor that he would hold to an old soldier's prayer, "Give that I do it diligently," amending it to a solemn, "Give that I do it *soon*."[59]

Goerdeler returned to his friends glowing with anticipation. Since Brauchitsch had wished to see one more point cleared up—whether

[56] Strünck-Gärtner interview, April 18, 1970. Gisevius, *Bis zum bittern Ende*, 299-300.
[57] Gisevius, *Bis zum bittern Ende*, 300.
[58] As related by Frau von Brauchitsch, wife of a cousin of the general. Hassell Papers, notation of June 17, 1938.
[59] Gisevius, *Bis zum bittern Ende*, 300.

# Echoes and Sequelae

Goering, too, had known of the January 15 visitation in the Ferdinand Strasse—Gisevius offered to supply the needed intelligence. Goerdeler sat down that evening and wrote the general suggesting that he summon Gisevius. This missive was personally delivered by Oster the next morning. He ran into disaster. Brauchitsch was seething with rage and declared that he had no thought of honoring the suggestion to call in Gisevius. The fright was great at Tirpitz Ufer and the first thought—including that of the unhappy Gisevius—was that his impetuosity had once again gotten the best of him somewhere. But a call from Oster to one of Brauchitsch's adjutants at least brought reassurance on that point. No, was the answer, his chief had nothing against Gisevius—it was Goerdeler whom he would never receive again.[60]

The story of what had occurred is an absorbing one and throws much light on the problem of Opposition efforts to develop contacts with Britain. More detailed treatment belongs to a future volume and only so much will be said here as is essential to the present narration.[61] During his recent stay in London Goerdeler had said in Bank of England circles that a major change was in the offing and that Brauchitsch would have a part in this. Through a chain of no fewer than *five* middlemen the story had that very morning reached the general and thrown him into a state that hovered between rage and blind panic. In the upshot he reported the affair to Hitler, who fortunately took it lightly and, more to satisfy Brauchitsch than because he wished to dignify it, directed an investigation by the Ministry of Justice. Largely through the help of Schacht, who pulled wires among his British connections, the investigation was steered into safe channels and brought to a comparatively happy conclusion.

The significance of the episode for the present account lies in the dampening effect on Brauchitsch, always quicker to respond to a braking than to an energizing impulse. From what we know of him, he was probably already frightened by his own temerity in the cordial receptions he had given the overtures of Gisevius, Helldorf, and Goerdeler. Here was a welcome excuse for drawing

[60] *Ibid.*, 300–301.

[61] The author is indebted for much insight into this tragicomedy of indiscretions to documentary and oral testimony supplied by William T. Roloff, Count Gerhard von Schwerin, Hans Bernd Gisevius, and a number of others. The story will be presented in detail in a coming volume on the period of Opposition history from spring 1938 to September 1939.

back and for brusquely warding off two new approaches, this time from party quarters.

Gisevius had continued to work on Helldorf, shifting the proposed target a few degrees from the Gestapo to Goering. The SS intriguers, he argued, were hiding behind the broad back of their accomplice in Karinhall. If he could be brought to a fall the Gestapo would automatically go down with him. Helldorf should present Hitler with a chronological account of the affairs of the two generals, stressing how Goering had misused the Fuehrer in the matter of witnessing Blomberg's wedding and in arranging the confrontation of Fritsch with Schmidt.[62]

Helldorf seems to have been adventurer enough to relish the idea of such a daring journey to the Reich Chancellery. But the trip would be useless if the generals did not follow it with representations of their own. Oster undertook to carry the plan and the appeal for collaboration to Brauchitsch and received a cold shoulder. Let Helldorf do what he thought proper. He, Brauchitsch, had his own plans and meant to pursue them. There was no need for help from the party.[63]

A similar rejection met an offer of alliance from one of the major segments of the party complex—the SA. Gisevius and his friends never had any doubts about how Röhm's successor, Victor Lutze, and the boon companions of his hard-drinking entourage felt about Himmler and the SS leadership. Their sentiments amounted to a primitive resolution: "They have murdered our friends, so we shall murder *them* if we get the chance."[64] After his first meeting with Lutze,[65] Gisevius had kept up a tenuous connection through Nebe. As soon as he learned of the tensions engendered by the Fritsch affair, Lutze had tried to find out from Nebe whether anybody was likely to do something to hit back at the SS. He was plainly itching to take a hand, though hoping that the Army would take the lead and the risks. The Abwehr group had shown no inclination to cooperate with him. There was little confidence in Lutze as an ally and he had the reputation of a clumsy operator.[66]

Lutze had obviously been both disappointed and exasperated when nothing seemed to develop as a counterstroke against the Gestapo. He had been enchanted by the rumor of Fritsch's challeng-

[62] Gisevius, *Bis zum bittern Ende*, 303.
[63] *Ibid.*, 303.
[64] Gisevius interview, July 11, 1971.
[65] See above, p. 246n32.
[66] Gisevius interview, July 11, 1971.

ing Himmler to a duel and had expressed his bibulous delight in so many places that Fritsch's friends had been much upset.[67]

As the weeks passed and nothing happened, Lutze decided to make a direct approach to the Army. As chief president of the Hanover government district he had official relations with the Wehrkreis commander, General Ulex, and knew enough of his political sentiments and devotion to Fritsch to be sure of his ground.

The laying of the cornerstone of the Volkswagen works at Wolfsburg on May 26 offered the occasion for an approach to the general, who, like the other dignitaries of the area, was expected to be present when Hitler came for the ceremony. While waiting at the railway station, Ulex discussed with Gauleiter Telchow of North Hanover the case of an ensign who had come to blows with some party members for their calling Fritsch and Blomberg "traitors." Telchow's remark that the men involved belonged to the SA was overheard by the nearby Lutze. Blazing with fury he roared: "What? SA men? In the SA every man knows that in the Fritsch affair all right is on the side of Fritsch and all wrong on that of Himmler." Ulex quickly ended the discussion, saying to Lutze: "We can say somewhat more about that later."[68]

After the ceremony and Hitler's departure, the prominent guests remaining went to breakfast at the nearby castle of old General von der Schulenburg. As they rose from the table, Lutze cornered Ulex in a niche in the thick walls to tell him with the greatest vehemence that the Fritsch case must be utilized to eliminate Himmler, who was making the SS into a private force for seizing power after Hitler's death. Neither the Fuehrer nor Goering was in the best of health, so one never could tell when one would be faced by such a situation.

Ulex interjected: "Let us assume—purely theoretically—that things are as you describe them and that the Wehrmacht took a position against Himmler, what would the SA do then?" Like a shot out of a pistol came the answer: "Unconditionally stand on the side of the Wehrmacht." Lutze then begged the general to tell Fritsch or Brauchitsch that he was prepared to work with them to get rid of Himmler. But what if Hitler should back Himmler, wondered Ulex. After some hesitation in framing his answer Lutze

[67] Gisevius, *Bis zum bittern Ende*, 285.
[68] This paragraph and the five following are based on the Ulex ms., 98-100. That the date was May 26 is recorded by the Schulthess Europäische Geschichtskalender. Krausnick, "Vorgeschichte," 297n247.

replied: "As much as possible, of course, the Fuehrer must be spared." This as much as said that if Hitler supported Himmler he would have to take the consequences.

Ulex next asked what incriminating material against Himmler could be provided by the SA leadership. Could Lutze, for example, prove that Himmler had used coercion to make Schmidt give his false testimony? This he could not do, said Lutze, though he could prove that Himmler had used coercion in other instances to make people perjure themselves. That was not enough, replied Ulex; he would need proof of this for the Fritsch case as such.

Lutze was not to be balked and he seems to have gone to work with a will. No more than a week or two had passed before he was able to send one of his lieutenants, a man named Meinecke, with the assurance that he could now furnish the desired proof. Ulex, feeling he had something to go on, first visited Fritsch in his new establishment of Achterberg at the training ground of Bergen. But Fritsch had learned much during his two months of reflection. There was no sense in submitting such evidence to Hitler, he said, since he surely knew all of it. He was just as guilty as Himmler.

Ulex then went to see Brauchitsch who shortly before had promised him: "I assure you that I will not give up till I have cleaned out this pigsty Himmler." Now his response was a total rejection of Lutze's proposal: "If these gentry want to do this, let them do it themselves."

Walther von Brauchitsch had spoken his final word in the matter. When he next saw Gisevius sitting at a nearby table at the Hotel Continental he gave no sign of recognition.[69]

[69]Gisevius, *Bis zum bittern Ende*, 307.

# CHAPTER XII

# The Rehabilitation Issue

On January 31 Hitler had grudgingly promised Rundstedt that if Fritsch were fully exonerated he would be granted an appropriate satisfaction. On March 18 that exoneration had been accomplished beyond argument. Thereby, as Goltz puts it, "the problem of the colonel general's rehabilitation stepped giant size into the foreground."[1] But precisely what should Fritsch and his backers demand, what pressures should they seek to mobilize, and how much could they wring out of an unwilling dictator?

### Hitler's Calculations

Hitler, in his many statements of the considerations which had guided his steps in the affairs of the two generals, had unintentionally defined the course an out-and-out rehabilitation ought to take. Again and again he had insisted that he allowed the charges to be raised only because Fritsch was the obvious successor to Blomberg and that it was imperative to clear the way to his becoming so without the threat of a new scandal hanging over all their heads. As late as mid-February he had delineated this position to Biron, Heitz, and Sack with so much emphasis that Sack wondered how he would evade appointing Fritsch War Minister once the charges against him had been conclusively disproved.[2]

It scarcely requires reiteration that Hitler did not for a moment entertain the thought of appointing Fritsch to this post. He would never have pursued this line of explanation with such fervor and

[1] Goltz, "Erinnerungen," 208.
[2] *Ibid.*, 208–209.

consistency had he realized that it might store up trouble for himself. He assumed, in short, that he would never be faced with the issue; that enough, at the very least, would be "left hanging" on Fritsch to condemn him to a moral and professional limbo. Certainly nothing would have been further from his mind than to resign to the general the War Ministry he had himself assumed and whose importance in his own hands must have become clearer every day.

There was, of course, the lesser but still substantial form of rehabilitation: reappointment of Fritsch to the Army command he had been obliged to vacate. For Hitler to do this after the execrable way he had gotten rid of the general before giving him a chance to clear himself would have meant a painful loss of face. Moreover, as he was later to say repeatedly, he had for a considerable time been determined to make a change in the Army command.[3] In fact, one explanation for the elaborate show of considering Fritsch as successor to Blomberg was the excuse it provided for reviving the 1936 charges and getting rid of him *entirely*. The dismissal also took so rude a form that it was made intolerable for a man of Fritsch's character to serve in his former capacity under the same chief of state. Only a "political general" prepared to contest openly for power could have accepted such a situation—a role for which Fritsch was least adapted. As already noted, he told several friends and associates that, after what he had experienced, it was impossible for him ever again to serve in an official capacity in Adolf Hitler's state.[4]

To make doubly sure, the dictator had made the dismissal irreversible by the appointment of Brauchitsch. Here, too, his procedure was heavily overlaid with pretense. Until the very day on which Brauchitsch assumed office, Keitel claims to have had the impression that the appointment was to be a temporary one to fill the gap until the fate of Fritsch was decided.[5] It is, of course, difficult to believe that even so credulous a person as Keitel could have been deceived on this point. The conditions imposed on Brauchitsch and the haggling that accompanied them showed all too

[3] Engel interview, May 11, 1970.

[4] Siewert interview, January 15, 1970. Goltz interview, July 8, 1971. Grosskreuz letter to the German Institute for the History of the National Socialist Period, December 28, 1950, 2. Letter to Baroness Schutzbar, April 4, 1938. Fritsch Letters. Fritsch also said as much to Raeder, II, 122-123.

[5] Keitel, 111.

384

clearly from the start that there was no question of a few weeks' stopgap appointment.

Fritsch, for his part, regarded no indemnification adequate which did not include castigation of the responsible parties.[6] This was also the strongly expressed position of Canaris and Hossbach in their Beck-inspired post-trial memorandum.[7] However, only Brauchitsch was situated to place such demands before Hitler or take direct action against the offending SS leadership. As we have seen, week after week he had been importuned and had repeatedly declared himself in principle ready to move. The last signs of such a resolution flickered out in May.

There were, of course, other forms of rehabilitation which would have gone far to placate the indignant generals even if they did not fully satisfy Fritsch or his most ardent supporters. What was desired was an act of recognition so dramatic that there could no longer be any question about his record having been wiped clean. However much the affair had been treated as a state secret, hundreds, probably thousands had learned that some kind of crisis involving Colonel General von Fritsch had arisen. One need think only of the numerous individuals in the War Ministery, the OKH, the Minstry of Justice, the SS formations rippling out from the Gestapo and SS headquarters, the Reich Chancellery, the Berlin police—not to speak of the military stables and the prisons—who came into contact with the affair in one way or another. In the Army, Fritsch's own partisans had done much to circumvent Hitler's orders for secrecy.

Another form of rehabilitation, less costly to Hitler's purposes than returning Fritsch to office or dismantling the terror apparatus, was one suggested by Canaris and Hossbach: a highly publicized visit of the Fuehrer to the general. But this to Hitler may have looked like going to Canossa. From various sides it was proposed that Fritsch be made a field marshal or appointed to an intermediate grade between that and his previous rank. Far down on the list in desirability was what in the end Hitler did ungraciously confer, the honorary colonelcy of his old regiment.

The plain fact was that if the dictator could have helped himself—could have afforded the price in terms of Army reactions—he would have ignored the outcome of the trial completely and sought to make others do so. This would have kept a cloud hovering over

[6] Goltz, "Erinnerungen," 209.
[7] See above, pp. 361-362.

Fritsch's reputation. Fritsch's exoneration was a defeat for Hitler if only because it had proved him to have judged wrongly. He resisted any step which smacked of formally recognizing this.

In discussion with Keitel the day after the trial, Rosenberger unerringly put his finger on the sensitive spot. Since their conversation of January 28, he had been a thorn in the side of this man who always endeavored to smooth things out in the way desired by the Fuehrer. When Rosenberger asked whether Hitler had furnished Fritsch any satisfaction or offered an apology, Keitel replied that, though the Fuehrer was much shaken, he did not intend to do either of these things. Keitel then directed that only the bare fact of the verdict was to be disseminated (in high Wehrmacht quarters?). When Keitel left the room, Rosenberger turned to another person present and remarked: "It looks as if after what has happened it will be necessary to revise the dogma of the Fuehrer's infallibility." These words were reported to Keitel and led a few weeks later to the removal of the too daring offical from his post.[8]

It was the blow to his conceit that Hitler probably found most difficult to forgive. Apart from other considerations, this dictated that as little attention as possible be given the fact that Fritsch had been done an injury. Clearly, the general had no hope of satisfaction that was not wrung from the dictator under irresistible pressure.

## The Forces for and against Fritsch

The array of forces prepared to exert themselves on behalf of Fritsch was at first glance formidable. To outward appearances, it was led by the Army hierarchy headed by the commander in chief and the chief of the General Staff. There were also sympathizers in other Wehrmacht, government, and even party quarters.

A major weakness was the lack of solidarity among the chiefs of the Wehrmacht services. Goering was no more inclined to magnanimity than Hitler and, like the latter, had to consider that anything done *for* Fritsch would highlight what had been done *to* the former Army commander. In particular Goering opposed any form of rehabilitation that might yet lead to Fritsch's re-employment.[9] His negative attitude is demonstrated by the way he left the verdict unsigned for at least three months while maneuvering to effect alterations

[8] J. A. Kielmansegg, *Der Fritsch-Prozess 1938*, 110-111.
[9] Engel interview, July 14, 1971.

which would further seem to justify the proceedings against Fritsch.[10]

Raeder, though in a different way and degree, also acted like a man with an uneasy conscience. He had no reason for pride in the lack of faith he had shown in his colleague, in the way he had allowed himself to be misused by Hitler, and in his passivity at the trial despite all the trouble that had been taken to coach him. In addition to his usual inclination to conserve his credit for promoting purely Navy interests, some psychological reaction of guilt can help explain his failing to do more for a man for whom he professed such high regard. He did make Fritsch an offer of help to get him reinstated as Army commander but followed a hands-off policy once this proposal, as might have been expected, was rejected.[11]

It was not for lack of stimulus or of the issue's being raised that Raeder maintained this negative course. As in late January, it was Commander von Puttkamer who brought the matter to him. The Navy adjutant had just failed to move Major Schmundt, who as Wehrmacht representative was best placed to act on his own. Schmundt had replied evasively that he was too young and too new in his assignment to act effectively.[12]

Puttkamer then went to Raeder and in his straightforward fashion proposed that, as the senior of the service commanders, he should take the lead in an appeal to Hitler. The startled Navy chief objected lamely that this was not his position. It was Goering who, by virtue of his rank as field marshal, was the senior. Puttkamer had the temerity to point out an inconsistency; usually Raeder, far from subscribing to the thesis of Goering's seniority, was annoyed when

[10]Ulex ms., 97. The existing copy of the verdict includes Hitler's confirmation of March 30 and attestations of the same day by Sack. Verdict, 415–416. The signatures of Sellmer, the nominal presiding judge and writer of the verdict, and of Goering, the usurping president of the court, do not appear. Conceivably Goering either belatedly signed only the original or entirely failed to do so. Ulex at this period was in constant and intimate touch with Fritsch and in a position to learn much about what was going on.

[11]Raeder's inadequate memoirs give a jumbled picture of affairs after the trial. He makes much of pleading with Fritsch to remain in a post from which he actually had been dismissed six weeks earlier and claims that the general rejected his offer "to take any measure which he thought suitable in the interest of his reputation." Raeder, II, 122–123. See also the testimony at Nuremberg of Admiral Walther Schulte-Mönting, IMT, XIV, 326. Raeder obviously later constructed for himself a picture of his conduct as he would have liked it to have been.

[12]The story of Puttkamer's efforts as related here is derived from an interview with him of June 27, 1970.

it was raised. Raeder then changed his line of evasion: "Why should I of the Navy do this? It is really the business of the commander in chief of the Army."

The persistent officer then begged an audience with Brauchitsch to whom he unfolded his arguments for the better part of an hour. The results of his effort he concisely summarizes: "Brauchitsch flatly declined to undertake anything whatever in the matter."

In justice to Brauchitsch, it should be recalled that at this stage he appeared to be considering a more radical solution of the rehabilitation problem than anything Puttkamer seems to have had in mind. The Navy adjutant was motivated by sentiments of human decency and something so drastic as moving against the SS or Gestapo hardly played a part in his calculations. Brauchitsch lacked the skill to fob him off without giving him the impression of total rejection. Such, at least, is the more charitable interpretation.

The conclusion of these pages will be that Brauchitsch was as much responsible for so little being done on behalf of Fritsch as he was for failing to proceed vigorously against "this pigsty Himmler." If this estimate is correct, it leads next to a query on the relative roles of lack of will and lack of finesse on his part. A close study of his conduct in the two to three months after the Fritsch trial leads to a conviction that he was sadly in need of both.

Brauchitsch was the victim of a psychological impasse that had many facets. He knew that in the view of the higher Generalität he stood or fell on his performance in promoting Fritsch's interests. He also suffered the pangs of a man who sat in the place of a deeply wronged predecessor and was, if not the architect, at least the beneficiary of his misfortune. Though Fritsch had urged that he take the position, if only to keep it from going to Reichenau,[13] the manner in which he had bought his way in must have troubled him. Despite the fact that neither then nor later was he happy in his post, at the moment it was indispensable to him. In March the settlement with his first wife was still several months away, and the final details on the transmission of Hitler's gift of money were not concluded until October.[14]

Brauchitsch was also caught between Keitel, the man to whom he owed his appointment, and Beck, the chief of staff he had secretly promised to eliminate by autumn. Keitel was frantically urging

[13] Siewert, "Unterredung,"
[14] Engel Diary, entry of October 18, 1938.

388

# The Rehabilitation Issue

him to go slowly and not to "place a burden on his prestige with Hitler in these delicate matters." His Nuremberg memoirs quiver with distress over the way Beck was pressing his commander to make every imaginable effort to secure "an early visible rehabilitation." Beck is stridently denounced as an "agitator" to whom he ascribes disappointed ambition, perhaps even the aim to slip into Brauchitsch's place. Where, he asks rhetorically, was the traditional cry, "Le roi est mort, vive le roi?" Brauchitsch should have made a clean sweep of Fritsch's men and brought in his own as Doenitz was to do when he succeeded Raeder in 1943. Instead he allowed the "old guard" of Beck, Hossbach, and Siewert to stay on his back. And so the tirade continues.[15]

Clearly, Brauchitsch was unable to free himself from either set of influences and to follow a clear line. He salved his conscience and sought to placate his critics by being generous to Fritsch in adding to the small amenities of his life, placing horses, adjutants, and an auto at his disposal and authorizing a collection among Army officers to build for him a small house in Berlin-Lichterfelde.[16] He doubtless would have liked to do more for him in things that carried weight but he lacked the passionate dedication, the persuasive power, and the drive to prevail upon Hitler to do something he did not want to do. Though Brauchitsch assured his top generals in June that he had been about to do so, there is no evidence that he seriously considered laying his position on the line. He also appears to have had a special talent for choosing the wrong moments to carry unwelcome proposals to Hitler and could be "incredibly maladroit" in trying to make his case.[17]

Brauchitsch's manner of dealing (or failing to deal) with the problem of Fritsch's rehabilitation was the more unfortunate since the Army had recently established a representative of its own in the Chancellery. The departure of Hossbach had left a serious gap, from the Army's standpoint, in the coverage of developments around Hitler and in the capacity to speak effectively when an Army voice in his entourage was needed. While Hossbach was there, no one had thought of copying the Navy and the Luftwaffe in assigning a special service representative. It was indicative of

[15] Keitel, 175-176.

[16] J. A. Kielmansegg, *Der Fritsch-Prozess 1938*, 112. Stülpnagel, 357. The strong-minded Stülpnagel felt Fritsch should not have accepted such purely personal favors as long as the larger issues of his rehabilitation remained unsettled.

[17] Engel interview, June 24, 1970. See p. 402 below on Brauchitsch's claim to the generals.

the Army's self-esteem as the senior and ultimately decisive military arm that it had taken for granted that the official representative of the Wehrmacht as a whole should be one of its own. In a sense, then, the creation of a separate post of Army adjutant recognized loss of status within the military configuration of Germany.

The decision on this course was dictated in part by Hitler's assumption of the direct command of the armed forces. Thereby the Wehrmacht adjutant was reduced to a link between functions now incorporated in the same person. On top of this, the change from so iron-willed a man as Hossbach to one as supine as Schmundt, coming just when the need of the closest possible coverage of developments in the Chancellery had become painfully evident, brought home to the Army leaders that they needed to be better served. In place of an independent-spirited officer, there was now one handpicked by Keitel to "get along with the Fuehrer."

The officer of the Army selected to perform the vital role of filling this gap was a captain of artillery named Gerhard Engel. This talented and energetic soldier had won the regard of Fritsch and had several times served him as aide. During the general's period of seclusion, while awaiting trial, he managed to inspire this appointment.[18] Aside from such obviously necessary qualifications as intelligence, alertness, and devotion to his profession, Engel possessed one vital advantage that others who might have measured up equally well in these respects did not have—he had caught Hitler's eye favorably.

During the so-called Mussolini maneuvers of 1937 Hitler had visited the "battle positions" of Engel's regiment. Its commander being absent, Engel as regimental adjutant directed the exercise and made the formal situation report. Hitler asked many questions and seemed impressed with the answers. In conclusion he turned to Hossbach and instructed him, "Please take note of the name of this officer."[19]

It was thus possible to inform Hitler that the officer selected was one about whom he had expressed a high opinion. This by no means served to allay his suspicion that the Army was sending someone to watch over him, but it did ease the situation for Engel personally. As it was, his reception in the Chancellery when he reported on March 10 was icy enough. With the single exception of another of the Fuehrer's adjutants, Brückner, who showed a

[18] Engel interview, May 11, 1970.
[19] *Ibid.*

pleasant, comradely manner, the entire Nazi entourage of the dictator treated him as an interloper. Himmler, to whom he was introduced two days later in Vienna, measured him with a hostile, mistrustful glance and left him standing without saying a word.[20]

Engel had been hauled away from his company and virtually
dumped in the Chancellery half an hour after arrival in Berlin;
this without a glimmer of information about the situation at hand
and what problems he might face. It was typical of the confusion
which reigned in OKH in the midst of the Fritsch trial and the
march into Austria that no one took the responsibility of orienting
an officer entering on so important a function. Brauchitsch told
him briefly that he was to represent the Army "over there" and
that he must recognize and report anything that spelled "danger."
But for almost two days he was left in the dark about what had
gone on during the previous six weeks. Schmundt, who was fast
shedding his Army loyalties, gave him no help, while a call on
the still seething Hossbach yielded nothing but wrathful railings
that revealed little of what inspired them. Finally the sympathetic
Puttkamer took pity on the bewildered officer and reviewed for
him what had been going on since the last week of January.[21]

Engel was thunderstruck and wanted to rush to Fritsch whose
trial had been adjourned the very day of his arrival. This was
vetoed by Schmundt, whose attitude in all that concerned Fritsch
was at best ambivalent. In the week that intervened before the
final exoneration of Fritsch, Engel could do no more than act the
part of bystander. In contrast to this, he thereafter was the spearhead
of the prolonged struggle for rehabilitation of the general. Major
Siewert, who continued in his post of first staff officer, gave him
the most help and encouragement. Brauchitsch himself went little
beyond the motions needed to salve his conscience and allay the
pressures from the Generalität. Some proposals on what might be
done for Fritsch Brauchitsch carried to Hitler personally. More
often he transmitted them through Engel who, with more justification than Schmundt, could have alibied that he was too young
and too new in his post to be very effective. Far from permitting
these handicaps and the suspicion with which the dictator continued
to treat him to intimidate him, Engel never wearied in the fight
for Fritsch. Of this his diary is as eloquent a witness as it is of

[20] Engel Diary, entries of March 11 and March 14, 1938.
[21] *Ibid.*, entries of March 11 and the night of March 11-12.

Hitler's obduracy:

*March 28.*  [Brauchitsch] is completely tensed up and resigned. His reports to the F[uehrer] are inhibited and hesitant. There is no relationship of trust whatever. After all, he now has a good observer in the Reich Chancellery, for I keep my ears open and learn everything. . . . Mostly the F[uehrer] talks and Brauchitsch does not dare to interrupt or contradict him. Siewert hints to me that Brauchitsch is spiritually burdened with family matters and cannot do what he sometimes wishes.

*April 10.*  I . . . described once again exhaustively how important it is to do justice to the offended [former] commander in chief and to rehabilitate him by honoring him in some special way. For the Fuehrer, as always when Fritsch's name is mentioned, it was all disagreeable. . . .

*April 20.*  [It is Hitler's birthday and the day's military parade has left a profound impression.] The birthday is over and I have night duty. In the antechamber I walk up and down with the Fuehrer for about an hour and half. . . . Since he was deeply impressed with the military show I again ventured an effort with respect to our old commander in chief. I told much of his life and how revered he was by the troops. Told of war games in Stettin in which he directed the artillery and much of his activities as commander of A[rtillery] R[egiment] 2 in Schwerin. The Fuehrer, who was in a softened mood today, listened to all quietly and for once did not interrupt. I begged in the name of the Army commander that he should receive Fritsch whose dearest wish this was. He wanted a personal reconciliation and clarification; this was more important to him than any reinstatement or employment.[22] Now the Fuehrer again became restless. In lengthy expositions he spoke of the disappointments he had experienced through Fritsch since 1934. He had been the inhibiting element in rearmament and, independent of what had happened, he would have had to part from him. . . .

*May 15.*  [After a long talk with Both.] Canaris is the only one in the OKW who applies himself in this matter. Canaris and the military judges deserve all honor.[23]

*May 20.*  Today I again made an effort in the question of the old commander in chief. Shortly before the flight to the Berghof I came across a table of rank insignia. On this I saw a general's

[22] Here Engel, who at no time had talked with Fritsch since becoming adjutant, assuredly took the line he thought would most conciliate Hitler. Actually at this period Fritsch had come to regard Hitler as guilty as he thought Himmler.

[23] Engel and Both evidently were thinking of Rosenberger and Sack, perhaps also of Biron. They certainly were not referring to Heitz who, when Rosenberger complained to him bitterly about the nonrehabilitation of Fritsch, said lamely: "We must bear what is unavoidable." Notes on a conversation with Rosenberger Kielmansegg Papers.

shoulder piece with four stars. It was that of a colonel general in the rank of a field marshal general. I told the Fuehrer of this and proposed that this honor be conferred on Fritsch if he had doubts, in consideration of Goering, about promoting him to field marshal. He listened with interest. Suddenly he became very sharp. Angry words were uttered about the old commander in chief and always again the same reproaches.
. . .

*May 21.* Today I talked with Schmundt about my unceasing efforts. Schmundt warned me not to overstrain the bow. As things were he could do nothing, this matter having been reserved by Keitel for himself. He [Schmundt] no longer mixed in the matter. In Keitel I have not the least confidence in this matter. He is much too afraid of Goering and Himmler.

*May 24.* It is sad that I must get hold of the files and basic materials in roundabout ways. In the staff of the commander in chief things are unpleasant. Siewert and Brauchitsch do not get along well. In the latter case there is a degree of resignation which makes it impossible to get anywhere. I do not understand it, and also said so to Siewert, that a young officer like I must in this high political and important matter take the initiative with the Fuehrer. No one supports me, unfortunately not even Schmundt, who otherwise is innerly entirely on our side.

*May ?* [from the context probably May 25 or 26]. Without battleworthy forces [says Hitler] political aims are not attainable. In this Fritsch had hindered him and for this reason it had been necessary to get rid of him.

*October 18.* Attempt in matter Fritsch. Try after midnight to begin conversation with F[uehrer] about Fritsch. The occasion was favorable as F[uehrer] voices praise of Army. The entry [into the territories annexed from Czechoslovakia] has gone fabulously and the troops have made an excellent impression. Say that this is all the fruit of the old commander in chief who is much revered. F[uehrer] listens attentively, at first says nothing, and then returns repeatedly to the lack of will of Fritsch in relation to rearmament. When I dare to argue, F[uehrer] breaks off conversation abruptly.

The absence in Engel's diary of any reference to Beck in the contest over Fritsch's rehabilitation may seem strange. Engel, of course was not present at sessions between the Army commander and the chief of staff and may have heard nothing of Beck's unceasing pressure on Brauchitsch of which Keitel complains with so much acerbity. It was not in the chief of staff's province to deal directly with the Chancellery in such matters or to give directions to the adjutant. Beck could exert influence only through Brauch-

393

itsch, a channel where the initial impulse was largely dissipated.

Only once do we learn of an exchange between Beck and Hitler pertaining to Fritsch after the agonizing night of January 26. It may well have been at one of those social affairs where leaders of party, state, and Wehrmacht uneasily communed together. For a brief moment the two faced each other and Beck seized the chance to voice what was closest to his heart. To his plaint that public action assuring Fritsch his honor was overdue, Hitler responded huffily: "It is I who determine how the honor is to be restored." Beck could only retort that "honor is unconditional and will not call a halt even before your person."[24]

## The Struggle for Rehabilitation

Fritsch justifiably felt that the campaign to secure him satisfaction belonged essentially in the hands of the Army leadership. His exoneration he owed entirely to himself and his volunteer supporters. Because he had regarded the issue as so personal a one, his sense of fitness and dignity had inhibited any appeal for broad Army support. Though he had said nothing, he probably felt keenly about this not having been forthcoming on its own. Now that he was cleared, there could no longer be any doubt about the duty of his peers to see that justice was done him. But he was sunk in depression and pessimism. In a letter of appreciation on the day after his trial he wrote Goltz: "Whether the Fuehrer will bring himself to rehabilitate me remains to be determined. I fear he will resist it with all his energy. Goering's concluding remarks already indicated so much."[25] Four days later he gave the Baroness von Schutzbar a summary of the proceedings and went on to say:

Finally the prize witness on whose testimony all had rested, the black-mailer, a convict hired by Himmler and Heydrich, admitted that he had lied in everything he had said about me. Herr Hitler has regarded my word of honor as commander in chief as a thing of no account. I shall never forget this. It remains a fact that on the basis of the lying accusation of a scoundrel and criminal without honor I was removed from my post with a kick.

Herr Hitler has for the time being not shown himself prepared to give me satisfaction. He has gone to South Germany and supposedly does not return until the end of the week. The background of this affair I see with complete clarity. Only proof is lacking at this time for my

[24] As related by Beck, in September 1938, to the then Colonel Hans Speidel, who was a relative. Speidel interview, November 3, 1969.

[25] Letter to the author, March 19, 1971.

conception [of things]. I shall continue to insist on punishment of the authors [of the intrigue].

. . . For the next period I must have complete rest. I am close to being at the end of my nerves. Perhaps no wonder when one reflects what tortured weeks lie behind me, what a fullness of rascality I have experienced. . . . Once more, many thanks for your faithfulness, but also the urgent entreaty not to undertake anything whatever on my behalf. What is needed will be done by the Army which is standing up for me fully.[26]

Fritsch seems to have known enough about the baroness to appreciate the need of this caution. In fact, the lionhearted lady was not to be curbed so easily. She apparently had less faith in the steadfastness of the Army leadership than Fritsch had expressed. Wishing to do her bit to spread the word on what had been done to the general and to firm up sentiment on his behalf among an officer group within her reach, she initiated a meeting with the officers of Armored Regiment 2 at nearby Eisenach. To them she gave a reading of Fritsch letters which stirred up sufficient dust to reach all the way to the Prinz-Albrecht-Strasse. With the repercussions of the Fritsch affair far from abated, it would have been a risky proposition to deal harshly with the embattled lady. Heydrich chose the roundabout device of sending a severe warning to State Secretary Otto Meissner, head of the presidential chancery, who was a relative of the baroness. Meissner wrote her in earnest entreaty and enclosed a copy of Heydrich's letter.[27]

Meanwhile Fritsch, it can be said, sat back and waited for the much-promised intercession of the Army leadership to have results. We know next to nothing of the contacts between Brauchitsch and Hitler in the last two weeks of March or what passed between them. That the subject of Fritsch's rehabilitation and something in the way of an indictment of the Gestapo were brought up by Brauchitsch may be deduced from the general's remark to Gisevius that he had warned Hitler that files were probably also maintained on him.[28]

It was less Brauchitsch than Schmundt who tipped the scales enough so that Hitler at least took personal notice of the outcome

[26]The letter as here given is quoted by J. A. Kielmansegg, *Der Fritsch-Prozess 1938*, 111-112.

[27]Copies of the two letters have been furnished the author by Count J. A. Kielmansegg. Interview, November 17, 1969.

[28]See above, p. 377.

of the case.[29] Little as Hossbach's successor would expose himself to intercede for Fritsch, he did persuade Hitler that some sign of awareness of the general's exoneration was unavoidable to forestall a strong reaction from the Generalität. The dictator therefore wrote and Schmundt carried to Fritsch a letter that expressed satisfaction with the course affairs had taken:

Cologne, March 30, 1938

Colonel General!

You know the verdict by which your complete innocence is proven. I have confirmed it with a thankful heart. For however terribly the frightful suspicion must have rested on you, I also suffered much from the thoughts raised thereby. I am more devoted to the young Wehrmacht, its generals, officers, and soldiers than most people realize.

You, Colonel General, were not incriminated in the eyes of the German people and above all have not appeared to be charged [with anything].

The commitment of the Army on March 12 of this year was the first ordered by me and furnished highest confirmation of the efficacy of your operation and your work!

I shall bring this to the attention of the nation.

With the most grateful and sincere wishes I am yours

[signed] Adolf Hitler[30]

So artless a soul as Schmundt may have discerned in this letter an expression of conciliatory sentiment. In reality it was more like a slap in the face, barren as it was of any word of apology or regret. Fate, if one were to judge from it, had merely dealt unkindly with both writer and recipient. The reference to the public having learned nothing of the affair, though expressed in terms of reassurance, was an artful way of negating the very existence of any problem of rehabilitation. Fritsch's honor never having been assailed before a wider public, it implied, there was nothing that had to be "restored."

Hitler, indeed, had at the end said something about public recognition of the former commander's great services and Fritsch could only assume that some declaration would be made on the occasion of the next meeting of the Reichstag. Raeder wrote on April 28 that the Fuehrer was giving thought to such a possibility and word of this also reached Hassell. If any such notion was ever entertained by Adolf Hitler, it can only have been a passing one quickly sup-

[29] Puttkamer interview, June 27, 1970. Fritsch himself believed that Hitler wrote because of Brauchitsch's "strong pressure." Letter to Baroness Schutzbar, April 4, 1938. Fritsch Letters.
[30] Foertsch, Schuld und Verhängnis, 126-127.

pressed in the next acid mood. Fritsch himself had no illusions that it could be brought about without the strongest pressure.[31]

Fritsch had just retired to a house placed at his disposal by Brauchitsch at Achterberg at the exercise ground of Bergen until the one to be built for him in Berlin from the funds of the officers' subscription should be ready. After some hesitation about answering Hitler at all, he decided to do so, if only to prevent the Fuehrer from saying that the general had never made clear his position on the problem of rehabilitation.[32]

The reply was dated April 7 and was dressed in the phraseology customary when writing to the head of state. Hitler, he noted, had made much of what his relationship with the Wehrmacht meant to him. He, Fritsch, had thought he had enjoyed the Fuehrer's confidence and it was the most painful disappointment of a life devoted to the service of the fatherland to learn that for years there had hovered over this relationship a shadow that was to lead to his removal from the Army. The criminal accusation had collapsed completely. There remained the deeply wounding circumstances which had accompanied it and which weighed the more heavily since wide circles of the Wehrmacht and the nation *had* learned something about them. He felt obliged to bring this to Hitler's attention, for he had to judge from the letter he had received that the Fuehrer had "apparently been incorrectly informed" about this.[33]

His own suffering, as well as that to which the Fuehrer had testified, said Fritsch, could have been avoided if the Gestapo had provided "timely and exhaustive information." At the trial the declaration under oath of Criminal Commissar Fehling had established that the Gestapo as early as January 15 had come across Captain von Frisch and examined his bank account. In ignorance of this, Hitler had set in motion measures after January 26 which had taken their course. Without waiting for the investigative procedure requested by Fritsch, the Fuehrer had taken the steps toward dismissal on the basis of the testimony of a criminal.

"In the interest of the Army and of the Fuehrer" himself, Fritsch concluded by asking that the persons whose duty it had been to

[31] *Ibid.*, 127. Hassell Papers, notation of April 30, 1938. Letter to Baroness Schutzbar, April 4, 1938. Fritsch letters.

[32] As expressed in a letter of April 15. Quoted by J. A. Kielmansegg, *Der Fritsch-Prozess 1938*, 114.

[33] The full text of Fritsch's letter is given by Foertsch, *Schuld und Verhängnis*, 127-128.

provide Hitler and Goering with timely and complete information be called to account. Hitler must personally assume the responsibility for the restoration of Fritsch's honor before the Army and the nation.

This epistle, which, short of a direct accusation against Hitler and Goering, went as far as it could to call things by their proper names, was never accorded a reply. Though formally polite it was cast in distinctly ironic terms which could not be lost on the recipient and must have stung him to fury. Fritsch had sent it to Siewert who delivered it for final transmission to Engel. The adjutant gave it to Hitler in the early morning hours (2:30 A.M.) of April 10, seizing the occasion as usual to speak of the imperative need of rendering justice to Fritsch. Not having been oriented on the contents of the missive, he was forced to grope in the dark. Hitler, who had become unpleasant as soon as Fritsch's name was mentioned, silently read and folded the letter and, without further word, went off to bed.[34]

The public, it is hardly necessary to stress, was not advised in any way of the exchange. To avoid any impression that Hitler was ignoring Fritsch completely, announcement was made that the Fuehrer had congratulated him "on the restoration of his health." This made Fritsch all the more eager to bring the contents of the two letters to the attention of key persons. On April 27 we find him in Berlin, where at least one of his callers, Hassell, was shown the communications and filled in on their background.[35]

Though specific evidence is lacking, it may be assumed that Fritsch also apprised of this exchange of letters any friends within the Generalität whom he encountered in Berlin or who made the pilgrimage to his retreat. As the weeks passed without any sign of action from the Reich Chancellery, uneasiness and indignation revived in Army quarters. Unfortunately surviving sources often fail to differentiate between sentiments at this stage and those prevailing earlier or during the Fritsch affair in general.[36] Yet both the logic of developments and specific references to the rehabilitation issue as such show that feeling was again reaching a high pitch.

[34] Engel Diary, entry of April 10, 1938.
[35] Hassell Papers, notation of April 30, 1938. Hassell expresses strong approval of Fritsch's letter.
[36] This confusion is particularly notable in one of the fuller accounts, that of Joachim von Stülpnagel, which tends to jump back and forth between the various stages of the affair. Stülpnagel, 357–359.

# The Rehabilitation Issue

Old Field Marshal von Mackensen, whom Hitler regularly exploited as a frontispiece at military shows, deluged him and prominent Army figures with letters and telegrams, to which the Fuehrer, at any rate, returned no answers.[37] Brauchitsch, who must have been the old warrior's major target, was being urged from all sides to exert himself to the utmost for Fritsch. To ward off such importunities, he assured all and sundry that he was already doing everything conceivable. Regimental commanders who were besieged by their troubled officers apparently were instructed to assert this emphatically and to say that specific proposals for rehabilitation were being presented.[38]

Brauchitsch at times felt so sorely beset that he sought refuge at the house of a cousin of the same name who had once served in the 2nd Regiment of Foot Guards. There he would unburden himself of his troubles and seek "recuperation." When his cousin's wife somewhat skeptically asked whether he would really persevere in the matter of Fritsch, he replied in injured tones: "You should know me well enough to be sure that I won't give up." [39]

Most disturbing to Brauchitsch and, insofar as they penetrated to him, Hitler, must have been the proliferation of signs of disaffection among the top commanders. By May it was becoming conceivable that there might yet be that "general strike of the generals" that had been the nightmare of Goebbels at the height of the crisis. The first individual ultimatum reached Brauchitsch from Fritsch's firm friend Ulex. Having waited as long as his impatience allowed—some five or six weeks—he determined to force the issue by a formal statement through established channels. To Fedor von Bock, who at Dresden commanded the army group to which his corps belonged, Ulex addressed a written notice that he would resign his command and quit the Army if Fritsch did not receive satisfaction commensurate with his own desires. A copy of this communication was sent to Fritsch.[40]

[37] As related by Mackensen. Winnig, 115. Mackensen also voiced his sentiments to Stülpnagel at the annual meeting of the Schlieffen Society, severely censuring the lack of support given Fritsch by the generals and stating that he would no longer participate in any state ceremonies. Stülpnagel, 359.

[38] This was, for example, the case with the regiment of Fritsch's own nephew, Count Kielmansegg. The officers were led to assume that their commander was addressing them in this fashion on orders from higher up. J. A. Kielmansegg, *Der Fritsch-Prozess 1938*, 112.

[39] Hassell Papers, notation of June 17, 1938. The quoted remark appears to have been made somewhat before this date.

[40] Ulex ms., 102.

Bock's reaction was typical of the man who, until dismissed in 1942, had an unbroken record of evading anything that threatened his career. In place of a formal reply, he begged Ulex orally to address himself directly to Brauchitsch. He himself, he protested lamely, was already so "burdened" in the matter that he did not want to "take a position" on his subordinate's demarche.[41]

Ulex thereupon went to Berlin to notify Brauchitsch of his intentions. Perhaps sensing the need to quiet this gadfly before he brought the entire Generalität down about Brauchitsch's ears, the latter outdid himself in assurances. It was the occasion on which he delivered himself of the pledge quoted earlier, that he would not rest until he had cleaned out "this pigsty Himmler."[42] That Ulex could indeed become a serious center of infection was soon demonstrated when he encountered the commander of the neighboring Wehrkreis, Günther von Kluge. Meeting at a field exercise of troops of the two corps, Ulex seized the opportunity of a pause by the roadside to relate what he had done. "Donnerwetter," exclaimed Kluge, "that is what I shall do too." He straightway proceeded to follow Ulex's lead, though the latter judged that Kluge made the mistake of passing his message to Brauchitsch through Keitel, who was an old regimental comrade.[43] Ulex's surmise that Keitel suppressed it receives support from the latter's general inclination to dampen any tendency of Brauchitsch to take a stronger tone on an issue whose very mention inflamed Hitler.

As May became June it was increasingly evident that tidings of Ulex's chivalrous lead were spreading among his military peers and making a considerable impact. From what follows Brauchitsch must have been inundated with protests and inquiries as the inclination to follow Ulex's example made headway. Brauchitsch was being pushed into exerting great pressure on Hitler. And Keitel, though probably withholding Kluge's ultimatum from Brauchitsch, may well have shown it as a warning note to Hitler. In short, matters were approaching a stage where the dictator could not hide from himself the danger of allowing them to drift further. It was again becoming imperative that he take a hand in shaping events.

Never was Adolf Hitler's keen sense of timing more in evidence than at this juncture. Once again he utilized a precarious interna-

[41] *Ibid.*

[42] *Ibid.* From the fact that this was "shortly before" Ulex went to Berlin to tell Brauchitsch of the overture of Lutze, we may assume that this incident occurred in the first half of May.

[43] Ulex ms., 102.

tional situation of his own making to master a critical stage of the Fritsch affair. On an uncertain date late in May he called in Brauchitsch and, in the presence of Keitel, told him of his intention to "proceed militarily against Czechoslovakia in the near future."[44] A few days later followed the well-known meeting in the conservatory of the Chancellery in which the dictator informed leaders of the Wehrmacht, party, and state that it was his "immovable purpose to sweep Czechoslovakia off the map."[45] Two days later, that pronouncement was reflected in a revision of Case Green, the plan of campaign against this southern neighbor, by the insertion of the statement "It is my unalterable decision to smash Czechoslovakia by military action in the near future."[46]

### Hitler's Coup at Barth

The bellicose turn in his policy Hitler now utilized to lay the final ripples of the Fritsch affair. He convoked on June 13 an assembly of the same Wehrmacht leaders to whom he had spoken with such effect on February 4. Ostensibly they were called to witness air exercises at Barth on the Pomeranian coast.

From Hitler's standpoint, the mood of the Army generals on the eve of the meeting was ominous. Eloquent testimony to this is the case of Eugen Ritter von Schober, commander of the Bavarian corps, one of those most devoted to Hitler in the higher levels of the Generalität. Hearing over the military grapevine of Ulex's threat of resignation, Schober called on his military colleague to compliment him and say that he was contemplating similar action.[47] Kluge, on his return to Münster, even told his chief of staff, Georg von Sodenstern, that the twelve Wehrkreis commanders were agreed "in sharpest protest" to demand the rehabilitation of Fritsch and to threaten collective resignation if this were rejected.[48]

It may be said that Hitler had his work cut out for him and he responded to the challenge with as superb a performance as this extraordinary actor could achieve. The stage was set, no doubt

[44] Foerster, 106. Since Hitler arrived at this decision only after May 20, the communication to Brauchitsch must have occurred between then and the wider pronouncement to the May 28 gathering in the Chancellery.

[45] Wiedemann, *Der Mann der Feldherr werden wollte*, 127. The larger implications of this meeting will be analyzed in a study that is scheduled to follow the present one.

[46] IMT, XXV, 434.

[47] Ulex ms., 103.

[48] Sodenstern and Winter, 5.

at Hitler's direction,[49] by Brauchitsch, who ordered the Army leaders present, mainly army group and Wehrkreis commanders, to assemble in the morning and addressed them. Brauchitsch began by stressing his overwhelming concern over what had happened to Fritsch and the delay in his rehabilitation. It had been his firm purpose to resign in protest against the treatment meted out to his predecessor. Now, however, the Fuehrer had informed him that an unavoidable clash with Czechoslovakia loomed in the near future. Orders had been issued for a vast acceleration of the fortifications in the West under the direction of General Adam. Given such circumstances he could not in conscience vacate his post and he could only beg those who had similar intentions to reconsider their decisions in the same way.[50]

Brauchitsch's audience, to which the news of an impending showdown with Czechoslovakia was a bolt out of the blue, was left reeling. Those who had threatened or contemplated resignation were faced with a harsh dilemma. If they allowed themselves to be ruled by their sense of obligation to Fritsch, they faced the heavy responsibility of evacuating their posts on the eve of foreign conflict. They were little equipped, nor had their commander in chief given them any lead, for judging the compulsions of the international situation or Hitler's role in forcing the issue.

It would contribute much to understanding Hitler's tactics and Brauchitsch's rather ambivalent role if there were an explanation for Beck's absence. Only the bare fact is known and not whether he was prevented from attending by duties or by the maneuvers of others (Hitler and/or Brauchitsch?). In argument with his commander he had taken sharp issue with Hitler's pronouncement of May 28 and relations between the two had entered a new phase of strain. If Beck had been at Barth he surely would have spoken against Hitler's claim that an early war with Czechoslovakia was unavoidable. His absence and Brauchitsch's statement without commentary left the generals in a quandary.

One can only speculate on what would have been done if things had been left at this point. That was far from the case. Hitler

[49] This view is based on both the logic of the situation and the arrangements for the day which provided that Hitler not appear until close to noon when a demonstration of antiaircraft fire was scheduled. The longer meeting with the Fuehrer came after lunch.

[50] Brauchitsch's remarks and the reactions of his hearers are recorded most fully in the Liebmann and Ulex manuscripts, pp. 2 and 102 respectively. Both men testify to their amazement at what they were told.

now provided them with exactly what was needed to reconcile conscience with passivity by furnishing a plausible-sounding explanation for the delay in Fritsch's rehabilitation frosted with reassurances for the future.

Our knowledge of what Hitler said that afternoon derives from testimony of six listeners that varies much in emphasis and completeness. The only strictly contemporary accounts are reports made to Beck immediately after the meeting by two of his quartermasters general, Halder and Karl Heinrich von Stülpnagel. The former is much the most extensive and, except where otherwise indicated, will be the basic source for the following narration of what Hitler said on June 13. General Liebmann set down his recollection a year later and Ulex shortly after the war. Raeder gives a brief account in his memoirs and Kluge's chief of staff, Sodenstern, told in 1950 and 1954 what he learned from his commander on the latter's return.[51]

To justify the charges against Fritsch having been raised and carried so far, Hitler began the meeting by calling on General Heitz as president of the Reich Military Court to read the verdict of the court-martial with its many implied alibis that Lehmann had woven in under Goering's insistent prodding. Despite the absorbing interest for this audience of the document, it must in the end have become rather tiresome. A year later Liebmann was under the impression that the reading required three hours, though the text familiar to us could have been disposed of in less than half that time.

Hitler then took over and spoke for about an hour and a half with a pathos and emotion that won him rapt attention. To a listener, such as Ulex, who was already initiated into the intricacies of the affair, it was obvious that "some things he concealed, some he distorted, on some he lied." Otherwise, even the most skeptical were convinced of his sincerity and depth of feeling.[52] To Raeder

---

[51] The reports of Halder and Stülpnagel were found among Beck's papers. That of the former is given at length by Foerster, 94–96. The Ulex memoirs set forth his account on pp. 103–104. Liebmann's is pp. 2–3 of his manuscript. Sodenstern's 1950 relation of what Kluge told him is contained in a letter quoted by Foertsch, *Schuld und Verhängnis,* 141. His briefer story of 1954 was told to Drs. Vogelsang and Krausnick of the IfZ (ZS 149). Testifying again to Raeder's naiveté in such matters is his brief account, I, 123.

[52] Liebmann (3) confesses as much for himself, though a year later, perhaps under the influence of what he had himself suffered at Hitler's hands, he was beset by doubts.

nearly two decades later his words still appeared "unequivocal and convincing."

The Fuehrer began by once more emphasizing the "spiritual shock" into which he had been thrown by the affair of Blomberg. Under the impact of this bitter disappointment it had seemed necessary to clear up the 1936 charges against Fritsch about which there was an extensive documentary file. The confrontation of Fritsch with Schmidt had then taken a form which had greatly shaken him and made him believe that "anything was possible."

All this was dressed in the embellishments in which he had become letter-perfect through constant repetition. He went on to say that the legal procedures Fritsch himself demanded had, "as the result of a fortunate accident," led to the general's complete exoneration. In a voice choked with tears he protested that, like Fritsch, he had been the victim of a shameless deception which brought home to him how he was ever more alone. After pausing for a moment in what seemed an effort to master his emotions (Kluge/Sodenstern), he went on forcefully to reject "absolutely" any idea that the accusations had been advanced frivolously or actually contrary to better knowledge in high official quarters (i.e., Himmler and/or Heydrich). In view of the regard which the Wehrmacht enjoyed in the new Reich anything like this was unthinkable. There had been mistakes on the part of "subordinate officials" who lacked the good sense to stop once they thought themselves on a hot scent, whatever the evidence to the contrary that was unturned. The Wehrmacht could be sure that such a thing would never happen again. The real villain in the "tragic case" was of course the blackmailer Schmidt. Since a judicial proceeding against this abominable wretch could yield no more than a prison sentence, far short of what was demanded by the infamy of the deed and its pernicious consequences, Hitler had *ordered him to be shot.*

While his audience was digesting this last amazing disclosure, Hitler went on to the problem of Fritsch's rehabilitation. True, the former commander in chief had received the fullest legal satisfaction but this could hardly compensate for the personal tragedy. In trying to deal with this he found himself in a bind owing to reasons of state. To safeguard the prestige of the Army, he had been compelled to choose the subterfuge that Fritsch's bad health forced his retirement. He could hardly now "disavow" himself before the nation by contradicting this. Also, in future situations where it might again be advisable to disguise developments in the Wehrmacht by such a formulation it would receive no public credence if the allegation were repudiated in this instance. (Here Hitler conveniently ignored that at the end of March the press had announced that Fritsch had been congratulated by him on "the restoration of his health.") It was the more important to stick to the chosen explanation because the general public thus far knew nothing of the suspicions raised against Fritsch and should continue in ignorance of them. With a show of great delicacy of sentiment, Hitler further said that he could not expect Fritsch to work with him again in any spirit of confidence after the charges against him had once been treated seriously (Raeder, Liebmann).

Thus, Hitler argued, it was necessary to seek means to rehabilitate Fritsch other than reappointing him to high office. He had been waiting for the next convocation of the Reichstag to compliment the Army on its fine showing in the entry into Austria and to give Fritsch credit for bringing it to this high point of efficiency. But no such occasion had yet offered itself or appeared in early prospect. Not wishing to wait longer, he had called together those who had heard the charges on February 4 in order to do Fritsch the fullest justice before them. For the time being, all that could be done in addition would be to inform the Army of the appointment of Fritsch to the honorary colonelcy of his old artillery regiment. They could be assured that Hitler would not rest in seeking further ways to show respect for this "irreproachable man of honor" whom he so greatly revered. In a Reich Defense Council which was in process of formation the advice of this distinguished specialist would prove even more valuable than it had when he was commander in chief (Kluge/Sodenstern).

Hitler then reiterated that in the National Socialist Reich any attack on the Wehrmacht from critics beyond its own ranks was out of the question. Changes in high military positions could only be effected by its own action and never, as in Russia, through "external [i.e., party] influences." He concluded by pleading with his hearers not to abandon the flag at so critical a time (Kluge/Sodenstern). He placed his entire trust in the Wehrmacht and begged it to bestow a similar confidence on him.

The logical and factual flaws of this presentation stand out glaringly today, but could not readily be recognized by an audience which, with few exceptions, was familiar only with the outline of the affair. Psychologically the speech must count among Hitler's masterpieces. The tissue of lies thickly woven into the fabric was

405

difficult to identify, the spirit appeared wholly generous, and the promises sounded sincere. Hitler had again shown his exceptional insight into the tendency of men torn between conscience and self-interest to welcome what made it easier to opt for the latter. The fable of a "Reich Defense Council," by which he made Goering's February suggestion of a "Secret Cabinet Council" to disguise the eclipse of Neurath do double duty, was helpful here. And the sop thrown to Fritsch's friends by bestowing a regiment on him was skillfully represented as only a payment on account.

## Sidelight: The Fate of Otto Schmidt

However shameful such an admission, it was a master stroke on Hitler's part to state that Otto Schmidt had been liquidated. The problem of what to do with the blackmailer demanded immediate attention from the intriguers once the trial had been concluded. It cannot have been easy to weigh all the factors in deciding whether he was now an asset or a liability. Neither Goering nor the SS chiefs could know what turn events would take in the weeks and months—nay years—ahead.

The anxieties of Himmler and Heydrich and their fear of being sacrificed to Army pressures by Hitler or Goering have been noted. A major effort might be made to reach Schmidt and question him on points not driven home in the concluding minutes of the trial. Such a move would be forestalled if the man were killed or assumed to be dead. Their appreciation of this after the trial is evidenced by an effort to spread among men who had caught the Gestapo's attention as Fritsch sympathizers the word that he had been shot. Such was the story told Judge Kanter by one of the Gestapo agents with whom he had dealt.[53] No doubt it was hoped that this would inhibit efforts to get at Schmidt.

In actual fact, Schmidt was sent to the concentration camp at Sachsenhausen, where, we may be sure, so talkative and boastful a fellow was kept in strictest seclusion. There he sat, almost but, to his misfortune, not quite forgotten, until July 1942. Curious as are the decrees of fate, the death knell appears to have been rung for Schmidt—as for the distant Czech village of Lidice—by the assassination of Heydrich. The incidence of Schmidt's liquidation a few short weeks after Heydrich's demise (June 4, 1942) argues that it was, as usually assumed, Heydrich who had been instrumen-

[53] Kanter interview, May 9, 1970.

tal in keeping him alive. One can picture the case of Schmidt being among matters brought to Himmler just then as unfinished business of his lieutenant.

Himmler decided that this no longer active account should be closed. Schmidt, however, must have been consigned to the camp in agreement with Goering and Hitler; to the former Himmler wrote on July 29, requesting his assent to a proposal to the Fuehrer that Schmidt be finally executed. A summary of the miscreant's criminal record and a medical statement that he was a schizophrenic and asocial were enclosed. Back from Goering came a brisk reply, "Why, that one has long been scheduled to be shot."[54] Thereby the fate of Schmidt was sealed—ironically by the man who on March 18, 1938, before a crowded courtroom had pledged his word of honor that the blackmailer's life was secure if he finally spoke the truth.

Beyond the obvious intent of removing lingering doubts about the elimination of Schmidt by "making it official," why did Hitler on June 13, 1938, stress that he was no longer among the living? An additional push may have come from the prying of Lutze's people in late May and early June. The attempts of the SA to gather compromising evidence against the SS and help Ulex to rouse Brauchitsch may not have been specifically identified, but it is not likely that the inquiries, notably those aimed at gaining insight into the Gestapo's dealings with Schmidt, passed unnoticed. It may be further assumed that Hitler consulted with Goering and Himmler about the declaration on the Fritsch affair he was planning for Barth. Can one believe that the fate of Schmidt was not discussed in that connection?

Once the chief of state had solemnly averred before the Wehrmacht leadership that Schmidt was dead, Fritsch's less sophisticated

<hr />

[54] EAP 104/3, Microcopy T-34, Roll 7, Frames 7215-7217, in NA. Gisevius, partly on the basis of Goering's comment, believes (recording, January 1972; letter of March 21, 1972) that Himmler told Hitler and Goering in 1938 that "the order" to shoot Schmidt had been carried out but that he had actually put Schmidt away in order to bring him out later for another assault on Fritsch. This thesis is rejected here in view of the following: (1) Himmler and Heydrich, except for compelling reasons, would hesitate to disobey a direct order of Hitler's. (2) Fritsch was too finished a man to be a further obstacle to SS aims. (3) If Himmler had violated Hitler's order he would hardly have called this to his and Goering's attention in 1942. (4) If Himmler had reported in 1938 that Schmidt was dead, why bother to secure authorization in 1942 to shoot him, revealing his deceit in the process? The request for approval makes it look more as though *Hitler* had directed him to send Schmidt to the concentration camp. In short, Hitler lied to the generals to forestall any efforts to get at this dangerous witness to embarrass the regime. If the Fuehrer gave any order it was to *keep the man alive.*

partisans probably closed their books on the blackmailer. The Abwehr-associated group was less prepared to let Hitler's word settle matters. Since the conclusion of the trial it had watched for signs on the fate of Schmidt and had developed two contrasting theses: (1) he would now be liquidated and (2) Heydrich would put him in storage. Nebe, Oster, and Gisevius leaned to the latter view and were not completely shaken in it when the news came from Barth. Their predominant reaction then had been outrage that no voice had been raised against cold-blooded murder or the crowning insult to Fritsch in this form of "rehabilitation."[55]

Soon Nebe had ferreted out that Schmidt was indeed alive and under heavy guard. When Canaris learned this from Gisevius, the admiral, just then in one of his elfin moods, decided to plague Keitel to whom he continued to feed items of information calculated to keep him alert to machinations of the Gestapo.

The effect proved the opposite to that anticipated. Perhaps Canaris overdid things. Keitel was as heartily sick of the two affairs as anyone else and desperately trying to close accounts on them; if the Gestapo had really failed to "carry out the order" to shoot Schmidt, he wanted to bring it to the Fuehrer's attention. The startled Canaris was forced to backtrack. After all, he told Keitel, his information thus far was based on hearsay and nothing should be done until he had talked to Heydrich. A few days later he reported that the execution had now taken place and Keitel declared himself satisfied.[56] The laughter at Tirpitz Ufer was good-natured but Homeric when Oster gave a highly relished report of the discomfiture of the crafty "little Greek."

Keitel later heard of the actual 1942 execution (from Goering in prison?) as he declared in his memoirs, together with his conviction that Canaris reported correctly in the first instance but retracted out of fear of Heydrich. A greater influence on Canaris may have been his apprehension that if Keitel ran to Hitler with the story, it might induce Hitler to go through with the execution. Canaris could only prefer to have Schmidt kept on ice to be available later as a witness at the trial of the leaders of the Third Reich which was becoming a major dream of the conspiracy then forming.[57]

An intruding question, and one most difficult to clarify, is why

[55] Letter from Gisevius to the author, March 20, 1972.
[56] The story as related here is based on Keitel, 381.
[57] *Ibid.* Gisevius was left with the impression that Schmidt was dead. Gisevius, *Bis zum bittern Ende*, 308.

Hitler, instead of troubling to lie, had not really had Schmidt shot. Keitel, in his simplistic fashion, concluded that the latter "must have been a hired tool who could hardly be shot as a reward for his deed." This is to pay too high a compliment to the scruples of the Gestapo. Schmidt may still have had value as a source of information on such men as Funk who, though at the moment not in the SS black books, were liable, like everyone else in the Third Reich, to land there at some future time. Or perhaps Goering had some qualms, later abandoned, about breaking his word. There can also have been some not easily fathomable motive that swayed Hitler.

### The Honorary Colonelcy

The first impulse of Werner von Fritsch on learning that he was nominated honorary colonel of Artillery Regiment 12 was to give a flat rejection.[58] He could not avoid being deeply wounded that the notification was accompanied with a deliberate slight. Brauchitsch, who brought him the notification the evening of June 15, presented him only the instrument of appointment, barren of any verbal, not to speak of the customary written, felicitation. Hitler, as Fritsch wrote bitterly two days later, had clearly yielded only to the sharpest pressure and knew how to make even this gesture offensive to him. Outwardly the gesture was a good and even necessary one but for him it was worthless.[59]

Beck's feeling, as he expressed it that same day to Hassell, was similar. On the basis of the reports of his two quartermasters general, he declared himself "horrified" at the "frivolity" with which Hitler had treated the rehabilitation problem, a frivolity which unfortunately had not been apparent to his audience. The bestowal of a regiment on Fritsch did not seem to Beck relevant in terms of what would have been demanded by a genuine rehabilitation.[60]

It was evident, however, that Hitler had brilliantly succeeded in clouding the eyes of virtually all the generals, that he had convinced them of his sincerity and good intentions, and that a rejection of the proffered honor would create confusion in their ranks and seem to many an act of petulance. It illustrates the state of mind of the generals that immediately after the Barth meeting, Bock

[58] Grosskreuz interview, January 15, 1970.
[59] Letter to his sister, Frau von Werner, June 17, 1938. Quoted by Foertsch, *Schuld und Verhängnis*, 133.
[60] Hassell Papers, notation of June 17, 1938.

had told Ulex that, after all they had learned that day, he should no longer hesitate to stick to his post. Ulex took the problem home for reflection and then went to Berlin to tell Brauchitsch of the message he had sent to Fritsch at the time of his first notice, threatening resignation, to Bock. He felt bound by this unless Fritsch offered to release him. The next trip was to Achterberg where, as might have been expected, he was told: "Neither you nor Brauchitsch can in the existing situation [Hitler's revelation of an imminent war with Czechoslovakia] do anything else than stay."[61]

To Grosskreuz, Both's successor as adjutant, Fritsch voiced the conclusion that at such a time he must do nothing which might sow dissension within the officer corps or between it and the head of state. Personal resentment must yield to the need of avoiding all that might reduce the effectiveness of the Army.[62] To Goltz he wrote that the appointment was a gesture made by Hitler purely for Army consumption: "I myself am dead and proscribed by the Fuehrer, the party, and the rest of official Germany."[63]

The ceremony of investiture which made Fritsch honorary colonel of Artillery Regiment 12 took place on August 11 at the exercise ground of Gross Born under the aegis of Brauchitsch. Nine days earlier Captain Engel, on Brauchitsch's direction, had asked Hitler whether he would not be present in view of his going to Gross Born in any event about then to attend some exercises. The answer had been a short and sharp "No."[64]

The occasion itself was as elaborate as military ceremonial could make it. It began with the investiture and a review and proceeded through a round of dinners and receptions to a closing with the traditional Grand Tattoo.[65] Hitler, without being ostentatiously ungracious, could not avoid a public message of congratulation and front-page treatment of the affair in the German press. "On the occasion of your appointment as chief of Artillery Regiment 12," he wrote, ". . . my heartiest congratulations, in grateful appreciation of your ceaseless work during the rebuilding of the German Wehrmacht. In expressing to you my best wishes for your personal

[61] Ulex ms., 103.

[62] Communication of Colonel (ret.) O. H. Grosskreuz to the IfZ, December 28, 1950.

[63] Letter to Goltz, July 7, 1938.

[64] Engel Diary, entry of August 2, 1938.

[65] Procedures were laid down in "Befehl für die Uebergabe des Artl. Regt. 12 an den Herrn Generaloberst Freiherrn von Fritsch." Generalkommando II. Armeekorps, Wehrkreis XIII/240, R.G. 1031, in N.A.

welfare . . ."[66] If Hitler grimaced with distaste as he dictated these reluctant words of felicitation, he may have drawn consolation from the thought that this treatment of the incident, whether intended or not, served to allay rumors abroad that all was not well between him and the Army. "The letter to General von Fritsch which Herr Hitler sent with the commission of appointment," pontificated the London *Times*, "leaves no doubt that, as far as the Fuehrer is concerned, the clouds which have at times overshadowed the General's career during the past few months have vanished."[67]

If the event raised in Fritsch any feeling of exhilaration it failed to outlive the occasion. The ceremony seemed to him a public funeral and a second interment at that. His depression and bitterness spoke eloquently in a letter to Baroness Schutzbar of August 13: "It is really best when one permits the dead to rest instead of exhuming still live bodies and burying them again."[68]

The affair thus descended for him to the level of a public show and he conducted himself accordingly. He has been blamed in various quarters for observing current political manners by including a reference to Hitler's role in rebuilding the Wehrmacht and concluding with a threefold "Sieg Heil." In contrast therewith was his address that evening at a banquet and convivial celebration to which 500 officers had been invited. This time, though the usual practice would again have called for it, the Fuehrer was not mentioned and was not included in the concluding toast to the Army which ended with the traditional "Hurrah."[69]

Fritsch left Gross Born for Achterberg the evening of August 12. The following morning Hitler arrived to observe a military exercise of no particular importance.

The undesired honor of the honorary colonelcy was the last granted by the Third Reich to Werner von Fritsch after his dismissal. The promises of Barth had served their turn and were now buried and forgotten.

[66] *Frankfurter Allgemeine Zeitung*, August 12, 1938.
[67] Quoted by J. A. Kielmansegg, *Der Fritsch-Prozess 1938*, 130.
[68] *Ibid.*
[69] *Ibid.*, 131. Criticism of Fritsch at times extends to his having accepted the honorary colonelcy at all. Thus Schacht before the E.P. colloquium, protocol of January 3, 1955, 3.

# CHAPTER XIII

# Conclusion: Looking Back–and Ahead

The torments of Werner von Fritsch did not end with the affair associated with his name but only with his death some fifteen months later. To all intents and purposes that affair terminated at the point of Hitler's meeting with the military leaders at Barth, the final occasion on which they might have confronted him on behalf of Fritsch. Thereafter his personal fate ceased to be an issue and the bestowal of the honorary colonelcy on him seven weeks later was no more than an anticlimax.

In his Achterberg retreat Fritsch had ample opportunity to pursue further the introspective thoughts which had lain so heavily upon him during his weeks of sorest trial. His letters to the Baroness Schutzbar convey much gloom and occasionally a flash of ill-temper, for which he would apologize in his next communication. Though making no effort to hide his bitter feelings against the dictator, he avoided comment that could be used against him or his friends. He was more than ever convinced that his mail was under surveillance and repeatedly cut short what threatened to become a condemnatory outburst with such words as "Since this letter, like so many others, will be opened, I will not write any more [about this]."[1]

Achterberg in no way became a focus of pilgrimage for Fritsch's

---

[1] Letter of August 7, 1939. Fritsch Letters. The general's letters only occasionally reveal something about the depth of his relationship with the Baroness Schutzbar. He undoubtedly appreciated the opportunity, which the correspondence gave him, to unburden himself more fully than he probably did to his male friends. Since Baroness Schutzbar's own letters appear to be lost, we can judge of her feelings only from some of his responses, such as that he felt unable to reciprocate the degree of affection she professed.

412

# Looking Back—and Ahead

old associates of the Army leadership. It was a frantically busy period for them and some may also have been deterred, as they were later in the case of the retired Beck, by awareness that Hitler disapproved of visits to the fallen star. His residence, Haus Dorfmark, was too small for large gatherings or for more than a few overnight guests. Individual close friends, like Dr. Nissen, however, came for days at a time.[2] The Bergen exercise ground, which was under the jurisdiction of Ulex's 11th corps area, enabled that trusted friend to come often. Such visits afforded the general his most pleasant hours and were often passed in considerable conviviality. Fritsch would also attend the Bergen exercises dressed in the uniform of his 12th Artillery Regiment.[3]

From time to time he would emerge from his isolation for a trip to Berlin or to take part in a hunt, sometimes to observe military exercises elsewhere. Raeder invited him to attend fleet movements on the *Gneisenau* at whose launching Fritsch had presided. On this occasion the honors shown him surpassed the demands of courtesy in the form of a seventeen-gun salute.[4]

Meanwhile Fritsch was engrossed with mentally reviewing the events which had made a shambles of his life as well as his own conduct with respect to them. To men wise in the practice of courts it is an axiom that the average man is his own worst defender, and Fritsch must have been aware that he had more than lived up to this rule.[5] His conviction that Hitler and Goering had been involved in one or another aspect of the plot against him from the start continued to grow.[6] To gain greater insight into the background of the affair, he sent Goltz to Best, who, as has been noted earlier, shoved the blame on Goering.[7]

Fritsch incorporated his reflections and inquiries into a historical analysis of some length which he directed his adjutant, Captain Grosskreuz, to deliver to the head of the Army Archives, General Friedrich von Rabenau.[8] It remains a mystery whether this vital document was destroyed with a large part of the Potsdam archives or now rests in East German or Soviet hands.

[2] Nissen interview, July 15, 1971.
[3] Ulex ms., 98.
[4] Raeder, II, 124.
[5] Müller interview, October 11, 1969.
[6] Nissen interview, July 15, 1971. Ulex ms., 98.
[7] Goltz interview, November 1, 1969. Goltz, "Erinnerungen," 212-213. Goltz, "Darstellung," 15.
[8] Grosskreuz interview, January 15, 1971.

At times Fritsch's discussions with his friends dwelt on the possibility of military employment outside of Germany. Though he obviously gave some thought to this, he does not appear to have considered the idea very seriously. He pointed out that another fallen Army commander, the renowned General von Seeckt, had not been happy with such an experience in China. The Spaniards would not care to depend in any way on a German officer. Furthermore, he would have to solicit Hitler's consent, a prospect he did not relish, especially since he believed that it would be withheld.[9]

As the war clouds gathered about Germany, Fritsch was filled with gloomy foreboding. On moving to his new house in Berlin in the spring of 1939 he was able to observe developments more closely and to compare notes and judgments with his friends. To Oster he said sadly on returning from some Army exercise: "What a wonderful instrument this Wehrmacht has become! But this criminal fool may yet manage to employ it for the destruction of Germany and the world."[10]

As the approach of war became all too evident in the summer of 1939, the problem of his own role was thrust upon the former Army commander. He never wavered in his innermost feeling that, whatever came, he could only share the fate of Germany. When asked by Colonel Mellinthin whether he would accept the command of an army, his reply was: "Yes, I would accept one but he [Hitler] will never give me any."[11]

Under the circumstances Fritsch could see no alternative to accompanying his regiment as a volunteer. "At least they cannot prevent my going along as an expendable adjutant," he said to Dr. Nissen.[12] A month earlier he had written to the Baroness Schutzbar: "In wartime I shall accompany my regiment as a target, since I cannot remain at home."[13] Upon the opening of hostilities he expressed himself similarly to Goltz: he would simply "go along as a target."[14]

Such utterances are often interpreted as betokening suicidal intentions. However, though Fritsch may have welcomed the *prospect* of death, there is no evidence that he deliberately exposed himself

[9] Letter to Baroness Schutzbar, April 29, 1939. Fritsch Letters.
[10] As related by Oster to Josef Müller shortly after Fritsch's death. Müller interviews, October 11, 1969, and January 17, 1970.
[11] Mellinthin, "Niederschrift," 13.
[12] Nissen interview, July 15, 1971.
[13] Letter of August 7, 1939. Fritsch Letters.
[14] Goltz, "Erinnerungen," 213.

to a bullet. When he did fall before Warsaw on September 22, he was actually engaged in leaving the immediate combat zone to keep an appointment.[15]

One cannot believe that Hitler, for so much as an instant, considered returning Fritsch to a post of high command. The claim that he did so draws support only from the questionable testimony of Keitel. According to his version, Hitler seriously weighed a proposal of Brauchitsch, energetically supported by himself, that Fritsch receive command of an Army group or at least of the independently led army in East Prussia. The Fuehrer is described as finally turning this down on the grounds that he would then also have to employ Blomberg, to which he could not agree.[16] Actually, it will be recalled that Hitler just then was being told in unusually strong terms that he must not consider employing Blomberg, especially since he had made no move to give a command to Fritsch.[17]

Hitler, though far more inclined to soften toward Blomberg than toward Fritsch, was no doubt glad to have the pressures on behalf of the two generals cancel each other out. At the same time he must have found it painful that Fritsch's soldierly conduct again thrust him into a certain limelight—not before an unknowing public, but for those in the Generalität who were reached by the military grapevine.

The soldier's death of the rejected general was announced to Hitler in a fashion particularly calculated to put him out of countenance. It was the reputedly cold-blooded Jodl who, swept by a surge of generous feeling, began his situation report of September 22 with the words: "Today there fell one of the finest soldiers Germany has ever had, Colonel General Baron von Fritsch." This was said with a certain heat and sharpness which left his listeners

[15] Probably the most convincing argument that Fritsch would not have placed himself in unnecessary jeopardy is one made by Grosskreuz, that he would never have put the adjutant who was always at his side into such a position. Interview, January 15, 1970. The most extensive and up-to-date treatment of the last phase of Fritsch's life is the study by Gerd Brausch in *Militärgeschichtlichte Mitteilungen.*

[16] Keitel (219) states that he was told of this decision and Hitler's alleged reasons by Schmundt.

[17] See above, p. 126. Warlimont ("Interpretation," 102) quotes a statement of Helmuth Greiner of November 8, 1939, that Hitler told him at the beginning of the war that there was no way of employing Blomberg without again taking on Fritsch. This is, of course, the exact reverse of what Keitel relates in his memoirs. There is no evidence beyond his own story that Keitel exerted himself in any way on behalf of Fritsch's receiving a command.

amazed. All noted how Hitler could not repress a start. Schmundt and Engel agreed to use what persuasive powers they had to induce him to attend the funeral but, as the latter foresaw,[18] it proved impossible to achieve this.

Karl Sack spoke for the men whose last cast of the dice was made on July 20, 1944, when he described the Fritsch affair as the point of departure for the conspiratorial activities of the next six years.[19] The men who rallied to Fritsch in the first half of 1938 were indeed, with rare exceptions, the same who fashioned the plot of September of that year and thereafter remained in the forefront of the battle. Some of them had detested the regime from its beginnings, while others had freed themselves of illusions about its goals and character. Before the Wehrmacht crisis of 1938 no more than a few of them—Oster and Witzleben, for instance—had commenced to explore the readiness of others to help end Hitler's rule. Even here there was little evidence of concrete plans or something like a timetable for action.

Hitler's virtual *coup d'état* against the autonomy of the Wehrmacht transformed this state of affairs. In every military and government sector there were men for whom this outrage was decisive in hardening their attitude toward the regime. "The Fritsch affair entailed my complete inner break with the system," wrote General Thomas in 1945.[20] He spoke for many others.

Perhaps more important than the widening of the disaffected circle was the change in outlook of those whose "inner break" antedated Blomberg's ill-fated nuptials. Hitherto their debates had usually revolved about the problem of mobilizing sufficient potency to *control* the dictator. The absence of any national tradition of defiance of authority explains why they usually shrank from such a course themselves and, in the case of the less squeamish, why they lacked confidence in persuading others to engage in it. One will recall Beck's reference to Schlieffen's dictum that "mutiny" and "rebellion" were not in the lexicon of the German officer.

Hjalmar Schacht had been among those who had hoped to find means to control Hitler in such areas as foreign policy and the expenditure for armaments. His efforts during the Fritsch crisis, like those of most others who sought to help Fritsch, had been

[18] Engel Diary, entry of September 22, 1939.
[19] Weinheimer interview, February 15, 1970.
[20] Thomas, "Gedanken und Ereignisse," 3.

to stimulate pressures sufficient to *oblige* the Fuehrer to render justice. The experience had proved enlightening from the standpoint both of attempting to deal with Hitler on such a basis and of hoping to persuade the generals to confront him directly. Once Hitler had a chance to talk, he outmatched the generals at every point.

Schacht resigned all thought of attempting to intimidate or outmaneuver the Fuehrer. A few days after the Fritsch trial had ended, he had that first meeting with Erwin von Witzleben which initiated the planning for a coup that nearly came off in September.[21]

The shift in outlook and intentions is less well illustrated by Schacht and Witzleben, men who even before 1938 were clandestinely agitating and enlisting support, than by such laggard converts as Fritsch and Beck. We have seen that the Army commander and his chief of staff had occupied the only posts in the military hierarchy, with the one exception of Rundstedt, from which a determined counterattack on the Army's enemies could have been launched. Neither of them came close to such a course.

The tragic aspect of their fatal hesitation as the hours of decision passed is heightened by their tardy conversion once it was too late. "Fritsch now regrets not having acted," former War Minister Wilhelm Gröner told the historian Meinicke shortly after.[22] "I wanted to avoid the shedding of blood for the sake of my person," Fritsch said to Joachim von Stülpnagel in his retreat at Achterberg. The trouble, he said, was that very few saw through the knavish machinations of "the adventurer," whereas the masses believed in him. And what would have been the further course of affairs, he asked, if a coup had succeeded? "It was not possible to rule a people like the Germans with bayonets." But his final conclusion contrasted with this profound pessimism: "Yet, if I had known how wholly this man is without scruple and how he gambles with the fate of the German people, I should have acted differently and taken upon myself the odium of having acted through egotistic motives."[23]

[21] Schacht interview, November 12, 1969. Though they would legitimately fall within the compass of the present study, it has sought, so far as possible, to omit mention of the first exchanges that eventuated in the plot of the late summer of 1938. They will be given more intensive treatment in a volume that is to follow.
[22] Meinicke, 144.
[23] Foertsch, *Schuld und Verhängnis*, 205, 236n6. To Grosskreuz, Fritsch also commented that "a people could not be ruled with bayonets." Interview, January 15, 1970.

In a similar vein Fritsch addressed himself to Lieutenant Grosskreuz, Both's successor as adjutant, and in a letter to the Baroness Schutzbar.[24] To Major Siewert he did not hesitate to speak of a possible coup that might have to involve the dictator's assassination.[25] A study scheduled to follow the present one will demonstrate the final conversion of Fritsch to tryannicide and his relation to the plot of September.

Beck's metamorphosis came earlier and reflected a more complete conversion and a greater determination to make up for the lost time and opportunity. The chief of staff was given to rigorous self-critiques and was a stranger to whatever smacked of alibiing. If anything, he was prepared to accept more than his share of responsibility for the fact that "the politically and psychologically right moment had been missed." He repeatedly told Baron von Lüninck that as chief of staff he—Beck—should have committed the Army to preventing the illegal expulsion from office of its commander in chief. Basically he had understood this but he had missed the right moment of decision.[26]

That Beck subsequently regarded the plans for a coup in September a belated substitute for what should have been done the previous winter may also be inferred from comments made early that month to a relative, the later General Hans Speidel. Visiting him at Mannheim, where Speidel was a divisional chief of staff, Beck voiced his keen disappointment that Fritsch had not chosen to march, by inference thus also condemning his own inaction.[27]

For Beck, as for so many others, the stark fact of Fritsch's exclusion from office was no less unsettling than the abominable means employed for its accomplishment. Fritsch's reputation for quiet strength and iron imperturbability had become all but legendary among conservative critics of the regime in the years immediately preceding his fall. In him, they had reasoned wishfully, they had the ultimate guarantee of intervention if Nazi excesses passed all tolerance. That he said little was taken as evidence that he was

[24] J. A. Kielmansegg, *Der Fritsch-Prozess 1938*, 122. Grosskreuz interview, January 15, 1970.

[25] Siewert interview, January 15, 1970.

[26] Baron Hermann von Lüninck to the Reverend Max Pribilla, S.J., January 9, 1950 (in IfZ, ZS 394). Foerster (169n57a) believes that such remarks by Beck reflected "passing moods" and not his real sentiments. In view of what Beck in early September told the later General Speidel (Speidel interview, November 3, 1969) it would appear that they did represent his final verdict.

[27] Speidel interview, November 3, 1969.

biding his time and conserving his key position to strike when the situation demanded. Actually, of course, the façade and the reality of the man corresponded closely. The great enigma was no enigma at all—he was a "sphinx without a riddle."[28]

Beck not only had counted upon Fritsch as a final recourse against Nazi tyranny, but had also judged his presence in office a vital brake on Hitler's more irresponsible impulses and plans. Like others who shared this illusion, he was awakened to reality by the tragic fate of his commander, and made to recognize that the Army as a power center in Hitler's Reich had suffered a staggering blow. Its role as a restraining influence, already on the downgrade, was thus largely played out. Put another way, the dike had been cracked to a point where it lacked the solidity to confine the flood waters when next they should rise.

There is nothing to indicate that Hitler sensed the danger this implied for his rule. His decapitation of the Wehrmacht, which went double for the Army by replacing a leader of some strength with a figurehead, compelled those who yearned to purge the state to perceive that their sole hope was toppling the regime itself. The dictator thus forced that flight into illegality in which plots were hatched against him.

The Fritsch affair also proved a dress rehearsal for bringing together elements hostile to the regime in key military and civil agencies, notably in the OKH and the Abwehr. Persistently, though in hit-or-miss fashion, the group attached to Oster and Canaris had strengthened its ties in every direction, spied out the land, and taken note of pockets of discontent all over Berlin. It also systematically went about consolidating its ranks within its own agency.

The role of Oster, Canaris, and Gisevius was central in this enterprise. Oster's new place in the scheme of things within the Abwehr was crucial in this. Canaris, whose own viewpoint of what had to be done was fundamentally altered, now exerted himself for the advancement of his dynamic lieutenant. In this he enjoyed the support of Keitel, who, though without the faintest notion of the scope and focus of Oster's efforts, appreciated the services Oster had rendered him in the way of information. It was at this

[28] Wheeler-Bennett, 358–359. The present writer agrees with this estimate so far as it deals with Fritsch before and during the affair that bears his name. As indicated earlier, he rejects the conclusion that Fritsch also failed at a later date to associate himself with any conspiratorial activity.

time that Oster undertook direction of what later grew into the Central Division of the Abwehr, a post to which only an officer with full General Staff status and activity could ordinarily have aspired.[29]

Gisevius, since his punitive transfer to Münster, had been under a cloud and the Abwehr leaders, mindful of Heydrich's animosity toward him, had been inclined to confine their contacts to obscurer places such as homes. In these troublous times his police and other contacts had proved so indispensable that now Canaris abandoned his objections to being seen with him.[30]

As the purpose of this group became more fixed and as its aim shifted from curbing the SS to eliminating the Third Reich itself, the circle of which it was the nucleus took in more of the kindred spirits whom Canaris had assembled in the Abwehr since taking command in 1935. In the organization in 1938 there was scarcely a single out-and-out Nazi. There was nothing like solidarity, however, with respect to political attitudes. The majority of the officers were politically disinterested, though inclined to criticize one or another aspect of the regime. Only a small, though strategically placed, group was prepared to engage actively against it.[31]

In the lively discussion over the affairs of Blomberg and Fritsch that inevitably arose in the best informed military agency in Berlin, it was easy to identify those prepared to commit themselves fully. Oster was soon organizing such elements within Abwehr ranks and perfecting ties leading to other agencies. The lines running to Gisevius's police helpers, to men like Dohnanyi and Sack in the Ministry of Justice and military courts, to men like the brothers Kordt (Erich and Theo) in the Foreign Office, and to men like Schacht and General Thomas in the economic leadership were drawn taut. "Of course you are coming to us," Oster had said to Dr. Kanter as the Fritsch trial came to its end.[32] To the strategically placed he must have had more concrete things to propose than to the somewhat isolated jurist.

Most vital, of course, was the campaign to win over officers in key positions. Beck was just then arriving at his own decision and the intimate link between him and Oster dates from the busy summer of 1938. Parallel to and intertwined with this relationship

[29] Gisevius recording, January 1972.
[30] *Ibid.*
[31] A good analysis of the situation in the Abwehr at this juncture is that of Commander Franz Liedig, in "Sonderbericht einer Vernehmung."
[32] Kanter interview, May 9, 1970.

was the consolidation of the Canaris-Oster and Witzleben groups which, even before the 1938 Wehrmacht crisis, had been thinking in terms of enlisting support for eventual "action."

Such activities might well have gone for nought or even been lost to history if Hitler had not stepped up that surge of international adventuring that began with the Anschluss. He had rid himself of such troublesome impediments to his foreign and military policies as Blomberg, Fritsch, Neurath, Schwedler, and Hossbach. Lesser obstacles like Hassell and the dismissed or transferred generals had also been swept from his path. Beck was slated to go and the days of the obstreperous Schacht as president of the Reichsbank were clearly numbered. In place of these "troublemakers" Hitler set such ready instruments of his will as Keitel, Brauchitsch, Schmundt, Funk, and Ribbentrop, all of whom had, for one reason or another, surrendered themselves to him. The dictator was also about to break his repeated promises by the creation of a Praetorian Guard in the shape of elite SS formations that were to form the nucleus of a fourth military arm.

So, though Hitler continued to feel that the Generalität was still largely against him,[33] he believed that he had it and the Foreign Office boxed in sufficiently to have much his own way in the pursuit of his policies. The contempt he had conceived for the generals, who virtually to a man had allowed themselves to be run over or hoodwinked, and his conviction that they had proved a collection of cowards would not permit him to contemplate serious resistance to his will. That they might yet resort to force does not appear to have occurred to him at all.

Given such fancies and intentions, Hitler, if he did not elect to draw back for other reasons, was on a collision course. He did recoil at the last minute in September and thus, although unwittingly, averted a showdown that had been in the making since spring. The Western appeasers and his own loss of nerve saved him in 1938 by frustrating the plans of his enemies. Yet the spark engendered by the Blomberg and Fritsch affairs was to glimmer on for six more years until it finally though futilely burst into flame in July 1944.

[33] As he maintained to Captain Engel. Engel Diary, entry of April 4, 1938.

# A Supplementary Note

After the text of this volume had gone to the printer, the author was given access, through the courtesy of Mr. David Irving, to documentary material of great importance and undoubted authenticity which cannot as yet be specifically identified or cited. In significant instances it supports or refutes suppositions advanced in this study. In rough chronological order the following appear to deserve mention:

1. During 1937 efforts were stepped up to influence Hitler against Hossbach and the Army leadership. In some measure Blomberg was involved in this, for he found Hossbach too much a man of independent mind. He seems to have wanted a man of his own as Wehrmacht adjutant and a separate Army adjutant of lesser stature, a line officer rather than a staff type.

How far Hitler had yielded to this agitation he showed in a two-hour talk with Fritsch on January 15, 1938, by grim coincidence the day on which the "reconstruction" of his dossier of 1936 was launched. Hitler claimed that "anarchism" was spreading in the Army and, when asked for evidence, said this could be supplied, if at all, only to Blomberg. Fritsch determined to demand an expression of full confidence or dismissal. Since the Fuehrer had gone to Berchtesgaden, no occasion for such a showdown offered itself before the surge of events which began on January 24.

2. It was Keitel who, on the afternoon of the 25th, was the first to inform Fritsch of the developments concerning Blomberg.

3. Hitler began the confrontation of the evening of the 26th by giving Fritsch the protocol of an interrogation of Schmidt to read. The general was so preoccupied with examining this that, upon

Schmidt's being led in, he did not even hear the rogue's statement, "Yes, it is him."

Goering then told Fritsch that Schmidt had readily identified him from a photograph, that he had told the truth in a hundred cases, and that both the male prostitute and a witness to the final blackmail incident had also recognized him from his picture.

4. The order to go to the Gestapo the next morning was given Fritsch then and there. It seems that, apart from the later Wannsee interrogation, he was questioned by the Gestapo only on the 27th.

5. Fritsch held off on the resignation Hitler had demanded until February 3, when the Fuehrer peremptorily insisted that it be submitted that day.

6. Hitler's speech to the generals (and thus also that to the Cabinet) was not on February 4 but on the 5th.

7. Contrary to the assumption of this study, Fritsch's statement of February 23 did have some association with the summoning of his former orderlies. Though questioning probably only began about March 1, by which time about ten of them had arrived, Fritsch knew on February 23 what lay before him and expressed his indignation in an introductory part of the statement that is missing from the versions used for this study.

8. On March 23 Brauchitsch wrote to the commanding generals to inform them of the verdict. He had to use heavy pressure before Hitler agreed to write to Fritsch.

9. Count von der Goltz formally requested the transfer of Schmidt from Gestapo to Justice Ministry custody. Goering turned this down saying Himmler might be offended by such a vote of no confidence.

10. The undelivered challenge to Himmler included a bill of particulars on such points as failing to inform the Fuehrer that the January 15 investigation had clearly shown there was no Fritsch case but only a Frisch case. Beck was first asked to carry the challenge but suggested Rundstedt, who agreed but on March 30 asked Fritsch to give up the idea.

11. By early June Fritsch had prepared the draft of a letter to the commanding generals, detailing the account of his Calvary. The main censure he placed on Himmler. Hitler he did not believe to have been in the plot at the beginning, judging from his despairing attitude in the evening of January 26. The missive was never sent because of Hitler's speech to the generals at Barth on June 13.

# List of Abbreviations, Bibliography, and Index

# List of Abbreviations

| | |
|---|---|
| E.P. | Europäische Publikation e. V. |
| FA | Forschungsamt (Department of Investigation) |
| GD | *Documents on German Foreign Policy* |
| IfZ | Institut für Zeitgeschichte |
| IMT | International Military Tribunal |
| NA | National Archives (Washington) |
| OKH | Oberkommando des Heeres (Supreme Command of the Army) |
| OKW | Oberkommando der Wehrmacht (Supreme Command of the Armed Forces) |
| PRO | Public Record Office (London) |
| RSHA | Reichssicherheitshauptamt (Reich Main Security Office) |
| SA | Sturm Abteilungen (Storm Troops) |
| SD | Sicherheitsdienst (Security Service) |
| SS | Schutzstaffel (Himmler's Elite Guard) |
| VfZ | *Vierteljahrshefte für Zeitgeschichte* |

# Personal Sources
# of Information and
# Bibliography

## Individuals Providing Oral Information

### INTERROGATIONS

The following persons, prisoners of war, were interrogated by the author on problems related to this study:

Jodl, Colonel General Alfred. Chief of operations, OKW, 1939-45. October 1945.

Keitel, Field Marshal Wilhelm. Chief of OKW, 1938-45. On two occasions in October 1945.

Warlimont, General of Artillery Walter. Deputy chief of operations, OKW, 1938-44. On some twelve occasions from August to October 1945.

### INTERVIEWS

Abshagen, Karl-Heinz. German newspaper correspondent in London in the 1930's; brother and uncle of members of the Abwehr. May 12, 1970.

Albrecht, Reverend Johannes. Opposition figure in the Benedictine abbey of Ettal. November 15, 1969, and April 14, 1970.

Astor, David. Editor of *The Observer* (London) and friend of German Opposition figures. February 26, 1970.

Baudissin, Lieutenant General (ret.) Count Wolf. Adjutant of Infantry Regiment 9 (Potsdam), 1938-39. June 28, 1970, and June 23, 1971.

Beck, Walter G. Brother of Colonel General Ludwig Beck. May 28 and June 9, 1970.

Becker, Walter G. Professor of law, Free University of Berlin, and former military judge. April 16 and June 9, 1970, and June 26, 1971.

Bürkner, Vice Admiral (ret.) Leopold. Deputy commander of the Abwehr, 1938-44. February 14, 1970.

Butler, Lieutenant General Peter von. February 27, 1973. In 1938 a lieutenant in Armored Regiment No. 2 at Eisenach.

Canstein, General (ret.) Baron Raban von. November 29, 1969.

Dohnanyi, Christine von. Widow of Hans von Dohnanyi and sister of Klaus and Dietrich Bonhoeffer. June 26, 1958.

Einbeck, Colonel (ret.) Eberhard. Biographer of General Count Sponeck. December 2, 1969, and various occasions in 1970.

Engel, Lieutenant General (ret.) Gerhard. Army adjutant of Hitler, 1938-42. May 4, May 11, June 24, and June 26, 1970, and July 15, 1971.

Etzdorf, Ambassador (ret.) Hasso von. Foreign Office Opposition figure. Various occasions in 1958, 1960, 1966, 1967, and 1970.

Falkenhausen, Baron Gottfried von. Member of the Paris Opposition group (Stülpnagel-Hofacker). February 21, 1970.

Finkenstein, Countess Carmen von. Contact of many Opposition figures. June 28, 1970.

François-Poncet, Ambassador (ret.) André. French ambassador in Berlin during the Hitler years until October 1938; then in Rome, October 1938–June 1940. May 5, 1967, and October 22, 1969.

Freytag-Loringhoven, Lieutenant General Baron Bernd von. November 3, 1969. In 1938 a lieutenant in Armored Regiment No. 2 at Eisenach.

Geyr von Schweppenburg, Lieutenant General (ret.) Baron Leo von. German military attaché in London. January 26 and February 11, 1970.

Gisevius, Hans Bernd. Close associate of Canaris and Oster. September 1945, February 11, 1967, October 17, 1969, and July 11, 1971. Tape recordings of July 1971 and January 1972.

Goerdeler, Carl. Lord mayor of Leipzig. June 1936.

Goltz, Count Rüdiger von der. Defending attorney in Fritsch case. November 1, December 9, 1969, February 17, 1970, and July 8, 1971.

Grosskreuz, Colonel (ret.) Otto Heinz. Adjutant of Colonel General von Fritsch after retirement. January 15, 1970.

Halder, Colonel General (ret.) Franz. Quartermaster general II, 1938, Army chief of staff, 1938–42. June 19, 1958, and August 9, 1960.

Hammerstein-Equord, Baron Kunrat von. Son of Colonel General Kurt von Hammerstein-Equord. May 9, 1970.

Hammerstein-Equord, Baron Ludwig von. Son of Colonel General Kurt von Hammerstein-Equord. June 24, 1971.

Hardenberg, Countess Margarete von, nee von Oven. Successively secretary of Generals von Blomberg, von Hammerstein, and von Fritsch. February 20, 1970.

Hassell, Ilse von. Widow of Ambassador Ulrich von Hassell. December 2, 1969, and April 30 and June 3, 1970.

Heinz, Lieutenant Colonel (ret.) Friedrich Wilhelm. Member of Abwehr Opposition group. August 24, 1958.

Hentig, Ambassador (ret.) Werner Otto von. July 14, 1971.

Herwarth von Bittenfeld, Ambassador (ret.) Hans von. Foreign Office Opposition figure. April 1967, and July 1, 1969.

Hevelke, Elwine, nee von Meerscheidt Hüllessem. Secretary of Colonel General von Fritsch and relative of Field Marshal von Blomberg. June 11, 1970, and June 27, 1971.

Hofmann, Major General (ret.) Fritz. Close friend of Judge Advocate General Karl Sack. April 13, 1970.

Hossbach, General (ret.) Friedrich. Wehrmacht adjutant of Hitler, 1934 to January 28, 1938. July 21, 1963 (with Helmut Krausnick), and July 1, 1971 (with Walter Bussmann).

Huber, Franz Josef. Regierungsdirektor in the Gestapo and general of police. November 20, 1969, and June 3 and July 1, 1970.

Huppenkothen, Walter. Regierungsdirektor in the RSHA and SS Standartenführer; chief of a special force assigned to investigate persons accused in connection with the plot of July 20, 1944. September 11, 1960, and May 29, 1970.

Jodl, Luise, nee von Benda. Widow of Colonel General Alfred Jodl; secretary successively of Generals Adam, Beck, and Halder. June 10, 17, 24, and 30, 1970, and July 7, 1971.

John, Otto. Opposition figure. July 8, 1971.

Kaczmarek, Georg. Member of Gestapo. June 1, 1970. (Conducted for the author by Edouard Calic.)

Kanter, Senate President (ret.) Ernst. Member of investigative panel of the court-mar-

# Bibliography

tial of Colonel General von Fritsch. May 9, 1970, and July 15, 1971.

Kessel, Albrecht von. Foreign Office Opposition figure. July 4, 1967, and February 6, 1970.

Kielmansegg, General (ret.) Count Johann Adolf. Nephew of Colonel General von Fritsch and author of the earliest work on the Fritsch trial. September 16, November 17, and December 8, 1969, April 14 and June 24, 1970, and July 12, 1971.

Kordt, Minister Erich. *Chef de Cabinet* of Reich Foreign Minister, 1938–41, associated with Abwehr group Opposition. On numerous occasions, 1945 to 1969.

Kuehlmann, Richard von. German Foreign Minister, 1917–18; friend of Konstantin von Neurath. On various occasions in 1930's and in September 1945.

Langbehn, Irmgard. Widow of Carl Langbehn. June 19, 1970.

Liedig, Edda. Widow of Franz Liedig. June 2, 1970.

Liedig, Commander (ret.) Franz. Member of the Abwehr Opposition group. August 9, 1960 (with Helmut Krausnick).

Müller, State Minister Dr. Josef. Member of the Abwehr Opposition group, 1939–43. On some thirty-five occasions, 1958–70 (frequently with Helmut Krausnick or Hermann Graml).

Neave, Airey, Former British intelligence officer; member of Parliament. July 6, 1970.

Neubauer, Gertrud. Daughter of Colonel General Ludwig Beck. May 28, 1970.

Nissen, Karl. Professor and famed internist; physician and friend of Generals von Fritsch and Beck; relative of Field Marshal von Blomberg. July 15, 1971.

Nostitz, Ambassador (ret.) Gottfried von. Opposition figure associated with Foreign Office and Abwehr. February 4, April 23, and May 18, 1969, and July 9, 1971.

Oster, Brigadier General Achim. Son of Major General Hans Oster. December 12, 1967, December 17, 1969, March 14 and 15, 1970, and February 18, 1973.

Pabst, Waldemar. Associated with Oster Opposition circle. May 12, 1970.

Pfuhlstein, Major General (ret.) Alexander von. Member of the Abwehr and commander of its Division Brandenburg. February 14, 1970.

Piekenbrock, Renate. Widow of General Hans Piekenbrock, an associate of Abwehr Opposition circle. February 21, 1970.

Puttkamer, Admiral (ret.) Karl von. Naval adjutant of Hitler. June 27, 1970, and July 10, 1971.

Reichenau, Alix von. Widow of Field Marshal Walther von Reichenau. May 3 and June 23, 1970, and July 7, 1971.

Roloff, William T. German Unilever representative and Opposition contact with British circles. June 14, 1971.

Sack, Helle. Widow of Judge Advocate General Karl Sack. April 20, 1970.

Salomon, Ernst von. Writer. May 5, 1970.

Schacht, Minister Hjalmar. Minister of Economics and president of the Reichsbank; associated with Abwehr Opposition group. October 9 and November 6, 1969.

Schlabrendorff, Fabian von. Associate of various Opposition groups. On many occasions in 1945, 1958, 1960, 1963, 1967, and 1970.

Schmid-Noerr, Frau. Widow of Professor Friedrich Schmid-Noerr, an Opposition figure. January 25, 1970.

Schneckenburger, Ilse. Widow of General Schneckenburger and secretary successively of Generals von Hammerstein, Beck, and Adam. May 27 and June 10, 1970.

Schulenburg, Countess Charlotte von der. Widow of Fritz-Dietlof von der Schulenburg. June 19 and 30, 1970.

Schultze, Erich. Former city councilor of Königsberg and provincial councilor of East Prussia as well as secret officer of the Reichswehr. December 5, 1969, February 15, March 5, May 8, and July 4, 1970, June 27 and July 13, 1971, and February 18 and 19, 1973.

Schwerin von Schwanenfeld, Countess Marianne von. Widow of Count Ulrich von Schwerin von Schwanenfeld. June 22 and 27, 1970.

Schwerin-Ziethen, Lieutenant General (ret.) Count Gerhard von. Opposition emissary to Britain, 1939. July 1, 1970, and July 3, 1971.

Siewert, Lieutenant General (ret.) Curt. First staff officer of Generals von Fritsch and von Brauchitsch. January 15, 1970.

Simonis, Consul (ret.) Susanne. Cousin of Erich and Theo Kordt. December 12, 1969, May 9 and July 7, 1970, and June 28, 1971.

Speidel, General (ret.) Hans. Relative of General Ludwig Beck and Opposition figure. November 3, 1969, and May 9 and July 7, 1970.

Strünck-Gärtner, Elisabeth. Widow of Theodor Strünck and Opposition figure in her own right. April 18 and 20, 1970.

Thomas, Lieutenant General Georg. Chief of the War Economy Department, OKW, 1938-44. September 1945.

Vauhnik, Milos. Brother of Colonel Vladimir Vauhnik, Yugoslav military attaché in Berlin, 1938-41. September 30 and December 17, 1969, and April 9, 1970.

Warlimont, General of Artillery (ret.) Walter. Deputy chief of operations, OKW, 1938-44. On various occasions in 1958, 1960, 1963, 1969, and 1970.

Weinheimer, Military Judge (ret.) Wilhelm. Friend of military judges involved in Fritsch trial. February 15, 1970.

Wiedemann, Captain (ret.) Fritz. Personal adjutant of Hitler, 1934-39. December 2, 1969.

Witzleben, Major General (ret.) Hermann von. Director of the Europäische Publikation e. V., Munich, and cousin of Field Marshal Erwin von Witzleben. On numerous occasions in 1958, 1960, 1963, 1966, 1969, 1970, and 1971.

Witzleben, Ursula von. Wife of Major General (ret.) Hermann von Witzleben. February 9 and 10, 1970.

Wussow, Botho von. Member of Foreign Office Opposition circle. June 22, 27, and 29, 1970.


# Unpublished Sources
## (* denotes copy in possession of author)

Note: Any unpublished manuscript cited in the footnotes that is not listed separately here is deposited in the IfZ archives; see the listing under IfZ in the section OTHER DOCUMENTARY SOURCES.

### BOOK-LENGTH MANUSCRIPTS

Adam, Wilhelm. "Erinnerungen." 600+-page manuscript in IfZ.

Becker, Walter G. "Als Artillerist und Divisionsrichter im Kriege 1939-1945." 668 pp. Lent by courtesy of the author.

*Bielschowsky, Ludwig. "Die Tragödie des deutschen Judentums. Ein Schuss vereitelte 1938 die vorbereitete Rettung. Ein Zeugenbericht." 176 pp.

* Engel, Gerhard. Extracts from General Engel's Diary of 1938 and 1939 bearing on the Blomberg and Fritsch affairs. Made available to the author by the courtesy of General Engel.

Goltz, Count Rüdiger von der. "Erinnerungen." 514 pp. Lent by courtesy of the author.

* Heinz, Friedrich Wilhelm. "Von Wilhelm Canaris zum NKVD." Written in the first postwar years. 203 pp.

Kessel, Albrecht von. "Verborgene Saat: Das 'Andere Deutschland.'" Written in

# Bibliography

Rome, late 1944–early 1945. 237 pp. Lent by courtesy of the author.

Stülpnagel, Joachim von. "75 Jahre meines Lebens." Militärarchiv/Freiburg, N5/27. About 550 pp.

° Transcript of testimony at the trial of Walter Huppenkothen, February 4–14, 1951, and verdict, February 22. Three bound volumes. 1613 pp.

Trott zu Solz, Clarita von. "Adam von Trott zu Solz: Eine erste Materialsammlung, Sichtung und Zusammenstellung." 304 pp. Lent by courtesy of Christobel Bielenberg.

Ulex, Alexander. Pp. 94–104 of memoir-type manuscript. IfZ, EDI.

Warlimont, Walter. "Interpretation and Commentary on the Jodl Diaries, 1937–1945." Part I, 1937–39. 317 pp. NA microfilm.

Weizsaecker, Ernst von. "Extracts from the Diaries and Papers of Ernst von Weizsaecker." Prepared and annotated by Leonidas Hill. 89 pp. Lent by courtesy of Professor Hill.

° Wussow, Botho von. "Erinnerungen." Written in 1945 in English and German. 107 pp.


### OTHER DOCUMENTARY SOURCES

° "Aktenvermerk [on the Fritsch case]" of March 21, 1938, signed by Military Court Judges Biron, Kanter, and Sack. 2 pp.

Beck, Ludwig. "Nachlass des Generaloberst a. D. Ludwig Beck." In IfZ, BAMA H 08-28 (I-V).

° Best, Werner. "Aktennotiz des General a. D. Hermann Foertsch über eine Unterredung mit Herrn Ministerialdirektor z. V. Dr. Werner Best über die Vorgänge der Heirat Blomberg und die Angelegenheit Generaloberst Freiherr von Fritsch im Frühjahr 1938, 13.9.52." 5 pp.

° Bielschowsky, Ludwig. "Eidestaatliche Erklärung von Dr. Ludwig Bielschowsky." Affidavit made at Frankfurt on March 24, 1954. 2 pp.

° Bonin, Erich von. Statement of September 2, 1966. 8 pp.

° [Canaris, Wilhelm, and Friedrich Hossbach.] "Stellungnahme zu dem Fall des Generaloberst Freiherr von Fritsch." Undated memorandum of March 1938. 10 pp.

° Dohnanyi, Christine von. "Aufzeichnungen über das Schicksal der Dokumentensammlung meines Mannes, des Reichsgerichtsrats a. D. Hans von Dohnanyi." N.d. 4 pp.

° ———. "Aufzeichnungen von Frau Christine von Dohnanyi, geb Bonhoeffer." N.d. 11 pp.

° Europäische Publikation e. V. (Munich). Protocols of its colloquia in 1952–55. Many hundreds of pages.

° Fritsch, Baron Werner von. "English Language Translations of Letters Written by Freiherr von Fritsch to Baroness Margot von Schutzbar, Pertaining to Routine Personal Matters, Fritsch's Dismissal from the German Army, Participation in Initial Stages of Campaign against Poland, February 18, 1938–September 18, 1939." NA. Record Group No. 242/1048. Roll No. T84/272.

° ———. "Protokoll der Venehmung von Generaloberst Werner von Fritsch durch Dr. Werner Best und Regierungsrat Franz Josef Huber." IfZ. 82 pp.

° Goltz, Count Rüdiger von der. "Darstellung Prozess Generaloberst von Fritsch." Written in 1945–46. IfZ, ZS 49. 18 pp.

° Gruhn, Eva. Gruhn Police File. A much-abbreviated file found in Berlin ruins in 1945. IfZ, Akz. 4490/70.

° Halder, Franz. "Antworten zum Fragebogen vom 10.11.1950 ('Fritsch Krise')." 4 pp.

° Hassell, Ulrich von. Extracts from unpublished papers dealing with repercussions

of the Blomberg and Fritsch affairs. 5 pp.
*Huppenkothen, Walter. "Canaris und Abwehr." N.d. 13 pp.
*_____. "Verhältnis Wehrmacht-Sicherheitspolizei." N.d. 15 pp.
IfZ archives. Documentation in the IfZ is grouped by individual: Wilhelm Adam, ZS 6; Karl-Heinz Bodenschatz, ZS 10; Leopold Bürkner, ZS 364; Christine von Dohnanyi, ZS 603; Gerhard Engel, ZS 222; Hasso von Etzdorf, ZS 322; Hermann Foertsch, ZS 37; Franz Halder, ZS 240; Friedrich Hossbach, ZS 74; Erich Kordt, ZS 545; Erwin von Lahousen, ZS 658; Hermann von Lüninck, ZS 394; Horst von Mellenthin, ZS 105; Alexander von Pfuhlstein, ZS 592; Bernhard Rogge, ZS 1449; Gerd von Rundstedt, ZS 129; Hans von Salmuth, ZS 133; Hjalmar Schacht, ZS 135; Walter Schellenberg, ZS 291; Fabian von Schlabrendorff, ZS 628; Curt Siewert, ZS 148; Georg von Sodenstern, ZS 149; Georg Thomas, ZS 310; Alexander Ulex, ZS 627; Maximilian von Weichs, ZS 182; Fritz Wiedemann, ZS 191; *Restricted file, ZS 1992.
Kanter, Ernst. "General Graf Sponeck." 5-page statement of February 7, 1968. Lent to the author by courtesy of Colonel Eberhard Einbeck.
Kielmansegg, Count Johann Adolf. Papers assembled in 1946–48 for the preparation of his volume Der Fritsch-Prozess 1938. Lent to the author by the courtesy of Count Kielmansegg.
*Lahousen, Erwin von. "Eidesstattliche Erklärung." June 27, 1948.
*Lehmann, Dr. Rudolf. Affidavit of August 4, 1947.
*Liebmann, Curt. "Persönliche Erlebnisse des Gen. d. Inf. a. D. Curt Liebmann aus den Jahren 1938/1939." Written in November 1939 and footnotes added in 1947. 41 pp.
*Liedig, Franz. "Sonderbericht einer Vernehmung (CSIR), No. 6, 4. Oktober 1945." An interrogation of Liedig, October 4, 1945. 23 pp.
*Pfuhlstein, Alexander von. "Die Ablehnung der Mitarbeit zum offenen Kampf gegen Hitler durch den kommandierenden General des XI. Korps, Hanover 1938." 2 pp.
*_____. "Meine Tätigkeit als Mitglied der Berliner Verschwörerzentrale der deutschen Widerstandsbewegung vom 1. Oktober 1936–Juli 1944." Written in May 1946.
Röhricht, Edgar. "Bericht über eine Aussprache mit Goerdeler während der Blomberg-Fritsch Krise, 22.2.51." IfZ, ZS 96.
Rundstedt, Gerd von. "Affaire Blomberg-Fritsch 1938." IfZ, ZS 129 (I). 5 pp.
*_____. "Niederschrift der Unterredung des Herrn General Feldmarschall Gerd von Rundstedt mit Herrn Freiherr von Siegler, 26. November 1951." 1 p.
*Sack, Karl. "Aktenvermark."
Schacht, Hjalmar. "Spruch in der Spruchkammersache des Dr. rer. pol. Hjalmar Horace Greeley Schacht, 1. September 1948." 28 pp. Lent to the author by courtesy of Dr. Schacht.
*Schultze, Erich. Letter to six Social Democratic Reichstag deputies. Dated Königsberg, March 17, 1933. 10 pp.
Siewert, Curt. "Unterredung mit General a. D. Curt Siewert, Hannover, 13.10.51." IfZ, ZS 148. 15 pp.
*Sodenstern, Georg von, and August Winter. "Niederschrift über Unterredung der Herrn Generale a. D. von Sodenstern und Winter mit den Herren Dr. Vogelsang und Krausnick am 23.6.54." IfZ, ZS 149. 5 pp.
*Thomas, Georg. "Gedanken und Ereignisse." Written at Falkenstein, July 20, 1945. 17 pp.
*_____. "Mein Beitrag zum Kampf gegen Hitler." Prepared in 1945. 18 pp.
*Warlimont, Walter. "Zur Persönlichkeit des Generalfeldmarschalls Keitel." Prepared at the request of the author. Written on September 28, 1945. 4 pp.
*_____. "Zur Persönlichkeit des Generalfeldmarschalls von Blomberg." Prepared

# Bibliography

at the request of the author. Written on October 2, 1945. 3 pp.

⁰_____."Zur Persönlichkeit von Dr. Hjalmar Schacht." Prepared at the request of the author. Written on October 1, 1945. 3 pp.

Wiedemann, Fritz. "Aufzeichnungen." IfZ, ZS 191.

_____. "Fragen zur Bearbeitung der Fritsch-Krise, 1. Dez. 1950." IfZ. 3 pp.

⁰Wolff, Karl. "Aktenvermerk des Generals der Waffen-SS Karl Wolff über die Blomberg-Fritsch Krise, 11.8.52." IfZ, 1182/53. 8 pp.

_____. "Niederschrift zu Unterredungen des ehem. SS-Obergruppenführers General der Waffen-SS Karl Wolff mit Herr Dr. Hermann Mau am 7/8 September 1952." IfZ.


## Printed Sources

### DOCUMENT COLLECTIONS

Akten zur deutschen auswärtigen Politik, 1918-1945. Series D, Vol. I. Baden-Baden, 1950. English ed., Documents on German Foreign Policy, 1918-1945. Series D, Vol. I. Washington, 1950.

Calic, Edouard, ed. Ohne Maske: Hitler-Breiting Geheimgespräche 1931. Frankfurt, 1968. English ed., Unmasked: Two Confidential Interviews with Hitler in 1931. London, 1971.

[Hitler, Adolf.] Hitler's Secret Book, with an introduction by Telford Taylor. New York, 1961.

_____. Hitler's Secret Conversations, 1941-1944, with an introductory essay on the mind of Hitler by H. R. Trevor-Roper. New York, 1953.

International Military Tribunal. Trial of the Major War Criminals before the International Military Tribunal, 14 November 1945-1 October 1946. 42 vols. Nuremberg, 1947-49.

Kempner, Robert M. W. Das Dritte Reich im Kreuzverhör: Aus den unveröffentlichten Vernehmungsprotokollen des Anklägers. Munich, 1969.

Nazi Conspiracy and Aggression. 8 vols. and 2 supplements. Washington, 1946-48.

Spiegelbild einer Verschwörung: Die Kaltenbrunner Berichte an Bormann und Hitler über das Attentat vom 20. Juli 1944. Geheime Dokumente aus dem ehemaligen Reichssicherheitshauptamt, ed. Karl Heinz Peter. Stuttgart, 1961.


### MEMOIRS, DIARIES, ETC.

Bor, Peter. Gespräche mit Halder. Wiesbaden, 1950.

Faber du Faur, Moritz von. Macht und Ohnmacht: Erinnerungen eines alten Offiziers. Stuttgart, 1955.

François-Poncet, André. The Fateful Years: Memoirs of a French Ambassador in Berlin, 1931-1938. New York, 1949.

Geyr von Schweppenburg, Baron Leo von. The Critical Years. London, 1952.

Gisevius, Hans Bernd. Bis zum bittern Ende. Enlarged ed. Zurich, 1954. English ed., To the Bitter End. Boston, 1947.

Görlitz, Walter, ed. Generalfeldmarschall Keitel, Verbrecher oder Offizier? Erinnerungen, Briefe, Dokumente des Chefs OKW. Göttingen, 1962.

Groscurth, Helmuth. Tagebücher eines Abwehroffiziers: Mit weiteren Dokumenten sur Militäropposition gegen Hitler, ed. Helmut Krausnick and Harold C. Deutsch in association with Hildegard von Kotze. Stuttgart, 1970.

Guderian, Heinz. Erinnerungen eines Soldaten. Heidelberg, 1951.

Hassell, Ulrich von. Vom anderen Deutschland: Aus den nachgelassenen Tagebüchern 1938-1944. Unabridged ed. Frankfurt, 1946. English ed., The Hassell

*Diaries, 1938-1944: The Story of the Fight against Hitler inside Germany.* New York, 1947.

Hedin, Sven A. *Sven Hedin's German Diary, 1935-1942.* Dublin, 1951.

Henderson, Sir Nevile. *Failure of a Mission: Berlin, 1937-1939.* New York, 1940.

Hossbach, Friedrich. *Zwischen Wehrmacht und Hitler 1934-1938.* 2nd rev. ed. Göttingen, 1965.

Jodl, Alfred. *Das Dienstliche Tagebuch des Chefs des Wehrmachtführungsamtes im OKW.* For the period January 4, 1937, to August 25, 1939, Document 1780-PS, IMT, XXVIII, 345-390.

John, Otto. *Zweimal kam ich heim: Vom Verschwörer zum Schützer der Verfassung.* Düsseldorf-Vienna, 1969.

Keitel, Wilhelm, *see* Gorlitz, Walter

Manstein, Erich von. *Lost Victories,* ed. Anthony G. Powell. Chicago, 1958. German ed., *Verlorene Siege.* Frankfurt, 1953.

Meissner, Otto. *Staatssekretär unter Ebert-Hindenburg-Hitler: Der Schicksalsweg des deutschen Volkes von 1918-1945, wie ich ihn erlebte.* Hamburg, 1950.

Müller, Vincenz. *Ich fand das wahre Vaterland,* ed. Klaus Mammach. Leipzig, 1963.

Papen, Franz von. *Der Wahrheit eine Gasse.* Munich, 1952.

Raeder, Erich. *Mein Leben.* 2 vols. Tübingen, 1957.

Röhricht, Edgar. *Pflicht und Gewissen: Erinnerungen eines deutschen Generals 1932 bis 1944.* Stuttgart, 1965.

Sauerbruch, Ferdinand. *Das war mein Leben.* Munich, 1950.

Schacht, Hjalmar. *Abrechnung mit Hitler.* Hamburg, 1948. English ed., *Account Settled.* London, 1948.

_____. *76 Jahre meines Lebens.* Bad Wörishofen, 1953. English ed., *My First 76 Years.* London, 1955.

Schellenberg, Walter. *The Schellenberg Memoirs.* London, 1956.

Schlabrendorff, Fabian von. *Offiziere gegen Hitler.* New rev. ed. Zurich, 1951.

Schwerin von Krosigk, Count Lutz. *Es geschah in Deutschland, Menschenbilder unseres Jahrhunderts.* Tübingen and Stuttgart, 1951.

Shirer, William. *Berlin Diary: The Journal of a Foreign Correspondent, 1934-41.* New York, 1941.

Speer, Albert. *Erinnerungen.* Berlin, 1969. English ed., *Inside the Third Reich: Memoirs.* New York, 1970.

Vauhnik, Vladimir. *Memoiren eines Militärattachés: Mein Kampf mit dem Fingerspitzengefühl Hitlers.* Klagenfurt, 1967.

Wagner, Elisabeth, ed. *Der Generalquartiermeister: Briefe und Tagebuchaufzeichnungen des Generalquartiermeisters des Heeres General der Artillerie Eduard Wagner.* Munich, 1963.

Warlimont, Walter. *Im Hauptquartier der deutschen Wehrmacht 1939-1945: Grundlagen-Formen-Gestalten.* Frankfurt, 1962. English ed., *Inside Hitler's Headquarters, 1939-1945.* New York, 1964.

Westphal, Siegfried. *Heer in Fesseln: Aus den Papieren des Stabschefs von Rommel, Kesselring und Rundstedt.* Bonn, 1950.

Wiedemann, Fritz. *Der Mann der Feldherr werden wollte: Erlebnisse und Erfahrungen des Vorgesetzten Hitlers im ersten Weltkrieg und seines späteren persönlichen Adjutanten.* Dortmund, 1949.

Winnig, August. *Aus zwanzig Jahren 1925 bis 1945.* Hamburg, 1948.

Young, Donald, ed. *Adventure in Politics: The Memoirs of Philip La Follette.* New York, 1970.

# Bibliography

## Secondary Works

### BIOGRAPHICAL WORKS

Abshagen, Karl Heinz. *Canaris, Patriot und Weltbürger.* Stuttgart, 1949.
Bösch, Hermann. *Heeresrichter Dr. Karl Sack im Widerstand: Eine historisch-politische Studie.* Munich, 1967.
Buchheit, Gert. *Ludwig Beck, ein preussischer General.* Munich, 1964.
Bullock, Harold. *Hitler: A Study in Tyranny.* Rev. ed. New York, 1962.
Colvin, Ian. *Chief of Intelligence.* (Canaris.) London, 1951.
Einbeck, Eberhard. *Das Exempel: Graf Sponeck. Ein Beitrag zum Thema Hitler und die Generale.* Bremen, 1970.
Foerster, Wolfgang. *Generaloberst Ludwig Beck: Sein Kampf gegen den Krieg.* Munich, 1953.
Gisevius, Hans Bernd. *Adolf Hitler: Eine Biographie. Versuch einer Deutung.* Zurich, 1967.
———. *Wo ist Nebe? Erinnerungen an Hitlers Reichskriminaldirektor.* Zurich, 1966.
Krebs, Albert. *Fritz-Dietlof Graf von der Schulenburg: Zwischen Staatsraison und Hochverrat.* Hamburg, 1964.
Manvell, Roger, and Heinrich Fraenkel. *Heinrich Himmler.* London, 1965.
Peterson, Edward H. *Hjalmar Schacht, for and against Hitler: A Political-Economic Study of Germany, 1923–1945.* Boston, 1953.
Ritter, Gerhard. *Carl Goerdeler und die deutsche Widerstandsbewegung.* Stuttgart, 1954.
Rudelsdorff, D. *Generaloberst Freiherr Werner von Fritsch, Chef des Artillerie Regiments Nr. 12: Leben und Schicksal eines grossen Soldaten. Kurzfassung eines Vortrags.* Kassel, 1968.
Schramm, Percy Ernst. *Hitler: The Man and the Military Leader.* Chicago, 1971.
Wighton, Charles. *Heydrich, Hitler's Most Evil Henchman.* Philadelphia, 1962.

### GENERAL WORKS

Bennecke, Heinrich. *Die Reichswehr und der "Röhm-Putsch."* Munich, 1962.
Bracher, Karl Dietrich, Wolfgang Sauer, and Gerhard Schultz. *Die nationalsozialistische Machtergreifung: Studien zur Errichtung des totalitären Herrschaftssystems in Deutschland 1933/34.* 2nd rev. ed. Cologne and Opladen, 1962.
Buchheit, Gert. *Der deutsche Geheimdienst: Geschichte der militärischen Abwehr.* Munich, 1966.
———. *Soldatentum und Rebellion: Die Tragödie der deutschen Wehrmacht.* Rastatt/Baden, 1961.
Carroll, Bernice A. *Design for Total War: Arms and Economics in the Third Reich.* The Hague, 1968.
Craig, Gordon. *The Politics of the Prussian Army, 1640–1945.* Oxford, 1955.
Demeter, Karl. *Das deutsche Offizierskorps in Gesellschaft und Staat 1650–1945.* 4th rev. and enlarged ed. Frankfurt, 1965.
Deutsch, Harold C. *The Conspiracy against Hitler in the Twilight War.* Minneapolis, 1968. German ed., *Verschwörung gegen den Krieg: Der Widerstand in den Jahren 1939–1940.* Munich, 1969.
Dulles, Allen W. *Germany's Underground.* New York, 1947.
Europäische Publikation e. V. *Die Vollmacht des Gewissens.* 2 vols. Munich and Frankfurt, 1956 and 1965.
Foertsch, Hermann. *Schuld und Verhängnis: Die Fritsch-Krise im Frühjahr 1938 als Wendepunkt in der Geschichte der nationalsozialistischen Zeit.* Stuttgart, 1951.
Geffen, William, ed. *Command and Commanders in Modern Warfare.* 2nd enlarged ed. United States Air Force Academy, Col., 1971.

Görlitz, Walter. *Der deutsche Generalstab: Geschichte und Gestalt 1657-1945.* Frankfurt, 1952. English ed., *The German General Staff.* London, 1953.

Herzfeld, Hans. *Das Problem des deutschen Heeres 1919-1945.* Schloss Laupheim, 1952.

Höhne, Heinz. *Der Orden unter dem Totenkopf: Die Geschichte der SS.* 2 vols. Frankfurt and Hamburg, 1969.

Hoffmann, Peter. *Widerstand, Staatsstreich, Attentat: Der Kampf der Opposition gegen Hitler.* Munich, 1969.

Kielmansegg, Count Johann Adolf. *Der Fritsch-Prozess 1938: Ablauf und Hintergründe.* Hamburg, 1949.

McCloy, John J., II. *Die Verschwörung gegen Hitler: Ein Geschenk an die deutsche Zukunft.* Stuttgart, 1963.

Manvell, Roger, and Heinrich Fraenkel. *The Canaris Conspiracy: The Secret Resistance to Hitler in the German Army.* London, 1969.

Meinecke, Friedrich. *Die deutsche Katastrophe.* Zurich and Wiesbaden, 1946.

Messerschmitt, Manfred. *Die Wehrmacht im NS-Staat: Zeit der Indoktrination.* Hamburg, 1969.

Müller, Klaus-Jürgen. *Das Heer und Hitler: Armee und nationalsozialistisches Regime 1933-1940.* Stuttgart, 1969.

O'Neil, Robert. *The German Army and the Nazi Party.* London, 1966.

Pechel, Rudolf. *Deutscher Widerstand.* Erlenbach-Zurich, 1947.

Prittie, Terence. *Germans against Hitler.* London, 1964.

Reile, Oscar. *Geheime Westfront: Die Abwehr 1935-1945.* Munich, 1962.

Roon, Ger van. *Neuordnung im Widerstand: Der Kreisauer Kreis innerhalb der deutschen Widerstandsbewegung.* Munich, 1966.

Rothfels, Hans. *Die deutsche Opposition gegen Hitler: Eine Würdigung.* Rev. ed. Frankfurt, 1964. English ed., *The German Opposition to Hitler: An Assessment.* London, 1961.

Schlabrendorff, Fabian von. *The Secret War against Hitler.* London, 1966.

Shirer, William. *The Rise and Fall of the Third Reich.* New York, 1960.

Siewert, Curt. *Schuldig? Die Generale unter Hitler. Stellung und Einfluss der hohen militärischen Führung im nationalsozialistischen Staat: Das Mass ihrer Verantwortung und Schuld.* Bad Nauheim, 1968.

Taylor, Telford. *Sword and Swastika: The Wehrmacht in the Third Reich.* London, 1953.

Thomas, Georg. *Geschichte der deutschen Wehr- und Rüstungspolitik (1918-1943/1945),* ed. Wolfgang Birkenfeld. Publications of the German Federal Archives No. 14. Boppard am Rhein, 1966.

Vogelsang, Thilo. *Reichswehr, Staat und NSDAP.* Stuttgart, 1962.

Weinberg, Gerhard. *The Foreign Policy of Hitler's Germany: Diplomatic Revolution in Europe, 1933-1936.* Chicago, 1970.

Weisenborn, Günther. *Der lautlose Aufstand: Bericht über die Widerstandsbewegung des deutschen Volkes 1933-1945.* Hamburg, 1953.

Wheeler-Bennett, John W. *The Nemesis of Power: The German Army in Politics, 1918-1945.* 2nd ed. London, 1964.

Zeller, Eberhard. *Geist der Freiheit: Der 20. Juli.* 4th rev. ed. Munich, 1963.

## PERIODICAL ARTICLES AND CHAPTERS IN BOOKS

Adler-Brosse, Marcelle. "Jugements allemands sur la Wehrmacht," *Revue d'Histoire de la Deuxième Guerre Mondiale,* No. 22 (April 1956), 10-23.

Assmann, Heinz. "Some Personal Recollections of Adolf Hitler," *U.S. Naval Institute Proceedings,* Vol. 79, No. 12 (December 1953), 1289-1295.

# Bibliography

Baum, Walter. "Marine, Nationalsozialismus und Widerstand," *VfZ*, Vol. 11, No. 1 (January 1963), 16-48.

Boehm, F. "Widerstandsbewegung oder Revolution? Zur Auseinandersetzung um Carl Goerdelers Kampf gegen Hitler," *Monat*, Vol. 8 (1955), 20-28.

Boeningen, D. "Hitler and the German Generals," *Journal of Central European Affairs*, Vol. 14 (1954-55), 19-37.

Boveri, Margret. "Goerdeler und der deutsche Widerstand," *Aussenpolitik*, Vol. 6 (1955), 73-85.

Brausch, Gerd. "Der Tod des Generalobersten Werner Freiherr von Fritsch," *Militärgeschichtliche Mitteilungen*, Vol. 1 (1970), 95-112.

Bussmann, Walter. "Zur Entstehung und Überlieferung der 'Hossbach Niederschrift,'" *VfZ*, Vol. 16, No. 4 (October 1968), 373-384.

Fletcher, Willard A. "'Dulce et decorum est pro patria mori': The Dismissal and Death of Generaloberst Werner Freiherr von Fritsch," *University of Colorado Studies, Series in History*, No. 2 (1961), 61-78.

Gackenholz, Hermann. "Reichskanzlei, 5. November 1937: Bermerkungen über 'Politik und Kriegsführung' im Dritten Reich," *Forschungen zu Staat und Verfassung: Festgabe für Fritz Hartung*, ed. R. Dietrich and G. Oestreich. Berlin, 1958. Pp. 59-84.

Graml, Hermann. "Der Fall Oster," *VfZ*, Vol. 14, No. 1 (January 1966), 27-39.

Hubatsch, Walter. "Die deutsche militärische Memoirenliteratur," *Historische Zeitschrift*, Vol. 171 (1951), 373-382.

Kielmansegg, Count Peter. "Die militärisch-politische Tragweite der Hossbach Besprechung," *VfZ*, Vol. 8, No. 3 (July 1960), 269-275.

Kluke, Paul. "Der deutsche Widerstand: Ein Literaturbericht," *Historische Zeitschrift*, Vol. 169 (1949).

Moltmann, Günter. "Weltherrschaftsideen Hitlers," in *Europa und Übersee, Festschrift für Egmont Zechlin*. Hamburg, 1961.

Montesi, G. "Der Krieg des Tantalus: Hitler und die Generale," *Wort und Wahrheit*, Vol. 4 (1949), 295-303.

Müller, Klaus-Jürgen. "Reichswehr und 'Röhm-Affaire.' Aus den Akten des Wehrkreiskommandos (Bayer.) VII," *Militärgeschichtliche Mitteilungen*, Vol. 1 (1968), 107-144.

Pribilla, Max. "Die Fritsch-Krise 1938 als deutsche Schicksalswende," *Stimmen der Zeit*, Vol. 147 (1951-52), 206-213.

———. "Ein grosser Gegenspieler Hitlers," *Stimmen der Zeit*, Vol. 145 (January 1950), 254-260.

Rosenberger, Heinrich. "Die Entlassung des Generalobersten Freiherr von Fritsch," *Deutsche Rundschau*, Vol. 69, No. 8 (November 1946), 91-96.

Schickel, Alfred. "Wehrmacht und SS," *Wehrwissenschaftliche Rundschau*, Vol. 19, No. 5 (May 1969), 241-264.

Sehmid, Peter. "Admiral Canaris," *Die Weltwoche* (Zurich), March 1, 1946, 7.

Stock, Ulrich. "Der Fritsch-Prozess 1938: Seine rechtlichen Beurteilungen und seine Lehren," *Festschrift für Heinrich Lehmann zum 80. Geburtstag "Das deutsch Privatrecht in der Mitte des 20. Jahrhunderts."* Berlin, 1956. Pp. 925-937.

# Index

438

# Index

absence from Barth, 402; on Fritsch's honorary colonelcy, 409; converted to conspiracy, 418-419; association with Oster, 420; asked by Fritsch to carry challenge to Himmler, 423; mentioned, 15n38, 18n49, 39n18, 50, 63, 67, 99, 115, 120, 152, 171, 176, 186, 204, 206, 209, 214, 218, 226, 232, 233, 234, 235, 238, 241, 248, 253, 256, 260, 261, 274, 276, 281, 282, 295, 299, 303, 305, 306, 313, 314, 332, 334, 337, 375, 385, 393, 403, 413, 416, 417, 421

Behlendorff, Colonel, 261

Benda, Luise von, *see* Luise Jodl

Best, Werner: claims Fritsch dossier assembled in late 1937, 143-144; role in Fritsch interrogation, 175-179; reproached by Goltz, 179; told by Huber of Fritsch's innocence, 181-182; argues with Himmler, 182; proposed for court-martial panel, 188; throws blame on Goering, 370; mentioned, 98n60, 104, 145, 146, 154, 162n87, 270, 271, 290, 291, 294, 308, 362, 413

Bielschowsky, Ludwig, 55n64

Biron, Judge: selected as investigative judge, 283; basic sympathies with Fritsch, 285; with Sack in Lichterfelde, 316-317; interrogates Frisch, 317-320; dressed down by Goering, 355-356; mentioned, 282, 284, 286, 287, 291, 303, 305, 313, 327, 328, 353, 383, 392n23

Blomberg, Axel von, 125

Blomberg, Dorothee von, 96n52, 101

Blomberg, Eva von, nee Gruhn: involvement with Blomberg, 81, 85-87; background, 82-84; Gestapo watch on, 89-90; marries Blomberg, 96-97; discovery of police files on, 99-100; mentioned, 91n40, 95n51, 99, 105, 107, 108, 109, 110, 113, 121, 122, 124, 125, 148, 149, 150, 190, 200n17, 201, 269, 278

Blomberg, Field Marshal Werner von: career before Reichswehr Ministry, 9; backs Reichenau for Army commander, 12-13; involved in June 1934 Blood Purge, 15; and oath to Hitler, 20-21; brings Wehrmacht closer to National Socialism, 23; agrees to separate Air Force, 24;

believed to have poisoned Hitler's mind against Fritsch, 31-32; appointed Minister of War, 33; weakening position, 33-35; Goering's jealousy of, 34; moves Reichenau to Munich, 34-35; appoints Keitel to head Wehrmachtamt, 35; anxieties about drift to war, 38-39; refuses to intervene against Nazi excesses, 40; restricts influence to military affairs, 41; tensions with Fritsch, 56-57; instigates November 5 conference, 59-60; responds to Hitler's comments, 63-64; leads criticism of Goering, 66; reactions to conference, 68-70; amends Case Green, 69; passivity after November 5, 1937, 74; characterization of, 80-81; involvement with Eva Gruhn, 81, 84-85; solicits aid of Goering, 85-87; Schultze tries to warn, 91; gains Hitler's consent to marriage, 92; defiant mood of, 93; and problem of wedding witnesses, 93-97; honeymoon interrupted by death of mother, 97; early association with Keitel, 101; and Goering on January 25, 111-113; meeting with Hitler, 116-119; informs Keitel about talk with Hitler, 120-121; pursued by Oster and Wangenheim to Italy, 121-123; Beck demands severe treatment of, 124-125; offers to annul marriage if returned to post, 125; blames Keitel, 125-126; Hitler declines to re-employ, 126; vents spleen against Army, 261; Hitler describes conduct, 263-264; mentioned, 1, 8, 17, 37, 39n18, 40n19, 40n20, 71, 78, 79, 89, 98, 99, 102, 104n76, 105, 106, 107, 108, 110, 128n157, 129, 131, 133, 134, 143, 145, 146, 147n34, 150, 155, 160, 161, 168, 191, 194, 195n5, 200, 201, 202, 203, 205, 216, 217, 219, 225, 228, 231, 232, 236, 240, 241, 256, 257, 260, 264, 268, 269, 270, 271, 272, 273, 274, 276, 277n21, 278, 290, 293, 331, 336, 338, 339, 361, 371, 380, 384, 404, 415, 421, 422

Bock, General Fedor von: fails to support Ulex's steps on behalf of Fritsch, 399-400; mentioned, 221, 361-362, 409-410

# Index

Argentina for Blomberg's rival, 87

Dietrich, Sepp, 370n32

Dirksen, Ambassador Herbert von, recalled, 263

Dirksen, Viktoria von, 272

Doenitz, Grand Admiral Karl, 389

Dohnanyi, Hans von: made Gürtner's delegate in Fritsch case, 186; checks Wannsee Station with Gürtner, 187; and Fritsch's challenge to Himmler, 366n12; 367; joins Oster circle, 375; mentioned, 157, 160, 197n10, 233, 289, 300, 305, 420

Dollmann, General Friedrich, 254

Drews, Lieutenant Colonel, 236

Duenkel, queried in Fritsch investigation, 302

Edward VIII, Duke of Windsor, 81

Eitel, Prince Friedrich, 334

Engel, Captain Gerhard: speaks for Army against command for Blomberg during war, 126; on Army attitudes during Fritsch affair, 250; appointed Army adjutant, 389-391; fights for Fritsch, 391-393; mentioned, 96n57, 106, 112n101, 117n115, 118, 216n1, 228n31, 229n36, 254, 274n13, 298n92, 332n2, 339, 361, 410

Etzdorf, Hasso von, 229n35

Faber du Faur, Colonel Moritz von: Hitler confides Austrian intentions, 339; mentioned, 343

Fehling, Criminal Commissar: guards "dossier on Fritsch," 146; investigates Frisch, 147; indiscreet, 316; bungles situation on Frisch, 318-319; tripped up by Sack, 326-327; mentor of Goering at Fritsch trial, 337, 357; testimony at Fritsch trial, 359; survives inquiry, 370-372; mentioned, 149n35, 184, 294, 305, 323, 330, 362, 397

Foerster, Wolfgang, on offer of Army command to Beck, 216-217

Foertsch, Hermann, 20n52

Foreign Office, German: regarded by Hitler as uncertain element, 40; mentioned, 420, 421

Forschungsamt (FA), role of, 79-80

Fouché, Joseph, Duke of Otranto, 46

François-Poncet, Ambassador André, judgment of Fritsch, 26

Frank, Hans, exchange with Adam, 194

Frederick the Great, view on integrity of courts, 185

Frick, Wilhelm, 342

Friedeburg, Corvette Captain Hans von, 96

Frisch, Captain Achim von: blackmailed by Otto Schmidt, 136-137; discovered and interrogated, 317-320; problem of protecting, 321-322; mistreated by Gestapo and transferred to Ministry of Justice, 328; firm conduct at Fritsch trial, 348; mentioned, 135, 139, 140, 147, 181, 184, 187, 189, 286n49, 294, 304, 323, 327, 331, 333, 350, 351, 352, 362, 366, 370, 371, 397

Fritsch, SA leader, 365

Fritsch, Colonel General Baron Werner von: becomes Army commander, 13; protests June 1934 Blood Purge, 16-17; opposes oath to Hitler, 21; strained relations with Blomberg, 24, 25, 56-57; warned by Ludendorff about Hitler, 25; background, character, and mode of life of, 25-27, 296-298; letters to Baroness von Schutzbar, 28; and regime, 29; last hope of anti-Nazi circles, 30; clashes with SS, 30-31; doubts about Blomberg, 33, 81; anxieties about drift to war, 39; acquaintance with Erich Schultze, 56; advised to vacation in Egypt, 56; Hitler's target in February 5 conference, 61; responds to Hitler's comments, 63-64; joins Blomberg in criticism of Goering, 67; joins with Beck and Neurath to oppose drift to war, 71; meeting with Hitler, 71; chief obstacle of Goering, 88; alliance of Goering and Himmler against, 88-89; evades acting as witness at Blomberg wedding, 93-95; intriguers' efforts to mobilize him against Blomberg, 98; ostensible candidate for succession to Blomberg, 107, 109; warned by Hossbach, 115; construction of 1936 dossier against, 141-145; charges against launched, 149-150; reaction to charges, 150-151; warnings and presentiments, 152-153; talk with Hossbach on morning of January 26, 153; Gürtner delivers opinion on,

441

# Index

# Index

talks with Hitler, 131-132; appointed chief of Wehrmacht command, 132-133; misled on role of Gürtner, 160; role in dismissal of Hossbach, 172; and Rosenberger, 184-186; opposes Reichenau for Army command, 218-219; summons Brauchitsch to Berlin, 219-220; role in Brauchitsch negotiations, 222-226; supports Hitler's efforts for secrecy, 231-232; needled by Canaris, 234; servitude to Hitler, 271-273; demoralization, 274; seeks to moderate Brauchitsch's support of Fritsch, 280; refuses to oppose Gestapo investigation, 291; informed of Fritsch's "double," 295; reproves Kanter, 310-311; refuses to intervene to protect Frisch, 322; acts as buffer for Hitler on March 11, 342; exchange with Rosenberger, 386; pressure on Brauchitsch, 388-389; probably suppressed Kluge's threat of resignation, 400; and problem of Otto Schmidt, 408-409; mentioned, 87n40, 91, 93n46, 97, 104n76, 108, 112, 116, 117, 121, 123, 154, 155, 156, 163, 168, 171, 174, 188, 199, 201, 208, 232, 236, 241, 259, 260, 261, 266, 275, 283, 306, 329, 338, 343, 361, 384, 390, 393, 401, 415, 419, 421, 422
Kielmansegg, Lieutenant Count Johann Adolf, 39, 95n52, 350
Kleist, General Erwin von, 46
Kluge, General Günther von: acquaintance with Gisevius, 52; worked on by Gisevius, 254-255; threatens resignation, 400; mentioned, 200n17, 264, 401
Koch, Gauleiter Erich, 46
Kordt, Erich, 420
Kordt, Theo, 420
Kress von Kressenstein, General, 261
Kükelhaus, Hugo, mediates between Helldorf and Schulenburg, 277-278
Kuntzen, Colonel Adolf, 216

La Follette, Philip, learns of conspiracy against Hitler, 42-43
Lahousen, Colonel Erwin von: recruited for Abwehr Opposition, 374-375; mentioned, 233
Lammers, Hans Heinrich, 132, 266
Laue, Frau von, 96n52

Leadbitter, Counsul General Jasper, 12n27
Leeb, General Ritter Wilhelm von, 118, 219, 221, 262
Lehmann, Judge Rudolf: selected for Fritsch's court-martial, 284; judge at Fritsch trial, 336, 350; sets up verdict under direction of Goering, 358; mentioned, 403
Liebmann, General Curt: reports on Barth meeting, 403-405; mentioned, 265
Liedig, Commander Franz: development as Abwehr Resister, 374; mentioned, 233
List, General Wilhelm: Goerdeler tries to stir up, 255-257; visits Beck, 257-258; mentioned, 361
Löffner, Criminal Secretary: questions Schmidt, 141; mentioned, 146
Loewenstein, Prince Hubertus zu, approached by agent of Reichenau, 11n26
Ludendorff, Supreme Quartermaster General Erich: warns Fritsch against Hitler, 25; death and memorial services for, 92
Lüninck, Baron Ferdinand von, 53, 254-255, 418
Luftwaffe (German Air Force): most pro-Nazi of services, 41; favored in government allocations, 60; ordered to prepare for war against Czechoslovakia, 70; mentioned, 87, 130, 212, 218, 244, 251, 257, 265, 275, 389
Lutze, Victor: succeeds Röhm as head of SA, 18; hatred of SS, 246; offers Brauchitsch alliance against SS, 380-382; mentioned, 157, 400n42

Mackensen, Field Marshal August von: protests to Hitler on police state, 245-246; comes to support of Fritsch, 399
Manstein, General Erich von, 221, 244n30, 261, 265
Manteuffel, General Hasso von, 244n30
Marogna-Redwitz, Count Rudolf von, 374n47
Martini, Colonel, 55
Meinecke, SA figure, 382
Meinecke, Friedrich, 210, 417
Meisinger, Criminal Councilor Joseph:

# Index

# Index

451